THE LITERATURE OF AL-ANDALUS

The Literature of Al-Andalus explores the culture of Iberia (present-day Spain and Portugal) during the period when it was an Islamic, mostly Arabic-speaking territory – from the eighth to the thirteenth century – and in the centuries following the Christian conquest, when Arabic continued to be widely used. This volume is path-breaking in its approach to the study of Arabic literature since it embraces many other related spheres of Arabic culture including philosophy, art, architecture, and music. It also extends the subject to other literatures – especially Hebrew and Romance literatures – that burgeoned alongside Arabic and created the distinctive hybrid culture of medieval Iberia. Edited by an Arabist, a Hebraist, and a Romance scholar, with individual chapters compiled by a team of the world's leading scholars of Islamic Iberia, Sicily, and related cultures, this is a truly interdisciplinary and comparative work that offers a radical new approach to the field.

María Rosa Menocal is R. Selden Rose Professor of Spanish and Portuguese and Director, Special Programs in the Humanities, at Yale University.

Raymond P. Scheindlin is Professor of Medieval Hebrew Literature at the Jewish Theological Seminary of America.

Michael Sells is Emily Judson Baugh and John Marshall Gest Professor of Comparative Religions at Haverford College.

THE LITERATURE OF AL-ANDALUS

EDITED BY

MARÍA ROSA MENOCAL
Yale University

RAYMOND P. SCHEINDLIN
Jewish Theological Seminary of America

AND

MICHAEL SELLS
Haverford College

CAMBRIDGE
UNIVERSITY PRESS

PUBLISHED BY THE PRESS SYNDICATE OF THE UNIVERSITY OF CAMBRIDGE
The Pitt Building, Trumpington Street, Cambridge, United Kingdom

CAMBRIDGE UNIVERSITY PRESS
The Edinburgh Building, Cambridge CB2 2RU, UK http://www.cup.cam.ac.uk
40 West 20th Street, New York, NY 10011–4211, USA http://www.cup.org
10 Stamford Road, Oakleigh, Melbourne 3166, Australia
Ruiz de Alarcón 13, 28014 Madrid, Spain

First published 2000

Printed in the United Kingdom at the University Press, Cambridge

Typeface 11/13 Adobe Garamond *System* QuarkXPress™ [SE]

A catalogue record for this book is available from the British Library

ISBN 0 521 47159 1

CONTENTS

ILLUSTRATIONS

NOTE ON TRANSLITERATION

Foreign-language words found in standard English dictionaries or used repeatedly throughout this book are printed in Roman type and spelled with none or the barest minimum of diacritical marks. In names, book titles, and less common Arabic and Hebrew words, our transliteration is largely consonant with that used by the *International Journal of Middle Eastern Studies.* Where phonetic pronunciation is vital to the literary quality of the material being discussed, we have used a system designed to represent elisions and other aural effects.

CHAPTER 1

VISIONS OF AL-ANDALUS

María Rosa Menocal

GRANADA

Come, spend a night in the country with me,
my friend (you whom the stars above
would gladly call their friend),
for winter's finally over. Listen
to the chatter of the doves and swallows!
We'll lounge beneath the pomegranates,
palm trees, apple trees,
under every lovely, leafy thing,
and walk among the vines,
enjoy the splendid faces we will see,
in a lofty palace built of noble stones.

Resting solidly on thick foundations,
its walls like towers fortified,
set upon a flat place, plains all around it
splendid to look at from within its courts.
Chambers constructed, adorned with carvings,
open-work and closed-work,
paving of alabaster, paving of marble,
gates so many that I can't even count them!
Chamber doors paneled with ivory like palace doors,
reddened with panels of cedar, like the Temple.
Wide windows over them,
and within those windows, the sun and moon and stars!

It has a dome, too, like Solomon's palanquin,
suspended like a jewel-room,
turning, changing,
pearl-colored; crystal and marble
in day-time; but in the evening seeming
just like the night sky, all set with stars.
It cheers the heart of the poor and the weary;
perishing, bitter men forget their want.
I saw it once and I forgot my troubles,
my heart took comfort from distress,

my body seemed to fly for joy,
as if on wings of eagles.

There was a basin brimming, like Solomon's basin,
but not on the backs of bulls like his –
lions stood around its edge
with wells in their innards, and mouths gushing water;
they made you think of whelps that roar for prey;
for they had wells inside them, wells that emitted
water in streams through their mouths like rivers.

Then there were canals with does planted by them,
does that were hollow, pouring water,
sprinkling the plants planted in the garden-beds,
casting pure water upon them,
watering the myrtle-garden,
treetops fresh and sprinkling,
and everything was fragrant as spices,
everything as if it were perfumed with myrrh.
Birds were singing in the boughs,
peering through the palm-fronds,
and there were fresh and lovely blossoms –
rose, narcissus, saffron –
each one boasting that he was the best,
(though we thought every one was beautiful).
The narcissuses said, "We are so white
we rule the sun and moon and stars!"
The doves complained at such talk and said,
"No, we are the princesses here!
Just see our neck-rings,
with which we charm the hearts of men,
dearer far than pearls."
The bucks rose up against the girls
and darkened their splendor with their own,
boasting that they were the best of all,
because they are like young rams.
But when the sun rose over them,
I cried out, "Halt! Do not cross the boundaries!"

(from Ibn Gabirol, "The Palace and the Garden,"
trans. Raymond P. Scheindlin)

As you stand in the astonishing gardens of the Generalife, there seem to be an unlimited number of vistas before you. First there are the layered views that take in every fine detail of the gardens themselves: the terraces and the courtyards, water visible and audible everywhere. At many turns you come upon the panoramas that are the dramatic views from the palaces themselves: the snow-capped mountains, the vivid city below. And occasionally, in crucial places scattered throughout this complex, you necessarily look out at the outcroppings of the great palaces, and understand immediately that while the Generalife may indeed have been the most splendid of summer retreats, the other great service it provided was to let you look at the Alhambra itself, from that vantage point half-hidden, on the other side of a ravine.

These inward and outward visions, all from this edenic promontory, capture all sorts of views of this pinnacle of the culture of al-Andalus. And just beyond the gardens what awaits the visitor is the Alhambra itself, that often breathtaking palatine city of the Nasrid kingdom of Granada, the locus, since Washington Irving, of the romantic Western vision of "Moorish Spain," as well as a powerfully evocative emblem, among Muslims and Arabs, of a precious moment of cultural dominion, subsequently lost. The complexity of the problem of vision was understood in crystalline fashion by the builders of the Alhambra, who dotted palaces and gardens alike with "miradores," as the carefully chosen and laid out lookout points are called, from the Spanish *mirar*, "to look." And those half-views of the Alhambra from the retreat of the Generalife can certainly trigger a version of that emotionally charged reaction, that blend of exhilaration and sadness in the student of al-Andalus, the object of this volume.

The story of the Alhambra, told in the fullness of its complexity, is a maze of superimposed memories that is a fitting emblem for the powerfully paradoxical and often unexpected cultural history of al-Andalus as a whole. Little is known about the original fortifications on the hill, although references to a "Red Castle" appear from as early as the end of the ninth century. It is not until the middle of the eleventh century that significant palaces and gardens are first built on the citadel: the first building on the site was begun by Samuel Ibn Nagrila (Samuel the Nagid), the powerful Jewish vizier of Granada, whose family had fled from Córdoba to Granada at the time of the overthrow of the Umayyads, in 1013. The construction was subsequently continued and elaborated by the Nagid's son, Joseph, and whereas the Nagid apparently rebuilt the fortifications of an original castle to protect the adjacent Jewish neighborhood, his son Joseph built on a more grandiose scale, perhaps working principally on elaborate gardens.[1] The layers of memory and exile are thick here, from the outset: the first real traces of the monument we see in Granada today were sketched out by members of an elite Jewish community in a common exile from the much-lamented Córdoba of the caliphate, and the sacked palaces of the Umayyads. And despite the fact that it is merely wishful thinking to see in Ibn Gabirol's poem – quoted above – a historical description of the unique fountain in the Court of the Lions, the intimately shared aesthetics of Hebrew and Arabic poetry, not just in this poem but throughout Andalusian letters, reveals many shared visions, among them that of Solomon as quasi-magical prince par excellence.[2]

If these foundational details are largely not remembered it is because the attention of all guidebooks – and in this category one can certainly include most general historical presentations – is per force, and with very good reason, turned to the Granada of the Nasrids, which between 1273 and 1492 was the last Muslim city-state of the peninsula. As this last outpost of what had been a brilliant civilization, during those last 250 years of Islamic dominion, the independent kingdom of Granada achieved the cultural and artistic heights manifest in the unrivaled Alhambra. But there is also an ill-remembered epilogue that, like the prelude, that story of the Ibn Nagrila family's first cultivation of a palatine complex where the ruined Red Castle had been, is hard to explain smoothly. And yet, without this long postlude we might hardly be able to see this memory palace, let alone name it the pinnacle of Islamic culture in Spain: in 1492, immediately upon taking control of the city from the last of the Nasrids (poor Boabdil, whose infamous "last sigh" is remembered as a sign of his pathetic inability to hold on to this precious place), Ferdinand and Isabella proclaimed the Alhambra a *casa real*, or royal residence, which it in fact remained until 1868. And whether this act of appropriation was simply to flaunt this trophy of the Christian conquest over Islam (as is normally maintained) or for more complex reasons as well, the undeniable effect of the royal protection and patronage was to keep the Alhambra relatively well preserved over the centuries. Paradoxically, and despite the much reviled Renaissance palace of Charles V that sits uncomfortably at the entrance of the Alhambra complex (which itself may be a part of the paradox), its absorption into the royal treasuries of the Catholic monarchs played a crucial role in making it a better preserved medieval palace than any other in the Islamic world.

But what might be paradoxes and juxtapositions in other historical or cultural circumstances are very often the bread and butter of al-Andalus. Thus, both the beginning and the end of the story of this Red Castle are powerful attestations to the unusually strong and complex relationships among the religions of the children of Abraham in this land. The role played by the Jewish community in the early chapter of the Alhambra speaks eloquent volumes: the telling intimacy of the Jews of Granada sharing power as well as that yearning for a lost homeland, where the layer of Córdoba and a sacked Madīnat al-Zahrā' would have mingled with others. And at the end, we see that Catholic preservation of the Alhambra after the end of the Reconquest, and throughout the period of the Inquisition, while countless Arabic manuscripts were destroyed (most notoriously in Granada), and while the descendants of the Muslims who had built the Alhambra were being forcibly converted, persecuted, and eventually expelled. The adoption of the palaces and gardens, in such a context, is perhaps a more complex phenomenon than is normally acknowledged: the reflection that the Islamic arts were immoderately admired, quite independently of religious and political ideologies, an attitude that will account for the wide range of surprising "mixed" forms so characteristic of al-Andalus, from the muwashshahs in literature to the Mudejar architecture of so much of post-Reconquest Toledo to the continued and continuous use of mosques as Catholic churches. I return shortly to all of these issues, and to the ways in which this volume is concerned with the details of these typically "mixed" Andalusi forms. But for the moment I want to reflect on the middle part of the story, the one that is most often told, for it is the one that has the most bearing on the picture we carry in our heads of al-Andalus.

The Alhambra is built with the wolves howling mightily at the door: In 1232, in the now obscure village of Arjona, one Ibn al-Aḥmar rebels against the Cordoban Ibn Hūd (a successor to the Almohads) and forms an alliance with Ferdinand III. Indeed, Ibn al-Aḥmar helps Ferdinand III take Córdoba itself, in 1236, in tacit exchange for being able to carve out his newly won territory. The foundation of Nasrid Granada – which Ibn al-Aḥmar enters the next year, in 1237 – as the last Muslim outpost of what had been al-Andalus for half a millennium, is thus rooted in what we might see as a typically unideological act of warfare, with a Muslim in military and political alliance with a Christian.[3] One of the many problems with the widely used word "Reconquest" is the suggestion that it means ideologically pure and politically uncompromising stances between Christian and Muslim in this land, and yet even at the most basic diplomatic and military levels, one sees, as late in the day as this, that political alliances in practice often overrode the supposed ideological dividing lines.

Nevertheless, and despite some easy suggestions in these kinds of breaches of ideological frontiers, this was unambiguously the beginning of the end, after all, and even then it was visibly so. This was the beginning of what was to be an Iliad-like 250-year-long siege against the kingdom of Granada. Deep inside their rugged mountain stronghold, the Banū Naṣr, those descendants of Ibn al-Aḥmar whom history calls the Nasrids, turned ever more inward and became progressively more Arabized. They existed culturally in a state of siege, isolated from the other cultures of al-Andalus in ways previously unimagined – it is, for example, the only significant moment in the history of al-Andalus during which an Islamic state exists without noteworthy *dhimmī* communities: scattered pockets of Jews and no Christians. And it is in this corner, and in a state of perpetual defensiveness that was palpably different from the cultural and political universe that had existed before the middle of the thirteenth century, that they build a fitting nearly sepulchral monument for themselves: the Alhambra celebrates what they seem to have always known they would lose since, as in the Trojan wars, the Achaeans may have rested or been distracted from time to time, but the lone, encircled city could only survive if the enemy decamped altogether, and permanently.

So it is that when you stand at those precisely built miradores, all of those lookout balconies and belvederes in the Alhambra, and especially so those in the gardens of the Generalife, you are struck by the terrible realization that, at that moment so blithely described by so many as the "heights" of Islamic culture in what was already more than halfway to being Spain, those who looked outward, which is mostly to the north, could see clearly the inevitability of loss. If glory lies behind you, there in the palaces half-hidden in the pine trees on the other side of the ravine, ahead of you, to the north, on the other side of the mountains, lies disaster. There was no good way out: Granada was, from beginning to end, a besieged vassal state. It is true, of course, that the Alhambra was built during the 150 or so years following the entry of Ibn al-Aḥmar into the city, years during which the Castilians, in effect, were still struggling to get their own house in order and the Granadan vassal state might be left essentially alone or might be a pawn in the extraordinarily complex and often brutal struggles that continued among the Christian states. But even then the wolves were always at the door.

In 1369, while Muḥammad V was hurriedly adding the finishing touches to the splendid Court of the Lions and the rest of the parts of the Alhambra that are most of what we marvel at today, Peter the Cruel of Castile was murdered by his half-brother Henry. It was Peter, an important patron of all sorts of Mudejar architecture throughout his kingdom, who had cultivated complex alliances with Granada and thus made available, inadvertently no doubt, the relative peace and financial well-being necessary to finish the building of the Alhambra. But the Grenadine death rattle began shortly after Peter's murder – an internecine and "interconfessional" act, as were so many of the most crucial violent moments of medieval Spain, including, of course, the sack of Madīnat al-Zahrā᾽ by Berbers that provides the first building block of memory for the Alhambra. It is not clear, in the end, whether it was because the end had begun that the monument itself could no longer be worked on, or whether it was because the living tomb was finally perfected that the true end could finally proceed.

It was, in any case, precisely at this moment, when the perfection of the palaces coincides with the harshest political revelations of the end at hand, that the soon-to-be-great historian Ibn Khaldūn passed through Granada – indeed, he was centrally involved in a diplomatic mission between Muḥammad V of Granada and Peter the Cruel himself.[4] It would be easy to speculate that it is there, in that extraordinary moment of Islamic history, when a visibly terminal political decline provoked unprecedented clarity of artistic vision, that the historian developed some part of his sense of the moral imperative to explain decline – that same sort of moral imperative that would be so echoed by Gibbon when he came upon the ruins of Rome. But of course unlike the ruined Rome of Gibbon, the plaster on the unparalleled walls and ceilings of the Alhambra was barely dry. So it is that while it is far more commonly ruins that evoke the poignancies of human loss, and stir those who contemplate them to tears or to the writing of the histories of what was lost, or both, the remarkably pristine Alhambra may be one of the only monuments built *avant la lettre* to monumentalize the inevitability of loss, and thus to nostalgia itself. From those miradores at the Alhambra we should be able to look out and see everything that the Nasrids saw, and feel their obligation to remember an al-Andalus already gone.

Cultivating the memory of al-Andalus from a wide variety of miradores, and for a wide variety of viewers, is the principal purpose of this volume, and it is undertaken with a distinct consciousness that al-Andalus itself has always been a powerful token of nostalgia.[5] This is done in an academic and intellectual context that is not exactly a vacuum, but that affords surprisingly few sight lines for viewing al-Andalus. And this despite the recent heightening of consciousness about its existence brought about by a disparate range of circumstances: the explosion of international tourism, and its spread to modern Spain in the post-Franquist era, that has made of places such as the Alhambra and the Great Mosque of Córdoba regular stops; the publication of nonacademic books that evoke it (Rushdie's *The Moor's Last Sigh*); and a variety of cultural and political circumstances that on occasion suggest there is a historical parallel for the existence of communities of Muslims in late twentieth-century Europe and America.

One of the causes for the relative scarcity of good miradores is almost certainly also one of the causes of its particularly poignant nostalgic power, for everyone from the seventeenth-century Arab historian al-Maqqarī to the nineteenth-century American Washington Irving: the cultural displacement, that special configuration of "European" and "Middle Eastern" elements it represents and evokes. If within an "orientalist" tradition this has meant the implicit conjuring of an exoticized version of the Arab within Europe itself, for Arabs, and for non-Arab Muslims, it has also represented that moment of cultural superiority over Europe, and the nostalgia that the loss of that necessarily represents, for poets and historians alike. And for Jews it is both more complex and more explicitly powerful a touchstone: Sefarad, the Hebrew name for al-Andalus, is the ultimate symbol of a certain exalted level of social well-being and cultural achievement. In all of these cases, of course, specific views are more nuanced and the values and judgments that accompany them vary widely, even wildly. (There is a particularly virulent strain of Spanish historiography that has viewed the Andalusian chapter as the cause of subsequent Spanish social ills, and much of the xenophobia of this view survives in Spanish culture to this day.) But in revealing the existence of this fundamental tripartite divvying up, these rival claims to some sort of heritage, we can immediately perceive the most fundamental problem of "vision": al-Andalus, by and large, has been divided along the single-language lines, derivative of national canons, that are in fact inimical to the Middle Ages in general and extravagantly noxious to al-Andalus.

If other volumes in this Cambridge series have been intended and written overwhelmingly for a public of fellow Arabists, this volume explicitly is not. This is not another reference volume for those who can already read the *Encyclopaedia of Islam*, nor is it another mirador that can look into the Alhambra only if the viewer can already decipher the writing on its walls, all the intricate court poetry as well as the verses from scripture, tokens of the limpid purity of this embattled Arabism, carved in heartbreakingly beautiful plaster. It is a joy, as well as a special sorrow, to stand in those courts and be able to read and recite. But to believe it is merely about that is to participate, at this historical remove, in the encircling and isolation of that place. Instead, we also embrace the fundamentally mixed linguistic and cultural makeup of so much of al-Andalus that preceded the Nasrids and that they are, there and then, memorializing. And we also believe it crucial to recognize the special historical circumstances that make al-Andalus central in the course of medieval history far beyond the confines of traditional Middle Eastern studies.

Clearly, fundamental scholarly material on Andalusi literary culture should be available to a range of readers that includes but ranges far beyond fellow Arabists, and indeed, our most idealistic goal is perhaps to make those now disparate academic communities less so. But even if we fall far short of that, we have tried to make this volume a useful and enjoyable resource for colleagues in widely disparate fields: from the French medievalist whose interest has been aroused by notices of Hispano-Arabic culture having some interaction with Provençal to the specialist in Hebrew poetry who may want to understand the Jewish Golden Age in its fullest context, from graduate students in European medieval studies who will not necessarily learn Arabic but will need to understand something of this central culture to the Ottomanist interested in the makeup and history of so many refugees in the sixteenth century. And a great deal in between.

Fellow Arabists will indeed find here essays on individuals and topics about which they may already know something or even a great deal (Ibn Ḥazm, the maqama, the Great Mosque of Córdoba) but many more on topics (Petrus Alfonsi, the Mozarabs, Judeo-Arabic) that are distinctly Andalusi – and yet traditionally fall outside most Arabists' purview. Indeed, a number of our fellow Arabists will no doubt protest that the object of our attention, or at least some of the objects of our attention, pace the title of the series, are not really "Arabic" literature at all, but something else altogether. But, that, indeed, is the vital question here: just what is "Arabic" in that extended, influential and much lamented historical moment? And isn't a great deal of what is lamented, what provokes the extraordinary and almost universal nostalgia for an Andalus that from the start was partially imaginary, rooted in its being a summary of the varieties of exile that explicitly leaves "nations" by the wayside? And is the literary culture and history of al-Andalus, even if we were to leave aside the question of its enduring nostalgia, really usefully understood in the single-language terms of modern national paradigms?

These are some of the arguments in progress that are the backbone of this volume, and they will arise again and again, implictly and explicitly. They cry out for further attention here – but not exactly here. These are matters probably better understood if we leave our mirador overlooking Granada, here where we listen to the waters of the melted snows of the Sierra Nevada – and take them up again in a different rocky citadel, in that city that (among other things) was once the benefactor to Europe of all that was Arabic.

TOLEDO

"One day I was in the Alcaná at Toledo, when a lad came to sell some parchments and old papers to a silk merchant . . . and [I] saw in it characters which I recognized as Arabic. But though I could recognize them I could not read them, and I looked around to see if there was not some Morisco about, to read them to me . . . I pressed him to read the beginning, and when he did so, making an extempore translation from Arabic to Castilian, he said that the heading was: History of Don Quixote de la Mancha, written by Cide Hamete Benengeli, Arabic historian . . . I then went off with the Morisco into the cloister of the cathedral, and asked him to translate for me into Castilian everything in those books that dealt with Don Quixote . . . I took him to my house, and there in little more than six weeks he translated it all just as it is set down here."

(from Miguel de Cervantes, *El Ingenioso Hidalgo Don Quixote de la Mancha*, pt. 1, chap. 9, trans. as *Don Quixote* by J. M. Cohen)

There are a handful of remaining instances of Arabic writing to be seen today in Toledo, and like the tattered manuscript that Cervantes's narrator finds in the old Jewish quarters of the city, they tell us a great deal about the complexities of "Arabic" here. One of the earliest is in the church that sits at the highest point of the citadel city of Toledo. When you enter San Román, which in recent years has been designated the Museum of Visigothic Culture, you are certainly bound to believe that this, like a number of other churches in Spain, was once a mosque, one of those mosques that in turn may itself have once been a Visigothic church and then readapted for Christian worship a second time, after the Reconquest. (And indeed, not far from San Román, at one of the city's gates, there is just such a place: the small "Cristo de la Luz" was, until the end of the twelfth century, the mosque of Bāb al-Mardūm, built on the ruins of a Visigothic church.) The interior of San Román is redolent of all the architectural features that those of us who are not experts would assume are, indeed, the traces of a mosque: the distinctive horseshoe arches, for example, and even, most eye-catching of all, fine Arabic script around all the window niches. But on closer inspection it turns out the Arabic writing is fake – and that this building was not only never a mosque but was built as the Church to commemorate the *defeat* of the Muslims in 1085.[6] It is, of course, quite remarkable that this Catholic church should be adorned in the unambiguous style of the culture whose defeat it is meant to memorialize, and that it highlights that simulacrum of Arabic writing, as if in uncanny anticipation of the sixteenth-century "secret language" that is the "Aljamiado" of the Moriscos evoked in Cervantes's Toledan scene. But no less remarkable is the fact that the most spectacular of the four surviving synagogues of Spain is decorated with something in and of itself the real thing but in a context that is, to say the least, unexpected: the Toledan synagogue now called El Tránsito, built in 1360 in resplendent echoes of the Alhambra, just then being finished, includes real Arabic, along with Hebrew, integrated into the complex stucco ornamentation. And not just any Arabic, nor even some bits of the considerable body of Jewish writing done in Arabic in al-Andalus, but lines from the Qur'an itself.

Within an academic universe that would want to define Arabic in certain ways neither of these examples really counts, of course, although for different reasons – and they are in any case manifestly not the same Arabic as the abundant inscriptions in the Alhambra proper, which include, famously, a classical qasida by Ibn Zamrak, as well as the obsessively repeated "wa-lā ghālib illā-allāh" (There is no conqueror but God). And yet, a clean and neat definition of Arabic here would, ironically, severely diminish our appreciation of the extraordinary cultural dominance of what some have suggested might be better called "Arabicate" – a term that is technically appropriate but has, in fact, never acquired widespread acceptance, perhaps because of how inelegant it sounds. To define Arabic *strictu sensu* to mean only that which is Islamic (which is a not uncommon way of defining "Arabic" in the Spanish context) or, as many Arabists might, as what was redacted according to normative models of "classicism," that is, as contemporary grammarians or other arbiters of high culture did – or for that matter as the religious-cultural purists such as the Almohads often did – is to end up occluding the suppleness of Andalusi-Arabic culture. And by "suppleness" here we mean an openness and flexibility that permeates all aspects of its relationship with "other" cultures: itself hungrily adoptive and adaptive, it also ends up wearing its own style, even at its most dominant and arrogant, in a way that is attractive, and thus influential, even in circumstances where one might imagine ideology to hold sway. It is that suppleness that did indeed lead to things such as the simulated Arabic around the windows of San Román, and the Qurʾanic verses on the walls of that most lavish synagogue of Christian Spain – and to Cervantes's conceit about the found manuscript that is the true story of the Quixote. These are all things that once al-Andalus was gone became and remained largely unintelligible – as Cervantes said, I could recognize them but could not read them – at least in part because we have defined the languages and literatures we study aligning them along either modern national lines or religious lines, neither of which can end up accounting for so much of what is characteristically Andalusian.

In this volume we have explicitly rejected the sort of orthodox definition of "Arabic" that would leave a reader – whether he is an Arabist specializing in Baghdadi poetry or a Latin Americanist interested in the cultural admixtures in which Spanish has been involved – still unenlightened, at the end of the day, on the question of the various "Arabic" inscriptions he will find on a visit to Toledo. The reader of this volume will come away with an appreciation of a range of Andalusi qualities, and of the remarkable combination of unrivaled ascendance and elasticity of Arabic at that time and place. A crucial part of this history is that of the Jewish communities of al-Andalus whose absorption of Arabic culture was so intimate that it fundamentally redefined their own relationship to Hebrew – which is in the end what makes intelligible the use of the Qurʾanic inscriptions on the walls of the synagogue built by Samuel Halevi Abulafia in Toledo – remarkable also because it takes place not in a city in al-Andalus proper, but about three hundred years after that city was no longer ruled by Muslims – and was in fact the capital of what history records as the enemy, Castile. Three hundred years begins to suggest the variety of ways in which cultural styles – in literature, mostly, but also in closely related areas such as music and architecture – flourished in modes that did not align themselves properly along political or religious frontiers. This Arabic was so expansive and inclusionary, often balancing carefully its relationship with the East – so utterly successful in its cultural imperialism, we are tempted to say – that it fully accounts for the phenomenon of a church built in that special imitation Arabic style (which we call Mudejar) to commemorate a crucial victory in what will be later called the Reconquest of Spain.

Using the word "Spain" here reminds us that Arabic is only one of many terms defined with difficulty, and indeed much of the nomenclature we must employ, and that all of our authors have had to employ throughout this volume, is imprecise or controversial, or simply reveals the vexed nature of identities here. How to refer to the geographical area itself? Hispania (the name inherited from antiquity) meant, for Christians, all the peninsula, and included the Muslim-occupied lands; while for the Arab historians its equivalent, Ishbaniya, was usually applied only to Christian Spain. Al-Andalus, for the Arabs, similarly could encompass either the whole peninsula or only the portion under Muslim rule. The common phrase "Arab" (or "Islamic") Spain seems to many undesirable, with its suggestion that there was a permanent, European "Spain" that has existed from Roman to modern times and that, incidentally, for some centuries, was ruled by Arabs. This Eurocentric view might be countered with equal validity by an Eastern one: al-Andalus was as embedded in the Arab/Islamic world as a country like Tunisia is today, but happened to separate from it earlier, and this view has obviously been the backdrop for the sort of poetry represented by the famous *Sīniyya* (Poem in S) of the Egyptian poet Aḥmad Shawqī.

But the name of the place itself is but the beginning of the terminological and nomenclature problems. To look closely and grapple with these difficulties of naming is instructive, however, precisely because we can see complexities that all too often are occluded by the facile or relatively unnuanced understanding of certain terms. Thus, for example, a term such as "Moor" or "Moorish" has acquired (among other things) a racial veneer that is quite misleading, and that in fact can easily play into a racist vision of interconfessional relations in al-Andalus, where it is imagined (for example) that the Muslims of premodern Spain were a racially distinct people. And yet it could also continue to be used as the word that authentically represents the original term to designate those Berber settlers from Mauritania, the Roman name for what we now call Morocco. The Spanish equivalent, *moro*, can also play this ambiguous or paradoxical role: used to designate, sometimes pejoratively, and almost always with appropriate vagueness, that "other" that was not Christian and was not Jewish, it clearly includes other aspects of identity – language and culture, for example – suggesting that there was more at stake than just religion.[7]

This is of course true, and it is precisely that messy admixture of ethnicities and linguistic communities and cultural traditions and even religion that we mean to cover here with the term "Arabic." After all, in al-Andalus we see a full range of communities and individuals, and not only Muslims, whose language is Arabic. And whether it is merely the maternal tongue or it is accompanied by a full command of all its literature (from philosophy to poetry and back) is of course more likely to be a function of class and education than it is of religion, let alone ethnic group. From the Mozarabs, those Arabized Christians who had to have their Bibles translated into Arabic, to the Jews of Granada, who helped establish the site of the Alhambra as a place for memorializing Syrian Umayyad culture in an exile at least twice removed, to the variety of post-Reconquest upper-crust Christians for whom it was as necessary a part of their cultural baggage to be able to read philosophy, these are all members of a community of Arabic language and culture first in al-Andalus and then in what will become Spain.

The anchors of that community are, unambiguously, the Muslims who maintained a complex and usually vital relationship with the East, and with the Arabo-Islamic culture of the heartland, taking and contributing, respecting and surpassing. The extraordinary vitality of that culture, in fact, in some measure explains its widespread prestige as a language and its texts – whether those texts are written or architectural or musical – and thus helps account for the whole range of converts that came to make up the Muslim community of al-Andalus. This community, among whom many would proudly and exaggeratedly or even falsely claim noble Arabian ancestry, included everything from the first-generation children of Berber settlers and Romanized or Visigothic women to descendants of Jewish and Christian converts to newly arrived Syrians in exile – to a half dozen other permutations. And that is while we are still talking about Muslims proper, before we get to the complex societies of observant Christians and Jews who are a part of the Arabicate community without being Muslims.

The editors of this volume believe that the brilliance of that civilization, not to speak of its enduring legacy – this a term much bandied about in discussions of al-Andalus – are far better understood when the larger and much messier understanding of Arabic is used, rather than the neater and narrower one that prevails in so many discussions and, indeed, in the canonical curricula. But it is also the case that within that traditionally defined framework of Arabic studies al-Andalus has, until recently, been a very poor cousin, despite the special nostalgic place it enjoys. In the curriculum of Middle Eastern Studies it has never been a fundamental requirement, to say the least, and one could read through any number of literary histories and easily get the sense that it is as if it were written from the Abbasid perspective after 750 – as if those renegade Umayyads had simply gone off and done their rebellious thing way out in the Wild West and only when what they wrote looks pretty much just like what was written in Baghdad is it part of the real Arabic universe.[8]

Of course, other fellow Arabists will argue, correctly, that the case of al-Andalus is far from unique and that in fact the sort of cultural adaptations and fluidity that have just been described are, or were, virtually universally true in the creation and expansion of all instances of Arabo-Islamic culture, from that in the Arabian peninsula itself to what one can still see in Iran or Pakistan. But it strikes us that this is an argument to be used to favor the writing of more literary histories that would emphasize this cultural fluidity, rather than, as is normally the case, the essential and classical Arabicness of Arabic literature. The premises of this volume are not necessarily arguments for the uniqueness, in this regard, of Arabicate culture in that place we now call Spain – although one has to wonder if that is not at times the veiled, or unarticulated, argument that explains why al-Andalus is an extraordinarily important locus of nostalgia for a certain Arabic past, and has always been, at least since the days of al-Maqqarī, the extraordinary seventeenth-century historian. More simply, we argue merely that something like *convivencia* was self-evidently the cultural case in al-Andalus, and that a literary history of that place can be neat in its dividing lines only at very high costs.

Convivencia is of course one of those much contested and vexed terms that does have to do with al-Andalus and Spain in particular, and like its equally vexed counterpart, *reconquista*, perhaps it is only problematic if we insist on some sort of uniformity and neatness, if we persist, despite our own likely observations of human nature, in expecting consistencies and purities of any sort. This is where the wonderful examples of Toledo's varieties of Arabic writing can illuminate the necessary contradictions involved: the creation, the very cause for the creation, of a church like San Román proves that from certain perspectives – the military, the religious-ideological – a Reconquest did indeed exist and in the end prevail. At the same time, the very style, the very aesthetics of the Church, proves prima facie the vitality of Castro's much debated *convivencia* – which literally means nothing more than "living together" but which of course has come to imply a certain level of cultural commingling that most people assume must be based on a certain level of religious tolerance.

But the Church of San Román is decorated with horseshoe arches and with the suggestion of Arabic writing around all the windows precisely because *convivencia* and *reconquista* could and did exist side by side, at the same time, in the same place. The conceptual error that has plagued all sides of the study of what some call medieval Spain, and others al-Andalus, and yet others Sefarad (and sometimes these are identical and sometimes they overlap in part and sometimes they are at opposite ends), is the assumption that these phenomena, reconquest and convivencia, are thoroughgoing and thus mutually exclusive – that, to put it directly to the example, those whose commitment to the military and religious victory of Christian state over Muslim state in Toledo would not be building a monument to that victory that said loudly and clearly that the culture of the vanquished was superior to, or perhaps indistinguishable from, their own. And yet that is exactly what happened.

San Román is far from a unique case: one need only wander the streets of Toledo with eyes open to the necessary contradictions to see the other examples in this city that will in fact cultivate Arabic far more after the Reconquest than before, and where the large and important Arabized Christian population, the Mozarabs, will feel more culturally persecuted in the aftermath of the accession to power of their coreligionists than they did under the rule of their coculturalists. All categories here are nothing more than arguments in progress, and this volume is dedicated to deepening the arguments rather than to eliminating them. It is thus that the reader will find here, alongside Andalusians with unimpeachable "classical" credentials – Ibn Ḥazm and Ibn Zaydūn and Ibn al-Khaṭīb – portraits of complex individuals such as Ramon Llull and Petrus Alfonsi, in their own ways not unlike the horseshoe arches of San Román.

This is the universe, not the nation, of Arabic in al-Andalus. And it is a universe so powerful that even after it is officially gone, banished, it manages to speak from time to time, and we have felt that this volume should also make some attempt to hear those voices that are among the most difficult to hear and yet speak so eloquently to the tenacity of that cultural memory. Like the raggedy manuscript that Cervantes's narrator finds in the Alcaná, about to be sold to the silk merchant, these are sometimes only the sad tatters of what had once been the most valued manuscripts in the civilized world. Cervantes's novel, it must be understood, was published in 1605, a century after the surrender of Granada and the beginnings of the forcible conversions that would make "Moriscos" out of the Muslims who chose to stay – and just a few years before the forcible expulsions of the Moriscos in 1609. What had once been the revered language of knowledge and the marker of the very best stylistic achievements in all the arts – in a universe in which taste and knowledge could and often were assiduously cultivated independently of religious belief or political circumstances – was now incomprehensible even to the Moriscos themselves. Despite their persecution, these forcibly converted Muslims kept writing in the Arabic script, but now as the vehicle for their native language, a form of Romance. They kept the alphabet, but Arabic itself they barely knew. Like the Sephardim, the Jews expelled shortly after the surrender of Granada, the Moriscos are testimony to the extraordinary memory of al-Andalus – even for those who never knew it.

There is a long list of ironies in the fact that, for many well-read individuals, including many of our colleagues in the study of the literatures of the West, that pivotal scene in the Quixote, certainly among the most canonical and oft-read texts of European literature, provides the only experience of seeing – and thus "reading" – Arabic. One of the various poignancies of this scene is how powerfully it suggests the way in which the Arabic universe of al-Andalus, once at the heart of many aspects of European culture in the Middle Ages, will be so driven from the consciousness of European history that only specialists will be able to read its texts and cultivate its memory. This volume contains few essays of the now traditional sort on the "legacy" or "influence" of al-Andalus on the rest of medieval Europe. Instead, we attempt to redress the problem by defining this Andalusi-Arabic universe in ways where Arabic is not easily separable from other strands of medieval culture, where it is often a part of a tight weave – as opposed to a proposed foreign "influence" – and by making the whole of the cloth expressly accessible to those who, like Cervantes's narrator, might recognize the language but not be able to read it.

CÓRDOBA

> Shrine of the lovers of art! Visible power of the Faith!
> Sacred as Mecca you made, once, Andalusia's soil.
> If there is under these skies loveliness equal to yours,
> Only in Muslim hearts, nowhere else can it be.
> Ah, those proud cavaliers, champions Arabia sent forth
> Pledged to the splendid Way, knights of the truth and the creed!
> Through their empire a strange secret was understood:
> Friends of mankind hold sway not to command but to serve.
> Europe and Asia from them gathered instruction: the West
> Lay in darkness, and their wisdom discovered the path . . .
> Even to-day in its breeze fragrance of Yemen still floats,
> Even to-day in its songs echoes live on of Hejaz.
>
> (from Muḥammad Iqbal, "The Mosque of Córdoba," trans. V. G. Kiernan)

By the banks of the Guadalquivir, that wide and muddy river, the young prince found refuge from the brutal and vengeful violence of the Abbasids that had ended the Umayyad caliphate of his ancestors. He was a grandson of Caliph Hishām, but also the son of a Berber woman, so when he fled Syria heading west, and to the far west, he was heading to his mother's land. ʿAbd al-Raḥmān would be exiled here, forever, in this al-Andalus that was at that point hardly more than an extension of his mother's lands, across the straits of Gibraltar, not so long before decisively crossed by the Ṭāriq who had given the mountainlike rock his name. And up the river a way, by the banks of the Guadalquivir, the half-Syrian, half-Berber Andalusian, and his sons, and his sons' sons, would always still remember the river Euphrates, and would create a culture in exile that was always part heartbreaking yearning for Damascus, for that land of palm trees forever left behind.

But this culture was also always part rivalry with the Abbasid Baghdad that had destroyed their family – and from the outset, from the beginnings of his building what would become the Great Mosque, ʿAbd al-Raḥmān appears to have understood that combining nostalgia with scrappiness could create something that was in part a memory, or the evocation of a memory, but also the dream of a distinctive and overwhelming future. And so it is that this most memorable mosque is in part the comforting allusion to the Umayyad mosques of Damascus and Jerusalem, and in part the very definition of this new time and place, a dream of a future time when it will be the marker of triumph in exile, which needs to become a place that rivals the home to which one cannot return. It is in these delicately balanced visions – of past and future, of East and West, of old power and new claims – of the exiled ʿAbd al-Raḥmān I and his successors that we can see the fundamental architecture of Andalusi culture: that fine Umayyad equilibrium between a powerful belief in the most traditional legitimacy, and those audacities of the self-made transplants that would allow them to build as if they were themselves the center of the universe.

And this is why, finally, there is no more distinctively Andalusi a sight than those unforgettable rows upon rows of superimposed horseshoe arches, with those never-boring alternating red brick and white stone voussoirs: part that almost overwhelming nostalgia that is present at the beginning, as well as at the end, and part the brilliant putting together in altogether more audacious ways the materials lying about in this new place. These conjunctions, along with its continuous expansions, which eventually made it the largest medieval mosque, so canonically defined the very essence of the mosque in the West that even today it is visited, and mostly seen and understood, as the Great Mosque, despite the vast Renaissance cathedral that has sat at its very center since the sixteenth century, and despite the barely noticed fact that it is still the working cathedral of the Catholic city of Córdoba, where masses are said daily.[9]

In the planning of this volume there was no greater challenge than finding some architectural structure for it that in some way echoed the complexity of this culture, that layered complexity that is nowhere better seen than in the monumental Great Mosque, where memory, invention, palimpsests, and borrowings all interlock. Even at the miniature and self-evidently minor level of a volume of literary history, it is no mean feat to face the challenges posed by depicting a part of the culture that has produced that particular kind of monument, to figure out how to balance tradition and authority, the measures of the sort of cultural continuities and values that make literary histories worth reading, with the sort of innovation that would in some measure reflect the heterodox definition of the field we have sketched out. The genre of literary history has, of course, no fixed forms but it certainly has canonical expectations and, far worse, formal limitations. It was clear early on that it was easier to imagine the sort of substantive innovations already discussed – defining "Arabic" in expansive and untraditional ways, and writing for a public wider than our own specialist colleagues – than to define concretely the basic forms that such a literary history might take.

The many competing demands on a literary historian include (but are scarcely limited to) chronological narrative, individual authors, salient genres, and, in our own volume, considerations of other linguistic and cultural affiliations. In the end what was clearest was that no single taxonomy would do – and so, at the end of the day, we insist on varied shapes, differently angled perspectives, for each of the four major sections of the book. None of these points of departure has transcendent authority or primacy, although we would argue strenuously that some are, indeed, vital for the realization of any Andalusian portrait. And the whole is in part painstakingly engineered – and also partly serendipitous and dependent on everything from the well-understood limitations of time and space to the even more uncontrollable vagaries of who might be available to write on a given subject during a given year. Every path taken is, self-evidently, a path not taken, and it is perhaps especially the editors, intimately familiar with so many of the vast range of possible subjects and perspectives on so complex a subject, who fantasize about other possibilities. We fondly call these our "shadow volumes," and to these I will return.

But first to the volume actually in hand. The first section, "The Shapes of Culture," approaches in a thematic way the sorts of materials that are, *grosso modo*, introductory and meant to give some global sense of salient cultural features. These are cross-sections of topics that are not necessarily canonical features of a literary history and yet they seem indispensable as foundational pieces of the puzzle, or at least of this puzzle. We wanted to engineer the section so that it would be informatively introductory to Andalusian culture, and to the rest of our volume, for both the Arabist and the non-Arabist. The distribution of these opening visions is necessarily quite varied: the "Love" and "Knowledge" sections may better serve the nonspecialist, providing some distinctive fundamentals of Arabic culture in general and its ties to Andalusi writing specifically, for those who approach al-Andalus from somewhere else in Europe. "Language" and "Spaces," in contrast, will open up largely unknown vistas onto the details of Andalusi exceptionalism and thus be of at least equal interest to Arabists, whereas "Music" is relatively equal portions of both. But all the subjects here are foundational, and we see these components as the columns – as different from each other as the Roman spolia that are the building blocks of the earliest section of the Great Mosque – on which so much of the literature of the society leans (*Language, *Spaces) and which can also be seen as surrounding it, and thus casting varied light and shadows on it, defining how it is heard and understood (*Knowledge, *Music, *Love). (Use of an asterisk [*] indicates a cross-reference to another essay in this volume.)

In "The Shapes of Literature" three genres receive pointed and detailed attention. A particular kind of challenge in organization and balance for a volume like this is posed by the primacy of poetry as the literary genre par excellence in Arabic. Poetry bears a kind of cultural centrality that makes it a part of the everyday texture of societies and histories in a way not necessarily immediately familiar to those nourished in other cultures, especially in the modern age, and that makes it altogether possible, and even reasonable, to imagine a volume such as this into which nothing other than poetry managed to find its way. Yet the very centrality of poetry guarantees that it is not isolated, and suggests that in writing its history it is important to buttress the ubiquity of poetry, and of certain poetic genres especially, with the reflections of poetry in other spheres. In this section, as a focused section that can give a detailed taste of specific and exemplary forms, we end up running the gamut from the quintessentially Andalusian (and exceptionally controversial) muwashshah, which was always of dubious canonical standing, to the unimpeachably classical qasida. The maqama shares elements of both kinds of status, as well as a complex intertwining with the Hebrew tradition.

But these and other kinds of poetry, as well as other kinds of writing, appear and reappear through the rather different prism of authorship in the "Andalusians" section. The vantage point provided by biography is distinctly contrapunctal to the more formal, generic vision of the previous section: the individual figures, the Andalusians, we have chosen are arranged in chronological order, and every effort has been made to locate them in their historical moment, as well as to display the characteristic way in which that individual contributes to the overall cultural texture of his moment. As in all other sections there is a conscious effort to balance the expected (Ibn Ḥazm) with the unexpected (Moses Ibn Ezra), but here more than anywhere else we faced the painful decision of setting aside some individuals of such overwhelming importance (Ibn Rushd) that they are exceptionally well known to all Arabists and who, unlike others we have included, have been written about extensively for the nonspecialist as well.

Our excursus "To Sicily" is itself structured as a miniature of the whole of the volume, with three essays each looking at Siculo-Arabic culture from a different formal vantage point. This small taste of this different European outpost of Arabicate culture reveals the ways in which al-Andalus is a powerful and shaping cultural icon within Europe and indeed throughout the western Mediterranean, even in the thirteenth century, when it was being cornered into the lone outpost of Granada. The starkly mixed iconography of

Sicilian culture also serves as an offshore prelude for the final section of this volume, "Marriages and Exiles."

Here the perspective provided on the Arabic culture of al-Andalus is the special and often bittersweet one of groups with ambiguous and yet substantial and influential relations with the dominant classical culture. These are not only different iterations of what was the extraordinarily ample Arabicate culture of the peninsula, but also varied tokens of memories that confirm and complement the "official" nostalgia of the classical histories from al-Maqqarī on. From the Mozarabs who resist Islam and yet embrace Arabic – and who in a city like Toledo would be the guarantors of both the most traditional Latin-Christian rite and Arabic as the visual and verbal language of high culture – to the Sephardim who will jealously guard crucial literary memories of the Spain of the three religions in an oral tradition still in direct contact with pre-1492 Spain, these are important witnesses to a remarkable chapter of Arabic cultural and literary history.

Many of the obvious and even not so obvious limitations of this book are in some measure authorized, or at least compensated for, by the existence of other books that cover that ground, and we gratefully acknowledge our indebtedness to those different resources, both for what they have taught us and for serving as work to which our own readers should also turn. Each essay that follows is accompanied by its own bibliography of essential resources for that subject, of course, but beyond that several books require special notice. The first is certainly the encyclopedic *Legacy of Muslim Spain* (Leiden, 1992), which defines its subject so indefatigably that the reader can turn to it for articles on dozens of subjects complementary to literary culture: a detailed political history, pieces on economic history, calligraphy, even culinary culture – and much, much else besides. Moreover, and most importantly, the volume is graced with several extensive essays on Arabic poetry, written by the editor and brilliant critic of Arabic poetry, Salma Jayyusi, and they provide a vision of al-Andalus and its poetry as essentially unaffected by the cohabitation with the other languages and cultures, no doubt a salutary counterpoint to our perspective.

In contrast, *Al-Andalus: The Art of Islamic Spain* (New York, 1992), edited by Jerrilynn D. Dodds, although it has a different material focus (art and architecture), offers a reading of the complex relationships among the various cultures that is virtually identical to our own. This lavishly illustrated catalog of a major exhibit, shown both in Spain and in the United States, provides not only a range of direct visual reinforcement of points made less directly with reference to nonvisual texts in this volume but also a theoretical and historical vision of cultural interaction that is far less constrained than literary studies tend to be by the demarcations of national languages. Finally, even though it deals only with the period from 1250 to 1500, L. P. Harvey's *Islamic Spain* (Chicago, 1990) is a model of a history that, via its focus on Muslims on either side of the political divide, captures a great deal of that complexity of a territory that was part geographic and part cultural.

These are, of course, books we don't need to wish we had created, but there are others we do wish we could have created as well – and in the perfect world our own volume would include its shadow, as well as itself. Some subjects and focuses are missing, for a range of different pragmatic reasons, even though they were originally planned: "The Shapes of Culture" section, for example, was to have had an essay on religion, which would have been an obvious way, although not the only available one, to focus explicitly on the cultural interaction we see in other spheres; in the end, its place was taken, in effect, by the final section, "Marriages and Exiles." "Andalusians" was to have included a portrait of Alfonso the Wise, who presided over so much of the translation of Arabic, but instead we included a portrait of the peripatetic and influential translator Michael Scot in the section on Sicily, so we see translation through the prism of a translator and from a less Toledan perspective. These are but two of a number of cases where practical circumstances forced us to rethink essentially abstract plans – and in all of these cases although we regret what we lost (or what we never had) the alternatives have ended up being rich and now indispensable parts of the volume.

There are also possible vantage points we might well have chosen but did not simply because every type of mirador cannot (and perhaps should not) be accommodated in any finite volume, any more than in any given building. Whole categories – historical writing, literary criticism, and philosophical traditions – potentially legitimate and revealing places from which to contemplate aspects of poetry in al-Andalus – are now only glancingly glimpsed instead. One might even, for example, have provided a series of other medieval perspectives of al-Andalus from a wide arc that would take a reader from Baghdad when the early Abbasids first contemplated the Umayyad emirate of Córdoba, on to Paris when Ibn Rushd's work is banned, and then back east to Alexandria and Cairo when Judah Halevi arrives performing the chic Andalusian muwashshahs. Or there would be the range of perspectives given by looking at some of the special historians whose work was dedicated to cultivating the memory of al-Andalus, from al-Maqqarī to Washington Irving. Or using the cities of al-Andalus, perhaps arranged in chronological order or even (in the tradition of some Arabic historiography) in backward chronological order. Or . . . Self-evidently, these are the trade-offs that lie at the heart of this kind of book-building project: whether, for example, the sort of philosophy and literary criticism written by Ibn ʿArabī or by Ibn Ḥazm is going to end up being revealed via the portraits of those individuals, or instead as part of an essay or a group of essays on philosophy and literary criticism or instead, yet again, inside a detailed portrait of Murcia in the thirteenth century or Córdoba in the years after the collapse of the caliphate. We detail all of these omissions and fantasies – and this is certainly not a full inventory, even by our own reckoning – not out of anything like regret or apology for the volume at hand but, on the contrary, to suggest the untapped richness of a subject that, like all other great subjects in literature and history, can only begin to be appreciated after reading extensive and varied, even contradictory, accounts. The more one reads and sees and hears the more one is intrigued and even mystified by this extraordinary moment in the cultural and literary history of the Arabic-speaking people.

The editors gratefully acknowledge the following funds and organizations for the ongoing and generous support that have made the preparation of this volume possible: the research funds from the Provost's office of Yale University, with very special thanks to Deputy Provost Charles Long; the Maxwell and Fannie E. Abbell Publication Fund of the Jewish Theological Seminary of America; the Haverford College Faculty and Research Fund; and the Guggenheim Foundation.

Among the clichés of book acknowledgments it may be that the most overused is the one that begins "This book could not have been written without . . ." But in this case the quite literal truth is that without the ongoing editorial participation of Kim Mrazek Hastings nothing resembling this book would exist. The editors are deeply indebted for her unmatched organizational and editorial skills, and perhaps even more for the pleasure and comfort of her company during most of the years devoted to this project.

NOTES

The author gratefully acknowledges the many discussions, and especially the occasional vigorous disagreements, on these subjects with three precious interlocutors: Jerrilynn D. Dodds, Dimitri Gutas, and F. E. Peters. And despite the single authorship of this essay, its every premise, and indeed its very existence, are the products of the exceptional and always happy collaboration with fellow editors Raymond P. Scheindlin and Michael Sells.

1 The recent translation of Samuel the Nagid's poetry by Peter Cole (Princeton, 1996) has brought some degree of mainstream attention to the extraordinary life and times and work of many Jews living in Islamic Spain. On the Nagid's family and Jewish involvement in the early stages of building the Alhambra, see the relevant essays in Jerrilynn D. Dodds, ed., *Al-Andalus: The Art of Islamic Spain* (New York, 1992).

2 The historical relationship of the Ibn Gabirol poem to the (disappeared) eleventh-century palace, and especially the historicity of the description of the fountain famously proposed by Frederick Bargebuhr in *The Alhambra: A Cycle of Studies on the Eleventh Century in Moorish Spain* (Berlin, 1968) is refuted by Raymond P. Scheindlin in "El poema de Ibn Gabirol y la fuente del Patio de los Leones," *Cuadernos de la Alhambra* 29–30 (1993–94): 185–89. For a detailed literary discussion of the poem itself, see also his "Poet and Patron: Ibn Gabirol's Palace Poem," *Prooftexts* 16 (1996): 31–47. The relationship of a variety of lyrical writings to the palaces themselves is brilliantly (and accessibly, for the nonspecialist) laid out by Oleg Grabar in *The Alhambra*, 2nd edn. (Sebastopol, Calif., 1992). See especially from page 99 on for the questions related to the Fountain of the Lions and the shared Jewish–Muslim image of Solomon as a near-magical king.

3 This, after all, was the land of the Cid, a historical figure reasonably well-documented by both Arab and Christian sources, who in the context of nineteenth-century Spanish nationalist ideology becomes one of the foundational figures of emergent modern Spain, in the popular imagination because of his efforts in the Reconquest. And yet, in both historical documentation as well as in the surviving epic poem celebrating his life and deeds, there is no attempt to hide the fact that he is a crucial ally to Andalusian Muslims against the Almoravid Berbers, that he is eventually ruler of a Muslim Valencia, and that his name is an Arabic honorific. See Richard Fletcher, *The Quest for El Cid* (New York, 1990), for a delightful and multidimensional narration of the complex history of the Cid and his times, a portrait that succeeds better than many broader histories in conveying the tangle of political and cultural filiations.

4 The introduction by N. J. Dawood to the Franz Rosenthal translation of the *Muqqadima* (Princeton, 1967) provides a brief but useful recounting of Ibn Khaldūn's trip to Granada in 1364: "In 1364 Ibn Khaldūn was put in charge of a mission sent to Pedro the Cruel, King of Castilla, with the object of ratifying a peace treaty between Castilla and the Arabs. He thus had an opportunity to visit Sevilla, the city of his ancestors. Pedro honored him highly and offered to take him into his service and to restore to him his family's former property, but Ibn Khaldūn declined" (viii).

5 The omnipresent nostalgia provoked by al-Andalus is wonderfully summarized by Robert Irwin in his review essay of *The Legacy of Muslim Spain* (*Times Literary Supplement*, 13 August 1993).

6 These details of the history of San Román are virtually impossible for any layman to ascertain, despite the monument's relative prominence; they are occluded in all guidebooks and general introductions to the monuments of the city, as well as in the official Toledan literature about the decommissioned church. I am indebted to my ever-generous teacher in these matters, Jerrilynn Dodds, for telling me the history of San Román and pointing me in the right direction in many related matters.

7 Among others, see the complementary discussion of these issues in the introductory remarks (9–10 esp.) by Richard Fletcher, in his *Moorish Spain* (Berkeley, 1992), a term he uses interchangeably with Muslim Spain and Islamic Spain,

rightly pointing out the pitfalls of believing any term is precise or could possibly be used uniformly. A comparison to the titles and nomenclature of two other basic books of this same vintage proves the point: Hugh Kennedy, *Muslim Spain and Portugal* (New York, 1996), and L. P. Harvey, *Islamic Spain, 1250–1500* (Chicago, 1990). (I have also profited from the delightful discussion of the history of the "Moor" terminology by Ross Brann, in "Andalusian Moorings," forthcoming in *Diaspora.*) Finally, of course, the often thorny terminological and "identity" issues as they affect the question of "Arab" and "Arabic" and "Islamic" are far from limited to the Andalusian sphere. See Dimitri Gutas, *Greek Thought, Arabic Culture* (Routledge, 1998), for a series of detailed discussions of the problem as it crystallizes in Abbasid Baghdad and through the translation movement, and especially the trenchant statements on page 191.

8 The relatively scant notice paid to al-Andalus in Albert Hourani's outstanding *History of the Arab Peoples* (Cambridge, 1991) is telling and reflects the inherent difficulties of assimilating the Andalusian chapter into the larger narrative of the Arab peoples, as per Hourani's almost Churchillian title. Salma Khadra Jayyusi, the editor of the vast *Legacy of Muslim Spain* (Leiden, 1992), devotes her several lengthy essays on Andalusi poetry in the volume to substantiating the clearly circular premise that the real canonical poetry was utterly unaffected by any aspect of its multicultural environment – and that the poetry that shows innovations and variations vis-à-vis the Eastern forms is not "formal" enough to be considered canonical (317–26). More problematic yet is her quick review, in these same pages, of the body of scholarship by Andalusianists on the subject, a discussion prefaced by her unfortunate and yet telling dubbing of this group as "non-Arab literary historians."

9 The remarkably layered history of the Great Mosque is told in illuminating detail and from a variety of perspectives in Jerrilynn D. Dodds, "The Great Mosque of Córdoba," *Al-Andalus: The Art of Islamic Spain*, ed. Dodds, 11–25; and in Robert Hillenbrand, "'The Ornament of the World': Medieval Córdoba as a Cultural Center," *The Legacy of Muslim Spain,* ed. Jayyusi, 112–35.

MADĪNAT AL-ZAHRĀ' AND THE UMAYYAD PALACE

D. F. Ruggles

A palm tree stands in the middle of Ruṣāfa,
born in the West, far from the land of palms.
I said to it: "How like me you are, far away and in exile,
in long separation from family and friends.
You have sprung from soil in which you are a stranger;
and I, like you, am far from home."

* * *

The power of this verse, establishing ʿAbd al-Raḥmān's roots in Syria and his success in al-Andalus, has reached subsequent historians, generations of whom have repeated the poem as proof of an ideological and cultural bridge between Syria and the Iberian Peninsula. It reminds us that the first emir of al-Andalus named his palace outside Córdoba for Ruṣāfa, the estate in Syria where he had spent his youth, and thus links the masculine enterprises of palace building and empire building.

The Umayyads of Córdoba were genetically and culturally the progeny of Muslim Arab fathers. Through a variety of visual and performative signs, they presented themselves entirely as Arab and Muslim, the sons of a pure, uncomplicated patriarchal genealogy. But their mothers were for the most part Christian, often of slave origin or won in diplomatic exchanges. The world of the chroniclers, imams, calligraphers, and architects was peopled largely by men – but family life, where the children were reared until daughters were sent in marriage and sons stepped into the public eye, was ruled by women. Nowhere were the intimate ties binding the ethnic and religious groups that comprised

1 Madīnat al-Zahrā', view into the Salón Rico

Andalusian culture more evident and more profound than in the domestic arena of the harem. The emirs, caliphs, and sultans who ruled al-Andalus grew up in the secluded family quarters of the royal palaces such as Madīnat al-Zahrāʾ in tenth-century Córdoba. Living among women and his younger brothers, the future ruler regularly observed Christian rituals, heard stories and ballads from Castile, León, Catalonia, and France, and moved in an architecture whose syntax and vocabulary was as intrinsic to his mother's heritage as to his father's. He was thus steeped in the true culture of al-Andalus: heterodox and multiethnic.

The walled palatine city of Madīnat al-Zahrāʾ consisted of residences, reception halls, barracks, mosques, baths, workshops, kitchens, gardens, a zoo, an aviary, and pools stocked with fish. Construction began in 325/936 (or 329/940–41), and lasted for decades under both ʿAbd al-Raḥmān III and al-Ḥakam II. ʿAbd al-Raḥmān personally supervised the initial planning and construction and became so engrossed in it that he missed prayer for three consecutive Fridays, provoking public criticism from the qadi of Córdoba.

The palace city was on one level a statement concerning Umayyad power, but it was also built in the classical, Mediterranean architectural vocabulary of the Iberian Peninsula, one shared by a dozen divergent ethnic and religious groups, a truly heterodox architectural language. It was composed of basilical halls and courtyard palaces, all held aloft by arches poised on marble columns and densely drilled Corinthian capitals. Organized in three stepped levels, the uppermost contained official residences and halls (including the military headquarters, the *dār al-jund*); the lowest and largest level contained the houses and workshops of the artisans, regular staff, and soldiers as well as the congregational mosque that served all residents. The middle esplanade was devoted to handsome reception halls such as the so-called Salón Rico that gave onto large four-part gardens with pools, fountains, and pavilions. These halls commanded extensive panoramic vistas, which expressed sovereign authority over both the physical land surveyed and, metaphorically, the kingdom as a whole. This middle level, devoted to court ceremonial, is the only part of the city that was seen by the chroniclers who described in awed detail the festivities and ambassadorial receptions held there.

Medieval historians recorded skilled artisans from Baghdad and Constantinople, and ten thousand slaves and paid laborers who worked there daily. The columns came from the African provinces, France, Rome, and elsewhere in al-Andalus, and some were sent as a gift from the Byzantine emperor. One third of the kingdom's revenues were devoted to its construction and upkeep, a staggering figure. The dominating site and rich, even exotic materials were carefully chosen to express dynastic authority and personal power. By summoning the best architects, artisans, and materials from all around the known world, ʿAbd al-Raḥmān brought the arts of Córdoba to a new, ambitious level of refinement. Just as his diplomatic alliances and conquests made al-Andalus the dominant power in the western Mediterranean, so too his program of architectural patronage served to transform Córdoba from a city of marginal political, economic, and cultural importance to one that could compete with the grandeur of contemporary Baghdad and Cairo.

Madīnat al-Zahrāʾ was followed by eleven other estates, the most magnificent of which was the similarly named al-Madīna al-Zāhira built by the *ḥājib* al-Manṣūr, who served as regent to the child-prince Hishām II beginning in 366/976. Its immense size, splendor, and location on the east side of Córdoba were calculated to draw attention away from the Umayyad palace where the young caliph was virtually imprisoned and ultimately forgotten.

The Amirid palace which, unlike Madīnat al-Zahrāʾ, has not been located or excavated by modern scholars, was reportedly a vast complex on an artificially leveled site near the river; its many tall buildings were so sumptuously adorned with gold, lapis lazuli, and costly revetments "that the sight wearied the eyes." It had ample gardens with pools and fountains, such as the pearl-garlanded lion figure of black amber that spewed water into a green basin with live tortoises. There was also a large pool of waterlilies where once, to impress the envoys of a rival, al-Manṣūr arranged to have pieces of silver and gold inserted at dawn. In the afternoon when the lilies opened to the sunlight, the envoys were amazed to see that the flora of al-Andalus yielded silver seeds and golden pollen, and by this bit of theater, al-Manṣūr skillfully displayed the natural bounty of his kingdom and the riches at his disposal.

Tales such as these reflect a post-Umayyad admiration for a lost golden age, when rulers seemed formidable and wise, and Islam dominated the Iberian Peninsula. In the light of architectural memory, the military triumphs of ʿAbd al-Raḥmān III and al-Manṣūr seemed divinely ordained, and the ideological basis for the Muslim rule of al-Andalus seemed more clearly defined.

PART I

THE SHAPES OF CULTURE

CHAPTER 2

LANGUAGE

Consuelo López-Morillas

No sooner had the expulsion decree of 1609 stripped Spain of its last Muslim inhabitants, the Moriscos, than the vicar-general of the Valencia cathedral wrote exultantly to King Philip III: "Hago gracias a Dios que en Valencia ya no se siente hablar en lengua aráviga" [I thank God that we no longer hear Arabic spoken in Valencia] (Fuster 113). Exactly nine hundred years had passed since Arabic had first been brought to the country's shores by the Muslim conquest of 711. During those centuries the Iberian Peninsula was home to Romance, Arabic, and Hebrew, languages both European and Semitic; to rural, urban, and regional dialects; to writing and untutored speech; to registers and styles suited to court and home, to cathedral, mosque, and synagogue, to harem, battlefield, countinghouse, wineshop, and farm. Any attempt to draw the peninsula's linguistic portrait not only must comprehend the complexities inherent in all multilingual societies, but must do so over a vast span of time, during which the fortunes of Iberia's languages rose, fell, and changed together with those of her people.

To a great extent all the major languages of the peninsula followed their own chronologies of development, but the historical events that brought their speakers together could alter this natural evolution. Contacts between peoples acted on the languages themselves, as when vocabulary and structures were borrowed from one to another; or they affected literary expression, as when Romance popular songs inspired new forms of Arabic verse, and Hebrew poetry remodeled itself on Arabic. The social and cultural roles assigned to languages also changed: forms of speech once prestigious grew isolated and were stigmatized; language shifted from a marker of ethnicity to one of religious affiliation. As happens everywhere that languages are in contact, linguistic phenomena in Spain were intimately entwined with political and demographic movements.

This subject requires an approach that combines the synchronic and the historical, discussing at some length developments in a peninsular language as if they had occurred in isolation, but always returning eventually to the contact between multiple languages, dialects, and styles that must in some degree have formed the common experience of the inhabitants. Although it is probably never accurate to claim that an entire population is bi- or multilingual, the peninsula certainly knew periods in which many individuals were. In a further complication, both of the principal languages, Arabic and Romance, showed a deep split between written and spoken forms that only some speakers were able to bridge. The case is therefore one of unusual complexity and requires departures from purely chronological order.

Like the names for the peninsula itself, the names of its various languages can convey misinformation. The traditional dichotomy between a "Latin" presumably written and spoken by an educated elite and the "Romance" of the common people is now called into serious question. Among the varieties of Hispano-Romance, the one long known as "Mozarabic" may need to be better named. And, in the medieval world as much as today, the linguistic range of the single term "Arabic" encompasses every level, from the illiterate peasant's vernacular to the court poet's classical verse, with most speakers capable of uncountable intermediate shifts of register. Here, "Andalusi Arabic" refers to the particular dialect of al-Andalus, in its spoken and written forms. Within Arabic it has long been customary to use the term "Judeo-Arabic" to designate the writings of the Jews in the Arabic language employing the Hebrew alphabet. The term might suggest that the Jews had their own distinctive dialect of Arabic, but although Jewish communities of other lands in later times had such dialects, the Jews of al-Andalus did not.

THE LANGUAGE OF HISPANIA UP TO AD 711

To a considerable extent, the Roman province of Hispania shared the early linguistic history of other portions of the empire. A mosaic of prehistoric local tongues, both Indo- and non-Indo-European, was displaced by Latin after centuries of occupation. Slowly a characteristic Romance dialect evolved, flavored by the speech of post-Roman invaders. The most important of these, the Visigoths, scarcely changed the local evolution of Latin speech. Having ruled the area of Toulouse between 475 and 507, they had replaced their native Germanic tongue with Latin even before moving southward, and contributed only isolated loanwords to Hispano-Romance. Visigothic Hispania in the seventh century was the source of the most distinguished intellectual production in Europe; its scholars, led by Isidore of Seville (c. 560–636), created a "Visigothic Renaissance . . . [that] was a constructive revival of Latin culture in a Christian context" (Wright, *Late Latin* 82).

If the thinkers of the Visigothic age wrote in correct and elegant Latin, what did they speak? Was their speech like or unlike that of the illiterate? The answers to these and related questions are among the most vigorously debated topics in contemporary Romance linguistics. Of course, the nature of "classical," "late," "medieval," and "vulgar" Latin, and the emergence of the various Romance languages or of a putative common "Proto-Romance," have been issues central to the field since its inception; and the discussions surrounding them have never been free of controversy. But until recent years there had existed an overall consensus, in spite of disagreements over nomenclature, about the relationship of Latin to Romance up to the appearance of the earliest written Romance texts in the ninth to tenth centuries. The traditional analysis of this relationship (in a summary unavoidably oversimplified), has been as follows (see Wright, *Late Latin* 1–4).

Alongside the written, "classical" Latin of the republic and the empire, a spoken form, most often termed "vulgar" (in the sense of "common" or "popular") Latin, throve. Vulgar Latin, though closely allied with the prestige model, diverged from it in a variety of features that later characterized Romance as a whole, including a subject-verb-object word order, blurring of case endings with increased use of prepositions, development of analytic verb forms, replacement of vowel quantity by quality or timbre, and evolution of new affricate and palatal consonants. Many "vulgar" characteristics can be identified in written sources. In some of these texts, like the comedies of Plautus (254–184 BC), the vulgar usages were presumably deliberate, an attempt to mimic everyday speech. But most often, lapses from strict classical style in writing were inadvertent, failures of education or of attention that fortuitously revealed traits of the spoken tongue. (Although common sense and sociolinguistic knowledge convince us that over Rome's broad dominions spoken Latin must have been differentiated to some degree, no textual or epigraphic evidence from imperial times distinguishes a "Gallic" from an "African" or even a "Dacian" [Romanian] Latin.)

The collapse of the empire hastened the diversification of popular speech. The individual Romance languages must have developed between about the fourth or fifth century AD and the ninth, when the first textual proof appears. But throughout this period, a Roman and then a Christian elite would have clung to "Latin" as a written and probably also a spoken norm. Thus a situation of diglossia or even bilingualism must have obtained: the uneducated masses would have only Romance speech, while a tiny lettered minority would be capable of shifting into a Latin that substantially retained classical phonology and morphology.

Thanks chiefly to the seminal work of Roger Wright, these venerable assumptions now appear ill-founded on many points. Wright argues that an eighth-century cleric was no more capable of speaking, or reading, Latin with a classical pronunciation than is a modern actor of declaiming Shakespeare in the accents of sixteenth-century London; the necessary phonological information was simply not available to him, and even if it had been, his hearers would not have understood him. On the contrary: in the first eight centuries AD, written texts (all, of course, in Latin), when read aloud, were pronounced just as the common speech was, in the only pronunciation anyone knew. It is highly unlikely that even the educated considered "Latin" to be a separate language; one spoke LATINU (pronounced [ladino], but with none of the connotations that the latter term bears today), but one had to write it in an odd and difficult way. In Hispania, for example, one would be taught that [dweño] must be spelled DOMINUS (or -UM, -I, or -O), and [kjere] as QUAERIT. (English and French schoolchildren similarly have to learn about "silent letters" [like the *k* and *gh* in *knight*] and even whole "silent morphemes" [like the endings of *aimai-s, aimai-t, aimai-ent*]; but different as the written norm may be from the spoken, no one assumes that they represent two independent languages.)

In this view, "medieval" Latin as we understand it today – enunciated with a full sound corresponding to each letter – was an artificial reading pronunciation introduced as part of the Carolingian reforms, that is, in about AD 800 in France, but not until after 1080 in Spain. It is significant that the reform was directed by Alcuin, who as an Anglo-Saxon had learned to read Latin as a foreign language and not, like Romance speakers, as a written form of familiar daily speech. And it is only at this point that "Latin" and "Romance" become conceptually differentiated. Once the Church converted to reading Latin phonetically, the Mass became unintelligible; the sermon, still delivered in the common tongue, was now in an unmistakably different language. It is no coincidence that the first written texts in Romance were produced soon after. "Latin" was no longer the way one wrote what one spoke; it was something entirely separate, and one's daily language had to develop a new system of written expression.

In the year 711, then, the Latin–Romance dichotomy still lay far in the future of Hispania. The invading Muslims found a population that spoke an evolved form of the language imported from Rome; Arabic speakers called the local language *laṭīnī*, or simply *ʿajamī*, 'foreign'. With the gradual consolidation of Islamic rule in what we may now call al-Andalus came, naturally enough, the spread of the Arabic language. What distinguished the Muslim invasion from the Visigothic one in linguistic terms was the status of Arabic as a vehicle for a higher culture, a literate and literary civilization. The prestige of Islam and its empire drew the sights of Andalusis eastward to Damascus and Baghdad; thus, for a full five centuries (the eighth to the thirteenth), the dominant forms of intellectual expression in the peninsula were non-Latin. Beside this cultural superiority, the fact that the superstratum language was a Semitic one pales into relative unimportance. It might appear that because the structure of Arabic is profoundly unlike that of Indo-European, Arabic must have given Spanish a particularly exotic twist. It has contributed abundant vocabulary, but lexicon is the most superficial of linguistic features, and in fact the ultimate impact of Arabic on modern Spanish has been no greater than that of Germanic on French – in some domains, such as the role of stress accent, probably less. What gave al-Andalus its unique linguistic character was not the "otherness" of Arabic, but the role of that tongue as the exemplar of all that was desirable, and worthy of imitation, in the cultural sphere.

THE LANGUAGES OF AL-ANDALUS BETWEEN THE ARRIVAL OF THE MUSLIMS AND THE RECONQUISTA

Muslims

The Arabic language complex has been included among the classic known examples of diglossia.[1] Classical or literary Arabic represents the high variety: it is no speaker's native language, requires years of special education to master, and is employed, in its purest form, in a strictly limited set of religious, literary, and intellectual contexts. The low varieties of Arabic comprise the daily colloquial speech of Arabs from the Atlantic coast of North Africa to Mesopotamia and the Arabian Peninsula; although these speakers universally believe that they use a single language called "Arabic," many of their dialects are mutually incomprehensible. In practice, however, all but the most illiterate speakers are capable of moving among a range of spoken registers that blur the classical/colloquial distinction, and even level out regional differences. In modern times these linguistic compromises have been labeled "(educated) modern standard" or "inter-" Arabic. But even in the first centuries of Islam, comparable adjustments would have been necessary. In Muhammad's time (d. AD 632), and only within the compass of the Arabian Peninsula, Arabic was already fragmented into eastern and western dialect groups, as well as a separate Yemeni one.[2] The prestige dialect in which pre-Islamic poetry, and later the Qur'an, was couched – what we now know as "classical" Arabic, the written form of the language – was an artificial literary koine, some of whose features were not shared by any spoken variety. Even the very first Muslim armies were therefore, to some degree, polyglot confederations whose members needed to accommodate to each other linguistically. The situation grew more acute with the speed and extent of the early conquests: to the mix of Arabian dialects was added the speech of large populations that learned Arabic as they dealt with the new rulers or converted to Islam. Uneducated speakers, not exposed to the prescriptive and classicizing pressures of the Arab elite, developed a "middle" Arabic that was spoken and, eventually, written; its principal traits were loss of grammatical case endings, abandonment of synthetic structures – features that it shared with the modern colloquials – and, in its written form, an abundance of pseudocorrections (Blau).

The troops that swept through North Africa and overran Hispania within a mere century after the Prophet's death included a small core of Arabic speakers of varied Eastern origin, and a preponderance of Berbers, many of whom spoke little or no Arabic. This population sowed the seeds of what was to grow into an indigenous Andalusi Arabic. Like the other colloquials, it did not derive from the classical Arabic koine, but was rather "the result of the evolution of Old Arabic stock and of the interference of foreign elements in a given sociolinguistic contour" (Corriente, *Grammatical Sketch* 8). Its character had essentially crystallized by the tenth century.

Like spoken Latin, Andalusi Arabic was in principle not to be accorded written status, yet a number of lucky factors have made it the best-recorded of the medieval Arabic colloquials. Al-Andalus proved unique in the medieval Arab world in cultivating its colloquial speech for literary purposes, particularly in zajal poetry and in proverbs and aphorisms. These genres manifest a consciousness of, and even pride in, the distinctiveness of the dialect, its suppleness and expressivity. In Spain and the Maghrib, works dealing with errors arising from the influence of vulgar speech (constituting a genre known as *al-laḥn al ʿāmma*) provide grammarians' proscriptions of linguistic solecisms through which, rather as in the famed late Latin *Appendix Probi,* traits of the common tongue may be glimpsed. Another source for this Arabic vernacular is Judeo-Arabic Geniza texts of Andalusi origin. Finally, since al-Andalus was a polyglot society, the local Arabic had on occasion to be taught to Romance speakers. A rich source for late Granadan Arabic is Pedro de Alcalá, whose *Vocabulista* and *Arte para ligeramente saver la lengua aráviga* of 1505 sought to explain the language of the conquered to the conquerors.

We owe to Federico Corriente, who draws on all these materials and more, the first complete linguistic description of Andalusi Arabic. He insists on its characterization as a "dialect bundle" because, although "the common core was predominant and the local features, minimal" (*Grammatical Sketch* 6–7), there is evidence of regional variation and of higher and lower registers in the colloquial, as well as the expected relationship of diglossia with the written language. Some of the most characteristic traits of the dialect were as follows. In phonology, there was a raising of vowels *ā> e, ā> i*; conservative retention of the diphthongs *aw* and *ay* (reduced in other Arabic dialects to *o, e*); development of the consonant phonemes /p/ and /*č*/, not only in Romance loans but in native Arabic words (Corriente, "Fonemas"); replacement of phonemic vowel length by phonemic stress, and a generally oxytonic stress pattern. (The stress shift in Andalusi Arabic has significant implications for the metrics of the zajal, muwashshah, and kharja.) In morphology, the prefix *n-* marked the first-person singular imperfect, requiring the development of an analogical first-person plural (e.g., *naqtul* 'I kill', *naqtulū* 'we kill'); uniquely among colloquial dialects, the internal passive was retained; and diminutive patterns proliferated. In syntax, a relic of the indefinite case ending *-an* survived between a noun and its adjective.

Accustomed as we are to enumerating the effects of Arabic interference on Spanish, we forget that contacts between Arabic and Romance speakers were reciprocal and left a Hispano-Romance imprint on Andalusi Arabic as well. (For García Gómez, "[El árabe andalusí] tenía las ventanas de par en par abiertas a todo polen fecundador, y la ventana más grande era la que daba al huerto romance" [3:327].) Of the dialectal features sketched above, the adoption of the phonemes /p/ and /*č*/ and the substitution of stress for length unquestionably owe their origin to such bilingualism. Other traits of Romance origin are (for all these see Corriente, *Árabe* 125–32)

in phonology, the trend toward creation of a phoneme /e/; splitting the Arabic phonemes /d/ and /*ḍ*/ into two allophones of a single sound; devoicing and merging of consonants in final position; loss of *ʿayn*;

in morphology, abandonment of the gender distinction in second-person pronouns and verbs; use of the passive participle in stative verbs (e.g., *matʿūb* with the meaning *cansado*); attachment of some twenty Romance suffixes (*-el[la]*, *-ón*, *-ic[a]*, etc.) to Arabic bases;

in syntax, changes of noun gender to match Romance (e.g., *ʿayn* and *shams* become masculine like *ojo*, *sol*), and many syntactic calques of phrases from the substratum language.

Most prominent of all, perhaps, was the wholesale borrowing of Romance lexicon into Andalusi dialect, just as hundreds of Arabisms were transmitted in the opposite direction. Corriente (*Árabe* 133–42) seeks to distinguish three chronological layers of such loanwords, in which Romance functions respectively as a substratum, adstratum, or superstratum language vis-à-vis Arabic. Borrowing was most concentrated in certain semantic fields such as plant and animal names, domestic objects, and agriculture. (Where a Romance word survived together with its Arabic synonym, e.g., *imlíq* < UMBILICU and *surra*, both 'navel', we recall the many households made up of Hispano-Roman women and Arab men.) Once adapted to Arabic morphology, many Romance loanwords would no longer be transparent as such to speakers of either Arabic or Spanish: they could receive sound plurals (*nibšāriuh* 'aniversario', pl. *nibšāriyāt*) or broken plurals (*lubb* 'lobo', pl. *lababah*), take on diminutive form (*conáidal* 'candil pequeño'), or be conjugated like an Arabic verb (*ničayyap* 'cazar con cepo' < CIPPU). This abundance of Romance vocabulary persists to the last days of Arabic in the peninsula. It is found in Pedro de Alcalá's works, even though Granada was monolingually Arabophone in the two centuries prior to its reconquest. And of course it became still more pronounced in areas where Arabic was in daily contact with Romance, as among the Valencian Moriscos. An Arabic letter written by a Morisco from that city in 1595 contains such phrases as *taʿmál alburšíblī* 'haz lo posible', *aquštiš matáʿī* 'a costa mía', and *aqbázah maʿalbunā buluntád* 'recíbelos de buena gracia'; these examples testify to the practice of Arabic–Romance code-switching (Harvey; Corriente, *Árabe* 201).

Berbers

The linguistic implications of the Berber presence in al-Andalus are not yet clearly understood. It is known that the original invasion force included many more Berbers than Arabs, and that the disproportion continued during the first century or two of settlement (Guichard 248–49). But what language did those Berbers speak, or come to speak? Although Wasserstein (4) believes that some of them would initially have spoken "Latin" (i.e., its African Romance descendant), the work of other scholars (Lewicki; Lancel) suggests that nomadic, as opposed to settled, Berber tribes in the Maghrib were never really Latinized or Christianized; and presumably it was the nomadic ones who were, at least initially, induced to accompany the Arabs across the straits. Thus the real question is whether, when, and how thoroughly speakers of Berber dialects adopted Arabic (either before or after their passage to Spain), and whether any of them came to speak Romance after 711.

The answers to both halves of the question still lie in the realm of speculation. The research of the past twenty years (Bosch Vilá; and especially Guichard) has undermined the long-held opinion that the invading Berbers were beginning to be Arabized at the time of the conquest, and became wholly so soon afterward. It now appears that the Berber clans showed a high degree of cohesiveness, reinforced by endogamy and by contacts with their North African kin; that they settled, in tribal groups, in clearly defined areas separate from those of Arab settlement (but not exclusively in remote and mountainous regions, as had generally been believed); and that they retained many of their customs for centuries. Under those circumstances it would not be surprising if they retained their native tongue as well.

Corriente ("Nuevos berberismos") has identified some fifteen Berberisms that entered Andalusi Arabic, a handful of which were still current in the early sixteenth century. He considers this number of preserved words very small in proportion to the extent of Berber presence in the country (in contrast, the number of words of Romance origin in Andalusi dialect was ten times as great), perhaps because of the Berbers' relative isolation from the larger society. The nature of this vocabulary, too, testifies to a certain exclusivity, as most of the forms are related to dress, implements, arms, and some social institutions. The number of words of Berber origin surviving in modern Spanish is negligible, with the important exception of toponyms.

The Almoravid and Almohad hegemony over al-Andalus from the eleventh to the thirteenth century brought a degree of re-Berberization in language, as well as in customs, political life, and religion. The first Almoravid ruler of al-Andalus, Yūsuf ibn Tāshfīn, may have known no Arabic at all. The founder of the Almohads, Ibn Tūmart (c. 1078–1130), composed a religious work, *ʿaqīda* or credo, in Berber for the guidance of his Maṣmūda tribesmen. Although the original does not survive, the *ʿaqīda* was translated into Spanish, and an Aljamiado version that circulated among the sixteenth-century Moriscos is extant. Wiegers (40–45) believes that a Spanish translation could have been made as early as the thirteenth century: the Almohads favored a policy of propagating Islam in the vernacular, and just as they employed Berber for this purpose in the Maghrib, they might have authorized the use of Romance in the peninsula. Precisely in the thirteenth century, many Muslims were passing from the rule of their coreligionists to Mudejar status under Christian monarchs, and it is not known whether the Spanish version of the *ʿaqīda* would have been made in Islamic or Christian territory. This text of Ibn Tūmart's stands as a unique demonstration of Berber–Romance linguistic contact in Spain, always within an Islamic milieu.

Jews

As the Islamic tide engulfed the eastern Mediterranean and North Africa, the Jews of those lands became Arabized together with the other indigenous populations.[3] Aramaic and the other languages that Jews had written and spoken were replaced by Arabic, at least in urban areas, by the late ninth century. Both Jews and Christians in the Islamic world wrote middle Arabic, the nonclassical, simplified form of the language already described. But Jews, when addressing themselves in writing to their own coreligionists, used the Hebrew rather than the Arabic script. The term "Judeo-Arabic" used by specialists in speaking of such Jewish writing up to about the thirteenth century should not be taken to mean that the Arabic-speaking Jews in al-Andalus had a distinctive dialect. Of course, when writing and speaking about matters pertaining to their traditional customs and cultural practices, Jews would employ Hebrew terminology; but their spoken language was otherwise identical with that of their neighbors. As for their written Arabic, the reason they preferred to use the Hebrew script was that people normally wrote in the script of their religious writings (Goitein 1:16). This practice is probably the result of the fact that the first and most generally available education was religious, so that the script of each community's religious writings was the one most familiar to its members and the most natural for internal use. Romance-speaking Muslims would later use the Arabic alphabet in the same way as Arabic-speaking Jews would use the Hebrew one. The same phenomenon occurs with the Mudejares.

The Arabic written by the Jews differs from the Arabic written by non-Jews in that it only rarely employs the classical register of the language, being couched ordinarily in one of the registers of colloquial Arabic. Thus, Judeo-Arabic texts are a prime source for knowledge of the vernacular. Jews did not normally write in classical Arabic (*fuṣḥa*) because they did not share the Muslims' veneration for that language as a religious and cultural ideal; for them, that status was reserved for Hebrew. Accordingly, when writing for internal purposes, even those who possessed a classical Arabic education and were capable of writing *fuṣḥa* had little reason to do so. Educated Jewish writers tended to write Arabic at a higher level than that of ordinary speech, but such writers' frequent mistakes of hypercorrection attest to the artificiality of this practice and survive as valuable clues to their actual manner of speech.

Jews used Arabic for everyday written communication of every sort – business documents, personal letters, community records – as well as for literary works of an expository nature. The origins of formal Judeo-Arabic literature (used here to mean Jewish writings in Arabic irrespective of alphabet) are in Iraq. Saadiah Gaon (d. 942), a rabbi of Egyptian origin active there, was one of the most important figures in the creation of this literary tradition; he is noted for his translation of the Pentateuch into Arabic, which some scholars believe he composed not in the Hebrew but in the Arabic alphabet (Blau 39–41). Andalusi Jews, like Jews throughout the Arabic-speaking world, continued to write expository prose in Arabic widely until the thirteenth century, and to some extent even thereafter; among the subjects of their Arabic books were philosophy, science, medicine, religious law, Hebrew grammar, and Bible commentaries.[4]

Jews had passed into Hispania with the Romans, especially after the destruction of the Temple in AD 70, and their presence there is documented from the Council of Elvira of c. 300. On the peninsula they spoke Latin, and eventually Romance. The Islamic invasion brought with it Arabic-speaking Jews from the East and the Maghrib, and also resulted in the speedy Arabization of native Jews. Yet the Jews of al-Andalus retained their hold on

Romance, while continuing to be literate in Hebrew; thus among the three cultures their linguistic range was probably the greatest.

Hebrew was not a spoken language; though it might occasionally be used for oral communication, as when travelers found themselves in a strange linguistic environment, it was normally used only for prayer and ceremonial writings. Most Jewish males must have known enough Hebrew to perform the textually complicated Jewish liturgy and to translate the parts of the Bible that were ceremonially read in the synagogue, but only a small elite could have had the extensive education in both Hebrew and Arabic literatures that would enable them to participate in the sophisticated Judeo-Arabic culture that became characteristic of the Andalusian Jewry beginning in the tenth century.

Among this elite emerged a new type of Hebrew poetry that is one of the most distinctive products of Andalusian Jewish culture and the most original development in medieval Jewish writing. It is the great cultural achievement of Andalusian Jewry and warrants the labeling of the tenth to twelfth centuries in al-Andalus as the Golden Age of Hebrew literature. The new poetry is a product of the impact of Arabic literary culture on Jewish literary culture, and therefore of the Arabic language on Andalusian Jewry.

The prestige of Arabic language and literary tradition so impressed the members of the Jewish upper class in tenth-century al-Andalus that they adopted first the various functions and genres of Arabic poetry, and finally Arabic prosodic conventions. This process of the assimilation of features of Arabic poetry had already begun in the Muslim East early in the century, but it was in al-Andalus that the Jews first wrote Hebrew poetry using Arabic prosodic models and adopted nearly the entire range of Arabic poetic genres and stylistic devices in Hebrew.

The choice of Hebrew for the new Jewish poetry was not an obvious one; there is no convincing reason why the Jews could not have written poetry for internal use in Arabic, for the members of the Jewish educated class were perfectly familiar with classical Arabic poetry, and some are known to have written poetry in Arabic. The reason for the choice of Hebrew seems to be that this was a literature designed as a vehicle for the self-expression of a newly self-confident and cohesive community. It was a new prestige literature suitable to express the prosperity, security, and self-satisfaction of a uniquely successful Jewish community, one that counted as its head a courtier in the service of the caliph ʿAbd al-Raḥmān III, and one that fancied itself a revival, admittedly on a reduced scale, of the ancient Jewish kingdom. To express these attitudes and to further its activities, the Jewish elite of al-Andalus turned to the language that was distinctively their own, the language of the ancient Jewish kingdom and the Jewish religious classics, the traditional language of Jewish ceremonial writing.

The example of *ʿarabiyya* must also have played a part in the choice of Hebrew. This was the strong conviction among Arabic literary people that the language of classical Arabic poetry and of the Qurʾan was the only appropriate language for the literature of prestige in Arabic. Adopting the principle, but replacing Hebrew with Arabic, the Jews came to look upon biblical Hebrew as their own classical language. Thus, the classicizing nature of the whole enterprise of poetry in the Arabic milieu was responsible both for the choice of Hebrew and for the choice of its biblical register from among the three distinct registers of Hebrew widely familiar at the time: biblical, rabbinic, and payyetanic (the Hebrew of liturgical poetry).

But the vocabulary of the Bible is quite small compared to the vastness of the vocabulary of Arabic poetry, and the poets refused on principle to supplement it with words from later strata of the language. To make up the deficiency, it became necessary to take some liberties. Biblical roots were used in conjugational patterns that they did not take in the Bible itself; rare forms of prepositions were preferred over the common forms that were less adaptable to Arabic metric patterns; rare words and words of uncertain meaning were pressed into frequent service; Arabic syntactic patterns were adopted; and inevitably, the meanings of Hebrew words were contaminated by the meanings of their Arabic cognates. Thus, although the poets were convinced that they were writing in biblical Hebrew, they really created a register of their own, founded on biblical Hebrew but with a distinctive flavor deriving from Arabic poetry.

Andalusian Hebrew poetry came into existence in a literary environment that favored a rhetorically ornate style. Poetry of the Hebrew Golden Age reflects this preference for wordplays, antitheses, parallelism, and figures of speech. If it could not compete with Arabic for richness of vocabulary (a problem that could easily have been solved had the poets been willing to have recourse to rabbinic or payyetanic Hebrew for vocabulary), it developed a device of its own that did not have an exact parallel in Arabic: the use of biblical quotations as a rhetorical device. Of course quotations and allusions to verses of the Qurʾan and earlier poetry occur in Arabic poetry, and such quotations are recognized by medieval critics as a rhetorical figure. But because the entire vocabulary of Andalusi-Hebrew poetry came from the Bible, nearly every word in a Hebrew poem could potentially suggest one or more passages from the Bible. Poets turned this limitation to advantage by making a constant practice of manipulating biblical quotations. The poet may force the reader to complete a half-stated thought by supplying the biblical context himself; he may achieve wit by distorting the meaning of a biblical phrase; or he may distort the meaning of a biblical phrase to create a significant ambiguity. On a larger scale, he may use biblical stories and characters as typologies, expecting the reader to be familiar with their traditional interpretation. In short, Hebrew poetry is saturated with the Bible in a way unparalleled in Arabic; it is fair to say that the Bible became the poets' sourcebook of rhetorical play, for both frivolous and serious themes.

The Hebrew language needed some retooling in order to become suitable for the new metrics. Despite the family relationship between Arabic and Hebrew, the phonology of the two languages differs sufficiently to necessitate certain distortions in Hebrew to accommodate Arabic metrics, and these distortions were the cause of a vigorous and lasting debate as to the propriety of the whole procedure. But the new metrics, introduced by Dunash ben Labrat in the mid-tenth century, quickly won over the Hebrew-writing public and even entered the synagogue, as many Andalusian poets began to use it for their liturgical poetry. Even those liturgical poems that did not make use of the new metrics simplified their diction considerably, virtually eliminating the old payyetanic register of Hebrew in favor of a biblicizing style similar, though not identical, to the language of secular poetry. The composition of poems to enhance the liturgy was an ancient tradition in Judaism with a long-established body of distinctive linguistic and compositional traditions; the sudden overthrow of this tradition through the introduction of Arabic metrics and poetic style must have seemed a daring innovation.

The flowering of Hebrew poetry in al-Andalus was in itself an affirmation of Jewish identity and communal cohesiveness. The combination of the Hebrew language with religious and biblical themes, or, in secular poems, with biblical phrasing, reflected some of the deepest longings of diaspora Judaism. The unique trilingual nature of muwashshahs by Jewish poets, incorporating Hebrew, and, in the kharja, Arabic and Romance as well, was emblematic of the Andalusi-Jewish community, linked by language to both East and West.

The development of Hebrew poetry and its particular linguistic register went hand in hand with a new and widespread interest in Hebrew grammar and lexicography. The discovery by Judah Ibn Quraysh, a North African Jew of the ninth or early tenth century, of the family relationship between Hebrew, Aramaic, and Arabic was followed by the Andalusi Judah Ḥayyūj's (c. 945–1000) theory that Hebrew resembles Arabic in being based on triliteral roots. (This theory has underlain all Hebrew grammatical scholarship until the present century.) The effects of such study are seen readily in Bible commentaries by Andalusi Jews, which dwell extensively on linguistic matters and draw on both Arabic cognates and Arabic syntax to explain the biblical text. A tendency to focus on problems of language and a rigorous linguistic discipline acquired from the systematic study of grammar are hallmarks of the Jewish religious literature of al-Andalus.

Christians and other Romance speakers

No conquered population adopts the language of its conquerors overnight, and it was several centuries before Arabic became dominant in al-Andalus. Alvarus of Córdoba, in the ninth century, famously lamented his countrymen's loss of Latin: "Alas! Christians do not know their own law, and Latins do not use their own tongue" (Colbert 301). Yet knowledge of Arabic spread chiefly with conversion to Islam, and the latter occurred only gradually. Bulliet's well-known study equating adoption of Arab/Islamic names with religious conversion in the conquered lands calculates that only half the population of al-Andalus would have converted by AD 961, 250 years after the first conquest, and that not until about 1100 would the proportion have risen to 80 percent. By the mid-thirteenth century only the kingdom of Granada remained in Muslim hands, and Arabic–Romance bilingualism seems to have been extinguished there: its inhabitants were monolingual in Arabic. In the same period Bulliet's conversion curve surpassed 90 percent, suggesting that only at this late date had the rulers of al-Andalus achieved an entirely Islamic, as well as Arabophone, state.

Use of Romance speech by Muslims is documented in the early centuries, although much of the evidence is anecdotal. Al-Khushanī's history of the Islamic judges of Córdoba (Ribera 118, 136, 171) shows a number of these high officials conversing in the local language. Ibn Ḥazm, in his *Jamharat ansāb al-ʿarab* (Genealogy of the Arabs) of the mid-eleventh century, notes in an oft-quoted passage (443) that in a family of ancient Eastern lineage near Córdoba, both women and men spoke only Arabic. This remark has always been taken to suggest that such ignorance of Romance was rare (though Guichard's work now casts doubt on that view).[5] From as early as the twelfth century there is evidence that even Islam was not impervious to the local Romance vernacular. Wiegers (30–31) has identified a fatwa or religious opinion of circa 1120 that reveals that the story of Joseph from the Qur'an was recited in Romance in al-Andalus at the time.

The time-honored name for the form of Hispano-Romance spoken in Muslim-held territory, "Mozarabic," now provokes dissatisfaction among some scholars. Since the Christians of those lands are also called Mozarabs (from Arabic *mustaʿrib* 'one who adopts the manners of the Arabs'), it has been objected that the term straddles ambiguously the realms of religion and language, and further implies, erroneously, that the dialect was spoken only by Christians. The very form of the word suggests (again a false perception) that it denotes a language somehow related to Arabic. Spanish scholars increasingly now call it *romance andalusí*. This can be rendered into English as "Andalusi Romance" in a neat parallel to "Andalusi Arabic," but with two caveats: first, it should not be confused with "Andalusian" (the adjective of the southern region of Spain, Andalusia, and the name of a distinctive dialect of modern Castilian), and second, it must not be assumed that Andalusi Romance was significantly different from the varieties of Romance vernacular spoken in most of the Christian north – at least in structure, though it would have had a larger proportion of Arabic loanwords.

The usual linguistic map of the peninsula for about the year 1000 shows the political frontier between Islamic and Christian lands running from northeast to southwest roughly one-third of the way down. North of that line, the territory is divided with vertical lines corresponding to the borders of the Christian kingdoms of Galicia, León, Castile, Navarre, Aragon, and Catalonia; the northern dialects are often labeled "Galician," "Leonese," "Castilian," and so on. South of the east–west line, the usual linguistic label is "Mozarabic dialects." (The presence of Arabic as an adstratum is usually not indicated.) Such maps make the common error of equating political with linguistic frontiers, and the impression of a territory fragmented into seven or more varieties of Romance speech is a deceptive one. Romance speakers from all over the peninsula, had they been asked, would have identified their spoken tongue as *ladino*, certainly not as *leonés*, *navarro*, or any other variety. All shades of Hispano-Romance share many linguistic features; only Castilian was anomalous, and in its eventual expansion southward it ruptured a fundamental unity of speech. East, west, and south of Castile, in both Islamic and Christian lands, the most characteristic traits of Hispano-Romance recur. Were it not for the historical accident of Castilian expansion, Spanish would sound very different today, and its contrasts with Portuguese and Catalan would stand out in less sharp relief.

The special status of Andalusi Romance lies, then, not in any individuality of its linguistic structure. Its only real distinction is that it has been recorded primarily in Arabic script. The Arabic alphabet, an imperfect one even for the recording of its own language, is unable to represent many of the sounds of a foreign one. The way that Arabic letters mask the phonetic reality of Hispano-Romance is particularly frustrating to philologists who would like to establish how far the vernacular of the time had evolved from Latin. Paradoxically, however, the Arabic script has the potential to reflect the speech of the time more accurately than the Roman, since it is not bound by the tradition of the Latin language. As mentioned above, "Latin" documents of this period in northern Spain and France are themselves often a mask for the evolving vernacular, and were likely to have been read aloud with vernacular phonetics.

Even in the earliest surviving texts recognized as Hispano-Romance, the *Glosas Emilianenses* and *Glosas Silenses* of the late tenth century, the scribes who glossed the Latin with vernacular forms were unable to shake off their training in Latin orthography, writing for example *lueco* and *katet* when they were almost certainly pronounced [lwego] and [kate]. Unfettered by this tradition, Arab writers who recorded Andalusi Romance for any reason could at least attempt an approximation of what they heard pronounced.

Until halfway into the twentieth century, no connected texts in Andalusi Romance had come to light. Information about its nature was chiefly phonological, since it consisted of individual words. Romance toponyms and personal names were preserved in a variety of medieval documents, some in Arabic and some in Latin script: most important are the *Repartimientos*, surveys of property made by Christians after the Reconquest (Galmés de Fuentes), and the legal documents, written in Arabic, of the Toledan Mozarabs of the eleventh through thirteenth centuries (González Palencia). Arab botanists recorded plant names in the various languages known to them, including Romance (e.g., Asín Palacios); and poets like Ibn Quzmān who wrote zajal verse in Andalusi Arabic incorporated isolated Romance words, mostly nouns, to humorous effect. The *Vocabulista* of Pedro de Alcalá, published in Latin script in Granada in 1505, shows many Romance forms adopted by the local Arabic dialect. But these scattered citations could tell virtually nothing about the morphology and syntax of this now extinct variety of Hispano-Romance.

The discovery in the late 1940s of kharjas attached to Hebrew and Arabic muwashshahs, and containing entire phrases in Romance, thus proved a treasure from a linguistic as well as a literary point of view. The texts are paleographically difficult, and many of their readings remain insecure, yet they have brought to light an abundance of previously unknown morphological and syntactic features. For the first time the rhythms, the phrasal and sentential patterns of Andalusi Romance, are made manifest. No matter how cautious some editors are in interpreting the unvocalized Arabic script, and despite disagreement about individual words and combinations, the bilingual kharjas resound beyond doubt with echoes of Romance-speaking Andalusis.

Although the dialect thus revealed has offered few genuine surprises to students of Hispano-Romance as a whole, the kharjas are unique in their habit of interweaving Romance with Arabic (and thus should be called "bilingual" rather than strictly "Romance"). Although many readings are still speculative, combinations such as these appear: *no me leša mobere aw limtu* 'he does not allow me to move or I am reprimanded'; *eš yuḥayyī bokel(l)a ḥulú mitl eš(e)* 'how a little mouth revives something sweet like that'; *mio al-furār* 'my lamb';

imši ad unione 'come to a meeting'. Arabic nouns receive Romance diminutive suffixes (*ḥil(l)ello* 'little flatterer'), while Romance nouns take Arabic possessive ones (*qorağonī* 'my heart', beside *mio qorağon*). Some scholars have suggested that such hybrids cannot possibly reflect popular speech, but must be macaronic creations coined for aesthetic or humorous purposes. Others see in them signs of the code-switching in which many bilingual speakers indulge. Current scholarship (though there are differences between individuals and schools) would probably agree that the kharjas may well be rooted in popular forms of speech, but that once grafted onto the muwashshah they were subject to such learned reworking to fit the aesthetics of the genre that their language became artificial and conventional.[6]

Christians who lived in Islamic territory, while continuing to speak Romance alongside Arabic, found it difficult to preserve Latin, their classical language of religion and high culture. (By contrast the Muslims, while they spoke and occasionally even wrote in Romance, remained fully in possession of literary Arabic; its cultivation had the weight of Arab-Islamic civilization behind it, and was nurtured by contact with the other Arabic-speaking lands.) As Wright ("Muerte") has noted, Latin literacy in the Christian north was reinforced by the practice of reading documents, both ecclesiastical and notarial, aloud (with vernacular pronunciation). In 839, the acts of a Church council in Córdoba were written in the "colloquialized" Latin that suggests a continuum between writing and speech. But when Eulogius of Córdoba traveled to the Pyrenean monasteries in about 850 and returned with a precious hoard of Latin manuscripts, those texts, Wright believes, had a paradoxically pernicious effect on Mozarabic Latinity. Rather than renewing the Latin culture of the Church, these much-studied works set up an impossible ideal, inspiring their imitators to a hermetic style that, for the average Christian, severed the link between the oral and written forms of his language.

Indeed, the first translation of a biblical text from Latin into Arabic must have been made not long after Eulogius's journey. This would be a prose version of the Psalms, now lost, but cited in 889 by Ḥafṣ ibn Albār al-Qūṭī when he made his own rendering into Arabic verse (Urvoy 273–75). From the late ninth through the mid-eleventh century, continuous activity by Mozarabs in translating books of the Bible into Arabic shows the extent to which the Mozarabic church was losing Latin. Two independent Arabic versions of the Gospels were in circulation: one, made by Isḥāq ibn Balashk al-Qurṭubī in 946, drew on the *Vetus Latina*, and the other, from the previous century, on the *Vulgata*. There was also a translation of the Pauline Epistles. While the Mass continued to be celebrated in Latin, the Epistles and Gospels may have been read in Arabic to the congregation (Koningsveld, "Christian-Arabic Manuscripts" 426). The codex *Sistemática mozárabe*, of 1050, shows us a Christianity deeply penetrated by Arabo-Islamic culture (Kassis). Written in Arabic by a priest, Vincentius, for his patron, Bishop ʿAbd al-Malik, it contains the code of canon law for the Arabic-speaking church in al-Andalus. While the text is dense with words of Latin origin (*aqulīṭ*, *liqtūr*, *qlārīqī*, etc.), it is equally so with phrases and cadences reminiscent of the Qurʾan. The priest is called imam, and the name of God is followed by the epithet *ʿazza wa-jalla* ('may he be exalted'), as is customary with the name of Allah. Yet, as the manuscript also contains a long Latin passage in the Visigothic hand, at least one scribe involved in its composition must have known how to write that language (Koningsveld, "Christian-Arabic Manuscripts" 445).

LANGUAGE AND THE RECONQUISTA

Andalusi Romance, virtually untouched by outside linguistic influences in the first centuries of its history, may have been doomed from the moment in 1085 when Alfonso VI and his Castilian troops entered Toledo. The dialect of Castile had been forged in the northern mountains, where Basque speakers had never been subjugated and the veneer of Latinization was thin, and many of its features were anomalous within Hispano-Romance. Yet Castile proved as vigorous and expansionist in language as it was in politics and arms. Like an advancing wedge, the kingdom and its language pressed into Arab-held territory. The neighboring kingdoms were also marching southward: Galicia moved down the Atlantic coast, conquering what was to become Portugal, and the Catalan speakers of the northeast expanded along the Mediterranean and across to the Balearic Islands. But Castile encroached on the territory to its west and east, gaining particularly at the expense of León and Navarre, so that the "wedge" soon became a bulge. Within it Castilian, once an isolated minor dialect, came to be the tongue of the whole central peninsula.

At the same time, Romance-speaking Mozarabic Christians were suffering at the hands of their Muslim overlords. The consolidation of Berber rule under the Almoravids, beginning just after Alfonso VI reconquered Toledo, was accompanied by persecution of non-Muslim minorities, swelling the number of migrants to the Christian north. In 1125–26, Alfonso I "the Battler" of Aragon, responding to an appeal from the Christians of Granada, led a daring raid all the way south to that city; though he failed to capture it, thousands of Mozarabs followed him north in his retreat. In reprisal, the Almoravids deported large numbers of Christians to North Africa. Thus, while the northernmost cities reconquered from the Muslims – Toledo in 1085, Huesca in 1096, Saragossa in 1118 – were full of Mozarabic Christians who still spoke Andalusi Romance, the great urban centers of Andalusia were empty of them by the time of their own reconquest: Córdoba in 1236, Jaén in

1246, and Seville in 1248. In that intervening century native Romance had expired, and Castilian moved in to fill the linguistic gap.

As it expanded into former Arabic-speaking lands, Castilian also absorbed the wealth of Arabic vocabulary that even today – much reduced by lexical loss – marks it off from the other Romance languages. The Arabs' contribution in speech ran in close parallel to their innovations in material culture. Arabic lexicon in Spanish is clustered in such areas as domestic architecture and furnishings (*albayalde* 'whitewash', *aldaba* 'door-knocker', *alfombra* 'rug'), agriculture and its products (*albahaca* 'basil', *alcachofa* 'artichoke', *berenjena* 'eggplant', alongside many other fruit and vegetable names), military activity (*acicate* 'spur', *algazara* 'raid', *jinete* 'horseman'), science (*alambique* 'distilling flask', *algebrista* 'mathematician; [arch.] bonesetter', *atutía* 'zinc oxide') and institutions (*cadí* 'judge', *alcurnia* 'lineage', *mazmorra* 'dungeon'). Borrowings other than nouns are rare, consisting of a handful of verbs (like *zahorar* 'to have a late-night snack'), adjectives (*baladí* 'useless'), and interjections (*ojalá* 'if only!'). Lexicon is, of course, the most easily absorbed element of an adstratum language. The morphological structure of Arabic is too different from that of Romance to allow for much borrowing, with the exception of a few derivational suffixes like the *-í* of *marroquí*, *alfonsí*. And while it is true, from the point of view of phonology, that no individual phoneme has come into Spanish from Arabic, the large-scale incorporation of Arabisms has broadened the rhythmic-accentual pattern of Spanish nonetheless. It has introduced, for example, many polysyllabic words (*zanahoria*), oxytones (*alhelí*), paroxytones ending in a consonant (*almíbar*), and proparoxytones (*almuédano*), giving modern Spanish a highly individualized "acoustic impression" (Malkiel 62).

The Reconquest brought church as well as state back into the former Islamic lands, where the Mozarabs had retained their Christian identity but, as we have seen, had made Arabic their principal written language. Now back within the fold of Western Christendom, they had to relearn Latin in order to ensure their assimilation. The city of Toledo was probably at the forefront of that enterprise. There, in the late twelfth century, the Latin–Arabic glossary now at Leiden was compiled; its purpose must have been "to enable Christian readers who had a working knowledge of the Arabic language to read and understand certain Latin texts by giving a list of basic Latin words in alphabetical order and an explanation or explanations in Arabic" (Koningsveld, *Latin–Arabic Glossary* 1). (Many of these "explanations" drew on the vocabulary of the Arabic Gospels and Epistles that had been read for centuries in the Mozarabic church.) Most surviving Visigothic manuscripts that contain Arabic glosses either still are or have been at one time in Toledo, suggesting that the city, in the twelfth and thirteenth centuries, was a center for

Mozarabs who were studying Latin (Koningsveld, *Latin–Arabic Glossary* 50–51). This intellectual activity must, of course, be associated with the many Arabic-to-Latin translations being made at the same place and time.

The role of Jews in rendering Arabic texts into Latin in the twelfth century and into Castilian in the thirteenth is well known. In post-Reconquest Castile, Jews were much more likely than Christians to be conversant with Arabic, and in all the Christian kingdoms often served in the capacities to which their multilingualism best fitted them: as translators, interpreters, ambassadors, and scribes.[7] Some Jews must have known Latin, as there were numerous Latin-to-Hebrew translations made, especially of philosophy and science, between the twelfth and the fifteenth centuries; but more frequently a Jew prepared a Romance version of an Arabic text, either oral or written, and a Christian then turned that version into Latin. (In the Alfonsine translations, whose end product was in Castilian, the final step never took place.)

In the Christian kingdoms at this time, with the receding of Arabic as their spoken language, Jews' use of Arabic as a literary language also began to recede, though Arabic literary models retained their hold on Iberian Jewish writing until as late as the expulsion. Poetry, of course, both secular and liturgical, continued to be written in Hebrew, in the quasi-biblical style that had been developed by the great poets of the tenth to the thirteenth centuries, and rhymed prose continued in use for maqama-like narratives as well as for the introductions to books and other short formal writings.[8] But discursive prose, somewhat unexpectedly, now came to be written not in the vernacular, as had been the practice of the major Jewish communities of the immediately pre-Islamic past (such as Greek-speaking Egypt, Aramaic-speaking Palestine and Iraq) but in Hebrew. The reasons for this development are unclear, but may be explained by reference to the status of the languages of the dominant society. Centuries of acculturation to Arabic literary and linguistic ideas had conditioned Jews to think of Hebrew not simply as the language of religious expression but as a language of religious and cultural prestige, by analogy to the Arabo-Islamic cultural ideal of *ʿarabiyya*. As long as Arabic was the dominant spoken language among the Jews, Jewish scholars used it for writing, just as Muslim scholars spoke and wrote in the same language (albeit in different registers of that language). But in Christian Iberia, to which the Jews were now becoming acculturated, Latin had not yet been replaced by Castilian as the language of serious intellectual life; learned books were written in a language that was not intelligible to ordinary people. By analogy, the Jews naturally avoided the vernacular for their learned writing and adopted Hebrew, their own prestige language, for that purpose.

This period also saw a great wave of translations of scientific and philosophical literature from Arabic into Hebrew, as reduced knowledge of Arabic made it harder and harder for Iberian Jews to hold on to their Arabized Jewish culture. Translations were also necessary to satisfy the demands of the Jews of Provence and Italy, whom the Christianization of Iberia had brought closer to the cultural sphere of Iberian Jewry. These Jews were eager to gain access to the prestigious literary achievements of al-Andalus and other parts of the Arabic world. This tendency was as strong within the Jewish community as it was in the non-Jewish intellectual community. The result for Christian scholars was the renaissance of the twelfth century. Among the Jews, there emerged a corpus of Hebrew philosophical, grammatical, and scientific texts that were studied widely for centuries, consisting of books either translated from Arabic or composed in a Hebrew heavily influenced by Arabic vocabulary and syntax and reflecting patterns of thought and literary composition derived from Arabic culture. Such works as Maimonides' *Guide of the Perplexed*, originally written in Arabic; Abraham Ibn Ezra's commentary on large parts of the Bible, written in Arabized Hebrew; and David Kimḥi's Hebrew dictionary, written in Arabized Hebrew on the model of Ibn Janāḥ's Hebrew dictionary written in Arabic, became classics that were studied throughout the Jewish world, and carried with them myriad features of Arabic syntax, lexical calques from Arabic, and intellectual concepts formerly unknown in the Rhineland and in central and eastern Europe. Such influences of Arabic were noticeable in written Hebrew until modern times. Meanwhile, in Christian Spain, the Jews continued to write scientific and philosophical works as well as commentaries on the Bible and treatises on Jewish law in Arabized Hebrew until the expulsion.

For students of the Sephardic Jews and their speech, a fundamental question has been whether before the expulsion of 1492 Jews in Spain spoke a Hispanic dialect different from that of Christians (e.g., Marcus). Laura Minervini's work, based on careful study of medieval Hebrew-letter Spanish documents, has helped dispel two of the most common beliefs about Jewish language: first, that there was a Judeo-Spanish koine, developed before 1492, that formed the basis for modern Judezmo; and second, that preexpulsion Jewish texts show particularly archaic features, attributed to the isolation or conservatism of Jewish groups. Minervini characterizes peninsular Judeo-Spanish as polymorphic: in phonology and morphology, in incorporation of popular and regional forms, and in indifference to the leveling and normative forces emanating from Christian environments such as royal chancelleries and monastic scriptoria. Without a long literary tradition, not subject to Latinizing and etymologizing fashions, Jewish speech and therefore writing was open to a range of linguistic registers and codes. Although not closed to learned forms, it incorporated popular elements; it accepted provincialisms and external influences, without losing sight of the contemporary trend toward the Castilianization of regional varieties. As to their presumed isolation, the Jews of Spain were neither confined to ghettos nor kept out of the normal currents of society. What few archaisms exist in their writings (e.g., preservation of final *-t/ -d* in the third-person singular of verbs, or imperfects in *-ié*) do not qualify the whole corpus as archaic; these merely point to an indifference to the sort of linguistic standardization that spread from Christian cultural centers, and to a schooling that relied less on traditional rhetorical models. Further, representations of Jewish speech in Christian literature point out no particularities of phonology or morphosyntax, such as were caricatured for groups like Moriscos, blacks, or gypsies. *Mutatis mutandis*, early Judeo-Spanish stood in much the same relationship to standard Spanish as Judeo-Arabic to classical Arabic; Judeo-Arabic also kept apart from the classicizing pressures that Islamic education and literature exerted, and was much readier to incorporate varied levels of expression and the spontaneity of the spoken language.

One argument for early Judeo-Spanish as a separate dialect has been that Jews incorporated Hebraisms into their Spanish, and, for example, converted *Dios* 'God' into *el Dió* to purge any suggestion of plurality or Trinity. But the ability of Jews to function in many linguistic registers suggests that they could easily tailor the 'Jewishness' of their speech to their interlocutors. Thus a Jew who wished to pass unnoticed as such could eliminate from his discourse those Hebraisms of vocabulary, syntax, and style that he would employ freely when communicating with fellow Jews (Vàrvaro 169). We have discussed above how Jews in the Arab world adapted Judeo-Arabic in just the same way, using standard Arabic outside their own group, but a greater proportion of Hebrew terminology within it.

To the extent that a Judeo-Spanish koine existed, it came into being in the Sephardic diaspora, forming gradually during the sixteenth and seventeenth centuries. That story does not belong to the present chapter, but the preservation of Spanish language and literature in Jewish communities throughout the world remains one of the greatest achievements of the Sephardim.

THE ALJAMIADO PHENOMENON

At the mid-thirteenth century, with all but the Nasrid kingdom of Granada retaken by Christians, the Reconquest paused, and the frontier remained stable for almost two hundred years. To a greater extent than before, the political separation between Christians and Muslims was a linguistic one as well: Granada was wholly Arabic-speaking, while to the north the Mudejares, or Muslims living under Christian rule, were abandoning their Semitic tongue in favor of Romance. At this period the "Aljamiado phenomenon" began to take shape.

The Arabic term for non-Arabic peoples is *al-ʿajam*, and for their language, *al-ʿajamiyya*; this was the name that the Arabs of al-Andalus gave to the local variety of Romance. Hispanized, it became *aljamía*, and with the addition of the past-participial ending, *lengua aljamiada* or *aljamiado*. The latter word acquired in Spain the specialized meaning of "Spanish written in the Arabic alphabet." We cannot now identify the precise date and circumstances of the first Aljamiado writing in Christian Spain. There was, of course, precedent for writing Andalusi Romance in the Arabic alphabet in Muslim-held lands, the kharjas being the best-known example. Further, it must have been common knowledge that the Jews in their writings often "crossed" language and alphabet, writing Spanish in Hebrew letters, Hebrew in Arabic, and, most important, Arabic in Hebrew. When the Mudejares chose the Arabic alphabet for Spanish it need not have been an articulated decision, but rather the outgrowth of a familiar cultural practice; as explained above, the script tends to follow the religion. The well-known reverence of Muslims not only for the Arabic language but for its very letters – of which one manifestation is the use of calligraphy in architecture and the other arts – would in itself have made Arabic script preferable to Roman, particularly for Islamic themes.

The earliest surviving examples of Spanish Islamic writing can now be placed with certainty in the late fourteenth and early fifteenth centuries. (For this whole paragraph, see Wiegers 62 ff.) The first securely dated document in Aljamiado is of 1451; other Mudejar manuscripts of the same period use Latin letters. These are, in the main, religious works – legal, devotional, or polemical – and, though not numerous, they do show that Muslims had been making a regular practice of composing in the Romance vernacular. Against this background the œuvre of the mufti Yça of Segovia (fl. 1450) can now be more accurately understood. At a time when the origins of Aljamiado were less clear, Yça was believed to be its originator; his fame and position, as well as his authorship of the first complete Spanish translation of the Qur'an, made such an inference seem logical. It now appears that he merely continued (though he may have sanctioned and popularized by virtue of his influence) a custom already established among the Muslims of Christian Spain.

Had the Christians not striven so hard to eradicate Islam from the peninsula after 1500 – that is, if the Mudejar situation had been allowed to continue, with relative tolerance perhaps leading to slow assimilation – Aljamiado might have known a different history. We have seen that Muslims of the fourteenth and fifteenth centuries, when they wrote in Spanish, used both the Arabic and the Latin alphabets, and perhaps they might have gone on doing so. But the forced conversion of the Muslims to Catholicism – in Castile in 1501–2, in Aragon in 1525–26 – by forcing Islam underground, may paradoxically have made the Arabic script more revered. With the virtual disappearance of education in Islam and the Arabic language, the new converts in these regions, now called Moriscos, had little recourse but to write in Spanish; yet they did so almost exclusively in Arabic letters during the next century. The script had become a symbol of cultural and group identity, an assertion of Islamic faith maintained even in the face of persecution. It was only shortly before the Moriscos' expulsion, in the first decade of the seventeenth century, that a few of their important works were penned in Latin letters; and in the Moriscos' North African diaspora the Arabic alphabet was definitively abandoned in favor of the Latin. In an Arabo-Islamic milieu it was no longer the Moriscos' Muslim identity that needed to be underscored, but their Spanish and European one; and at least one exile to Tunisia looked back with longing on the Romance language and literature of his homeland.[9] The same nostalgia, of course, helped preserve Spanish among the Sephardim in their own diaspora.

Although Aljamiado texts were produced and copied continuously up to the expulsion of the Moriscos in 1609–10, most of them originated in Aragon, where the crypto-Muslim population was concentrated in the Ebro valley, and to a lesser extent in Castile; these were the areas where Arabic had ceased to be spoken and written. In Valencia, in contrast – both in the city itself and in its hinterland – Arabic was a living language to the end of the Morisco period. Aragonese Morisco youths were sent to Valencia to acquire an Arabo-Islamic education. The Valencian Moriscos negotiated a truce in 1528 that allowed them a forty-year delay in the forced adoption of Romance, yet at the end of that period their linguistic situation continued much as before, and aroused extreme anxiety in the Christians of the region. The latter saw, correctly, the link between language and belief: they understood that although the Moriscos were nominal converts, their refusal to abandon Arabic boded ill for their loyalty to Church and Crown. Moreover the Church, though it proselytized native Americans in their own languages, was unwilling to preach to the Moriscos in Arabic, a tongue too closely identified with heresy. So solid was the linguistic barrier between crypto-Muslims and Christians in Valencia that it hampered even the Inquisition. Many Moriscos brought before the Holy Office required interpreters to understand the charges against them; others, already condemned, were summoned from their cells and forced to translate the Arabic documents that would doom still more of their coreligionists. Christians came to believe that only the total expulsion of the Moriscos could uproot both an alien creed and an alien language from Spanish soil.

In drawing the linguistic portrait of the peninsula we must therefore add the final strokes not in the iconic year of 1492 but nearly a century and a quarter later: only in the early seventeenth century were the Semitic tongues finally silenced in Spain. Just as Juan del Encina had rejoiced in 1496, "Ya no se sabe en sus señoríos e reinos [de Fernando e Isabel] qué sean judíos" [In the lands of Ferdinand and Isabella we no longer know what Jews are] (Resnick

58), the vicar-general of Valencia in 1610 could thank God that he need no longer hear Arabic spoken in his city. The Inquisition and Counter-Reformation then joined forces to ensure that Hebrew and Arabic not only would not be heard, but would not be studied or taught by Spanish scholars. Early modern Spain felt the rejection of its Jews and Muslims not only in the realms of economics and culture but also in that of language, and was greatly diminished by the loss.

NOTES

The parts of this chapter dealing with Judeo-Arabic and Hebrew were contributed by Raymond P. Scheindlin.

1 On diglossia, see Ferguson; for later refinements, Fishman. Kaye and Mitchell fine-tune even further the concept of diglossia as applied to Arabic.

2 "ʿArabiyya," *Encyclopaedia of Islam*, 2nd edn. (Leiden, 1954–), 1:564.

3 On the complex of Hebrew–Arabic interactions and the seminal role played by Arabic in the development of Hebrew letters, see *Muwashshah, *Maqama, *Moses Ibn Ezra, *Judah Halevi, and *Arabized Jews.

4 For a thorough inventory of such writings, see Moritz Steinschneider, *Die arabische Literatur der Juden* (1902; rpt., Hildesheim, 1964).

5 The question of what language Muslim women in al-Andalus spoke is intimately related to the history and role of women in that society as a whole. It has long been believed that since the all-male invading armies formed families with local women, and continued to import female slaves from the Christian north, the new generations born in al-Andalus were Romance-speaking, and culturally more Hispano-Roman than Arab, through their mothers' influence. Guichard's work undermines these assumptions. He finds decisive the social organization of Arabs and Berbers into patrilineal, agnatic clans: these tended to travel and settle in extended family groups, bringing their women and children with them, and to marry endogamously, with a preference for marriage between paternal cousins. In this system, "foreign" women would have been absorbed into the established order without altering it (Guichard esp. chaps. 1–4).

6 For bibliography on all issues, literary and linguistic, related to the kharjas, see Hitchcock; Hitchcock and López-Morillas.

7 There is ample evidence that the Jews preserved Arabic when they migrated to the Christian north, especially after the Almohad invasions of the 1140s: there were Arabic-speaking Jews in Huesca as late as 1190, and Judeo-Arabic documents from Saragossa date from the 1220s. Only by the late thirteenth century were most Jews Romance-speaking, though not necessarily monolingual (Wexler 175).

8 Cf. Raymond P. Scheindlin, "The Hebrew Qasida in Spain," *Qasida Poetry in Islamic Asia and Africa*, ed. Stefan Sperl and Christopher Shackle, 2 vols. (Leiden, 1996), 1:121–35.

9 He was the anonymous author of the astonishing Gayangos S-2 manuscript. See Oliver Asín; López-Baralt.

BIBLIOGRAPHY

Asín Palacios, Miguel, ed. *Glosario de voces romances registradas por un botánico anónimo hispano-musulmán (siglos XI–XII).* Madrid, 1943.

Blau, Joshua. *The Emergence and Linguistic Background of Judaeo-Arabic.* 2nd edn. Jerusalem, 1981.

Bosch Vilá, Jacinto. "A propósito de la berberización de al-Andalus." *Les cahiers de Tunisie* 26 (1978): 129–41.

Bulliet, Richard W. *Conversion to Islam in the Medieval Period: An Essay in Quantitative History.* Cambridge, Mass., 1979.

Colbert, Edward P. *The Martyrs of Córdoba, 850–59.* Washington, D.C., 1962.

Corriente, Federico. *Arabe andalusí y lenguas romances.* Madrid, 1992.

"Los fonemas /p/, /č/ y /g/ en árabe hispánico." *Vox Romanica* 37 (1978): 214–18.

A Grammatical Sketch of the Spanish Arabic Dialect Bundle. Madrid, 1977.

"Nuevos berberismos del hispanoárabe." *Awrāq* 4 (1981): 27–30.

Drory, Rina. *The Emergence of Judeo-Arabic Literary Contacts at the Beginning of the Tenth Century* [Hebrew]. Tel Aviv, 1988.

Ferguson, Charles. "Diglossia." *Word* 15 (1959): 325–40. Rpt. in *Language and Social Context.* Ed. P. P. Giglioli. London, 1972. 232–51.

Fishman, Joshua A. "Bilingualism with and without Diglossia; Diglossia with and without Bilingualism." *Journal of Social Issues* 23 (1967): 29–38.

Fuster, Joan. *Poetes, moriscos i capellans.* Valencia, 1962.

Galmés de Fuentes, Álvaro. *Dialectología mozárabe.* Madrid, 1983.

García Gómez, Emilio. *Todo Ben Quzmān.* 3 vols. Madrid, 1972.

Goitein, S. D. *A Mediterranean Society: The Jewish Communities of the Arab World as Portrayed in the Documents of the Cairo Geniza.* 5 vols. Berkeley, 1967.

González Palencia, Ángel. *Los mozárabes de Toledo en los siglos XII y XIII.* 3 vols. Madrid, 1926–28.

Guichard, Pierre. *Structures sociales "orientales" et "occidentales" dans l'Espagne musulmane.* Paris, 1977.

Harvey, L. P. "The Arabic Dialect of Valencia in 1595." *Al-Andalus* 36 (1971): 81–115.

Hitchcock, Richard. *The Kharjas: A Critical Bibliography.* London, 1977.

Hitchcock, Richard, and Consuelo López-Morillas. *The Kharjas: A Critical Bibliography: Supplement 1.* London, 1996.

Ibn Ḥazm. *Jamharat ansāb al-ʿarab.* Ed. ʿAbd al-Salām Muḥammad Hāṣūn. Cairo, 1962.

Kassis, Hanna. "Arabic-Speaking Christians in al-Andalus in an Age of Turmoil: Fifth/Eleventh Century until A.H. 478/A.D. 1085." *Al-Qanṭara* 15 (1994): 401–22.

Kaye, Alan S. "Modern Standard Arabic and the Colloquials." *Lingua* 24 (1970): 374–91.

Koningsveld, P. van. "Christian-Arabic Manuscripts from the Iberian Peninsula and North Africa: A Historical Interpretation." *Al-Qanṭara* 15 (1994): 423–51.

The Latin–Arabic Glossary of the Leiden University Library. Leiden, 1977.

Kutscher, Eduard Yechezkel. *A History of the Hebrew Language.* Jerusalem, 1982.

Lancel, Serge. "La fin et la survie de la latinité en Afrique du Nord: Etat des questions." *Revue des études latines* 59 (1981): 269–97.

Lewicki, Tadeusz. "Une langue romane oubliée de l'Afrique du Nord: Observations d'un arabisant." *Rocznik Orientalistyczny* 17 (1951–52): 415–80.

López-Baralt, Luce. *Un Kāma Sūtra español.* Madrid, 1992.

Malkiel, Yakov. Rev. of *Historia de la lengua española,* 2nd edn., by Rafael Lapesa. *Romance Philology* 6 (1952): 52–63.

Marcus, Simon. "A-t-il existé en Espagne un dialecte judéo-espagnol?" *Sefarad* 22 (1962): 129–49.

Minervini, Laura. *Testi giudeospagnoli medievali (Castiglia e Aragona).* 2 vols. Naples, 1992.

Mitchell, T. F. "More Than a Matter of 'Writing with the Learned, Pronouncing with the Vulgar': Some Preliminary Observations on the Arabic *Koine.*" *Standard Languages, Spoken and Written.* Ed. W. Haas. Manchester, 1982. 123–55.

Oliver Asín, Jaime. "Un morisco de Túnez, admirador de Lope: Estudio del ms. S-2 de la Colección Gayangos." *Al-Andalus* 1 (1933): 409–56.

Resnick, Seymour. "The Jew as Portrayed in Early Spanish Literature." *Hispania* 34 (1951): 54–58.

Ribera, Julián. *Historia de los jueces de Córdoba por Aljoxaní.* Madrid, 1914.

Sáenz-Badillos, Ángel. *A History of the Hebrew Language.* Trans. John Elwolde. Cambridge, 1993.

Urvoy, Marie-Thérèse. "La culture et la littérature arabe des chrétiens d'al-Andalus." *Bulletin de littérature ecclésiastique* 92 (1991): 259–75.

Vàrvaro, Alberto. "Il giudeo-spagnolo prima dell'espulsione del 1492." *Medioevo romanzo* 12 (1987): 155–72.

Wasserstein, David J. "The Language Situation in al-Andalus." *Studies on the Muwaššaḥ and the Kharja.* Ed. Alan Jones and Richard Hitchcock. Reading, 1991. 1–15.

Wexler, Paul. "Ascertaining the Position of Judezmo within Ibero-Romance." *Vox Romanica* 36 (1977): 162–95.

Wiegers, Gerard. *Islamic Literature in Spanish and Aljamiado: Yça of Segovia (fl. 1450), His Antecedents and Successors.* Leiden, 1994.

Wright, Roger. *Late Latin and Early Romance in Spain and Carolingian France.* Liverpool, 1982.

"La muerte del ladino escrito en al-Andalus." *Euphrosyne* 22 (1994): 255–68.

Wright, Roger, ed. *Latin and the Romance Languages in the Early Middle Ages.* London, 1991.

CHAPTER 3

MUSIC

Dwight Reynolds

Medieval Islamic Spain bequeathed to Europe and the Middle East a rich and enduring heritage in architecture, belles lettres, philosophy, poetry, religious thought, and science. This is no less true in the realm of music. The musical traditions of al-Andalus were celebrated in their own day, influenced the musical traditions of their northern neighbors, eventually relocated to and flourished in North Africa, and also spread to eastern Arab lands where they rapidly took root and thrived. At the easternmost boundaries of the Arabic-speaking world, however, their diffusion stopped; few traces of Andalusian poetic or musical forms are to be found in Persian or Turkish culture.

Along with the Ottoman and Persian classical music traditions, the Arabo-Andalusian musical legacy constitutes one of the great art music traditions of the Middle East, and indeed ranks as one of the oldest continuously performed art music traditions in the world. Arabo-Andalusian music (*al-mūsīqā al-andalusiyya*) subsumes a variety of historically distinct subtraditions that can be briefly identified as follows.

Iberian: These include the Arab musical traditions that originated in medieval Islamic Spain, specifically, the muwashshah and zajal, the two strophic vocal genres that emerged uniquely in Muslim Spain, and their associated instrumental genres. Although sometimes portrayed as a courtly tradition of the Muslim elite, the medieval song tradition of muwashshahs and zajals extended across sectarian and social boundaries. Jewish musicians performed in Muslim courts and Jewish poets composed Hebrew and Arabic muwashshahs. The tradition was probably also popular among Arabized Christians, Berbers, and the less elite Arab social classes, but historical evidence for this is sparse. Ibn Khaldūn (d. 1406) notes that muwashshahs "were appreciated by all the people, both elite and masses, due to the ease of understanding them and the familiarity of their style" (2:767).

Of musical traditions in languages other than Arabic, substantial evidence survives from the Iberian Christian Mozarabic musical liturgy, the origins of which extend back to Visigothic times. It endured until shortly before 1100 when it was replaced by the Roman liturgy during the reign of Alfonso VI. Mozarabic music is known through a variety of documentary remains, chief among them the Antiphoner of León (c. 1069), that reveal a complex and sophisticated transcription system of neumes, the interpretation of which has engendered a great deal of scholarly discussion. In Jewish communities, liturgical and secular music in Hebrew, Arabic, and later Ladino, collectively referred to as Sephardic music, flourished, as well. Modern traditions of Sephardic Ladino song offer a glimpse of a popular musical tradition descended, albeit remotely, from the time of Islamic rule in Spain. Otherwise, little musical historical evidence exists from the various folk/popular musical traditions of the Christian, Muslim, or Jewish communities of al-Andalus. Even less is known about the presence and possible influence of Berber music in medieval Iberia.

Post-Iberian: The effects of the musical fluorescence of Islamic Spain beginning in the ninth century were soon felt throughout the Maghrib and Ifriqiya; many famous composers and performers traveled back and forth among these regions. Although the muwashshah and zajal seem to have spread to North Africa even before the fall of Toledo and Córdoba, the post-Iberian Andalusian musical traditions received their greatest impetus from the waves of immigration precipitated by the Christian conquests and the subsequent forced expulsions of massive numbers of Jews and later Muslims. Over several centuries, Andalusian music in North Africa expanded into new social contexts including Sufi confraternities and, geographically, spread even to regions that did not possess large communities of Iberian refugees. Though the style, repertory, and language of these traditions harken back to a historical past, they were, and continue to be, performed at weddings and public festivities, in local cafés, and in many other contexts, such that in the breadth of their appeal and their role in daily life, they are equally as popular as they are classical.

The post-Iberian tradition flourished as a creative tradition for several centuries. The earlier repertory was added to in a manner that retained the basic literary style of the poetic corpus and – we can infer, but not historically prove – retained many of the musical features of the earlier tradition as well. Eventually, regional traditions of Andalusian music came into being in nearly all the urban centers of the North African littoral and in some cities of the eastern Mediterranean, notably Cairo, Aleppo, and Mosul. The traditions of North Africa are closely related to each other, sharing musical structures, melodies, technical terms, and other practices; the muwashshah traditions of the eastern Arab countries, however, are more tenuously related both to each other and to the earlier Iberian tradition.

The post-Iberian traditions eventually ceased to create new repertory (with very few exceptions) and devoted themselves to the preservation, performance, and transmission of an established canon. The conservative nature of these traditions in recent centuries has been noted by scholars, as have the meticulous methods developed for teaching and transmitting the accepted repertory.

Modern: Composing "in the Andalusian style" has remained a living tradition well into the twentieth century among Arab composers. Songs such as "Yā shādī l-alḥān" (O Singer of Songs) written early in this century by the Egyptian composer Sayyid Darwīsh (d. 1923) and the modern compositions included in the popular *Andalusiyyāt* concerts of the Lebanese singer Fayrūz are the best-known examples of this artistic impulse.

Hybrid: In addition, a number of musical traditions of the Arab Middle East are understood to be the result of cross-fertilization between local musical forms and Andalusian music of Iberian and post-Iberian origin. In these cases, the Andalusian tradition is typically seen as high culture by virtue of its historical pedigree and its expression in a more classical idiom, whereas the "hybrid" tradition is understood to be more popular, in no small part due to its expression in colloquial Arabic. Examples of these traditions include the Moroccan *melḥūn*, the Algerian *ḥawzī* of Tlemcen, and the *qudūd* tradition of Aleppo in Syria. *Melḥūn* means "colloquial" or "sung" (since the Arabic word *laḥn* can mean either "melody" or "dialect"), and *ḥawzī* derives from a term for the region surrounding Tlemcen. The Aleppan term *qudūd* is more problematic, but most likely derives from the idea of contrafactum composition in which new lyrics are "set to" (*ʿalā qadd*) the melody of an existing song, in this case to melodies of the regional muwashshah repertory. These derived traditions are understood to be Andalusian in inspiration and style, but local in origin and language.

Thus, only a small portion of the "Andalusian" musical tradition within Arab culture lays claim to being historically transmitted from al-Andalus itself. Andalusian, in its Arabic musical usage, refers rather to a vast family of traditions from a period of a thousand years extending from Spain to Iraq. These traditions share a common historical reference point in the musical traditions of medieval Islamic Spain. In practice, the traditions are linked by a handful of shared poetic structures, a typical stylistic lexicon reflected most directly in the imagery of the texts, and a number of shared musical ideas and forms.

The musical dimension of these Andalusian traditions, however, has received far less attention than their literary texts despite the fact that the muwashshah/zajal tradition was from its very inception a tradition of song (Monroe, "Tune"). This lacuna in scholarship is due in part to the paucity of musical evidence available in comparison to the relative abundance of historical materials for the study of Andalusian literature. Historical work on Andalusian music is greatly constrained by the absence of musical notation in medieval Islamic culture. Although medieval musical theorists writing in Arabic developed methods for the representation of pitch (using, for example, diagrams of the lute's fingerboard) and for conveying rhythms, these devices were rarely applied to the representation of melody. The primary sources for constructing a musical history of the Andalusian tradition are therefore literary in nature. Unfortunately, no medieval scholar of Andalusian culture left us a work of either the scope or richness of the monumental chronicle of musical life in medieval Baghdad, the *Kitāb al-aghānī* (Book of Songs) of Abū l-Faraj al-Iṣfahānī (d. 967). Although the thirteenth-century Andalusian scholar and composer Abū l-Ḥusayn ibn Ḥāsib is said to have written a multivolume work on music, it has not survived.

A limited reconstruction of musical practice in the Arabo-Andalusian tradition from medieval times to the present can thus be undertaken; however, the melodies and rhythms of the early songs are not fully recuperable and their major characteristics can be deduced only very partially and tentatively from modern repertory.

THE IBERIAN TRADITION

If contacts among Christian Iberians, Berbers, Arabs, and Jews produced musical traditions of a distinctive nature in the first centuries after the Islamic conquest of Iberia, history has not recorded mention of them, although musical contact appears to have preceded the conquest itself (Grunebaum). The Arab elite of the new western Islamic territories maintained a general cultural dependence on the high traditions of the eastern Mediterranean. Al-Maqqarī (d. 1632), drawing on earlier sources, cites eighty-six intellectual and artistic luminaries who immigrated to Andalusian Spain of whom eight – 10 percent – are musicians and singers. These include female singers of the late eighth and early ninth centuries such as Qamar, who was trained in Baghdad, and al-ʿAjfāʾ, as well as a group of three women singers – Faḍl, ʿAlam, and Qalam – all trained in Medina. Qalam was of Basque or Navarrese Christian origin and had been captured at a young age and sent to Medina, where she received training in music, dancing, calligraphy, and the recitation of Arabic poetry. She was later purchased for the Umayyad caliph ʿAbd al-Raḥmān II and brought back to Spain where she performed as a favorite in the Cordoban court. Three male singers from the early ninth century are also cited: ʿAlūn and Zarqūn, who arrived during the reign of al-Ḥakam (r. 796–822), and were said to be the first great singers to travel to al-Andalus from the East, and finally, the figure who eclipsed all of his peers, Ziryāb. The Umayyad court patronized musical traditions imported from the East, yet figures such as Qalam also suggest that local Iberian musical traditions may occasionally have been performed even in the highest circles of Andalusian Muslim society.

The arrival in Muslim Spain of Abū l-Ḥasan ʿAlī ibn Nāfiʿ, commonly known as Ziryāb (Blackbird, or Lark), in 822 provides Andalusian musical history with a symbolic starting point. Biographical accounts of Ziryāb provide conflicting information about even the most basic dates and events of his life (Wright 556–59). He was probably raised in Baghdad and trained there as a musician and singer, possibly by the great Isḥāq al-Mawṣilī (d. 850). In the earliest known account, that of Ibn ʿAbd Rabbih (d. 940), Ziryāb came from the East to North Africa where he offended his new patron, the Aghlabid ruler Ziyādat Allāh I (d. 838), and thereafter fled to al-Andalus. A slightly later account by Ibn al-Qūṭiyya (d. 977) similarly informs us that Ziryāb incurred the wrath of a powerful figure, but that this occurred before his sojourn in North Africa while he was a member of the circle of al-Amīn (d. 813) in Baghdad. He is reported to have angered his patron's brother al-Maʾmūn (d. 833) and at the latter's accession to power departed for al-Andalus. Finally, according to a still later work by Ibn Ḥayyān (d. 1076) cited by al-Maqqarī, Ziryāb attracted the anger of his mentor Isḥāq al-Mawṣilī after a spectacularly successful debut before the Abbasid caliph Hārūn al-Rashīd and left Baghdad under threat of death from his own jealous teacher. Thus, as Ziryāb's prominence in Andalusian history grew, the events of his life appear to have been resituated so as to bring him into direct contact with two legendary names in the history of Arab music, the musician Isḥāq al-Mawṣilī and the caliph Hārūn al-Rashīd; no mention of Ziryāb, however, is to be found in al-Iṣfahānī's *Kitāb al-aghānī.*

Once in Córdoba, Ziryāb established himself as an intimate of the ruler and arbiter of courtly manners and quickly emerged as a central figure in the Umayyad court. He was supposedly accorded a salary so large that it caused even the royal exchequer to object and ʿAbd al-Raḥmān II was forced to pay it out of his own privy funds. Al-Maqqarī reports that before his arrival, men and women in al-Andalus wore their hair parted in the middle, hanging loose on both sides; but in imitation of Ziryāb's elegant coiffure, the entire court cut their hair with bangs clipped straight across the forehead, level with the eyebrows, with the remainder pulled back behind the ears except for "love-locks" left flowing at the temples. At his dictum, courtiers began to use protoxyde of lead to ward off underarm odors. He also directed them how to bleach their white clothing, to change the color of their dress with each of the four seasons, to serve drink in fine glassware rather than heavy gold or silver vessels, and to serve food on leather rather than wood since it could be wiped clean more easily. He brought about a culinary revolution introducing new cooking techniques and new delicacies including asparagus (certain recipes in modern North Africa are still attributed to him). His innovative, refined, and luxurious tastes harmonized well with Umayyad aspirations to create a cultural rival to Baghdad in Córdoba. The prince may have ruled in matters of state, but Ziryāb ruled in all matters of taste. Ziryāb is Muslim Spain's most visible icon to its own emerging cultural independence from the East.

Ziryāb's fame, however, ultimately rests on his reputation as a musician, singer, and teacher. His vocal and instrumental abilities soon overshadowed those of previous favorites at the court. He is said to have known by heart more than ten thousand songs, in addition to being well versed in history, astronomy, poetry, and geography. In music, too, he is portrayed as an innovator, redesigning the lute, for example, in both shape and materials, selecting at times precious, rare substances such as lion cub's gut for the lower strings, silk for the higher strings, an eagle's quill for the plectrum, and thin, expensive woods for the body. If this experimentation was conducted in search of greater clarity of sound and expanded technical possibilities, given the costs involved, it could have affected only a small circle within the court. Another of Ziryāb's innovations was the addition of a fifth string to the lute, a practice that was not continued, however, by later Andalusian musicians.

Ziryāb is also credited with the establishment of a distinctive musical style that survived long after his death. Not only did all eight of his sons and his two daughters become musicians of note, but he trained numerous students and devised novel teaching techniques to improve the strength and quality of singers' voices. Modern tradition and scholarship sometimes credit Ziryāb with having created the "suite" (*nawba*; *nūba* in modern pronunciation), the fundamental form for Andalusian musical performance. If so, he could have created only a basic paradigm, for the poetic genres that constitute the actual content of the Andalusian tradition, the muwashshah and zajal, did not come into existence until after his era. Although modern writers at times see his influence even in modern practice and repertory, a commentator far closer to his time, the Tunisian author Aḥmad al-Tifāshī (d. 1253) reports that Ziryāb's influence was predominant only until the close of the eleventh century.

Aḥmad al-Tifāshī's two chapters on music from his encyclopedic *Faṣl al-khiṭāb fī madārik al-ḥawāss al-khams li-ʾūlī l-albāb* (Final Say for Intelligent Minds: On the Capacities of the Five Senses), the remainder of which is lost, offer a glimpse of how the history of music in al-Andalus was understood in the Islamic Middle Ages. Citing a chain of authorities going back to Ibn Bājja, or Avempace (d. 1139), the famous philosopher, musician, and minister of state, al-Tifāshī records that the earliest musical traditions among the people of al-Andalus were either in the style of Christian songs or in the style of the ancient Arab camel-drivers. After the rise of the Umayyad dynasty in Iberia, and specifically during the reign of al-Ḥakam I, singers and musicians came from the East. Ziryāb then developed a new style that became so popular and so widely adopted that all others were abandoned. Ziryāb's highly innovative – yet still essentially Eastern – style reigned supreme until it was replaced by a new style created by Ibn Bājja in the early twelfth century.

For al-Tifāshī, the songs of al-Andalus are of four types: *nashīd*, *ṣawt*, *muwashshah*, and *zajal*. The first two types were classical monorhymed poems whereas the latter two were strophic genres. The *nashīd* consisted of two elements, *istihlāl* and *ʿamal*; the *ṣawt* included only *ʿamal*. The *istihlāl* appears to have been a vocal prelude, probably with instrumental responses, and the *ʿamal* a composition combining voice and instruments. That the *istihlāl* was precomposed rather than improvised is clear from the fact that al-Tifāshī attributes certain examples to specific composers; it may have resembled the modern *mawwāl* of the Mashriq or the *istikhbār* or *baytayn* of the Maghrib, which, although allowing a high degree of improvisation, are performed from a set text and a known, though unmeasured, melody.

In his discussion of regional singing styles, al-Tifāshī refers only to songs with classical lyrics and not to the new strophic genres. This mirrors the practice of contemporary compilers of poetic anthologies who did not include strophic poems in their collections since they were not composed according to classical rules of prosody and form. Al-Marrākushī (d. 1249), for example, did not include the muwashshahs of Ibn Zuhr (d. 1198) in his work, though they were well known to him, since it "was not customary to do so in sizeable respectable works" (Zwartjes 41). In classical practice a poem circulated first as a poem and was only later set to music by a composer; the muwashshah and zajal, in contrast, seem to have been composed directly as songs, at least in the early period. This characteristic may have further strengthened the distinction between the strophic genres and classical *shiʿr* (poetry).

Al-Tifāshī describes the singing style of al-Andalus as a continuation of that of the ancient Arabs featuring a repertory of pre-Islamic poems. That of Ifriqiya featured primarily lyrics from poets of the early Islamic period, was lighter or faster than that of al-Andalus, and yet was more embellished (i.e., contained more notes) than that of the East. Of the Maghrib, he says that audiences there rarely appreciated the work of modern poets, and even then, only if the new lyric had been set to the melody of a well-known song. Ibn Bājja attempted to compose new poems with new tunes, but these songs did not achieve any lasting popularity and were, already in al-Tifāshī's time, almost forgotten. Apparently the combination of new poetry and new music found little appreciation, the implication being that in successful songs either the text or the melody was already established and well known.

Al-Tifāshī refers both to precomposed songs and to fabulous feats of improvisation. In one case, he cites an Andalusian singer who improvised for two hours on a single line of poetry and in another a singer who added seventy-four embellishments (*hazzāt*) to a single phrase. These passages indicate that some singers, perhaps only the most highly trained, engaged in extensive improvisation and ornamentation. Al-Tifāshī writes that Seville was the major center for this style and that singing girls trained there were sold far and wide. Interestingly, he often cites songs for which he names both the original composer as well as a later composer or singer who made additions or improvements to the piece, demonstrating that musical composition was accorded a level of individual attribution similar to poetry.

Then, in a cryptic but now famous passage, al-Tifāshī describes the emergence of a new musical style in al-Andalus. Ibn Bājja accomplished this, al-Tifāshī says, by devoting himself to the project for several years during which time he reworked the *istihlāl* and the *ʿamal*, and, working with skilled singing girls, combined "the songs of the Christians with those of the East, thereby inventing a style found only in Andalus, toward which the temperament of its people inclined, so that they rejected all others" (Liu and Monroe 42). But did this mixing of Christian and Eastern styles occur at the level of the music, the lyrics, or both? Did it involve only the performance of classical monorhymed poetry (the only examples al-Tifāshī provides), or does it refer to the singing of muwashshahs and zajals? Before Ibn Bājja, the muwashshahs had been known for more than two centuries, and zajals had been circulating for at least one century (and probably much longer in oral tradition), so the reference can scarcely be to the creation of the genres themselves. Or, is this an example of historical "telescoping" such that – seen from al-Tifāshī's later historical date – the origin of one or the other of these genres is indeed being attributed to Ibn Bājja? Yet why then does al-Tifāshī make no reference to the muwashshah or zajal in this passage? Whatever the case, al-Tifāshī reports that Ibn Bājja's new style was carried on and developed by a series of composers including Ibn Jūdī, Ibn Ḥammāra, Ibn al-Ḥāsib, and others. All of the forty-four attributed examples in al-Tifāshī's chapter on the principal musical modes of Andalusian singing were composed by members of this new stylistic school.

Al-Tifāshī mentions the muwashshah and the zajal as genres of song but is concerned only with the more respected classical poetic forms. Unfortunately, most medieval texts that treat the muwashshah and the zajal as literary genres provide little information of a musical nature. One exception is the Egyptian scholar Ibn Sanāʾ al-Mulk (d. 1211), who wrote the most detailed treatise on the muwashshah to survive to modern times. He wrote as a devotee of the tradition and as a gifted writer of muwashshahs, yet also as an outsider. He notes apologetically that "Your brother [the author] was not born in al-Andalus, nor was he raised in the Maghrib, nor did he live in Seville, nor did he ever disembark in Murcia or pass through Meknes, nor did he ever hear the *urghun* [organ] . . . he could not find a teacher from whom to acquire this knowledge, nor even a book from which to learn this art" (53). Rather, he explains, he himself deduced or extrapolated everything in his work from the examples he heard in Cairo. This may not, however, have been entirely true if we are to believe a recently uncovered notice on Ibn Sanāʾ al-Mulk in a biographical compendium by Ibn Abī ʿUdhayba (d. 1355) that states, "In his gatherings there was a Moroccan man who engaged in the composition of Maghribi-style muwashshahs and zajals. He acquainted [Ibn Sanāʾ al-Mulk] with their secrets and discussed them with him until [Ibn Sanāʾ al-Mulk] produced in their composition what was even more beautiful than those produced by the people of the Maghrib" (Raḥīm 134).

Ibn Sanāʾ al-Mulk begins his work with a categorization of muwashshahs by their rhyme schemes and structures. His description then proceeds by dividing the corpus of muwashshahs into contrasting categories noting, for example, that some possess an introductory common-rhyme couplet (*maṭlaʿ*) and others do not. Regarding meter, he notes that some follow the rules of classical Arabic prosody, but that the vast majority do not. He himself attempted to ascertain their metric system, but declared that this was impossible. In a passage that plays on the Arabic technical terminology for prosodic meters originally derived from the parts of the Bedouin tent (a "tent peg" is a triconsonantal foot and a "tent rope" is a biconsonantal foot) and the parts of musical instruments, he concludes: "They have no prosody but that of the music, no meter but that of the rhythm, no 'pegs' but the pegs [of the instruments], no 'ropes' but the [instruments'] strings, and only with this [musical] prosodic system can one know a well-formed muwashshah from an uneven one, a perfect one from a defective one" (47).

Ibn Sanāʾ al-Mulk appeals many times to the music of the muwashshahs as critical to understanding their form and structure. He notes that in al-Andalus they were composed and performed to melodies on the *urghun* and that singing them without the *urghun* is incorrect, although singing them to the accompaniment of an equivalent instrument is acceptable. At another point he notes certain pitfalls for the inexperienced composer of muwashshahs, stating that faults in their compositions would be apparent as soon as they were sung, due to the forced retuning of the instruments as the performers moved back and forth between the sections. He also states that sometimes the correct pronunciation of a muwashshah, such as whether to sing a word with a stop or a short vowel, is clear only from the melody. In his final section, Ibn Sanāʾ al-Mulk points out that some muwashshahs have lyrics that fit their melodies (i.e., syllabically or by use of melisma) and others require nonsense syllables such as "lā lā lā" to fill out their melodic line. The latter practice, incidentally, survives until the present and in songbook manuscripts lyrics that require such syllables are labeled *shughl*, or "worked." Though some of his musical references are as yet poorly understood, throughout his treatise Ibn Sanāʾ al-Mulk refers to the sung, musical tradition of muwashshahs as authoritative.

CONTACT WITH NORTHERN IBERIAN MUSICAL TRADITIONS

Debates over the amount of influence Arabo-Andalusian music may have had on the musical traditions of its northern neighbors, and in particular the role it played in the emergence of the troubadours and trouvères, have continued for more than two centuries. Unfortunately, whereas contact is often easy to document, influence is notoriously difficult to prove and, at times, even to define. Although some translated Arabic treatises on music theory, particularly that by al-Fārābī (d. 950), circulated widely in Europe between the twelfth and sixteenth centuries, they had little impact on musical practice.

Historical evidence, however, documents numerous contexts for direct interaction between Arab and Christian musical traditions in medieval Iberia (Boase 462–66), including certain clearcut cases of transmission, and provides the grounds for some limited inferences concerning the thorny issue of influence. The most prominent contexts for musical contact included royal and noble intermarriages, political negotiations involving the exchange of delegations and ambassadors, periods of extended captivity among nobles of all camps, the movement of trained singing girls and professional musicians among various courts, and finally, though with the least amount of substantive proof, the vast numbers of Iberians of all confessions who lived in daily contact with other communities. Contact, however, does not necessarily imply influence, for although music can at times cross sectarian and linguistic borders with an ease far surpassing that of other cultural phenomena, it can equally well be resolutely maintained as a significant element in a community's identity in the face of outside influences.

The most famous cases of intermarriage took place in the first generations of the Umayyad dynasty in Spain, many of whom married, or possessed as concubines, Christian women from northern Spain. ʿAbd al-Raḥmān II (d. 852) fathered his son, ʿAbd Allāh, by his Christian wife Ṭarūb; his grandson, ʿAbd Allāh (d. 912), married the Navarrese princess Onneca or Iñiga; she gave him a son, Muḥammad, who never ruled, but married a Christian girl, Maria, who bore him ʿAbd al-Raḥmān III (d. 961), the first Umayyad ruler to assume the title of caliph; and ʿAbd al-Raḥmān's son, al-Ḥakam II (d. 976), also married a Navarrese girl who became the mother of the third Umayyad caliph, Hishām II (r. 976–1009 and 1010–13). The case of the Umayyad royal family is the most prominent example of a pattern that is also reflected in other noble families among the Arab elite such as that of the Amirid chamberlains (*ḥājib*) who ruled al-Andalus during the caliphate's weaker periods. These numerous intermarriages at the highest level of Andalusian society imply delegations, negotiations, celebrations, the arrival of large retinues and entourages, and musical performances.

Medieval sources also tell us of Christian and Muslim nobles who spent months and even years in foreign courts while acting as ambassadors negotiating treaties or while held in gentile captivity as collateral for outstanding ransoms or other payments. The father of the above-mentioned Princess Onneca, Fortun Garcés of Pamplona, for example, spent twenty years in Córdoba as a captive. Al-Rashīd, an accomplished musician and son of the poet-king al-Muʿtamid of Seville (d. 1095), spent an extended captivity in the court of Count Ramón Berenguer II of Barcelona in the early eleventh century as human collateral for a payment to be paid the latter by his father. These and other cases provide examples where nobility of both sides had ample opportunity to hear musical performances from the other culture and, due to the length of their sojourns, to become passingly familiar with the major themes of the songs they heard performed.

No predilection for Christian music seems to have ever taken hold among the Muslim upper class; however, the courts of northern Spain did acquire a taste for the performance of Arabo-Andalusian music, even to the extent of hiring and maintaining ensembles of professional Arab musicians. A document from nine years after the death of Alfonso X notes the presence of thirteen Arab musicians and one Jew among the twenty-seven professional musicians in his son's household (Touma 147). Similar groups of musicians were part of the entourages of Sancho IV of Castile (1284–95), Peter III of Aragon (1276–85), James II (1291–1327), John I (1387–95), John II (1406–54), Alfonso IV (1327–36), and Peter IV (1336–87).[1] Most of these musicians appear to have been instrumentalists.

There is equally abundant evidence for another class of professionally trained performer, the female vocalists or singing girls, who moved from court to court, and noble household to household, bought and sold as gifts and even as war booty. Seville became well known for the musical education to be had there at the hands of older women singers. Al-Tifāshī records that a female vocalist was usually sold with a certificate that attested to her knowledge of calligraphy and Arabic, as well as her repertory of memorized songs, her expertise on various instruments, in dance, and even in shadow puppetry (Liu and Monroe 37–38). Such artists brought prices in the thousands of dinars.

Many historical accounts refer to the purchase, exchange, or capture of singing girls, but one particularly fascinating incident involved a Christian raid against the Muslim-held fortification of Barbastro in 1064. On one hand, from a Muslim source, we have the following story. After the conquest, a Jew was commissioned by a Muslim family to go into the city and negotiate with the Christian nobleman who had seized their house and daughters as his part of the war booty. The Jew found the Christian count comfortably ensconced in the Muslim's former home and even wearing the latter's clothes. The count remained adamant in his refusal to ransom the daughters at any price and the Jewish go-between discovered that the count had even taken one of them as his wife. Before the Jew departed, the count, in broken Arabic, asked one of the girls to sing and play the lute for them. As she did, he wept openly, so moved was he by the verses she sang though he did not fully understand them. The Jew left, amazed at what he had seen.

On the other hand, according to a contemporary Christian source, the booty after the raid on Barbastro included one thousand slave girls, many of whom were singers and musicians. One of the major participants in this expedition was William VIII of Aquitaine, father of William IX, often referred to as the first troubadour. William VIII would have received a large share of the prize for his prominent role in the expedition and thus, presumably, a number of singing girls. The young William IX inherited his father's estate while still a teenager; it is probable, therefore, that William IX not only spent his formative years in a household that included Andalusian singing girls, but that he came to possess them in his own right upon his father's death (Boase 465–66). Legal records from northern Spain also offer testimony to the penetration of Arabo-Andalusian music into the very heart of Christian culture – the Church. In 1322, the Council of Valladolid felt it necessary to reprimand churches for the custom of employing Muslim musicians and went so far as to institute harsh penalties for those churches that did not cease this practice.[2] Other legal records show that Arabo-Andalusian music was prevalent in Spain even as late as the sixteenth century: a commission investigating the question of the Moriscos under the authority of Charles V recommended the prohibition of Moorish music and dance (*leylas* and *zambras*) and this prohibition was reissued and strengthened during the reign of Philip II (Mármol y Carvajal).

The most telling evidence of musical exchange between the Christian north and the Islamic south, however, lies not in such historical accounts, but in the vast number of musical instruments that, along with their Arabic names, were assimilated into Spanish culture and then transmitted to other parts of Europe. The forty famous miniatures of the thirteenth-century *Cantigas de Santa María* depict seventy-two instrumentalists performing on every conceivable instrument, nearly half of which are deemed to have been introduced into Spain by the Arabs. The lute (Ar. *al-ʿūd*), the rebec (Ar. *rabāb*), and the nakers (Ar. *naqqāra*) are but three examples whose Arabic names reached as far as English. The fourteenth-century *Libro de buen amor* by Juan Ruiz, the archpriest of Hita, demonstrates the author's familiarity with a large number of Arab musical instruments including the square tambourine (Sp. *adufe*; Ar. *al-duff*); the horn (Sp. *albogón*; Ar. *al-būq*); the long straight trumpet (Sp. *añafil*; Ar. *al-nafīr*), the plural of which – *anfār* – is the origin of the English word "fanfare" via Spanish and French; a round drum (Sp. *atabal*; Ar. *al-ṭabl*); and many others. Beyond the names of instruments, medieval Spanish possessed dozens of musical terms and words for sounds derived from Arabic (the Arabic–Castilian dictionary of Alcalá, a rich source for this lexicon first published in 1505, contains 239 musical terms).

The transmission of such a broad-ranging and numerous instrumentarium, including strings, woodwinds, and percussion instruments, and their subsequent adoption at all levels of musical performance in Christian Spain and then Europe, implies a variety of different levels of musical contact rather than a narrowly bounded context such as the royal courts.

THE POST-IBERIAN TRADITIONS

In 1492, with the fall of Granada, the exodus of fleeing Muslims, and the expulsion of the Jews, Arabo-Andalusian music came to reside primarily in North Africa, but also in centers of the eastern Arab world where the tradition had taken root. In addition, Sephardic Jewish exiles carried elements of the tradition to non-Arab regions of the Ottoman Empire, and in Spain, Arabo-Andalusian music continued to be performed in Morisco communities until their final suppression in 1610.

The North African traditions are conceived of by their modern practitioners as maintaining a musical patrimony traceable directly to medieval Iberia, often even to specific cities. In popular attribution, for example, Fez is said to maintain the style of Granada, Tlemcen the style of Córdoba, and Tunis that of Seville. Historically, however, there is little evidence of regional styles within Islamic Spain, and the great mobility of musicians, composers, and singing girls even offers an argument against such distinct regional schools of performance. These traditions use a variety of terms to refer to their repertories and styles: *al-āla* ("instrumental" or "singing with instruments") in most cities of northern Morocco such as Tétouan, Meknes, and Fez; *gharnāṭī* ("Granadan") in the western Algerian cities of Tlemcen and Oran and in the Moroccan cities of Oujda and Rabat; *ṣanʿa* ("art/craft" music) in Algiers; and *malūf* ("customary" music) in Constantine and Tunisia. The traditions of the eastern Mediterranean, in contrast, refer to the Andalusian repertory simply by the term for its primary poetic form, the muwashshah. They also assert with far less emphasis the idea of direct inheritance from medieval Iberia.

Some traditions recognize the gradual historical development and expansion of their repertory. In Tlemcen, for example, it is commonly asserted that the "great suites" (*nawbas*) represent the oldest material while a secondary repertory known as "transformations" or "rotations" (*inqilābs*) represents more recent additions. Andalusian music in Morocco, Algeria, Tunisia, and Syria became intimately associated with Sufi brotherhoods. This connection may have its roots in the strophic poetry of two famous Andalusian mystics, Ibn ʿArabī (d. 1240) and al-Shushtarī (d. 1269), both of whom immigrated to the East and may have been instrumental in the rise of Sufi use of the strophic genres. In certain regions these brotherhoods served as the primary conduit through which the Andalusian repertory was preserved (Jones). Along with the Sufi orders, however, professional and nonprofessional singers and musicians continued performing as well, and in some areas, "genealogies" of master musicians through several generations of teachers are well known. In the twentieth century, new institutions have been formed for the preservation and performance of Andalusian music including private schools, clubs, amateur orchestras, regional and international competitions, festivals, government-supported conservatories, and national ensembles.

Regarding the diffusion of Andalusian poetic and musical forms into the Mashriq, scholars have identified a number of candidates as the first figure to transmit the art to the East: the above-mentioned Ibn ʿArabī, who traveled to the East in 1202 and spent the rest of his life there; ʿAbd al-Munʿim al-Jilyānī al-Andalusī, who died circa 1207 in Damascus and composed both a diwan that included muwashshahs and another work that may have dealt with the composition of muwashshahs; and Abū l-Salṭ Umayya (d. 1134), who immigrated from al-Andalus to Egypt in 1096 and spent twenty years there, mostly in prison, before returning to Ifriqiya. Most likely, however, the Andalusian tradition was first disseminated by professional singers and musicians rather than by poets or theorists.

In any case, the Andalusian poetic and musical traditions rapidly gained a footing in the urban centers of Egypt, Syria, and Iraq. The earliest known muwashshahs composed by a native poet of Shām appear to be two poems by Ibn al-Dahhān al-Mawṣilī (d. 1175), one of which may date to 1160. Only a handful of poets in Syria and Iraq are known to have composed muwashshahs in the twelfth century, but by the thirteenth century the genre had become well established in Aleppo and Mosul. The production of muwashshahs by local poets continued unabated well into the nineteenth century; Aleppo, in particular, grew famous for its Andalusian music.

From the fifteenth to the nineteenth century, few sources similar to al-Tifāshī or Ibn Sanā᾽ al-Mulk provide substantial information on the history of Andalusian music. In their place, however, are numerous anthologies of poetry containing hundreds, even thousands, of muwashshahs and zajals, and, more significantly, songbooks that include not only texts but indications of the melodic mode and rhythm for each song. Among the most significant of the anthologies are *Jaysh al-tawshīḥ* (The Striking Army of Stanza Poetry) by the Andalusian Lisān al-Dīn ibn al-Khaṭīb (d. 1375), *ʿUddat al-jalīs* (The Table Companion's Provision) by ʿAlī ibn Bishrī (dates unknown; sometime after 1375), and *Tawshīʿ al-tawshīḥ* (The Spool of Muwashshahs) by Ṣalāḥ al-Dīn al-Ṣafadī (d. 1363). Among the most important songbooks figure the *Kunnāsh* (Anthology) by the Moroccan Muḥammad ibn al-Ḥusayn al-Ḥā᾽ik (written c. 1786), *Safīnat al-mulk wa-nafīsat al-fulk* (The Vessel of State and the Treasure of the Ark) by the Egyptian Muḥammad Shihāb al-Dīn al-Miṣrī (pub. 1854), the *Majmūʿ* (Collection) published in Algeria by Nathan Edmond Yafil in 1904, and the Algerian *al-Muwashshaḥāt wa l-azjāl* (Muwashshahs and Zajals) published by Yelles and al-Ḥifnāwī (1972–82).

FORMS AND STRUCTURES

The melodic dimension of premodern Arabo-Andalusian music may be for the most part unrecuperable, but a sense of musical practice from medieval times to the present can be gleaned from evidence concerning three different aspects of the tradition: (1) the individual songs, (2) the Andalusian suite known as *nūba*, and (3) the instrumentarium.

Song forms

From the Islamic conquest until the time of al-Tifāshī, the most formal and most common song form in courtly circles was the classical Arabic monorhymed ode – the qasida – set to music by a later composer who was most often himself a singer and/or musician. These compositions were performed by trained singers, usually solo vocalists who accompanied themselves on the lute or were accompanied by several musicians on diverse instruments.

Eventually the postclassical strophic forms gained popularity among the elite. Whether they displaced the older qasida song form during the Iberian period or only in the post-Iberian tradition is not known; however, these forms came to be viewed in later centuries as the core of the Andalusian musico-poetic tradition. It is not clear that Arabo-Andalusian poets or musicians of the Middle Ages would have placed such singular focus on the new strophic song forms. However, al-Tifāshī lists fifty-six classical poems in the old style representing a selection of those still sung in his day and then forty-five examples of classical poems set to the new Andalusian style founded by Ibn Bājja that he says represented all the Andalusian songs known to him. A comparison of these with his claim immediately thereafter that singers in al-Andalus often knew five hundred songs from the four types (*nashīd*, *ṣawt*, *muwashshah*, *zajal*) may constitute evidence that the strophic forms already commanded a large portion, perhaps even the greater part, of the repertory of his day.

When and how the muwashshah and the zajal emerged have been the subject of lengthy scholarly debate and numerous conflicting theories (Zwartjes 23–40; *Muwashshah). Suffice it here to say that in the period from the ninth to the eleventh century, experimentation with multiple rhymes, refrains, and strophic forms was taking place simultaneously in Arabic, Hebrew, and Persian literatures, and probably in the Romance oral traditions of Iberia as well. Although written records of muwashshahs predate the earliest written zajals, it appears that the zajal may be the older of the two forms (Monroe, "*Zajal*").

The primary structural element of both genres – in contrast to the classical monorhymed ode – is that the text moves back and forth between two distinct elements: one maintains the same rhyme throughout the poem (the common rhyme A) whereas the other presents a new rhyme in each stanza (the independent rhymes B, C, etc.). From remarks by Ibn Sanāʾ al-Mulk, it appears that the common-rhyme and independent-rhyme sections were musically distinct and transitions may have entailed modulation between different melodic modes (*ṭubūʿ* or *maqāmāt*). This accords with modern practice in which there are at least two, and sometimes as many as four, distinct melodic sections corresponding to the contrasting textual elements.

Scholars have suggested that the opening common-rhyme section – the *maṭlaʿ* – was repeated in medieval performances as a refrain at the end of each strophe. The evidence for this, however, is indirect and the issue remains open to some debate (Monroe, "Tune"). There is almost no use of textual refrains in modern practice on which to support this theory, and the issue of the "bald" muwashshahs (those lacking a *maṭlaʿ* to use as a refrain), nearly a third of the medieval corpus, remains problematic. However, the Hebrew tradition of muwashshahs possessed a refrain even in the medieval period, so the existence of a parallel practice in Arabic is certainly a possibility. The final common-rhyme section – the kharja – was usually in a different linguistic register, voice, or even a separate language. The question therefore arises as to whether it was musically distinct and acted as a final cadence or coda. No evidence for this has yet appeared, however, which may support the theory that it represented a reference to an extant song and indicated the melody for its performance (similar to the modern phrase "Sung to the tune of x") (Monroe, "Tune").

Comparison to modern Andalusian traditions at times poses more problems than it resolves. Almost no modern examples possess a kharja of the type found in medieval texts, so the issue of a distinct musical coda remains unanswered. In addition, most songs in modern repertory are of types that evolved from the earlier strophic forms but whose antiquity is unknown. There are a large number of different rhyming patterns; the following are two common structures drawn from the Moroccan songbook of al-Ḥāʾik (late eighteenth century):

Ex. 1 "Complete"	Ex. 2 "Bald" (with no *maṭlaʿ*)
-------y -------A	-----x ------B
-------y -------A	-----x ------B
------x -----B	-----x ------B
------x -----B	----y ----A
------x -----B	----y ----A
-------y -------A	
-------y -------A	

The basic elements of contrasting rhyme sections and the use of internal rhyme are preserved here; however, these songs are quite often only a single stanza in length. Whether they represent fragments of earlier multistanza poems or were created as complete compositions is not clear. The musical setting of these texts falls into several basic patterns (al-Faruqi 2–4; Liu and Monroe 20–25; Pacholczyk 11–13; Raḥīm 177–84). Contrasting melodies are used in the different rhymed sections. Within each line, there may be a single melodic phrase repeated twice (once for each stich), but it is more common to find a separate melodic unit for each stich. Additionally, most songs incorporate an instrumental response (*jawāb*) at the end of each line except those leading into a new rhyme at which point the singers move directly from the last line of one section to the first line of the next.

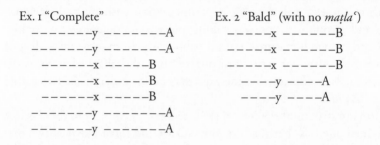

In later centuries, particularly in the Mashriq, the basic binary structure of contrasting common-rhyme and independent-rhyme sections in the strophic forms underwent further elaboration with the addition of a third contrasting rhyme section, the *silsila*, consisting of a rapid series of very short rhymed phrases. By the early nineteenth century, as seen in Shihāb al-Dīn al-Miṣrī's *Safīnat al-mulk*, larger strophic songs include sections labeled *khāna*, *dawr*, *silsila*, *dūlāb*, and *qafla*. Except for the *silsila*, these terms are grounded in musical practice rather than textual form. These developments seem to have been driven by the melodic expansion of the genre from two to as many as four, and even five, contrasting melodic sections. Further musical developments created forms in which each return to the common-rhyme section was performed in a different melodic mode and other forms that featured contrasting drum rhythms in different sections (Erlanger 6:173–78). Although these later forms are musically far more complex than their predecessors, they have as yet attracted little scholarly attention.

Contrafactum composition – setting new words to old music or the reverse – played a role in Andalusian traditions for centuries, parallel to the Arabic literary concept of *muʿāraḍa*, in which a poet composed a new poem utilizing the rhyme, structure, and theme of an older, more famous poem. As a result, it is not surprising to find a single text performed to different melodies and cases of a melody being used for several different texts. Despite these variables, it is not unthinkable that study of the musical structures of muwashshahs and zajals in modern Andalusian performance traditions will provide valuable insights into medieval Andalusian performance practices, but that work has yet to be accomplished.

Nūba

The most characteristic element of Andalusian music in North Africa is the *nūba*, or suite. Suitelike structures are typical of Middle Eastern art music in general and the Andalusian *nūba* bears resemblances to the *waṣla* form of the Mashriq, to the Ottoman *fāṣil*, and the Iraqi *faṣl*. In North Africa, the Andalusian repertory is contained almost entirely within these *nūba*s, whereas in the Mashriq, Andalusian-style muwashshahs and zajals were incorporated as individual songs into a variety of contexts including into the local *waṣla* suite form.

In Abbasid Baghdad the term *nawba* expressed the idea of taking one's turn when performing in a gathering with more than one singer (Sawa). It is likely that this "turn" included a standard sequence of elements including an instrumental solo, a vocal improvisation, and a precomposed song. Ziryāb's performances in al-Andalus consisted of a slow opening *nashīd* section, then a *basīt*, a more lively *muḥarrak*, and finally a *hajaz* section, but it is unclear whether these sections constituted distinct song types, musical genres defined by rhythms and tempi, or sections within a single composition.

In modern North Africa, the *nūba* has evolved into a highly complex structure. Each *nūba* is tied to a specific melodic mode (*ṭabʿ*, *maqām*). In medieval treatises on music theory, each mode was tied to a specific time of day, and tradition claims that twenty-four Andalusian modes existed, one for each hour of the day. These may never have existed, however, in actual musical practice. Modern Andalusian traditions, varying from region to region, possess approximately half that number, a fact usually explained by a decline of the tradition resulting in the loss of many modes along with their repertory.

Although each regional tradition possesses a slightly different format, there are larger general resemblances that unite them. The most commonly shared elements are one (or more) opening instrumental piece(s) followed by five vocal "movements," each of which contains one or more separate songs. The vocal movements proceed generally from slow to fast and the rhythms from longer rhythmic cycles to shorter ones. The slow opening vocal movements typically display a high degree of melisma and proceed to a more syllabic setting in the faster movements. At various points in the *nūba* there are instrumental and vocal solo improvisations. The balance between solo and choral singing and between solo and ensemble instrumental performance differs a great deal from region to region. In addition, the Andalusian traditions of Algiers, Constantine, and Tunisia demonstrate varying degrees of influence, particularly in the instrumental genres, from Ottoman art music with which they came in contact between the sixteenth and nineteenth centuries. Detailed descriptions of specific regional *nūba* structures are available in a number of works (Davis; Erlanger; Guettat; Schuyller).

Contrasting nūba *traditions: Fez and Tlemcen*

One meaning of the term *nūba* is shared throughout North Africa: the entire known repertory within a single melodic mode. Thus *nūbat ramal māya* can refer to all of the known songs and instrumental pieces in the mode of *ramal māya*. The *nūba* as a unit of performance, however, differs from region to region. To hear performances of *nūbat ramal māya*, for example, in Fez and Tlemcen is to hear two very different musical events. In Tlemcen, the master musician or leader of an ensemble creates the *nūba* to be performed by selecting among the known examples of each movement. The ensemble performs the instrumental introductions to the *nūba*: first the unmeasured *mshāliya* or *metshāliya*, if there is one (only two modes, *zīdān* and *muwwāl*, currently have an *mshāliya* in modern Tlemcen repertory), followed by the rhythmic *tūshiya*, the orchestral overture (only one mode, *dhīl*, possesses more than one *tūshiya*).

Next the maestro selects the core of the performance, the songs – one or more examples from each of the five movements: *mṣaddar*, *bṭayḥī*, *derj*, *inṣirāf*, and *mkhlaṣ*. Here the maestro has far more freedom of choice for in some modes there are numerous options within particular movements. There are, for example, at least fifty-four *inṣirāf* songs for the mode *ḥsīn* in current repertory. By combining melodic and textual elements according to his own taste, he may create an entirely new combination or he may choose to re-create a traditional sequence. The structure is in theory infinitely expandable, but in practice the performance of a full *nūba* in Tlemcen almost never exceeds two hours in length.

By contrast, in Fez a full *nūba* is simply never performed, for the term refers only to the larger concept of all known pieces in a single mode; a full performance would take many hours. In Fez the known repertory has been written down and codified and all known songs are understood to be part of a single canonical order (though musicians are at liberty to skip pieces occasionally in order to shorten a performance). If a specific vocal piece is being sung, locally trained musicians and educated listeners know what song comes next.

The unit of performance in Fez is the *mīzān*, or "movement" (literally "rhythm" or "measure"). After an instrumental introduction, an entire *mīzān*, or sometimes half a *mīzān*, is performed. Thus, although the Fez *nūba* is also defined as consisting of a series of five vocal movements (*basīṭ, qā'im wa-nuṣf, bṭayḥī, draj*, and *quddām*), much as in Tlemcen, this progression is never performed. Rather, the entire known repertory of *bṭayḥī*s from a particular mode is performed at one sitting, and, after a break, the musicians might return to perform another "movement" from an entirely different *nūba*.

	Tlemcen	Fez
Instrumental	*mshāliya*	*mshāliya*
	tūshiya	*bughya*
		tūshiya
Vocal	*mṣaddar*	*basīṭ*
	bṭayḥī	*qā'im wa-nuṣf*
	derj	*bṭayḥī*
	inṣirāf	*draj*
	mkhlaṣ	*quddām*

The diagram above is greatly simplified and ignores the instrumental pieces between movements as well as the improvised solo sections; however, it illustrates that in Tlemcen the performance of a *nūba* proceeds "vertically" by playing one or more examples from each of the five vocal movements, whereas in Fez a performance consists of a "horizontal" presentation of a single movement.

Instrumentarium

Although the Andalusian traditions are assiduous in their efforts to transmit melodies and poetic texts unchanged, they have accepted great modifications in their instrumentarium. Medieval sources indicate the presence of a variety of percussion, woodwind, and string instruments not commonly found in modern practice, including a brass instrument with a reed mouthpiece (*al-būq*) that both al-Tifāshī and Ibn Khaldūn deemed the most beautiful of Andalusian instruments, the organ, the plucked zither (*qanūn*), the lyre (*rōta*), and several forms of flute. Flutes, the *qanūn*, and even the Persian hammered zither (*santūr*) appear in photographs of Andalusian ensembles as recently as the nineteenth century. The modern addition of the Western violin (played vertically on the knee), viola, mandolin, the slightly larger mandol, banjo, and even cello have created the string-dominated sound typical of most contemporary Andalusian performances. The central elements of continuity are the lute, the bowed *rabāb*, the drum, and the small tambourine. The lute is found in several different forms including the *ʿūd sharqī* (the larger eastern Mediterranean lute), the *ʿūd ʿarabī* (a smaller North African lute), and the *kwītra* (a small ovoid lute with only four courses of double strings). The boat-shaped North African *rabāb* (not to be confused with other instruments of the same name but different forms found from Egypt to Indonesia) is considered by many to be the heart of the Andalusian tradition. It was parent to the medieval European rebec, has remained essentially unchanged in form since the Middle Ages, is not used in the performance of any other repertory, and indeed is not even known in eastern Arab regions. Often the leader of an ensemble plays the *rabāb*, the sound of which – as it "growls" its deep unembellished version of the melodic line – not only sets the pace for the ensemble, but adds a distinctive aural cachet that links modern Andalusian performances to those of their predecessors in medieval Islamic Spain a millennium ago. Though the *rabāb* remains a potent symbol of the tradition as a whole, its role is diminishing, and it is currently found in only a small number of ensembles.

NOTES

1 Ramón Menéndez Pidal, *Poesía juglaresca y juglares* (Madrid, 1924), 139, 249, 264.

2 Joseph Sáenz de Aguirre, *Collectio maxima conciliorum omnium Hispaniae et Novis Orbis* (Rome, 1694), 3:567, para. 68.

BIBLIOGRAPHY

Alcalá, Pedro de. *Arte para ligeramente saber la lengua aráviga.* 1505. Fac. edn. New York, 1928.

Boase, Roger. "Arab Influences on European Love-Poetry." *The Legacy of Muslim Spain.* Ed. Salma Khadra Jayyusi. Leiden, 1992. 457–82.

Davis, Ruth F. "Modern Trends in the Ma'luf of Tunisia, 1934–84." Diss., Princeton University, 1986.

al-Dulamī, Muḥammad Nāyif. *Dīwān al-muwashshaḥāt al-mawṣiliyya.* Mosul, 1975.

Erlanger, Baron Rodolphe d'. *La musique arabe.* 6 vols. Paris, 1930–59.

Farmer, Henry G. *History of Arabian Music.* London, 1929.

al-Faruqi, Lois. "*Muwashshaḥ*: A Vocal Form in Islamic Culture." *Ethnomusicology* 19 (1975): 1–29.

Grunebaum, Gustave von. "'Lírica románica' before the Arab Conquest." *Al-Andalus* 21 (1956): 403–5.

Guettat, Mahmoud. *La musique classique du Maghreb.* Paris, 1980.

al-Ḥā'ik, Muḥammad. *Kunnāsh.* Ed. Driss Bengelloun Touimy as *al-Turāth al-ʿarabī al-maghribī fī l-mūsīqā.* Casablanca, 1980.

Ibn Khaldūn, ʿAbd al-Raḥmān. *al-Muqaddima.* 2 vols. Tunis, 1989.

Ibn Sanā' al-Mulk. *Dār al-ṭirāz fī ʿamal l-muwashshaḥāt.* Ed. Jawdat al-Rikābī. 2nd edn. Damascus, 1977.

Jones, Lura Jafran. "The ʿIsāwīya of Tunisia and Their Music." Diss., University of Washington, 1977.

Liu, Benjamin M., and James T. Monroe. *Ten Hispano-Arabic Strophic Songs in Modern Oral Tradition.* Berkeley, 1989.

Marouf, Nadir, ed. *Le chant arabo-andalou (Colloque international Lille 6–8 décembre 1991).* Paris, 1995.

al-Maqqarī. *Nafḥ al-ṭīb min ghuṣn al-andalus al-raṭīb (Analectes sur l'histoire et la littérature des arabes d'Espagne).* Ed. Reinhart Dozy, Gustave Dugat, Ludolf Krehl, and William Wright. 2 vols. 1855–61. Rpt., Amsterdam, 1967.

Mármol y Carvajal, Luis del. *Historia del rebellión y castigo de los moriscos del reino de Granada.* 1600. Rpt., Madrid, 1941.

Monroe, James T. "The Tune or the Words? (Singing Hispano-Arabic Strophic Poetry)." *Al-Qantara* 8 (1987): 265–317.

"*Zajal* and *Muwashshaḥ*: Hispano-Arabic Poetry and the Romance Tradition." *The Legacy of Muslim Spain.* Ed. Salma Khadra Jayyusi. Leiden, 1992. 398–419.

Pacholcyzk, Jozef. "The Relationship between the Nawba of Morocco and the Music of the Troubadours and Trouvères." *World of Music* 25 (1983): 5–16.

Poché, Christian. *La musique arabo-andalouse.* Arles, 1995.

Raḥīm, Miqdār. *al-Muwashshaḥāt fī bilād al-shām mundhu nash'atihā ḥattā nihāyat al-qarn al-thānī ʿashar al-hijrī.* Beirut, 1987.

Ribera, Julián. *Music in Ancient Arabia and Spain.* Stanford, 1929. English trans. of *La música de las cantigas* (Madrid, 1922).

Sawa, George D. *Music Performance Practice in the Early ʿAbbasid Era 132–320 A.H./750–932 A.D.* Toronto, 1989.

Schuyller, Philip D. "Moroccan Andalusian Music." *World of Music* 20 (1978): 33–46.

Shihāb al-Dīn, Muḥammad ibn Ismāʿīl. *Safīnat al-mulk wa-nafīsat al-fulk.* Cairo, 1864.

Stevenson, Robert. *Spanish Music in the Age of Columbus.* The Hague, 1960.

al-Tifāshī, Aḥmad. "al-Ṭarā'iq wa l-alḥān al-mūsīqiyya fī ifrīqīya wa l-andalus." Ed. Muḥammad ibn Tāwīt al-Ṭanjī. *Abḥāth* 21 (1968): 93–116.

Touma, Habib Hassan. "Indications of Arabian Influence on the Iberian Peninsula from the 8th to the 13th Centuries." *Revista de musicología* 10 (1987): 137–50.

Wright, Owen. "Music in Muslim Spain." *The Legacy of Muslim Spain.* Ed. Salma Khadra Jayyusi. Leiden, 1992. 555–79.

Zayas, Rodrigo de. "Musicology and the Cultural Heritage of the Spanish Moors." *Musical Repercussions of 1492: Encounters in Text and Performance.* Ed. Carol E. Robertson. Washington, D.C., 1992.

Zwartjes, Otto. *Love Songs from al-Andalus: History, Structure, and Meaning of the Kharja.* Leiden, 1997.

CHAPTER 4

SPACES

Jerrilynn D. Dodds

In the beginning of his account of the martyrdom of the priest Perfectus at the hands of officials of ʿAbd al-Raḥmān II's court in Córdoba, the author – and saint – Eulogius, who would soon himself be martyred, paused to contemplate the caliph's contribution to Córdoba as a city: "since his rise to the throne, he has covered it with honor, strewn it with glory and accumulated riches, multiplied the pouring in of all the pleasures of the world, with an amplitude surpassing the imagination, of a kind that crushes in its radiance all the royal predecessors of his race in all that touches secular display, while on the other hand the orthodox church trembled under his terrible yoke" *(Memoriale sanctorum* 2:1, *Patroligia latina* vol. 115). In this expansive digression to the story of a Mozarabic martyr can be found a nod to the virtues of asceticism, but Eulogius reserves the most lavish, powerful language for the grandeur of the physical transformations of Córdoba: as he deplores the execution of the priest, Eulogius cannot help but take personal pride that the city now "crushes in its radiance all the royal predecessors."

If there were ever a moment in the history of al-Andalus during which one would expect a cultural identity to polarize along the lines of religion, ninth-century Córdoba of the Mozarabic martyrs would be that time, that place. This particular group of Mozarabs had resisted acculturation, had chosen nothing less than voluntary martyrdom as a kind of theater of resistance to Umayyad culture. This violent act and the Mozarabs' nostalgia for Christian hegemony of the past, in fact, were the centerpiece for a kind of Christian cultural revival. The Mozarabic Christians feared the decimation of their traditional and historical identities in the face of the juggernaut of opulent, complex cosmopolitan literary and visual culture. "The Christians love to read the poems and romances of the Arabs," mourned Alvarus of Córdoba. "For every one who can write a letter in Latin to a friend, there are a thousand who can express themselves in Arabic with elegance" (*Indiculus luminosus* 35, *Patroligia latina* vol. 121).

And yet, Eulogius did not see this extravagant embrace of the glories of

2 San Miguel de Escalada, interior

Umayyad Córdoba as contradictory: he was Cordoban; he participated in its glories and was complicit in the caliph's competitive zeal. For all their polemic writings and rhetorical gestures, the identities of the participants of the Mozarabic martyr movement could not be defined completely by religious difference. It was probably in fact their own degree of identification with the cultural fabric of Córdoba, with a visual world fashioned according to the Umayyad imagination, that gave birth to their passionate, separatist zeal.

Urbanism and monumental architecture became the natural ground for this dialogue; they were the stage for public acts, and – further – monumental construction was, on one level, almost uniquely dedicated to the symbolic task of positioning. Thus the Great Mosque of Córdoba, the first and most important public project of ʿAbd al-Raḥmān I, appropriated the city center, inscribed public meeting space with its signs: horseshoe arches falling on Corinthian capitals fashioned or painted with alternating voussoirs. These forms evoked both Umayyad hegemony in Damascus (alternating voussoirs) and Umayyad oneness with local identity and tradition (horseshoe arches, Corinthian capitals), but it placed the player in a space clearly structured, parented, by the new regime. This gesture was accompanied by legislation aimed at limiting the Mozarabs' capacity to use building as rhetorical expression.

The Umayyads' use of architecture as a public stage, combined with their control and strict limitation of church building, heightened the symbolic importance of the act of building. Thus, when the most politicized Mozarabs

3 The Great Mosque of Córdoba, prayer hall

built on their immigration to the Christian kingdoms of the north, the effect was a kind of strict historicism wound tight around the notion of resistance to the vibrant power of Umayyad visual culture. San Miguel de Escalada was constructed in 913 by monks who had come "from Córdoba," their "*patria*" (García Lobo). It is an austere, wooden-roofed, horseshoe-shaped Visigothic basilica: in arch profile, the partitioning of liturgical space, and lighting and capital type, San Miguel evokes the building of the Visigothic period of two hundred years before, a time when the church and its teaching had controlled much of the political and cultural vision of society on the Iberian Peninsula.

That San Miguel suggests not only a yearning for the past, and the kind of pure, unmediated Christian identity it implies, but also a resistance to the cultural power of Umayyad Córdoba is suggested in a page of the Morgan Beatus, a tenth-century manuscript sometimes associated with San Miguel de Escalada itself. On the page depicting the feast of Balthasar from the Book of Daniel, the artist Maius pictures the king and his court reclining at a table, while Daniel points to a disembodied hand, inditing the "writing on the wall" that warns of the fall of Balthasar's impious kingdom. Maius uses specific architectural reference to link Umayyad Córdoba to the impious rule: alternating red and white voussoirs, the most salient non-Spanish feature of the decoration of the Great Mosque of Córdoba. He was able thus to transform a well-known biblical story into a contemporary morality play, using architecture as his primary point of reference. Maius and his audience understood that polychrome masonry distinguished this horseshoe arch from Visigothic and Mozarabic ones – understood what made this arch a carrier of ideological meaning.

The notion is continued in the image of Babylon from the Morgan Beatus, but here it is layered with ambivalence. The doomed city, shown in flames, is a fantastic representation of an Islamic palace: covered with polychromy, geometric designs, and niches that display precious Islamic objects of the sort in heated demand in the northern Christian kingdoms. The image bristles at once with an opulence and otherness that permit the parallel between Córdoba and Babylon. And yet, it is a vibrant, beautiful image exhibiting a high level of attention to those formal issues that distinguish Umayyad architecture: it carries the pride and admiration of Eulogius's laudatory text.

This same layered meaning can be read in other churches constructed by Mozarabic immigrants in the north, as well as in those built for indigenous patrons taken up in the Mozarabs' polarized political message. The apse opening of the monastic chapel of San Miguel de Celanova is enframed with an *alfiz* like the doors of the Great Mosque of Córdoba, and San Cebrain de Mazote, otherwise a quite conservative, Visigothic-type basilica in plan, elevation, and arch type, was decorated with alternating red and white voussoirs.

A dialogue between these two positions – the idea of a pure, embattled separate identity anchored in Christian historicism, and the notion of a layered identity that acknowledges history, belief, and the rich texture of a multicultural world embedded in a powerful, cosmopolitan Umayyad hegemony – characterizes much of the architecture of Christian patronage of the Iberian Peninsula during the years of its many Islamic hegemonies. Thus, the plan chosen to create a sense of hierarchy and culmination in both Madīnat al-Zahrā᾽ under the new caliph ʿAbd al-Raḥmān III and the new *maqṣūra* of the Great Mosque of Córdoba under his son al-Ḥakam II were drawn from Christian basilicas. A sense of drama and mystery was added with a procession that seems equally to be drawn from Mozarabic sources (Dodds, *Architecture*). Creative growth, the awakening of desire and the forms that issued from it, was not limited to subalterns. The experience of living with a group perceived as alien was one of constant change for all parties involved – for the refashioning of identities both expansive and embattled.

In the northern Christian kingdoms, the impact of the Umayyads and the Taifa kingdoms that followed was even more profound for its mythification, for the strength of the resistance it inspired. As Church chronicles fashioned a vision of two peoples deeply alienated by virtue of religion and ethnicity ("On our side, Christ, God, and Man. On the Moors', the faithless and damned apostate, Muhammad. What more is there to say?" the Latin Chronicle of the Kings of Castile would later declare [Barrau-Dihigo 43]), northern Christians still made artistic choices that revealed fragments of

4 Illustration from the Morgan Beatus

more complex cultural identities. Bones of saints and kings were wrapped in the finest silks from Córdoba and Almería – often covered with Qur'anic inscriptions – and church treasuries were flooded with precious objects of ivory, silver, and bronze, all demonstrably manufactured in al-Andalus. Even those considered trophies shimmered with the admiration of the authors of the display. Objects of northern Christian manufacture are wound in false Kufic inscriptions; Spanish Islamic culture came to galvanize the religious and hegemonic aspirations of callow Christian rulers and churchmen in a way local culture could not.

This sense of interdependence with indigenous Islamic culture – one visually drawn most clearly by the presence of Mozarabic monks and the architectural style they introduced – gave way on the public stage to a violent and purposeful ideological distancing from Islamic material culture in the eleventh century. Monarchs began to look to France and the papacy for a uniquely Christian identity, and to reject any parts of themselves that did not conform with the purity of the ideal. Under Alfonso VI the traditional Hispanic – or Mozarabic – rite was suppressed in favor of the Roman liturgy, and at about the same time horseshoe-arched churches were destroyed, renovated, or replaced with monumental churches constructed in the Romanesque style. Memory faded; no distinction was made concerning Visigothic- or Islamic-style arches. The otherness of the horseshoe arch from French and Roman tradition marked a kind of cultural individuality and insularity that seemed to the Spanish Christians to set them apart from those Christian lands whose experience was unmediated by intercultural tensions.

Thus the architectural space of the north of Spain was transformed, made French. It was homogenized with smooth ashlar masonry, and rational orders linking semicircular arches and barrel vaults. The purposeful effect was an artistic expression that proclaimed an unsullied, unchallenged Christian identity, that wove all a culture's complexities of identity and yearnings for the other into fragile silks folded deep in the reliquaries and tombs of these Romanesque crypts.

To enforce this unnatural image of cultural purity, appreciation of the arts of Spanish Islam was tightly controlled; when it could not be encased in a context that exteriorized Islam through themes of victory and domination, it spilled over into the margins of ornamental reliefs, or was locked deep into tombs. Grand Islamic visions mushroomed from time to time in Romanesque Spain, but nearly always with the justification of underlining a political polarity: so the tiny oratory at Torres del Río, an entire building fashioned around a masterful austere ashlar interpretation of the mihrab dome of the Great Mosque of Córdoba, became a victory trophy for the members of the Templar order who built it. A symbolic replica of the Holy Sepulchre, it linked the justification for the Crusades to the Church's crusade on the

Iberian Peninsula. Spanish Muslims were, by this architectural gesture, swept up into the vast cosmic polarity designed by the Church in the interests of Christian domination of the assets of the peninsula. Both the Church and the kingdom were given a sharper, more forceful identity by virtue of the existence, the physical and spatial representation, of the created enemy.

Official attempts to link the struggle against a vilified, reductive Islam with the pilgrimage to Santiago de Compostela constituted an extension of this same idea. As early as the eleventh and twelfth centuries, St. James the Apostle became Santiago Matamoros, and he began to appear in monumental sculpture, as he was reported by Spanish monarchs, "on a white horse, with a white standard, and a great shining sword"[1] with which to lead Christians in battle against Muslims. He appears in this guise in the Romanesque apostolic church, with both mangled and submissive Muslims at his horse's feet.

These visions masked, of course, a time when the political and social alliances between Christians and Muslims were "kaleidoscopic," as Thomas Glick has put it. Taifa kingdoms like that of Saragossa were struggling to stay within the myth of their own uncontested hegemony as well, though they, like the Christian kingdoms, experienced a high degree of cultural and social interdependence with northern Christians on a number of levels. The insularity of the spaces of palaces like the Aljafería in Saragossa, and the elaborate nostalgia for architectural morphemes and compositions that recall the great years of Umayyad rule in Córdoba reflect a kind of architectural embattlement in the past, one designed to create a space where the act of denial might be maintained a few years longer. The elegance and sophistication of this art possessed, like the complex interwoven forms of the decoration of the Aljafería, no rational architectonic foundation, just as the political aspirations of their patrons were rooted neither in territories nor in the military resources necessary for their realization. So the Taifa kings of Saragossa made Christian alliances, hired Christian mercenaries, and created a mythic space of desire, of undisturbed Umayyad cultural hegemony.

The bipolar image of Christians and Muslims facing off at a single frontier is a mythic image born of Spanish Christian fear and Taifa despair. For the Spanish Christians, these gestures include a repulsion of the complexity of their own cultural identity. Even today, the act of imagining a pure Spanish Christian identity is acted out in urban space and architectural fantasy. On the eve of the saint's feast, a temporary facade inscribed with the words "Al Patrón de España" is built in front of the Cathedral of Santiago. It is an impertinent, carnivalesque palace, one whose structure mirrors eerily the image of Babylon/Córdoba from the Morgan Beatus. More specifically, it is a web of horseshoe arches and red and white polychrome masonry, providing the viewer with an easily recognizable, reductive vision of "Islam" in polarized architectural terms. On the stroke of midnight this vision of all that was Islam

5 Santiago de Compostela with temporary facade

in Spanish Christian cultural myth erupts into gaudy fireworks and is extinguished in seconds. A visual image of Islam in Spanish culture is controlled, trivialized, and erased: that is perhaps what Spanish Christian monarchs of the early Middle Ages wished to do with that part of their identity shared with Spanish Muslims.

Not until the intervention of the Almohads and Almoravids did the same level of polarization, of yearning for a pure religious and cultural product, rear its head in a Spanish Islamic hegemony. Because the official identities of both groups were founded in the notion of an unmediated Islam, their justification for moving on Spain was rooted in the alleged corruption of the Umayyads and Taifa kingdoms by worldly Christian culture. The most pronounced and public expression of this ideology was architecture: buildings were whitewashed or destroyed and replaced with new, austere brick structures with conservative hypostyle plans and restrained, austere ornamentation. At the Almohad Great Mosque of Seville, brick keel arches were originally whitewashed, and decoration grew from the thin, cool edge of a reveal here or a hidden *muqarnas* vault there. The interlace that adorns its famous minaret exists entirely in two flat planes; enframed in a rectangular reveal, it is a controlled field of repetitive surface ornament, far from the dizzying trompe l'œil composition of the Taifa period to which it is remotely related. Though these structures were made without any reference to the presence of Christians and Christian building, they are intimately related to them: one of their meanings is to protest the influence of Christians, and Christian culture. Their austerity is a moral rebuke to those who would look too closely at Christians as anything more than a religious other.

The architectural ideology of the Almohads and Almoravids included the periodic destruction of churches, and the complete remodeling of mosques, not only as a military measure but as a cultural statement as well. The destruction of churches, although not permitted according to the precepts of the Covenant of ʿUmar (the early document that outlined the appropriate treatment of Peoples of the Book in the *dar al-islām*), had occurred at several moments in al-Andalus, when the power of a vanquished Christian population was felt to be threatening to urban order and Islamic cultural hegemony (Dodds, *Architecture*). Thus, in the most heated moments of the Mozarabic martyr movement, churches built outside the stipulations of the covenant were destroyed.

The dialogue that surrounds towers, minarets, and bells is a potent one that spans the entire history of al-Andalus. Eulogius pits the call to prayer against the ringing of church bells in one account, and complains of the pulling down of towers that had exceeded a legal height. It is possible that the minaret as a tower from which the call to prayer is made rather than a low platform (*ṣawmaʿa*) grew in al-Andalus and North Africa not only as a defiant gesture to the Fatimids (Bloom) but in some measure from a dialogue of interaction and competition with Andalusian Christians.

Al-Manṣūr, who destroyed churches in punitive raids to the north, burnt an early church at Santiago de Compostela and was said to have sent its bells to Córdoba on the backs of Christian prisoners. In the Almohad period and after, bells captured from Christian churches were reworked as lamps to light mosques like the Qarawiyyin mosque in Fez. Their clappers removed, they hover silently in the air, mute and transfixed in a cage of worked bronze bands, bearing luminous testimony to the victory of Islam over a mythic, reductive Christianity on the Iberian Peninsula. It is against this backdrop that minarets like that of the Great Mosque of Seville ought to be seen; and its subsequent conversion into a bell tower and victory monument for Sevillian Christians – La Giralda – after that city's conquest was but the next parry in the match.

Not all architectural gestures were so enmeshed in dualistic political values. The twelfth century saw the conquest, by Christian hegemonies of the north, of numerous multicultural cities that had for five centuries functioned under Islamic rule. Though new Christian rulers at times emulated the religious toleration established by the Umayyads in al-Andalus, mosques were occasionally destroyed and replaced with churches, while new churches were constructed on a large scale and antiquated Christian structures renovated. The building traditions that resulted are today collectively called Mudejar.

Though the term "Mudejar" suggests that it is the architecture of subjected Muslims, it is a blanket term that embraces the traditions of profoundly interdependent collectives. The buildings were constructed by Muslims, Christians, and Jews, for patrons of all three religions. The term is often used to provide a classification for architecture of ambivalent political or religious parentage, and it has been employed as a catchall for the orphans of a tradition of scholarship that unwittingly continues the mythic religious borders that princes and the church hierarchy would have us imagine divided society on the peninsula.

In fact, there is a surprising formal consistency to Mudejar architecture, one that grows from the restrained, inexpensive formulas introduced under the Almohad regime. Churches like San Román in Toledo, synagogues like the one later converted to a church for the convent of Santa María la Blanca, bell towers, and palaces share the use of brick to create fields of planar ornamentation that derive from architectural morphemes. Some churches have detached bell towers that evoke the placement of minarets. Polylobed arches, interlace, and planar reveals transform the skin of building exteriors and must have given a sense of formal consistency to Toledo, a city of three lively, engaged religious traditions. Mudejar is, in fact, a visual document to formal values shared, a tradition so potent that it is not transformed but eventually continued by northern Christians who came to dominate politically and economically these Islamic multicultural cities.

At times Mudejar buildings can carry a political meaning as a kind of overlay to the collective values revealed in its style. The mosque of Bāb al-Mardūm was converted into the chapel of Santa Cruz sometime after 1186. The small brick nine-bay oratory was given an enormous apse embellished with striking figural paintings. On one hand, the apse clearly identifies the building as Christian, and the way it outscales the small neighborhood mosque structure that serves as its nave suggests transformation and dominance in clear, readable urban language. And yet, the apse is constructed in a local style steeped in Almohad – and even in local Umayyad – ornamental traditions, which use architectural morphemes as the basis for decoration. Blind arcades composed of brick reveals, pointed and horseshoe arches, and interlacing forms all declare that those who would appropriate this space for Christianity also desired ardently to be part of an established urban tradition. That tradition was one in which architectural style was Toledan, in which – though interiors might be rich in religious symbolism – the style of buildings were conceived to integrate them into a culture in which certain taste and formal values were shared by groups of divergent religious belief and political hierarchy. In Mudejar, taste did not constitute the expression of a religious boundary, as it did very purposefully in the Romanesque period: it rather bore witness to shared culture as it must have existed in most cities in al-Andalus before the twelfth century.

The style was applied to a more voluminous, Romanesque elevation and imported north to Sahagún, perhaps as an emblem of the capture of the old Visigothic capital of Toledo. And it grew unfettered for centuries in the city of Teruel through multiple political transformations. The towers of San Salvador and San Martín in Teruel, like Almohad minarets set with jewels, combine planar, aniconic ornamentation with ceramic and colored stone. As a style it marked this city's character: integrated, multiconfessional – a city whose physical urban aspect spoke more of the complexity of its population and history than of a single political or religious ideology.

The synagogues of Toledo bear witness to the dynamic presence there of an active, integrated Jewish community, and synagogues in Granada and Córdoba, and those documented in Segovia, Gerona, Barcelona, and nearly every other major city of al-Andalus, remind us that Jews, as well, flourished under the long periods of religious tolerance there. The synagogue that is now in the convent of Santa María la Blanca not only uses aniconic decoration that can be traced to North African Almohad tradition, but its plan is hypostyle, suggesting the impact of mosque design. Architectural style here is clearly dissociated from religious belief and practice; it becomes part of a shared visual language of Jews and Muslims without religious or symbolic political implications. This was probably a synagogue type, for a strikingly similar synagogue survived in Segovia until a fire in 1900 (Dodds, "Synagogues").

The Mudejar of the Toledo synagogues signals how closely Jewish architectural culture is linked to developments in al-Andalus. Interestingly, that orientation does not wane with the political dominance of Spanish Muslims after the fall of Toledo. Samuel Halevi Abulafia, a rich and powerful courtier, and the treasurer and adviser of King Peter I "the Cruel" of Castile, constructed a synagogue as a private residential oratory, much as a Christian king would construct a palace chapel. Woven into the skin of this simple, monumental rectangular space are the arms of his master, and inscriptions in Hebrew and Arabic. But the decoration itself – a skin of delicate, colorful, and complex vine scrolls carved in plaster bas-relief – is Nasrid, and reflects the deep links, the social, political, and cultural interdependence between Halevi, Peter, and the last Islamic hegemony on the Iberian Peninsula.

Among the many, stratified meanings that emerge from the Nasrid masterpiece, the Alhambra in Granada, is a sense of history and desire. In its plan, certain ornamentation, and symbolism, and perhaps in the celebrated lion fountain, can be found evocations of great palaces of past hegemonies and the brandishing of cultural history as a weapon of defiance in the final struggle for the survival of an Islamic Spain (Grabar; Ruggles). With the exception of a series of paintings that take a marked competitive stance toward Christians and Christianized northern culture (Dodds, "Paintings"), the entire city of the Alhambra is remarkably insular in style and reference, as proud and defiant as it is embattled, nostalgic, and controlled.

The power of Nasrid culture and the seventh-century history of Spanish Islam it celebrates would not be marked in the survival of the kingdom of Granada, or even of Islam on the peninsula. Its survival would be the mark of Islam on the victors who would polarize it: its survival would be found in the Alcazar of Seville, where Peter the Cruel, in his Christian monarch's interpretation of an Islamic palace, would find Nasrid style the most powerful manifestation of royal dignity and power. It would be found in massive urban acts of resistance to a culture already jettisoned from the peninsula: in Charles V's massive Renaissance palace, which seeks to defy the delicate beauty of the royal palace with the muscle-flexing rationality of Italian Renaissance geometry; in the Renaissance cathedral grafted onto the sprawling carcass of the Great Mosque of Córdoba, a triumphal marker still required a generation after the expulsion.

But the force and authority of al-Andalus were not the only memories feared and desired after 1492. Within Córdoba's mosque-turned-cathedral is an ornamental scheme of minute complexity, which spreads a skin of infinite aniconic geometry over its vaults and walls; in Salamanca and Teruel, churches would experiment with architectonic and aniconic forms. Deep within the folds of popular culture, ceramic, wall painting, woodworking, metal arts, and textile weaving would all continue to reflect a culture shared, a culture born of tensions and dialogue, of resistance and admiration. Beyond the posturing of princes and churchmen, beyond the brutal amputation of inquisition and exile, the arts still bear witness to a single culture without borders.

NOTE

1 *Crónica general, España sagrada,* ed. E. Flórez et al. (Madrid, 1747–1918), 19:331.

BIBLIOGRAPHY

Barrau-Dihigo, L. *Chronique latine des rois de Castille.* Bordeaux, 1913.
Bloom, Jonathan. *Minaret: Symbol of Islam.* Oxford, 1989.
Borras Gualis, Gonzalo M. *El islam de Córdoba al mudéjar.* Madrid, 1990.
Dodds, Jerrilynn D. *Architecture and Ideology in Early Medieval Spain.* University Park, 1990.
"The Arts of al-Andalus." *The Legacy of Muslim Spain.* Ed. Salma Khadra Jayyusi. Leiden, 1992. 599–620.
"Islam, Christianity, and the Problem of Religious Art in Spain." *The Art of Medieval Spain, A.D. 500–1200.* Ed. Jerrilynn D. Dodds, Charles Little, and John Williams. New York, 1993. 27–37.
"Mudejar Tradition in Architecture." *The Legacy of Muslim Spain.* Ed. Salma Khadra Jayyusi. Leiden, 1992. 592–97.
"The Paintings in the Sala de Justicia of the Alhambra: Iconography and Iconology." *Art Bulletin* 61, 2 (1979): 186–97.
"The Synagogues of Medieval Spain: Cultural Identity and Cultural Hegemony." *Convivencia: Art and Society in Medieval Iberia.* Ed. Jerrilynn D. Dodds, Thomas Glick, and Vivian Mann. Cambridge, 1992. 113–31.
Dodds, Jerrilynn D., ed. *Al-Andalus: The Art of Islamic Spain.* New York, 1992.
García Lobo, Vicente. *Las inscripciones de San Miguel de Escalada: Estudio crítico.* Barcelona, 1982.
Gómez-Moreno, Manuel. *Iglesias mozárabes: Arte español de los siglos IX a XI.* Madrid, 1919.
Grabar, Oleg. *The Alhambra.* 2nd edn. Sebastopol, Calif., 1992.
Pavon, Basilio. *Arte toledano: Islámico y mudéjar.* Madrid, 1988.
Ruggles, D. Fairchild. "The Gardens of the Alhambra and the Concept of the Garden in Islamic Spain." Dodds, *Al-Andalus* 163–71.
Valdés Fernández, Manuel. *Arquitectura mudéjar en León y Castilla.* León, 1984.
Williams, John. *Early Spanish Manuscript Illumination.* New York, 1977.

CHAPTER 5

KNOWLEDGE

Peter Heath

> The pleasure of the intellectual in his rational discernment, of the religious scholar in his knowledge, of the sage in his wisdom, and of the legal expert in his interpretive judgment is greater than the pleasure of the eater in his food, the drinker in his beverage, the walker in his stride, the acquirer in his gain, the player in his game, and the commander in his decree.
>
> (Ibn Ḥazm, "Risāla fī mudāwāt al-nafs" 1:335)

In Ibn Ḥazm's enumeration of categories of knowledge and those who master them, knowledge is clearly a polysemous and multivalent phenomenon. Each area required its own terms and territories: the rational discernment (*tamyīz*) of the intellectual (*ʿāqil*), the tradition-based knowledge (*ʿilm*) of the religious textual scholar (*ʿālim*), the abstract wisdom (*ḥikma*) of the sage (*ḥakīm*), and the interpretive legal judgment (*ijtihād*) of the jurisprudent (*mujtahid*). Ibn Ḥazm's categories warn us against presuming too narrow a conception of "knowledge" in Andalusi culture. Ibn Ḥazm also assigns relative priority to the divisions of knowledge, valorizing intellectual over physical pleasure in consonance with much Mediterranean ethical discourse since the age of Plato and Aristotle (cf., for example, Aristotle *Ethics* 1.1729–42).

THE DIVISIONS OF KNOWLEDGE

The pursuit of knowledge is a structured endeavor, and each community (Muslim, Jewish, Christian) developed its own taxonomies. Such organizational formats are not constant; they carry within themselves individual histories, fault lines, and courses of development. Nevertheless, Ibn Ḥazm, who lived around the midpoint of Andalusi history and who devoted a treatise to "The Division of the Sciences" (*Marātib al-ʿulūm*), can offer a good introduction.[1]

Ibn Ḥazm begins his survey with a discussion of elementary education. Parents should entrust the child to a teacher who will instruct him in reading and writing until the child can profit from "any book that should fall into his hand in his mother language" (4:66, trans. 194). Memorization of the Qur'an is recommended for its effect on linguistic fluency, stylistic eloquence, and good morals. The student should study the basics of grammar, lexicography, and poetry, followed first by elementary mathematics – arithmetic, geometry, and basic astronomical calculation – and then by the introductory study of logic and the natural sciences, such as knowledge of "atmospheric conditions, composition of the elements, zoology, botany, and mineralogy," and anatomy (4:72, trans. 198–99). Finally, the student should become proficient in history.

Ibn Ḥazm then considers advanced study of the same fields:

> The prevailing sciences today are divided into seven, and are the same for all people in all places and at all times. They are: (1) the religious law of every nation, which is always there, since every nation believes in something, either affirming or denying it; (2) the science of history of a nation; (3) the science of language of a nation. Nations differ from one another by virtue of these three sciences. As for the remaining four sciences, they are common to all nations and consist of: (4) philosophy, which is the knowledge of things as they are and according to their definitions from the highest genera to particulars; it also includes the knowledge of metaphysics; (5) astronomy; (6) numbers; (7) medicine, which deals with the body.
>
> (4:78, trans. 204, slightly amended)[2]

For Ibn Ḥazm, Islamic religious law (sharia) consists of (1) knowledge of the Qur'an, including its seven readings (*qira'āt*) and commentary (*tafsīr*); (2) the study of prophetic tradition (hadith), in regard to both its texts and their transmitters; and (3) jurisprudence (fiqh) and theology (kalam). Language consists of the above-mentioned fields of grammar and lexicography. Approaches to history vary according to whether they (1) focus on the history of individual dynasties, (2) offer general annalistic accounts, (3) treat specific areas, whether cities or countries, (4) deal with the lives of classes of individuals arranged in biographical dictionaries, or (5) employ a general, mixed arrangement. Included in the study of history is the science of genealogy (4:79, trans. 204).

After touching on the philosophical and natural sciences, Ibn Ḥazm discusses the advanced study of poetry, rhetoric, and dream interpretation. He finally observes that although all the previously described sciences are those usually designated as "knowledge," any area of specialization – "commerce, tailoring, weaving, navigation, agriculture, forestry, horticulture, construction, and other crafts" – can constitute a type of knowledge (4:81, trans. 206).

In addition to suggesting how fields of knowledge interact, Ibn Ḥazm, ever the theologian, ranks them. Although admitting that many sciences retain practical value, he remarks on the limited nature of such practical value, adding that "an incurable malady, a grave censure, and a ruinous loss will be the lot of one who acquires the loftiest sciences and spends his knowledge for the purpose of acquiring wealth and not for the purpose for which they were intended" (4:64, trans. 192–93; cf. 4:84–85, trans. 209–10). The primary reason to pursue knowledge is to achieve success in the afterlife, which one gains through dedicated cultivation of religious sciences.

Ibn Ḥazm also warns against the ignorance of the semieducated who believe that a little knowledge qualifies them as experts. Similarly, he notes the fallacy shared by specialists in the Arabic sciences and in the rational sciences, that is, that they deem their areas of study to be superior to other branches of investigation and sufficient unto themselves. Unable to disprove the efficacy of astrology, Ibn Ḥazm still distrusts it deeply. Nevertheless, his discussion of astrology probably testifies to its contemporary popularity.

Ibn Ḥazm's treatise on the classification of knowledge is only one of several that appeared in the fourth/tenth and fifth/eleventh centuries in the Islamic world. Their congruence suggests that by this time a degree of consensus on this subject had evolved. The durability of this consensus is confirmed by comparison with classification offered later by Ibn Khaldūn (d. 808/1406), whose theory of civilization (*ʿumrān*) was heavily influenced by evidence drawn from Andalusi and Maghribi history.

Ibn Khaldūn divides the sciences into two main groups: "one that is natural to man and to which he is guided by his own ability to think, and a traditional kind that he learns from those who invented it" (2:385, trans. 2:436). The first consists of the intellectual sciences (philosophy and the natural sciences); the second of sciences based on religious law, where the place of reason is to elaborate the details of already accepted religious premises. Ibn Khaldūn's subdivision thereafter accords in general structure with that offered by Ibn Ḥazm. To the religious sciences listed by Ibn Ḥazm, he adds mysticism (Sufism), which was more developed in his day. Like Ibn Ḥazm, Ibn Khaldūn respects dream interpretation for its kinship to religious prophecy. He then enumerates the intellectual sciences, followed by the occult sciences: sorcery, talismans, letter magic, alchemy, and astrology. Ibn Khaldūn entertains even deeper reservations about alchemy and astrology than Ibn Ḥazm. He admits the theoretical possibility of the manipulation of the supernatural, but he distrusts its practical application, warning against trusting practitioners of letter magic (*al-sīmiyāʾ*, onomatomancy), for example (3:146, trans. 3:182). Finally, he warns against the potentially corrupting effects of philosophy on those without prior knowledge of Muslim religious sciences (3:220, trans. 3:257–58).

As useful as they are, the divisions of knowledge by thinkers such as Ibn

Ḥazm and Ibn Khaldūn pay relatively little attention to the social contexts and modes of transmission of knowledge. To incorporate such perspectives, this essay begins with a summary discussion of modes of transmission, both public and private, and then constructs a historical and socially contextualized overview of the accomplishments of Andalusians, within the realm of three categories of knowledge: the sacred (religious), the profane (political), and the rationalist (scientific and philosophical). In concrete historical contexts, of course, participants in these spheres often interacted and interlapped, as witnessed by a figure such as Ibn Rushd (d. 595/1198), who was a well-known qadi, a sometime adviser to his Almoravid ruler, and a noted philosopher and physician. Despite such practical overlap, considering these spheres of knowledge separately has the organizational advantage of clarifying general demarcations of intellectual pursuit.

ACQUISITION AND TRANSMISSION OF KNOWLEDGE

For Muslims in al-Andalus, education consisted of three stages: elementary, advanced, and specialized. The first centered around the school (*maktab* or *kuttāb*), the second around study in the mosque, and the third around lengthy apprenticeships (*ṣuḥba, mulāzama*) with scholars in one's chosen field, apprenticeships that frequently entailed extensive travel.

The general structure of premodern Islamic education was private and personal. Individuals from one generation transmitted knowledge to those of the next on an oral, interactive basis. As a result, the particular geographical or institutional venue of instruction mattered much less than it did in the university system that developed in Christian Europe. Although famous centers of education existed in Córdoba, al-Qayrawan, Mecca and Medina, Nishapur and Bukhara, and later in Cairo, Fez, and Tunis, these cities were more renowned for their concentration of well-regarded scholars than for the presence of institutions famous in themselves (ʿĪsā 211–16; Berkey 21–43).

Elementary education was the responsibility of parents. Wealthy parents hired tutors or occasionally took charge of their children's education themselves. Most parents, however, sent their children to private elementary schools, diverse in size, quality, and cost. Children began school usually between the ages of five and eight, and studied reading, writing, the Qur'an, and basic levels of language, literature, history, the religious sciences, mathematics, and the sciences. Those taking the full course of elementary study completed it between the ages of thirteen and fifteen, at which time they entered their chosen professions or undertook advanced training (ʿĪsā 216–20).

The private nature of education limited it to those who could afford it.

Consequently, more children received education in times and places of prosperity than in areas of poverty or eras of economic distress and dislocation. Venue also varied. Some schoolmasters ran schools, others taught in their homes, while wealthy families hired tutors. There is little explicit reference to girls attending schools, but educated women, perhaps taught mainly in their parents' homes, are mentioned (ʿĪsā 220–23, 261–62).

During the second stage, advanced education, venue depended on field of study. The most common site for study of the religious sciences or related fields, such as early Arabic literature and history, was the mosque, while teachers of medicine and science or of such profane arts as adab would train students privately in their houses or on the job. In the mosque, instruction was specialized; students attended classes with masters in individual subjects, with each teacher guiding them through the study of books essential to their respective fields. Progress proceeded book by book; after mastering a book or set of books in a field, students received a certificate (*ijāza*) in which the teacher attested to their mastery of the book and to their competency in teaching it to others. Thereafter, a student moved to the next level, either with the same teacher or with one better qualified for a higher level of study. In this way, students both completed their advanced general education and began to specialize in one or more areas (ʿĪsā 263–81; Makdisi, *Rise of Colleges* 10–27).

Remuneration was essentially private; students paid individual fees to their teachers. Occasionally, a scholar received a royal or government stipend or was provided with a salary through the mosque in which he taught, but such instances were not the rule, especially early in Andalusi history. Some teachers helped support themselves by taking supplemental employment, becoming the muezzin or imam of a mosque, for example. Gradually, there developed the tradition of dedicating religious bequests (*hubūs* or *waqf*) to mosques, which could provide regular stipends for faculty and advanced students, increasing the level of institutional support. In al-Andalus, most such endowments were donated to mosques, since, unlike other parts of the Islamic world (including the Maghrib), the advanced college (or *madrasa*) remained a minor institution, with only that founded in Granada in the mid-fourteenth century achieving any note. A perplexed al-Maqqarī (d. 1041/1632) remarked that

> Notwithstanding the proficiency of the Andalusis in all the departments of science, we are informed that there were no colleges in that country where the youth might be educated and inspired with the love of science, as is the case in the East; there seem to have been instead several professorships attached to every mosque, and numerous professors who delivered lectures on various subjects for a fixed salary which they received; and had it not been so, science could not have flourished as it did.
>
> (1:208, trans. 1:140–41)

Those who wished to specialize in nonreligious studies sought their teachers from among recognized specialists. Those desiring to enter government bureaucracy became apprentices in chancelleries or other governmental departments, where they received on-the-job training. Those interested in medicine or the sciences attached themselves to one or more masters who guided them through the theory and practice of their disciplines. Often fields became family specialties, so that sons of courtiers and officials entered governmental administration, and children of physicians, such as those of the famed Banū Zuhr, were trained by their fathers and even replaced them in their positions when they retired.

With mysticism, instruction also assumed a master–student format, but progress was measured in spiritual development as well as mastery of texts. In the context of this personal system, the emergence of such specialized physical institutions as the Sufi convent (*ribāṭ*) in the fourth/tenth and fifth/eleventh centuries or the religious college (*madrasa*) in the mid-eighth/fourteenth century represented only avenues for providing institutional support – scholarships and stipends for students and salaries and benefits for teachers – for what remained an essentially private and decentralized system of education.

For the final stage of specialized study, students often traveled to centers of learning in North Africa and the East. Such journeys were essential for maintaining the quality and prestige of regional centers of education. Studying with and comparing one's level of education and expertise with masters and colleagues in other areas of the Islamic world boosted one's own career and validated the quality of education received in al-Andalus. For the religious scholar, Mecca and Medina were central. For the profane scholar, first Baghdad and then post-Fatimid Cairo were equally important. By this time, the student had also become a qualified teacher and could support himself by transmitting the learning he had acquired in al-Andalus.

Oral transmission was essential to the structure of Islamic education and is exemplified by the model of hadith. In transmitting the accepted corpus of prophetic tradition, oral communication was more highly valued than studying written hadith collections. Written versions existed from the third/ninth century, but specialists in hadith regarded them as secondary aids to the more valid form of knowledge learned and memorized through oral instruction. In this way, specialists in hadith transmitted the prophet Muhammad's very words from one generation to the next without dilution or alteration. The voice of the Prophet echoed through the centuries to reach each new generation of Muslims with a force that replicated, to the extent possible, its original verbal authenticity and spiritual force (Goldziher 2:164–66; Berkey 23–27; Makdisi, *Rise of Colleges* 99–105; Nasr 57–58).

Similar models existed in the other traditional sciences, whether linguistic, literary, or religious. Muslim biographical dictionaries devoted to the lives of scholars focus on two areas: (1) the place the individual holds in this chain of transmission, that is, the identities of his teachers and his students, and (2) the rank he holds in mastery of his fields of specialization. By knowing the scholar's teachers and professional reputation, readers can evaluate his trustworthiness as a transmitter. Attestation of competency was demonstrated by the conferral of an *ijāza* testifying that on the ideal, and often enough on the practical, level the scholar had committed the book studied to memory, and thus truly knew it.

This expectation of personal oral transmission explains the importance of travel. When scholars returned to al-Andalus after study in the East, or when prominent scholars from the East traveled to settle and teach in al-Andalus, their arrival signified the importation of new or renewed authentic lines of scholarly transmission extending back to the founders and acknowledged masters of each field. A specialist in grammar could trace his pedagogic lineage back to such masters as al-Sībawayhī or al-Kisāʾī; an expert of prosody or lexicography to al-Khalīl ibn Aḥmad; a scholar in early Arabic literature to al-Aṣmaʿī and Abū ʿUbayda – all early masters from the second/eighth and third/ninth centuries. Students traveling to obtain *ijāza*s were in fact accumulating scholarly pedigrees.

Despite ideals of oral transmission, learned individuals did value books. Some scholars accumulated extensive libraries, and anecdotes attest that wealthy individuals valued books as items of social prestige. Large libraries were crucial for the development or survival of certain fields. The bibliophile caliph al-Ḥakam II developed a library that reputedly encompassed more than four hundred thousand volumes. This influx of books provided a basis for the development of philosophy and the sciences in al-Andalus. Even after the library was sold off, looted, and dispersed in the postcalifate period, sufficient volumes survived to ensure the continued study and teaching of the rational sciences (Ṣāʿid al-Andalusī 162–65, trans. 61–62). Libraries and booksellers were also places where scholars and bibliophiles met informally to discuss subjects of mutual interest (Makdisi, *Rise of Colleges* 24–27; Makdisi, *Rise of Humanism* 54–57).

Learned interchange also took place in assemblies and soirees. These were regular meetings held in mosques or in private homes, sponsored by wealthy intellectuals or members of the court. Although these groups might consist of friendly study groups and seminars in which social interaction was an important element, it was not unusual for professional competitiveness to infuse into them a strong degree of disputational asperity (ʿĪsā 349–52; Makdisi, *Rise of Colleges* 129–47; Makdisi, *Rise of Humanism* 210–12).

Because scholars earned their livelihood from fees paid them by their students, social affluence played an important role in education. If the surplus social wealth that underpinned education decreased, so did the number of students and subsequently the number of teachers and scholars. It took decades for Andalusi society to establish the network of flourishing cities necessary to accumulate this wealth. Once achieved, however, the important cities and their relative proximity to one another provided a base to support a rich intellectual and cultural tradition, even in the face of the political factionalism and tumult of the Taifa, Almoravid, and Almohad periods.

The loss of Muslim political control to Christian states, however, ultimately undercut the economic and social foundations of centers of learning outside Granada. Even in Granada, where a high level of culture was maintained, the small size of the Nasrid territories could not provide a base broad enough for many new intellectual endeavors; the center of gravity for Muslim education moved to North Africa, while the focus of Jewish and Christian education moved to cultural centers in Christian Europe.

HISTORICAL OVERVIEW OF ACHIEVEMENTS

The first period (92/711–350/961)

The arrival in 138/756 of the Umayyad prince ʿAbd al-Raḥmān I ibn Muʿāwiya to al-Andalus, after four decades of political instability, fostered a desire for political unity. Although this desire often remained more ideal than reality, during the ensuing century and a half, it nonetheless promoted the flow of intellectual ties with the East and increased the cultural and political prestige of the pursuit of knowledge. The creation of the caliphal state in 316/929 provided a century of relative political stability that ensured a harmonious and nurturing environment for the pursuit of knowledge and laid the foundation for the period of cultural efflorescence that followed.

Sacred knowledge

The production of religious knowledge in the early centuries of Andalusi history is closely connected with the establishment of independent political rule under the Umayyad dynasty. During the first forty years of Muslim rule, the Umayyad caliphs of Damascus appointed a series of governors who thereafter appointed judges or other religious authorities. During this period there was apparently neither desire nor need to create a distinctly Andalusi policy of religious practice or legal doctrine. The most prominent legal *madhhab* was that of al-Auzāʿī (d. 157/774), the imam of the school of jurisprudence followed in Damascus at the time. Al-Auzāʿī based his teachings on the orally transmitted traditions of the Prophet and his companions, relying as little as possible on personal legal judgment (*al-ra'y*).

With the establishment in al-Andalus of an independent Umayyad polity, however, its princes saw an advantage in adopting a *madhhab* untainted by the political failure of the collapse of the Umayyad dynasty in the East and yet distinct from the Hanafi school favored by the new Abbasid regime. They selected the Medina-based *madhhab* established by Mālik ibn Anas (d. 179/796), who considered the customary practice of Medina as the normative foundation for legal practice. As Ibn Khaldūn states:

> Mālik was of the opinion that by virtue of their religion and traditionalism, the Medinese always necessarily followed each preceding generation of Medinese, in respect to what they cared to do or not. The (process would have gone back) to the generation that was in contact with the actions of the Prophet, and they would have learned from him (what to do and not to do). In (Mālik's) opinion, the practice of the Medinese, thus, is the basic legal evidence. (3:5, trans. 3:7)

According to al-Maqqarī, sources provide slightly varying explanations for this change of *madhhab.* He prefers the explanation that several Andalusi doctors encountered Imam Mālik in Medina, heard his doctrines from his own mouth, and began to spread them. When al-Ḥakam I heard of these ideas, he held several conferences with their exponents, then ordered the establishment of the *madhhab* of Mālik ibn Anas throughout his dominions (4:217, trans. 1:113, slightly modified).[3]

Al-Maqqarī's account sheds light on the interaction between the professional aspirations of the ulama and exigencies of state politics. Those ulama who advocated the Maliki *madhhab* undertook the burden of traveling to Mecca and Medina for the purposes of pilgrimage and study, and once there they were sufficiently astute to recognize the advantages of becoming Mālik's disciples. They were attracted enough to his doctrines to work to spread them in distant al-Andalus, yet they no doubt understood the extent to which their being his students and thus promoting the religious authority that stemmed from their direct personal and scholarly links with the imam would enhance their own prestige among their colleagues on their return. This process had already begun in the reign of Hishām I, when returnees from the East, such as ʿAbd al-Raḥmān Shabṭūn, known as the Faqih of al-Andalus, propagated Mālik's opinions (2:255, trans. 1:100–101).

Similarly, al-Ḥakam I was intelligent enough to recognize the advantage of allying himself with this energetic group of ulama growing in prestige and number, and adopting a legal school directly connected with the traditionalist, pietist, and latently anti-Abbasid tendencies of Medina that Mālik's school represented. Hence, the desire for religious authenticity and authority, professional careerism, and the interests of politics intermeshed in a manner that was to establish the uncontested authority of the Maliki school for the remainder of Andalusi (and Maghribi) history (cf. ʿĪsā 82–88). Among the many prominent disciples of Mālik at the courts of al-Ḥakam I and ʿAbd al-Raḥman II were Yaḥyā ibn Yaḥyā al-Laythī, Ibn Ḥabīb, author of the authoritative Maliki textbook *Kitāb al-wāḍiḥa* (Book of Clarification), whose student al-ʿUṭbi wrote another standard textbook, *al-Mustakhraja* (The Supplemented, i.e., *al-Wāḍiḥa* with additional *isnād*s (ʿĪsā 83; Ibn Khaldūn 3:10, trans. 3:14).

The alliance between al-Ḥakam I and the newly elevated party of Maliki jurists did not prove to be completely harmonious. In 202/818, a group of the *fuqahāʾ* participated in a failed revolt against the prince. The ruler punished the leaders and exiled thousands of Cordoban families from al-Andalus; nevertheless, he forgave several religious scholars (such as Yaḥyā ibn Yaḥyā and Ṭalūt ibn ʿAbd al-Jabbār al-Maʿāfarī) who had rebelled and, in the process, taught the Maliki ulama a lesson about the relative power of political and religious authority that they never forgot. Despite this brief rupture, the alliance between the court and the Maliki ulama established both the dominance of this *madhhab* and the religious scholars who led it. Ibn Ḥazm's discussion of Yaḥyā ibn Yaḥyā illustrates how this group of Maliki *fuqahāʾ* extended their influence:

> Having gained the favour of the Sultan, who approved of his doctrines, [Yaḥyā] was consulted upon every occasion; and no qadi was appointed without his consent, with this singularity, that Yaḥyā himself would never accept office; so that in a very short time the administration of justice was completely in the hands of the friends and disciples of Yaḥyā, or those who, like him, professed the *madhhab* of Mālik. Man being naturally inclined to improve his position in this world, when the students of law perceived that there was no other way of obtaining place than conforming with the doctrines of Yaḥyā, they unanimously adopted his innovations, and in this manner was the rite of al-Auzāʿī rejected, and that of Mālik ibn Anas introduced into this country.
>
> (al-Maqqarī 2:222, trans. 2:123–24)

Yaḥyā's descendants, the Banū Yaḥyā, continued to live in Córdoba, where they remained numerous and prominent; thus were scholarly dynasties formed (cf. Makkī 128–32, 163–67).

Early Andalusi Malikis relied on Mālik's legal work, *al-Muwaṭṭaʾ* (The Level Path), and their personal scholarly tradition of interpreting it. Yet as Dominique Urvoy points out, the use of hadith, the basis of Mālik's approach, was neglected in favor of special rulings *(furūʿ)* worked out by the first successors of the master and "the idea of submission (*taqlīd*) to the authority of the competent man capable of 'personal effort' (*ijtihād*) was blindly and mechanically repeated, whereas the whole idea of *ijtihād* was proscribed." Indeed, devotional literature (*manāqib*) concerning Mālik overshadowed his actual teaching ("'Ulamā'" 853; cf. Fierro, "Heresy" 896–97).

Maliki ulama continued to resist the intrusion of other legal schools (Shafii or Zahiri) or theological movements (such as Mutazilism or Shiism), while incorporating those innovations (reliance on *'ilm al-ḥadīth*, early Sufi asceticism) they could not resist. Here again, the attitude of the individual ruler could play a central role. Hence under Muḥammad I the dominance of traditional Andalusi Malikism was loosened and new ideas arose with the return from the East of scholars like Baqī ibn Makhlad (d. 276/889) and Muḥammad ibn Waḍḍāḥ (d. 287/900).

Both had traveled widely. Ibn Makhlad reportedly had studied with 284 scholars in cities such as Mecca, Medina, Cairo, Damascus, Baghdad, Kufa, and Basra. Both discovered that the East was several generations into the legal revolution introduced by al-Shafii (d. 204/820), who had laid the foundations for a new juridical methodology that, among other things, explicitly promoted the authority of prophetic hadith in legal judgments. On their return both espoused a more formal reliance on hadith. As a result, Ibn Makhlad, the author of an esteemed *tafsīr* and known for his piety, found himself charged with heresy by Cordoban ulama opposed to the organized use of hadith in Andalusi fiqh – even though he was teaching the hadith collection (*muṣannaf*) of a fellow Maliki scholar (albeit an Eastern one), Ibn Abī Shayba. Only the personal intervention of Muḥammad I saved him from execution (Fierro, "Introduction" esp. 77–83).

The Andalusi ulama grudgingly came to accept the formal use of hadith in legal decisions. In fact, Qāsim ibn Aṣbagh, student of both Ibn Makhlad and Ibn Waḍḍāḥ and the author of major hadith works, became the most prominent faqih of 'Abd al-Raḥmān III's reign. In general, however, the ulama were successful in suppressing larger religious tendencies of which they disapproved. Despite the presence of individual exponents of Shafiism and Zahirism, as well as of Shiism or Mutazilism, proponents of these schools could not gain enough followers to establish an institutional base. Even as forceful a personality and prominent a scholar as Ibn Ḥazm left no permanent school to carry on his Zahiri teachings (cf. Makkī 140–49).

Only in the realm of Islamic mysticism (Sufism) were *fuqahā'* eventually to give ground. Yet there is little evidence for any organized mystical activity during this first period. One possible example involves Ibn Masarra (d. 319/931). Ibn Masarra was born in Córdoba and studied the religious sciences, especially hadith, with his father, 'Abd Allāh, and with Ibn Waḍḍāḥ, who, like Ibn Makhlad, was celebrated for his piety. On returning from study in the East, Ibn Masarra attracted a small following, with whom he eventually moved to a retreat in the mountains outside Córdoba. The nature of Ibn

Masarra's ideas has been a matter of dispute; they appear to be a combination of asceticism and Mutazilism spiced with doses of hermeticism and esoteric (*bāṭinī*) thought. His few followers survived his death and suffered some persecution, while his writings were burned by the ulama in 350/961. His influence on the history of Sufi thought in al-Andalus appears to have been relatively minor.

Profane knowledge

The court was the center of profane knowledge, which during this period was characterized more by a reception of ideas, genres, and fashions from the East than by the creation of an outstanding body of indigenous writings. Nevertheless, the importance of this period of initial intellectual investment should not be underestimated, since by the end of this period, the cultural environment of al-Andalus matured to the point where it produced a remarkable burst of creative literary activity.

Being a successful member of the court elite required sharp intelligence, personal charm, wit and charisma, good political instincts, and a fair measure of luck. A courtier also need fluency in classical Arabic for purposes of sophisticated and cultivated conversation and the delivery of formal orations, a refined and elegant prose style for compositions and epistles, and ready access to a store of cultural knowledge based on the body of literary traditions and cultural norms that came to be termed adab, a realm of practical knowledge that Ibn Khaldūn defined as "expert knowledge of the poetry and history of the Arabs as well as the possession of some knowledge regarding every science" – including, one might add, the sciences of good manners, elegant deportment, polite behavior, and witty conversation (3:295, trans. 3:340).

Initially, this body of knowledge was an integral part of Arab tribal tradition that youths learned from their elders. With the passage of time, Arab elites living in metropolitan areas together with highly cultured non-Arabs began to lose touch with the tribal customs of their forefathers. In reaction to this process, urban-based scholars and philologists undertook to collect, review, and rework pre-Islamic Arab traditions. Scholars and writers also began to appropriate areas of pre-Islamic Persian and Hellenistic literary and intellectual traditions. By the end of the third/ninth century, these cultural strains were united in a new Islamic synthesis of interrelated fields of knowledge that encompassed and combined such genres as poetry, belles lettres, grammar, genealogy, history, biography, proverbs, ethics, wisdom and advice, and examples of behavior recognized as models worthy of emulation. These bodies of knowledge and remembered experiences came to constitute both the particular materials for individual specializations as well as the larger base of cultural capital upon which writers of adab drew. Adab consisted therefore of theory and practice: funds of knowledge and the wise and sophisticated behavior that mastery of such should produce. The models for such behavior were ideally the rulers themselves. ʿAbd al-Raḥmān I (d. 172/788), for example, was described by the historian Ibn Ḥayyān as kind-hearted, disposed to mercy, eloquent, endowed with quick perception, slow in his determinations, but constant and persevering in carrying them into effect, exempt from weakness, prompt and active. In addition,

> He would never lie in repose or abandon himself to indulgence; he never entrusted the affairs of the government to any one, but administered them himself, yet he never failed to consult, on such difficult cases as occurred, with people of wisdom and experience; he was a brave and intrepid warrior, always the first in the field; he was terrible in his anger, and could bear no opposition to his will; he could speak with much fluency and elegance; he was likewise a good poet, and composed verses extempore; he was, in short, a beneficent, generous, and munificent prince.
>
> (al-Maqqarī 4:37, trans. 2:87)

Given the proximity of the eastern lands to the Arabian Peninsula with its ready access to Bedouin traditions as well as to indigenous Persian and Hellenistic cultures, it is not surprising that inhabitants of these areas initially dominated the creation of this cultural synthesis. Those Andalusi wishing to improve their knowledge of profane Islamic and Arab culture naturally looked to the East. Some traveled to study with prominent Eastern scholars. Suwwār ibn Ṭārik al-Qurṭubī, for example, traveled to Basra, where he met al-Aṣmaʿī and other philologists and then returned to be appointed tutor to the sons of al-Ḥakam I. Alternatively, Eastern experts who ventured west in search of employment were welcomed with open arms.

Two such immigrants attained special fame: the musician Ziryāb, and the philologist-*adīb* Ismāʿīl al-Qālī. Ziryāb arrived in al-Andalus in 206/821. ʿAbd al-Raḥmān II, newly ascended to the throne, welcomed the musician. Ziryāb's Eastern styles of music took the court by storm and continued to be taught and propagated by his many sons. Ziryāb also provided a model of what a good courtier should know and how he should act. ʿAbd al-Raḥmān took him as a boon companion, drinking with him and allowing him to "sit by his side, as if he were an equal" (al-Maqqarī 4:122, trans. 2:118). Nor did Ziryāb attain the status of royal favorite on the basis of musical genius alone.

> He was like learned in astronomy, in geography or the division of the earth into seven climates. . . . Ziryāb, moreover, was gifted with so much penetration and wit; he had so deep an acquaintance with the various branches of polite literature; he possessed in so eminent a degree the charms of conversation, and the talents requisite to entertain an audience; he could repeat such a number of entertaining stories; he was acute and ingenious in guessing at the wants of his royal master – that there never was either

before or after him a man of his profession who was more generally beloved and admired. Kings and great people took him for a pattern of manners and education, and his name became forever celebrated among the inhabitants of al-Andalus.

(al-Maqqarī 4:124, trans. 2:120, slightly modified)[4]

Ziryāb's ascendancy was challenged by other courtiers, such as al-Jayyānī, known as al-Ghazāl (the gazelle) for his handsomeness, whom the historian Ibn Ḥayyān calls "the sage, poet, and polymath (*al-ʿarrāf*) of al-Andalus" (al-Maqqarī 3:20, trans. 1:116). Al-Ghazāl lived to be ninety-four years old and served under five rulers, from ʿAbd al-Raḥmān I to Muḥammad I. He was renowned for his poetry (ʿAbd al-Raḥmān II was compelled to forbid him from lampooning Ziryāb in his verse) and composed a verse history of al-Andalus. He was also valued as a diplomat and was dispatched on important legations to destinations as diverse as the Norsemen and the Byzantine court.

A cultural epiphany comparable to the arrival of Ziryāb occurred with al-Qālī's arrival in 330/941 during the reign of ʿAbd al-Raḥmān III. Al-Qālī was famed for his knowledge of ancient Arabic poetry, language, and lore, for which his *al-Amālī* (Dictations) remains a primary source to this day. He also composed commentaries on collections of pre-Islamic poems and a well-known dictionary. He brought his large library with him, but equally important, he personified the instructional lineages of his masters in the East, having studied with many Eastern teachers, including Ibn Durayd, a student of al-Aṣmaʿī and acknowledged leader of the Basran school of philologists. Al-Qālī's arrival in al-Andalus brought both his vast personal expertise and prominent Eastern academic lineages that he thereafter transmitted to his own students.

This point explains the veneration in which al-Qālī was held as compared to his predecessor, Ibn ʿAbd Rabbih (d. 328/940), court poet to Muḥammad I and ʿAbd al-Raḥmān III, but best known for his large adab encyclopedia *al-ʿIqd al-farīd* (The Unique Necklace). This work is divided into twenty-five books organized according to topic, beginning with government, war, and generous men, and ending with natural history, food and drink, and witty anecdotes, jokes, and riddles – encompassing basic cultural knowledge about which well-educated people should be acquainted. This fund of knowledge, all of which concerns matters of the East, was obtained secondhand, since Ibn ʿAbd Rabbih himself never traveled in search of knowledge. Hence, important as the *ʿIqd* is for the study of adab, neither it nor its author enjoyed the prestige and sense of authenticity that al-Qālī and his *Amālī* attained among Andalusis.

By the end of his reign, ʿAbd al-Raḥmān III's court in Córdoba was a dazzling center of sophisticated culture in the world. Andalusi profane culture had attained a state where it had absorbed and integrated the traditions of the

East, and its indigenous scholarly and literary traditions were sufficiently mature that in the following centuries scholars and writers of al-Andalus produced cultural landmarks in all fields of knowledge rivaling anything found in the East.

Scientific knowledge

Ṣāʿid al-Andalusī (d. 462/1070), a key source for the early history of the sciences in al-Andalus, remarks that there was little formal scientific inquiry among Muslims until the middle of the third/ninth century (158–59, trans. 59). Before that, specialists in mathematics, medicine, and astronomy-astrology certainly existed. Hishām I (d. 180/796), for example, consulted an astrologer who had studied the writings of Ptolemy (al-Maqqarī 2:321, trans. 2:96), and Ibn Juljul provides anecdotes about several early physicians. Our sources agree, however, that even through the following century serious interest in scientific research was slight. This situation began to change late in the reign of ʿAbd al-Raḥmān III and especially during that of his son and successor, al-Ḥakam II, who both spurred the importation of scientific writings from the East and was himself an enthusiastic proponent and patron of these fields of research. Although original achievements in these fields occurred only in the following period, popular science in such areas as folk medicine, magic, and astrology doubtlessly thrived in al-Andalus during this early period.

The second period (350/961–636/1238)

The accession of al-Ḥakam II al-Mustanṣir marks the beginning of an era in which internally produced forms of knowledge began to compete with and outshine those from abroad. Political changes – the dissolution of the caliphate and the rise of the party kings, and the ensuing establishment of Almoravid and then Almohad dominance – sometimes hindered these currents and sometimes helped, at times promoting work in some fields while discouraging or curtailing it in others. Nevertheless, the cultural base of Andalusi society produced sufficient numbers of sophisticated scholars, teachers, and writers to ensure an extended period of cultural efflorescence. This was correspondingly the period of the Golden Age for the Jewish community, and the period in which the pursuit of knowledge among intellectuals of the increasingly powerful Christian states to the north became established.

Sacred knowledge

Bedrock Malikism is the most prominent aspect of these centuries but not the most interesting. More fascinating are the challenges that mainstream

Malikis faced, whether from individuals (such as Ibn Ḥazm from within al-Andalus or al-Ghazālī from without), from political conditions (whether from the unity of the caliphate, the rivalries of the Taifa rulers, or the incursion of religio-political reform movements from the Maghrib, such as the Almoravids and Almohads), or from competing internal religious orientations (such as various forms of rationalism, mysticism, or esotericism). Nevertheless, while discussing these challenges, we must remember that with the exception of the influence of Sufism, which one could justifiably argue complements rather than competes with Malikism, Maliki fiqh emerged from this period as strong, influential, and uncontested as it entered it.

Malikism maintained this position less because of the brilliance of its exponents than from the coherence of its institutional structure. Each generation produced enough outstanding scholar-teachers to train enough students to fill the necessary legal and scholarly positions. Changing the system did not serve the interests of scholars, jurisprudents, or politicians, so religious corporate cohesion withstood both political tumult and transformation and intellectual and spiritual challenges. A number of religious scholars from this period deserve mention, Abū Āmr al-Dānī for Qurʾanic readings, Ibn ʿAbd al-Barr, al-Bājī, Abū Bakr ibn al-ʿArabī, al-Ṭurṭushī, the two Ibn Rushds – the grandfather and grandson – and the qadi ʿIyāḍ in fiqh and hadith. The outstanding religious thinkers of this period were Ibn Ḥazm and the speculative mystic Muḥyī l-Dīn ibn ʿArabī, the first of whom left no prominent followers and the second of whom only became influential after his departure to the East.

The central point of controversy during this period was the question of how to define religious authority. For mainstream Malikis, authority rested in the tradition of interpretations developed by core members of their school: a position of traditional-based imitation (*taqlīd*). Rationalist and spiritual approaches to religious interpretation arose to dispute this view.

The rationalist challenges appeared in jurisprudence and theology. In jurisprudence, the major rival was Shafii use of legal analogy (*qiyās*) to formulate juridical judgments. Several jurists, including Ibn Ḥazm and Ibn ʿAbd al-Barr, were attracted to Shafiism in their youth, although they later rejected it – Ibn ʿAbd al-Barr to return to Malikism and Ibn Ḥazm for the Zahiri school. Ibn ʿAbd al-Barr's decision may be partly adduced to professional considerations: in order to attract students and wield influence, he rejoined the majority faction. Ibn Ḥazm's choice signaled a more radical rationalism. Having been exposed to logic and philosophy, Ibn Ḥazm based his Zahiri literalism on the rational principle of refusing to interpret religious texts beyond what they themselves specifically stated. According to the Zahiri view, when the Qur'an or hadith permitted or forbade something, it referred to only that particular practice without either allowing or banning any analogous situation (hence grape wine [*khamr*] is forbidden since it is expressly banned in the Qur'an whereas intoxicants not specifically mentioned are deemed permissible). According to this position, other interpretations, whether based on *qiyās* or *taqlīd*, avoid awarding ultimate authority to religious texts themselves. The Zahiri position attracted few adherents (among them the mystic Ibn al-ʿArabī) and never developed into a full-fledged school. Among the Maliki *fuqahā'*, the extent to which *qiyās* should be used remained a matter of contention – favored by a rationalist such as Ibn Rushd, bitterly opposed by such traditionalists as Qadi ʿIyāḍ.

The theological dispute centered on the concept of individual interpretation, *ta'wīl*, justified on the basis of either personal charisma or rational insight. Al-Ghazālī, well versed in Aristotelian logic and philosophical rationalism, promoted both justifications of *ta'wīl* in speculative theology (kalam). Simultaneously, he espoused reliance on mystical inspiration for personal interpretation of religion – stances that ran counter to the Maliki jurists and the reformist conservatism of the Almoravid dynasty.

The Almoravids were a religio-political movement intent on removing religious innovation (*bidʿa*), first among the Berber tribes of al-Maghrib and then in the cities of al-Andalus, by imposing strict interpretations of the provisions of early Islam (as they understood them). Many Maliki scholars in al-Andalus initially welcomed Almoravid stringency as an antidote to the religious laxity of the upper classes. They later regretted their enthusiasm, becoming disenchanted with the Almoravids' combination of uncivilized behavior, narrow religious interpretation (they criticized the Maliki reliance on *furūʿ*, for example), and, later on, corruption. The Almoravids banned the teaching of kalam and persecuted its practitioners, at one point (503/1109) publicly burning some of al-Ghazālī's writings. They considered reliance on *ta'wīl* reprehensible.

A contrasting attitude emerged with the Almohad dynasty that succeeded the Almoravids first in the Maghrib and then in al-Andalus. This movement's primary tenet was the essential unity (*tawḥīd*) of Islamic doctrine as taught by their charismatic founder, Ibn Tūmart (d. 524/1130), whom they regarded as the Mahdi. If issues remained unresolved by recourse to the teachings of Ibn Tūmart, religious leaders could then resort to the intellect. As part of their rationalist inclination, some Almohad rulers permitted the study of philosophy at their courts, even employing Ibn Ṭufayl and Ibn Rushd as personal physicians and political advisers. Such rationalism never extended to public arenas, however, where the Almohads continued to rely on the support of the Maliki establishment. Royal patronage of philosophy disappeared with the decline of the Almohad dynasty, although its study remained an option for members of the elite who wished to pursue it privately, as the writings of Ibn al-Khaṭīb and Ibn Khaldūn reveal.

If the Malikis resisted rationalist interpretation, they ultimately accommodated themselves to Sufism. Piety and asceticism had long characterized Andalusi figures such as Ibn Makhlad and Ibn Waḍḍāḥ. The transition from asceticism to Sufism occurs when abstemious practices and supererogatory acts of worship are conceived as means to a closer personal relationship with God. Communal Sufism had existed in al-Andalus at least since the time of Ibn Masarra; this period witnessed its intellectual and popular development. The Almoravids arrested three prominent Sufis of Almería, Ibn Barrajān, Ibn al-ʿArīf, and al-Mayūrqī, apparently on suspicion of political provocation, and crushed the revolt of their Sufi contemporary Ibn Qasī (d. 546/1151). Yet, despite this occasional friction between individual Sufis and the ruling regime, this was a seminal period for Andalusi Sufism.

Two final developments in this period deserve mention. The first is the emergence of a regional self-awareness among the religious establishment. This is evidenced by a remarkable series of biographical dictionaries of prominent ulama: the *Taʾrīkh ʿulamāʾ al-andalus* (History of the Ulama of al-Andalus) by Ibn al-Faraḍī (d. 403/1013), continued by Ibn Bashkuwāl, then by Ibn al-Abbār, Ibn al-Zubayr, and Ibn ʿAbd al-Mālik al-Marrākushī (d. 703/1303–4). The second is the integration, through the conquests of the Almoravids and Almohads, of the Andalusi and Maghribi religious establishments and their religious views, orientations, and levels of sophistication.

Profane knowledge

By the reign of ʿAbd al-Raḥmān III, all disciplines of Arabic literary creation and philological study had reached maturity in al-Andalus, and they continued to be cultivated under the rules of his successors, his son al-Ḥakam II and the Amirid viziers, until the final collapse of the caliphate in 422/1031. Court life and governmental bureaucracy in Córdoba provided a center for the patronage of elite prose, both chancellery and literary. In philology and grammar, Ibn al-Qūṭiyya wrote the first treatise on verb conjugation, and al-Zubaydī, a student of al-Qālī, authored a biographical dictionary on grammarians. The epistolary art also thrived; Ibn Darrāj al-Qasṭallī and Ibn Zaydūn, for example, were famous poets much admired as well for their fine prose styles. Rhymed prose (*sajʿ*) increasingly dominated literary style. A century of political stability provided the economic and cultural framework for a literary golden era during the Taifa period. Ironically, it can be argued that the sudden political disintegration and process of governmental decentralization of that period sparked cultural efflorescence. Al-Shaqundī (d. 629/1231–32) writes that when

> the kings of the small states, divided among themselves the patrimony of the Banū Umayya, the cause of the sciences and literature, instead of losing, gained considerably by the division, since every one of the usurpers disputed with each other the prize of prose and poetical composition, and overstocked their markets with all departments of science; encouraged literature, and treated the learned with distinction, rewarding them munificently for their labours; their principal boast was to have people say, the learned man such a one is held in great esteem by the king so and so – or the poet such a one is much beloved by the king so and so; so that not one is to be found among them who has not been distinguished by the most brilliant qualities, or who has not left behind him traces that the hand of time will never obliterate.
>
> (al-Maqqarī 4:182–83, trans. 1:35)

This was the highwater mark of Andalusi literary production. Ibn Ḥazm wrote *Ṭawq al-ḥamāma* (The Dove's Neckring), a classic of Arabic love literature. His cousin, Ibn Shuhayd, composed *Risālat al-tawābiʿ wa l-zawābiʿ* (Treatise of Familiar Spirits and Demons), in which he embarks on an imaginary journey to interview the creative demons of poets and prose writers from the past and cites his own poetry and prose to prove his artistic superiority. Ibn Gharsiya wrote his treatise on *shuʿūbiyya* (anti-Arabism) for his princely Slav patron, al-ʿAmirī (d. 436/1044), while Ibn Burd al-Aṣghar composed essays on varied literary topics. Several rulers of the period, members of the Banū ʿAbbād in Seville, the Banū Hūd in Saragossa, and the Banū ʿAmir in Denia, proved to be major patrons of and even active participants in literature and learning. Political rivalry fanned the flames of culture.

This is also the great age of Andalusi political, cultural, and literary history as written by Andalusis themselves. Ibn Ḥayyān (d. 469/1076), the greatest historian of medieval Spain, wrote the *Muqtabis* (The Selection, in ten volumes) and *Matīn* (The Solid, in sixty volumes), the surviving fragments of which were preserved by later writers through lengthy quotes. Combined political and cultural history was continued by ʿAbd al-Wāḥid al-Marrākushī, Ibn Saʿīd al-Maghribī, and Ibn ʿIdhārī, who incorporated the works of predecessors such as Ibn Ḥayyān and continued their narratives through the Almoravid and Almohad periods.

Ibn Ḥazm, staunch supporter of the Umayyads, authored a series of short dynastic histories. His book on heresiography and religious history, *al-Fiṣal fī l-milal wa l-ahwāʾ wa l-niḥal* (Book of Schisms and Sects), is perhaps the world's first work on comparative religion. In answer to a North African scholar's inquiry of why Andalusis never praised their cultural achievements, Ibn Ḥazm also composed the first of the series of essays on the virtues of al-Andalus, praising Andalusi accomplishments in all fields of learning, a topos continued in treatises by Ibn Saʿīd and al-Shaqundī (all included in al-Maqqarī 4:149–211, partial trans. 1:168–99). Similarly, Ṣāʿid al-Andalusī devoted a chapter to al-Andalus in his *Ṭabaqāt al-umam*, an overview of the philosophical and scientific endeavors of various nations.

Defense of the greatness of al-Andalus was also prominent in literary history. The greatest Andalusi literary historian, Ibn Bassam (d. 543/1147), complained of his countrymen's failure to give credit to Andalusi writers because of their fascination with things Eastern. As a remedy, he offers his *al-Dhakhīra fī maḥāsin ahl al-jazīra* (Treasury of the Best of the Andalusian Peninsula), a literary history and anthology in four parts, each devoted to the poets and writers of a particular region of the country. Ibn Khāqān (d. c. 529/1134) contributed to this tradition of literary biography/anthology with two works surveying poets by professional class, as did later scholars such as Ibn Saʿīd al-Maghribī and al-Maqqarī. Such anthologies, often composed in styles admired by lovers of belles lettres, themselves fall within the genre of adab.

Scientific knowledge

This period begins with almost all branches of science and philosophy being imported from the East. By the era's end, however, al-Andalus is a major exporter of knowledge, to the lands of the Islamic south and east and to the Christian north. As such, al-Andalus should be viewed less as a passive east to west conduit of Greek science than as an active participant in a Mediterranean intellectual tradition that begins with the Greeks but is continued by Romans, Byzantines, Persians, subjects of the Muslim empires (whether Muslim, Christian, or Jew), and then intellectuals in the West.

The basis of this tradition is rationalism: the belief that the intellect is a universal, defining element of human nature and that by means of the intellect human beings are able to acquire knowledge of universal validity and relevance; differences in language, culture, or religion are of noteworthy but not defining importance. In fact, participants in this intellectual tradition have often believed that they shared more with corresponding members of other cultures or communal groups than with nonintellectual members of their own communities. This is one reason that this tradition so effectively crossed boundaries of time, space, and culture. Greek philosophy and science provided the basis on which later practitioners then built. The Hellenistic, Roman, and then Muslim *oikoumēnēs* thereafter charted their own intertwined intellectual courses within a transcultural intellectual endeavor.

Beyond its universalist vision, the great appeal of this rationalist tradition is its unified method of inquiry, based on reliance on Aristotelian logic and a uniform curriculum of study. The configuration of this curriculum is evident in Ibn Ḥazm's division of the sciences. It begins with the study of logic, which provides a standard terminology, approach, and frame of reference, continues with study of the natural sciences, and culminates with metaphysics. Philosophy has both theoretical and practical dimensions. Metaphysics is the inquiry into first principles, while the natural sciences investigate the fundamental and ancillary principles of the laws of nature and material phenomena, including the study of human beings and how they can most happily live, whether in groups (politics), as individuals (ethics), or as physical entities (medicine).

Intrinsic to the popular acceptance of this tradition are the hermetic analogues that accompanied these scientific endeavors. Although they had distinct underlying (if sometimes seemingly overlapping) operational principles and goals, philosophy and the sciences shared with the occult corresponding areas of interest (medical treatment versus thaumatology, astronomy versus astrology, chemistry versus alchemy, and metaphysics versus demonic cosmology). Fascination with these occult sciences was usually more prevalent than interest in their more serious analogues and, as a result, stimulated the latter's social acceptance and financial support. Many a ruler became a patron of astronomy because astrology was part of the bargain. *Ghāyat al-ḥakīm* (Aims of the Sage, the Latin *Picatrix*), the magical treatise falsely attributed to the astronomer al-Majrīṭī, had a larger audience than anything written by the historical al-Majrīṭī.

Philosophy and science were the domain of the few. They were taught and communicated privately, with the socially useful practical fields of mathematics, astronomy, and medicine presenting the public rationale for the study of logic, psychology, and metaphysics. Not all physicians were philosophers, but many philosophers practiced medicine, both to earn their livelihoods and to protect their lives. Many were also attached to courts, where their intellectual skills occasionally elevated them to the highest levels of government service. The three greatest Muslim philosophers of the West all served as ministers and shared the risks that high government service presented to courtiers. Ibn Bājja, for example, was imprisoned twice by princes whom he served and died poisoned by court rivals; Ibn Rushd was forced into retirement and saw his books banned due more to changes in political policy than to true royal disapproval of his thought.

The process of translating Hellenistic science and philosophy into Arabic was largely completed in the East by the end of the fourth/tenth century. By this time, a philosopher such as al-Fārāb īor Ibn Sīnā could have access to the major works of Aristotle, Euclid, Ptolemy, Galen, and Hippocrates, along with important Hellenistic commentaries, with more limited exposure to the original works of Plato, mainly the *Timaeus* and the *Laws*, and summaries or secondary accounts of *The Republic.* All of these works, the translations from the Greek and original works of the great philosophers of the Muslim East, arrived in al-Andalus throughout the fourth/tenth and fifth/eleventh centuries. Ibn Ḥazm, Ibn Juljul, and Ṣāʿid al-Andalusī show how this appropriation of knowledge transpired.

The main sciences cultivated in al-Andalus until the sixth/twelfth century were practical: mathematics and astronomy (essential for determining the accurate direction and times of prayer), and medicine. Ṣāʿid mentions the early activities in these areas of Ibn Firnās, Abū ʿUbayda al-Laythī, and Yaḥyā ibn Yaḥyā (d. 316/927). First ʿAbd al-Raḥmān III and then even more intensively al-Ḥakam II began to import books in all scholarly fields on a massive scale, a process that solidified and broadened knowledge of science and philosophy in al-Andalus (Ṣāʿid 158–63, trans. 60–61). Exemplary of this process is Abū l-Qāsim al-Majrīṭī (d. 397/1007), who introduced the philosophic compendia of the Ikhwān al-Ṣafāʾ (Brethren of Purity) into al-Andalus, and was a major mathematician and astronomer who trained a circle of students (Ibn Samḥ, al-Zahrāwī, and al-Kirmānī) who carried on his research into the next century. Later mathematicians and/or astronomers include al-Muʾtaman, Hudid ruler of Saragossa, Ibn Sayyid, teacher of Ibn Bājja, al-Jayyānī, Ibn Zarqullāh, the greatest Andalusi astronomer, and Abū l-Ṣalt (d. 529/1134). The activities of these scholars and their successors centered on geometry and spherical trigonometry, the improvement of astronomical tables (*zījes*), and development of astronomical instruments.

In the middle of the fourth/tenth century, the Byzantine emperor presented ʿAbd al-Raḥmān III with a Greek copy of Dioscorides' *Materia medica*, an essential work of pharmacology. The translation of this work from Greek into Arabic spurred investigation as local physicians and pharmacologists reviewed native plants to learn their medical uses. Abū l-Qāsim al-Zahrāwī (Abulcasis, d. c. 404/1013), a friend of Ibn Ḥazm, composed his medical encyclopedia, *al-Taʿrīf li-man ʿajaz ʿan al-taʾlīf* (Aid to Whomever Is Unable to Compose Treatises), which remained a major surgical textbook in al-Andalus and in Europe even after the arrival of Ibn Sīnā's *Qānūn* (Canon on Medicine) early in the sixth/twelfth century. Perhaps the most famous Andalusi physicians were the the Banū Zuhr: ʿAbd al-Malik ibn Zuhr (d. 470/1078), personal physician of Mujāhid al-Amirī, ruler of Denia; his son Abū l-ʿAlā ibn Zuhr, who served al-Muʿtamid ibn ʿAbbād of Seville and then the Almoravid Yūsuf ibn Tāshfīn; and his grandson Abū Marwān ibn Zuhr, a contemporary and esteemed colleague of the philosopher Ibn Rushd.

Andalusi philosophy reached a high point in work of Ibn Bājja (Avempace, d. 533/1139), Ibn Ṭufayl, Ibn Rushd (Averroes), and Maimonides. Ibn Bājja was born in Saragossa, where he also served as vizier until the city's fall to

Alfonso I of Aragon. After a period that combined governmental service with short periods of political imprisonment, he served for twenty years (until his death) as vizier to the Almoravid governor Yaḥyā ibn Yūsuf ibn Tāshfīn. Ibn Bājja was well trained in all branches of knowledge and was an able poet, but his renown stems from his philosophical compositions, such as *Tadbīr al-mutawaḥḥid* (Rule of the Solitary). In his epistemology, Ibn Bājja explores the relationships among sensual, imaginative, and intellectual forms of knowledge and the modalities of their acquisition and interaction. Like most philosophers, he holds that the apperception of pure intelligibles constitutes the highest level of human perfection, although few individuals attain this state. The question he thereafter poses is how such individuals should relate to the rest of society, consisting as it does of imperfect human beings. Unlike al-Fārābī, who otherwised influenced his thought, Ibn Bājja had little faith in human ability to achieve a perfect society. Hence, although he believes this to be a praiseworthy goal, he advises that on a practical level intellectuals should only discuss philosophical topics with one another and refrain from making their views known to other classes of people.

Ibn Ṭufayl did not know Ibn Bājja personally, but like him he served important rulers (in his case the Almohads) as both a physician and political adviser. Influenced by Ibn Bājja's writings, along with those of Ibn Sīnā and al-Ghazālī, IbnṬufayl also focused on the issues of knowledge and the relationship of the philosopher with society, dealing more explicitly than his predecessor with the relationship between philosophy and religious revelation in his philosophical novel *Hayy ibn Yaqẓān* (Alive, Son of Awake) (*Ibn Ṭufayl).

Ibn Ṭufayl's thought on the relation between philosophy and religion influenced that of his protégé at the Almohad court, Ibn Rushd (Averroes), who succeeded him as court physician. Nevertheless, Ibn Rushd treated this subject differently. As the scion of a family of religious scholars, being the son and grandson of famous Cordoban qadis (a position he also attained) and himself the author of a well-regarded introductory textbook on Muslim jurisprudence, Ibn Rushd was intimately aware of the complexities and opportunities offered by Islamic religious discourse. As a result, he confronted the arguments of religious opponents to philosophy directly. He wrote a detailed response to al-Ghazālī's critique of peripatetic philosophy, *Tahāfut al-falāsifa* (The Incoherence of the Philosophers), which he titled *Tahāfut al-tahāfut* (The Incoherence of the Incoherence). In *al-Faṣl al-maqāl* (Decisive Treatise), he discussed the concordance of religion and philosophy in the format of a fatwa.

That Ibn Rushd was prepared to defend philosophy from religious critics did not mean that he fully agreed with the ideas of earlier Muslim philosophers. He was especially critical of Ibn Sīnā, preferring instead to return directly to the writings of Aristotle. These he knew intimately, since he presented them to his contemporaries in a series of synopses, renditions, and full-scale lineal commentaries (known respectively as the short, middle, and great commentaries). Through first Hebrew and then Latin translation, these works helped introduce Aristotle's thought to Christian Europe.

Similar to Ibn Rushd in his masterly command of both the religious (in this case Jewish) and the philosophical traditions was Mūsā ibn Maimūn, better known as Maimonides. He was contemporary to Ibn Rushd and knew of him, although they did not directly influence each other's thought. Maimonides also wrote on the relation between philosophy and religious revelation in his *Guide of the Perplexed,* originally composed in Arabic. He was less aggressive than Ibn Rushd and less mystical than Ibn Ṭufayl, relying instead more on the ideas of Ibn Bājja and al-Fārābī in his interpretation of how philosophy and religion relate. For him religion was a social necessity and a moral imperative that the truths of philosophy underlie but cannot replace.

This period also witnessed the beginning of the translation movement that transmitted Greek and Islamic science and philosophy to Western Europe. From the sixth/twelfth century through the seventh/thirteenth, this process of translation paralleled similar movements from earlier times, such as the Muslim appropriation of Greek and Hellenistic science and philosophy in the East or the movement of such knowledge from the East to al-Andalus. In each case, members of the acquiring communities first actively sought out works of magic and astrology, followed by those dealing with mathematics, astronomy, and medicine, and finally, in a more organized fashion, appropriated the full philosophical curriculum, from logic to metaphysics. Of less interest to European scholars was Muslim religious or profane knowledge. In general, translations in these areas circulated on the popular level and consisted of tales such as those found in the *Thousand and One Nights* or works of popular adab, such as *Kalīla wa-dimna.*

The third period (636/1238–897/1492)

The reduction of Muslim al-Andalus to the Nasrid kingdom of Granada undercut the cultural and economic infrastructure needed to support the pursuit of knowledge. It also resulted in the emigration of the highly educated Muslim classes who comprised the religious, political, and intellectual elites to beyond al-Andalus, whether to North Africa or farther to the lands of the East. Ambitious individuals now traveled to serve the new Marinid dynasty in Morocco, the Hafsids to the west, or the Mamluk rulers of Egypt. Andalusi scholars had long accustomed themselves to obtaining employment in Marrakech or Fez. With the loss of most of al-Andalus by the middle of the seventh/thirteenth century, such individuals and their families now assumed permanent residence in the Maghrib or in the East.

The political and military victories of the Christian states stimulated a corresponding intellectual and cultural flowering in these kingdoms, as exemplified by the creative activities at the court of Alfonso the Wise of Castile-León (d. 1284), and an even greater efflorescence in France and Italy, where scholars and intellectuals, armed with the newly acquired knowledge of Muslim–Hellenistic traditions of philosophy and science, took the lead. Jewish communities in lands now controlled by Christian rulers became increasingly embattled and their cultural impetus ultimately shifted to the European-based Jewish communities north of the Pyrenees and in Italy.

The declining state of Andalusi culture is typified by several careers. The philosopher and mystic Ibn Sabʿīn was born in Murcia. When his controversial intellectual views necessitated his departure from his home city, he moved to Ceuta in Morocco. He continued East, finally ending in Mecca where he died in 668–69/1269–71. Similarly, Ibn Saʿīd al-Maghribī was born in Granada, spent his youth in Seville, then left with his father to perform the pilgrimage and find his fortune. In the East, he attained fame as the author of *Kitāb al-mughrib fī ḥulā al-maghrib* (Wondrous Book on the Ornaments of the Maghrib), a biographical dictionary and poetical anthology of cultural figures of al-Andalus started by Ibn Saʿīd's grandfather and continued by his father and uncle. Renowned as an authority of Andalusi culture for this and other works, Ibn Saʿīd never returned home, dying in Tunis in 685/1286. Andalusis had often traveled in the East; now once they left their homeland, there was little reason to return.

Al-Andalus produced one final polymath in *Ibn al-Khaṭīb (d. 776/1375). Trained among other things as a physician, he rose to become vizier to the Nasrid ruler of Granada, Muḥammad V. Celebrated for the quality of his chancellery letters and for his writings on medicine, history, adab, and mystical philosophy, Ibn al-Khaṭīb was also friend and patron to the great historian Ibn Khaldūn, who came to Granada from Tunis to serve him. Al-Maqqarī composed the first two-thirds of his great compilation of Andalusi history and culture, *al-Nafḥ al-ṭīb* (The Breath of Perfume), as a prolegomenon for his biography of Ibn al-Khaṭīb, which comprises the final third of the book. It is eminently appropriate that the biography of this great man also became the history of the brilliant culture of which he was final representative and worthy heir.

The capture of the final independent Muslim political entity in al-Andalus, Granada, marked the end of formal traditions of intellectual pursuit. Informal and popular traditions continued to exist for another century among the Mudejar and Morisco communities until their final expulsion in 1609–12. The contours of this type of knowledge may be seen in the surviving body of Aljamiado literature, texts written in Romance in Arabic script (*Moriscos).

CONCLUSION

There is a tendency to mourn the disappearance of the brilliant culture of al-Andalus. Given the impressive intellectual achievements of Andalusi culture, such feelings of loss and remorse are understandable. Nevertheless, one should also celebrate the accomplishments of members of this culture who excelled in so many fields of endeavor. We should also appreciate the extent to which their contributions continued to enrich Islamic civilization in North Africa and the Muslim East, Christian civilization to the north, and Jewish culture throughout the Mediterranean for centuries thereafter. Relatively few cultures have in fact seen their achievements in the field of knowledge so thoroughly and efficiently incorporated by those who came after. Despite the existence of some unfortunate gaps and regretful losses, a remarkable amount of the contributions of Andalusi scholars and intellectuals remain extant. Together, they comprise an extraordinary book of knowledge open for all who wish to consult it, learn from it, and enjoy.

NOTES

1 English trans. in Chejne, *Ibn Hazm* 189–214. Cf. Ibn ʿAbd al-Barr's *Jāmiʿ bayān al-ʿilm* (Comprehensive Exposition of Knowledge) and Ṣāʿid al-Andalusī's *Ṭabaqāt al-umam* (Categories of Nations). On earlier approaches, see Rosenthal, esp. 70–96.

2 Compare this framework with the medieval European curriculum of the seven liberal arts: grammar, dialectic, rhetoric (the trivium), then arithmetic, music, geometry, and astronomy (the quadrivium).

3 A second version focuses on a direct link between al-Ḥakam and Mālik. Imam Mālik heard from an Andalusi scholar of the exemplary conduct of the Andalusi rulers of the house of Marwān, which contrasted to the oppression by Abbasid caliphs, especially al-Manṣūr, who were persecuting the descendants of ʿAlī and had earned Mālik's constant denunciation. When Mālik heard of al-Ḥakam's conduct,

> he is said to have exclaimed in rapture, "God grant that he may be one of ours," or words to that purport. This wish having been communicated to the sultan by the *ʿālim* in whose presence it was

> expressed, they say that al-Ḥakam, who was already informed of the great reputation which his virtues and sanctity had gained him, decided immediately upon adopting the *madhhab* of Mālik and forsaking that of al-Auzāʿī.
>
> (al-Maqqarī 4:217–18, trans. 113, slightly amended)

4 For more on Ziryāb, see *Music.

BIBLIOGRAPHY

ʿAbd al-Wāḥid al-Marrākushī. *al-Muʿjib fī talkhīṣ akhbār al-maghrib.* Ed. M. al-Uryān. Cairo, 1963.

Addas, Claude. "Andalusī Mysticism and the Rise of Ibn ʿArabī." Jayyusi 909–33.

Quest for the Red Sulphur: The Life of Ibn ʿArabī. Trans. Peter Kingsley. Cambridge, 1993.

Atiyeh, George N., ed. *The Book in the Islamic World: The Written Word and Communication in the Middle East.* Albany, 1995.

Berkey, Jonathan. *The Transmission of Knowledge in Medieval Cairo: A Social History of Islamic Education.* Princeton, 1992.

Chejne, Anwar G. *Ibn Hazm.* Chicago, 1982.

Islam and the West: The Moriscos, a Cultural and Social History. Albany, 1983.

Muslim Spain: Its History and Culture. Minneapolis, 1974.

Ḍaif, Shauqī. *ʿAṣr al-duwal wa l-imārāt: al-Andalus.* Vol. 7 of *Taʾrīkh al-adab al-ʿarabī.* Cairo, 1989.

Fierro, Maria Isabel. "Heresy in al-Andalus." Jayyusi 895–908.

"The Introduction of *Ḥadīth* in al-Andalus (2nd/8th–3rd/9th Centuries)." *Der Islam* 66 (1989): 68–93.

Glick, Thomas F. *Islamic and Christian Spain in the Early Middle Ages.* Princeton, 1979.

Goitein, S. D. *A Mediterranean Society: The Jewish Communities of the Arab World as Portrayed in the Documents of the Cairo Geniza.* Vol. II, *The Community.* Berkeley, 1971.

Goldziher, I. *Muslim Studies.* Trans. S. M. Stern and C. R. Barber. 2 vols. London, 1971.

Hernández, Miguel Cruz. *Historia de la filosofía española: Filosofía hispano-musulmana.* Madrid, 1957.

"Islamic Thought in the Iberian Peninsula." Jayyusi 777–803.

Ibn al-Abbār. *al-Takmila li-kitāb al-ṣila.* Ed. ʿI. al-Ḥusainī. 2 vols. Cairo, 1963.

Ibn ʿAbd al-Barr, Yūsuf. *Jāmiʿ bayān al-ʿilm wa-faḍlih.* 2 vols. Cairo, n.d.

Ibn ʿAbd al-Malik al-Marrākushī, Muḥammad ibn Muḥammad. *al-Dhayl wa l-takmila.* Edition under preparation.

Ibn ʿAbd Rabbih, Abū ʿUmar Aḥmad. *al-ʿIqd al-farīd.* 9 vols. Beirut, 1983.

Ibn (al-)ʿArabī. *Sufis of Andalusia: The Rūḥ al-quds and al-Durrat al-fākhira of Ibn ʿArabī.* Trans. R. W. J. Austin. Berkeley, 1971.

Ibn Bājja. *Risālat ittiṣāl al-ʿaql bi l-insān.* Ed. and Spanish trans. Miguel Asín Palacios. *Al-Andalus* 7 (1942): 1–47.

Risālat al-wadāʿ. Ed. and Spanish trans. Miguel Asín Palacios. *Al-Andalus* 8 (1943): 1–87.

Tadbīr al-mutawaḥḥid/El régimen del solitario. Ed. and trans. Miguel Asín Palacios. Madrid, 1946.

Ibn Bashkuwāl, Khalaf ibn ʿAbd al-Malik. *al-Ṣila fī taʾrīkh aʾimmat al-andalus.* Ed. ʿI. al-Ḥusainī. 2 vols. Cairo, 1955.

Ibn Bassam. *al-Dhakhīra fī maḥāsin ahl al-jazīra.* Ed. Iḥsān ʿAbbās. 4 pts. in 8 vols. Libya, 1979.

Ibn Faraḍī, ʿAbd Allāh ibn Muḥammad. *Taʾrīkh ʿulamāʾ al-andalus.* Ed. I. al-Abyārī. 2 vols. Cairo, 1983.

Ibn García, Abū ʿAmir. *The Shuʿūbiyya in al-Andalus: The Risāla of Ibn García and Five Refutations.* Trans. and intro. James T. Monroe. Berkeley, 1970.

Ibn Ḥayyān, Ḥayyān ibn Khalaf. *Kitāb al-muqtabis min anbāʿ ahl al-andalus.* Ed. P. Chalmeta, F. Corriente, and M. Sobh. Madrid, 1979.

Ibn Ḥazm. *al-Fiṣal fī l-milal wa l-ahwāʾ wa l-niḥal.* 5 vols. Cairo, n.d.

Rasāʾil ibn ḥazm al-andalusī. Ed. Iḥsān ʿAbbās. 4 vols. Beirut, 1987.

"Marātib al-ʿulūm" (*Rasāʾil* 4:61–90).

"Risāla fī faḍl al-andalus wa-dhikr rijālihā" (*Rasāʾil* 2:171–88).

"Risāla fī mudāwāt al-nafs" (*Rasāʾil* 1:333–414).

Ṭawq al-ḥamāma fī l-ulf wa l-ullāf (*Rasāʾil* 1:84–319).

Ibn ʿIdhārī al-Marrākushī, Abū l-ʿAbbās Aḥmad. *al-Bayān al-mughrib fī akhbār al-andalus wa l-maghrib.* Ed. E. Lévi-Provençal, G. S. Colin, and I. ʿAbbās. 4 vols. Beirut, 1983.

Ibn Juljul, Sulaymān ibn Ḥassān. *Ṭabaqāt al-aṭṭibāʾ wa l-ḥukamāʾ.* Cairo, 1955.

Ibn Khaldūn. *Prolégomènes d'Ebn-Khaldoun (Arabic Text).* 3 vols. Paris, 1858. English trans. Franz Rosenthal. *The Muqaddimah: An Introduction to History.* 3 vols. New York, 1958.

Ibn Khāqān, al-Fatḥ ibn Muḥammad. *Maṭmah al-anfus wa-maṣraḥ al-taʾannus fī mulāḥ ahl al-andalus.* Cairo, 1916.

Qalāʾid al-ʿiqyān fī maḥāsin al-aʿyān. Cairo, 1905.

Ibn Maimūn, Mūsā (Maimonides). *Dalālat al-ḥaʾirīn.* 3 vols. Cairo, n.d. English trans. and intro. S. Pines as *The Guide of the Perplexed.* 2 vols. Chicago, 1963.

Ibn al-Qūṭiyya, Abū Bakr ibn ʿUmar. *Kitāb al-afʿāl.* Ed. ʿAlī Fauda. Cairo, 1953.

Ibn Rushd. *Bidāyat al-mujtahid wa-nihāyat al-muqtaṣid.* 2 vols. Beirut, n.d. Trans. I. A. K. Nyazee and M. Abdul-Rauf as *The Distinguished Jurist's Primer.* 2 vols. Reading, 1994–96.

Faṣl al-maqāl fī-mā bayna l-ḥikma wa l-sharīʿa min al-ittiṣāl. Ed. M. ʿImāra. Cairo, 1972. Trans. G. F. Hourani as *On the Harmony of Religion and Philosophy.* London, 1976.

Tahāfut al-tahāfut. 2 vols. Ed. S. Dunyā. Cairo, 1971. Trans. Simon van den Bergh as *Averroes's Tahāfut al-tahāfut (The Incoherence of the Incoherence).* 2 vols. London, 1954.

Ibn Saʿīd al-Maghribī, Abū l-Ḥasan ʿAlī. *al-Mughrib fī ḥulā al-maghrib*. Ed. S. Ḍayf. 3rd edn. 2 vols. Cairo, 1978.

Ibn Shuhayd, Abū ʿAmir. *Risālat al-tawābiʿ wa l-zawābiʿ: The Treatise of Familiar Spirits and Demons*. Trans. and intro. James T. Monroe. Berkeley, 1971.

Ibn Ṭufayl. *Ḥayy ibn Yaqẓān*. Ed. and French trans. by Léon Gauthier. Beirut, 1936. English trans. by Lenn E. Goodman. 3rd edn. Los Angeles, 1991.

Ibn Zubayr, Aḥmad ibn Ibrāhīm. *Ṣilat al-ṣila*. Partial ed. Évariste Lévi-Provençal. Rabat, 1938.

ʿĪṣā, Muḥammad ʿAbd al-Ḥamīd. *Ta'rīkh al-taʿlīm fī l-andalus*. Cairo, 1982.

Jayyusi, Salma Khadra, ed. *The Legacy of Muslim Spain*. Leiden, 1992.

al-Majrīṭī (Pseudo.). *Ghāyat al-ḥakīm (Picatrix)*. Ed. H. Ritter as *Das Ziel des Weisen*. Leipzig, 1933.

Makdisi, George. *Religion, Law, and Learning in Classical Islam*. Hampshire, 1991.

The Rise of Colleges: Institutions of Learning in Islam and the West. Edinburgh, 1981.

The Rise of Humanism in Classical Islam and the Christian West, with Special Reference to Scholasticism. Edinburgh, 1990.

Makkī, Maḥmūd ʿAlī. *Ensayo sobre las aportaciones orientales en la España musulmana y su influencia en la formación de la cultura hispano-árabe*. Madrid, 1968.

al-Maqqarī. *Nafḥ al-ṭīb min ghuṣn al-andalus al-raṭīb*. Ed. Yūsuf al-Shaikh Muḥammad al-Baqāʿī. 11 vols. Beirut, 1986. Partial English trans. by Pascual de Gayangos as *The History of the Mohammedan Dynasties in Spain*. 2 vols. New York, 1840–43; rpt. 1964.

Nasr, Seyyed Hossein. "Oral Transmission and the Book in Islamic Education." Atiyeh 57–70.

O'Callaghan, Joseph F. *A History of Medieval Spain*. Ithaca, 1975.

The Learned King: The Reign of Alfonso X of Castile. Philadephia, 1993.

al-Qālī, Ismāʿīl ibn al-Qāsim. *Kitāb al-amālī*. 2 vols. Beirut, 1980.

Rosenthal, Franz. *Knowledge Triumphant: The Concept of Knowledge in Medieval Islam*. Leiden, 1970.

Ṣāʿid al-Andalusī, Abū l-Qāsim. *Ṭabaqāt al-umam*. Ed. Ḥayāt al-ʿīd Bū ʿAlwān. Beirut, 1985. Trans. Semaʿan I. Salem and Alok Kumar as *Science in the Medieval World: "Book of the Categories of Nations."* Austin, 1991.

Samsó, Julio. "The Exact Sciences in al-Andalus." Jayyusi 952–73.

Sirat, Colette. *A History of Jewish Philosophy in the Middle Ages*. Cambridge, 1985.

Urvoy, Dominique. *Ibn Rushd (Averroes)*. Trans. Olivia Stewart. London, 1991.

Le monde des ulémas andalous du V/XIe au VII/XIIIe siècle: Etude sociologique. Geneva, 1978.

Pensers d'al-Andalus: La vie intellectuelle à Cordoue et à Séville au temps des empires berbères (fin XI siècle–début XIII siècle). Toulouse, 1990.

"The ʿUlamā' of al-Andalus." Jayyusi 849–77.

Vernet, Juan. *La cultura hispanoárabe en Oriente y Occidente*. Barcelona, 1978.

"Natural and Technical Science in al-Andalus." Jayyusi 937–51.

Wasserstein, David. *The Rise and Fall of the Party Kings: Politics and Society in Islamic Spain, 1002–1086*. Princeton, 1985.

Wiegers, Gerard. *Islamic Literature in Spanish and Aljamiado: Yça of Segovia (fl. 1450), His Antecedents and Successors.* Leiden, 1994.
al-Zahrāwī, Abū l-Qāsim. *al-Taʿrīf li-man ʿajaz ʿan al-taʾlīf.* Still unedited.
al-Zubaydī, Abū Bakr Muḥammad. *Ṭabaqāt al-naḥwiyyīn wa l-lughawiyyīn.* Ed. M. Abū l-Faḍl Ibrāhīm. Cairo, 1973.

CHAPTER 6

LOVE

Michael Sells

One day during his pilgrimage to Mecca and while circling the Kaaba, the Murcian Ibn ʿArabī (d. 1240) recited the following verses:

I wish I knew if they knew
  whose heart they've taken
Or that my heart knew
  which high-ridge track they follow
Do you think they're safe
  or do you think they're perished
The lords of love are bewildered
  in it, ensnared.[1]

Ibn ʿArabī, who went on to become known as the grand master (*al-shaykh al-akbar*) of Sufi thought, recounts that a young woman appeared and objected to each verse in turn, asking how such a famous and respected sheikh could have so badly misunderstood the workings of love. With the final verse, she lost all patience:

> Amazing! How could it be that the one pierced through the heart by love had any remainder of self left to be bewildered? Love's character is to be all consuming. It numbs the senses, drives away intellect, astonishes thoughts, and sends off the one in love with the others who are gone. Where is bewilderment and who is left to be bewildered? (Ibn ʿArabī 11–12)

This encounter under the shadow of the Kaaba – the central shrine within Islam – is a sign of the role of poetry in the language of love as well as the interplay of religion and love within Arabic poetry. The poets of al-Andalus brought together these two realms of infinity (religion and love) at the intersection of three major religious traditions, at the culmination of the classical Arabic tradition of love poetry, and within the development of the tradition's first extensively recorded popular and strophic poetic forms. In the area of ghazal ("love talk"), the poets of al-Andalus achieved a depth and power of expression that, within the Arabic and non-Arabic worlds alike, still astonishes.

Arabic ghazal as a poetic form originates in the *nasīb*, the first movements of the pre-Islamic qasida. The *nasīb* opens out of a meditation on the *aṭlāl*, the ruins of the beloved's campsite, or an encounter with the *ṭayf* or *khayāl*, the phantom of the beloved. As the Bedouin poet stands over the campsite, a moment of recognition occurs. These marks in the sand or blackened cooking stones are not simply ruins of a campsite, but the ruins of *her* campsite, the connection to her and the sign of her absence. This moment of discovery often incites a reverie, a vision of past times with her and the transformation, in memory or imagination, of desolation into a lost garden: cold, running water, lush vegetation, wild animals at peace. At some point the reverie is broken and the poet reminds himself that the beloved is gone and the garden wasted. He may recall the *ẓaʿn*, the departure of the beloved with the other women of her tribe and their movement off into the distance, recounting each station of their journey with ritual solemnity. Throughout the *nasīb*, it is *dahr* (time, fate) that is viewed as responsible for the separation, and indeed fate ties together the *nasīb*, the journey section that follows, and the final tribal boast.

The *nasīb* contains its own world of poetic sacred space and sacred time. The *aṭlāl* echo in their symbolic density the *ḥimā*, the hallowed tribal grounds and the *ḥaram*, any sacred area within the fluid, animistic world of the Bedouin. Fate is represented in part by the jinni, those semispirits of the desert that provide poetic inspiration, cause love madness, and swallow up the wayward desert traveler. The states or conditions (*aḥwāl*) of the beloved are often compared to the protean shifting guises of the *ghūl*, a particular species of jinni. The stations (*manāzil, maqāmāt*) of the beloved's journey away from the poet echo in emotive and ritualized solemnity the stations of pre-Islamic pilgrimages, including the pre-Islamic hajj.

During the period of Muhammad, independent love poems grew out of the *nasīb* section of the qasida. In the *ʿudhrī ghazal* (named after the tribe from which many of the poems came) the lover goes mad through his unrequited love. The semilegendary Qays ibn al-Mulawwiḥ was given the epithet Majnūn Laylā (Mad for, or, literally, Jinned for, Laylā). The love-mad ʿUdhrite can never break from the remembrance. He is an incessant wanderer (*hāʾim*) in the wake of a beloved who is nowhere yet everywhere. Majnūn talks to the trees, the rocks, the streams, addressing them as Laylā. He is too far gone to help; ultimately he perishes from love. In contrast, the erotic ghazal, exemplified by ʿUmar ibn Abī Rabīʿa, centers on love talk as banter, wit, flirtation, and the hints and codes of the lovers used to achieve a secret rendezvous. The eroticism can also be deadly; the face of the beloved becomes an arena of nature and danger – her eyes piercing arrows, her teeth flashes of lightning – that not even the most adept knight can always survive. The Umayyad-era poet Ghaylān (Dhū al-Rumma) perfected a third independent love lyric, the *nasīb*-qasida. Ghaylān kept the formal structure of the qasida with its *nasīb*, journey, and boast, but incorporated all three elments into the wider sensibility of the *nasīb*.

Islam was almost immediately incorporated into the love lyric. Muhammad's companion-poet, Ḥassān ibn Thābit, for example, transformed the *nasīb* remembrance of the beloved into an elegy for the Prophet, with the *aṭlāl* as Muhammad's pulpit and prayer yard in Medina. The stations of Islamic pilgrimage were added to the itinerary of the departing beloved and the wandering lover and within a century the full range of Islamic ritual and terminology had been integrated into the love lyric. By the eleventh century, prose writers were placing the different experiences or conditions (*aḥwāl*) into fully elaborated lists and categories drawn from the poetry, even as Sufi writers were drawing on the same store of poetry for many of their own categories of the conditions of mystical experience (Giffen; Sells, *Islamic Mysticism* 56–74, 99–150).

COURTLY LOVE

The most famous Andalusian love poet, Ibn Zaydūn (d. 1070), who was born in Córdoba and died in Seville, proclaimed the "religion of love" within the context of the lover's wasting away (74, ll. 3–9):

In desiring you, I play my destiny away,
  in loving you, I worship.

Wishings of passion, save me!
  At my back is death's shade.

Keep the oath that I, by God,
  won't be the one to betray.

Console a mournful lover
  sorrow thinned away,

His nights sickness, sighs,
  worry, and care.

Love wasted him and he became
  too thin to see.

He became, for desires, the prey.
  From him, all eyes were pulled away.

Here are brought together the realms of poetry (exemplified by *dahr*) and religion (exemplified by *dīn*).[2]

bi-hawāka d-dahra alhu	In desiring you, I play my destiny away,
wa bi ḥubbayka adīnu	in loving you, I worship.

Here, the theme of the poet's martyrdom to love is reinforced, as always with Ibn Zaydūn, with brilliant acoustical resonance:

shaffahu l-ḥubbu fa-amsā saqaman lā yastabīnu	Love wasted him and he became too thin to see.
sāra li-l-ashwāqi nahbun fa-nabat ʿanhu l-ʿuyūnuʾ	He became, for desires, the prey. From him, all eyes were pulled away.

The first words of the last hemistich, for example, exploit wickedly the variant of the *ramal* meter that begins with two short beats – *fa-na* – to create a sudden rapidity that re-creates aurally what is described (a sudden turning away or repelling of the eyes) – as if we just couldn't bear to look.

The quintessential Arabic love poem, Ibn Zaydūn's *Nūniyya* (Poem in N) (9–13), employs similar sound effects to heighten an ambiguity within the simple rhyme word for "us" (*nā*). The emotive power of the poem is compounded by the ambiguity between "we" as poetic and courtly plural (lover addressing the absent beloved), and the "we" of mutuality and ongoing relations that the poet-persona attempts to create. The poem opens (ll. 1–5):

Morning came – the separation –
substitute for the love we shared,
for the fragrance of our coming together,
falling away.

The moment of departure
came upon us – fatal morning.
The crier of our passing
ushered us through death's door.

Who will tell them
who, by leaving, cloak us
in a sorrow not worn away with time,
though time wears us away,

That time that used
to make us laugh
when they were near
returns to make us grieve.

We poured for one another
the wine of love. Our enemies seethed
and called for us to choke
– and fate said let it be.

The "morning of departure" of the classical Islamic *nasīb*, when the beloved leaves the poet-persona behind, is presented here with an intensity that will facilitate allusions later in the poem to the Qur'anic expulsion from the garden and day of reckoning. At first, the "us" seems to refer to both the lover and the beloved sharing the sufferings of separation. In verses 3–5, however, the poet-persona asks for an intermediary to tell those who left what sorrow they have caused. Those who left must include the beloved, and thus the primary referent of the "us" in "by leaving / cloak us in a sorrow" must refer to the poet-persona alone. As occurs throughout the poem, personifications are used with a haunting power. The abstract "distancing" is personified as standing in for the prior intimacy. Time (*dahr*) "returns" *(ʿāda)*, bringing sorrow in place of laughter. And when the "enemies" call for love's destruction, *dahr* is only too happy to satisfy the demand.

It is around the theme of the lover's secret that the poem develops its greatest intensity. For example (l. 13):

When our secret thought
whispered in your ear,
sorrow would have crushed us,
had we not held on to one another.

Does the beloved share the lover's grief, or is the lover speaking once again of himself in the courtly plural? And is it the lover's lonely secret thought or a thought shared with the beloved that is whispered? Underlying this ambiguity are allusions to the Qur'anic virtue of patience (*ṣabr*) and the quintessential whisperer, *al-shaytān* (the satan). These allusions to the world of religion thicken later in the poem, but they continue to be balanced by the language of the classical *nasīb*. For the Andalusi poet, the topoi of the Arabian desert such as the east wind – the perfumed, life-bearing messenger between lovers from the world Najd – are now rediscovered as marks of longing for the lost Cordoban court and for the beloved who both inhabits and represents it (ll. 20–23):

Night-traveler, lightning,
go early to the palace
and offer a drink to one
who poured us her pure love freely,

And ask if thoughts of us
trouble a lover
as the memory of her
possesses our troubled mind.

O fragrant breath of the east wind
bring greetings to one,
whose kind word would revive us
even from a distance.

Will she not, through the long
pass of time, grant us consideration,
however often, however
well we plead?

The last verse here might well be part of a panegyric, in which the poet addresses a prince asking for a particular dispensation. Here the royalty is the beloved and this class marking becomes a repeatedly deepened theme within the *Nūniyya.*

The anguish of love is more and more read through the vocabulary of religion, both Islamic and esoteric, from the proclamation that the beloved is the only creed (*iʿtiqād*) the lover takes and the only religio-legal opinion (*ra'y*) he follows, to the depiction of the beloved in terms of alchemical and astrological allusions to the creation of gold and silver and to the engraving of star signs on amulets. Toward the end of the poem, *dīn* becomes especially prominent as the poet-persona addresses the good life gone by (ll. 33–35):

We cannot name you.
In station you transcend
all names, freeing us
of the obligation.

You are unique, the one and only.
Your qualities cannot be shared.
We are left to describe you
as best we can.

O garden never dying,
your lote tree and spring of Kawthar
are now for us the tree of skulls
and the drink of the damned.

The past bliss is unique and none can share it (*yushārikuka*). The word for "share" is based on the same root as the word for idolatry (*shirk*) and to look to any other happiness would be a form of lovers' *shirk.* The former bliss transcends all names, clearly an allusion to theological disputes about whether the infinite God can be delimited by names. The lote tree (*sidr*) is the tree over which Muhammad saw his original prophetic vision (Qur'an 53:1–18) and the waters of Kawthar are the waters of paradise promised to those who keep the faith. The skulls and drink of the damned, on the other hand, are found within Qur'anic depictions of the fate of those who betray the faith.

There follow verses of poetic magic, in which mastery of conventions and a brilliant originality are combined (ll. 36, 38, 40):

> Did we not spend the night,
> making love our third companion,
> when our good luck weighed
> on our informer's eyes,
>
> Two secrets
> hidden in the whisper of darkness,
> until the morning's tongue
> was about to reveal us . . .
>
> We read our sorrow,
> that dawn of parting
> as Qur'an, reciting it by heart
> from the verse of patience.

Here, lovemaking (*waṣl*) becomes the third and welcomed party in this ménage-à-trois, as the normal, intrusive third party, the *wāshī*, slumbers. The power of this spectral personification of sexual union is enhanced by the tension within the "our" of "our good luck" between reference to the individual lover or to the lover–beloved relationship that the language continually strives to conjure.

The moment stolen from the night and from fate is soon lost. The classical dawn of parting that the poem had opened with is here combined with Qur'anic revelation and predetermination. Sorrow is learned as a sura and recited by heart. When the poet-persona exclaims that "we read our sorrow," the "we" can refer either to the lover only or to both lover and beloved – an ambiguity that fades three verses later when the lover protests of himself, "Not by our choice did we / withdraw from so near! / Time's twist, destiny / turned us against our will."

The final verses of the poem deepen the combination of classical *nasīb* and Qur'anic themes within the religion of courtly love (ll. 46, 49–51):[3]

> Be true to our vow
> as we have been.
> The noble give back,
> loyally, as given . . .

I am left sad, keeping the faith
though you have shut
me out. A phantom
will be enough, memories suffice.

Though in this world
we could not afford you,
we'll find you in the stations
of the last assembly, and pay the price.

A response from you
would be something!
If only what you offered
you gave.

God bless you
long as our love for you still burns,
the love we hide,
the love that gives us away.

Here the lover speaks directly to the beloved in the second-person singular: "dūmī ʿala l-ahdi" [be true to the vow]. The poetic tradition had long associated the oath (*ahd*) of lovers with prophetic covenants in the Qur'an, as well as the pre-eternal covenant implicit in the conversation that took place between God and the souls of all humanity before the creation (Qur'an 7:172). After such solemn associations and given the earlier use of either the high-discourse masculine or the second-person plural to refer to the beloved, the shift to the second-person feminine singular toward the end of the poem is striking. The linguistic register is transformed from formal address and circumlocution to a language of direct, immediate, and intimate encounter.

The final reference to a secret the lovers hide but which gives them away (in the dual sense of revealing and betraying them) eerily inverts the previous (and more common) themes of the secret being betrayed by the lover or by an outside agent. First it was distance and alienation that had been personified as a "stand-in" coming between the lover and the beloved. Later, lovemaking was the third party, while good fortune weighed down the eyes of the informer. Here, love itself has become the informer, exposing the lovers. Toward the end of the *Nūniyya*, the poet-persona argues that the phantom of the beloved will be enough for him. But the poem also creates its own phantom throughout, a third-party personification of separation, of fate, of a lovemaking (*waṣl*), and finally of the passionate love (*ṣabāba*) itself. This creation of a phantom third presence throughout the *Nūniyya* echoes the pre-Islamic phantom (*ṭayf, khayāl*) who appears to the poet-lover to engage in pleadings, excuses, and recriminations, but also manages to evoke that presence as a poetic force slipping through various guises as the poem unfolds.

At the end of the poem, the poet-persona reverts to the "us" in such a way that, syntactically and poetically, the beloved is implicated in it, harkening back to the previous reference to the happy secret they shared. Throughout the poem, the poet-persona had continually urged that the relationship not end, that the beloved offer at least a reply, and in that undertone of hope, the "us" is a final prayer. Within the poem, the religion of love has its own parallel sacred scripture, ritual, law, theology, mythic allusions of expulsion, eschatology (future or realized), and mysticism – as well as alchemy, astrology, and magic – channeling the conditions and experiences of love through the interplay between the realm of *dīn* and the realm of *dahr*. Finally, the poet, by revealing the love in one the world's most popular and enduring love poems, becomes the *wāshī* as well, immortalizing the relationship and extending the conversation and complaint about its brokenness into the realm of the timeless.[4]

BACCHIC LOVE

The wine of Arabic lyric is an ancient vintage, as well as a potion that offers escape from age-old time (*dahr*) itself. In the classical qasida, wine appeared as *tasliya*, distraction from the pain and longing for the beloved and from time itself, which caused the separation. The wine, the singing girl, the wine bearer (*sāqī*), and drinking companions evoke and imitate time and fate, as the wine cups are almost ritually passed in circular motions, filled and refilled, in a motion as endlessly recurring as that of the heavenly spheres. The effects of drink are contradictory; the poet drinks to forget the beloved, but sometimes, as in the famous *Muʿallaqa* (Hanging Ode) of Labīd, he can be found still drinking as dawn breaks and protesting all too much to an absent beloved how well he has forgotten her.

It was left to Abū Nuwās (d. 810), of Basra and Kufa, those two ancient centers of Arabic philology and literary criticism, and then of the caliphal courts of Baghdad, to achieve a more central role for wine within love talk. While the windswept ruins of the Bedouin campsite were retained – and indeed would be retrieved in striking new ways – wine became for the new urban cultures and for the non-Arabic ghazal tradition the most immediate and culturally portable sign of remembrance.

It has been said that "the *nasīb* is like a catalyst or like a filter through which new aspects, or purer filtrations, are achieved. It is through this realization, or one may say discovery, that we may begin to understand the genesis of symbolic language in Arabic poetry: everything that touches the *nasīb* becomes a symbol" (J. Stetkevych 62). With Abū Nuwās, wine is no longer an ingredient only, but has taken on the role of that elixir. Not only is it ancient, like the wines of the pre-Islamic poets; it is as old as time itself, as the daughters of Time (*banāt al-dahr*) or the mother of the Mother of Time (*umm al-dahr, umm al-zamān*). It is of the vintage of Noah or it preceded the creation of Adam (see citations in Kennedy 237). Wine remains both a momentary escape from the relentless ravages of *dahr* as well as a potion that can confer immortality. But this immortality bears suspicious resemblance to the timelessness of remembrance (*dhikr*) itself, remembrance of the beloved and the lost garden that is her symbolic analogue. As the jazz lyric has it, "If blues was whiskey, I'd be drunk all the time."

Abū Nuwās's wine can take over the entire classical qasida. In one poem (43–44), he begins by mocking the spring meadows of *nasīb* reverie:

> Forget the meadows. There's nothing
> in them for you. I've never yet
> been captivated by Zaynab or Kaʿub.

The quest becomes a journey to the wine tavern. The wine is presented in a quasi-ritual fashion. It is brought out ceremonially in a procession and solemnly unveiled. It becomes the *mamdūḥ* or object of panegyric praise and its names and qualities are recited. It has magic powers. It can seep through bones, change the flow of time, make the cautious man reveal his secret. Yet even as the classical *nasīb* is mocked, it often comes back at the end with its classical lyricism:

> He sang to the tune of
> "the lightning flashed that night from the West
> and the stranger yearned."
>
> The tears of a lover among us flowed
> though he had long seemed happy.
>
> Some laughed. Some wept.
> As what was hidden was revealed.
>
> Sirius passed over and set
> and the stars of the Pleiades
> appeared and adorned the coming dawn.

To the wine of *dahr*, Abū Nuwās added the wine of *dīn*. In his poetry, his *qibla* or direction of prayer faces toward wine. His belief is in the vine. In every mode from gravitas to the mockery, the poet-persona is repenting, thinking of repenting, and repenting of repenting. His repentance (*tawba*) in Islamic terms parallels his various stances on return to *ḥilm* (self-control) after the wine bouts taken in the state of *jahl* (Kennedy 86–148).

The references to the religion of wine – transgressive already in an Islamic tradition where wine is prohibited – were spiked further in the poetry of debauchery (*mujūn*). Abū Nuwās's verse continually alludes to Qur'anic depictions of paradise such as 56:17: "Surrounding them will be male youths to serve them in their perpetual freshness, with goblets, shining beakers, and cups filled from flowing fountains." In the *mujūn* poems these allusions form a parody of the Qur'anic heaven; the object of the poet-persona's desire is portrayed as one of the *sāqīs* of paradise come down to earth. Similarly, the obligation of jihad becomes making *hilāl* (permitted) the indulgence of passion, drinking a yellow wine spraying fire, and sex with boys in their youth, as their beards sprout, and in their ripe old age. For some, the reward for such a jihad is paradise; just as the *mujūn* lover conquers paradise through his transgression, in the realm of *dīn*, as Abū Nuwās proclaims in mock heroic boast, these "proud and penetrating men" overpower *dahr* in their pleasure. Abū Nuwās writes of a perfected religion in which the fivefold prayer becomes five obligatory fornications (Wright 10–13; Wafer 70–73).

We are tempted to call the *mujūn* poetry of Abū Nuwās and his many followers in al-Andalus blasphemous. Yet these poets have not been charged with blasphemy and the poems of Abū Nuwās to this day can be found sold amid books on religion, morals, and law. For some, the transgressive nature of *mujūn* love differs only in degree, not in kind, from any expression of eros – Ibn Qayyim al-Jawziyya chastised Ibn Ḥazm for allegedly banning a second look at a woman, but not the first (Giffen 129–32). Particularly striking is the prominence of Abū Nuwās's verse as a source of citation and allusion within Sufi literature.

Thus the Egyptian mystic poet Ibn al-Fāriḍ (d. 1235) begins his famous *Khamriyya* (Wine Song) with an allusion to Abū Nuwās's ancient vintage (cf. Homerin 11): "In memory of the beloved / we drank a wine / we were drunk with / before the creation of the vine" [sharibnā ʿalā dh-dhikri l-ḥabībi mudāmatan/sakirnā bihā min qabli an yukhlaqa l-karmu]. The commentators explain that this wine refers to the mystical intoxication that can be achieved when the boundaries of the ego-self are dissolved and the divine beloved appears in the heart of the human. This mystical intoxication was related by Ibn al-Fāriḍ and his commentators to the pre-eternal covenant between God and the precreated souls of humans.

Samuel the Nagid (d. 1056), the poet, scholar, and vizier of Granada, works the ancient wine into a biblical frame of reference (Cole 63; see also Scheindlin, *Wine* 54–59).

Bring me wine from a cup
held by a girl
who excels on the lute;
a mature vintage, made by Adam,
or new, from Noah's fields.
Its hue like living coral
and gold, its bouquet
like calamus and myrrh –

like David's wine that queens prepared,
impeccably, or graceful harems.
The day it was put in his pitcher,
he sang to Jerimoth's harp
unsurpassingly, saying:
this should be sealed and stored
in casks in the cellar –
for those who drink with excellent hearts

The Cordoban Ibn Quzmān (d. 1160) also rejects the "chaste love" of the *ʿudhrī* poets and then proclaims himself the disciple of Abū Nuwās (no. 123; Monroe, "Striptease" 113). Elsewhere, he draws on the religion of love. He dismisses those who are content with a kiss, and proclaims himself to be of the *madhhab* (school of religious thought) of *ʿishq khumārī* (bacchic love), ending his declaration with a bawdy double entendre (no. 30). The term *madhhab* elicits a context of religion: "Say O disbelievers, I do not worship what you worship and you do not worship what I do."

My mores are not those mores / that's not by school or style /
Bacchic love, stand and rise!
[Lays akhlāqi fi-dha l-akhlāq / wa lā kān madhhabī wa la stiḥsānī/
ʿishqan khumārī, qum, atlaʿ.]

In the above verse, we can sense beneath the phrasing of Ibn Quzmān a play on the Qur'anic verses 109:1–3.

A famous poem of the Cordoban Ibn Shuhayd (d. 1035), another self-proclaimed disciple of Abū Nuwās, combines bacchic love with a seduction. The seducer is portrayed as a kind of serpent creeping up on his victim. Here the weighing down of the eyes of the watcher and the betrayal of the lovers by the dawn twist into the leering smile of the seducer and collaborator (trans. Franzen 22; García Gómez, *Poemas* 100):

When the wine he drank
put him to sleep and the eyes
of the watchmen closed also

I approached him timidly
like one who seeks to come close,
but on the sly, pretending not to.

I crept toward him imperceptible
as a dream, moved myself close
to him, softly as a breath.

I kissed his throat, a white jewel,
drank the vivid red of his mouth

and so passed my night with him
deliciously, until darkness smiled,
showing the white teeth of dawn.

Ibn Shuhayd introduces another poem he categorizes as *mujūn* by explaining how he and his friends would frequent the mosque in Córdoba, not to pray, but to prey, looking for sexual adventure. When a woman comes to worship, she reads their intent and leaves: "Immediately she turned away, and the musk from her hem left / upon the ground a trail like the back of a serpent" (*Risāla* 67; trans. Monroe, "Striptease" 108). The final verse is ambiguous. The trail like the back of a serpent could be a reflection of the poet-persona's intentions, or it could indicate that the woman has been affected by them as well. Here the *mujūn* nature of the poem has become a matter of intention hidden within the motion of the hem of the woman's dress as she turns away.

The Hebrew poets enjoyed the game fully; in a muwashshah extolling promiscuous sex and drink, Granadan Moses Ibn Ezra (d. 1138) invokes the biblical Ram of Consecration sacrifice. The sacrificial breast and thigh offered in the consecration of Aaron's priesthood are transformed into symbols of the beloved as objects of desire (Scheindlin, *Wine* 91–95):

You too deserve a portion of the Ram
of Consecration, like your people's chiefs.
To suck the juice of lips do not be shy,
But take what's rightly yours – the breast and thigh!

Elsewhere, the same poet embeds the lover's exclamation "Adonai is there" [Adonai shamma] within a graphic scene of sexual play. These are the last words of Ezekiel and the culmination of Ezekiel's vision of the messianic Jerusalem, marking the phrase as particularly sacrosanct. The term "Adonai" had been used in the medieval period as a circumlocution for the even more sacrosanct tetragrammaton YHWH, but when the sacrality attached itself by contagion to the word "Adonai," it had to be protected by another circumlocution, *Ha Shem* (the name), which was then protected by the convention of using the letter *H* to stand in for the name The Name. The trangressive mixture of *mujūn* love and religion is amplified through the Ezekiel subtext and the embedded layers of sacrality around the divine name *Adonai shamma* (Scheindlin, *Wine* 96–101).

Bacchic love moves through an almost limitless range of cultural permutations. In his love lyrics, Sufi master Ibn ʿArabī combines bacchic images, classical ghazal (perishing in the beauty of the beloved), and the lover's defense (if I love to excess, God or *dahr* determined that I do so). He often makes no effort to distinguish between earthly and heavenly varieties of wine and love (173–75):

Who is here for a braveheart
  who halts at Sálʿin and hopes
Who for a braveheart
  lost in the hollow desert,
  love-burned, love-mad, gone sad
Who for a braveheart
  drowned in his tears
  drunk from the wine
    of her open mouth

Who for a braveheart
  burned by his own sighs
  led astray and abandoned
  in the beauty of the glow between her eyes.

The hands of desire
  played on his heart
What is there to hold against him
  Where is his crime?

The mutability of bacchic and *mujūn* love is also shown in an obscene muwashshah by al-Abyaḍ that became the model for a chain of contrafactions or poems playing on the meter, vocabulary, and kharja of the original – the last of which was a purely devotional muwashshah by Abraham Ibn Ezra (*Muwashshah).

Just as wine was culturally adaptable, it often attached itself to other culturally portable images. In a short, exquisite wine song, Samuel the Nagid invokes the *sāqī* and the wine, and then alludes to the henna on the female *sāqī*'s hands as the blood of the lover (Scheindlin, *Wine* 74):

Take from a fawn the crystal filled with blood
  Of grapes, as bright as hailstones filled with fire.
Her lips are a scarlet thread; her kisses, wine;
  Her mouth and body wear the same perfume.
Her hands are crystal wands with ruby tips –
  She tints her fingers with her victim's blood

The association of henna with the blood of the lover is one of the most common images in the ghazal. It is commonly used in plays on wine and on blood; indeed, it is one of the most culturally portable images in the poetry of the Islamic world, appearing in Hebrew, Persian, Arabic, and Ottoman lyric.

POPULAR LOVE

With the evocation of henna and the world of women, the wine song moves into popular dimensions of love. In the strophic muwashshah, the passing round of the cup of wine appropriates with complete ease the place formerly held by the *aṭlāl*, and forms the core of much of the love lyric. Even in muwashshahs that are panegyrics, the bacchic and love lyric elements are far more than simple introductions. They are woven through the poem, with a full exploitation of the analogies among the praise of the beloved, praise of the wine, and praise of the prince or patron.

The strophic muwashshah inherited from al-Andalus and still widely used within the Arabic world evokes popular culture in various ways. The refrain offers a kind of people's chorus, offering encouragement, criticism, or wisdom to the lover. The chorus echoes the timeless voice of the proverbs found in the early qasida, but its wisdom is more exclusively concerned with love. The refrain as vox populi is intensified when it is sung as a chorus, frequently in response to the predicament of the lover. In a muwashshah attributed to al-Aʿmā of Tudela (d. 1126) or Ibn Baqī of Córdoba (d. 1150), the choral voice commands the passing round of the cup of wine – the ancient ritual of cure, forgetfulness, and remembrance, the timeless turn of *dahr*. The chorus sings about the poet's party companions (*jullās*), but in another sense, members of the chorus are the *jullās*, forming an infinitely reduplicating act with each performance down through the generations to the North African ensembles that perform the same muwashshah today – evoking and perhaps also representing the timeless round of *dahr*. The chorus then commands the lover to "take love as your religion, your law!" [din bi l-hawā sharʿā] and to take as his *ḥukm* (religious injunction or obligation) a headlong rush to the cup of wine (Arabic text from Liu and Monroe 54):

Pass the cup around! In it the trance is forgotten.
Bring in the companions! The love is finished.

Take love as your religion, your law,
  friend! long as you're alive
Don't listen to the
  slanderer's persuasion.
Hurry! – that's your obligation –
  Here for you is the cup of wine!

The kharja brings a return to the religion of love, with the poet-lover now said to have repented (*tāb*):

> Our drinking companion has repented! Sing to him, recite,
> and show him a cup of wine. Perhaps he'll change his mind!

The play on repentance is compound; the *jullās* are urging and hoping that their friend will repent from his repentance, and they set about with their own time-word activities of proselytization or *daʿwā*.

Arabic dialect brings into recorded Arabic love lyric for the first time sustained examples of the diglossia essential to Arabic culture. The dropping of grammatical suffixes and the movement toward a more stress-based acoustics opens the lyric to a play of registers. Thus Ibn Quzmān opens a poem with the ruins of the beloved's campsite – ironically the mark of high classicism and solemn melancholy within the urbane world of al-Andalus – but adds a comic gesture through the use of dialect and an extravagant use of long-*a* assonance, achieving the aural equivalent of the sad face of the clown (Arabic text in Zwartjes 107–9):

> dār al-ḥabīb mudh bān   mahduma li-l-qāʿ
> ʿala ḥabar ad-dār   li-l-wuddi narjaʿ
>
> [the dwelling since my baby left me   rubble to the ground
> In the tracings of the ruin   we return to the love
> we had]

Later in the poem, the poet-persona, no choice left after his defeat in love, announces, with theatrical mockery, his own repentance, even as he figures his days of wine and women as *ʿīd*s or holy days.

> qad tāb aban quzmān ṭūba lu in dām
> qad kānat ayyāmu aʿyād fi-l-ayyām
>
> [Ibn Quzmān's repented. Good for him if it lasts!
> Oh, the days gone by were ʿIds among days!]

In the muwashshah form, the kharjas extend the effect through contrast with the classical Arabic in the body of the poem. A kharja by al-Aʿmā plays on the classic vow of the lover not to take any substitute for his lost beloved. With minor dialectal changes, this language and this comic vignette can be heard on the streets of Cairo today (text in Compton 98):

> wāsh kān dahānī   How he stunned me!
> yā qawmu wāsh kān balānī   O tribe! How he tried me!
> wāsh kān daʿāni   How he provoked me
> nabdal ḥabībī bi-thānī.   I'll trade in my lover for
> another.

Mixed dialect kharjas compound the shift in registers with a dynamic between Romance and Arabic. In addition, kharjas containing Romance vocabulary frequently represent the voice of the beloved. In the classical tradition the beloved speaks through the phantom, the east wind, the lightning, and the delirium of the lover's overheated brain, but seldom as herself. The Romance kharjas construct a female persona who speaks in person, in an unusually direct manner. The lover addressing his social superior, as with Ibn Zaydūn, is here balanced by the voice of the beloved in the language of the folk.

Thus the beckoning *jī ʿandī* (come to me) is intensified by the Romance *adúname*, a combination that appears in several kharjas with minor changes. Or the Arabic *khalīl* (intimate friend), a word associated with as daunting a figure as the Qur'anic Abraham is given a Romance diminutive and a new context: "Non kero, non, un khillelo / illa as-samarello" [The brunette's the only pal I desire]. The word *habībī* (my beloved), placed in the register of dialect and Romance, takes on a particularly popular touch (texts in Compton 105, 95, and 97). The last example reads:

ké fareyo o ké serad de mibe	What'll I do or what'll I be
ḥabībī	Darling
non te tolgash de mibe	Don't leave me!

A muwashshah by Judah Halevi (d. 1141) pushes the conventions of the classical erotic ghazal to the edge of parody. Her heart of stone is guarded by two breasts, like lances, their fiery nipples burning or piercing into the lover's heart. Then "one day as my hands were grazing in the garden [*janna*] / and I fondled her breasts, / she said to me *non me tangas yā habībī* [don't touch me, baby]." She then complains that her breasts are too sensitive for the rude hands of the lover – a devastating reversal of the earlier martial images (Carmi 342–43; Stern 193; cf. Ibn Ruhaym in García Gómez, *Jarchas* 214–21).

MEADOWS AND GARDENS: LIVED, LOST, AND MELANCHOLY

If, as Ibn Khaldūn suggested, Arabic civilization is the result of a dialectic between Bedouin and urban cultures, then we might say that the *locus amoenus* of the Arabic lyric inhabits at once the spring meadows of the Arabian desert and the enclosed garden, the *hortus conclusus*, of the city. The meadows have traces within them of the garden, and, particularly in al-Andalus, the gardens hold the flora of the deserts of Najd and Hejaz. This interplay between meadow and garden brings a combination of delicacy and passion to nature's reflection of the visions of the lost beloved, the moods of the lover, and the yearning for the homelands (*ḥanīn ilā l-mawāṭin*), the longing to belong.

In the classical *nasīb*, nature mediated the emotions of love, both expressing and disguising them. Apparent descriptions of the beloved would veer off, through digressive chains of similes, into a depiction of the lush beauty of the lost garden, the beloved's symbolic analogue. In the classical erotic ghazal, images of the garden and the features of the beloved's idealized face were put into a more direct relation. The Andalusians intensified this human–nature world of emotive sympathy, even as they transformed the Bedouin meadow into an enclosed garden encoded with a delicate lyricism. No one reads the human through the natural and the natural through the human like Ibn Khafāja (d. 1139), the great poet of Alcira near Valencia (trans. Franzen 15; García Gómez, *Poemas* 162):

Her glance, like a gazelle's,
her throat, that of a white deer,
lips red as wine,
teeth white as sea foam.

Tipsiness made her languid.
The gold-embroidered figures
of her wrap swirled round her,
brilliant stars around the moon.

During the night love's hands
wrapped us in a garment of embraces
ripped open
by the hands of dawn.

Like Ibn Zaydūn and Ibn Quzmān, Ibn Khafāja brings a distinctive genius to the conceit of dawn revealing the lovers. Here, the poem opens with the beloved compared to nature and her clothing compared to the night sky. But the poet ends by inverting the relation as the hands of dawn rip open the garment of embraces that concealed the lovers.

Ibn Shuhayd uses the Bedouin convention of the sleepless poet "pasturing the stars" to project onto the heavens the brilliant array of the enclosed garden. The long extravaganza of verses depicting the "tottering, leaning, tumbling Throne" of the astral garden end with a sudden interiorization: "as though night's darkness were my care, / its stars my tears" (J. Stetkevych 154–55). With Ibn Ḥazm of Córdoba (d. 1064), the final interiorization of the astral garden is reversed, the stars projected outward from the poet's consciousness (30; J. Stetkevych 157, commentary 157–61):

I pasture the stars as though entrusted
To tend all fixed constellations
  and planets that incline to set

For, when the night's ablaze
  with passion's flames, they seem
To have ignited out of the darkness of my mind,

And I become like a green meadow's keeper,
Its grasses cross-garlanded with narcissus.

Were Ptolemy alive, he'd vouch
  that of all men
I am the ablest one to chart
  the movement of the stars.

The first hemistich, arʿā an-nujūma kaʾannanī kulliftu [I pasture the stars as though entrusted], is a quotation, an allusion, and a brilliant subtle shift on the pre-Islamic elegist al-Khansāʾ: "I tend the stars, although not tasked to tend them / Throwing at times about me the flaps of my rags" [arʿā an-nujūma wa mā kulliftu].

Ibn Ḥazm is able to place an objectivizing exterior over undertones of uncontrollable emotion evoked in his subtext from al-Khansāʾ. In the second hemistich of the first verse, the poet compounds the effect with a play of etymology and archaic vocabulary. He refers to the stars as *al-khunnas*, a word etymologically related to the name al-Khansāʾ; the *khunnas* can refer to gazelles or antelope moving through the meadows or the antelope stars moving across the sky, even as al-Khansāʾ means, in what for the Bedouin carried no irony, only affection, "the gazelle-nosed or oryx-nosed beauty."

Three verses later, he rhymes *khunnas* with the relatively obscure *kunnas* (running ghazals, fast moving stars), a dead giveway allusion to the Qurʾan (1–6, 15–20). That passage begins by evoking the Qurʾanic day of reckoning not only in cosmic terms – the overturning of the sun, the strewing of the stars, the boiling over of the seas – but also in pastoral terms of birthing camels and beasts of the desert. It swears to the authenticity of Muhammad's prophetic vision by invoking (and employing as rhyme words) the *khunnas* and the *kunnas*: the stars wandering like gazelles, streaming across the sky. To the oaths by these pastoral stars, the Qurʾan then swears by other *nasīb*-like signs – by the night as it slips away and by the fragrant breath of morning – that the Prophet was not mad (*majnūn*) and was not speaking out of desire (*hawā*). The references to the Prophet and to not speaking of our desire allude to the Qurʾanic vision text par excellence (53:1–18), which begins with another divine oath: "by the star when it falls" [wa n-najmi idhā hawā]. The word for "falls" (*hawā*), in turn, is a homonym and etymological twin of the word for desire.

Beneath this urbane and apparently objectivized garden of Ibn Ḥazm there opens up the archaic ground of Arabic literature, antelope and gazelles of the desert rocklands and sleepless starry night, the ancient and by now immortalized grief of al-Khansā' for the loss of her brother, and the Qur'anic meditations on destiny, revelation, and the end of time. It is commonly said that the value of *Ṭawq al-ḥamāma* (The Dove's Neckring) resides in the prose analysis of the states of love, that the poetic examples are only there from convention, and that Ibn Ḥazm's own poetry is of little intrinsic merit (Giffen 23–35). Yet his sole comment on his poem is to state the obvious: that it represents the theme of lover's insomnia (Ibn Ḥazm 30). But the deeper meanings within the sleeplessness of love and the claim that Ptolemy would vouch for the poet's star-charting ability are not even suggested within his prose narrative.

The Bedouin pasturing the stars was integrated by Samuel the Nagid into a biblical universe. He gazes at the stars, seeing the tent of the sky, clasps joined by loops (Tabernacle hangings, Exod. 26:6), moon and stars like a shepherdess grazing her flock in a pasture. Then, projecting his meditation back to the earth, his thoughts grow somber: "But the earth's inhabitants are like an army pitching its tents for a night, looting the local granaries. And all flee before the terror of death – like a dove chased by a hawk" (Carmi 295; see also Scheindlin, *Wine* 148–51).

In returning the garden back from the sky to earth, Ibn Khafāja, like no one else, sees the emotive reflections of nature and human reverberating and amplifying one another like two facing mirrors. After alluding to both the ruins of the beloved's campsite and her phantom, he shifts to the now mostly mythological topography of the Arabian lovers (124–25; trans. J. Stetkevych 188):

Should all I forget, I shall not forget
   a night over Hima,
Aquiver with moonlight, in beauty dissolved . . .

Rain clouds were generous there
   both morning and eve
Tossed about on strong winds till exhaustion.

One nightly cloud darkness led astray,
But a refulgent lightning lit it for a wick.

And in the early morning, my God, how sadly
   the dove cooed there,
And how dew-laden were the shadows
   of the Arak tree!

Then the easterly breeze teased
   at the stem of the hillock
And it swayed and bent over the rump-curve
   of the dune.

The chill of morning stirred
narcissus' lid.
A tear of dew first gleamed on it
and then rolled down.

Ibn Khafāja finds the symbolic language for his yearning within the Arabian desert: the east wind (*al-ṣabā*) of gentle showers, perfumed air, and lovers' murmurs; al-Ḥimā, a proper name that means "sacred tribal meadows"; and the *arak* (thornberry), a desert shrub of Najd. These and other features of ancient Bedouin lovers had become through centuries of symbolic condensation the perfect vehicle for the Andalusian longing for the homeland. In particular, that very specific east wind that brought rain, perfumed air, and messengers from the far-flung beloved to the pre-Islamic Ṭarafa and Imru' al-Qays, through Ibn Abī Rabīʿa strikes Valencia's most famous poet with the immediacy of a cloud that has picked up moisture over a long journey: "When the east wind rises I cry out / longing for al-Andalus" (Ibn Khafāja 136; see also J. Stetkevych 125–32).

The plasticity of the *aṭlāl* for expressing longing is further illustrated in Ibn Zaydūn's famous ode to the caliphal palace of al-Zahrā' (*Madīnat al-Zahrā'). There, the ruins of the palace take the place of the ruins of the abandoned campsite. The reverie of times with the beloved ends not in a desert meadow, but within the most delicately cultivated Andalusian garden (46–47; trans. Franzen 34–37; García Gómez, *Poemas* 119–20):

The blossoms are eyes.
They see my sleeplessness
and weep for me;
their iridescent tears overflow
staining the calyx.

The Hebrew poets again illuminate the play of allusion within the Arabic poetic tradition as they integrate it into a biblical context. The Granadan Moses Ibn Ezra begins with the classical *aṭlāl*, but the ruins of the beloved's camp, the Temple, and the lair of wild beasts are all brought together through the use of the word *maʿon* (Scheindlin, *Gazelle* trans., 65, commentary 66–68; *Moses Ibn Ezra).

Hasten to the lovers' camp,
dispersed by Time, a ruin now;
Once the haunt of love's gazelles
Wolves and lions' lair today.

From far away I hear Gazelle,
From Edom's keep and Aram's cell,

Mourning the lover of her youth,
Sounding lovely, ancient words:
"Fortify me with lovers' flasks,
Strengthen me with sweets of love."

The final cry of the beloved is based on the Song of Songs. The temple in ruins reflects the poet's captivity within a cultural universe only partially made his own. Yet he also finds within that same culture not merely a vehicle to express his longing but a poetic language in which that longing, at least, is perfectly at home.

While Ibn Ezra was still able in his old age in the Christian-ruled north to look to Granada with longing, Judah Halevi shifted orientations on a wider arc. Born in the border areas between Christendom and Islamdom, Halevi soon mastered the intricate Arabicate culture of al-Andalus – but not without ambivalence about abandoning the East (the Christian-ruled territories). In one poem, the poetic figure of the blamer upbraids the poet for moving to the "idolatrous West" of al-Andalus. In that poem, the poet-persona defends his attachment to al-Andalus. By the end of his life, however, the East beckoned again, now redefined as the ruin of the beloved abode in Jerusalem: "My yearning love is stirred when I remember the East of yore, / Your Glory exiled, your Shrine ruined" (trans. Brann, *Judah Halevi).

With the expulsion from the garden of al-Andalus, it was inevitable that this civilization of love song and exile would itself become the object of longing generations of Arabic poets, musicians, and *jullās.*

MYSTICAL LOVE

The Egyptian Ibn al-Fāriḍ, called the Sultan of Love (*ṣultān al-ḥubb*), was known as a love poet long before he became considered a Sufi sheikh. According to his hagiography, during a Sufi session of *dhikr* and poetry, someone recited verses of a lover's complaint that on the day of separation, his tears had left his heart behind in the Hejaz (Homerin 25). On hearing the verses, the poet went into *wajd* (ecstatic trance). The intensity of his *wajd* in turn convinced those around him that he was indeed a *walī*, an intimate friend of God.

The anecdote illustrates a frequently resisted relation between love lyric and Sufi mysticism. A verse, indistinguishable from other *nasīb* lyrics, provokes the future sheikh into a state of ecstatic trance. It has been characteristic of mystical poetry within Islam that the most loved poems are those that refuse to give away their referent and refuse to distinguish between earthly and heavenly longing – though generations of commentators are more than willing to make the distinctions. The state of *wajd*, as experienced by the Cairene poet and mystic, is itself the Sufi analogue to the state of *ṭarab*, that indescribable state that occurs when the tears begin to well up in the eyes of even the most self-controlled members of the party circle – as remembrance is circulated in the cup of *sāqī* and the *bayt* (abode, verse) of the poem.

Like Ibn al-Fāriḍ, his contemporary Ibn ʿArabī merged the realms of love and hajj. In his collection of *nasīb*-qasidas, the *Turjumān al-ashwāq* (Translator of Desires), the Murcian grand master of Sufism rediscovered in new key the archaic analogy between stations of the beloved's journey away from the poet and the stations of religious pilgrimages (33–34):

> Meet us at the spring of Zamzam
>   after circumambulation,
> near the middle tent,
>   near the boulders,
>
> There a man thinned away
>   by the fever of love
> is cured by the fragrance
>   of the women that made him yearn.
>
> When disquieted
>   they loosen their hair
> and let it fall
>   folding themselves in veils of darkness.

Elsewhere Ibn ʿArabī explicitly merges with the stations of the hajj, the stations of Bedouin Arabia, such as Najd, Kathīb and Laʿlaʿ. The request to his "two friends" to turn aside at the ruins of the beloved's campsite evoke the opening of Imruʾ al-Qays's *Muʿallaqa*, the most famous poem of pre-Islamic Arabia. The stations and rituals (the casting of stones and the great sacrifice in memory of Abraham) are then interiorized (20–24):

> O my two friends –
>   turn aside at al-Kathíb,
> pull off the track at Láʿlaʿ,
>   and seek the waters of Yalámlami.
>
>   There you'll find
> those you came to know.
>   To them belong my fastings,
> my pilgrimages, my festivals.
>
> May I never forget what happened
>   at the stoning grounds at Mina,

that day, at the fields of sacrifice,
 at the Zamzam's blessed spring,

 Their stoning ground, my heart
Let them cast their pebbles there!
 their field of the sacrifice, my soul,
their sacred spring, my blood.

The *Turjumān* continually weaves *dīn* and *dahr* together. A pun on the term for red roan camels that bear the beloved away (*ʿīs,*) and the word for Jesus (*ʿīsā*) – whom Ibn ʿArabī viewed as the mediator of his inspiration – allows him to blend the two together. And although it was conventional for Sufi verse to figure the divine beloved as female, Ibn ʿArabī's conception is particularly bold. In one poem, the ghazal theme of the fatal beauty of the beloved accompanies references to the Qur'anic queen of Sheba and the prophet Idrīs who represent the world of the divine throne and the seven heavens crossed by Muhammad in his ascent to it (16–19).

She takes possession
with a glance that kills,
like the Shéban queen
 Bilqís on her throne of pearl.

When she walks
on the polished tiles of glass
you see a sun on a sphere
 in the stone of Idrís.

What her glance kills
her speech revives,
bringing the dead to life,
 like Eissa.

The poem then depicts this fatal beauty dumbfounding the sages of all tradition. At times the depiction is made with irreverent humor, only to shift back to the dead serious:

A hint from her
she wished the gospel
and just like that! you'd think us priests,
patriarchal highnesses in flowing robes.

The day they left me
I set loose squadrons,
squadrons along the path,
 the armies of my patience.

As my soul rose to my throat
I begged that beauty,
that grace:
  Save me.

The poem ends with the classical *ẓaʿn,* departing company of the beloved, with a pun on the red roans and Jesus:

As they saddled her camel
mare for departure, I cried:
driver of the red roans,
  don't take the Eis' away!

Another lyric is structured in the form of a hadith (54–56) and blends traditional religion, mystical religion, and the religion of love. It begins with lightning flashing in the East, an image that comments on and echoes other verses back through the tradition to the pre-Islamic *nasīb*:

He saw the lightning flash
and yearned toward the East.
If it had flashed in the West
west he would have turned.

It then cites the tradition and its chain of authorities, which are the various states of love, ending with the beloved's statement (*matn*) that the one he searches for is within his heart. This is a rare instance of a hadith-type statement where the message is returned by the recipient back through the chain of transmitters. The poet-persona sends a response that it was the beloved who kindled the fire in his heart, that only lovemaking (*waṣl*) can quench it, and that if it continues to burn, a lover can never be blamed for loving. The poem, without calling itself a hadith, used the form and thus manages to blend traditionalist religion, mystical religion, and the religion of love.

Ibn ʿArabī's most cherished expression of the religion of love occurs in the eleventh poem of the collection (41–44). He begins with the *arak* (thornberry), the moringa thicket, and the cooing of the dove (always a sign of loss within the Arabic lyric), and in the second verse, offers his own version of the exposure of love's secret. The poem is composed around several complex and intertwined thematic movements. It begins and ends with *nasīb* themes, especially the *ẓaʿn,* the journey of the beloved and her female companions away from the poet. In the fourth verse, the Sufi condition of *fanāʾ*, the passing away or annihilation of the self of the Sufi in union with the divine beloved, is signaled through a subtle wordplay in reference to the spirits "passing him away." As throughout the *Turjumān*, the stations of the desert lovers (Ghadā, Naʿmān) and the stations of the hajj (Minā) are placed into the same pilgrimage. Finally, in the center of the poem there is a perspective shift grounded in the Sufi claim that the greatest Kaaba is the heart of the divine lover at the moment of *fanāʾ*.

Gentle now, doves of the thornberry
and moringa thicket,
don't add to my heartache
your sighs.

Gentle now,
or your sad cooing
will reveal the love I hide,
the sorrow I hide away.

I echo back, in the evening,
in the morning, echo,
the longing of a lovesick lover,
the moaning of the lost.

In a grove of Gháda,
spirits wrestled,
bending the limbs down over me,
passing me away.

They brought yearning,
breaking of the heart,
and other new twists of pain,
putting me through it.

Who is there for me in Jámʿ,
and the Stoning-Place at Mína,
who for me at Tamarisk Grove,
or at the way station of Naʿmán?

Hour by hour
they circle my heart
in rapture, in loveache,
and touch my pillars with a kiss.

As the best of creation
circled the Kaaba,
which reason with its proofs
called unworthy.

He kissed the stones there –
and he bore the pronouncement!
What is the house of stone
compared to a man or woman?

They swore, and how often!
they'd never change – piling up vows.
She who dyes herself red with henna
is faithless.

A white-blazed gazelle
is an amazing sight,
red-dye signaling,
eyelids hinting,

Pasture between breastbones
and innards.
Marvel,
a garden among the flames!

My heart can take on
any form:
gazelles in a meadow,
a cloister for monks,

For the idols, sacred ground,
Kaaba for the circling pilgrim,
the tables of the Torah,
the scrolls of the Qur'an.

I profess the religion of love;
wherever its caravan turns
along the way, that is the belief,
the faith I keep.

Like Bishr,
Hind and her sister,
love-mad Qays and the lost Láyla,
Máyya and her lover Ghaylán.

The "passing away" occurs in the grove of tamarisks in which spirits were wrestling, bending down the limbs over the poet. The word here for spirits (*arwāḥ*) is a central term in Ibn ʿArabī's writings, commonly referring to those bewildered spirits that encircle the divine throne (itself envisaged as a celestial Kaaba). The word for winds or breezes (*riyāḥ*) is closely related to *arwāḥ*, and the poem plays on both senses. The list of pilgrimage stations places side by side the stations of the hajj and those of the Arabian Bedouin lovers.

In midpoem, the relationship of poetic voice to the stations is inverted. The poet-persona had been following in the wake of the stations and the visions of the beloved that occupy them. But with the words "Hour by hour /

they circle my heart," he is the center of the circumambulation, speaking from the place of the divine abode or house (*bayt*), the Kaaba. If even the "best of creation" (Muhammad) found a rock (the Kaaba) worth kissing, he argues, how much more worthy of devotion must be the heart of the lover.

The henna-dyed beloved, the gazelle, and the meadow all evoke the classical *nasīb*. The fickleness of the beloved is tied to the perishing of the lover, a perishing that in turn evokes perishing of the self in *fanāʾ*. There follows the famous verse "I profess the religion of love" [adīnu bi d-dīni l-ḥubb]. The forms that the heart can take on are listed in a manner reminiscent of the listing of the pilgrimage stops earlier: the meadow for the gazelles, the sacred home of the idols, the Kaaba, the Torah, the Qurʾan. The rhythm of the poem has changed, becoming as measured as that of the pilgrim moving through the stations of the pilgrimage, combination of calm measure and increasingly fevered intensity. The poem ends with a tribute to the martyred lovers of the classical ghazal as role models.

In his preface to the *Turjumān*, Ibn ʿArabī dedicated the poems to Niẓām, the young woman who had confronted him at the Kaaba. He was then attacked by another kind of critic, who saw his poetry as unbefitting a Sufi sheikh not because he didn't understand love, but because he was writing erotic verse in the first place. His response was a new preface and a commentary linking an allegorical reading of the poems to his wider mystical theophany.

The *Turjumān* has suffered in the study of Arabic literature precisely because many critics took the allegorical commentary as if it exhausted the meanings of the poems, thus falling into the fallacy that Sufis simply used the conventions of love poetry as a vehicle to express mystical theologies they had attained independently of them (see Sells, "Bewildered Tongue"). In many cases, the technique is identical to contemporaneous Jewish commentaries on the Song of Songs by writers such as Ezra Ben Solomon of Gerona (Ben Solomon 38–146). Yet there are places where the commentary connects the poem to the mystical theology in ways that do not delimit the meaning of the poem.

Thus in commenting on the verse "My heart can take on every form" [qābil li kulli ṣūra], the Murcian sheikh links the verse to his mystical philosophy of the constant transformation of the heart. For Ibn ʿArabī, the infinite cannot be known in any one manifestation in time, and its manifestations are constantly changing. It is the normal activity of the intellect and of language to bind or delimit (*qayyada*) things, to mark out their boundaries. But when this delimitation is applied to the infinite, the primal error occurs: each belief (*iʿtiqād*) binds the deity into the image formed within that system and denies the images manifested within other beliefs. The result is a double error: an idolatry in which the "god of belief" is worshiped not as a manifestation of the divine, but as the deity itself; and a disbelief (*kufr*) in which the one deity is denied in its authentic manifestations in other beliefs.

The antidote to the error is found within the hadith of love, in which God announces: "When I love my servant . . . I become the hearing with which he hears, the seeing with which he sees, the feet with which he walks, the hands with which he touches [and in some versions], the tongue with which he speaks." This hadith is the ground of Sufi understanding of *fanā'* or passing away (Sells, *Islamic Mysticism* 216, 234, 258). The divine cannot be known as an objectified entity. It can be known only when the ego-self (*nafs*) of the Sufi, with its delimiting intellect and projecting will, passes away. At that moment the heart of the Sufi becomes like a combination of polished mirror and prism in which the undifferentiated unity of the divine light is reflected and refracted (Sells, *Languages* 63–115).

The temptation is to grasp or possess the image with that reflection and refraction. But the manifestations are constantly changing. One whose heart (*qalb*) can take on every form is open to continual transformation (*taqallub*), in each moment receiving the new manifestation giving up the prior manifestation. In poetic terms, the constantly moving caravan of the beloved, always just behind the poet, in memory, or just ahead of him, in the stages of her journey, offers a lyrical understanding perfectly consonant with this mystical philosophy. Majnūn was right in his madness; those rocks, those trees, those riverbeds are Laylā, but she cannot be confined or seized within them. The beloved is held within the heart, but never possessed. The images of her are constantly changing, driving the lover to bewilderment (*ḥayra*). Playing on the dual meanings of *ʿaql* as either rope or mind, Ibn ʿArabī conceives of the *ʿaql* as the faculty that delimits reality into bound categories. When the lover is driven out of his wits (*ʿaql*), he no longer binds the divine into a particular image. In the shifting images, lyrically evoked in the fickle states and moods of the beloved, he perishes.

Herein lies the elegiac lyricism of Ibn ʿArabī's understanding of mystical union. The heart that is receptive to every form must be willing to give up each image, each form, each beloved, in order to be receptive to the next form. Thus in announcing the religion of love, Ibn ʿArabī evokes the mournful cooing of the doves, and the *ẓaʿn*, the movement of the beloved and her companions away from the poet. At the end, the poetic voice speaks from out of the Kaaba of the heart. The beloveds (or different manifestations of the beloved) combine both centripetal and centrifugal forces in their circling motion around the Kaaba of love.

Of all Andalusians, the Murcian sheikh is most rooted in the Bedouin paradigm of constant wandering. "He saw the lightning flash / and yearned toward the East. / If it had flashed in the West / west he would have turned." He spoke of his own life and mystical itinerary as *siyāḥa*, perpetual wandering. The act of losing the beloved, the garden, the homeland, and the simultaneous act of retrieving them is, simply put, the human condition. The poet does not spend time identifying or delimiting the beloved as earthly or heavenly. Such distinctions to the lover (*ʿāshiq*) would be obtuse, given that the one who is loved is beyond all categories and cannot be excluded from any aspect of reality. Even to raise the question about the identity of the beloved would be indiscrete, a violation of adab or the proper conduct of the lover.

It is fitting also that it was under the Kaaba that Ibn ʿArabī was moved to recite a love lyric, that he found a young woman taking him to task for not understanding that the highest state of love is a bewilderment (*ḥayra*) in which there is no piece of the self left to speak of its own bewilderment, and that he began the composition of his great collection of love odes. According to one legend, the seven prizewinning pre-Islamic qasidas were embroidered in black cloth and hung from the walls of the Kaaba. According to another legend, the Kaaba stone is a remnant of the paradise of being with the divine beloved, the paradise from which Adam and Eve were expelled, the cosmic *ṭalal* or ruin. Attempts have been made to find the philosophical sources of Arabic love traditions, and Andalusians have distinguished themselves in such work. But just as Ibn Shuhayd's and Ibn Ḥazm's poems open onto an almost limitless ocean of allusion, intertextual play, and subtleties that their philosophical commentaries cannot capture, so Ibn ʿArabī's prose attempts to delimit, categorize, explain, or paraphrase the names of love such as *ʿishq, hawā*, and *ḥubb* are melted away within the intensity of the poems. It is in that tangle, where even the lords of love (*arbāb al-hawā*) are bewildered and ensnared, that the expression of love is deepest.

NOTES

1 All translations from the Arabic are mine unless otherwise noted.

2 This poetic balance was often defended by reference to the famous hadith in which God forbids the cursing of *dahr* and states "I am *dahr.*" In such a hadith, the realm of *dahr* and its poetic ruminations on love, fate, and mortality are appropriated rather than rejected.

3 The verses of the *Nūniyya* are notoriously unstable in the order and number in which they appear in different sources. Verse 49 on finding the beloved in the afterlife does not appear in the *Dīwān* manuscripts. Rather, it is found in Ibn Khāqān as verse 37, but that placement is awkward and has been rejected by some modern editors. I have placed it where I find it most compellingly belongs. See Monroe, *Poetry* 184.

4 The conceit of the secret revealed echoes Qurʾanic references to Allah as *al-khabīr, al-samīʿ*, and *al-baṣīr*, the one who hears, sees, and searches out every inner secret. In some theological interpretations, with the day of reckoning, the world will be turned inside out and that which was held interior and secret will be exteriorized and revealed.

BIBLIOGRAPHY

ʿAbbās, Iḥsān. *Taʾrīkh al-adab al-andalusī.* 2 vols. Beirut, 1960, 1962.

Abū Nuwās. *Dīwān.* Beirut, 1982.

Ben Solomon of Gerona, Rabbi Ezra. *Commentary on the Song of Songs and Other Kabbalistic Commentaries.* Selected, trans., and annotated by Seth Brody. Kalamazoo, 1999.

Brann, Ross. *The Compunctious Poet: Cultural Ambiguity and Hebrew Poetry in Muslim Spain.* Baltimore, 1991.

Carmi, Ted. *The Penguin Book of Hebrew Verse.* London, 1981.

Cole, Peter. *Selected Poems of Shmuel HaNagid.* Princeton, 1996.

Compton, Linda Fish. *Andalusian Lyrical Poetry and Old Spanish Love Songs: The Muwashshaḥ and Its Kharja.* New York, 1976.

Franzen, Cola. *Poems of Arab Andalusia.* Trans. Cola Franzen from the Spanish versions of Emilio García Gómez. San Francisco, 1989.

García Gómez, Emilio. *Las jarchas romances de la serie árabe en su marco.* Madrid, 1965.

Poemas arábigoandaluces. Buenos Aires, 1940.

Ghāzī, Sayyid. *Dīwān al-muwashshaḥāt al-andalusiyya.* 2 vols. Alexandria, 1979.

Giffen, Lois. *Theory of Profane Love among the Arabs: The Development of the Genre.* New York, 1971.

Gloton, Maurice, trans. *Traité d'amour* by Ibn ʿArabī. Paris, 1986.

Hatto, A. *Eos: An Enquiry into the Theme of Lover's Meetings and Partings at Dawn in Poetry.* The Hague, 1965.

Homerin, Emil. *From Arab Poet to Sufi Saint: Ibn al-Fāriḍ, His Verse, and His Shrine.* Columbia, S.C., 1994.

Ibn (al-)ʿArabī. *Turjumān al-ashwāq.* Beirut, 1966.

Ibn al-Fāriḍ. *Dīwān.* Beirut, 1957.

Ibn Ḥazm. *Ṭawq al-ḥamāma.* Ed. aṭ-Ṭāhir Aḥmad Makkī. Cairo, 1984.

Ibn Khafāja. *Dīwān.* Alexandria, 1960.

Ibn Khāqān. *Qalāʾid al-iqyān.* Tunis, 1966.

Ibn Quzmān. *Dīwān.* Ed. Federico Corriente. Madrid, 1980.

Ibn Saʿīd al-Maghribī. *Kitāb rāyāt al-mubarrizīn wa ghāyāt al-mumayyazīn.* Damascus, 1987.

Ibn Shuhayd. *Risālat al-tawābiʿ wa l-zawābiʿ.* Ed. Buṭrus al-Bustānī. Beirut, 1951.

Risālat al-tawābiʿ wa l-zawābiʿ: The Treatise of Familiar Spirits and Demons by Abū

ʿAmir ibn Shuhaid al-Ashjaʿī al-Andalusī. Introduction, trans., and notes by James T. Monroe. Berkeley, 1971.

Ibn Zaydūn. *Dīwān.* Beirut, 1957.

Jayyusi, Salma Khadra. "Andalusī Poetry: The Golden Period." *The Legacy of Muslim Spain.* Ed. Salma Khadra Jayyusi. Leiden, 1992. 317–66.

"Nature Poetry in al-Andalus and the Rise of Ibn Khafāja." Jayyusi. 367–97.

Kennedy, Philip. *The Wine Song in Classical Arabic Poetry: Abū Nuwās and the Literary Tradition.* Oxford, 1997.

Liu, Benjamin M., and James T. Monroe. *Ten Hispano-Arabic Strophic Songs in the Modern Oral Tradition.* Berkeley, 1989.

Lug, Sieglinde. *Poetic Techniques and Conceptual Elements in Ibn Zaydūn's Love Poetry.* Washington, 1982.

al-Maqqarī. *Nafḥ al-ṭīb min ghuṣn al-andalus al-raṭīb.* Cairo, 1949.

Menocal, María Rosa. *Shards of Love: Exile and the Origins of the Lyric.* Durham, 1994.

Monroe, James T. *Hispano-Arabic Poetry.* Berkeley, 1974.

"The Striptease That Was Blamed on Abū Bakr's Naughty Son." Wright and Rowson 94–139.

al-Nowaihi, Magda. *The Poetry of Ibn Khafāja: A Literary Analysis.* Leiden, 1993.

Noorani, Yaseen. "The Lost Garden of al-Andalus: Islamic Spain and the Poetic Inversion of Colonialism." *International Journal of Middle East Studies* 31 (1999): 236–54.

Pérès, Henri. *La poésie andalouse en arabe classique au XI siècle.* Paris, 1953.

Scheindlin, Raymond P. *The Gazelle: Medieval Hebrew Poems on God, Israel, and the Soul.* Philadelphia, 1991.

Wine, Women, and Death: Medieval Hebrew Poems on the Good Life. Philadelphia, 1986.

Sells, Michael. "Bewildered Tongue: The Semantics of Mystical Union in Islam." *Mystical Union in Judaism, Christianity, and Islam.* Ed. Moshe Idel and Bernard McGinn. New York, 1996. 87–124.

Early Islamic Mysticism. New York, 1996.

Mystical Languages of Unsaying. Chicago, 1994.

Stations of Desire: Love Elegies from Ibn ʿArabī and New Poems. Jerusalem, 2000.

Stern, Samuel M. *Hispano-Arabic Strophic Poetry.* Ed. L. P. Harvey. Oxford, 1974.

Stetkevych, Jaroslav. *The Zephyrs of Najd: The Poetics of Nostalgia in the Classical Arabic Nasīb.* Chicago, 1993.

Stetkevych, Suzanne Pinckney. "Intoxication and Immortality: Wine and Associated Imagery in al-Maʿarrī's Garden." Wright and Rowson 210–32.

Stetkevych, Suzanne Pinckney, ed. *Reorientations: Arabic and Persian Poetry.* Bloomington, 1994.

Vadet, Jean Claude. *L'esprit courtois en Orient: Dans les cinq premiers siècles de l'hégire.* Paris, 1968.

Wafer, James. "Sacred and Profane Love in Islam." Thesis. Indiana University, 1986.

Wright, J. *Masculine Allusion and the Structure of Satire in Early ʿAbbāsid Poetry.* Wright and Rowson 1–24.

Wright, J., and Everett Rowson, eds. *Homoeroticism in Classical Arabic Literature.* New York, 1997.

Zwartjes, Otto. *Love Songs from al-Andalus: History, Structure, and Meaning of the Kharja.* Leiden, 1997.

THE GREAT MOSQUE OF CÓRDOBA

D. F. Ruggles

In eighth-century Córdoba, a public architecture emerged that – like the Palace of Madīnat al-Zahrā' – blended Roman, Visigothic-Christian, and Syrian-Muslim elements. Córdoba's congregational mosque exemplifies the integration of different architectural traditions. It was built on the site of a Visigothic church that, according to legend, stood on the ruins of a Roman temple. Centuries after the founding of the mosque, chroniclers described a church that was first divided into Muslim and Christian halves and then bought and replaced with a new mosque in 169/785–170/787. That this closely resembles the story of the adaption and rebuilding of the Damascus mosque casts doubt on the authenticity of the Córdoba account but indicates that even several hundred years later, the Syrian origins of the mosque resonated.

The Great Mosque consisted of a walled courtyard and a rectangular prayer hall of nine or eleven aisles running perpendicular to the *qibla* wall. A taller and wider central aisle led to the mihrab, a niche in the *qibla* wall that indicated the direction of Mecca and hence the orientation of prayer. However, in actuality the orientation was incorrectly skewed to the south, either in deference to an earlier mosque on the site or as a mirror of the correct orientation of Damascus, the home of the Umayyads and first great Islamic center.

The prayer hall was a large airy space with a flat timber ceiling supported by double-tiered horseshoe arches springing from Corinthian and composite white marble capitals on reused Roman and Visigothic columns. The simple interior was enlivened by alternating light-hued marble and

6 The Great Mosque of Córdoba, *maqsura* of al-Ḥakam II

gray granite columns with rows of rose-colored columns along the central aisle; overhead these bore horseshoe arches and a second tier of semicircular arches of contrasting white stone and red brick voussoirs. The nearest model for bichromy and doubled arcades was a Roman aqueduct in Mérida: a monumental triple-arched structure of multiple courses of pale stone and red brick that, if impressive today, must have been awesome in the eighth century. The horseshoe arch was a Visigothic motif that predated and survived the advent of Islam; yet it was also known in pre-Islamic Syria and Asia Minor and appeared in the Great Mosque of Damascus. Likewise, the doubled arcades may have owed a visual debt to the stacked arcades of the prayer hall at Damascus. It is quite clear that ʿAbd al-Raḥmān I set out to re-create the monumental architecture of Damascus, realizing his copy in the regional idiom of the Iberian Peninsula.

In the next 150 years, a staircase was added to the roof for the call to prayer, the mosque was extended southward, an ornamental portal was added, and a bridge was built to link the prayer hall with the emir's palace. This bridge (*sābāṭ*) ostensibly protected the emir from assassination attempts, but as the figure of the prince was seen less and less often by the people, it contributed to the political machinery that elevated and set him apart as a remote and increasingly mysterious being. The caliphs ʿAbd al-Raḥmān III and his son, al-Ḥakam II, who worked beside him for several decades, planned a new expansion of the mosque in which the courtyard was enlarged, a new minaret built, and the prayer hall extended to the south. Al-Ḥakam II doubled the *qibla* wall and built a new mihrab in the form of a faceted chamber with ornamental stuccos and faced with a monumental program of mosaics containing Qur'anic inscriptions. The mihrab bay was topped by a complex ribbed dome completely surfaced with dazzling gold, red, and blue mosaics; flanking it were ribbed ornamental domes above smaller mosaic frames. These geometrically conceived domes suggest celestial vaults, and indeed, as the sunlight filtering in through the colored glass windows gradually moved from east to west during its daily course, the domes themselves might have seemed to rotate overhead. These three domed bays – which formed a reserved space, or *maqṣūra* – were fenced at floor level, and at the level of the arcades the horseshoe arches were transformed into a complex web of intertwining polylobed arches further enriched by the color and texture of the carved voussoirs.

The last phase of the mosque before the Christian conquest was the eastward expansion of the prayer hall and courtyard under the regent-vizier Ibn Abī ʿĀmir, called al-Manṣūr (the Victorious), in 377/987–378/988; although ambitious in size, it was entirely conservative with respect to style. The architects of the Córdoba mosque, despite building it in four stages over the course of two hundred years, remained faithful to the original orientation and decorative scheme – a telling demonstration of the profound symbolic power of the original edifice and its Umayyad patrons.

The hypostyle plan and various elements such as the mihrab, *maqṣūra*, and minaret create a dedicated place for prayer and congregation according to the tenets of Islam. But in other respects, the mosque of Córdoba, although admired as a pinnacle of early Islamic architecture, is an amalgam of Roman-inspired engineering and Visigothic and Islamic architectural forms. Its trademark horseshoe arch was learned either from pre-Islamic sources in Syria and Asia Minor or from regional Visigothic architecture. Its most spectacular feature – the *maqṣūra* zone and brilliant mosaic mihrab – was the work of Byzantine artisans whose skills and materials were sent as a diplomatic courtesy from distant Constantinople. The visual strength and energy of early Islamic architecture comes from this eclecticism; but the Córdoba mosque was unusual in Islamic architecture because even while it adapted local architectural techniques and motifs, it cast itself unequivocably as the heir to the mosque of Damascus built by the Hispano-Umayyads' forebears. It is an early example of a deliberately historicizing architecture; yet despite its backward gaze, it became the progenitor of subsequent mosques in Spain, such as the congregational mosque built for the palace city Madīnat al-Zahrāʾ in 956 and the diminutive neighborhood mosque called Bāb al-Mardūm in Toledo in 999–1000.

PART II

THE SHAPES OF LITERATURE

CHAPTER 7

THE MUWASHSHAH

Tova Rosen

THE GENRE

Of all the forms known to Arabic literature in al-Andalus, only strophic poetry is known to have originated on the peninsula. Despite certain characteristic thematic features, the Andalusian qasida and maqama remained principally products of the Muslim East, but strophic poetry is a quintessentially Andalusian creation and the most complete literary embodiment of the multiethnic and multilingual fabric of Andalusian society. The pride that Andalusians and Maghribis took in these genres is echoed well into the fourteenth century by Ibn Khaldūn, whose survey of Arabic literature culminates in an account of Andalusian strophic poetry. In both its varieties, the muwashshah – the prosodically more complicated form, employing classical language in all but its concluding couplet – and the zajal – which is simpler in form and vernacular throughout – Andalusian strophic poetry is indeed the most distinguished contribution of the Muslim West to the history of Arabic poetry, and its forms are most explicitly involved with the universe of incipient Romance lyrics.

But which form came first? The muwashshah – of which the earliest examples to have reached us date from the eleventh century – or the zajal – which appears as a literary form a little more than a hundred years later? Was one derived from the other? Or were these cognate forms both derived from an earlier type, the traces of which have vanished? Are those modern critics who follow Ibn Khaldūn right in considering the zajal to be the popularization and hybridization of the muwashshah? Or are those critics who see the muwashshah as the product of the literary elevation of the zajal correct? These questions are treated briefly below, in the survey of scholarship. Our present discussion is limited to the muwashshah.

The Andalusian strophic genres were admired not only in the west of the Arabic-speaking world but in the east as well, as attested by the Egyptian poet Ibn Sanāʾ al-Mulk (1155–1211), who, in the introduction to his treatise on the poetics of the muwashshah, called the muwashshah "Time's beauty, Babylon's magic, al-Shihr's amber, India's aloes-wood, al-Qufs's wine, the gold of the West." In a similar vein, Ibn Diḥya, an Andalusian in thirteenth-century Baghdad, wrote: "The muwashshah is the cream of poetry and its choicest pearl; it is the genre in which the people of the West excelled over those of the East."

In its beginnings, the muwashshah was not regarded with such enthusiasm, but with time it gained recognition and wide popularity among all Andalusians, Jews as well as Arabs. The large number of muwashshahs written in Hebrew during the Andalusian period (and later in the East) constitute an important part of the Andalusian legacy, and indeed, the Arabic and the Hebrew corpora of muwashshahs constitute a single body of literature. Around the mid-twelfth century, both the Arabic and the Hebrew muwashshah spread to North Africa and the Middle East, where they enjoyed a second renaissance, and they are still very much alive in the sung repertoire of North Africa and the Middle East.

The muwashshah is both the product and a microcosm of the cultural conditions peculiar to al-Andalus. Its linguistic complexity reflects the fluid and diverse linguistic situation of the peninsula's population. The muwashshah embodies the flexible and changing relation between the written languages (classical Arabic, Hebrew), as well as between these languages and the oral forms (the Arabic spoken in Andalusia; Romance; and Mozarabic, the dialect formed from the mixing of Romance and Arabic). It reflects life in the court and on the streets; the sociocultural relations between various ethnic groups, and between the sexes; and even the tensions and rapprochements between secular and religious interests. Despite its status as an Arabic literary genre, it serves as a junction within a cultural space that encompassed non-Arabs as well. According to the testimony of Ibn Bassam (d. 1147) in his survey of Andalusian poetry, *al-Dhakhīra fī maḥāsin ahl al-jazīra* (Treasury of the Best of the Andalusian Peninsula), the genre from its very inception included Romance, non-Arabic elements, and popular-vernacular traits. Hebrew poets maintained its linguistic hybridness in their secular poetry. The similarity between the muwashshah and endogenous Hebrew liturgical strophic forms even rendered it appropriate for religious poetry.

Thus, the muwashshah exemplifies a pluralistic cultural politics that allowed for difference and plurality, clashes and juxtapositions. It admits non-Arabic and nonlearned cultures, recognizes the female voice, and expresses both secular sentiments and religious yearnings. If the muwashshah continues to fascinate us today, it is precisely because of the cultural hybridness that it embodies. It is appropriate to reiterate this fact because of those who would reduce the muwashshah to a product of a "pure" and prescriptive poetics.

Modern research into the muwashshah (which began about a hundred years ago) was and sometimes continues to be hard pressed to accept this cultural diversity. Largely divided along the national-philological lines of nineteenth-century philology, it interested itself mainly in the matter of the muwashshah's national affiliation: was it Arabic or Spanish-Romance? Scholars of Arabic literature generally saw the muwashshah as an essentially Arabic form that arose through the strophization, Romanization, and vulgarization of the classical qasida. Romance scholars either ignored the muwashshah's Arabic character altogether or viewed it as an essentially Romance genre that was rendered compatible with the majority culture by a process of Arabization and literary elevation. But posing the national question with respect to a multiethnic and prenationalist culture did an injustice to the genre's essential heterogeneity. The partnership of philology and nationalist ideologies discouraged a holistic view of the muwashshah, focusing on its segmentation into an Arabic "body" and a Romance "tail" in support of claims regarding the "original" or "pure" nature of this form. Any recognition of the hybrid nature of the muwashshah, and of Andalusian culture as a whole, would have reconfigured traditional disciplinary boundaries. It is not surprising, therefore, that the initial breakthrough made to the study of the muwashshah came from Samuel M. Stern, a scholar who was acquainted with all its cultural sources and did not find it difficult to recognize and admit their interaction.

The muwashshah is defined vis-à-vis the qasida first and foremost by its strophic organization and its peculiar system of rhymes; the difference in form also entails a difference in function, for whereas the qasida is meant to be recited, the muwashshah is a song. Unlike classical poetry, the muwashshah is made up of strophes (called *bayt*; pl. *abyāt*), usually five in number, and is polyrhyme. The form is said to owe its name to the *wishāḥ*, a girdle encircling the body and embroidered with alternating colors; indeed, two elements do alternate regularly throughout the poem. These are the *aghṣān* (branches; sing. *ghuṣn*), whose rhyme is uniform within each strophe but changes from one strophe to another; and the *asmāṭ* (threads on which pearls are strung; sing. *simṭ*), whose rhymes are common to all strophes. The first *ghuṣn* may be preceded by a freestanding *simṭ,* known as a *maṭlaʿ*. The most basic rhyme scheme is thus: [XX] *aaa*XX, *bbb*XX . . . (or [XY] *aaa*XY, *bbb*XY . . .), but the patterns can get quite complicated.

A muwashshah poet had more liberty than the author of a qasida in choosing the poem's prosodic scheme, for a muwashshah might be written in classical meter or, more commonly, in a meter unrecognized by classical metrics. Yet he was hampered by the requirement that he follow that initially chosen pattern meticulously, for the metrical correspondence of homologous units in a given poem is mandatory. The genre was therefore attractive to poets as a sphere in which they could display technical virtuosity, either by inventing a completely new and even eccentric prosodic pattern or by contrafaction, the imitation of an illustrious model from the past.

The origins of the muwashshah's meters are a topic of intense controversy. Are they offshoots of the classical Arabic system, did they derive from Romance syllabic meters, or are they a coproduct of both systems? Since even the simplest account of the muwashshah's metrics is inevitably theory-dependent, it has become impossible to describe the muwashshah's meters in neutral terms.[1] For this reason, we postpone the subject to our survey of scholarship on the muwashshah. Another distinctive feature of the muwashshah is the manner in which the poems end. The final *simṭ,* called the *kharja* (exit), or *markaz* (center), is distinguished by the fact that it is often composed in the vernacular dialect, in most cases in vulgar Arabic, or in Mozarabic.[2] This poetic diglossia makes the muwashshah a literary embodiment of the coexistence of the different languages and ethnic groups of al-Andalus; it is what makes these poems so quintessentially Andalusian. Ibn Sanāʾ al-Mulk correctly views the kharja as the muwashshah's most remarkable feature apart from its prosody. He stipulates that even when it is in the classical language, "it should be erotic and moving, enchanting, alluring and germane to passion" (40–44). "It should be garrulous, like naphtha and cinders and in the manner of the Gypsies," he adds.

Kharjas are generally represented as the song or the utterance of a speaker other than the main speaker of the poem; the new speaker may be "he," "she," or "I"; a dove or a gazelle; or, more rarely, a group of people, a town, or an allegorical figure. All these levels of otherness necessitate the use of a transitional device. Ibn Sanāʾ al-Mulk describes the kharja as a quotation in direct discourse, introduced by an expression like "he said," "I said," "he sang," or "she sang." Though not every muwashshah follows this practice, the vast majority do.

According to Ibn Sanāʾ al-Mulk, the kharja is also quotational in the sense that it is borrowed from another poem. He says that the poet builds his muwashshah on a kharja taken from an existing poem, "holding the tail fast and putting the head on it." This initially chosen kharja determines the prosody of the rest of the poem. He recommends the practice of borrowing an existing kharja because only the very talented poets are able to invent a vernacular kharja. Whether or not this is the reason for the practice, his account of the procedure is in full agreement with Ibn Bassam's remark that the poet of the first *washshāḥ,* the blind poet of Qabra, "took vernacular and Romance phrases . . . and built the muwashshah upon them."

It has been maintained that Ibn Sanāʾ al-Mulk's description applies more to the late Eastern muwashshah than to early Andalusian practices and that his poetics constitute "ideal rules" of the art rather than an accurate account of an extant corpus of poetry. Yet his statements are generally corroborated by the Arabic and Hebrew material of the Andalusian and early oriental period and may be taken as general guidelines.

The themes of the kharjas – like those in the muwashshahs themselves – fall roughly into two large groups: love/wine and panegyric. Panegyric kharjas are in classical Arabic or Hebrew and continue the laudatory contents of the preceding parts of the poem. Erotic kharjas may occur at the end of poems on either love or panegyric and tend to be in simple, unembellished style, with a strongly sentimental tone. When a kharja is taken out of context, it is often hard to determine the sexes of the speakers; in fact the same kharja can be read differently in different poems. Thus it is the kharja's function in the poem that determines our understanding of the speech situation in the kharja, not the kharja's theme per se. Kharjas in Arabic and Romance do not differ significantly in their contents. Both lament unfulfilled love; both urge the beloved to return and complain about his disloyalty; both declare the lover's loyalty and complain of his longing and lovesickness. At times, they invoke not the lover himself but another figure – a mother, a messenger, a sorcerer, a judge, a neighbor, a townsperson, a friend, an enemy – often employing formulaic diction, especially in terms of address like *mamma* (mother), *yā rabb* (O God), *yā qawm* (O people), *al-ḥabīb* (lover), *al-raqīb* (watcher). These features (sentimentality, simplicity, invocation, "feminine" tone) are especially present in the Romance kharjas pronounced by women. The kharjas have been the main battleground between the Arabic and the Romance schools of scholarship, as explained below.

Muwashshah poems manifest a marked preference for themes of love (*ghazal*), panegyric (*madīḥ*), and wine (*khamriyya*), and totally exclude other important themes of Arabic poetry, such as lament over the dead, war, and invective. Muwashshahs may be dedicated to a single theme or may combine two or three themes; the tripartite thematic structure – love–panegyric–love – is quite common, but many panegyric muwashshahs omit the erotic theme. The theme of wine (instead of love) may dominate the introduction or the ending. The beloved gazelle may be a woman in the introductory strophes and a man at the end of the poem, or vice versa. When the beloved in the erotic parts is male, the shift from the amatory to the laudatory theme is smooth (e.g., "The gazelle I love is no other than my patron"), whereas when it is a woman, more complicated transitional devices have to be employed (e.g., "When the patron I love ignored me, I sang to him the song that I once heard a loving maiden singing to her departing lover"). The treatment of love in the concluding strophe and the kharja tends to be more passionate than in the ghazal, and may even be bawdy. Isolated motifs from other thematic genres may occasionally appear without dominating the whole composition.

A typical polythematic poem is tripartite. It usually begins with one or two introductory strophes addressing a beloved man or woman or singing the praises of wine. Then, employing some transitional device, the speaker shifts for the next one or two strophes to the eulogy of his patron. There follows a second transition, so that the poem concludes with one or two strophes elaborating the themes of love or wine. These last strophes furnish the context for the erotic or impudent kharja that ends the poem. Whereas the first shift, from love to praise, corresponds to the *takhalluṣ* of the qasida, the second shift, from praise back to love, is peculiar to the muwashshah. This typical tripartite structure results from the combination of the conventional two-part qasida with the requirement that the muwashshah end with an erotic theme culminating in the kharja.

The passage from Ibn Bassam's *Dhakhīra* referred to above is our earliest source on the muwashshah. Although written when the genre had already reached its full flowering, it contains valuable information about its origins, the first poets, and their achievements. According to Ibn Bassam, the genre was invented by the blind poet Muḥammad Maḥmūd al-Qabrī (c. 900)[3] or Ibn ʿAbd Rabbih (d. 940); in either case, the first author of a muwashshah was not a popular bard but a learned poet who also had an ear for colloquial Arabic and Romance expressions, which he used as endings (*markaz*es) to his poems. Two other famous poets, Yūsuf al-Ramādī (d. c. 1016) and ʿUbāda ibn Māʾ al-Samāʾ (d. 1028 or 1031), are praised for having contributed formal improvements to rhyme. From Ibn Bassam, we also learn that the early muwashshahs were originally intended as love poems, and only later were adjusted to serve as panegyrics.

Though the muwashshah is a literary genre written by professional poets and intended for learned audiences, its character lies in its performance: it is, unlike the qasida, a song as well as a poem. In the luxurious courts of al-Andalus, panegyric muwashshahs were improvised and sung by the poets, or were taught to and sung by female slave singers, in praise of princes, patrons, and other notables. Wine and love songs in the muwashshah form served as entertainment music at banquets and other social events. From the courts they spread to wider audiences.

There is a discrepancy, however, between the muwashshah's popularity and the negative attitude toward it of literary critics, anthologists, and even the poets themselves, who did not include the muwashshahs in their mainstream collections of classical poems, either because they deviate from classical metrics or on account of their use of vulgar language. Accordingly, the lyrics of the muwashshahs were at first transmitted only orally (together with their melodies), and only occasionally copied on single sheets; this is why our knowledge of the early muwashshah poets and their poems comes from occasional references to them in literary histories and from fragmentary quotations. Not until the twelfth century were the muwashshahs gathered in special collections and included in diwans.

Despite the secular origins of the form and its overwhelmingly secular functions and themes, the form, surprisingly, came to be used for religious purposes in both Islamic and Jewish communities. In the first half of the eleventh century, Jewish poets writing in Hebrew adopted the muwashshah for secular as well as religious purposes. Its reception by Hebrew poets was much easier and swifter than that of the Arabic muwashshah, possibly because the Jews already had an ancient tradition of strophic liturgical poetry. The muwashshah was also less provocative for Jews than for Arabs; since the Jews had absorbed within a few decades virtually all aspects – formal, thematic, and rhetorical – of the dominant Arabic literature, the muwashshah was only one novelty among many. Finally, Jews did not have the same cultural stake in classical Arabic literary models as Muslims did: they could absorb nonclassical forms with the same ease as classical ones, just as they were content to use nonclassical Arabic, alongside classical, as their written language (*Language). The first extant Hebrew muwashshahs, written by Samuel Ibn Nagrila (d. 1056) and his contemporaries, are of roughly the same period as the earliest extant Arabic poems by ʿUbāda ibn Māʾ al-Samāʾ,[4] and already show the mature style of the classical period.

Since no notation is left, theories about the music to which muwashshahs were performed are based on conjecture (*Music). What is known about the performance of muwashshahs in modern Egypt, Palestine, and Yemen (where it is still performed by Muslims, and was performed by Jews until the mid-twentieth century) cannot serve as direct evidence about the Andalusian situation. However, there is reason to believe that the Maghribi collections of muwashshahs, which include a great amount of Andalusian material and were still in use by popular singers in North Africa at the end of the twentieth century, may still, to a certain extent, reflect the Andalusian musical tradition.

A unique source on Andalusian music, the Tunisian al-Tifāshī (d. in Cairo, 1253), attests that "the songs of the people of al-Andalus [before the rise of the Umayyad dynasty in 756] were either in the style of the Christians or in the [Eastern] style of the Arab camel drivers."[5] The composer Ibn Bājja (d. 1139), "after locking himself up to work for several years with skilled singing girls," succeeded in combining the Eastern and the "Christian" musical traditions. An anecdote about him by Ibn Khaldūn tells of the occasion when he taught a female slave singer (or, according to another interpretation, to a chorus of slave girls) the lyrics and melody of a panegyric that later became a famous muwashshah.

Musical instruments mentioned in the texts of the muwashshahs – the lute, the flute, and the tambourine – may allude to the kind of accompaniment used in the actual performances. Ibn Sanāʾ al-Mulk refers to a certain unidentifiable organ (*urghun*) that accompanied the muwashshahs in al-Andalus. (See also López-Morillas.)

It is debatable whether the muwashshah originally had refrains. Hebrew manuscripts from the same period as that of the classical Andalusian muwashshah insert the word *pizmon* (refrain) after each strophe as a singing instruction. This word is sometimes followed by the initial word or words of the *maṭlaʿ*, an indication that it was the *maṭlaʿ* that served as refrain after each strophe. This practice is also corroborated by the entry "pizmon" in a dictionary compiled in Egypt by a Jewish lexicographer. The same source also indicates that a soloist sang the strophes and the audience joined in the refrains. Modern scholars (especially those associated with the Romance theory; see below), noting the formal similarities between the muwashshah and European strophic genres with refrains, have inferred by analogy that the muwashshah was also performed with refrains.[6] Ibn Sanāʾ al-Mulk refers to the subordination of the muwashshah's meters to music. Since word accent and musical beat (*darb*) often conflict with each other, it may be the music that explains and justifies the muwashshah's anomalous meters.

Several muwashshahs may be sung to the same tune. This is attested by the manuscripts, which often indicate the *laḥn* (melody) of a muwashshah by citing the first words of another muwashshah. Writing new lyrics to a famous melody ensured the future popularity of a poem. Adopting the melody of an existing muwashshah entailed the poet's imitating the exact metrical scheme, the rhyme pattern, and the kharja of the poem that served as the model.

Though not uncommon in classical Arabic poetry, *muʿāraḍa* is specifically associated with the traditions of the muwashshah (*Ibn Zaydun and the *muʿāraḍa* of the *Nūniyya*). Imitation was part of the entertainment in poetic gatherings, where poets contended with each other, trying to outdo each other. The fact that imitation was practiced publicly, extensively, and by poets of stature shows that it was not considered plagiarism but rather a mark of skill and a title to fame. The practice of *muʿāraḍa* also led to the development of religious muwashshahs in both Arabic and Hebrew.

Besides reproducing the prosodic mold, contrafaction involved incorporating the kharja of the model poem in the new poem. Kharjas might be based on other parts of an older poem than its kharja: often it was the *maṭlaʿ* of a muwashshah or of a zajal,[7] or even the incipit of a classical poem that was taken over. Thus, several poems with identical kharjas[8] may constitute a "family" of muwashshahs. Such a family may include Arabic and Hebrew, secular and religious, early and late, Andalusian as well as Eastern poems. The intertextual levels involved in *muʿāraḍa* are potentially vast, crossing the borders of genres, languages, and cultures; oral and written; sacred and secular.

A unique document attesting to the practice of contrafaction is a letter written by the seventeen-year-old Judah Halevi (c. 1075–1141) to the man who was to become his mentor and lifelong friend, Moses Ibn Ezra (c. 1055–after 1138). While traveling from his birthplace in Christian Spain to Granada, which was Ibn Ezra's hometown and a major center of Jewish culture in al-Andalus, the youthful Halevi stopped in a border town, where he was invited to a wine party. The company was entertaining itself by singing and imitating muwashshahs. When no one was able to imitate a certain poem with a particularly complex form, the participants challenged Halevi to attempt an imitation of his own. Halevi succeeded where everyone else had failed, and hastened to report his achievement to Ibn Ezra by letter, attaching his *muʿāraḍa* (*Judah Halevi).

The poem Halevi imitated was a muwashshah written by another Hebrew poet, Joseph Ibn Zaddiq (d. 1149), itself a *muʿāraḍa* of a famous Arabic muwashshah by Abū Bakr al-Abyaḍ (d. c. 1130). This is the first strophe of al-Abyaḍ's poem:

> I only enjoy drinking
> by beds of daisies
> with one slim of waist
> who, upon getting drunk in the morning,
> or at noontime,
> speaks up and says: / "Why did the good wine / strike my cheek? /
> And why did the north wind / blow and bend / that upright
>   branch / that my cloak enfolds?"

Ibn Zaddiq's poem reproduces al-Abyaḍ's intricate rhyme scheme and its unusual meter and, like it, lacks a *maṭlaʿ*. Like its model, it begins with the combination of love and wine.

Judah Halevi's imitation plays on Ibn Zaddiq's theme. Having nothing to lose after his secret passions for wine and young boys have been revealed, the speaker taunts his critics and vows to pursue delights. The middle part of all three poems is devoted to the praise of a notable; each of the poems reverts to the erotic theme in the final strophe, which culminates in the same kharja in all three. Let us observe how each of the poets approaches the kharja. Al-Abyaḍ introduces a "maiden" to sing the kharja:

How dear is the cheerful maiden
Who secretly sent the messenger of sleep
To the timorous gazelle
And sang softly to him:
"By God, O messenger, / tell my beloved / the path / and let him sleep at my place. / I'll give him the curls / beyond the curtains, / and despite the pain / I'll also give my breasts."

Ibn Zaddiq allegorizes the passionate maiden (while also alluding to the epistolary aspect of his poem):

Lady Wisdom will announce her love.
She will declare it by a song
Sent by a messenger, whom she will adjure,
On behalf of her beloved:
"By God, O messenger . . ."

And Halevi follows:

For loving of him she sings
a love song and a chant.
To get him to lie in her bosom like a bundle of myrrh,
so she adjures the faithful messenger:
"By God, O messenger . . ."

The series of imitations did not stop here but was carried into the religious sphere by Abraham Ibn Ezra (d. 1164). His Hebrew poem is intended for the morning service. Not only is its form identical to that of the secular members of the family; it is also sung, according to the instructions in the manuscript, to the melody of al-Abyaḍ's poem. As is the rule in liturgical muwashshahs, there is no non-Hebrew kharja. The erotic imagery symbolizes the believer's passion to unite with cosmic intellect and, ultimately, with God.

To him, a beloved whom I never called by name,
I have appealed since my youth.
I acquired his love with my soul,
And I have abided within his heart.
My soul's abode / is the heavenly sphere [of Intellect] / where angels dwell; / all I desire / Is that my soul will adhere to / God, whom I will thank / with a legion / of songs for ever more.

It is amazing that a genre quintessentially secular, at times even bawdy, could have been put to the service of religion, yet this is exactly what happened in both Arabic and Hebrew poetry through quite independent developments. The Jewish poets adopted the muwashshah for their synagogue poetry about two centuries before any religious Arabic muwashshah is known. The first to employ the form for devotional purposes was Solomon Ibn Gabirol (d. c. 1058). His innovation was soon followed by a host of major and minor Hebrew poets, among whom we find Moses Ibn Ezra, Judah Halevi, and, as we have seen, Abraham Ibn Ezra. The last two composed several hundred religious muwashshahs each, many of which are imitations of known secular Arabic or Hebrew poems. The manuscripts often have inscriptions explicitly indicating the opening of the secular Hebrew or Arabic poem to whose tune the religious piece was to be sung in the synagogue. Though devotional poems did not use Arabic kharjas, they did tend to preserve the quotational nature of the kharja by quoting or paraphrasing earlier Hebrew texts, typically a biblical verse in slightly altered form.

The Hebrew devotional muwashshahs were designed to be incorporated within the texts of the various benedictions of the prayer service, with their content more or less related to the theme of each benediction. Thus, the morning benediction eulogizing God the creator of light would be elaborated in a muwashshah as a Neoplatonic allegory on the theme of the light of reason. A benediction blessing God who loves his people Israel would be accompanied by an allegorical-erotic muwashshah linking the secular theme of the ghazal to the imagery of the biblical Song of Songs. Sufi-like muwashshahs in which erotic motifs fuse with mystical ideas were written in Hebrew at least a century before Ibn ʿArabī (d. 1240).

Within Islam, the spiritual vogue of Sufi muwashshahs, initiated by Ibn ʿArabī in his great mystical diwan, aimed at superseding the secular genre. Themes of longing for the beloved, capturing him in one's heart, seeking erotic union with him to the point of self-oblivion, or themes of wine drinking and intoxication assume mystical meanings in his Sufi muwashshahs. Each of his poems imitates a secular model and quotes its kharja, which, coming at the end of the poem, now appears in a spiritual light. However, it was not Ibn ʿArabī's esoteric muwashshahs but those of his successor, Ibn al-Sabbagh (d. 1266), that acquired broad popularity. All his muwashshahs were allegorical love poems addressed to the Prophet. The poet yearns to visit his beloved's abode (i.e., make a pilgrimage) and unite with him. The erotic kharja, borrowed from the secular source poem, is introduced by an admonition to the readers to abstain from profane verse of this type, or to ask forgiveness for its author. Al-Shushtarī (d. 1269) extended this form of imitation to his mystical zajal poems.

Ibn Sanāʾ al-Mulk speaks of another subgenre of the muwashshah, called *mukaffir* (atoning), a muwashshah by which poets "atoned" for their worldly sins. The poet would take the structure and kharja of a famous muwashshah and base on it a new muwashshah dedicated to the theme of contempt for this world (*zuhd*). But such muwashshahs have not come down to us.

THE HISTORY OF SCHOLARSHIP

The study of the muwashshah, now more than a century old, has, as mentioned, generally been divided among the proponents of the Arabist and the Romance schools, each with its own hypotheses about the origin and nature of the genre. Recent years, however, have seen a tendency toward a more integrated approach to the subject, as a number of scholars have tried to view the muwashshah as a product of a multiethnic, multilingual culture.

Modern Western interest in the muwashshahs seems to stem from two distinct moments: the publication of Heinrich Brody's edition of Judah Halevi's diwan in Berlin in 1894 and the publication of Martin Hartmann's comprehensive book *Das arabische Strophengedicht: I. Das Muwaššaḥ* in Weimar in 1897. The publication of Hartmann's book actually set off the literary and historical investigation of the muwashshah. Brody's contribution was much more modest. In his commentary on Halevi's poems, Brody called attention to certain kharjas that were indecipherable and suggested that "those who know old Castilian might understand them."[9] The challenge was met the same year by the Spanish medievalists Francisco Fernández y Gonzales and Marcelino Menéndez y Pelayo, who produced their respective readings of Halevi's garbled kharjas. Menéndez y Pelayo was the first to suggest that such verses may belong to the realm of neo-Latin vulgar poetry. It is interesting to note that the two main directions of modern investigation of the muwashshah – the Arabist theory, starting with Hartmann, and the Romance theory coupled with kharja studies, inadvertently initiated by Brody – both emerged independently, though in proximity of place and time.

Until the appearance of Hartmann's book, the muwashshah had been almost totally ignored by Arabic literary criticism and was virtually unknown to Western scholarship. Hartmann brought to light Ibn Sanāʾ al-Mulk's book on the poetics of the muwashshah, *Dār al-ṭirāz fī ʿamal l-muwashshaḥāt* (The House of Brocade: On the Making of Muwashshahs) and on it he based his own description and literary analysis of the genre, as well as a detailed historical survey. Hartmann viewed the genre as the product of a development internal to classical Arabic poetry. Reducing the rich rhyme schemes of the muwashshah to their basic patterns (*aaa*XX or *aaa*XY), Hartmann called attention to their resemblance to the classical rhyme scheme of poems known as *musammaṭ*, in which the basic two-hemistich structure of the qasida is altered from *a*X, *b*X, *c*X (where *a*, *b*, *c* are the nonrhyming ends of the first hemistichs and X is the common rhyme of all verses of the qasida) to *aaa*X, *bbb*X, *ccc*X. The analogy with the muwashshah pattern (*aaa*XX, *ccc*XX) is obvious; in both forms, there is a common rhyme that alternates with the changing rhymes. This resemblance led Hartmann to view the classical line (*bayt*) of the *musammaṭ* as the embryo of the muwashshah's stanza (also called *bayt*). Hence, for Hartmann, the *musammaṭ* served as a mediating phase between the Eastern monorhymed qasida and the innovative strophic Andalusian muwashshah.

In the absence of either Eastern or early Andalusian texts attesting to this intermediate stage, Hartmann turned to the Hebrew poetry of the second half of the tenth century, where a form apparently identical to the *musammaṭ* existed.[10] Hartmann's assumption was that the Hebrew *musammaṭ* poems reflect the lost Arabic model that must have existed before, and simultaneously with, the emergence of the muwashshah. He was not aware that the Hebrew *musammaṭ* followed indigenous models of strophic poetry in the Jewish Eastern liturgy known as piyyut, and was not necessarily an imitation of an Arabic model.

Hartmann described the meters of the muwashshah and classified each as well as possible according to its affiliation to specific classical meters. In that, he departed from Ibn Sanāʾ al-Mulk's assertion that some muwashshahs have "nothing to do" with the meters of *shiʿr*. Hartmann also failed to note that the necessary rhythmic changes that must have occurred as a result of line splitting, internal rhyming, and ultimately of strophization must have also affected the very definition of the metrical line.

Some fifteen years later, the genre caught the attention of the Spanish scholar Julián Ribera, who elaborated a theory of the Romance roots of Andalusian strophic poetry. In his 1912 address to the Academia Real, Ribera suggested that the Quzmanian zajal imitated a popular poetry of a Romance origin that must have existed in Muslim Spain. Relying on the resemblance between the strophe of the zajal and that of thirteenth- and fourteenth-century Galician strophic poetry,[11] Ribera hypothesized that Galician oral poetry had been imported to Córdoba in the eighth century by captive women brought home by the Muslim conquerors; this poetry had inspired the blind poet from Qabra. According to Ribera, the zajal imitated this native Romance poetry not only in its mixture of Arabic and Romance diction, but also in its strophic structure. In his *Épica* (1928), Ribera published for the first time Ibn Bassam's famous paragraph about the incorporation of Romance expressions by the inventor of the muwashshah. Thus, Ribera offered a single explanation for both the muwashshah and the zajal, without establishing a clear formal distinction between the two strophic forms. With all the difficulties posited by Ribera's hypotheses, his creative suggestions were extremely fruitful and inspired scholars to carry on their research in similar directions.

Ramón Menéndez Pidal (*Poesía*) also attributed the invention of the zajal to the poet of Qabra, positing, however, a slightly different route of transmission. In his view, the Arabs took the form from their Christians neighbors in al-Andalus who, in turn, reappropriated it and spread it to Castile, Provence, France, and Italy. José María Millás Vallicrosa's "liturgical theory" explored strophic arrangements in the Hebrew piyyut as well as in Latin liturgical poetry. In his view, both underwent similar procedures of strophization that reached their fullest development around the tenth century. He conjectured that the postulated early Romance secular strophic poetry was an imitation and parody of the Latin liturgy. He thus viewed the emergence of the Andalusian muwashshah as influenced by these processes of secularization and strophization.

But it was Samuel M. Stern's unrivaled erudition in all three relevant cultures and his profound understanding of the complex multicultural situation in medieval Spain that enabled him to decipher twenty Romance kharjas that he had found in Hebrew poems. His 1947 article, where he first published his findings, contributed both to a more rigorous and grounded approach to the Romance theory and to the establishment of what became the field of kharja scholarship.[12] In that article, Stern published the kharjas in their original Hebrew script, transliterated them to Roman characters, and then provided his interpretation. By doing so, Stern was able to trace the first written evidences of the vulgar dialect that Menéndez Pidal designated as "Mozarabic" (*Language). This dialect was spoken by Muslims, Christians, and Jews in al-Andalus prior to the Reconquista, and included varying measures of Arabic and Romance elements. Based on these twenty kharjas, Stern reconstructed the basic lexicon as well as the grammar of this dialect. Stern's "discovery" was a sensation in various parts of the scholarly world and it encouraged other scholars to find more Romance kharjas in Hebrew as well as in Arabic poems.

Stern's starting point in his discussion of the kharjas is their "otherness," the fact that the kharja is spoken in another language by a speaker other than that of the rest of the poem. Stern then asks whether the kharjas were composed in imitation of popular poems (in Romance or vernacular Arabic), or whether they are authentic quotations from popular poems. Stern also calls attention to the feminine-erotic nature of the kharja and its resemblance to other alleged feminine genres in medieval Europe. He suggested that these sentimental expressions of women may go back to pre-Islamic, perhaps even to Roman, times; and, adducing evidence that these poems were sung in the courts by choruses of palace girls, he proposes that they might be of feminine origin. The Arabic poets would have appropriated such Romance oral lyrics to the endings of their courtly muwashshahs. Stern conjectured that these postulated Romance poems were not short, independent couplets like the kharja, but were longer strophic structures, like the muwashshah or the zajal.

Regarding the kharjas, Stern was clearly in favor of the Romance theory, but he was quite ambivalent in his discussion of prosody. He conceded that the rhyme schemes of the muwashshahs might have evolved from the Arabic *musammaṭ*; at the same time, he maintained that the Arabic and the Romance theories are not mutually exclusive, and he also left room for the assumption that the lost Spanish oral poetry from which the kharjas originated might have influenced the rhyme, meter, and music of the muwashshah (126–27). As to metrics, Stern accepted Hartmann's metrical approach as a method rather than as a theory; in his own detailed metrical analysis (27–32), Stern used logical criteria to arrange the various techniques for modifying the classical meters on a graduated scale from classical to nonclassical schemes; but he avoided drawing from this analysis any inferences regarding the origins of meters or their evolution.

Stern's revolutionary findings encouraged the publication of anthologies of muwashshahs as well as of separate collections of kharjas. The unearthing of unknown Romance kharjas and the industry of deciphering their script and determining their meaning dominated the field from the 1950s to the 1970s. Though not Stern's own intention, his findings resulted in a disproportionate emphasis on the kharja, sometimes at the expense of the muwashshah itself. Soon after Stern's publication of the Romance kharjas in Hebrew poems, Arabic poems containing Romance kharjas were also discovered and published. Stern's work also highlighted the importance of the Hebrew corpus for the investigation of the Arabic muwashshahs. Students in various fields began to view the evidence of the kharjas from the unique perspective of their respective fields, at the same time abandoning Stern's cautious, even tentative approach, and devising a host of – often contradictory – theories and hypotheses. Ironically, Stern's remarkable enterprise of bringing together disparate bodies of knowledge did not result in the propagation of an integrative approach but, paradoxically, stimulated recurring waves of debates and partisan attitudes, a battlefield tainted with cultural bias and nationalistic ideologies (see Menocal, *Arabic Role* 18–19 n. 5).

Dámaso Alonso's claim that the kharjas are the earliest known traces of Romance lyric was the first attempt by a Spanish scholar to place Stern's discovery of the kharjas in the context of European lyric and to readjust the older versions of the Romance hypothesis to the new findings. Another early reaction to Stern was that of Francisco Cantera, who emphasized the role of the Jewish poets. Menéndez Pidal ("Cantos") used the Romance kharjas to recapitulate his former views about the preexistence of lost poetic traditions, according to which the *canciones mozárabes*, the Portuguese *cantigas de amigo*, and the Castilian *villancicos* are viewed as three branches of the same trunk. Margit Frenk Alatorre established an analogy between the kharjas and French refrains. Her 1975 work is considered the most thorough and balanced evaluation of the Romance theory. A more skeptical voice is that of Pierre Le Gentil, who, while making formal and musical analogies between the Spanish *villancico*, the Provençal *dansa*, the French *virelai*, and the Italian *lauda*, was much more cautious than other Romance scholars in establishing links between the old Romance genres and Hispano-Arabic poetry.

Emilio García Gómez, a Spanish Arabist, became the most extreme advocate of the Romance theory. He went beyond the earlier advocates of the Romance approach by claiming metrical affinity between the muwashshah and Romance poetry. He hypothesized that if the Mozarabic kharjas represent traces of an older popular Romance poetry, then its meter, too, must be syllabic, like that of the poetry it follows; and since the meter of the kharja dictated the meter of the whole muwashshah, that, too, must originally have been syllabic. He interpreted Ibn Bassam's and Ibn Sanāʾ al-Mulk's statements on the nonclassical nature of the muwashshahs' meters as affirming their isosyllabism; Ibn Sanāʾ al-Mulk's statement that muwashshahs are composed in both classical and nonclassical meters he interpreted as meaning that the nonclassical (syllabic) stage preceded the introduction of classical meters. He applied Romance scansion to large corpora of strophic Andalusian poetry (all of Ibn Quzmān's zajals and all Hebrew and Arabic muwashshahs known to him), in order to demonstrate their syllabism. Later, he even suggested that the Arabic kharjas, too, must have obeyed syllabic metrics. (See his *Jarchas* and *Métrica*.)

Finally, García Gómez hypothesized that, as the muwashshahs were admitted to the canon of Arabic literature, their originally syllabic meters underwent assimilation into the classical, quantitative system. As a parallel development, Romance diction in the kharjas was gradually abandoned in favor of vernacular Arabic diction, and eventually, poets began also to counterfeit kharjas in vernacular Arabic. This process of Arabization ended in the composition of kharjas in classical Arabic.

James T. Monroe and David Swiatlo hailed García Gómez's "discovery that the muwashshah prosody is stress syllabic" and attempted to apply his approach to the scansion of the Hebrew muwashshah by analyzing ninety-three Arabic kharjas in Hebrew muwashshahs and the muwashshahs to which they belong. The meter and the stanzaic formation (i.e., couplets, tercets, or quartets) of each poem are compared with a parallel from a Latin poem, a Galician *cantiga de amigo*, an old French refrain, or a Castilian *villancico*, in order to illustrate their close prosodic affinity to other Romance traditions. The authors claim that although the muwashshahs had been adjusted to conform to the "orthographic" conventions of the quantitative meters, their underlying rhythm was stress-syllabic, reflecting the pronunciation of the Andalusian dialect, where the quantity of the Arabic has been replaced by stress. Hence, each poem is doubly scanned – once as having syllabic meters (whose stress is marked by acute accent marks), and once as obeying an imposed quantitative meter. Certain classical meters were, the authors theorize, more popular in the muwashshah than others, because they allowed for certain Romance metrical patterns (i.e., deca- and dodecasyllable meters in the *khafīf*, and trochaic octosyllable in the *ramal*). Being aware that the hypothetical rhythm of a poem often conflicts with the accents that words take in normal speech, the authors suggest that in practice these irregularities were disguised by musical rendition.

Based on their prosodic analyses, Monroe and Swiatlo conclude that the muwashshahs contained elements deriving from both the high and the low cultures. The dominant elements that they borrowed from below were the prosody, the occasional feminine lyrical voice, and some colloquial forms of expression and stylistic features. These popular elements were applied by cultured poets to thematic material derived from the classical Arabic tradition of panegyric and love poetry. Monroe and Swiatlo maintain that even if none of the kharjas can be proved to be an authentic oral composition stemming directly from a popular milieu, they at least offer us an indirect glimpse into what that folk tradition might have been like. The Arabic kharjas thus represent two trends. On one hand, Romance poetry influenced Arabic poetry from below, leading to a development of Arabic folk lyric in Spain; on the other, this Arabic folk lyric was, in turn, influenced by classical Arabic poetry from above. The fact that there is little textual variation in classical kharjas suggests a stable written tradition; conversely, the variant readings of certain colloquial kharjas suggest an unstable oral source rather than a written tradition. Thus, when a kharja appears in multiple poems, it does not necessarily follow that it imitated an earlier poem, for it could have been borrowed from a common oral source.

Monroe is also in favor of the feminine view of the kharjas. The fact that the feminine tone is more dominant in Romance kharjas than in the Arabic ones leads him to associate the Romance kharjas with the feminine lyric and the Arabic with its masculine counterpart. Romance was the language of women, while Arabic was spoken by the Muslim conquerors. In mixed marriages, Romance was the intimate family language spoken among women, and by women to their children. Hence, the recurrence, in Mozarabic kharjas, of the word *mamma* discloses a feminine situation of a girl speaking to her mother, while the Arabic *ḥabībī* occurs when a male lover addresses his beloved in Arabic.

But these varieties of Romance theories did not go unchallenged. The first attack on García Gómez came from T. J. Gorton, who proposed traditional Arabic scansion for Ibn Quzmān. This was countered by an undignified rejoinder by García Gómez, disguised by the pseudonym Ramírez Calvente, defending his own positions and suggesting that non-Spaniards stay out of the field. García Gómez's publications were then criticized by the Romance scholar Richard Hitchcock, who blamed him for taking liberties with the Arabic texts by altering consonants, inventing vowels, and making other additions and omissions in order to make the text fit his theories. Hitchcock suggests that some "Romance" words might actually be in colloquial Arabic, and recommends eschewing Romance solutions until all the Arabic possibilities have been excluded.

Another critique, foreshadowing the revival of the Arabist theory in the 1980s, was that of Jarir Abu Haidar. He blamed scholars for focusing on the marginal phenomenon of the Romance kharja; for him, the muwashshah is an Arabic genre, stemming from Arabic origins and written by Arabs for Arabs. Hence, it has to be exclusively understood against the background of traditional Arabic poetry. Hypotheses about Romance origins, and postulating of Romance meters, he insisted, had derived from the "misleading" statements made by Ibn Bassam and Ibn Sanā᾽ al-Mulk about the kharja being the basis of the whole muwashshah. Additionally, he aimed to show that there is nothing new in the vulgar (i.e., both vernacular and obscene) traits of the kharja; the kharja is simply part of the literary tradition of *hazl*, a style well rooted in Andalusian writing consisting of the use of informal, often ungrammatical language with farcical effects. In order to achieve their purpose, the kharjas often employed Romance or Berber terms, obscene and foul words, and impudent erotic expressions. The bilingual Arabic audience could enjoy the occasional foreign words; but the meters and rhyme schemes, the virtuosity and formal perfection remain unquestionably Arab. This approach was taken also by Sayyid Ghāzī, who in his edition of *Dīwān al-muwashshaḥāt al-andalusiyya* meticulously applied Hartmann's metrical methods to the whole corpus.

But it was Alan Jones who became the most ardent adherent of the Arabist theory. Joining in Hitchcock's attack on García Gómez's misleading editorial practices, he called for the publication of responsible editions – a task that he himself undertook, maintaining that García Gómez's metrical theory introduces more problems than the system it proposes to supplant. Although Ibn Bassam was correct in stating that the meters of the majority of muwashshahs fall outside the classical Arabic metrical schemes, Jones asserts that their meters do conform to the basic quantitative principles of Arabic prosody, if allowances are made for such modifications and expansions of the khalilian meters as would have been inevitable once the poets began splitting up lines and hemistichs. Thus, Jones's views on rhyme and meter are not essentially different from those of Hartmann. Jones added that kharjas containing Romance words actually total less than 10 percent of the whole kharja corpus, and the six hundred extant kharjas contain only about four hundred Mozarabic words. Though admitting that Romance kharjas were more susceptible to being lost than purely Arabic ones, Jones insisted on the marginality of the Romance element. He concluded that the muwashshah is unequivocally Arabic.

Support for Jones's critique of García Gómez came, unexpectedly, from a Romance linguist. Federico Corriente rejected the Romance scansion and advocated the theory of extended *ʿarūḍ*, but using different arguments from those adduced by Jones. Corriente explains that the meters of the muwashshah evolved from the basic *ʿarūḍ* system in order to suit the particular phonemic features of Spanish Arabic. Classical Arabic was spoken by the ruling class and clerics, while vernacular Arabic was influenced by the Romance substratum; in this dialect bundle, stress, rather than quantity, was phonemic. When Spanish Arabs started to compose Arabic poetry in classical meters, quantity was theoretically observed, but some long syllable slots in the classical line were marked as stressed while others remained unstressed. That evolution, facilitated by a local mode of recitation of classical Arabic poems, led to the interpretation of the feet of the classical Arabic meters as nuclei with just one stressed syllable and one to three unstressed or neutral syllables. Muwashshahs emerged when some poets freed themselves, at least partially, from those traditional constraints, by taking as their rule that theoretical quantity would not matter as long as the accentual structure of feet and meter were not altered. This meant the occurrence of unstressed short syllables in long slots and vice versa. But since the concept of stress was unknown to Arab grammarians, it was difficult for writers on the muwashshah, in East and West, to describe the phenomenon. Ibn Bassam's "somewhat confused" statement about meters reflects, according to Corriente, two views: that of the conservatives, who rejected these new improper meters; and that of the liberals, who accepted them as adapted *ʿarūḍ*.

During the 1980s, the Romance periodical *La Corónica* hosted a continued and heated debate focused principally on the metrical aspect of the Arabist versus Romance theories. It began with Samuel G. Armistead, who focused mainly on developments in the Romance school, and was followed by Jones, who claimed that the Romance hypothesis was based on imperfect assessments of medieval authorities and on too small a sample of poems. Facts do not allow us to conclude affinity to Romance feminine lyric, priority in time of the Romance kharjas, or a dichotomy between Arabic and Mozarabic kharjas (that were, after all, composed by the same poets). Jones criticized Monroe and Swiatlo for treating Romance and Arabic kharjas as separate subsets, and charged them with having too much faith in García Gómez's editions. In response, Monroe ("Pedir") admitted that García Gómez had tampered with the texts, but insisted that this did not justify the wholesale dismissal of the Romance stress-syllabic theory. According to Monroe, there are at least two Romance schools: the more conservative (that of Monroe himself), which assumes that Hispano-Arabic metrics are not necessarily completely regular, and the more radical (that of García Gómez), which assumes that these meters are perfectly regular, thereby giving itself license to emend the texts in order to prove their uniformity. Monroe welcomes Jones's project to restore the texts, in his future editions, to their pristine syllabic irregularity, since this will provide further support for the more conservative school.

Philip F. Kennedy's arguments in support of the Arabist cause are mainly thematic. Like Abu Haidar, he seeks precedents for the style of the muwashshah in the Arabic poetic tradition. Eastern monorhymed poetry can also be bawdy, narrative at times, loosely composed from the thematic point of view, quotational, and "feminine." In his words, these themes are "not alien to the eastern stock of lyrical themes, of which they are . . . consciously derived"; they are "part of the hinterland of the kharja poet's poetical experience" (71, 82). For Kennedy, the thematic homogeneity of the kharja and its muwashshah is additional proof for the historical continuity between the muwashshahs and classical Arabic poetry. Hence, he proposes that the Romance kharjas be viewed as "a Romance rendering of Arabic lyrical themes" (76) rather than vice versa. Kennedy's fine critical observations, which, unlike most writings in the field, are not based on philology and history, but on principles of literary analysis, are somewhat marred by being put at the service of polemics on the origin of the genre. Another work written from a literary-structural approach is Tova Rosen's book on the Hebrew genre, which offers an analysis of the dynamic relationship between prosodic form and thematic composition, structural patterns and meaning, conventions, and aesthetic effects.

After the acrimonious debates of the 1980s, the field seems to be enjoying a reduction of hostilities due to the inability of the antagonists to produce new arguments, and their having fought themselves to a standstill. Two "ecumenical" symposiums, held in Exeter (1988) and Madrid (1989), signaled the need for more tolerant dialogue and the hope for new modes of collaboration. This new spirit seems also to be part of the contemporary zeitgeist of postmodernism and deconstruction, and the rejection of the purist philological approach that has so far dominated kharja studies with its aim to present definitive, purged, and stable texts, the essentially "modernist" task of finding the national origins of texts and traditions. The new approaches call for a more integrated and multilevel view of the subject.

María Rosa Menocal requires that the muwashshah be seen as participating in both the medieval Arabic/Hebrew cultural orbit and the Romance /Latin world simultaneously and to the same degree. Consequently, she asserts that it has to constitute part of the modern literary canon of all relevant literatures. Her reading of the muwashshah is anchored in the dialectics of the genre itself. She views its inner-conflicting literary elements as metonyms, or as a microcosm, of its cultural polyphony, and its many voices (Arabic/Hebrew/ Romance, male/female, courtly/popular) as reflecting the multilingual, multiethnic context in which it functioned. Thus, the muwashshah is a metapoetic restatement of its own state. Whereas the amputation of the kharjas from the poems' bodies served nationalistic claims, the integrative-dialectical approach that treats the muwashshah both as poem (susceptible to literary, not just philological, analysis) and as performed song bridges the gap between muwashshah and kharja, and between the cultures involved. Paraphrasing Anthony Esposito's metaphors, the conclusion follows that rather than being obsessed with borders, we should see the muwashshah as a busy crossroads; by presenting traditions as separate islands, we may miss the "peninsular" (pun intended) nature of the subject.

NOTES

1 Meters that resemble those of classical Arabic poetry are easier to describe in quantitative terms. A single meter may run throughout a muwashshah, or two different meters may alternate in the *aghṣān* and in the *asmāṭ*. The most common classical meters are rare in the muwashshah; rare classical meters (usually modified) are more common. Only occasionally is an exact classical meter fully employed. A muwashshah's line often consists of a single classical hemistich. Internal rhyme may occur within this hemistich, "chopping" the classical pattern into small subunits. A classical hemistich might be prefixed by, suffixed by, or have inserted in it an extra foot of that same meter, or a foot alien to the meter. The line may consist of two (or more) hemistichs of two (or more) different classical meters. Classical feet may also be arranged in altogether new combinations, not reminiscent of any of the authorized meters. Although all the preceding cases may be considered as unorthodox variations on, or as deviations from, classical metrics, a large proportion of the muwashshahs' meters cannot be related to any of the classical meters.

2 Out of about 600 Arabic secular muwashshahs, almost 300 kharjas are in colloquial Arabic, more than 200 are in classical Arabic, and about 50 have kharjas in

Romance (or include Romance elements); the rest fall into the gray area between classical and vulgar language. Some of the "colloquial" Arabic pieces are basically classical with added vulgar gloss. This inherent bilingualism may mar the statistics. The parallel corpus of secular Hebrew poems includes more than 250 pieces. Half of them have Arabic kharjas, about 50 have Hebrew (always classical, since there was no vernacular) kharjas, and in 25 poems the kharjas are Romance. In a handful of kharjas, there is a combination of Hebrew and Arabic. About 20 Hebrew poems appear in manuscripts so fragmentary as to leave the language of their ending uncertain.

3 Another tradition (followed also by Ibn Khaldūn) ascribes the invention to Muqaddam ibn Muʾāfa al-Qabrī, a poet from the period of the emirate of ʿAbd Allāh. These may be not two poets but one.

4 Discovered recently by Jones (see his introduction to Ibn Bishri's *ʿUddat* 2 n. 33) is an earlier text by the Sevillian grammarian Abū l-Qāsim ibn al-ʿAttār (d. 997), whose name is unmentioned by Ibn Bassam.

5 For English translation, see Monroe ("Pedir" 134–36).

6 Armistead and Monroe suggest that it was the kharja that was sung as refrain (230).

7 The latter fact is the basis for Monroe's ("Poetic Quotation") hypothesis that prior to its emergence as a literary form, the zajal existed orally alongside the muwashshah, and that many colloquial-bilingual kharjas are traces of lost *maṭlaʿ*s of zajals.

8 In rarer cases, a certain muwashshah would be copied, in different manuscripts, with totally different kharjas.

9 See, e.g., his notes to 1:111, later known as Stern's kharja no. 5.

10 Hartmann relies, in fact, on a single dubious Arabic example attributed to Imruʾ al-Qays. Others pointed to a possible precedent by Abū Nuwās.

11 Ribera's theory also embraces troubadour poetry on the basis of resemblance between the Quzmanian strophe and that of the Provençal poets. This theory (known as the Arabic theory of troubadour poetry) was later elaborated by Menéndez Pidal, Le Gentil, and Nykl. It was rejected by Stern (*Poetry* 211), and recently revived and revised by Menocal (*Arabic Role* 83–88, 91–92, 101–9). Menocal laments "the conceptual schism between East and West [that] has in turn resulted in the creation of fundamentally separate fields of inquiry" (21). The essentially hybrid muwashshah and its kharja, instead of becoming a forceful lever in unifying these fields of study, fell victim to this very same compartmentalization.

12 Stern (*Poetry* 133) gives credit to Brody, who in his 1894 edition of Halevi's poems surmised that the indecipherable elements at the endings of Hebrew poems might be in the Old Castilian. Similarly, he mentions Menéndez y Pelayo, Baer, and Millás Vallicrosa as pioneers of kharja readings. The 1947 article is republished in the posthumous volume edited by Harvey. For simplicity's sake, all references to Stern's doctoral thesis and other early works are quoted from this volume.

BIBLIOGRAPHY

Abu Haidar, Jarir. "The Kharja of the Muwashshah in a New Light." *Journal of Arabic Literature* 9 (1978): 1–14.

al- ʿAdara l-maʾisat. Ed. Muḥammad Zakarīyā ʿInani. Alexandria, 1986.

Alonso, Dámaso. "Cancioncillas de amigo mozárabes: Primavera temprana de la lírica europea." *Revista de filología española* 33 (1949): 297–349.

Armistead, Samuel G. "A Brief History of Kharja Studies." *Hispania* 70 (1987): 8–15.

"Some Recent Developments in *Kharja* Scholarship." *La Corónica* 8 (1980): 199–203.

"Speed or Bacon? Further Meditations on Professor Alan Jones' 'Sunbeams.' *La Corónica* 10 (1981): 148–55.

Armistead, Samuel G., and James T. Monroe. "Beached Whales and Roaring Mice: Additional Remarks on Hispano-Arabic Strophic Poetry." *La Corónica* 13 (1985): 206–42.

Brody, Heinrich. *Diwan Judah ha-Levi.* 4 vols. Berlin, 1894–1920.

Cantera, Francisco. "Versos españoles en las muwaššaḥas hispano-hebreas." *Sefarad* 9 (1949): 197–234.

Compton, Linda Fish. *Andalusian Lyrical Poetry and Old Spanish Love Songs: The Muwashshaḥ and Its Kharja.* New York, 1976.

Corriente, Federico. "Again on the Metrical System of Muwashshah and Zajal." *Journal of Arabic Literature* 17 (1986): 34–49.

"The Metres of the Muwashshah: An Andalusian Adaptation of ʿArūḍ (A Bridging Hypothesis)." *Journal of Arabic Literature* 13 (1982): 76–82.

Corriente, Federico, and Ángel Sáenz-Badillos. *Poesía estrófica: Actas del Primer Congreso Internacional sobre Poesía Estrófica Árabe y Hebrea y Sus Paralelos Romances.* Madrid, 1991.

Dīwān al-muwashshaḥāt al-andalusiyya. Vols. I and II. Ed. Sayyid Ghāzī. Alexandria, 1979. Vol. III. Ed. Muḥammad Zakarīyā ʿInani. Alexandria, 1986.

Esposito, Anthony P. "Dismemberment of Things Past: Fixing the Jarchas." *La Corónica* 24 (1995): 4–14.

Frenk Alatorre, Margit. *Las jarchas mozárabes y los comienzos de la lírica románica.* Mexico City, 1975.

García Gómez, Emilio. "Estudio del *Dār aṭ-ṭirāz*: Preceptiva egipcia de la muwashshaha." *Al-Andalus* 27 (1962): 21–104.

Las jarchas romances de la serie árabe en su marco. 2nd edn. Barcelona, 1975.

"La 'ley de Mussafia' se aplica a la poesía estrófica arábigoandaluza." *Al-Andalus* 27 (1962): 1–20.

"La lírica hispano-árabe y la aparición de la lírica románica." *Al-Andalus* 21 (1956): 303–38.

"Métrica de la moaxaja y métrica española: Aplicación de un nuevo método de medición completa al Gaish de Ben al Hatib." *Al-Andalus* 39 (1974 [1975]): 1–255.

"Veinticuatro jaryas romances en muwashshahas árabes (Ms. G. S. Colin)." *Al-Andalus* 17 (1952): 57–127.
Gorton, T. J. "The Metre of Ibn Quzmān: A 'Classical' Approach." *Journal of Arabic Literature* 6 (1975): 1–29.
Hartmann, Martin. *Das arabische Strophengedicht: I. Das Muwaššaḥ.* Weimar, 1897.
Heger, Klaus. *Die bisher veröffentlichten Harǧas und ihre Deutungen.* Tübingen, 1960.
Hitchcock, Richard. *The Kharjas: A Critical Bibliography.* London, 1977.
Hitchcock, Richard, and Consuelo López-Morillas. *The Kharjas: A Critical Bibliography: Supplement 1.* London, 1996.
Ibn (al-)ʿArabī. *al-Dīwān al-akbar.* Bulaq, 1271 A.H.
Ibn Bassam. *al-Dhakhīra fī maḥāsin ahl al-jazīra.* Ed. Iḥsān ʿAbbās. 8 vols. Beirut, 1979.
Ibn Bishri. *The ʿUddat al-jalis of ʿAli ibn Bishri: An Anthology of Andalusian Arabic Muwashshahat.* Ed. Alan Jones. Cambridge, 1992.
Ibn al-Khaṭīb. *Jaish al-tawshih.* Ed. Hilāl Naji and Muḥammad Madur. Tunis, 1967.
Ibn Sanāʾ al-Mulk. *Dār al-ṭirāz fī ʿamal l-muwashshaḥāt.* Ed. Jawdat al-Rikābī. Damascus, 1949 [1977].
Jones, Alan. *Romance Kharjas in Andalusian Arabic Muwassah Poetry: A Paleographical Analysis.* London, 1988.
"Romance Scansion and the *Muwashshaḥāt*: An Emperor's New Clothes?" *Journal of Arabic Literature* 11 (1980): 36–55.
"Sunbeams from Cucumbers? An Arabist's Assessment of the State of *Kharja* Studies." *La Corónica* 10 (1981): 38–53.
Kennedy, Philip F. "Thematic Relationships between the *Kharjas*, the Corpus of *Muwashshaḥāt*, and Eastern Lyrical Poetry." *Studies on the Muwaššaḥ and the Kharja: Proceedings of the Exeter International Colloquium.* Reading, 1991. 68–87.
Latham, Derek. "The Prosody of an Andalusian *Muwaššaḥ* Re-Examined." *Arabian and Islamic Studies.* Ed. Robin Leonard Bidwell and Gerald R. Smith. London, 1983. 86–99.
Le Gentil, Pierre. *Le virelai et le villancico: Le problème des origines arabes.* Paris, 1954.
López-Morillas, Consuelo. "Was the Muwashshah Really Accompanied by the Organ?" *La Corónica* 13 (1985): 40–54.
al-Maqqarī. *Nafḥ al-tīb min ghuṣn al-andalus al-raṭīb.* Ed. Iḥsān ʿAbbās. 8 vols. Beirut, 1968.
Menocal, María Rosa. *The Arabic Role in Medieval Literary History: A Forgotten Heritage.* Philadelphia, 1990.
"Bottom of the Ninth: Bases Loaded." *La Corónica* 17 (1988–89): 32–40.
Menéndez Pidal, Ramón. "Cantos románicos andalusíes, continuadores de una lírica latina vulgar." *Boletin de la Real Academia Española* 31 (1951): 187–270.
Poesía árabe y poesía europea. Madrid, 1941.
Millás Vallicrosa, José María. *La poesía sagrada hebraico-española.* Madrid, 1948.

Monroe, James T. "Pedir peras al olmo? On Medieval Arabs and Modern Arabists." *La Corónica* 10 (1982): 121–47.

"Poetic Quotation in the Muwashshaha and Its Implications: Andalusian Strophic Poetry as Song." *La Corónica* 14 (1986): 230–50.

Monroe, James T., and David Swiatlo. "Ninety-three Arabic Hargas in Hebrew Muwassaḥs: Their Hispano-Romance Prosody and Thematic Features." *Journal of the American Oriental Society* 97 (1977): 141–65.

Nykl, A. R. *Hispano-Arabic Poetry and Its Relations with the Old Provençal Troubadours.* Baltimore, 1946.

Rosen-Moked, Tova. *The Hebrew Girdle Poem (Muwashshah) in the Middle Ages* [Hebrew]. Haifa, 1985.

al-Ṣafadī. *Tawshīʿ al-tawshīh.* Ed. Albīr Habib Mutlaq. Beirut, 1966.

Solà-Solé, J. M. *Corpus de poesía mozarabe: Las hargas andalusies.* Barcelona, 1973.

Las jarchas romances y sus moaxajas. Madrid, 1990.

Spitzer, Leo. "The Mozarabic Lyric and Theodor Frings' Theories." *Comparative Literature* 4 (1952): 1–22.

Stern, Samuel M. *Les chansons mozarabes: Les vers finaux (kharjas) en espagnol dans les muwashshahs arabes et hébreux.* Palermo, 1953.

Hispano-Arabic Strophic Poetry. Ed. L. P. Harvey. Oxford, 1974.

Whinnom, Keith. "The Mamma of the Kharjas, or Some Doubts Concerning Arabists and Romanists." *La Corónica* 2 (1981): 11–17.

CHAPTER 8

THE MAQAMA

Rina Drory

THE ARABIC MAQAMA

Few classical Arabic literary phenomena have achieved as much fame, both inside and outside the Arabic world, as the maqama. The maqamat are collections of short independent narratives written in ornamental rhymed prose (*saj*ʿ) with verse insertions, and share a common plot-scheme and two constant protagonists: the narrator and the hero. Each narrative (maqama) usually chooses one familiar adab-topos for elaboration; each tells of an episode in which the hero, a vagrant and mendicant who is also a man of letters and eloquence, appears in some public place (a market, mosque, cemetery, public bath, traveling caravan, etc.) in different guises, and tricks people into donating money to him by manipulating their feelings and beliefs. Usually the narrator witnesses the hero's adventures, and at the end of each episode, the narrator exposes the hero's identity, the hero justifies his behavior, and the two part amicably. This scheme appears in many variations, depending on the author and his age.

The maqama appeared on the Arabic literary scene in the tenth century, when the literary system was already well established, when bodies of knowledge constituting the core of Arabic education and learning had crystallized in the form of adab literature. Favored by the courts and scholars attached to the courts, of whose activity it was a product, adab was the alma mater of the maqama genre, serving as a literary fund from which the maqama drew practically everything, from literary models to particular themes, motifs, situations, verses of poetry, figures of speech, clichés, and ready-made rhymed-prose formulas. Specific texts were sometimes drawn from adab literature to serve as the principle on which an entire maqama is structured (e.g., the maqama of the lion by al-Hamadhānī 35–46). The maqama reshapes these literary materials into a new literary model distinct from traditional adab models in that it overtly proclaims itself to be fictional.

Governed by powerful religious-poetic norms, canonical classical Arabic literature in general insisted on the historicity of its texts; fiction, when discussed at all, was usually condemned as a "lie." The introduction, via the maqama, of a literary model that was deliberately fictional was thus an innovation, although it was announced very cautiously, in a way that tended to obscure rather than herald the fact. In the introductions to their works, maqama authors often stated that "they themselves gave the names to the hero and the narrator, who otherwise never existed," meaning that they employed fictional, rather than historical, characters. But at the same time, they were careful to relate their works to accepted literary traditions such as the fables of *Kalīla wa-dimna*, or love poetry, in order to prove the legitimacy of their writings.

The first maqama texts were created with obviously humorous intent by Badīʿ al-Zamān al-Hamadhānī (d. 1008) in 995 or 997 (al-Ḥuṣrī 2:369; al-Thaʿālibī 4:257), in Nishapur, Khurasan, as a sort of comic relief at learning sessions in which serious adab materials were circulated and discussed. A tradition cited by al-Sharīshī, the famous Andalusi, states that at the end of such sessions al-Hamadhānī used to challenge his fellow companions to suggest a theme, or topos, on which he would improvise a "maqama" (1:24; cf. also the opening passage of the 1880 Constantinople edition of al-Hamadhānī's maqamat). His texts were thus created as parodic variations on familiar, often much-studied pieces of adab knowledge. In order to mark the improvisations as mere "fun" and distinguish them from "genuine" educational texts by and about real historical figures, fictitious characters had to be introduced, and their fictionality, to a certain degree, openly admitted.

The maqama hovered on the periphery of canonized Arabic literature for about a century, until the maqamat of al-Ḥarīrī (d. 1122) appeared. Al-Ḥarīrī openly modeled his maqamat on those of al-Hamadhānī. However, although the similarity is apparent, the basic cultural model has been changed: whereas al-Hamadhānī composed his narrations publicly as oral improvisations at the end of adab sessions, and apparently did not trouble to arrange for an authorized collection (various manuscripts have different numbers of maqamat), al-Ḥarīrī composed his privately, in writing, and presented them in an authorized version of fifty pieces. A different conception of "text" underlies his work, which, unlike that of oral composition, regards the work as finalized and therefore unchangeable. Thus, although he admitted that a suggestion by a colleague improved the work, he refused to correct it, claiming that he could not alter a text that he had already authorized in seven hundred copies (Yāqūt 4:599–601). The function of the maqama also changed with al-Ḥarīrī: al-Hamadhānī's maqamat were created as parodies on high literature circulated in courtly circles, whereas al-Ḥarīrī's maqamat became scholarly material from the moment of their inception, and were studied and transmitted as such. Their function as amusement became subordinate to their function as instruction.

Al-Ḥarīrī's maqamat quickly captured the literary taste of the age, as evidenced by the praise of the critics, the many commentaries written on them almost from the time of their first publication in Baghdad, and the testimonies of learned men who came from distant places, including Spain, to hear the authorized version from al-Ḥarīrī's own mouth (Yāqūt 16:266–67; al-Maqqarī 2:509 n. 193). Their exemplary status created a model for the maqama genre that overshadowed all previous models (al-Qalqashandī 14:110), including al-Hamadhānī's, whose collection seems to have been rearranged to conform with the new model. Al-Ḥarīrī's maqamat became a symbol of Arabic eloquence and stylistic dexterity, and preserved this status until modern times, but at the cost of relegating fictionality, the maqama's great innovation, to a secondary position, and the conferring of priority on erudition. With the success of al-Ḥarīrī's maqamat a "real," historic biography was invented for their fictional hero Abū Zayd al-Sarūjī.

It took al-Hamadhānī's writings, at least in the form of samples, only twenty years or so to reach the Muslim West. One traceable channel was the adab anthology *Zahr al-ādāb* (Blossom of Culture) by the Qayrawani scholar al-Ḥuṣrī (d. 1022). This anthology, based on a collection of contemporary compositions recently brought back from the East, included excerpts from al-Hamadhānī's *risālas* and seventeen maqamat, together with a note explaining their origins (1:261). The literary novelty of the maqamat must have intrigued Andalusi men of letters, as both Ibn Bassam (d. 1147), in his great anthology *al-Dhakhīra fī maḥāsin ahl al-jazīra* (Treasury of the Best of the Andalusian Peninsula), and his contemporary al-Kalāʿī, in *Iḥkām ṣanʿat al-kalām* (The Perfection of the Art of Prose Writing), quote the note from *Zahr al-ādāb* explaining the inception of al-Hamadhānī's maqamat.[1]

Al-Hamadhānī's epithet, Badīʿ al-Zamān (Wonder of the Age), became a synonym for refined eloquence and stylistic dexterity in al-Andalus. Andalusi authors often expressed their admiration for a colleague's high prose standards by stating that he "has exceeded Badīʿ al-Zamān" (see, e.g., Ibn Bassam index; al-Maqqarī index).

An interesting testimony to the impact of al-Hamadhānī's maqamat on early eleventh-century Cordoban literati is preserved in the *Risālat al-tawābiʿ wa l-zawābiʿ* (Treatise of Familiar Spirits and Demons) by Ibn Shuhayd (d. 1035). In this piece of literary criticism set in a fictional framework, Ibn Shuhayd challenges texts of some canonical poets and prose writers (mostly Eastern), in order to prove his own superiority, and among these is al-Hamadhānī. Ibn Shuhayd meets al-Hamadhānī's jinni, Zubdat al-Ḥiqab (Cream of the Years, an obvious parody on Wonder of the Age), and asks him to set a theme for improvisation, just as al-Hamadhānī used to ask of his companions. The jinni proposes a description of a slave girl, and approves of Ibn Shuhayd's improvisation on this theme. There follows a short improvisation contest on the description of water, in which Ibn Shuhayd puts in the jinni's mouth an actual quotation from a maqama by al-Hamadhānī (al-Hamadhānī 136–37). Ibn Shuhayd then offers a piece of his own, which apparently surpasses al-Hamadhānī's, as upon hearing it the distraught jinni strikes the ground with his foot; then the earth opens and swallows him up. Ibn Shuhayd thus demonstrates his acquaintance with both the text of al-Hamadhānī's maqamat and the story of their initiation, while challenging their ornate style.[2]

Several eleventh-century writers in al-Andalus cite al-Hamadhānī's maqamat as their inspiration, and others quote his maqamat extensively.[3] Yet the fact that al-Hamadhānī's name is absent from the *Fahrasa* (Index) of Ibn Khayr (d. 1179) is significant, as this book is taken to be a reliable report on contemporary Andalusi curriculum; and the frequent mention of al-Hamadhānī would lead one to expect more conspicuous traces of his work in Andalusi literary output. Although his works were known there, it is difficult to discern to what extent they were read and transmitted and to what extent they inspired new local writing. It seems that al-Hamadhānī's early fame in al-Andalus neither made his maqamat an identifiable productive model for narration nor gave them exemplary status. The early interest in his maqamat apparent throughout the eleventh century seems to have faded, perhaps because of al-Ḥarīrī's success. Yet the style of al-Hamadhānī's rhymed prose, whether inspired by his maqamat or *risāla*s, had a clear impact on Andalusi writings,[4] and his epithet remained a symbol of stylistic sophistication in Andalusi culture.

As noted, al-Ḥarīrī's maqamat marked a cultural enterprise quite different from that of al-Hamadhānī. As opposed to al-Hamadhānī's maqamat, which were the variable product of a series of public oral interchanges, al-Ḥarīrī's maqamat were composed privately and then officially introduced in a complete text of fifty pieces. The earliest manuscript of al-Ḥarīrī's maqamat, which we are fortunate to have (MacKay), was copied in the year of their completion. It contains a fascinating record of the first public reading of the maqamat in Baghdad over the course of a month in 1110[5] in the presence of al-Ḥarīrī himself and thirty-eight named distinguished scholars. The manuscript was endorsed by the author and became an authorized master copy for later copyists and scholars. Its records of another twenty-nine scholarly readings held over 180 years allow us to follow the exact channels by which the maqamat of al-Ḥarīrī were transmitted.

Introduced in this way, al-Ḥarīrī's maqamat thus became scholarly merchandise from the start, and they quickly found their way into al-Andalus. Educated Andalusis frequently traveled to the East in search of such scholarly merchandise, studying under prominent authorities in different fields and gaining authorization to transmit the texts thus acquired. Several Andalusis were present at the very first public readings of the maqamat, which were conducted by al-Ḥarīrī himself. Abū l-Ḥajjāj Yūsuf ibn ʿAlī al-Quḍāʿī (known as Ibn al-Qaffāl) heard the maqamat at al-Ḥarīrī's home in Baghdad only about one month after their first reading and again in Basra; he also read them in front of al-Ḥarīrī, another way of getting permission to transmit them (Ibn Khayr 387). Abū l-Qāsim ibn Jahwar also attended al-Ḥarīrī's reading in Baghdad. Other known Andalusis either were present at these readings or heard the maqamat from someone who was. Al-Quḍāʿī transmitted al-Ḥarīrī's maqamat to Ibn Khayr in Almería (Ibn Khayr 387, 451), and Ibn Jahwar transmitted them in Jerez to Abū Bakr ibn Azhar al-Ḥujrī and Ibn Lubbāl al-Sharīshī (d. 1187). Ibn Lubbāl wrote a commentary on al-Ḥarīrī's maqamat (Ibn Sharīfa 61–66; it is apparently lost) and transmitted them to Aḥmad ibn ʿAbd al-Muʾmin al-Sharīshī (d. 1222), the famous commentator of al-Ḥarīrī's maqamat. The scholarly community of Jerez thus seems to have established a school for the study of al-Ḥarīrī's maqamat, issuing authorized versions of the text and compiling commentaries.

Aḥmad ibn ʿAbd al-Muʾmin al-Sharīshī wrote three versions of his commentary: a large, adab commentary; a middle-length, linguistic volume; and a small, abridged edition (Ibn al-Abbār, *Takmila* 136; al-Sharīshī 1:10, where only the abridged version is mentioned). Al-Sharīshī's working method included reporting on each of his five channels of transmission; meticulous verification of the correct and authorized text; building on existing commentaries while adding annotations on persons and places; identifying verses of Qurʾan and poetry, as well as hadiths and proverbs; elaborating on larger issues like figurative language; and comparing al-Andalus and the East. Other scholars are known to have composed commentaries as well. All this testifies to the distinct status of al-Ḥarīrī's maqamat in comparison to those of al-Hamadhānī. Instead of becoming a model and inspiration for new writing, al-Ḥarīrī's book became part of the scholar's curriculum, to be manipulated in scholarly practices to process bodies of knowledge. It was deemed worthy of preservation and study, but not necessarily imitation.

An outstanding exception to this attitude is the book of maqamat by Abū l-Ṭāhir Muḥammad ibn Yūsuf al-Tamīmī al-Saraqustī, known as Ibn al-Ishtarkūnī (from Estercuel; d. 1143). His *Maqāmāt al-luzūmiyya* (or *al-Saraqustiyya*) (Maqamat of Constraint), written in Córdoba, were explicitly intended to challenge al-Ḥarīrī's maqamat. Like the maqamat of al-Ḥarīrī, it is a collection of fifty narrations in rhymed prose, sharing the same two protagonists: a narrator (al-Sāʾib ibn Tammām; the name of a second narrator, al-Mundhir ibn Ḥummām, is occasionally added to create the rhyme) and a hero, a witty old rogue (Abū Ḥabīb al-Sadūsī, from ʿUman) who gains alms by tricking his audience with the help of impostures and eloquence. Both names obviously imitate those of al-Ḥarīrī's protagonists, al-Ḥārith ibn Hammām and Abū Zayd al-Sarūjī. Each maqama ends with the hero being exposed by the narrator, and ultimately departing, but not before leaving behind a note in verse describing the unfortunate consequences of his life and his subsequent philosophy. Al-Saraqustī's intention of outdoing al-Ḥarīrī is manifest in his choice of a particularly difficult pattern for his rhymed prose, requiring a two-consonant rhyme, though the norm is only one. Although this pattern was a recognized refinement of rhyme (known as *luzūm mā lā yalzam*, "undertaking the nonobligatory"), it was rarely used because it severely limits the choice of rhyming words. The collection derives its name from its rhyme pattern.

Al-Saraqustī's maqamat are very Eastern in character, rarely touching on Andalusi subjects. Their geography spans the entire Islamic world from China to al-Andalus, but the scenery in each maqama tends to be fictional rather than realistic. Al-Saraqustī actually seems to be more interested in Yemen, the location of four of his maqamat, than in al-Andalus or the Maghrib, where he sets one maqama each. His maqamat draw heavily on the Eastern literary repertoire, even elaborating on fantastic themes and curiosities (e.g., *al-Maqāma al-ʿanqawiyya* [The Maqama of the Phoenix], no. 44) not found in al-Ḥarīrī's or other Eastern maqamat. In *Maqāmat al-shuʿarāʾ* [The Maqama of the Poets], only Eastern poets are discussed. Al-Saraqustī seems to have invested all his literary effort in surpassing al-Ḥarīrī's maqamat rather than in creating his own (perhaps Andalusian) model; he did so mainly by elaborating on the prosodic form, rather than on the content.[6]

Al-Saraqustī's imitation of al-Ḥarīrī's fifty-maqama model remained unique. Abū ʿAbd Allāh ibn Abī al-Khiṣāl (d. 1146) made a more daring attempt, though on a smaller scale, to develop the Haririan model. His hero and narrator are named after al-Ḥarīrī's protagonists and act in the same way, but the story combines two encounters of Abū Zayd al-Sarūjī and al-Ḥārith ibn Hammām, apparently in an attempt to create a longer and more complex narration than that of al-Ḥarīrī. In two other exercises Ibn Abī al-Khiṣāl interestingly exploits the new concept of fiction using a bird (*zurzūr*) to address an audience, in a manner similar to that of the rooster in Ibn al-Shahīd's maqama described below (Nemah 84–86).

Nevertheless, composition of occasional maqamat became part of Andalusi epistolary practice in the courts of the party kings and their Berber successors. Eleventh- and twelfth-century Andalusi literati composed both maqamat and *risālas* – a *risāla* is an epistle in ornate prose, sometimes rhymed, treating any of a wide variety of topics – without distinction, for social occasions. As a result, we are able to reconstruct a maqama corpus of about twenty authors who wrote over a period of two hundred years.[7] Most of these texts have survived only in anthologies and often in partial form; some are still unpublished. This supports the impression that like much of the period's high-society correspondence, they were usually composed to celebrate social occasions or promote courtly interactions and interests rather than for educational purposes and therefore for preservation. For example, parts of two maqamat from the court of al-Muʿtaṣim ibn Ṣumādiḥ, the governor of Almería (r. 1051–91), are preserved in Ibn Bassam's literary anthology. The first, written by Abū Ḥafṣ ʿUmar ibn al-Shahīd, was composed for a certain dignitary, Ibn al-Ḥadīd, in commemoration of Ibn al-Ḥadīd's trip to the countryside (Ibn Bassam 2:674–85; cf. S. Stern, "Arabic Source"); the second was written by Abū Muḥammad ibn Mālik al-Qurṭubī to celebrate a military victory (Ibn Bassam 2:741–52). Al-Muʿallim, one of al-Muʿtaḍid's administrators, composed a panegyric maqama, presumably in honor of his king al-Muʿtaḍid (Ibn Bassam 3:113–18). *Al-maqāma al-qurṭubiyya* (The Maqama of Córdoba), attributed to al-Fatḥ ibn Khāqān (d. 1134), criticizes and mocks the distinguished scholar and man of letters Ibn al-Sīd al-Baṭalyawsī and must have caused a row among literati, as several refutations were written in reply (Nemah 86–88).

The social context of the Andalusi maqamat largely determined the way in which this corpus developed its specific poetic framework. Unlike the maqamat of al-Saraqustī, Andalusi court maqamat entirely abandoned specific Eastern characteristics such as the mendicancy theme, two constant protagonists, scheme-based plots, and final exposure. They even relinquished intertextuality and overt reference (whether serious or caricaturing) to established literary models, so intrinsic to Eastern-type maqamat.

They did, however, retain the fundamental novelty of the Eastern maqama: its overt fictionality. And since their frame of reference was life, rather than bodies of knowledge and texts, they exploited fictionality in a different way from that of the Eastern maqamat.

The Haririan models of maqama (adopted by al-Saraqustī) offered a fictional concept designed for processing erudition and knowledge. It provided scholars, who routinely cited and transmitted earlier texts, with a novel means of elaborating on the established stock of literary materials without actually citing from it. Creating fictional protagonists who could speak and act allowed for the reproduction of knowledge in a way that would both display erudition and offer an enjoyable play to the learned. The Andalusi maqamat-*risālas*, in contrast, offered a concept of fiction designed for referring to and commenting on courtly life. They were created by court poets and literati whose task was to depict and extol events in their patron's career, the traditional task of court poets. But instead of continuing the tradition of descriptive-laudatory discourse, they created fictional scenes in which the patron, his entourage, and sometimes the authors themselves appeared as main protagonists. Giving the patrons a part in a fictional scene was much more effective than merely composing a panegyric, for it granted them a second, nontemporal existence, and rewarded them for the remuneration they paid their protégé-writers with something that only artists could offer: a chance to be immortalized through fictional life in a work of art. The audience undoubtedly distinguished fact from fiction in a maqama describing an actual trip to the countryside or a battle, but it was precisely this magical confusion of reality made into fiction and fiction made into reality that was so enchanting. Playing on representations that challenged the borders of reality and fiction, these texts served as both amusing and flattering entertainment for the royal company, including a promise of immortality.

Of all Arabic modes of writing, Andalusi maqamat were the closest to poetry, which likewise operated within a social context and played on the opposition between reality and fiction. But while poetry thrived on contradiction, declaring that it was in no way committed to conveying reality, yet posturing as a report on an actual state of affairs, the maqamat-*risāla*s thrived on combination: while fully admitting fictionality, they nevertheless invited actual figures to play a part in their invented world. In both modes of writing fictitious names would substitute for actual figures, but whereas poetry both invites and denies the reference to reality, the maqamat-*risāla*s encourage the reference and even celebrate it. Thus it is within this framework of modes of representation that the maqamat (whether Andalusi or Eastern) should be assessed, rather than within the framework of literary genres, which seems to project an anachronistic conceptualization onto a corpus of texts sharing a name but stemming from diverse cultural activities and fulfilling different social functions.

THE HEBREW MAQAMA

Throughout most of their history, Jews have been a multilingual community in which several languages coexisted, each language often serving for different functions. Hebrew enjoyed a privileged status in this language setting due partly to the fact that basic books of the Jewish canon had been written in Hebrew. This was also the case with the Hebrew literature produced within the context of Arabic culture. From ninth-century Persia and Iraq until fifteenth-century Christian Spain and Provence (where Jews no longer lived under Muslim rule) most texts produced by Jews were written either in Judeo-Arabic or in Hebrew. The Hebrew literary production of this period cannot be properly understood without taking into account its contacts with Arabic; likewise, the study of the Arabic maqama would benefit from taking the Hebrew works into account.

While both Hebrew and Judeo-Arabic served for writing, they maintained a clear-cut division of functions that was established in the Jewish communities of the Muslim East by the middle of the tenth century. Arabic served for lucid, straightforward expression, while Hebrew served for festive and exalted writing, often at the expense of clarity and specificity. Writing in Hebrew was designed to demonstrate the author's command of the language and to produce a text that would arouse admiration for its beauty and elegance; writing in Arabic was intended to produce a clear and understandable text. Thus it was always easier for Jewish authors to relate to reality in Arabic rather than in Hebrew.

This functional division between Arabic and Hebrew was largely maintained throughout the Andalusi phase of Jewish contact with Arabic culture, a period characterized by an abundance of Hebrew secular poetry produced according to Arabic poetic models by Jewish courtiers and literati (*Language). Biblical Hebrew was effectively re-created as a written language both by experiments in poetry and by formulation of the rules of Hebrew grammar. But since it served mostly for poetic purposes, Hebrew was still associated with elevated style and linguistic display rather than with precise meaning and the representation of reality. Like Arabic court poetry, Hebrew poetry was composed for connoisseurs in celebration of public and private occasions and to amuse patrons and colleagues by dazzling displays of linguistic skill. Nonpoetic writing, such as scholarly treatises, even those dealing with Hebrew grammar, continued to be written only in Judeo-Arabic.

It was not until the relocation of Jewish cultural centers to Christian Spain and Provence following the Almohad invasions of al-Andalus (after 1146) that this division of functions began to break down. Hebrew took over more and more functions that had traditionally been fulfilled by Arabic and gradually replaced Arabic as the major written language of Jewish literature. As a result, new literary genres developed in Hebrew; Arabic models were introduced through both the translation of Arabic texts and the creation of Jewish equivalents in Hebrew. The new Hebrew literature was based on Arabic models, but it was embedded in a cultural figuration quite different from the one that had prevailed in the Jewish literature of the Muslim period. This Spanish-Christian context is easily overlooked when its literary products, bearing the unmistakable imprint of Arabic culture, are examined.

With the emergence of universities in Europe, the Arabic philosophical-scientific corpus gained prestige; with the growing demand for faithful reproductions of imported texts, translation thus became a recognized scholarly activity. The high status of Arabic texts in the Christian areas, as well as the development of book culture there, may account for the fact that for the first time Hebrew contacts with Arabic assumed mainly the form of translation of specific texts rather than of appropriation of underlying models. Scientific and philosophical writings were intensively translated from Arabic into Hebrew, as well as into Latin. Artistic texts, like adab compilations or maqamat, were also either translated or adapted into Hebrew.

Hebrew maqamat and other rhymed narratives flourished in Christian Spain and Provence from the mid-twelfth to the fifteenth century (there is one possible early example from al-Andalus in the first half of the twelfth century, the stories of Solomon Ibn Ṣaqbel). They thus proliferated in a non-Muslim cultural atmosphere about a hundred years after the establishment of their Arabic models in Andalus. From the thirteenth century onward, rhymed narratives became a normal part of Jewish writing, as is evidenced by the extant texts from Italy, Egypt, Yemen, Turkey, and Greece (Pagis, "Variety"). Many of these compositions are clearly modeled on Arabic exemplars, both the Hamadhani-Haririan and the Andalusi ones. But they also diverge from these models in ways that suggest inspiration by local, non-Arabic models. Further research is required to assess the non-Arabic contribution to the emerging Hebrew models.

Considerable effort has been invested in recent years in defining the genre and drawing neat borderlines between proper maqamat and other rhymed narratives. Contemporaries often did not make such distinctions. A broad, inclusive definition may permit us to discern connections and contrasts within the heterogeneous corpus of Hebrew rhymed prose better than classification bordering on taxonomy.

Pagis's description of this heterogeneous corpus, comprising maqamat inspired by al-Hamadhānī and al-Ḥarīrī, philosophical and satirical tracts, animal fables, allegorical works, and more, is worth repeating here:

> Whatever their main trend, all of those works introduced a wealth of new themes absent from the preceding classical [i.e., Andalusi] period – journeys and battles, amorous intrigues, adventures in palaces and market places, discussions of philosophical and scientific issues, descriptions of literary soirées, of types and professions, of town and country – a tapestry of medieval life, both general and specially Jewish.
> ("Variety" 80–81)

When Jewish authors began experimenting with Hebrew rhymed narratives modeled on Arabic maqamat, the challenge they faced was not the use of rhymed prose – rhyming had long been established in Jewish culture – but the representation of reality in fictional texts. Hebrew writers were confronted with a literary model that, although claiming to be fictional, was nevertheless based on faithfully reporting on reality. Writing in Hebrew was traditionally not expected to report on reality or to create realistic effects; meaning tended to be produced by relating each particular text to the stock of canonical texts rather than to reality. Such links often hinged on intertextual allusions and multiple meanings, not on the overall image of reality conveyed in a text. Hebrew writing, lacking both the necessary mental habits and textual tools, had structural difficulty representing reality in fiction as embodied in the Arabic maqama.

Traditionally, Jewish literature – reflecting perhaps some basic bias of Jewish culture – was not so much interested in portraying reality as in representing the correct order of things. Its main concern lay in theological and moral paradigms rather than in their particular, transient, historical manifestations, and the truth claim of a text stemmed from its agreement with the paradigm, rather than from any claim to depict reality faithfully. Thus, certain pretenth-century rabbanite texts, such as *Pirqe derabbi eliᶜezer* or *Tana devei eliyahu*, refer to contemporary reality in mishnaic-talmudic terms, and consequently conceal concrete reality items behind ancient vocabulary with nonspecific denotations. Such speculations require further study and refinement. But the case of the Hebrew rhymed narratives seems relatively clear: whereas in Arabic literature the major difficulty in accepting the maqamat consisted in the novelty of overt fiction, which violated the norm of faithfully reporting on reality, in Hebrew literature it was the very report on reality that was hard to accept.

Arabic maqama authors would declare fictionality by stating in their prefaces that they themselves gave the names to the hero and the narrator, who otherwise never existed, indicating thereby that they employed invented, fictional – rather than historical, real – characters. These statements were apparently taken by the Hebrew writers to be an indispensable part of the maqama model, for almost all of them addressed the subject of invented personae in the preface or the epilogue to their works. Yet although similar in wording, the Arabic and Hebrew statements actually reveal opposed conceptions of fiction, derived from different cultural attitudes toward representing reality in written texts.

When Arabic authors state that they "have created the stories from their own heart" and named their characters themselves, they mean that, in conscious deviation from the official literary norm, they have invented their own personae (in both narration and transmission chain) rather than resorting to historical figures; they are not denying that their fiction is founded on plausible representation of reality. But when Hebrew writers make the same statements, they are firmly asserting not only that the stories are false, but that they are not even plausible. Numerous variations on the talmudic saying "[It] never was and never happened, but is only a parable" (Babylonian Talmud, Baba Batra 15a) recur in Hebrew rhymed narratives in order to remind the audience that the stories are imaginary events illustrating a moral or spiritual lesson, not actual reality. Solomon Ibn Ṣaqbel, for example, ends his maqama with the words "Enjoy my charming story, gentle friends, / But don't be taken in by what you've heard. / A tale of lover's folly this, no more, / A pack of lies – I made up every word" (264). And al-Ḥarīzī declares in the preface to his *Sefer taḥkemoni* (Book of Tahkemoni), "All the words of this book I have put upon the tongue of Heman the Ezrahite, and in the name of Ḥever the Qenite I have founded and built them, though neither of them lives in our generation; and everything that I have mentioned in their name never was and has never happened, but is only fiction (literally, a parable)" (*Taḥkemoni* 1:40).

It is interesting to note how the similar statements assume opposite functions in the two literatures. In his preface to *Masāʾil al-intiqād* (Issues in Literary Criticism), the Arab writer Ibn Sharaf al-Qayrawānī writes about his protagonist: "I ascribed [the stories] to Abū l-Rayyān al-Salt ibn al-Sakan ibn Sulaymān" (2). He then outlines a sort of biography of Abū l-Rayyān, which, though imaginary, is obviously intended to grant the hero a realistic existence. The Hebrew writer Jacob Ben Eleazar refers to himself in almost the same words in the preface to his *Sefer ha-meshalim* (Book of Parables):

> Rather than lend my name to the stories, I narrated them instead in the name of Lemuel Ben Itiel, and thus I concealed my own. This I did in the manner of the Ishmaelites, whose habit is to disguise their names in their stories. Nevertheless, I now declare that I am indeed Jacob Ben Eleazar, in order that "no stranger shall draw near." (That is, plagiarize my work; the quotation is taken from Num. 17:5. David 14)

Ben Eleazar thus recognizes the "naming-of-the-hero declaration" as a convention of the preface to an Arabic-type maqama collection, but he completely misconstrues its raison d'être, treating it, perhaps in line with a Jewish convention, as a device for disguising the identity of the real author.[8] But since a work by a fictional author might fall to the public domain, he makes a point of declaring his own authorship. His statement discloses how Jewish authors understood the idea of the fictional hero: as a disguised appearance of themselves in the text, not of some plausibly existing person, as was the case in the Arabic maqamat. This is further supported by the way other Hebrew authors, especially al-Ḥarīzī, designed their fictional hero (see, for instance, S. Stern, "Unpublished Maqama" 202–10). Whereas Arab writers employed fictional names in the maqamat within the framework of decoding reality, Hebrew writers seemed to have conceived employing fictional names within the framework of encoding it.

While Arabic declarations of fiction thus reveal difficulty in fictionalizing reality, Hebrew declarations reveal difficulty in rendering it. Hebrew authors even seem to display a kind of "realism anxiety" that leads them to disclaim the veracity of their fictions, as when Judah Ibn Shabbetai intervenes in his own story to declare that none of the figures truly existed, but were merely creations of his imagination.

Abandoning realism in the Hebrew maqamat in favor of fictionality opened many nonrealistic options for the Hebrew writers. They chose to develop mainly two: the interplay of fictional plot and real protagonists, and the allegorical mode. The favorite play on representations challenging the borders of reality and fiction, as developed in the Arabic Andalusi maqamat in the context of court culture, was enhanced and enriched in the Hebrew maqamat, which were also produced within the framework of a Jewish version of courtly patronage. Hebrew writers made the patron and members of his family, as well as themselves and sometimes their family, active participants in the narration. In Ibn Shabbetai's story of the misogynist, the trial is held before "the king Abraham," none other than Ibn Shabbetai's real patron Abraham Ibn al-Fakhkhār, and, when Abraham condemns the misogynist to death, Judah himself intervenes to explain to the judge that all characters are fictitious anyway. In *Milḥemet haḥokhma veha'osher* (Strife of Wisdom and Wealth), Ibn Shabbetai also makes Todros ha-Levi, to whom the work is dedicated, a judge between the two fictional rivals, Peleg and Yoqtan. Isaac, the author of *'Ezrat ha-nashim* (Women's Assistance), has Todros ha-Levi appear in the shape of an angel to explain that Isaac has modeled the heroine, Rachel, on his wife; Todros begs Isaac to go and present his work to her. Isaac immediately admits that all his protagonists in the work are fictitious, and were only invented to praise and honor Todros ha-Levi's wife, to whom the work is dedicated. Likewise, in some of his maqamat, Judah al-Ḥarīzī (1170–1225), the most famous writer of Hebrew maqamat, has his fictional protagonist Ḥever the Qenite recount al-Ḥarīzī's real journeys in Spain and the Muslim East and his encounters with Jewish dignitaries there. A little later, around 1300, Immanuel of Rome stages himself and many of his friends and colleagues in fictional scenes in his maqamat.

In contrast to this new interplay of fiction and reality, Hebrew writers had many precedents to follow in pursuing the second option, that of allegory. Allegory had a long Jewish tradition in both canonical and apocryphal literatures. Supported by mystical and Neoplatonic trends current in contemporary Jewish communities in northern Spain and Provence, Hebrew writers produced highly elaborate allegories on body and soul, on wisdom and intellect. Many of these allegorical maqamat introduce intricate plots based on the spirit and etiquette of courtly love, as developed in the Abbasid culture and refined in the Andalusi courts, but inspired perhaps also by European romance. But these love plots are developed in ways that suggest a nonallegorical reading as well; their true meaning is still to be deciphered.

The difficulty faced by Hebrew writers in accommodating the Arabic model for the presentation of reality as embedded in the Arabic concept of fiction can be demonstrated by comparing Hebrew adaptations of Arabic maqamat to their sources. Al-Ḥarīzī adapted an episode from a long maqama by Ibn al-Shahīd into Hebrew and incorporated it into his *Sefer taḥkemoni* (Ibn Bassam 2:674–85; al-Ḥarīzī, *Taḥkemoni,* no. 10; cf. S. Stern, "Arabic Source"). Ibn al-Shahīd's maqama tells of a trip by a dignitary named Ibn al-Ḥadīd and his entourage to the countryside. They arrive at the abode of a Bedouin,[9] who hurries to make order, greets his guests warmly, and invites them in. The house is neat as a pin, spread with country-style mats, and decorated with varied ribbons (in the manner of the stage decor of the shadow theater); colorful fabrics, clothing, scarves, and different kinds of spices are stored in various kinds of vessels. The guests react to the sight with barely concealed mockery. The Bedouin recites a poem in praise of the tradition of Bedouin hospitality and sends his servants to catch an aged rooster to make a meal for the guests. The rooster escapes and a chase ensues. The rooster flies to a rooftop, where he recites a poem in honor of his escape. At his voice, a congregation gathers for prayer, for the people of the place are in the habit of setting the times for prayer by the rooster's crowing. He complains about the ingratitude practiced toward him after he had served the congregation so long and well. He has waked them for prayer, reproduced, and raised generations of chicks, yet now that he is old they want to slaughter him. The people beg the host to spare him; he explains that he has no choice but to perform the rites of hospitality in accordance with his ancestors' tradition. The rooster answers that he is wrong if he thinks that the flesh of an aged rooster will satisfy the demands of royal hospitality, for it is more like poison than like food; he recommends substituting one of his chicks for himself, making the medical claim that their flesh is good for the blood. The people are impressed with his knowledge and immediately appoint him their doctor. The Bedouin accepts the verdict and makes his guests a fine meal. They thank him and go on their way.

While following closely this basic plot, al-Ḥarīzī's rooster maqama is significantly different in several ways. First, the Arabic maqama was written to commemorate a pleasant episode of courtly life, and the story is therefore introduced in the manner of a report of a real adventure, though couched in high and humorous style. In the Hebrew reworking, the episode is introduced as a tale, recounted in the framework of a conversation between al-Ḥarīzī's two constant protagonists; Ḥever the Qenite, unreliable as ever, tells this marvelous story at the request of the transmitter Heman the Ezrahite, who is always eager to hear Ḥever's stories. At the end of the maqama, the veracity of the story is denied, as is often the case in the Hebrew maqamat. A story within a story, the episode is thus twice removed from "actual reality." Second, although both versions of the story are founded on the theme of hospitality, the model of hospitality in each version is different. The Arabic version plays on the common motif of the Bedouins' unlimited generosity, whereas the Hebrew version has as its model the biblical story of Abraham welcoming the three angels (Gen. 18). This is why in the Hebrew the host bows to his guests, when no such gesture is mentioned in the Arabic, and why he serves them first curds and milk, then a lamb and a meat stew. In the Arabic, the rooster was the only available food, due to the poverty of the host, which stands in contrast to pretensions of a proud Bedouin; the proposal to slaughter the rooster was therefore a necessary part of the plot. In the Hebrew, after the mention of the abundance of food dictated by the biblical model, a different reason had to be concocted to slaughter the rooster. Al-Ḥarīzī's hero therefore asks the host to slaughter his rooster because its voice had disturbed his sleep during the previous night, a weak excuse necessitated by the desire to bring the biblical story of Abraham's hospitality into conformity with the portrayal of a multifaceted situation of country hospitality. Third, in the Arabic maqama the humor is built on constantly changing social points of view. The Bedouin tries to make an impression on his noble guests according to what he imagines to be their criteria of noble virtues and their expectations of him. He thus boasts of a "noble" Bedouin origin with a long family tradition of generosity (while being in fact very poor), and is eager to show the company the overly decorated interior of his house (which the guests find merely pretentious). When the rooster pleads for his life, the Bedouin justifies himself by arguing that he is obliged to act according to the noble code of generosity, to which the rooster answers that the Bedouin shows gross misunderstanding of royal etiquette if he presumes that an old rooster's meat is fit for kings. None of these social insights is to be found in the Hebrew maqama, which dwells instead on stereotyped rural scenes of hospitality and elaborates on the lengthy sermon of the rooster. Concrete reality items, like the long list of cloths, garments, and perfumes decorating the interiors of the Bedouin's home, which are used to create funny, realistic effect in Arabic, are, characteristically, ignored in the Hebrew. The Hebrew maqama gave up on context-dependent humor exploiting divergent social perspectives and contradictory cultural images in favor of a joke constructed on archetypes, playing, in almost each phrase, on sophisticated intertextual references.

Numerous examples can be cited to demonstrate the tendency of Hebrew writers to abstain from concretization, and this trend stands out when we compare Hebrew to Arabic maqamat. A concrete description of a several-course meal at a Baghdad market in al-Hamadhānī is reduced in al-Ḥarīzī's Hebrew adaptation to only one item – roast meat – and ready biblical quotations are cleverly interwoven to produce shadowy elevated imagery (no. 12 in al-Hamadhānī's collection; no. 21 in al-Ḥarīzī's collection); a minute account by a nouveau riche merchant in al-Hamadhānī of how he cunningly managed to purchase his house and furniture becomes, in al-Ḥarīzī's adaptation, a pastiche of the biblical description of the Tabernacle and its furniture (no. 22 in al-Hamadhānī; no. 34 in al-Ḥarīzī). Hebrew readers, for their part, are so accustomed to this nonconcrete character of the Hebrew maqamat that they do not expect the texts to refer to actual reality. When concrete reality items are referred to in some maqamat that depict actual travels, it often takes deciphering efforts to identify these items.[10]

Hebrew maqamat thus seem to be more successful in constructing nonrealistic fiction than in constructing reality. They did open to Jewish literature in Hebrew the option of conveying actual reality, but, as is the case with the Arabic maqamat, cultural habits managed to enforce themselves on the new models. In the Hebrew maqamat concretization continued to be concealed behind elevation and festiveness for generations; in the Arabic maqamat, veracity and historicity eventually prevailed.

Al-Ḥarīzī is not only the most famous but also the most productive maqama writer in Hebrew. His career as a Jewish intellectual spans the territory from Christian Spain and Provence to the Muslim East, and from Hebrew to Arabic. His career also marks the movement of the Hebrew maqamat from their inception in Spain to the Jewish culture of the Muslim East.

Born in Toledo to a family that apparently originated in Jerez, as his name suggests, al-Ḥarīzī was living in northern Spain during the second half of the twelfth century, when an interest in Arabic texts began to flourish in Jewish as well as Christian circles. He became an Arabic–Hebrew translator, translating several Arabic and Judeo-Arabic works, usually at the invitation of distinguished patrons or scholars of the Jewish communities of northern Spain and Provence. Among his translations are some of Maimonides' works, including his *Moreh nevukhim* (Guide of the Perplexed), as well as Arabic works like Ḥunayn ibn Isḥāq's *Adāb al-falāsifa* (Dicta of the Philosophers) and ʿAlī ibn Riḍwan's *Epistle on Morals.* While still in northern Spain or in Provence, he translated al-Ḥarīrī's maqamat, under the title *Maḥberot iti'el* (Maqamat of Itiel). He then traveled to the Muslim East, where, sometime after 1216, he composed his own Hebrew maqamat (*Sefer taḥkemoni*), which he modeled on al-Ḥarīrī's Arabic maqamat.[11] There, he also composed a Judeo-Arabic maqama, describing his journey in the East. Nothing was known of his later life (whether he stayed in the East or returned to Spain; when he died) until recently, when Joseph Sadan discovered an entry on him in an Arabic biographical dictionary by a younger contemporary, a Muslim named Ibn al-Shaʿʿār of Aleppo.[12] From this precious biography we learn that after much wandering al-Ḥarīzī finally settled down in Aleppo, where he died in 1225. He is portrayed as somewhat eccentric in appearance and behavior, and distinguished by his Maghribi accent. Four Arabic poems of his are quoted, of which one is a panegyric in honor of the Ayyubid prince al-Ashraf Mūsā (d. 1237).

Al-Ḥarīzī's maqamat are traditionally regarded as a highly typical (perhaps the most typical) example of Arabic influence over Hebrew literature: he first translated al-Ḥarīrī's Arabic maqamat into Hebrew, then composed his own maqamat on the same model. Moreover, he openly declared in his preface that he had been inspired by al-Ḥarīrī's maqamat. Yet an examination of the cultural context within which this work was composed – in the Muslim East – reveals that it took a non-Muslim and non-Arabic cultural atmosphere, that of Christian Spain and Provence, to produce a literary work so notably Arabic-Hebrew in nature. Coming from a place where Hebrew was replacing Arabic as the major Jewish written language and Hebrew literature proliferating, al-Ḥarīzī's encounter in the Muslim East with a Jewish public who was not as much interested in Hebrew writing and probably highly taken with Arabic culture might have been quite striking for him. His motivation for composing the Hebrew maqamat was to prompt Eastern Jews to be interested in Hebrew, rather than mere admiration for what was considered to be the peak of Arabic eloquence.

Al-Ḥarīzī himself describes in the preface to *Sefer taḥkemoni* how he was asked while still in Spain to translate al-Ḥarīrī's work into Hebrew: "For the nobles of Spain, when they heard the words of the Arab's book [al-Ḥarīrī's maqamat], marveled at them. And they sought of me while I was still among them to translate this book for them and I was not able to turn them away" (*Taḥkemoni* 1:39). But when he composed his own Hebrew maqamat in the Muslim East, he had to "seek of the patrons of the world, from Egypt to Babylon, [for] one with whose name I might adorn the book and it would be sealed with his seal. I searched him among the leaders of the time, and sought for him but found him not, and no one answered me when I called" (1:41), until at last a patron was found.

The fact that while still in the East, but apparently after he had composed *Sefer taḥkemoni*, al-Ḥarīzī also wrote a Judeo-Arabic maqama, seems to indicate that he himself realized that there was no great public for Hebrew writing there and that he would have to write in Arabic in order to make his voice heard. Explaining why he wrote in Arabic, he notes, "When I visited Baghdad the Jewish community there turned its back on me and treated me rudely. I have therefore decided to compose a maqama in Arabic about them, in which I will expose some of their hidden feats . . . let me quote here from this maqama, so that it serve to commemorate what they have done" (S. Stern, "New Description" 150–51). His decision to switch to Arabic (in Hebrew characters) reflects his feeling that Hebrew is too exalted for straightforward writing, and that one should write in Arabic if one wants the message to be clearly conveyed and understood by all. His words also reveal disappointment, even alienation, from the Jewish cultural ambience of the Muslim East.

The fact that al-Ḥarīzī's later life was considered worth telling about in an Arabic biographical dictionary by a Muslim demonstrates that he was sufficiently involved in Arabic circles to be acknowledged as an Arabic poet. Though we have no way of knowing whether or not he continued to write in Hebrew at that period of his life in Aleppo, or even in Judeo-Arabic, we do know for certain that he composed poems for an Arabic audience. It is highly interesting, then, to find this ardent crusader for Hebrew ending his life as an Arabic poet, composing poems and panegyrics for a local Muslim ruler in northern Syria and Mesopotamia. Through all of his known life al-Ḥarīzī seems to have known how to accommodate his literary output to changing demands.

NOTES

1. Ibn Bassam 8:585; al-Kalāʿī 125–26. Al-Sharīshī presents a short version of this passage in his commentary on al-Ḥarīrī's maqamat (1:24). For the scholarly debate that followed, see Drory, "Introducing Fictionality." For *Zahr al-ādāb* in al-Andalus, see Ibn Khayr 380.
2. From the literary circle of Ibn Shuhayd we also have a *muʿāraḍa* to a *risāla* of al-Hamadhānī by Abū Mughīra ibn Ḥazm (d. 1046) (Ibn Bassam 1:140–42) and a reference to al-Hamadhānī's eloquence (*balāgha*) by Abū Muḥammad ibn Ḥazm in his *Kitāb al-balāgha* (Book of Eloquence) (Ibn Ḥazm al-Andalusī, *Rasā'il*, ed. Iḥsān ʿAbbās [Beirut, 1983], 4:352).
3. Among those who imitate him are Ibn Sharaf al-Qayrawānī (d. 1067) in his twenty hadiths (4); al-Kalāʿī (early twelfth century) (124–25, 196–204); and Ibn Shammākh in a *risāla*, no longer extant (Ibn Bassam 2:827, 840–41).
4. Cf., e.g., Abū Mughīra ibn Ḥazm's *risāla* mentioned in n. 2.
5. AH 504 (MacKay 6–11); Ibn al-Zubayr 206 (no. 400) gives the year as AH 505.
6. For an English description of al-Saraqustī's maqamat, see Nemah 88–92.
7. For surveys of this corpus and its contents, see Nemah; Granja; Iḥsān ʿAbbās 280–326; ʿAwad 268–311; Ḥasan ʿAbbās 99–146.

8. Saadiah Gaon (882–942) recognizes this practice in his comments on Rabbi Ishmael's supposed authorship of the esoteric book *Shiʿur qomah* (The Dimensions of the Godhead) (S. J. Halberstam, *Commentar zum Sepher Jezira von R. Jehuda b. Barsilai aus Barcelona* [Berlin, 1885], 21).
9. In Arabic literature, *badawī* usually denotes Arab Bedouin, but in Andalusi texts, *badawī* can also mean somebody from the countryside. It is hard to tell which is the correct meaning here; probably both the literary and the local meanings apply.
10. Thus, Joseph ben Simeon, a contemporary of al-Ḥarīzī's, in a maqama in praise of Maimonides, describing his arrival at the port of Alexandria, uses the common Hebrew word for lamp, *menora,* to denote the famous lighthouse; even experienced scholars had trouble deciphering this denotation of the Hebrew word, primarily because they did not expect a work in such exalted style to refer to realia. See Joseph Yahalom, "'Sayeth Tuviyyah ben Zidkiyyah': The Maqama of Joseph ben Simeon in Honor of Maimonides," *Tarbiz* 66 (1997): 543–77.
11. Only part of *Maḥberot iti'el* has survived.
12. In *Book on the Poets of the Age . . .* by Ibn al-Shaʿʿār al-Mawṣilī. See Joseph Sadan, "Rabbi Judah al-Ḥarīzīa's Cultural Junction" [Hebrew], *Peʿamim* 68 (1996): 16–67.

BIBLIOGRAPHY

Arabic maqamat

ʿAbbās, Ḥasan. *Fann al-maqāma fī l-qarn al-sādis.* Cairo, 1986.

ʿAbbās, Iḥsān. *Taʾrīkh al-adab al-andalusī.* Beirut, 1974.

ʿAwad, Yūsuf Nūr. *Fann al-maqāmāt bayna al-mashriq wa l-maghrib.* Beirut, 1979.

Beeston, A. F. L. "Al-Hamadhānī, al-Ḥarīrī and the *Maqāmāt* Genre." *The Cambridge History of Arabic Literature: ʿAbbasid Belles-Lettres.* Ed. Julia Ashtiany et al. Cambridge, 1990. 125–35.

al-Dāya, Muḥammad Riḍwān. *Taʾrīkh al-naqd al-adabī fī al-andalus.* Beirut, 1968.

Drory, Rina. "Introducing Fictionality into Classical Arabic Literature: The Maqāma." *Models and Contacts: Medieval Arabic Literature and Its Impact on Jewish Culture.* Leiden, forthcoming.

Granja, Fernando de la. *Maqamas y risalas andaluzas.* Madrid, 1976.

al-Hamadhānī, Badī al-Zamān. *Sharḥ maqāmāt badīʿ al-zamān al-hamadhānī.* Ed. Muḥammad Muḥyī al-Dīn ʿAbd al-Ḥamīd. Cairo, 1962.

al-Ḥuṣrī, Abū Isḥāq al-Qayrawānī. *Zahr al-ādāb wa-thimār al-albāb.* Ed. ʿAlī Muḥammad al-Bajāwī. 2 vols. Cairo, 1953.

Ibn al-Abbār. *Kitāb al-ḥulla al-siyarāʾ.* Ed. Ḥusayn Muʾnis. Cairo, 1963.

Kitāb al-takmila likitūb al-ṣila. Ed. Alfred Bel and M. Ben Cheneb. Algiers, 1920.

Ibn Bassam. *al-Dhakhīra fī maḥāsin ahl al-jazīra.* Ed. Iḥsān ʿAbbās. 8 vols. Beirut, 1979.

Ibn Khayr. *Ben Khair, Abou Bequer: Index des livres et maîtres.* Ed. F. Codera and J. R. Rarrago. Beirut, 1979.

Ibn Sharaf al-Qayrawānī. *Masā'il al-intiqād (Questions de critique littéraire).* Ed. Charles Pellat. Algiers, 1953.

Ibn Sharīfa, Muḥammad. *Ibn lubbal al-sharīshī.* Casablanca, 1996.

Ibn Shuhayd al-Andalusī. *Risālat al-tawābiʿ wa l-zawābiʿ.* Ed. Buṭrus al-Bustānī. Beirut, 1976.

Risālat al-tawābiʿ wa l-zawābi ʿ: The Treatise of Familiar Spirits and Demons by Abū ʿĀmir ibn Shuhaid al-Ashjaʿī al-Andalusī. Introduction, trans., and notes by James T. Monroe. Los Angeles, 1970.

Ibn al-Zubayr, Aḥmad. *Kitāb ṣilat al-ṣila.* Ed. Évariste Lévi-Provençal. Rabat, 1937.

al-Kalāʿī, Muḥammad ibn ʿAbd al-Ghafūr. *Iḥkām ṣanʿat al-kalām.* Ed. Muḥammad Riḍwān al-Dāya. Beirut, 1985.

MacKay, Pierre A. *Certificates of Transmission on a Manuscript of the Maqamas of Ḥarīrī (Ms. Cairo, Adab 105).* Philadelphia, 1971.

al-Maqqarī. *Nafḥ al-ṭīb min ghuṣn al-andalus al-raṭīb.* Ed. Iḥsān ʿAbbās. 8 vols. Beirut, 1968.

Nemah, H. "Andalusian Maqāmāt." *Journal of Arabic Literature* 5 (1974): 83–92.

al-Qalqashandī. *Subḥ al-aʿshā fī ṣināʿat al-inshā'.* 14 vols. Cairo, 1913–19.

al-Saraqustī, Abū l-Ṭāhir Muḥammad ibn Yūsuf. *Al-maqāmāt al-luzūmiyya.* Ed. Aḥmad Badr Ḍayf. Alexandria, 1982.

al-Sharīshī, Abū l-ʿAbbās Aḥmad ibn ʿAbd al-Mu'min. *Sharḥ maqāmāt al-ḥarīrī.* Ed. Muḥammad Abū l-Faḍl Ibrāhīm. 5 vols. Beirut, 1992.

al-Thaʿālibī. *Yatīmat al-dahr fī maḥāsin ahl al-ʿaṣr.* Ed. Muḥammad Muḥyī al-Dīn ʿAbd al-Ḥamīd. 4 vols. Cairo, 1979.

Yāqūt. *Muʿjam al-udabā'.* 20 vols. in 10. Beirut, 1991.

Hebrew maqamat

Brann, Ross. "Power in the Portrayal: Representations of Muslims and Jews in Judah al-Ḥarīzī's Taḥkemoni." *Princeton Papers in Near Eastern Studies* 1 (1992): 1–22.

David, Yona. *Sipure ahava shel yaʿaqov ben elʿazar.* Tel Aviv, 1992–93.

Drory, Rina. "Al-Ḥarīzī's Maqamas: A Tricultural Literary Product?" *Medieval Translator* 4 (1994): 66–85.

Fishman, Talya. "A Medieval Parody of Misogyny: Judah ibn Shabbetai's 'Minḥat Yehudah Sone Hanashim.'" *Prooftexts* 8 (1988): 89–111.

al-Ḥarīrī, al-Qāsim ibn ʿAlī. *Maḥberot iti'el.* Trans. Judah al-Ḥarīzī. Ed. Yitsḥaq Peretz. Tel Aviv, 1951.

al-Ḥarīzī, Judah. *Taḥkemoni.* Ed. Y. Toporowsky. Tel Aviv, 1952.

The Taḥkemoni of Judah al-Ḥarīzī. Trans. V. E. Reichert. 2 vols. Jerusalem, 1965–73.

Ibn Ṣaqbel, Solomon. "Asher in the Harem." Trans. Raymond P. Scheindlin. Stern and Mirsky 253–67.

Ibn Shabbetai. "The Misogynist." Trans. Raymond P. Scheindlin. Stern and Mirsky 269–94.

Pagis, Dan. "Trends in the Study of Medieval Hebrew Literature." *Association of Jewish Studies Review* 4 (1979): 125–41.

"Variety in Medieval Rhymed Narratives." *Scripta Hierosolymitana* 27 (1978): 79–98.

Scheindlin, Raymond P. "Fawns of the Palace and Fawns of the Field." *Prooftexts* 6 (1986): 189–203.

Schirmann, Ḥayim. *Hebrew Poetry in Spain and Provence* [Hebrew]. 4 vols. Jerusalem, 1961.

New Hebrew Poems from the Genizah [Hebrew]. Jerusalem, 1965.

Studies in the History of Hebrew Poetry and Drama [Hebrew]. 2 vols. Jerusalem, 1979. 1:342–438.

Schirmann, Jefim. "Les contes rimées de Jacob ben Eléazar de Tolède." *Etudes d'orientalisme dédiées à la mémoire de Lévi-Provençal.* 2 vols. Paris, 1962. 1:285–97.

Die hebräische Übersetzung der Maqamen des Hariri. Frankfurt am Main, 1930.

The History of Hebrew Poetry in Christian Spain and Southern France [Hebrew]. Ed. Ezra Fleischer. Jerusalem, 1997.

"The Love Stories of Jacob Ben Eleazar" [Hebrew]. *Studies of the Research Institute for Hebrew Poetry* 5 (1939): 209–66.

Segal, David S. "Maḥberet Ne'um Asher ben Yehudah of Solomon Ibn Ṣaqbel: A Study of Scriptural Citation Clusters." *Journal of the American Oriental Society* 102 (1982): 17–26.

Stern, David. *Parables in Midrash.* Cambridge, Mass., 1994.

Stern, David, and Mark Mirsky, eds. *Rabbinic Fantasies.* Philadelphia, 1990.

Stern, Samuel M. "The Arabic Source of al-Ḥarīzī's Rooster Maqama" [Hebrew]. *Tarbiz* 17 (1946): 87–100.

"A New Description by Judah al-Ḥarīzī of His Tour to Iraq" [Hebrew]. *Sefunot* 8 (1964): 145–56.

"An Unpublished Maqama by al-Ḥarīzī." *Papers of the Institute of Jewish Studies London* 1 (1964): 188–210.

CHAPTER 9

THE QASIDA

Beatrice Gruendler

The qasida belongs to those crucial areas in which the Andalusian literary universe is an extension of the classical Arabic one. The qasida is a formal multithematic ode addressed to a member of the elite in praise, in admonition, or in quest of support. Poets and scholars traveling in both directions imported the Eastern heritage into Andalusia, and by the fourth/tenth century, the distant province became the home to centers of patronage that attracted even Eastern poets. The affiliation manifested itself in Andalusian emulations of famous Eastern qasidas by Abū Nuwās, al-Mutanabbī, and others. Only as a second step did Andalusians give up vying with their Eastern cousins to find their own paths, as evidenced by the emergence of the muwashshah. At first excluded from the poets' official collected works (diwans), the muwashshah gradually conquered high literature, eventually rivaling the qasida in its own sphere of panegyric. But while giving due credit to Andalusian self-assertion within the Arabo-Islamic literary universe, one must also recognize that al-Andalus first earned its legitimacy by excelling in qasida poetry.

Not surprisingly, the study of Andalusian Arabic literature has been dominated by the study of the distinctively Andalusian zajal and muwashshah or the question of literary influences between Muslims, Jews, and Mozarabs. As a result, research on classical poetry in Arabic, a major unifying field in this culture, has suffered (Schmidt 66). Moreover, scholarship on classical Andalusian poetry has tended to focus on genres perceived as typically Andalusian, such as nature poetry, or on personalities differing from the mold of the courtier-poet, such as the doomed last Abbadid king, al-Muʿtamid, and the independent Valencian aristocrat Ibn Khafāja (Jayyusi, *Legacy* 317–97; al-Nowaihi; Scheindlin, *Form*). As a result, their roles as a patron and a panegyrist respectively have been deemphasized (ʿAbbās 3:76–77; Khāliṣ 83–90). Both tendencies have highlighted distinctively Andalusian phenomena, leaving the qasida in darkness: neither of two recent surveys of al-Andalus and qasida poetry discusses it.[1]

Ideally, an overview of Andalusian qasida poetry should be able to draw on literary analyses of individual diwans and poetic anthologies for the fourth/tenth to the ninth/fifteenth centuries. Such groundwork being as yet uncompleted, the present study selects qasidas by three poets from different periods, poets of varied social status, circumstances, and literary styles. Without claiming comprehensiveness, it aims to enable the reader to gauge the genre's play between constraint and variety.

HISTORY, APPROACHES, AND DEFINITION

The historical evolution leading to the Abbasid (and the Andalusian) qasida falls into two larger stages: the first extends roughly from the time before Islam to the early Abbasid era (sixth to late second/eighth century); the second moves from the period of political and cultural preeminence under the Abbasids to the initial disintegration of their empire and the rise of Turkish military elites, such as the Ghaznavids and the Seljuqs (third/ninth to fifth/eleventh century).[2]

During the first period, poems containing a single theme (*qiṭaʿ*; sing. *qiṭʿa*) were joined to odes containing several themes (*qaṣāʾid*; sing. *qaṣīda*) through a gradual, dialectic process of poets' innovation and audience response. In a first phase, during the first part of the sixth century, amatory verse (*nasīb*) was joined to the camel description (*raḥīl*); in a second phase, which ended with the *Jāhiliyya* (Age of Ignorance), the camel description was connected to boasting (*fakhr*) or praise (*madīḥ*). At first, the themes were linked only by rhyme and meter, but later thematic transitions emerged. The resulting tripartite poem was named, according to its final part, a boasting qasida, panegyric qasida, or message qasida, though other thematic combinations continued to exist (Jacobi, "Origins" 1:24–34).[3] In the Umayyad era, the panegyric qasida (familiar from Ibn Qutayba's description) became the dominant tripartite ode. Its love–journey–panegyric sequence was reinterpreted as a narrative of the poet's mental and physical journey to his addressee (*mamdūḥ*), most evident in the change of the *raḥīl* from a camel description to the poet's travelogue (Jacobi, "Camel-Section" 14–19). This need to link the two time-honored themes of *nasīb* and *madīḥ* would challenge poets' inventiveness again and again. But the tripartite structure remained only one of many options. In terms of function, the Jāhilī qasida had served as a register of social events of Bedouin society and the collective celebration of its moral code. In the Umayyad era, personal loyalties increasingly supplanted tribal ones and more poets became panegyrists.

In the second period, three major changes produced the Abbasid panegyric qasida – in which form it would reach al-Andalus. First, the qasida now celebrated and commemorated the religious and political ideals of the Muslim community. It extolled the ideal Islamic ruler and offered a vision of the Arabo-Islamic past and future. Its themes were "reforged" to fit this new function (Stetkevych, *Abū Tammām* 232–35). In general, urban themes supplanted nomadic elements. Descriptions of spring, gardens and wine, blame of fate, and lament for lost youth very often replaced the traditional *nasīb*. The *raḥīl* was frequently dropped, and in the panegyric proper, battles with unbelievers superseded tribal skirmishes. Description of palaces, parades, and religious festivals supplied new themes of praise. The qasida's central figure became the perfect ruler, God's instrument and recipient of his grace, guarantor of right guidance, and mediator between God and his subjects. But despite all the innovation, a skilled poet could still resurrect and adapt any older theme, even one temporarily eclipsed.

Second, through its quasi-official function, the qasida became a court genre and its author a court poet, dependent on the caliph or another patron. But the poet might still exert a limited moral hold over a patron through modes of address, ranging from praise and felicitation (*tahniʾa*), to admonition (*waʿẓ*) and reprimand (*ʿitāb*), to implied threat of slander. Thus the eloquent poet might balance his weaker position by publicly placing a qasida's recipient under moral pressure – a strategy perfected by Ibn al-Rūmī (d. 283/896), who developed for this purpose a specific dramatic style (Gruendler, "Redemption" 120–61, 355–65, and "Ethics").

Finally, the relationship of poetry to reality was redefined in the "new" (*muḥdath*) style, aptly rendered as mannerism (Heinrichs, "'Manierismus'"; Sperl, *Mannerism* 155–80). As the Abbasid poet worked with existing images, he created effects by combining these, transferring them between themes or overlaying them with rhetorical figures, such as paronomasia (*jinās*) and antithesis (*ṭibāq*). The binary character of the last two figures facilitated expansion into a larger dialectic structure, one fit for contrasting the just government of a divinely instated caliph with the chaotic injustice of fate (Sperl, *Mannerism* 19–27; Badawī, "Rhetoric"; Meisami). The intellectual, and sometimes surreal, nature of his new style first drew the poetic critics' protest, but gradually, with the acclaim of its illustrious representatives, Abū Tammām and al-Buḥturī, it became the panegyric standard. In sum, the Islamization of the qasida's worldview, its role as a nexus between poet and patron, and its new mannerist attire show the genre's consummate adaptation to the caliphal court and its literary circles.

During this second stage of the qasida's development, it took hold in al-Andalus. It may have existed already during the emirate of ʿAbd al-Raḥmān I (r. 138/756–172/788), but the fragmentary state of surviving poetry precludes a study of the genre in that period. Only from the time of the Cordoban caliphate through the Nasrid period do we possess poets' collected works, which yield at least sporadic insight. Among them, the diwans of Ibn Darrāj al-Qasṭallī (d. 421/1030), Ibn Zaydūn (d. 463/1070), Ibn Khafāja (d. 533/1139), Ibn al-Zaqqāq (d. c. 528/1134), and Ibn Sahl al-Isrāʾīlī (d. 648/1251) contain substantial shares of praise qasidas (Schmidt 69 n. 21).

But the Andalusian qasida was joined by two other genres in dispensing *madīḥ*. In the late fourth/tenth century, the *nawriyya* came into fashion. This short panegyric consisted of few verses of varying complexity, describing a flower, and ending with a reference to the addressee attached by an image or figure. Ibn Darrāj al-Qasṭallī and Ṣāʿid al-Baghdādī composed *nawriyyas*, and the regent ʿAbd al-Malik al-Muẓaffar (r. 392/1002–399/1008) even preferred them to long qasidas (Blachère, "Pionnier" 32–34; Blachère "Vie" 107). Al-Ramādī, while in prison, changed the genre to a short bird description, concluding with a plea for forgiveness. The qasida's second rival, the muwashshah, was first reclaimed for classical Arabic *madīḥ* in the mid-twelfth century, by Ibn al-Labbāna (d. 507/1113) in praise of al-Muʿtamid ibn ʿAbbād. It either contained praise alone or connected with another theme, such as a festive occasion or the description of wine, love, or gardens. Ibn Sahl composed more panegyric muwashshahs than qasidas. Ibn Zuhr (d. 595/1198) and Ibn Zamrak (d. 795/1393) also used the genre, the latter stretching a muwashshah in praise of the Nasrid king Muḥammad V to seventy verses.

Besides the rival panegyric genres, the Arabic Andalusian qasida itself became the model for a Hebrew variant. As early as the tenth century, Dunash, a protégé of Ḥasdai Ibn Shaprut, a Jewish courtier of ʿAbd al-Raḥmān, adapted the prosody of the Arabic qasida to his own sacred language. Other poets, such as Ibn Gabirol (d. c. 1058), Ibn Nagrila (d. 1056), Moses Ibn Ezra (d. c. 1138), and Judah Halevi (d. 1141), bestowed on the Hebrew qasida a literary character of its own, substituting overtly Islamic motifs with biblical ones, and using it for the praise and advice of illustrious coreligionaries (Scheindlin, "Hebrew Qasida"; Schippers). With the irony of history, the Andalusian Hebrew qasida even outlived its Andalusian Arabic ancestor, for Judah Abravanel (d. c. 1523) still composed a specimen in Naples in 1503 before switching to Italian vernacular (Scheindlin, "Judah"). At the same time, in the East of the Islamic *umma* and under the tutelage of the Samanids and Ghaznavids, the qasida entered the realm of Persian literature, imparting praise or moral advice.

Subsequently during the sixth/thirteenth century, the Arabic qasida would be yet again transformed and appropriated, this time for pious admonition, praise of the Prophet, and Sufism, the latter kind reaching a high point in al-Andalus with Ibn ʿArabī (d. 638/1240) and al-Shushtarī (d. 668/1269). The

Sufi qasida as well as the other devotional variants existed side by side with the panegyric one, though addressing different audiences.

The qasida as a genre enjoys growing scholarly interest. The fact that it supports diverse, and even mutually exclusive, readings confirms it to be a "classic" of Arabo-Islamic literature. Furthermore, the variety of approaches highlights the modern reader's difficulty in appreciating this product of a normative poetic tradition, one designed to be practiced before highly educated hearers. With increasing familiarity, however, the modern reader may approach an impression of the fulfilled or flouted expectations that thrilled earlier audiences (Jayyusi, "Persistence" 1:2). A broad survey of the history of research of the qasida has been given by Michael Sells. Recent qasida scholarship has advanced in three general directions. First, the various themes, motifs, figures, and styles of the qasida – as opposed to the monothematic *qiṭʿa* – have led to studies of its textual unity with special regard for the way in which these elements contribute to the qasida's overall coherence (Jacobi, *Poetik*; Hamori; Scheindlin, *Form*). Second, the diachronic position of the qasida within the literary tradition has been examined in intertextual studies. These pursue the development of single themes or motifs across poems, so as to delimit a poet's share in a reused motif as well as the audience's pleasure occurring *between* works and not *within* one monolithic work (Montgomery, "Deserted Encampment"; Bauer; Jacobi, "Camel-Section"). Third, the qasida has given rise to broadly synchronic studies that complement a close reading of the poetry with the search for an underlying (ritual, ethical, or ideological) rationale, thus motivating a qasida's play on the tradition by its function (Stetkevych, *Abū Tammām*; Gruendler, "Redemption"; Montgomery, "Dichotomy"; Meisami; Sperl, *Mannerism*; Scheindlin, "Poet"). Many of these approaches identify a situational meaning at the intersection of historical context and poetic text. The present study falls essentially within the third group.

The broad definition of the qasida as a genre formulated by Sperl and Shackle allows for variations in structure, themes (*aghrāḍ*), motifs (*maʿānī*) and style, along with changes in the qasida's status and social function. In order to safeguard the practical use of their dynamic definition they distinguish between "core features" and nonessential "intermediate" and "peripheral features." These core features coincide with those of the Abbasid panegyric qasida, posited as the basis of further developments, and fall into two sets of norms.

The textual norms include a courtly, ornate, and formal register of speech, the Arabic lexicon and motifs, and a prosody employing one of sixteen meters with a single rhyme. The structure is flexible but generally linear and transformational (e.g., ascending from the physical to metaphysical world), containing several themes arranged into two or three parts. Over time, the recurring themes and motifs have themselves become polysemic or symbolic, conveying secondary, situational meanings. The cultural norms include performance in a public setting with a ceremonial or celebratory purpose, the moral code of Islamic statehood and Arabo-Islamic morality, and the social function of praising those who wield God-given power, chastising their adversaries and admonishing their subjects to respect it.

The intermediate and peripheral features accommodate other qasida types that develop out of the core version (such as the religious qasida, the Sufi qasida, and the modern nationalistic qasida), and whose languages include among others Hebrew, Persian, Turkish, Malay, and Swahili (Sperl and Shackle 2:32–61).

The definition accommodates widely diverse traditions, with the Abbasid tradition at its center. Because of its importance to Andalusian developments, the Abbasid qasida deserves a more detailed description. It had sprung up in the East only briefly before it was imported into al-Andalus (ʿAbbās 2:35–36). This qasida did not result from a wholesale discarding of pre-Islamic or Umayyad elements, but rather their selective marshaling as a prestigious tribute to members of the Islamic elite. This function necessarily affected the poets' status and dominated their œuvre. Moreover, poets inscribed their panegyric qasidas not only with the portraits of their addressees but also with their own literary personae, with all their aspirations. The Abbasid panegyric qasida was then at the center of, and conditioned by, a social and literary exchange. Its material value, iconographies, and modus vivendi place this qasida type in a class of its own – in the same way qasidas serving devotional, didactic, or ideological functions warrant consideration in light of their context.

In this study I use "qasida" in the narrow sense of the Abbasid panegyric subtype described. In referring to its parts, I apply Sperl's terms of "strophe" and "antistrophe" (*Mannerism* 19–27). His strophe encompasses all introductory themes, such as remembrance of love or youth, description of spring, wine poetry, and so forth, and their combinations. They involve the personae of the poet as hero and his beloved or fate. The antistrophe revolves around the ruler for (and about) whom the qasida was composed, describing his various, warlike, or peaceful attributes. According to Sperl, the poetic worlds of strophe and antistrophe form an antithesis. I modify his concept in two respects. First, I do not assume between the two parts an antithetical relationship, which is in fact often absent. Second, I isolate the qasida's end as a separate metastrophe. As the Greek prefix *meta-* indicates, this part says something about the qasida itself: it describes and dedicates it and sometimes discusses the patronage relationship it belongs to. The three terms are meant to be helpful headings for the major qasida sections and the themes, protagonists, and attitudes one is likely to encounter there. Not every qasida contains all of them; al-Mutanabbī often skipped the strophe, and only a few poets, such as Ibn al-Rūmī, fully exploited the metastrophe (Gruendler, "Redemption" 93–97). A given qasida might then consist of a strophe and an antistrophe, or of an antistrophe and a metastrophe, or of a metastrophe alone. In two of the Andalusian qasidas discussed below, strophe and metastrophe elements are even merged. (This qasida terminology should not be confused with the strophe and refrain of the muwashshah and zajal.)

At this point the reader may expect a characterization of the Andalusian qasida per se. In other genres, certain features have indeed been characterized as "Andalusian," for example, in nature poetry, where nature is infused with a human soul, or in love poetry, where a refined, almost spiritual feeling is expressed. For qasida poetry, such an undertaking is at best premature, for even the Eastern qasida has been only partially studied, and there is as yet little consensus as to its character. Moreover, characterization of the Andalusian qasida presupposes a theoretically posited standard Eastern qasida, yet such a construct would do injustice to such an inherently fluid genre. Even qasida parodies were already part of the Abbasid development, and when Andalusian poets mocked some Eastern motifs for being out of touch with their own reality, they followed Eastern precedent. Thus Ibn Ḥazm followed Abū Nuwās in mocking the *aṭlāl* motif, and Ibn Quzmān followed Bashshār ibn Burd in ridiculing selfless *ʿudhrī* love (Badawī, "ʿAbbāsid Poetry" 163). At the worst, the quest for an Andalusian qasida might miss the point. While Andalusian poets did develop other regional genres, in the qasida, they were appropriating an Eastern classic in which they needed to establish their repute. At the heights of Andalusian literary activity during the Cordoban caliphate, Western and Eastern qasida poets alike faced the challenge of living up to a poetic tradition that had developed over centuries. Rather than distancing themselves from a literary past, both strove to remain connected with it. In the following sections, I show how three Andalusian voices took part in this dialogue.

IBN DARRĀJ AL-QASṬALLĪ AND THE NEOCLASSICAL QASIDA

The productive life span of Ibn Darrāj al-Qasṭallī (347/958–421/1030) fell into two distinct periods. First he enjoyed sixteen years of lavish patronage by the energetic and powerful regent al-Manṣūr and his son al-Muẓaffar (382/992–399/1008) in Córdoba. As an official court poet and scribe, he accompanied al-Manṣūr on his numerous military campaigns, composing thirty-two odes on victories over Christian rulers and other momentous occasions.[4] In a second period (399/1008–421/1030), the poet lived through the political fragmentation of the realm, the Hammudid usurpation, then died shortly before the collapse of the caliphate. While still in Córdoba, Ibn Darrāj approached in vain the Umayyad caliphs al-Mustaʿīn and al-Murtaḍā and then ʿAlī ibn Ḥammūd in Ceuta in 1014; the following years saw him wandering between the Amirid clients ruling Almería, Valencia, Tortosa, and Jativa,[5] without a single one of them making his stay worthwhile. Finally he found a haven with the Tujibid al-Mundhir of Saragossa and his son Yaḥyā (Viguera). Praises for them fill a third of the poet's diwan[6] and celebrate such remarkable occasions as al-Mundhir's arranging the wedding between the son and daughter of two Christian royal neighbors. Ibn Darrāj concluded his wanderings at the court of the Amirid Mujāhid in Denia (9–70; Sezgin 699–700; Blachère, "Vie" 100–115; ʿAbbās 2:191–213).

The poet stood firmly in the Abbasid neoclassical tradition of Abū Tammām and al-Mutanabbī. Ibn Darrāj thrived on the challenge of recreating the intricate but malleable themes and motifs and strewed his qasidas with bits of knowledge of legendary and early Islamic history, astronomy, grammar, and other disciplines. His remarkable sense for composition is exemplified in his introductory qasida to al-Manṣūr, one skillfully fitted to the occasion. A long strophe is followed and rounded out by a short antistrophe, with a metastrophe omitted. The strophe boasts a variegated list of themes; some pre-Islamic (description of campsite traces or *aṭlāl*, camel journey), others more modern (lament of lost youth, wine song, farewell from his family), with the style ranging from archaic (campsite description) to proselike (lament and farewell scenes) and mannerist (wine song). With great skill Ibn Darrāj articulates across this assortment the progress of the poet's persona from foolishness to sobriety and service. He welcomes, for instance, gray hair (a metonym for old age) as the "dawn of reason." Yet gradually he reveals its pernicious nature as a man's shame and the end of all love, which leads him to admit his loss. This is dramatized as his bidding farewell to the personification of youthful love. The remnants of this departed and abstract beloved become the subject of the *aṭlāl* motif. With the camel journey the addressee al-Manṣūr enters the poem. In its first part, the poet's persona repeatedly urges on exhausted fellow travelers and his own camel mare with the mention of al-Manṣūr's name (no. 3, ll. 26–27, 32–33). At the outset of the journey's second part, the Amirid's call wrenches the poet away from his family. Meanwhile, the poet effaces himself step by step as he approaches al-Manṣūr in the movement of the qasida. Once he reaches him, a mere "brief glance" from the patron's "satisfied eye" fulfills the poet's aspiration. This is followed by hyperbolic praise of al-Manṣūr and his ancestors so extreme as to eclipse the poet's persona, as if al-Manṣūr's mere presence obliterated his poet's self-awareness.

This "vanishing" persona responds to the qasida's occasion as a first offering to al-Manṣūr. It advertises the poet's skills in an impressive array of themes in the strophe. To claim any prior relationship with the addressee, as is often done in a metastrophe, would be presumptuous for Ibn Darrāj. Therefore, the poet uses, in the transition (*takhalluṣ*), a less telling place to adumbrate his loyalty. His farewell scene conflates two older motifs, the departure from the beloved, which Abū Nuwās had already used as transition, and al-Aʿshā's farewell to his daughter.[7] Yet Ibn Darrāj introduces major changes: he parts from a wife, not a lover, is motivated by duty, not thirst of adventure, and, most important, suffers from the separation as much as his family. He sets the scene by introducing his wife and daughter in the third person, emphasizes the impossibility of staying at home, and pleads with his daughter to release him, then names the patron as his destination, completing the transition to the antistrophe (ll. 35–45; cf. Monroe, *Risāla* 8). The compositional necessity of the *takhalluṣ* is brilliantly accomplished, when the poet dramatizes the personal sacrifice his allegiance cost him. In another rendering of this motif, he even leaves behind a wailing baby son (no. 78, ll. 9–11; Jayyusi, *Legacy* 335). The depiction within the qasida, in a self-reflexive way, of its surrounding circumstances is an old panegyric ploy (Gruendler, "Redemption" 82–83, 319–64). But this variation of a migrant panegyrist as a family father is a novelty. Its domestic tone sounds a strange note, for poets usually spoke their feelings in less private themes, such as a fictional lover or former youth. Ibn Darrāj here gave the qasida tradition a twist bespeaking maturity and confidence. (He did not yet know that this poetic motif would become a tragic reality in his later life.)

Our first example showed how confidently Ibn Darrāj mastered the challenge of the qasida tradition in a thematic variation. But he also enjoyed the challenge of contrafaction, emulating qasidas by Abū Nuwās, al-Mutanabbī, as well as Ṣāʿid al-Baghdādī and himself. Such an emulation (*muʿāraḍa*) consisted of composing a new qasida based on the themes, figures, and prosody of an existing one, while vying with it in length and virtuosity. Ibn Darrāj was, in turn, emulated by his contemporary Ghassāniyya (no. 33; Garulo 66–67).

Ibn Darrāj was charged with plagiarism (*intiḥāl*) by his fellow poets. To resolve the dispute, al-Manṣūr tested him by requiring that he improvise a description of a floral arrangement; Ibn Darrāj passed with flying colors, though improvisation was not his forte. Yet, his reward of one hundred dinars and his inclusion in the poets' payroll left him unsatisfied, and he vindicated his name with a second, prepared qasida whose thematic layout differed starkly from the introductory piece. This qasida begins immediately with an antistrophe, thanking al-Manṣūr for reinstating justice, followed by a metastrophe mixed with hyperbolic praise, establishing the poet's innocence and his triumph over his detractors. The metastrophe's central part refutes the plagiarism charge in four well-formulated points. First, Ibn Darrāj recapitulates the events. Then, as a first argument, he lists mock analogies "proving" the plagiarism allegation to be absurd. The poetic analogies of the sea and pearl, spring and rose, the sun and light, musk and fragrance, a weapon and thrust, claim a similar relationship of cause and effect for Ibn Darrāj and his poetry. The second argument is based on ethical grounds and cites the poet's indebtedness to al-Manṣūr as the reason precluding dishonesty with him. He crowns the argument with a causal hyperbole, reducing his poetry to a necessary consequence of the patron's favors and nobility. As a third argument, the poet adduces historical precedent: the famous pre-Islamic poets Imruʾ al-Qays and al-Aʿshā also faced false allegations, and al-Aʿshā, too, challenged his patron to test him – and triumphed like Ibn Darrāj. As his fourth and last argument Ibn Darrāj asserts that his literary prowess makes him dispense with other people's verses, and he positively dares his accusers: "Here I am prepared, waiting for a manifest test" (no. 100, l. 36). He triumphantly concludes with a praise of the present qasida and a renewed declaration of his loyalty. In this qasida, the poet has constructed logical, ethical, historical, and literary motifs from the tradition to serve the defense of his poetic integrity.

On two different occasions, Ibn Darrāj uses extremely diverse qasida structures, adapting old themes and motifs to the new personae, such as the itinerant panegyrist and family father, or plying them in new situations, such as the defense against plagiarism. Our sample falls far short of representing a poet whose diwan is brimming with qasidas on multifarious subjects, who excelled in epistle writing, and was called the Mutanabbī of the West. Sadly though, the lavish and stimulating patronage that made him flourish dwindled already during his lifetime and soon became a thing of the past.

IBN SHUHAYD AL-ANDALUSĪ AND THE AMBIVALENT QASIDA

Although Ibn Shuhayd (382/992–426/1035) scarcely outlived Ibn Darrāj, his birth twenty years later destined him to experience the demise of the caliphate while still a young man at the outset of his literary career. Unlike Ibn Darrāj, he belonged to the Cordoban aristocracy and kept close family ties to the Amirids, specifically with the grandson of the regent al-Manṣūr and governor of Valencia, ʿAbd al-ʿAzīz al-Muʾtamin (r. 412/1021–453/1061). Ibn Shuhayd treated poetry primarily as an inspired art and not as a source of income. In his *Risālat al-tawābiʿ wa l-zawābiʿ* (Treatise of Familiar Spirits and Demons), he defended originality (*iqtirāḥ*), chastised poetic stagnation, and rejected the idea of poetry as something that can be taught (Sezgin 697–98; Monroe, *Risāla* 17–47; Monroe, "Theory and Practice" 138–45; Jayyusi, *Legacy* 335–42). But although Ibn Shuhayd applied his theories in his shorter poems, especially those composed during his long agony, he still left behind a (partial and fragmentary) diwan at least half of whose verses consisted of panegyrics. Why did Ibn Shuhayd avail himself of the qasida, if no material need prompted him? His qasidas themselves often enough hint at their function, through a depiction of the addressee and poet as well as direct statements about the occasion, as is shown in the following three cases.

To his friend and frequent addressee al-Muʾtamin of Valencia, Ibn Shuhayd sent a letter and a qasida with a rich thematic layout. Its strophe takes up half of its verses and contains a description of campsite traces and departing women, a lamentation of lost youth, and a meditative gaze at the stars. In the antistrophe the poet's persona pledges his loyalty to the Amirids, followed by general and ancestral praise, after which a terse metastrophe conveys the poet's gratitude and dedicates the piece.[8] The wide array of descriptive episodes in the strophe resembles that of Ibn Darrāj's introductory qasida. But Ibn Shuhayd's persona does not gradually fade, like that of Ibn Darrāj; it dominates both the antistrophe (in the role of an Amirid supporter) and the metastrophe (in the role of the author). Moreover, Ibn Shuhayd does not treat the different themes as stations for his persona's progress, as does Ibn Darrāj, but as points of departure for flights of mannerist imagery, as, for example, in his treatment of the *aṭlāl* theme:

An abode in which I knew [women's] youthful love
  As a big tree, under whose branches
  I sought the shade of joys . . .
When supple boughs with [radiant] suns
  walked there in swaying gait,
  I gathered their pomegranates.

[dārun ʿahidtu bihā l-ṣibā liya dawḥatan
atafayyaʾu l-faraḥāti min afnānihā . . .
wa-idhā tahādat bi l-shumūsi nawāʿiman
fihā l-ghuṣūnu janaytu min rummānihā]
(no. 68, ll. 3, 5 [Pellat/Dickie])

Lexicalized metaphors, such as sun for face and pomegranate for breast, abound. They are a familiar feature of *muḥdath* poetry, and their true appeal lies in their combination, as shown by Heinrichs ("Metaphors"). Line 5 gives a classic example of overlaying one semantic field (women) with metaphors taken from another (nature). Yet the figurative level has no meaning on its own. This is not so with the tree image in line 3: the noun metaphor "big tree" for the time of youth is an extension of the verb metaphor "seeking a thing's shade" for enjoying its presence. Both are combined with the preceding lexicalized metaphor "branches" for female figures. The resulting verse conveys two independent meanings: on the level of reality, the still-youthful poet is dallying with women; on the figurative level, he sits underneath a tall tree enjoying the shade of its branches. Ensuing verses (5, 7) develop the tree image, but more importantly it recurs in the antistrophe, where Ibn Shuhayd describes himself as a branch of the Amirid tree, the Amirids having taken the place of love and youth. (Ibn al-Zaqqāq will be shown to use the image of the illuminated night in a similar way in both strophe and antistrophe.) Such metaphoric links balance the thematic contrast between these two qasida parts.

The strophe displays Ibn Shuhayd's command of mannerism; the antistrophe in turn throws light on his motives. Briefly hailing the Amirid family as the recipients of his loyalty, Ibn Shuhayd devotes nine verses to extolling this loyalty. Only in the metastrophe does he turn to his addressee al-Muʾtamin, to thank him for an earlier epistle the prince wrote in support of the poet against his Cordoban detractors (ll. 34–35). This acknowledgment of al-Muʾtamin's support heralds the qasida's dedication to him. First, the qasida is offered as a token of gratitude and as the fruit of the poet's intellect. Then, Ibn Shuhayd sets his qasida apart from all other poetry in a twofold distinction; it is free, not enslaved like other poetry, and it is royal, not outlawed like the poetry of brigands (ll. 36–38; Pellat 121). Hence Ibn Shuhayd's qasida acts as a voluntary royal countergift. Only its lavish fabric – and not the short, simple *ikhwāniyya* that Ibn Shuhayd reserved for his closest friends – befitted an aristocrat and governor like al-Muʾtamin. Furthermore it endorsed the high status of its giver, claimed in Ibn Shuhayd's self-portrayal.

When asking, already for the second time, a similar favor from a more difficult patron, the caliph Sulaymān ibn al-Ḥakam al-Mustaʿīn (r. 399/1009 and 403/1013–407/1016), the poet chose a simple, dramatic style.[9] The qasida consisted of a metastrophe in two scenes, the first, a dialogue of the neglected poet with his soul, the second, his imagined departure for another court. In the opening scene, the poet's soul urges him to abandon the caliph for a better patron, while the poet himself still protests allegiance. The (feminine) soul tries to instill reason in the poet – a common action of female fictional personae, such as the beloved, the blamer, and the neighbor. But their usual place is the strophe, where they offset with rational argument the passionate behavior of the poet as hero. Ibn Shuhayd transplants this dramatic device to his relationship with the caliph. The soul's practical advice of trading the heedless

Sulaymān for a better patron only gives the poet an opportunity to show his inner struggle between his devotion to the Umayyads and his fear of compromising his nobility (no. 62 [ed. Pellat]/no. 61 [ed. Dickie], ll. 1–8; Monroe, *Risāla* 90). But the poet reserves for himself the option of departure, should the patron fail to retain him. This is dramatized in the second scene, a monologue in which the poet visualizes his celebrated arrival at another court – probably the Berber Hammudid rulers of Málaga – whose rulers are "observing the due of high exploits better than previous nations [sc. the Umayyads, v. 13]." Both scenes, the poet's despair with the caliph and his juxtaposition with a better patron, denigrate Sulaymān by showing his deviation from the qasida's ideal patron. By flouting expectations of positive depiction, inherent to the genre, this "counterqasida" delivers a sophisticated reprimand.

No response of Sulaymān al-Mustaʿīn is recorded and soon afterward the Hammudids under ʿAlī ibn Ḥammūd al-Idrīsī (r. 407/1016–408/1018) unseated the Umayyad caliphs – as if Ibn Shuhayd had foreseen history. But the poet erred regarding his own fate: a prison sentence awaited him, allegedly due to his licentious verse. From prison he addressed to a member of the Ḥammūd family a qasida that contained a remarkable defense of poetic freedom (no. 15 [ed. Pellat]/no. 18 [ed. Dickie]).[10] Like the previous example, it is a metastrophe with dramatic scenes, blended with elements from the strophe and antistrophe. A first movement leads from the poet's lament of his state to a defense of his poetry and a description of his sadness. The poet begins the qasida referring to himself in the third person, but when defending his poetry, he switches to the first (ll. 3–9; Monroe, *Risāla* 67).[11] He gives licentious poetry, the reason for his confinement, a triple defense: as an invented, not real, indecency – an old excuse – as a creative necessity (Pellat 122–23), because a poet's word should not be confined to his actions, and as an emotional relief. The subsequent themes leave rational argument for emotional persuasion, depicting the poet as suffering from his jilted loyalty. They culminate in a scene in which Ibn Shuhayd addresses a dove (a frequent motif for the projection of inner grief). Again, an element of the strophe, commonly used with the poet's fictional persona, is readapted to render Ibn Shuhayd's actual sadness, caused by his patron. The dove's response reflects and amplifies the poet's sufferings, and even the inanimate wall and doors of his prison cell come alive with compassion. At the climax of their collective lamentation, the theme changes abruptly to the praise of the caliph's fate-defying omnipotence and his ambivalent powers, as a cloud dispensing both rain and thunder. In a final, sketched dialogue with a female persona, the poet admits the impact of these very powers on himself. The qasida's crescendo of dramatic scenes delivers rationalized and emotional pleas for release. Ibn Shuhayd quotes it in his *Risāla,* and has it move the poetic jinni of Abū

Nuwās to tears (Monroe, *Risāla* 67), but from the poem's historical addressee, whose Arabic was poor, no answer is recorded and the poet may have lingered in prison (Dickie 265–66).

Ibn Darrāj had mastered diverse occasions by adapting traditional and modern themes and motives; Ibn Shuhayd instead altered his styles, choosing a manneristic style for a qasida conveyed as a countergift and a dramatic style for qasidas delivering a reprimand or a plea. In the latter style, he moved dialogue scenes from the strophe to the metastrophe for dramatic effect. Both poets deployed their greatest ingenuity in fighting their own causes, the former poetic originality, the latter poetic freedom. But only Ibn Shuhayd insisted that his qasida reflect the royal nature of both author and recipient.

IBN AL-ZAQQĀQ AL-BALANSĪ AND THE MATURE QASIDA

Under the Taifa kings and even more so under the Almoravids, literary patronage waned and the status of poets fell beneath that of other professions. The Abbadids in Seville, the Aftasids in Badajoz, the Banū Ṣumādiḥ in Almería, and the Banū Mujāhid in Denia continued to patronize literature, but only the Abbadids hosted and sponsored poets in an official way. The Aftasid and Amirid rulers alienated poets by criticizing them publicly. Other princes neglected poetry in favor of scientific, religious, or linguistic study. As a result, poets without positions as scribes or courtiers found themselves hard-pressed for survival; some became wandering beggars, and others gave up panegyrics (ʿAbbās 3:71–92).

But a different kind of panegyrist survived in Valencia, in the person of Ibn al-Zaqqāq. Early settled by Arabs, with a rooted aristocracy, Valencia had risen to become a provincial capital during the Taifa period. With its Almoravid governors caught up in campaigns at the Upper Frontier, the Valencian elite assumed the city's administration and patronage. The judiciary and lower civic positions circulated among three families, among two of which Ibn al-Zaqqāq found patrons (nos. 1, 5, 6; Guichard, "Social History" 701; Guichard, *Musulmans* 2:291–99). Other identifiable addressees were a governor (no. 17) – whom he later lampooned (no. 142) – a family of Almoravid dignitaries (nos. 2, 7, 52), probably the supreme judge of the East (no. 28), and perhaps the Almoravid ruler ʿAlī ibn Yūsuf himself (no. 111).

Valencia's rich intellectual life had attracted among others the prolific philologist Ibn al-Sīd al-Baṭalyawsī (d. 521/1127), who became Ibn al-Zaqqāq's teacher. The presence of a thoroughly Arabized and Islamized urban aristocracy explains why Ibn al-Zaqqāq – like his maternal uncle Ibn Khafāja (d. 533/1139) – never left his homeland to pursue knowledge or patronage (17–24). Ibn Khafāja's ample panegyric activity in the Almoravid period also deserves attention; though without an official position, he availed himself of *madīḥ* for personal benefits (Guichard, *Musulmans* 1:84, 94). The local elite appreciated the classical Arabic poetry of these two poets and later al-Ruṣāfī (d. 572/1177). For the same reason no famous muwashshah poet arose in the city during the Hispano-Maghribi regimes, despite the great popularity of music and song. Ibn al-Zaqqāq's financial situation remains uncertain; his frequent belittling of material values may point to his concern about them, but despite that he was rather choosy with his addressees, as his relatively few panegyric qasidas (11 of 150 poems) show (27–45).[12]

One of his patrons was Abū Ḥafṣ ʿUmar (d. 557/1161–62), the son and deputy of judge Abū l-Ḥasan Muḥammad ibn Wājib (r. c. 507/1118–519/1125) (Guichard, *Musulmans* 2:297, doc. 60). The qasida dedicated to him resembles in its proportions the first example by Ibn Shuhayd, with a strophe of twenty-six verses slightly longer than the antistrophe and metastrophe combined. It groups traditional motifs around the poet as hero. The departure of beloved women occasions his grief; he accepts this as his lot, but also as befitting his past, which he then recalls by boasting of former conquests. Awakened to his present solitude, he checks his grief and meditates on the treachery of time and people – in contrast to his own constancy, frugality, and high aspirations. In a reprise of the initial departure motif he displays aloofness to everyone but his addressee, whom he now introduces. Abū Ḥafṣ's praise is duly fulfilled in a brief antistrophe, after which the poet returns to his own values and virtues in a longer metastrophe. The qasida distinguishes itself from previous examples by the poet's dominating persona and the merging of mannerist and dramatic styles.

To take up the latter point first, the strophe's numerous metaphors all amplify inner feelings or experiences of the poet's persona. They derive from three semantic fields: water, weaponry, and the contrast of light and darkness. Water, for instance, as an image for the night, engulfs the departing beloved, real water appears in the tears and the rain that bring no relief to the abandoned lover (no. 5, ll. 3–4, 11). The second semantic field derives from weaponry. The poet prefers real lances to the lover's piercing glance. The women's glances peer out from under brows compared to a legendary bow that a pre-Islamic tribal chief named Ḥājib once pledged for a high sum to a Sassanian king (ll. 9–10, 13–14). The third semantic field, the contrast of light and darkness, appears in a reference to a gloomy night as an image for deep sorrow. In another passage, that night's darkness cloaks the lover on his way to the women, and, in an inverted comparison, its stars pale before their shining décolletages (ll. 16–17). The hyperbole of the illuminated night and its eclipsed stars recurs in the antistrophe as an attribute of both addressee and qasida (ll. 27, 37). While the night equals sorrow, the lightning brings solace to the sleepless lovesick poet (ll. 5, 7). The strophe's metaphors do not comprise an independent layer of meaning, as was the case in Ibn Shuhayd's first example; rather, they connect phenomena from the outer world to the poet's inner self, in an amplification of his feelings. Hence the images perform a dramatic function, similar to that of the light–darkness contrast and the humanized night in Ibn Khafāja's poetry (al-Nowaihi 154–58).

Let us return to the first point of contrast between this qasida and the previous examples: the poet's self-portrayal. Wearied from his experiences in the strophe, the qasida's protagonist collects himself in the transition (*takhalluṣ*). But instead of prefacing the praise with the expected account of hardship and suffering, the poet extols his independent virtue. He keeps his faith to love and high aspirations and relies solely on himself and his sword, rejecting any favors. His praise is not servile but voluntary, though imperative (*wājib*), punning with the addressee's patronym.

The dusty earth has not born anything nobler
  Than a man who aims with noble acts
  At the unattained marks of high achievements . . .
Nor has a reed on fingertips been asked
  For anything more vital [*wājib*]
  Than decorating the memory of Ibn Wājib!

[fa-lam taḥmili l-ghabrā'u anjaba min fatan
ramā ghubra aʿlāmi l-ʿulā bi l-najā'ibi . . .
wa-lā ntudibat fawqa l-banāni yarāʿatun
li-awjaba min taḥsīni dhikri bni Wājibi] (no. 5, ll. 24, 26)

The ensuing praise is brief and limited to the essential virtues of the Banū Wājib as a group: erudition, generosity, high civic ranking in the Almoravid state, and the righting of time's wrongs, specific to their holding of the judgeship. Abū Ḥafṣ is named only at the openings of antistrophe and metastrophe and referred to as administering judicial decisions (*aḥkām*). The metastrophe in which the poet speaks about himself is more elaborate. It begins with a dedication extolling in many images the verses' beauty and power. The poet's pride in his work makes him restrict it to people with proper esteem for it.

Too honored are they [sc. my verses] for their shielded reputation
To be profaned by the rudeness of an aloof sovereign
  Or by the scowl of a doorkeeper.

[mukarramatun ʿan an yudhāla maṣūnuhā
bi-ghilẓati maḥjūbin wa-ʿabsati ḥājibi] (l. 40)

Then, resuming the ideas of the transition, the author constructs a poetic persona that observes only ethical motives (ll. 41–45). The poet's frugality concedes material favors no power over him. He honors reward as a gesture irrespective of its quantity (l. 43), while he likens himself in his moral aspirations to his addressees (l. 34). Truthfulness is to him a prerequisite, but one easy to observe with the present addressee's family; their record not only spares poetry exaggeration but ennobles it (ll. 46–47). This last pair of verses recaptures the earlier dedication (ll. 36–40), in which the poet had described his verses as "brides raised from reason," "well-built," and "clear." He makes no claim but that of eloquent diction and expects nothing in return but the respect the qasida itself conveyed. What is more, the worthy content enhances its poetic form. In sum, the poet draws from the classical tradition a scintillating array of images, bringing to life a poetic persona with a strong sense of self as an artist and member of the elite, foregrounding the ethical side of panegyrics.

Ibn al-Zaqqāq thus secured for the panegyric qasida a respected home in his native Valencia, while panegyric poetry disappeared elsewhere from rulers' payrolls. Poetically, he merged classical imagery with a dramatization of the poet's persona in a novel way, not unlike the style of his relative Ibn Khafāja. Both poets took new paths in creating a mature qasida style, deservedly singled out as "Levant lyricism" by García Gómez (11–13) and the "Valencian school of poetry" by Dayrānī (Ibn al-Zaqqāq 24).

CONCLUSION

The multifarious choices and challenges of the Andalusian panegyric qasida tradition have been demonstrated, albeit not exhaustively. Poets adapted old themes and motifs to new situations, chose between, or merged, descriptive and dramatic styles. The antistrophe, or praise proper, being the official part, poets reserved their ingenuity for the remaining sections of the poem, strophe and metastrophe, offering more freedom and less risk of offense. Yet, however inventive, the aesthetic experience their qasidas provided was located in the derivation from a known pattern (Jauss 342–43). Moreover, the qasida's reflexive nature, that is, its depicting *within* its text of the *outer* situation of its delivery, allowed poets to portray themselves in a variety of roles, whether as supplicants, refugees, courtiers, professional artists, or aristocrats, claiming either dependence from a patron or autonomy. As a result, the declared function of a qasida could be a plea, counsel, service, or reprimand directed to a superior, or a homage to a friend. In sum, while the qasida's textual and intertextual dimensions ensured its continued prestige among the elite, its situational pliancy made it an efficacious tool of formal communication with this audience. Receiving and responding to a qasida was a mark of social grace Arab and non-Arab leaders would cultivate alike, which contributed to making it in the West as enduring a literary genre as in the East.

NOTES

1. Jayyusi, *Legacy;* Sperl and Shackle. See the latter for a translated Arabic Andalusian qasida with remarks on its syntax (vol. 2, no. 9; vol. 1, 12, 16) and two translated and discussed Hebrew qasidas (vol. 2, nos. 13, 14; vol. 1, 123–24, 127–28).
2. On periodization, see also Gregor Schoeler, "Ein Wendepunkt in der Geschichte der arabischen Literatur," *Saeculum* 35 (1984): 293–305; and Wolfhart Heinrichs, "Literary Theory: The Problem of Its Efficiency," *Arabic Poetry: Theory and Development*, ed. G. E. von Grunebaum (Wiesbaden, 1973), 24–26.
3. For another view, see Suzanne Pinckney Stetkevych, *The Mute Immortals Speak: Pre-Islamic Poetry and the Poetics of Ritual* (Ithaca, 1993), and her "Structuralist Interpretations of Pre-Islamic Poetry: Critique and New Directions," *Journal of Near Eastern Studies* 43 (1983): 85–107.
4. They include delegations (nos. 107, 112, 117) and battles (nos. 4, 18, 111, 126), especially Santiago de Compostela (nos. 102, 120, 128) under al-Manṣūr, and raids against the caliphate (nos. 7, 8, 122), as well as concerns of the poet (nos. 5, 14, 23, 24) under al-Muẓaffar. La Chica Garrido has drawn from this an iconology of al-Manṣūr.
5. For his poems dedicated to them, see no. 33 (Khayrān of Almería), nos. 35 and 155 (the brothers Mubārak and Muẓaffar of Valencia), no. 36 (Labīb of Tortosa), and no. 34 (al-Fatḥ ibn Aflaḥ of Jativa).
6. For his poems dedicated to them, see nos. 43 and 44; see also nos. 39, 41, 45, 46, 54 (al-Mundhir), and nos. 50 and 132 (Yaḥyā).
7. See Abū Nuwās, *Dīwān,* ed. Iliyā al-Ḥāwī, 2 vols. (Beirut, 1983–87), vol. 1, no. 422, ll. 10–14; and al-Aʿshā, *Dīwān,* ed. Muḥammad Ḥusayn (Cairo, 1950), no. 4, ll. 50–59.
8. The paraphrase follows Pellat's verse order after al-Thaʿālibī (19–24, 28–33). Dickie advances l. 21 before ll. 29–33. Al-Muʾtamin also received nos. 8, 31, and 63 (ed. Pellat)/nos. 10, 32, and 69 (ed. Dickie), the last boasting seventy-nine verses.
9. *Dīwān* no. 26 (ed. Pellat)/no. 30 (ed. Dickie). This caliph also received no. 45 (ed. Pellat)/nos. 38 and 46 (ed. Dickie).
10. This may have been ʿAlī, his successor al-Qāsim (r. 408/1018–412/1021 and 413/1022–414/1023), or Yaḥyā (r. 412/1021–413/1022 and 416/1025–418/1027) before he became caliph; see *Dīwān* (ed. Dickie), 30–31. The latter subsequently received nos. 21, 41, 42, 44, and 57 (ed. Pellat) /nos. 24, 43, 44, 49, and 63 (ed. Dickie).

11. The translation of ll. 3, 4, and 8 follows Pellat's edition.
12. This includes nos. 37 and 101 dedicated to an identifiable recipient and corrects the number given by ʿAfīfa Dayrānī (Ibn al-Zaqqāq 39).

BIBLIOGRAPHY

ʿAbbās, Iḥsān. *Tāʾrīkh al-adab al-andalusī.* 3 vols. Beirut, 1960–67.

Badawī, M. M. "ʿAbbāsid Poetry and Its Antecedents." *The Cambridge History of Arabic Literature: ʿAbbasid Belles-Lettres.* Ed. Julia Ashtiany et al. Cambridge, 1990. 146–66.

"The Function of Rhetoric: Abū Tammām's Ode on Amorium." *Journal of Arabic Literature* 9 (1978): 43–56.

Bauer, Thomas. *Altarabische Dichtkunst: Eine Untersuchung ihrer Struktur und Entwicklung am Beispiel der Onagerepisode.* 2 vols. Wiesbaden, 1992.

Blachère, Régis. "Un pionnier de la culture arabe orientale en Espagne au Xe siècle, Ṣāʿid de Baġdād." *Hesperis* 10 (1930): 15–36.

"La vie et l'œuvre du poète-épistolier andalou Ibn Darrāǧ al-Ḳasṭallī." *Hesperis* 17 (1933): 99–121.

"Le vizir-poète Ibn Zumruk et son œuvre." *Annales: Institut d'Etudes Orientales* 2 (1936): 291–312.

Dickie, James. "Ibn Shuhayd: A Biographical and Critical Study." *Al-Andalus* 29 (1964): 243–310.

García Gómez, Emilio. *Ibn al-Zaqqāq: Poesías.* Madrid, 1956.

Garulo, Teresa. *Dīwān de las poetisas de al-Andalus.* Madrid, 1986.

Gruendler, Beatrice. "Ibn al-Rūmī's Ethics of Patronage." *Harvard Middle Eastern and Islamic Review* 3 (1996): 104–60.

"The Patron's Redemption: The Praise Poetry of Ibn al-Rūmī Dedicated to ʿUbaydallāh b. ʿAbdallāh b. Ṭāhir." Diss., Harvard University, 1995.

Guichard, Pierre. *Les musulmans de Valence et la Reconquête (XIe–XIIIe siècles).* 2 vols. Damascus, 1990–91.

"The Social History of Muslim Spain from the Conquest to the End of the Almohad Régime (Early 2nd/8th–Early 7/13th Centuries)." Jayyusi, *Legacy* 679–708.

Hamori, Andras. *The Composition of Mutanabbī's Panegyrics to Sayf al-Dawla.* Leiden, 1992.

Heinrichs, Wolfhart. "'Manierismus' in der arabischen Literatur." *Islamwissenschaftliche Abhandlungen Fritz Meier zum sechzigsten Geburtstag.* Ed. R. Gramlich. Wiesbaden, 1974. 118–28.

"Paired Metaphors in *Muḥdath* Poetry." *Occasional Papers of the School of Abbāsid Studies* 1 (1986): 1–22.

Ibn Darrāj al-Qasṭallī. *Dīwān.* Ed. Maḥmūd ʿA. Makkī. Damascus, 1961. Rpt. 1968.

Ibn Shuhayd al-Andalusī. *Dīwān*. Ed. Charles Pellat. Beirut, 1963.
Dīwān. Ed. Yaʿqūb Zakī (James Dickie). Cairo, 1969.
Ibn al-Zaqqāq al-Balansī. *Dīwān*. Ed. ʿAfīfa M. Dayrānī. Beirut, 1964.
Jacobi, Renate. "The Camel-Section of the Panegyrical Ode." *Journal of Arabic Literature* 13 (1982): 1–22.
"The Origins of the Qasida Form." Sperl and Shackle 1:21–34.
Studien zur Poetik der altarabischen Qaṣide. Wiesbaden, 1971.
Jauss, H. Robert. "Der Leser als Instanz einer neuen Geschichte der Literatur." *Poetica* 7 (1975): 325–44.
Jayyusi, Salma Khadra. "The Persistence of the Qasida Form." Sperl and Shackle 1:1–23.
Jayyusi, Salma Khadra, ed. *The Legacy of Muslim Spain*. Leiden, 1992.
Khāliṣ, Ṣalāḥ. *La vie littéraire à Séville au XIe siècle*. Algiers, 1966.
Kratchkovsky, Ignatius. "Une anthologie magribine inconnue à Leningrad." *Al-Andalus* 2 (1934): 197–205.
La Chica Garrido, Margarita. *Almanzor en los poemas de Ibn Darrāŷ*. Saragossa, 1979.
Massignon, Louis. "Investigaciones sobre Shushtarī: Poeta andaluz enterrado en Damieta." *Al-Andalus* 14 (1949): 29–57.
Meisami, Julie. "Uses of the Qaṣīda: Thematic and Structural Patterns in a Poem of Bashshār." *Journal of Arabic Literature* 16 (1985): 40–60.
Monroe, James T. *Hispano-Arabic Poetry*. Berkeley, 1974.
"Hispano-Arabic Poetry during the Caliphate of Córdoba: Theory and Practice." *Arabic Poetry, Theory and Development: Third Giorgio Levi Della Vida Biennal Conference*. Ed. G. E. von Grunebaum. Wiesbaden, 1972. 125–54.
Risālat al-tawābiʿ wa l-zawābiʿ: The Treatise of Familiar Spirits and Demons by Abū ʿĀmir ibn Shuhaid al-Ashjaʿī al-Andalusī. Introduction, trans., and notes. Berkeley, 1971.
Montgomery, James E. "The Deserted Encampment in Ancient Arabic Poetry: A Nexus of Topical Comparisons." *Journal of Semitic Studies* 40 (1995): 283–316.
"Dichotomy in Jāhilī Poetry." *Journal of Arabic Literature* 17 (1986): 1–20.
al-Nowaihi, Magda M. *The Poetry of Ibn Khafāja: A Literary Analysis*. Leiden, 1993.
Pellat, Charles. *Ibn Shuhayd ḥayātuhū wa-āthāruhū*. Amman, 1965.
Pérès, Henri. *La poésie andalouse en arabe classique au XI siècle*. Paris, 1937.
Scheindlin, Raymond P. *Form and Structure in the Poetry of al-Muʿtamid ibn ʿAbbād*. Leiden, 1974.
"The Hebrew Qasida in Spain." Sperl and Shackle 1:121–35.
"Judah Abravanel to His Son." *Judaism* 41 (1992): 190–99.
"Poet and Patron: Ibn Gabirol's Poem of the Palace and Its Gardens." *Prooftexts* 16 (1996): 31–47.
Schippers, Arie. *Arabic Tradition and Hebrew Innovation*. 2nd edn. Amsterdam, 1988.
Schmidt, Werner. "Die arabische Dichtung in Spanien." *Grundriss der arabischen Philologie*. Vol. 2, *Literaturwissenschaft*. Ed. H. Gätje. Wiesbaden, 1987. 64–77.
Sells, Michael. "The Qaṣīda and the West: Self-Reflective Stereotype and Critical Encounter." *Al-ʿArabiyya* 20 (1987): 305–57.

Sezgin, Fuat. *Geschichte des arabischen Schrifttums.* Vol. 2, *Poesie bis ca. 430H.* Leiden, 1975.

Sperl, Stefan. "Islamic Kingship and Panegyric Poetry in the Early 9th Century." *Journal of Arabic Literature* 8 (1977): 20–35.

Mannerism in Arabic Poetry: A Structural Analysis of Selected Texts. Cambridge, 1989.

Sperl, Stefan, and Christopher Shackle, eds. *Qasida Poetry in Islamic Asia and Africa.* 2 vols. Leiden, 1996.

Stetkevych, Suzanne Pinckney. "Abbasid Panegyric and the Poetics of Political Allegiance: Two Poems of al-Mutanabbī on Kāfūr." Sperl and Shackle 1:35–63.

Abū Tammām and the Poetics of the ʿAbbāsid Age. Leiden, 1991.

"The Qaṣīdah and the Poetics of Ceremony: Three ʿĪd Panegyrics to the Cordoban Caliphate." *Languages of Power in Islamic Spain.* Ed. Ross Brann. Bethesda, 1997. 1–48.

Viguera, María J. "La corte Tuŷībīde Zaragoza en el Dīwān de Ibn Darraŷ." *Actas del IV Coloquio Hispano-Tunecino.* Madrid, 1983. 243–51.

7 Aljafería, Saragossa, intersecting arches in courtyard

THE ALJAFERÍA IN SARAGOSSA AND TAIFA SPACES

Cynthia Robinson

Beginning with the *fitna* (civil war) (c. 1010), early Taifa literary and visual culture directly engage the Cordoban court, through either emulation or manipulation of topoi. Surviving palatial spaces date largely to a second period, however, which begins around 1040. These later Taifa spaces can be divided into two categories: settings for official events that affirmed the ruling dynasty through traditional displays of riches and "marvelous things," and spaces that served as the backdrops against which sovereign and *nudamā*ʾ (drinking companions) indulged in the arcane excesses of the royal *majlis* (chamber). No complete official spaces survive, but the *majlis* is represented in the central zone of the Aljafería at Saragossa.

In accounts of official and private palatial spaces, two distinct visual languages might be seen as paralleling the two Taifa approaches to space. In a description of a complex of pavilions and rooms constructed by al-Maʾmūn of Toledo, Ibn Jabir communicates the orchestrated nature of the celebration in a matter-of-fact tone. The features that most attracted the author's attention were the lavish ornamentation and textiles in salons and pavilions, and their formality and exclusivity. Accounts of "lifelike" ornament and opulent use of rare and luxurious materials – carefully listed in texts along with their provenance and ostentatiously displayed – are characteristic of the ornamental idiom used to address the conservative audience (*quwwād*, *fuqahā*ʾ, and other upholders of the Maliki school) for which these official spaces were created. Likewise, straightforward prose is adequate to the purposes of recording, enumerating, and thus further securing the value of luxurious furnishings.

The central zone of the Aljafería – including two shallow salons preceded by porticoes that mirror one another across a rectangular garden – is the only surviving example of a space constructed as a backdrop for the more private, intimate *majlis*. Its small size is made even more intimate by the high walls surrounding it: vistas onto the surrounding countryside were not planned. *Majlis* activities were confined to this pair of salons and to the lush garden that separated them. The gazes of participants, thus, were directed toward the forest of densely ornamented, interlacing polylobed arches that wound their way, "like lovers intertwined," toward the roof.

This setting is "described" in a densely metaphorical rhymed prose anecdote. It consists of an introductory paragraph and a poetic composition, often panegyric, which combines themes from *khamriyya*, *wasf*, and *ghazal*, portraying palace and garden as an earthly paradise filled with sensual delights and the prince as diety. Flowers are transformed into their own images in brocade: "[It was] in the time of the [paradise] of his well being, when his stars spread happiness, and the garden had masterfully woven the embroidery of its brocade, and the water had run its serpentine course between green grasses. The pond was filled like a bride revealed to her husband."

Both literary and architectural manifestations of the *majlis* spaces represent closed, cryptic entities. The literature and its densely metaphorical language is accessible only to a small, erudite, informed public, limited largely to the circle of the king and poet-companions. *Majlis* anecdotes, in their structure, are closed literary spaces, beginning with a description of a space then terminated or annihilated by the author's announcement of the arrival of dawn, the breaking of the spell. The architectural manifestation of the *majlis* is also hermetically closed, both from the rest of the palace and from the world outside. Twin salons, garden, and high walls form the limits of this world, yet the multivalent ornamental motifs – largely architectural and vegetal – imply other spaces that, in the imagination of an informed audience, transformed stone, gesso, and paint into paradise on earth.

PART III

ANDALUSIANS

CHAPTER 10

IBN ḤAZM

Eric Ormsby

A powerful member, briefly, of a moribund dynasty, an insider and yet simultaneously an exile, Ibn Ḥazm was a loyal upholder of the waning Umayyad caliphate of Spain, itself in exile from the place of its origins. Indeed, as the caliphate of Córdoba crumbled, Ibn Ḥazm's loyalty intensified; in the chaotic period of savage bickering among the party kings, his fidelity to the extinguished dynasty became a fixed principle, at one with the high status accorded to faithfulness (*wafā'*) throughout his thought. Ibn Ḥazm's allegiance to Umayyad claims was quixotic and stood in inverse proportion to his hopes. Though banished more than once because of his Umayyad sympathies, Ibn Ḥazm viewed his exile in purely transcendent terms. It was, he declared, the out-of-placeness of the man who no longer sets hope in the life of this world that occasioned his estrangement. His unwavering reliance on reason in the face of fanaticism isolated him still further. To an old friend he wrote, in a treatise on the true nature of belief, "this is what attaches us one to the other for we are strangers [*ghurabā'*] among those fanatically opposed to anyone who concedes this world to them so that his belief may be vouchsafed" (*Risālat al-bayān* 3:187).[1]

Arguably the greatest writer al-Andalus produced, Abū Muḥammad ʿAlī ibn Aḥmad ibn Saʿīd ibn Ḥazm occupies a unique position in the literary history of Muslim Spain. The magnitude of his literary output alone, as well as its wide range, sets him apart from most of his compatriots. A mediocre poet in an age and place in which poetry commanded universally high esteem, Ibn Ḥazm was a superlative craftsman of Arabic prose, one of the supreme stylists after al-Jāḥiẓ. Ibn Ḥazm's style, or range of styles, distinguishes him even more radically. In certain works he encompasses and conveys the most delicate and refined nuances of human feeling with an exquisite lyricism; in others he engages, and revels, in harsh and scathing polemic as well as vituperative ad hominem attacks. "The tongue of Ibn Ḥazm and the sword of al-Ḥajjāj ibn Yūsuf are brothers" became proverbial (Ibn Khallikān 3:15). He is a master of the succinct, highly formulaic phrasing of the jurisprudent but he is also adept at long, passionate, cadenced sentences full of powerful feeling. Even more unusually among medieval authors, Ibn Ḥazm often writes with an unmistakable individual voice; his personality seems vividly present in every sentence. This gives him at moments a deceptively contemporaneous accent.

An acute psychologist of the inner life, and in particular of the magical spheres of memory and the lost past, Ibn Ḥazm was an uncompromising adversary in the outer, and public, aspects of his life. In his early masterpiece *Ṭawq al-ḥamāma* (The Dove's Neckring), written when he was around thirty, Ibn Ḥazm offers insights into love and sexual passion that remain startling and persuasive even today.[2] This is, however, the same Ibn Ḥazm who soon became the ferocious polemicist attacking individuals – Ibn Nagrila and al-Bājī, among others – as well as whole groups, the Maliki *fuqahā'* and the Asharite theologians, in particular. Against Ibn Nagrila – otherwise known as Samuel the Nagid (993–1056), one of the greatest medieval Hebrew poets – Ibn Ḥazm uses no fewer than a dozen distinct terms of abuse of which "ignoramus" is perhaps the mildest.[3] This harshness in debate cast a shadow over his memory after his death. His books were burnt and though in the East Abū Ḥāmid al-Ghazālī (d. 505/1111) in his treatise on the divine names praised Ibn Ḥazm, al-Ghazālī's pupil Abū Bakr ibn al-ʿArabī (d. 543/1148), a fellow Andalusian, delivered a detailed critique on a number of points and accused Ibn Ḥazm of outright slander.[4]

Born in Córdoba in 384/994 into a family of wealth and influence, Ibn Ḥazm enjoyed a privileged childhood. His early years are remarkable in numerous respects but particularly with regard to his education, for he was raised and taught exclusively by women. In *Ṭawq al-ḥamāma* Ibn Ḥazm describes his upbringing and says, "I have observed women at first hand and I am acquainted with their secrets to an extent that no one else could claim, for I was raised in their chambers and I grew up among them and knew no one but them." He continues, "They taught me the Qur'an and recited many poems to me and drilled me in calligraphy" (*Ṭawq* 1:166). It is worth noting in this respect that Ibn Ḥazm is unusual among medieval Islamic authors in his sensitivity to women; for example, he takes the minority position in arguing that women feel desire in the exact measure that men do (*Ṭawq* 1:123). Later, too, he argues famously that women have prophetic capability (*Fiṣal* 5:17–19: "nubūwwat al-nisā'").[5] Nevertheless, while his uncommon upbringing is sometimes thought to account for Ibn Ḥazm's extreme sensitivity, it may also partially explain his acerbity. Among women, he writes, he learned about "violent jealousy" (*ghayra shadīda*), which "stamped" his nature, and in observing their intrigues, he came to know suspicion and mistrust.[6] "I have forgotten nothing," he writes dryly, "of what I witnessed among them."

Ibn Ḥazm had the dubious good fortune to grow up in such circumstances just as his entire world was about to capsize forever. The realm of his childhood was sealed off from the circumstances of his adult life and in that life, as in his official careers, he ascended abruptly to unexpected eminence only to be plunged, with equal abruptness, into disgrace, imprisonment, and banishment. Thus, in 403/1013 he fled Córdoba for Jativa after the destruction of his family estate. In 407/1016, upon the overthrow of the caliph Sulaymān, Ibn Ḥazm was imprisoned by Khayrān, governor of Almería, on suspicion of Umayyad sympathies and then banished. A few years later he served as vizier to the caliph of Valencia, ʿAbd al-Raḥmān IV al-Murtaḍā, and fought in the battle of Granada, where he was taken prisoner. In 409/1019 he returned to Córdoba and in 414/1023 became the vizier of the ill-fated ʿAbd al-Raḥmān V al-Mustaẓhir, the last Spanish Umayyad caliph. The twenty-three-year-old Mustaẓhir was an unprepared, somewhat dandified, and ineffectual ruler; he reigned for a mere seven weeks before being betrayed and murdered. Ibn Ḥazm was again imprisoned. The reversals of his official career are captured in a well-known verse by him, which his biographer cites: "The worthy man [*dhū l-faḍl*] is like gold: now you find him flung into the dirt, now you see him, a crown on the head of a king" (al-Maqqarī 2:82). After 415/1024 (or 418/1027 in some accounts), he withdrew completely from public life. Rather unusually, he devoted himself to the career of an independent author unattached to any patron or court. His isolation did not prevent Ibn Ḥazm from becoming embroiled in vehement disputes. At first an adherent of the Maliki *madhhab*, he abandoned this school because of its excessive reliance on *taqlīd*, or unquestioning obedience to authority. He then became a Shafii and wrote a celebrated treatise on theoretical jurisprudence, his *al-Muḥallā* (The Embellished [Book]). Finally, around 418/1027, he adopted the Zahiri school of law, founded in Baghdad by Abū Sulaymān Dāʾūd al-Iṣfahānī (d. 884), which stressed interpretation of the exoteric (*ẓāhir*) meaning of scripture. It was from a Zahirite perspective that Ibn Ḥazm created his greatest theological and legal works. Dāʾūd al-Iṣfahānī had rejected the use of *raʾy* (individual insight) as one of the "roots" of jurisprudence and had sought to reduce the reliance on *qiyās* (analogy). Ibn Ḥazm went further and rejected the use of analogy altogether. He delivered stinging attacks on the Maliki jurists (not sparing even the sacrosanct figure of Mālik ibn Anas himself) that eventually led to his flight to Majorca in 430/1038, where he found followers for his own school of law, the Hazmiyya. There Ibn Ḥazm became part of the brilliant court of Mujāhid, ruler of the Balearics, and in 439/1047, at the court of his son ʿAlī Iqbāl al-Dawla, Ibn Ḥazm engaged in a celebrated debate with the formidable Maliki scholar Abū l-Walīd al-Bājī. Apparently at the contrivance of al-Bājī, Ibn Ḥazm was again banished. He passed his last years in a form of "house arrest," forbidden to teach or to have students, at his family estate in Manta Līsham. Goldziher characterized Ibn Ḥazm in his last years memorably as "the embittered recluse of Niebla, forsaken by the world" (*Gesammelte Schriften* 5:339). He died there on 30 Shaʿbān 456 (16 August 1064).

In general, scholars (apart from Goldziher) have found Ibn Ḥazm appealing, despite his choleric temperament. Lévi-Provençal, for example, considered him "le type achevé de l'Arabe andalou, aristocrate et savant, de la fin de l'époque du califat" (*Civilisation* 139). For García Gómez, he is the "acerbic intellectual globe-trotter" (5). Pérès speaks of his "aristocratic style" and his "modesty" (459–60). It should be noted that Ibn Ḥazm was keenly aware of his own defects of character – anger and pride, in particular. In a remarkable "confession" in his ethical treatise he dwells mercilessly on his own failings and singles out his furious need to be always in the right as especially reprehensible (*Epître* paras. 96–114).

The contradictions of his personality spill over into his work. Ibn Ḥazm is the systematic and erudite author of a comprehensive work on religions and sects – his monumental *Kitāb al-fiṣal fī l-milal wa l-ahwāʾ wa l-niḥal* (Book of Schisms and Sects), begun around 418/1027 when he became a Zahiri – which shows him to have possessed an uncommon familiarity with Hebrew and Christian scriptures as well as with other non-Islamic traditions. A rigorous advocate of reason, he provides a detailed and nuanced exposition and critique of Aristotelian logic in his *Taqrīb li-ḥadd al-manṭiq* (Approach to the Definition of Logic). A man of somewhat shadowy lineage – al-Maqqarī (2:78–79) refers to him regularly as "Persian" in origin[7] – he penned an exhaustive treatise on genealogy, his *Jamharat ansāb al-ʿarab* (Genealogy of the Arabs). Though steeped in traditional Arabic literature from the East, he was nevertheless proudly and consciously Andalusian and argued vigorously for the superiority of his homeland in his *Risāla fī faḍl al-andalus* (Treatise on the Excellence of al-Andalus). According to Abū Rafīʿ al-Faḍl (d. 479/1086), one of his three sons, Ibn Ḥazm left more than four hundred works at his death, of which only some thirty-six survive today (Brockelmann 1:505ff.; supp. 1:692ff.).

No doubt it is part of Ibn Ḥazm's continuing attraction as thinker and as writer that he encompasses so many apparent contradictions. His vehement detachment from the world gives him unusual tenderness in describing and evoking the world. To be sure, this is a world that exists for Ibn Ḥazm more in remembrance than in actuality; we often feel in reading him that it is the pull of the past he is resisting most even as he summons it. At the same time, the "quixotic redresser of theological wrongs," as García Gómez so aptly described him, is always much in evidence. There is something perpetually youthful and freshly outraged in even his harshest tirades. This makes him intriguing to modern readers, as well as dangerous: it is all too easy to read our own contradictions, in what is perhaps anachronistic retrospect, into this monumental figure of Muslim Spain.

REASON AND THE DOUBLE NATURE OF MAN

For Ibn Ḥazm, man is a being possessed of two contradictory natures, a creature of sundered extremes. At one pole resides man's self (*nafs*), driven by passion and the furies of appetite. At the opposite pole stands reason (*ʿaql*), which is guided by justice, and which alone can guide man rightly. The only bridge between the two extremes is formed by spirit (*rūḥ*). This view occurs early in Ibn Ḥazm, in *Ṭawq al-ḥamāma*, and he hews closely to it thereafter. Ibn Ḥazm writes about this with an accent of conviction, which suggests that he was himself well acquainted with the inner struggle that this division, created by God himself, sparks within man. Indeed, Ibn Ḥazm is perhaps the best embodiment of his thesis that man is a radically divided being.

Reason's prime instrument is discernment, the faculty of discrimination (*tamyīz*). Discernment enables us to distinguish between what is good and what is evil in the virtually inextricable tangle that is human existence. In his treatise on the classification of knowledge, Ibn Ḥazm remarks, "God ennobled the sons of Adam and showed them preference over much of what he created, and he distinguished them from the rest of his creation by the faculty of discrimination [*tamyīz*] with which he enabled them to have mastery in the sciences and the practical arts" (*Marātib al-ʿulūm* 4:61). At times Ibn Ḥazm accords to reason a virtually supreme status: "He who follows what sound reason has illumined for him is saved and in bliss whereas he who deviates from [reason] perishes" (*Iḥkām* 1:6).

Existence is best characterized as a "mixture" (*mizāj*), a texture within which good and evil in all their gradations and degrees are subtly interwoven. This notion, already old in Islam by Ibn Ḥazm's time, owes much to early dualistic conceptions of existence; it entered Islamic theology at the hands of the early Mutazilite masters, such as Ibrāhīm ibn Sayyār al-Naẓẓām (d. between 835 and 845) and his brilliant pupil al-Jāḥiẓ (d. 869).[8] Ibn Ḥazm appropriates this notion. Consider, for example, the following small allegory Ibn Ḥazm introduces near the beginning of his masterwork on Zahiri *uṣūl al-fiqh*, the celebrated *al-Iḥkām fī uṣūl al-aḥkām* (Precision in the Precepts of the Law). The topoi are well worn but Ibn Ḥazm makes them unmistakably his own:

> Suppose a man were to be given the choice, in this earthly life of his, between two abodes, one hundred years in an elegant castle which was spacious and provided with orchards and streams, gardens full of trees and blossoming flowers; with servants and retainers in attendance; a place of pervasive peace, manifest possession and abundant affluence. Suppose, however, that on his way toward that castle, he had to walk for a whole day on a road in which there were some rough patches, even if not all were rough. And as he was walking on that day, there were pleasing fields with places of danger interspersed between them, frightening things together with agreeable shades, and also in the intervals, terrors as well as desert places. Suppose too that at the close of this day he arrived at a narrow house, a seat of penury, full of misery and toil and fear and destitution and scarcity, and that he then dwelt there for one hundred years. Suppose, then, that he *chose* this tight-cramped house solely because of the pleasure of a day mixed with the flaws of affliction which he encountered on his way there. Were a man so to choose, would he not be, in the opinion of all who heard report of him, severely impaired in his power of discrimination, quite crippled of intellect, manifestly imbecilic, corrupted of will, a man to be censured, ostracized and upbraided? (1:7)

The allegory appears all too obvious. The elegant castle represents the life of the hereafter and is contrasted with the narrowness of the grave. The grave is a place of cramped oppressiveness and as such, represents an extension of earthly life stripped of all its delights; this is the traditional *barzakh*, the isthmus between worlds where the dead await judgment in squeezing confinement. Elsewhere in the same work Ibn Ḥazm terms the world "a house of affliction" [*dār ibtilāʾ*] (1:8). The sense of the narrowness of human existence, the almost palpable feeling of oppressive stricture, is hardly unique to Ibn Ḥazm. Indeed, his great contemporary, and adversary, the Jewish poet and prince Samuel the Nagid (Ibn Nagrila) expressed it succinctly and memorably in comparing life on earth to "a prison," in which the very sky itself hems man in.[9] Certainly, too, the notion of man as a wayfarer in this world, the medieval *homo viator*, is a well-known topos in Islamic as well as in Western texts. Ibn Ḥazm himself uses the image of the journey elsewhere on several occasions. At the beginning of *Ṭawq al-ḥamāma*, for instance, he writes to his friend, the unnamed addressee of the treatise: "and you came to me yourself, despite the distance of the journey, the remoteness of our houses one from the other, the far-flung location of the place you were visiting, the tedium of the trip itself and the perils of the road" (1:85). But the interest of the allegory lies elsewhere.

Ibn Ḥazm raises the possibility, on the face of it absurd, that a person could choose to remain in the cramped house merely on the basis of his recollection of the mingled pleasures of the journey that led to it. The possibility that a person could choose the cramped quarters of the grave over the vast palace of the afterlife draws Ibn Ḥazm's denunciation. The very vehemence of his denunciation is itself significant, as are the reasons he gives for the possibility. To be sure, Ibn Ḥazm is always vehement in the face of stupidity ("stupidity" is one of his favorite terms of abuse). But the reason he gives for the choice is odd and interesting. The man defective in discernment chooses the "narrow house" because of "the pleasure of a day mingled with the flaws of affliction" [*li-surūr yawm mamzūj bi-shawāʾib al-balāʾ*]. In this account, a person would be stupid to choose the narrow house as a permanent abode on any grounds but most especially on the basis of his memory of the mixed pleasures of the world that he encountered on his way there. It is the mingling of pleasure with affliction that here tempts the man lacking in discernment, and not either unmixed misery or unadulterated bliss. The faculty of discrimination (*tamyīz*), which occupies an important place in Ibn Ḥazm's anthropology – indeed, he considers it equivalent to "logic"[10] – enables us to sort out the waste places from the pleasure gardens in the course of our experience. It is the faculty by which we separate good from bad, the deleterious from the beneficial. Ibn Ḥazm seems to be saying that only a person insensate to the gradations of experience could choose a narrower existence because of the mixture of things that occurs naturally in human life. Yet it is presumably just this enticing mélange, or the remembrance of it, that most fully engages the power of discernment.

What is perhaps most interesting in this text is the tacit allowance Ibn Ḥazm makes for the possibility of such a temptation. It is, we may infer, the nuanced and diverse nature of earthly life, its chiaroscuro alterations, that constitute it as a temptation – a temptation so powerful, in fact, that it can cause even the discerning to prefer it over the promise of limitless bliss. This is a subtle insight; and as such, it is fully characteristic of Ibn Ḥazm. Few writers have had so refined a sense of the varying textures of human experience as Ibn Ḥazm.

EXCURSUS: THE PALACE OF MEMORY

The passage quoted above may be considered in another light and in a manner more personal to its author. It then gains a heightened resonance. Perhaps the soul on its way to the confines of the grave has lost the imagination of splendor and so clings to the paltry and compromised pleasures of the path, instead of to those of the castle at its end. That Ibn Ḥazm himself retained such an imagination, however, seems beyond doubt. It is powerfully displayed in a famous passage in *Ṭawq al-ḥamāma* in which he evokes the memory of his childhood house:

> One who came from Córdoba told me . . . that he had seen our house at Balāṭ Mughīth in the western quarter . . . I remembered my days in that house, my delights. I remembered the months of my youth there, amid full-breasted young girls who excited even the shyest man. I pictured their bodies beneath the dust or in far-off countries and distant regions. The hand of exile had dispersed them; the claws of displacement had ripped them to bits. To my inner eye the extinction of that lofty house was vividly present after I had known it in all its beauty and opulence. I had grown up within its well-arranged routines. I envisaged the vacancy of those inner courtyards once close-packed with occupants! And I fancied that I heard the voice of owls upon it after the bustling commotion of those groups of people among whom I had grown up. Night had followed day for them as they separated and then came together again; but now, day succeeded night for them in soundlessness and estrangement. (1:227–28)

Ibn Ḥazm was around nineteen years old when this destruction took place. He himself witnessed the Berber rampage that leveled much of Córdoba in May 1013. According to some reports, he knew of at least sixty scholars put to the sword during this reign of terror.

In a curious sense, the rhetorical embellishments of this beautiful passage are guarantors of its authenticity, for Ibn Ḥazm here uses all the literary means at his disposal to convey a powerful emotion. Indeed, the passage is in effect a prose rendition of the pre-Islamic convention of lamenting over "the ruins" (*aṭlāl*); this is all the more interesting in that Ibn Ḥazm, at the very beginning of *Ṭawq al-ḥamāma*, rejects all such reliance on, and reference to, the tales of the desert Arabs with the dismissive remark "Leave me be with your tales of the ancient Arabs! Their way is not ours and reports about them are already too plentiful." And he continues proudly: "It is not my manner to wear down anyone's riding beast but my own, nor to deck myself out in borrowed finery!" (1:87). In this passage, however, he not only evokes the pre-Islamic convention but transforms and surpasses it.

The memory of the destroyed house of his childhood prompts Ibn Ḥazm to a renunciation of this world because it makes plain the world's fleetingness. At the same time, the house, resurrected in memory and in language, becomes an image of all that existence, an enlarged existence, can promise; it becomes a prefiguration of that spacious house of the hereafter.

The two poles of self and reason are complemented as well by the twin pulls of time between past and future. The past is the realm of childhood, which Ibn Ḥazm evokes repeatedly in vivid detail, whereas the future is the realm of the world to come. Ibn Ḥazm is an exile of time, ejected forcibly from the privileged and sensuous world of his childhood and not yet eligible for entry into the life to come. His exile is multiple and unfolds in time as well as in physical location.

THE TRUE QUIDDITY OF LOVE

It is perhaps a commonplace to note that Ibn Ḥazm's conception of love is resolutely Platonic. Indeed, he himself, by temperament as well as by inclination, appears, and portrays himself, as the very type of the "Platonic lover." His love feeds on distance and idealization. At the same time, however, we owe to Ibn Ḥazm's pen a passage on the joys of sexual union that is perhaps unsurpassed in all Arabic literature.

Ibn Ḥazm's originality on this topic derives from his willingness to draw on his own personal experience with startling frankness rather than from mere theoretical views on the nature of love. Love, he writes, begins in lighthearted joking but ends in seriousness (*awwaluhu hazl wa-akhīruhu jadd*) (*Ṭawq* 1:90). Its various senses and significations surpass description; its reality can be understood only through experience. In the end, love is somehow beyond the scope of either religion or the sharia, since "hearts are in the hand of God" [*al-qulūb bi-yad allāh*].

The "quiddity" (*māhīya*) of love Ibn Ḥazm explains in quasi-Platonic fashion: It is "the union between the separated parts of selves in this creation in the transcendent source of their natures." Moreover, genuine passionate love is something intrinsic to the self (*shayʾ fī dhāt al-nafs*), not something that affects it merely from without, as in other forms. Ibn Ḥazm distances himself explicitly from the more blatantly Platonic definition of his Zahiri master Dāʾūd al-Iṣfahānī (*Ṭawq* 1:94).

Ibn Ḥazm's definition is Platonic in that it relates to the reunification of previously divided selves, but it also draws on occult and alchemical notions. He lays great emphasis on the concept of a hidden affinity (*munāsaba*) between selves and on magnetic attractions and repulsions. This is reminiscent in part of one notion of love we find transmitted in the work of his Andalusian predecessor (and fellow Cordoban) Ibn ʿAbd Rabbih (d. 328/940). According to the latter, "when the essences of two separate selves strike together by the union of mutual affinity, a flashing spark is emitted from them through which the inner organs are illumined; because of their illumination the vital natures are set in motion and from that there takes shape an entity present to the self and linked with its thoughts, [and this] is named 'love'" (2:167).

Nevertheless, Ibn Ḥazm is no partisan of unrequited love. For him union with the beloved offers the highest and most joyous experience accorded to human beings. The chapter on union (*waṣl*) remains one of the most exquisite in *Ṭawq al-ḥamāma* and is the true culmination of the entire treatise. Physical union is a near-perfect state: "not the sprouting of new leaves on plants when the rain has ended, nor the glistening of blossoms after night-traveling clouds have passed in the time between darkness and dawn, nor the murmur of waters running through a profusion of flowers, nor even the elegance of white palaces encircled by green gardens, is lovelier than union with a beloved" (1:180–81).

THE DIVINE GIVENNESS OF LANGUAGE

In the long debate over the nature and origin of human language, Ibn Ḥazm takes the view that language is divinely established: *al-kalām tawqīf min allāh* (*Iḥkām* 1:28) and opposes the notion that language occurs by "convention" (*iṣṭilāḥ*). God taught Adam the names of all things (Qur'an 2:31). The knowledge of names distinguishes men, angels, and jinn from other creatures (*Taqrīb* 4:94). Whoever fails to understand this cannot understand the nature of God's language, nor the Prophet's, and is enslaved by mere blind obedience (*taqlīd*), which is reprehensible (4:95).

Ibn Ḥazm offers two arguments, one scriptural, as in the above-mentioned verse, and the other a "necessary proof" (*burhān ḍarūrī*). If language emerged by convention and mutual accord among people, he argues, this would presuppose a perfection of intellect and a state of learning that is complete and exhaustive. People would then be in a position to agree on the designations of all objects in existence, and they would know their definitions. We are aware, however, that many years must pass before an infant comes to maturity; it even takes a year for a human being to learn to stand upright. In addition, social life requires communication between its members. But those who advocate the origin of language by convention tacitly assume that some interval occurred before which language did not exist. But if language did arise in this way, there must have been some moment at which it arose; and yet, how would those who agreed on the names for things be able to agree in the absence of a common language? Furthermore, in a kind of linguistic argument from design, Ibn Ḥazm notes that human language is made up of "composite letters" (*ḥurūf mu'allafa*). Such composites, or compounds, however, must be the work of an agent. Every such action, moreover, has a moment in which it commences. Language must then have been created by a creator in a given moment. In any case, man as such cannot exist in its absence. The notion of man is inconceivable without language. Those who argue for the origin of language by convention ignore the fact that language is itself necessary in order to arrive at a mutually comprehensible convention; they pursue, in effect, a *petitio principii*.

In his discussion of language, Ibn Ḥazm's Zahiri convictions are evident. The language God taught Adam in Eden may have been Syriac, Hebrew,

Greek, or Arabic – the evidence is inconclusive (Ibn Ḥazm seems to favor Syriac) – but whatever language it was, it was clear, literal and univocal. In our primal tongue words were still untinged with ambiguity. Words meant precisely what they said (*Iḥkām* 1:30f.). This respect and concern for the exterior meanings of words is connected too with Ibn Ḥazm's sense of divine compassion; to admit the validity of esoteric teachings would restrict God's mercy exclusively to the initiated.

EXCURSUS: IBN ḤAZM AS DON QUIXOTE

García Gómez, Ibn Ḥazm's most sympathetic interpreter, has described him as "quixotic" (5), and it is easy to see why. His passionate and uncompromising temperament wedded to a kind of unappeasable longing for justice and righteousness put him squarely, if *avant la lettre*, in the company of the Knight of the Mournful Countenance. It would seem too that there is some indefinable quality in Ibn Ḥazm's temperament, as perceived through his writings, that resonates particularly for Spanish readers. Perhaps it is a certain "shock of recognition," however anachronistic, that links Ibn Ḥazm with the love for "la verdad de los extremos" so dear to certain Spanish intellectuals, such as Miguel de Unamuno (1864–1936), another *quijotesco* whose phrase this is.[11] Indeed, Ibn Ḥazm could, it seems, have taken Unamuno's motto as his own: "Either renew oneself or die . . . Thought that does not renew itself dies."[12]

The history of this unexpected assimilation goes back to 1841 when Reinhart Dozy first described the unique manuscript of *Ṭawq al-ḥamāma* in his great catalog of the Arabic collections of the University of Leiden. Twenty years later Dozy translated the affecting anecdote of Ibn Ḥazm's love for a slave girl in his monumental *Histoire des musulmans d'Espagne* and was moved by the delicacy of Ibn Ḥazm's sentiments to comment:

> It must be borne in mind that this writer – the chastest, and, we had almost said, the most Christian of Moslem poets – was not an Arab of pure blood. Great-grandson of a Spanish Christian, he had not entirely lost the modes of thought and feeling characteristic of his ancestors. (580)

In 1914 the Russian scholar of Romance languages D. K. Pétrof published the Arabic text of *Ṭawq al-ḥamāma* for the first time; not until 1931 did A. R. Nykl, another Romanist, publish the first English translation. Russian, German, French, and Italian translations followed over the coming years; though García Gómez began publishing separate chapters of his translation in 1934, his complete Spanish translation did not appear until 1952. This version, which almost at once achieved the status of a *Spanish* classic, effects the transformation of Ibn Ḥazm into an author who is indubitably Muslim while also Spanish. Indeed, García Gómez, whose translation came crowned with a magisterial and affectionate prologue by none other than José Ortega y Gasset, presents Ibn Ḥazm explicitly as a Muslim Don Quixote, albeit a "conquered Quixote." For García Gómez, Ibn Ḥazm is a "bitterer and more pessimistic Quixote and yet equally the victim of his dreams" (*Collar* 47). Moreover, he is a "paladin of orthodoxy" and also a "champion of Umayyad legitimacy, forever vanished." Ibn Ḥazm's courage in particular appealed to García Gómez; he cites the ethical treatise where Ibn Ḥazm declares that "the definition of courage is to expend oneself to the point of death in defense of religion, of women, of the mistreated neighbor, of the oppressed who clamors for protection" (*Epître* para. 90).

But for García Gómez the Spanishness of Ibn Ḥazm goes even deeper than Quixotism. It lies in the radical synthesis of disparate and warring elements within the soul, between exquisite sensibility and fierce asperity, between sentiments that are "delicate and ferocious," and he sees this trait as somehow fundamentally Hispanic, exemplified in Góngora and Quevedo, as well as in Cervantes (*Collar* 49). Beyond this, beyond even "Spanish pride" so characteristic of Ibn Ḥazm, García Gómez sees a kind of "Adamic solitude" that is quintessentially Spanish. Ibn Ḥazm represents "one of the purest incarnations of the soul of Muslim Spain." In this curious way Ibn Ḥazm, perhaps alone among authors of Muslim Spain (though Ibn Quzmān might qualify), has entered into the history and the lifeblood of Spanish, as well as Andalusian, literature.

CONCLUSION

If one were to seek a single thread that links Ibn Ḥazm's thought and personality throughout his many works, it might well be the virtue of faithfulness, though fierce honesty would come a close second – both, it may be noted, preeminently quixotic virtues. Despite his many vicissitudes, self-inflicted or not, Ibn Ḥazm remained constant to certain principles and to certain institutions; whether the latter were extinct or not was in a sense immaterial. The theme of fidelity runs through *Ṭawq al-ḥamāma* like a hidden leitmotiv, for loyalty is also a form of love. In that work Ibn Ḥazm writes: "The safekeeping of former loyalties is a positive duty for intelligent men. A nostalgia for what is past – not to forget what is finished and whose span has expired – is the strongest sign of a real fidelity" (1:207). Fidelity, to the sovereign uses of human reason, to love and the empire of the affections, to language given whole and complete by God himself, is the unwavering fixed star in the firmament of his exile.

NOTES

1. Such notions of estrangement were not unique to Ibn Ḥazm. Compare the remark of his later compatriot the philosopher Ibn Bājja (d. c. 533/1139): "These are those whom the Sufis mean in speaking of 'strangers' [*ghurabā'*] because although they are in their native lands and among their companions and neighbors, they are strangers in their views and they journey in their thoughts into other levels which are their true native lands" (11, Spanish trans. 42).
2. Interestingly (and no doubt rightly), in the Library of Congress system *Ṭawq al-ḥamāma* is classified with works by such writers as Georges Bataille, Havelock Ellis, Masters and Johnson, and Kinsey.
3. See *Risāla fī l-radd* 3:43; also, García Gómez 3 n. 7.
4. al-Ghazālī 190; Ibn al-ʿArabī 2:336–37, 350ff., 363ff. Goldziher's judgment is even harsher: "Fanaticism, irreconciliability, offensive recklessness, a mania that attempted to stamp as heresy all rival opinions, these traits, which represent the dominant features of the literary image of our Ibn Hazm, were not conducive to his endeavors in attracting friends or followers from the opposing camps" (*Ẓāhirīs* 156). See also Goldziher's remarks in *Gesammelte Schriften* (5:340). Ibn Khallikān attributes Ibn Ḥazm's troubles to his harshness of tongue (3:15).
5. See the excellent treatment in Turki, "Femmes privilégiées et privilèges féminins dans le système théologique et juridique d'Ibn Ḥazm" (*Théologiens* 101–58).
6. Elsewhere, however, Ibn Ḥazm praises jealousy as a virtue compounded of courage and justice, and he remarks that when jealousy diminishes, so, too, does love (*Epître* paras. 171–72).
7. Brockelmann, however, posits a "Gothic" or "Celto-romanesque" origin for his family (supp. 1:693).
8. See the discussion in van Ess (2:31). Also, my *Theodicy* (223ff).
9. See, e.g., the brief poem translated by Carmi as "The Prison": "The earth is a prison to man all his life./ Therefore I say this truth to the fool: / though you rush about, the sky / surrounds you on all sides. / Try to get out, if you can" (292). Cf. also the little poem its translator titles "Man's Sojourn" in Weinberger: "Man's sojourn in the mother's womb is a life in cramped quarters until the time of exit . . ." (132–33).
10. "Among [human faculties] is the faculty of discrimination [*tamyīz*] which the Ancients called 'logic' [*mantīq*]" (*Iḥkām* 1:6).
11. See "Arabesco pedagógico sobre el juego," *De mi vida* (Madrid, 1979), 87.
12. Ibid.: "O renovarse o morir . . . Pensamiento que no se renueva se muere."

BIBLIOGRAPHY

ʿAbbās, Iḥsān. *Ta'rīkh al-adab al-andalusī.* Beirut, 1972.

Arnaldez, Roger. *Grammaire et théologie chez Ibn Ḥazm de Cordoue: Essai sur la structure et les conditions de la pensée musulmane.* Paris, 1956.

"Ibn Ḥazm." *Encyclopaedia of Islam.* 2nd edn. Leiden, 1954–. 3:790–99.

Asín Palacios, Miguel. *Abenhazam de Córdoba y su historia crítica de las ideas religiosas.* 5 vols. Madrid, 1927–32.

Brockelmann, Carl. *Geschichte der arabischen Litteratur.* 2nd edn. 5 vols. Leiden, 1943–49.

Carmi, Ted. *The Penguin Book of Hebrew Verse.* New York, 1981.

Dozy, Reinhart. *Spanish Islam: A History of the Moslems in Spain.* Trans. Francis Griffin Stokes. London, 1913.

Fletcher, Richard. *Moorish Spain.* London, 1992.

García Gómez, Emilio. "Polémica religiosa entre Ibn Ḥazm e Ibn al-Nagrīla." *Al-Andalus* 4 (1936–39): 1–28.

al-Ghazālī. *al-Maqṣad al-asnā fī sharḥ asmāʾ allāh al-ḥusnā.* Ed. Fadlou Shehadi. Beirut, 1971.

Giffen, Lois A. "Ibn Ḥazm and the *Ṭawq al-ḥamāma.*" *The Legacy of Muslim Spain.* Ed. Salma Khadra Jayyusi. Leiden, 1992. 420–42.

Goldziher, Ignaz. *Gesammelte Schriften.* Ed. Joseph Desomogyi. 6 vols. Hildesheim, 1970.

The Ẓāhirīs: Their Doctrine and History. Ed. and trans. Wolfgang Behn. Leiden, 1971.

Ibn ʿAbd Rabbih. *al-ʿIqd al-farīd.* 9 vols. Beirut, 1987.

Ibn al-ʿArabī. *al-ʿAwāṣim min al-qawāṣim: Arāʾ abī bakr ibn al-ʿarabī al-kalāmiyya.* Ed. ʿAmmār Ṭālibī. 2 vols. Algiers, [1974].

Ibn Bājja. *Tadbīr al-mutawaḥḥid/El régimen del solitario.* Ed. and trans. Miguel Asín Palacios. Madrid, 1946.

Ibn Ḥazm. *Epître morale (Kitāb al-akhlāq wa l-siyar).* Ed. and trans. Nada Tomiche. Beirut, 1961.

al-Fiṣal fī l-milal wa l-ahwāʾ wa l-niḥal. 5 vols. in 3. Beirut, 1975.

al-Iḥkām fī uṣūl al-aḥkām. 2 vols. Ed. Aḥmad Shākir. Cairo, n.d.

Jamharat ansāb al-ʿarab. Ed. Évariste Lévi-Provençal. Cairo, 1948.

Rasāʾil. Ed. Iḥsān ʿAbbās. 4 vols. Beirut, 1980–83.

Marātib al-ʿulūm (*Rasāʾil* 4:61–90).

Risāla fī faḍl al-andalus wa-dhikr rijālihā (*Rasāʾil* 2:171–88).

Risāla fī l-radd ʿalā ibn al-naghrīla al-yahūdī (*Rasāʾil* 3:39–70).

Risālat al-bayān ʿan ḥaqīqat al-īmān (*Rasāʾil* 3:185–203).

al-Taqrīb li-ḥadd al-manṭiq (*Rasāʾil* 4:93–357).

Ṭawq al-ḥamāma fī l-ulfa wa l-ullāf (*Rasāʾil* 1:84–319).

Translations:

Arberry, A. J. *The Ring of the Dove: A Treatise on the Art and Practice of Arab Love.* London, 1953.

García Gómez, Emilio. *El collar de la paloma: Tratado sobre el amor y los amantes de Ibn Ḥazm de Córdoba.* Prologue by José Ortega y Gasset. 2nd edn. Madrid, 1967.

Nykl, A. R. *A Book Containing the Risālah Known as The Dove's Neck-Ring about Love and Lovers.* Paris, 1931.

Ibn Khallikān. *Wafāyāt al-aʿyān wa-anbāʾ abnāʾ al-zamān.* 6 vols. Ed. M. Muḥyī al-Dīn ʿAbd al-Ḥamīd. Cairo, 1367AH.

Lévi-Provençal, Évariste. *La civilisation arabe en Espagne: Vue générale.* Paris, 1948.

Histoire de l'Espagne musulmane. 3 vols. Paris, 1950–53.

al-Maqqarī. *Nafḥ al-ṭīb min ghuṣn al-andalus al-raṭīb.* Ed. Iḥsān ʿAbbās. 8 vols. Beirut, 1968.

Monroe, James T. *Hispano-Arabic Poetry.* Berkeley, 1974.

Ormsby, Eric L. "Ibn Ḥazm." *Dictionary of the Middle Ages.* Ed. Joseph Strayer. New York, 1985. 6:117–18.

Theodicy in Islamic Thought: The Dispute over al-Ghazālī's "Best of All Possible Worlds." Princeton, 1984.

Pérès, Henri. *La poésie andalouse en arabe classique au XI siècle.* Paris, 1953.

Turki, ʿAbd al-Majīd. *Polémique entre Ibn Ḥazm et Bāgī sur les principes de la loi musulmane: Essai sur le littéralisme ẓāhirite et la finalité mālikite.* Algiers, n.d.

Théologiens et juristes de l'Espagne musulmane: Aspects polémiques. Paris, 1982.

Urvoy, Dominique. *Pensers d'al-Andalus: La vie intellectuelle à Cordoue et à Seville au temps des empires berbères (fin XI siècle – début XIII siècle).* Paris, 1990.

van Ess, Josef. *Theologie und Gesellschaft im 2. und 3. Jahrhundert Hidschra.* 6 vols. Berlin, 1990–97.

Watt, W. Montgomery, and Pierre Cachia. *A History of Islamic Spain.* Garden City, 1967.

Weinberger, Leon J. *Jewish Prince in Moslem Spain.* University, Ala., 1973.

CHAPTER 11

MOSES IBN EZRA

Raymond P. Scheindlin

Of all the Arabized poets of the Hebrew Golden Age in al-Andalus, Moses (Abū Hārūn) Ibn Ezra is the one whose poetry most resembles that of an Arabic poet.[1] Yet his literary career was more varied than that of most Arabic poets, reflecting the interests of the Jewish aristocrats of his age. The interplay of Arabo-Islamic and Jewish elements, a fascinating feature of the lives and careers of all the leading Hebrew poets of al-Andalus, is so fully developed in him as to render him a model case of an Andalusian Jewish intellectual.

Ibn Ezra's life is known only in outline (Ibn Ezra, *Selected Poems* xxiii–xxxix; Schirmann 380–420). He was born in Granada, around 1055, to a distinguished family, several of whose members were, like Samuel and Joseph Ibn Nagrila in the preceding generation, in the service of Ḥabbūs and Bādīs of Granada. Moses' elder brother Isaac (Abū Ibrāhīm) seems to have been married to one of the Nagid's daughters. As a young man, Moses studied at the academy of Lucena, training ground for many of al-Andalus's courtier-rabbis. The academy was headed at the time by Rabbi Isaac Ibn Ghiyāth, the premier rabbinic authority of al-Andalus and the premier liturgical poet of his generation. As an adult, Moses lived in Granada, where he held a title of dignity; he enjoyed wealth and tranquillity until 1090, when the Almoravid invasions disrupted the lives of Jewish and Muslim courtiers alike. The family fortune was confiscated and his three brothers fled. Moses, who by this time was married and the father of several children, remained behind. Later, he too fled, apparently under some threat to his life, leaving his family behind.

Ibn Ezra spent the rest of his life in the Christian north, where he died sometime after 1138. The second half of his life was as miserable as his early years had been happy. From the very beginning of his exile, he wrote poems pleading to his brothers for financial help and complaining of their refusal. But his need for material support is only one of the subjects of his many poems of complaint from this period. He complains of being separated from his children and of their coldness to him; of the death of family members and the death of friends; of the hard-heartedness and ignorance of the people among whom he had to live; of being imprisoned; and of having to flee for safety from military zones. Above all, he bewails his loneliness. He describes the Christian north as a place without culture, and its inhabitants, Jews and Christians alike, as crude and stingy. He expresses his yearning for Granada in terms that were traditionally used in speaking of the stateless condition of the Jewish people:

> How long will my feet be sent wandering
> in exile [*galut*], finding no rest?[2]

Thus Ibn Ezra diverts the language of Jewish aspiration for national restoration to his personal longing for al-Andalus, the home of the Judeo-Arabic synthesis. Such interweaving of Arabic and Jewish elements may stand as a model for Ibn Ezra's entire career.

As a young man, Ibn Ezra wrote a book of poems that adumbrates key aspects of his literary career and may serve as a model of the entire Judeo-Arabic literary enterprise. *Sefer haʿanaq* (Book of the Necklace), known in Arabic as *Zahr al-riyāḍ* (Blossom of the Garden; Ibn Ezra, *Diwan* 1:235–404; selections translated in Ibn Ezra, *Selected Poems* 66–92), consists of 573 short Hebrew poems (mostly two to four lines long) by Ibn Ezra himself, in Arabic quantitative meters, forming a miniature encyclopedia of poetic themes that surveys virtually the entire repertoire of Golden Age courtly poetry. Thematically, the book covers on a microscopic scale the ground covered in Arabic by the famous and voluminous poetic anthology by Ibn ʿAbd Rabbih, the *ʿIqd* (Necklace), and the Hebrew title of Ibn Ezra's little work could well have been intended as an allusion to the much larger one. The *ʿAnaq* is also a rhetorical tour de force, for the poems are so constructed that the rhyming words of each poem are homonyms. Plays on homonyms and other kinds of paronomasia (the generic term in Arabic is *tajnīs*) are the backbone of the *badiʿ* style typical of Andalusian Arabic and Hebrew poetry in the Taifa period. The identification of homonyms and the classification of the various kinds of *tajnīs* was a regular theme of books on rhetoric and poetics (including Ibn Ezra's own book, the *Muḥāḍara*, discussed below), and the composition of epigrams based on homonym rhyme was common in both languages.

The book's first theme is panegyric – specifically, praise of the Sevillian Jewish astrologer and courtier Abraham Ibn al-Muhājir, to whom it is dedicated in an elaborate introduction in classical Arabic rhymed prose[3] and in a dedicatory qasida. The great length of the first chapter and its placement immediately after the introduction accurately reflect the relative importance of panegyric in the repertoire of genres cultivated by Hebrew and Arabic poets alike. Panegyric was one of the most important vehicles of social relations among the Jewish elite class, as it was among the Muslim elite; Ibn Ezra wrote many long panegyric qasidas in the course of his career.[4]

The final chapter contains verses in praise of poetry and excellent poets. This theme, less central to the Arabic literary tradition than the others, but often found near the end of panegyric qasidas in both Arabic and Hebrew (Schippers, *Spanish Hebrew Poetry* 302–3; Pagis, *Shirat haḥol* 193–96),[5] enables Ibn Ezra to conclude the book with praise of his own work and to renew the book's dedication. The last chapter, especially the last poem, with its allusion to the book's title, thus serves as a kind of envoi to the entire work.

Between the chapters of panegyric and envoi, the successive chapters illustrate the representative themes of the courtly poetry of the age in a sequence that represents an idealized biography for both Muslim and Jewish literary figures, from youthful pleasure through the experience of loss to resignation and late piety. The literary commonplace that dictated the contents and organization of the *ʿAnaq* was realized in Ibn Ezra's actual life story, as we shall see.

Ibn Ezra's diwan is replete with short poems on all the themes surveyed in the *ʿAnaq*, but it is also notable for its many long poems, especially those of the qasida type. As is the case with most Hebrew poets of the age, his qasidas are addressed to friends and family members, to social equals or potential social equals rather than to potential patrons. Even when his purpose is to ask for financial assistance, as in some of the poems written during his exile, or to complain of an addressee's failure to render him such assistance, the tone is not ordinarily that of a supplicant.

True to the conventions of the form, Ibn Ezra shapes his qasidas out of two parts linked by a transitional verse (*takhalluṣ*). Here is the opening of a qasida of twenty-four verses (Ibn Ezra, *Diwan* 1:90–91):

> The abodes of lovers remain desolate,
>   and their palaces have become like deserts.
> They had been designated feeding grounds for girl-fawns,
>   and had been called a tramping ground for young bucks,
> but today, instead, leopards crouch in them,
>   and in them, lion-cubs roar . . .
> Is it for my friends I am weeping, or is it
>   for the wandering of brothers and the absence of sisters? . . .

This last line sets up the transition, a few verses later, to the poem's second part:

> Or am I lamenting the separation from Solomon,
>   whose friendship is like honey to the mouth? . . .

By beginning this and several other qasidas with the ruined-campsite motif – one that derives from pre-Islamic Arabic poetry and was not common among Andalusi-Arabic poets – Ibn Ezra might appear to be somewhat more conservative than his Andalusi-Arabic contemporaries. Yet, from a Jewish point of view, his frequent use of a nostalgic literary motif so tied to Arabic literary memory and tradition and not deriving from the lived reality of al-Andalus might be judged a stroke of originality against the background of the by now well-established usage of the Hebrew poets. Since most of the poems in which he incorporates it are those in which the panegyric is connected to a lament on his own isolation, it seems that his intention was to use the nostalgia of the ruined-camp motif to establish the tone that would dominate the second part of the qasida.

Thus, in the poem just quoted, Ibn Ezra follows the lament over the desert encampment with a passage on his separation from various friends and relatives before naming the specific person, Solomon, the subject of the panegyric. After the verses of panegyric that follow, the poem concludes with a complaint against Time for separating him from this friend. The two halves of the qasida are thus complementary, and the classical qasida's antithesis between *nasīb* and panegyric has become attenuated, as it has in most of the qasidas of Ibn Ezra (full discussion in Levin, "Habekhi" and *Meʿil* 1:28–33; examples in Schippers, *Spanish Hebrew Poetry* 158–62; Scheindlin, "Hebrew Qasida" 1:124–27).

Another striking feature of the qasida just quoted is the prominent role of the poet's own person in the second part. In panegyrics addressed by an inferior to a superior, especially in hope of payment, the poet naturally effaces himself (though there are, of course, exceptions, as in the case of al-Mutanabbī). But Ibn Ezra ordinarily writes as an equal to equals and tends to feature himself quite prominently in the second part of many of his qasidas, especially those composed during his exile period.

Finally, the density of rhetorical devices in the lines quoted is typical of the style of Andalusi-Arabic poets. The synonymous and antithetical parallelism may be observed in the translation, but the paronomasia so often used to reinforce such parallelisms may not. An example may be cited from another qasida beginning with the ruined-camp motif (Ibn Ezra, *Diwan* 1:99):

meʿonot meʿanoti neʾelamot
veʾoznehem shemoaʿ li ʿarelot

[The encampments are mute and do not answer me;
their ears are covered and do not hear.]

Each of the great Andalusi-Hebrew poets composed, alongside a body of poems of standard type – qasidas, both panegyric and funerary, short poems on themes of pleasure and asceticism, epigrams and riddles – a body of poems in which they created a distinctive literary persona. Many of these poems, though adhering to all the rules of Arabized Hebrew poetics, break through the genre categories of the Arabic literary tradition (Pagis, *Hebrew Poetry* 5–23). Thus, the outstanding feature of the diwan of Samuel the Nagid is the series of poems he composed in connection with his career as the vizier of Bādīs of Granada, describing specific historical events and his complex personal attitudes toward them and his role in public life (examples in Cole 39–47; Constable 84–90). For all the dependence of these poems on Arabic literary traditions, they do not have exact models in Arabic literature; though some may be related in form to the war poems of al-Mutanabbī (Schippers, *Spanish Hebrew Poetry* 227–43; Scheindlin, "Hebrew Qasida" 1:122), they are actually sui generis. Similarly individualistic are the anguished poems in which Ibn Gabirol describes his personal ambitions, frustrations, and rages and the poems written by *Judah Halevi in connection with his pilgrimage to the Land of Israel.

Ibn Ezra, too, wrote poems reflecting biographical events and personal attitudes, but even in these poems, he hewed more closely to the Arabic genre tradition than did the others. Because the drive to shape an individual persona is somewhat less marked in his work than in that of the other poets, his work provides the best model for studying the ways in which Hebrew poets adapted Arabic literary conventions for their own use, as he was, in fact, studied in a now classic book by Dan Pagis (*Shirat haḥol*). Nevertheless, a desire for self-expression is evident in Ibn Ezra's qasidas, even in many of those that formally belong to a regular genre, such as the panegyric quoted above. This tendency is naturally most marked in those qasidas that are not formally addressed to others. Most of these are poems of complaint, dealing with his exile and the problems associated herewith.

An outstanding example is an impressive qasida that begins with forty dense and rhetorically elaborate verses describing wine, wine drinking, and lute playing, leading up to the following *takhalluṣ* (the only complete translation of the entire poem into English in Ibn Ezra, *Selected Poems* 16–22; a few verses in Carmi 329):

> . . . even mourners take joy at the sound of lutes and flutes
> and get relief from sorrow, but not I –
> my brothers dead, friends wandered off.

After this transition follow twenty-two verses lamenting the poet's loneliness and complaining of the treachery of the people around him in his exile. That the poem should take this turn is not unexpected, for the first part, the description of wine and other pleasures, is shot through with intimations of pain. All these motifs of sorrow are standard ones that can be found in many wine poems (for a beautiful example by Ibn Ezra, see Scheindlin, *Wine* 142); but here, the literary conventions are used to prepare the ground for a complaint in the second part, founded less in literary tradition than in autobiography. Though in qasida form, the poem is not addressed to anyone in particular, creating the impression of being pure self-expression. True, Ibn Ezra does not provide the kind of biographical detail that we are avid to know; such detail would not have been in accord with the decorum of medieval Hebrew and Arabic verse. But the intensely personal tone of the second part of the poem makes abundantly clear that the lavish description in the first part was designed not only as a rhetorical tour de force but as preparation for a poem of personal complaint. This is the genre in which Ibn Ezra made his most distinctive literary statement.[6]

Like most of the poets of the Hebrew Golden Age, Ibn Ezra devoted at least as much attention to religious poetry as he did to courtly poetry. Much of this poetry belongs to the ancient tradition of synagogue poetry, and some to the new Andalusian type.

Although the forms of Hebrew liturgical poetry changed gradually throughout its history, its tradition was extremely conservative. In all periods, it retained its collective voice and its standard themes, granting virtually no purchase for the expression of the poet's individuality, which is such an outstanding feature of Andalusi secular poetry and of Jewish writing in the Arabic sphere in general. Traditional liturgical poetry did change somewhat in al-Andalus, abandoning the recondite diction of the older tradition, and to some extent adopting ascetic themes from Arabic *zuhd* poetry as well as philosophical and scientific themes. But while the traditional liturgical poetry was undergoing these modifications, a wholly new kind of liturgical poetry appeared at its side. In a radical break with tradition, this new poetry used Arabic verse types – both monorhymed verse in quantitative meter and muwashshahs – and the neobiblical, Arabic-accented diction of secular poetry. As if to call attention to their innovative character, the new poems were often inserted in parts of the liturgy that had never before been embellished with poetry.[7]

One typically Andalusian type of liturgical poetry takes up and modifies the ancient theme of Israel's exilic condition. Jewish religious writers had for centuries depicted Israel as a woman abandoned by her lover and hoping for his return; this theme was ripe for reworking by Andalusian poets, who were busy writing Hebrew secular love poetry based on Arabic models. They now began to incorporate the themes of secular love poetry into their liturgical poetry, writing erotic *qiṭʿa*s portraying Israel and God as lovers (full discussion of this theme in Scheindlin, *Gazelle* 33–51). Though such poems were designed to be attached to parts of the service dealing with the themes of God's love for Israel and Israel's hope for redemption, they can also be read as freestanding love poems in which the lovers are God and Israel. Ibn Ezra distinguished himself in this genre by adding to its repertoire of themes the ruined-encampment motif, which, as we have seen, he also introduced into the Hebrew qasida. In this quotation, the "lover's camp" is Jerusalem:[8]

Hasten to the lovers' camp
  dispersed by Time, a ruin now;
Once the haunt of love's gazelles,
  Wolves' and lions' lair today . . .

The preoccupation of most of the Hebrew poets of al-Andalus with philosophy also found an outlet in their liturgical poetry, especially because of the central place of the soul in the philosophical speculations of the age. This provided the impetus for the composition of poetic meditations on the nature of man and his relation to God and the universe, as interpreted along Neoplatonic lines. Typically, this theme appears in *reshuyot,* short monorhymed poems in Arabic meters or strophic poems designed to introduce certain prayers in the weekly liturgy; the poems often seem only marginally related to their liturgical context, and are sometimes couched in a tone so personal and intimate that they, like the national love poems illustrated above, can often be read as freestanding poems – as devotional poetry rather than as liturgy. A particularly warm example is a strophic poem by Ibn Ezra (Scheindlin, *Gazelle* 121), the tone of which is so intimate that in the final stanza it is unclear whether the plea for help is that of Israel in exile or of the soul trapped in the body and longing to be restored to the divine realm:

Can God's compassion be exhausted?
Can comfort and support be far off?
Can Gilead's balm afford no healing
Or help to hold upright a stumbling child,
  Who knocks upon Your gates,
  Who pleads to You for aid?

The Jewish intellectual's fascination with philosophy led Ibn Ezra to preface his book the *Ḥadīqa* (discussed below) with a lengthy cosmological poem that has some points of resemblance with an Arabic poem by Ibn Ḥazm.[9] But the artistic culmination of his philosophical poetry is his magnificent meditation "I roused my sleeping mind,"[10] dealing with the contrast between the external and the internal senses. As long as our bodies are awake to sensual pleasures, our minds are asleep; but when we put our bodies to sleep and waken our minds, we become aware that we possess a set of spiritual tools, especially an inner sense of vision, that enables us to perceive the light of our own souls. This light, in turn, affords us access to the divine world and to the bliss that results from contact with that world and knowledge of God.

The lamp is a figure for the rational soul; that it is of divine nature is proved by the fact that it does not fail as the body ages but, properly cultivated, actually burns more brightly with time. One of the means of activating the internal senses and achieving spiritual perfection is the study of the writings of the ancient sages – Ibn Ezra does not specify whether he is referring to the writings of the sages of Israel or the Greek philosophers or both – and the resulting engagement with the spiritual world instills in the poet the power to compose poetry.

Ibn Ezra is reported to have written a number of prose works in Arabic, but only two are extant, both written in his later years: the *Kitāb al-muḥāḍara wa l-mudhākara* (Book of Conversation and Deliberation) and the *Maqālat al-ḥadīqa fī maʿnā l-majāz wa l-ḥaqīqa* (The Garden: On the Figurative and the Literal).[11] The *Muḥāḍara* is a treatise on the Hebrew poetry of al-Andalus; the *Ḥadīqa* is a treatise on the theological implications of figurative language. Neither book fits perfectly into established genres; both are loosely organized works that draw heavily on anecdotes and quotations from Hebrew and Arabic literary and philosophical writings in poetry and prose. In view of their tendency to ramble, both books are usually described as adab works rather than as specialized treatises on poetry or theology and rhetoric. This looseness of structure may be a kind of clue to the nature of Ibn Ezra's literary career in general.

The *Muḥāḍara*, the most important medieval book about Hebrew poetry, purports to be the answers to eight questions about poetry that had been put to Ibn Ezra by a friend in Christian Spain; but describing the work in its opening sentence, the author is explicit about its miscellaneous character. Successive chapters deal with the definitions of poetry and artful prose: on why the Arabs are naturally gifted poets, while other peoples have to master it by training; on whether the Jews of preexilic times knew of metrical poetry; on why the Jews of al-Andalus are preeminent in the composition of poetry among the Jews (this chapter includes an invaluable chronological survey of the great Hebrew poets of al-Andalus down to the age of the author); on his personal reflections about poetry; on whether it is possible to compose poetry in a dream; and on the techniques employed in composing poetry. This final chapter includes a lengthy and systematic conspectus of figures of speech with examples drawn from the Bible, from Arabic poetry, and from Andalusi-Hebrew poetry.

The *Ḥadīqa*'s contribution to Jewish letters consists of bringing together the theological-exegetical issue of anthropomorphism in Scripture with the literary and grammatical studies developed by Andalusian Jews under the influence of Arabic scholarship. In this effort, Ibn Ezra was not the first, but he was the most thorough and the most inclined to resort to literary materials for his models. The book is divided into two parts, the first philosophico-theological, and the second exegetical. Part 1 begins with a chapter devoted to the definition of figurative and literal speech, continues with several chapters on theology, exploring the unity of God, the negation of his attributes, the negation of divine names, motion, the createdness of the cosmos, God's laws, and the composition of man, nature, and the soul. Part 2 is a detailed exploration of the Hebrew and Arabic terms used to describe the parts of the human organism, and a minute demonstration of the variety of metaphorical usages that are attributed to corporeal terms in biblical Hebrew and in Arabic and Hebrew poetry. The *Ḥadīqa*'s organization is a bit clearer and more focused than that of the *Muḥāḍara,* but it, too, abounds in digressions on matters literary, philosophical, scientific, and exegetical.

Both works reflect a broad familiarity with Arabic and Arabo-Greek culture typical of Andalusian Jewish intellectuals. They demonstrate Ibn Ezra's familiarity with works on poetry and belles lettres by such Arabic literary masters as Qudāma, Ibn al-Muʿtazz, al-Ḥātimi, Ibn Rashīq, Ibn Qutayba, and al-Jāḥiẓ, with Arabic poets from the pre-Islamic to the Abbasid period such as Imruʾ al-Qays, Zuhayr, Ṭarafa, al-Farazdaq, Abū Tammām, Abū l-ʿAtāhiya, al-Mutanabbī, and al-Maʿarrī; works by Plato, Aristotle, Plotinus, and other Greek philosophers; and also statements attributed to, and anecdotes about, these and other sages of antiquity such as Galen, Hippocrates, and Porphyry. But much of his information about Greek philosophy seems to be derived from Arabic anthologies and encyclopedias or from Arabic works by Jewish philosophers rather than from primary sources (Fenton 196; Halkin in Ibn Ezra, *Kitāb* xxvi).

In both poetry and philosophy, Ibn Ezra seems more at home with the literature of the Islamic East than with that of al-Andalus; he knows pseudo-Empedocles and the Ikhwān al-Ṣafāʾ, but not Ibn al-Sīd al-Baṭalyawsī and Ibn Bājja (Fenton 5), and he does not mention a single Andalusian Arabic poet (except the Mozarab translator of the Psalms into Arabic). His explanation for the preeminence of the Jews of al-Andalus in composing poetry over all other Jewish communities is consistent with this neglect of Andalusian culture: he sees the superiority of Andalusian Jewry not as a result of any superiority of locally available Andalusian Arabic models, but as a consequence of the supposed descent of the Andalusian Jews from the aristocracy of Jerusalem. In his poetic practice, Ibn Ezra writes in the *badiʿ* style favored by Andalusi-Arabic poets and he composes in the distinctively Andalusi form of the muwashshah; but in his theoretical writings, his Arabic culture seems to represent the mastery of Abbasid culture rather than personal involvement with current Andalusian literary and philosophical developments.

Ibn Ezra's two prose works show him to be less a professional scholar than a broadly educated man of letters. The *Muḥāḍara* is not a systematic treatise on literary history and criticism like some of the books on poetry that he cites; it is really a book of literary table talk. In its elegiac reflections and frequent autobiographical reminiscences, it recalls somewhat the style of Ibn Ḥazm in *Ṭawq al-ḥamāma* (The Dove's Neckring), evoking as author a cultivated man whom time has passed by, who has achieved resignation, and who writes out of sheer love of letters. The *Ḥadīqa* is less personal in tone (after the opening pages), but it is no less enthusiastic about its subject. As the *Muḥāḍara* shows Ibn Ezra not as a professional literary critic but as a cultured person, so the *Ḥadīqa* shows him not as a philosopher but as an intellectual who is so committed to philosophical writings that he can quote approvingly from the Ikhwān al-Ṣafāʾ the opinion that the philosopher ranks higher than the prophet (Fenton 92).

The three bodies of Ibn Ezra's work – Hebrew secular poetry, Hebrew religious poetry, and Arabic prose writings – combine to form a picture of a well-rounded Andalusi-Jewish intellectual in exile. In his poetry, he comes across as a bit stiff and classical, expert in the manipulation of rhetorical devices, and fluent in handling familiar themes, but, compared with the other great Hebrew poets, less individualistic. In his writing about poetry, he shows himself a bit conventional in his cautioning against extremes and in his disparagement of lampooning poetry. Much of Ibn Ezra's most personal poetry projects the persona of a man full of complaints about the treatment he has received at the hands of life and men. But even when these poems sink to a tone of self-pity, they are redeemed by superb craftsmanship and by a spiritually sustaining philosophical optimism that was stronger than any temporal misery. These qualities enabled Ibn Ezra to turn his bitterness into a poetry of pious resignation (Scheindlin, "Old Age"):

> And so I scorn this world and shun her lure,
> so that she not pile sins on me –
> abandon her, lest she abandon me,
> untie my shoe, fling spittle in my face.
> And though she were to make the sun my crown,
> the moon an ornament to wear,
> the Bear a chain of honor round my arm,
> its stars a medal encircling my neck
> I would not want her glory, no, not even
> if she were to build a palace for me,
> set among the spheres! . . .
> The ancient books are everything I want;
> their wisdom is the balm that soothes my pain.

With them I keep sweet company,
my own true circle, and my trusty friends.
They are my sea of wisdom, where I plunge
and bring up pearls to ornament the throat of Time.
My heart and eyes get true delight from them,
and to them in return my lips give hymns.
Incense, sweetness, light, and song
to breath and tongue, to ear and eye;
they elevate me, give me pride;
my thoughts are all of them until I die.

NOTES

1. He is not to be confused with the later poet, scientific writer, and Bible commentator Abraham Ibn Ezra (1093–1164 or 1167), who is much better known to non-Hebraists. It may be assumed that the two belonged to the same extended family, but the nature of their relationship has never been clarified.
2. My translation; the complete poem with an English translation is in Ibn Ezra, *Selected Poems* 2–5.
3. This introduction, though written in Hebrew characters, like nearly all Arabic works written by Jewish writers for use within the Jewish community, is in classical Arabic. It is thus an excellent example of the point made in the *Language essay in this volume that a text is defined as Judeo-Arabic not by its script but by its grammar and diction.
4. The Hebrew panegyric is generally slighted in modern discussions of medieval Hebrew poetry, despite the centrality of this genre to the craft and to the social setting. The same disregard has traditionally attended the Arabic qasida, as noted forcefully by Suzanne Pinckney Stetkevych, in "Abbasid Panegyric and the Poetics of Political Allegiance: Two Poems of al-Mutanabbī on Kāfūr" (Sperl and Shackle 1:35–36), though this imbalance is being corrected in contemporary scholarship through such works as the volume in which that paper appeared.
5. For a parallel phenomenon in Arabic, see the discussion of "metastrophe" in the *Qasida essay in the present volume.
6. For comparison with Arabic poetry of personal complaint, see Schippers, "Two Andalusian Poets."
7. This type of poetry is the subject of Scheindlin, *Gazelle*.
8. Translation from *Gazelle* 65, q.v. for discussion. Edom is a standard epithet, in medieval Hebrew poetry and rabbinic writing generally, for Christendom; this line makes the allegorical reading of the poem certain. Fleischer, in Schirmann 408 n. 162, questions whether the poem was intended for the liturgy.
9. For thorough bibliography on this important poem, see Tanenbaum. Ibn Ḥazm's poem was published in ʿAbbās 370–74.

10 Text with my translation and notes in Scheindlin, "Lamp"; the end of the poem is quoted at the end of this essay. See also Pagis, *Shirat haḥol* 308–9; Scheindlin, "Old Age."

11. For additional discussion of the former work, see the *Arabized Jews essay in this volume. The publication of the latter by Professor Paul Fenton is imminently expected. A brief fragment of a third work is also extant. For a survey of the Arabic works attributed to Ibn Ezra, see Fenton 26–40.

BIBLIOGRAPHY

ʿAbbās, Iḥsān. *Taʾrīkh al-adab al-andalusī*. 2nd edn. Beirut, 1981.

Brann, Ross. *The Compunctious Poet: Cultural Ambiguity and Hebrew Poetry in Muslim Spain*. Baltimore, 1991.

Carmi, Ted. *The Penguin Book of Hebrew Verse*. Harmondsworth, 1981.

Cole, Peter. *Selected Poems of Shmuel HaNagid*. Princeton, 1996.

Constable, Olivia R. *Medieval Iberia: Readings from Christian, Muslim, and Jewish Sources*. Philadelphia, 1997.

Fenton, Paul B. *Philosophie et exégèse dans le jardin de la métaphore de Moïse Ibn Ezra, philosophe et poète andalou du XIIe siècle*. Leiden, 1997.

Ibn Ezra, Moses. *Diwan*. Ed. Hayim Brody. Vol. I. Berlin, 1938. Vol. II. Jerusalem, 1941.

Kitāb al-muḥāḍara wa l-mudhākara. Ed. and trans. Abraham S. Halkin. Jerusalem, 1975.

Selected Poems of Moses Ibn Ezra. Trans. and ed. Solomon Solis-Cohen and Ḥayim Brody. Philadelphia, 1934.

Levin, Yisraʾel. "Habekhi ʿal ḥorvot hameʿonot vehademut halelit hameshoṭeṭet." *Tarbiz* 36 (July 1966): 278–95.

Meʿil tashbeṣ. 2nd edn. 3 vols. Tel Aviv, 1994.

Pagis, Dan. *Hebrew Poetry of the Middle Ages and the Renaissance*. Berkeley, 1991.

Ḥidush umasoret beshirat haḥol. Jerusalem, 1976.

Shirat haḥol vetorat hashir lemoshe ibn ʿezra uvene doro. Jerusalem, 1970.

Scheindlin, Raymond P. *The Gazelle: Medieval Hebrew Poems on God, Israel, and the Soul*. Philadelphia, 1991.

"The Hebrew Qasida in Spain." Sperl and Shackle 1:121–35.

"The Lamp Within." *Prooftexts* 17 (1997): 260–65.

"Old Age." Forthcoming.

"Rabbi Moshe Ibn Ezra on the Legitimacy of Poetry." *Medievalia et Humanistica*, n.s., 7 (1976): 101–15.

Wine, Women, and Death: Medieval Hebrew Poems on the Good Life. Philadelphia, 1986.

Schippers, Arie. *Spanish Hebrew Poetry and the Arabic Literary Tradition: Arabic Themes in Hebrew Andalusian Poetry*. Leiden, 1994.

"Two Andalusian Poets on Exile: Reflections on the Poetry of Ibn ʿAmmār (1031–1086) and Moses Ibn Ezra (1055–1138)." *The Challenge of the Middle East.* Ed. Ibrahim A. El-Sheikh et al. Amsterdam, 1982. 113–21, 201–4.

Schirmann, Ḥayim. *Toledot hashira haʿivrit bisefarad hamuslimit.* Ed. Ezra Fleischer. Jerusalem, 1995.

Sperl, Stefan, and Christopher Shackle, eds. *Qasida Poetry in Islamic Asia and Africa.* 2 vols. Leiden, 1996.

Tanenbaum, Adena. "Nine Spheres or Ten? A Medieval Gloss on Moses Ibn Ezra's 'Beshem El Asher Amar.'" *Journal of Jewish Studies* 47 (1996): 294–310.

CHAPTER 12

JUDAH HALEVI

Ross Brann

As a historical figure, Judah Halevi (Abū l-Ḥasan) (before 1075–1141) approaches iconic status in Jewish culture. Medieval Franco-German pietists, German Romantics, nineteenth-century Wissenschaft des Judentums historians, Zionist historiographers, modern Hebrew poets, and, more recently, critical scholars of Judaica all embrace Halevi as one of their own, seeing something of themselves in him and his work and occasionally reinventing Judah by projecting their own values onto him. One can scarcely identify another figure of the so-called Golden Age of Jewish culture in al-Andalus acclaimed in so many diverse quarters as the embodiment of literary artistry, sophisticated religious conviction, mystical piety, or protonationalist commitment – a clear testament to the enduring appeal of Halevi's poetic and religious genius and to the ambiguity of his literary identity.

By all accounts, Halevi was a foundational figure in Andalusi-Jewish culture. A now famous personal letter written in 1130 and preserved in the Cairo Geniza testifies that canonical status was conferred on Halevi during his own lifetime. The correspondent refers to Halevi as "the quintessence and embodiment of our country" – meaning al-Andalus – "our glory and leader, the illustrious scholar and unique and perfect devotee" (Goitein, "Judaeo-Arabic Letters" 341, 343). Literary references to Halevi amplify the homage preserved in the documentary record. The seminal biblical exegete Abraham Ibn Ezra cites Judah's textual interpretations in his commentaries on biblical books (Weiser 1:52–58). Admiring accounts of Halevi, enthusiastic assessments of his work, and intertextual references to him are found in such disparate literary intellectuals as Moses Ibn Ezra (78), Solomon Ibn Ṣaqbel (Schirmann, *Hebrew Poetry* 2:558), Abraham Ibn Dā'ūd (Cohen 73–74, trans. 103), Joseph Ibn ʿAqnīn (176–78), and Judah Alḥarizi (Schirmann, *Hebrew Poetry* 3:113–14). More than any of the major Andalusi-Hebrew poets, Judah Halevi occupies a revered place in the Andalusi-Jewish and subsequently Sephardi cultural pantheon in Christian Spain and in exile after 1492. For that particular communal audience of readers, Halevi's devotional poetry gives singular voice to the religious and historical longings of his community. His elegant secular verse represents an unrivaled lyrical achievement in the canon of Andalusi-Hebrew poetry; widely read as the most significant document of medieval Jewish thought, Halevi's *Kitāb al-khazarī* (Khazarian Book) resolutely affirms the centrality of rabbinic tradition and the essential truth of biblical revelation in the face of Karaite provocations, Aristotelian threats, and an untenable historical predicament; and Judah's mystical devotion sets him apart as a model of Jewish piety. The Jews of al-Andalus and their successors as well as various arbiters of Jewish culture over time and place have thus designated Halevi as a cultural authority.

But much as the inhabitants of Cervantes's La Mancha tell of encounters with various fictional Quixotes, tradition relates more than one Halevi, calling into question the nature and significance of the cultural authority he represents. Paradoxically, Halevi retained his standing as a paragon of Andalusi-Jewish culture even as he began to turn away from its conventional discourse, poetic forms, and values, even as he challenged its assumptions and then assailed them in his poetry and the Judeo-Arabic *Kitāb al-khazarī*. He scandalized an adoring society with his iconoclastic views, shocked his circle by planning to leave Spain, and according to the report of his disciple Solomon Ibn Parḥon, "Before his death, he repented (and resolved) never to compose poetry again" (fol. 5a). Halevi's ambivalent attitude toward Jewish life in twelfth-century al-Andalus (and Christian Spain) might well have turned him into a controversial, even divisive figure in Andalusi-Jewish cultural history. Instead, his "rejection" of Andalusi-Jewish courtly culture and society appear to have deepened the esteem in which he was held and with which he has been remembered.

How could such a manifestly transgressive figure simultaneously maintain the status of a foundational and authoritative figure? Readings that would firmly anchor Halevi within a specific literary or intellectual circle or within a narrowly defined cultural orbit (i.e., courtly aesthetic; mystical; antirationalist; protonationalist) tend to obscure more than illuminate him: Halevi's manifold literary production situates him in each of these cultural camps, and his literary life followed a trajectory that cannot be reduced to simple formulas. I therefore prefer to think of the contradictions in Halevi's work and his struggle to define himself in relation to Andalusi-Jewish culture as a sign of that culture's own contradictions and evolution at a critical moment of historical transition for the Jews of al-Andalus – as evidence of the dialectical process according to which the cultural system, its literary forms, and its values are challenged by its very own methods of expression and discourse.

Born in northern Spain (probably in then Muslim Tudela near the frontier with Christian Spain [Fleischer, "Yehuda Halevi" 241 ff.]), Halevi frequently traversed the shifting border between Christendom and Islam in eleventh- and twelfth-century Iberia. His movements across linguistic, religious, cultural, and political boundaries suggest that these borders were considerably more fluid and permeable than is commonly thought. In any case, from the moment he arrived in al-Andalus via Toledo as a young man sometime before 1090, Halevi came to be intimately associated with Andalusi-Jewish courtly circles. Halevi's first personal letter to Moses Ibn Ezra (d. c. 1138), the reigning literary figure of the period, describes Judah's initiation into the Andalusi scene in a charming anecdote about a competition among poets. A well-known muwashshah was named, whereupon members of the company began to improvise strophic songs of their own according to the prosodic requirements of the specified poem. When the others faltered, they turned to Halevi – who proved more than equal to the challenge (Abramson 405).

Although Halevi's letter offers an unassuming, self-effacing account of his poem's origin, his accompanying muwashshah (Sáenz-Badillos and Targarona 186–88) is sufficiently dazzling to demonstrate the poet's uncommon lyric power. The poem represents Wisdom as an exuberant beauty who speaks invitingly of the exquisite pleasures she has reserved exclusively for Moses Ibn Ezra. The tantalizing erotic description of her body parts seems to strike a discordant note with textual allusions that suggest a correspondence between Ibn Ezra and two dignified characters of biblical Israel: Moses the prophet-lawgiver (Num. 12:7), and Heman, a sage counselor and singer of songs in the Jerusalem Temple (1 Kings 5:11):

> Wisdom calls him Heman,
> Moses, entrusted over all my house.
> For you the pleasure of my breasts is reserved
> Along with my scarlet lips like manna,
>
> Honey cake, perfect beauty, my dress's loops
> Undo, and uncover a breast rising like a heap, like breasts of a
> lovely woman, and press the nipples! (ll. 19–24)

Wisdom's erotic persona and posture are not quite as improper as might seem. The reader understands that "she" is in fact a completely appropriate counterpart to the addressee: this Moses Ibn Ezra, dean of Andalusi-Hebrew poets, is surely her most fitting suitor.

Some eight hundred of Halevi's poems (including love and wine poetry, elegies, panegyric and friendship songs, epithalamia, and religious meditations, many intended for liturgical use) have come down to us, but the poet's lyric voice, above all, sets him apart from his contemporaries. In another poem

(Schirmann, *Hebrew Poetry* 2:440; Sáenz-Badillos and Targarona 42–43), for example, Halevi turns the conventions of love poetry to humorous effect, stamping his singularly witty lyric style on the experience of a jilted lover:

> Graceful gazelle, you've captured me with your beauty,
> enslaved me ruthlessly by your captivation.
> Ever since parting came between us
> I've not found one as beautiful as you.
> So I take comfort in a reddish apple,
> whose fragrance is like the frankincense of your breath,
> Its shape like your breasts, its color
> like the blush visible upon your cheeks.

Halevi's technical mastery of convention and style and surpassing lyrical sensibility merits him an honored place in the literary history of al-Andalus despite his northern origins.

Halevi's roles as a communal leader and prosperous court physician (and apparently related lucrative business ventures) frequently carried him from Lucena, Córdoba, and other Andalusi towns back to Christian Toledo where his ongoing involvement in the cultural, political, and social life of that Jewish community is attested in Geniza documents (Goitein, *Mediterranean* 5:462 ff.) and poems to Jewish notables at the court of Alfonso VI of Castile (Sáenz-Badillos and Targarona 174). Notwithstanding Halevi's close identification with literary society in the Muslim south, the poet as well as his many admirers remained conscious of his northern origin on the frontier with Christian Spain. Moses Ibn Ezra marvels at his protégé's skill in an epistolary poem applauding the youthful poet as having "shone forth from the East," that is, from Christian Spain, in apparent reference to Judah's stay in Toledo prior to his initial encounter with the Jews of al-Andalus (Brody and Pagis 1:23 [l. 14]). Another important poet, scholar, and lifelong friend, Judah Ibn Ghiyāth, also greets Halevi as a "foreigner" (Brody 190 [l. 36]). Halevi, too, identifies himself as "the immigrant from Christendom" in the aforementioned letter to Ibn Ezra (Abramson 404–5; Fleischer, "Sources" 898–99) and in several poems (Brody and Habermann 1:20 [l. 42]; Jarden, *Liturgical Poetry* 1:57–63).

Apart from their biographical significance, poetic allusions to Halevi's connection to Toledo and Castile evince the Andalusi literary intellectuals' delight in rhetorical formulas based on conceptual opposition. As evident in his verse and prose, Halevi and his circle gave expression to the irony that he appeared on the Andalusi-Jewish scene as an outsider, became an Andalusi by choice, so to speak, and suddenly came to loom large in their society and culture. Yet this "outsider" arrived fully versed in Judeo-Arabic learning and manners, was quickly embraced as an insider, and ultimately was deemed the epitome of the Andalusi-Jewish ideal.

Halevi's association with Christian Spain and the acquired identification with al-Andalus have yet another meaning. If we think of Andalusi-Hebrew poetry as representing a cultural process of translation – of rewriting the form and content of Arabic culture into Hebrew (*Arabized Jews) – Halevi the "outsider" can be said to have greatly advanced the process of adaptation begun in mid-tenth-century Córdoba. Contrefaction (*muʿāraḍa*), that is, imitation of the prosodic and melodic pattern of several Andalusi-Arabic muwashshahs, incorporation of Arabic kharjas in Hebrew muwashshahs, intertextual references to Hispano-Arabic poets such as Ibn Zaydūn, Hebrew translations of Arabic lyrics by al-Mutanabbī and others, and devotional lyrics informed by the language and conceptual framework of Islamic piety are only the most accessible examples of the complex process of cultural adaptation and appropriation evident in the prosodic forms and musicality, metaphorical layers, and rhetorical structures of Halevi's verse (Brody and Habermann 1:169–71, 199–201; Stern 171–74; Sáenz-Badillos and Targarona 78, 98, 185, 189; Monroe and Swialto 145–57; Hamori, "Reading" 123–25; Schirmann, *Hebrew Poetry* 2:446; Scheindlin, *Wine* 122–23; Scheindlin, *Gazelle* 133). The repeated identification of Halevi as having come from northern Spain reminds the reader of the powerful allure of al-Andalus and thus amounts to an ironic indication of his origins rather than a sign of the poet's cultural otherness.

Halevi upheld Andalusi cultural ideals with brilliant conviction until sometime around 1125, when he apparently began to think of himself more as a religious devotee than a lyric poet and communal notable (Sáenz-Badillos and Targarona 468–74; Schirmann, *Hebrew Poetry* 2:494–97; trans. Goldstein 134–36):

> Are you, at fifty, pursuing your youth,
> as your days prepare to fly away?
>
> Do you run from the service of God,
> and yearn to serve only men?
>
> Do you seek the crowd's company and forsake
> the presence of the One whom all who will may seek?
>
> (ll. 1–3)

Religious disillusionment with the classical and Arabo-Islamic foundations of aristocratic life in al-Andalus is addressed in one of the poet's argumentative lyrics (Schirmann, *Hebrew Poetry* 2:492–94; Sáenz-Badillos and Targarona 438–43) and signified there by the poet's attitude toward *ḥokhmat yevanit* ("Be not seduced by Greek thought that has only flowers but no fruit" [l. 27]). A similar attitude is evident in Halevi's ornate formal letter to a North African scholar (Ratzaby, "Iggeret" 270):

I've named this place "toil" for it has me preoccupied . . . It goads me to Hippocrates, forces me to abandon the Prophets. Greece and its wisdom have drowned me in mucky grease; Islam and its language have painted me dark, and Christendom has dissected and destroyed me!

Halevi's disenchantment with al-Andalus had a communal as well as a personal dimension. According to a poem in which the poet recounts a prophetic dream (Sáenz-Badillos and Targarona 318; Schirmann, *Hebrew Poetry* 2:480; trans. Scheindlin, *Gazelle* 109), Halevi seems to have received, calculated, or imagined an esoteric (messianic) tradition that the year 1130 was to bring a general redemption and a reversal of fortune for Jews of Islam:

You dozed and fell asleep and rose in fear;
  What was this dream you dreamt, already unclear?
Perhaps your dream revealed to you your foe –
  You the master; he, humbled and low.

Tell Hagar's son, "Let down your haughty hand
  From Sarah's son, the rival you have scorned,
For I have seen you in my dream, a ruin;
  Perhaps in life you really are undone.
Perhaps this year, eleven-hundred thirty,
  Will see your pride thrown down, your thinking thwarted . . ."

When the expected deliverance did not materialize, disappointment seems to have catalyzed deepening doubts about the meaningfulness of Jewish life in al-Andalus and Toledo. Halevi subsequently appears to have directed his thinking and efforts toward realizing a more strictly personal redemption: he formulated a plan to abandon al-Andalus for the sacred precincts of Jerusalem where he would spend the remainder of his life in religious devotion.

As Halevi's ruminations became public, tensions emerged between the poet and his circle. These strains and Halevi's own ambivalence contributed to one of the most creative periods in the poet's career in which he risked taking issue with the artistic and intellectual foundations of Jewish life in al-Andalus. Ironically, Halevi dared to channel his mastery of Andalusi-Hebrew poetic convention and style into lyrics in which he repeatedly renounces aristocratic life and in which he chronicles in poetic form his abandonment of al-Andalus, in effect turning the culture against itself. In 1140 Halevi finally set sail for Jerusalem via Egypt. There, once again, he assumed the role of the outsider embraced as the ultimate cultural authority. Moreover, Halevi seems to have confronted a devoted attitude toward Egypt among the Jews of that land comparable to the sentiments of the Andalusi Jews (Jarden, *Liturgical Poetry* 4:956–57). Halevi thus became an exile from his adopted home, one of many intellectually and spiritually earnest Andalusis, like *Ibn ʿArabī (d. 1240), who left al-Andalus for the East.

Exile, even the self-willed exile Halevi boldly envisioned, involves transformations of art as well as life (Edwards 23). Halevi's most significant departures from literary tradition and from cultural convention date from the period between 1125 and 1140–41, when he was preoccupied with the idea of leaving al-Andalus and going East. These deviations involve the production of culturally subversive discourse that revises normative forms of expression and replaces the dominant values established by the Andalusi Judeo-Arabic cultural synthesis of the tenth and eleventh centuries. Some thirty-five "Songs of Zion" and "Sea Poems" (imagining or rendering in poetic form the journey from Spain to Egypt and subsequently from Alexandria to Palestine in 1141) blur the formal and conceptual distinctions between devotional and secular verse and between personal and communal compositions. Halevi's expressly liturgical compositions frequently appropriate the language of national redemption to address the longings of the individual soul to return to its sublime source (Scheindlin, *Gazelle* 46–47). But in the cycle of poems devoted to his spiritual quest and journey, the poet speaks of a yearning to "go East" in images of frustrated desire drawn from the conventional love lyric. Consider the expressive urgency of "Yefe nof mesos tevel" (Fair-Crested, Cosmic Joy) that depicts the poet's imaginary visualization of the "Enthroned Glory" in Jerusalem, a poem also predicated on the Arabic topos of *al-ḥanīn ilā l-waṭan*, the poet's longing for his lost homeland:

> Fair-crested, cosmic joy, city of the great King,
> My soul yearns for you from the edge of the West,
>
> My yearning love is stirred when I remember the East of yore,
> Your Glory exiled, your Shrine ruined.
>
> Would that I were borne to you on eagle's wings
> So I could drench your dust with my tears until they blend.
>
> I seek you even though your King is away, and in place of
> Your balm of Gilead are venomous snakes and scorpions.
>
> Shall I not cherish and kiss your stones,
> The taste of your clods sweeter to my mouth than honey?
> (Sáenz-Badillos and Targarona 430; Schirmann, *Hebrew Poetry* 2:489)

Readers of Andalusi-Hebrew verse could not miss the poet's inventive reapplication of conventional "separation" motifs, so reminiscent of al-Muʿtamid's lyric plea to die in Seville (al-Maqqarī 4:275) or Moses Ibn Ezra's yearning for restoration to Granada's soil (Brody and Pagis 1:155; Schirmann, *Hebrew Poetry* 2:379).

Related texts of this cycle also address the religious problem implicit in the historical predicament of the Jews of twelfth-century al-Andalus. Seemingly relegated to the margins of history, the Jews were displaced and shaken by the upheavals of the Almoravid Berber occupation in the south beginning in 1091, and they were cast as bystanders to the political and military contest between Islam and Christendom in Iberia after 1085 (and in the Holy Land after 1099). Liturgical poems by Halevi (and Ibn Gabirol before him) had addressed the historical-theological aspect of this problem as framed by piyyut tradition. But until Halevi began to contemplate the journey to Zion in verse, the problem of the Andalusi Jew in relation to the Exile of Israel had rarely been so sharply framed in social and personal terms, at least not since it had been raised in poetic form by Dunash ben Labrat in the mid-tenth century (Scheindlin, *Wine* 40–45). It was apparently no longer sufficient for Halevi as a devotional poet to speculate on behalf of the community about the status of the covenant between the God of history and Israel. Rather, the poet now wonders about the commitments of the community of believers, including himself: how could an intellectually and spiritually minded Jew presume to remain religiously earnest while seduced by the comforts and pleasures of al-Andalus and bound by the obligations of public service?

His opponents' dissuasions resound about him
But he listens in silence like a man of no words.

What is the use of reply or refutation,
Why make them all angry when they are all drunkards?

They congratulate him for being in the service of kings,
Which to him is like the worship of idols.

Is it right for a pious and worthy man
To be glad that he is caught, like a bird by a child,

In the service of Philistines, Hittites, and descendants of Hagar,
His heart is seduced by alien deities

To do their will, and forsake the will of God,
To deceive the Creator and serve his creatures?

(Schirmann, *Hebrew Poetry* 2:497–500;
trans. Goldstein 137–38; cf. trans. Carmi 347)

One intertextual emblem of the conflicting cultural forces and impulses that shaped the poet's literary existence can be found in the geographical signs that figure prominently in Halevi's poetry. For example, in four poems written in 1141 as the anxious pilgrim awaited favorable gusts to take him by ship from Alexandria to the coast of northern Palestine, the poet employs terms previously used to indicate al-Andalus and Christian Spain (*ma'arav* [west] and *mizraḥ* [east]) to signify the western and eastern winds respectively.[1] In particular, the motif of geographic orientation lies at the center of a cluster of poems such as "Libi vemizraḥ veanokhi vesof ma'arav" (My Heart Is in the East) (Schirmann, *Hebrew Poetry* 2:489; trans. Carmi 347; Goldstein 128), composed sometime after Halevi began to doubt the meaningfulness of spending the final years of his life in Spain. Drawing on references to prophetic passages and to the Book of Psalms, the poem sets up an escalating series of oppositions between the poet's spiritual ideal and the very real geographical, political, and personal obstacles impeding his quest:

My heart is in the East but I am at the edge of the West.
  How can I savor what I eat, how find it sweet?

How can I fulfill my vows and obligations while
  Zion is in Christendom's fetter and I am in the shackle of
    Islam?

It would be easy for me to leave behind all the opulence of Spain;
  It would be glorious for me to see the dust of the ruined
    Shrine!

"Libi vemizraḥ" employs images and motifs developed more fully in the ode "Ṣiyyon halo tish'ali" (O Zion, Will You Not Ask?) (Schirmann, *Hebrew Poetry* 2:485–89; partial trans. Carmi 347–49) as well as in other poems of the cycle (cf. "Yefe nof mesos tevel" above; and "Hayukhlu fegarim" [My Body Is a Room], Schirmann, *Hebrew Poetry* 2:497–500; trans. Goldstein 137–39). It represents in miniature the poet's struggle to escape from Andalusi-Jewish courtly society and repudiate its manners and values in preparation for his pilgrimage to the land of Israel. Yet the lyric nearly succeeds in casting the poet backward to the "opulence of Spain" as well as projecting him forward to the life of religious devotion he imagines for himself in Jerusalem. That the poem and the poet (who referred to himself as one "whose country is Spain but whose destination is Jerusalem") point in more than one direction is suggested by the chiastic semantic and rhetorical structure of lines one and two (1a = 2b; 1b = 2a), a structure that works at cross-purposes with the supposed thematic progression of the poem away from Spain and toward Palestine. Dramatization of the poet's conflicting feelings also figures prominently in other compositions where the pilgrim appears at cross-purposes with his roles and responsibilities as father, grandfather, and member of the Andalusi-Jewish community.[2] Furthermore, Halevi's investment in the Andalusian ethos is very much evident in documentary accounts of his career including his Judeo-Arabic autograph letters, his formal rhymed-prose Hebrew epistles, and in the Hebrew lyrics he composed prior to and even during and after his departure for the East.

Although "Libi vemizraḥ" memorialized both motifs in Hebrew literary history, the opposition between West and East and the heart's longing for restoration to its desired place were not Halevi's innovations but two of the many themes Hebrew poetry absorbed from the Arabic verse that served as its model. It is important to note that in Hispano-Hebrew poetry the east–west opposition acquired a specific significance not found in the Arabic, in that in Halevi's time *mizraḥ* and *maʿarav* were sometimes applied to connote Christian and Muslim Spain respectively (Brody and Pagis 1:70 [l. 13], 124 [l. 21]). Aristocratic poets such as Moses Ibn Ezra viewed the Christian north with such disdain that the rhetorical opposition between east and west takes on the quality of an ontological antithesis. Hebrew literary intellectuals such as Samuel the Nagid and Moses Ibn Ezra tended to regard the political and cultural achievements of the Jews of al-Andalus as signs of divine favor, perhaps even election (Cohen 287 ff.). Their devotion to Sefarad as the center of Jewish life took various literary forms, as, for instance, in a poem in which Halevi addresses Moses Ibn Ezra as "ner ha-maʿarav" (the Lamp of the West, i.e., of al-Andalus).

The theme of the heart's separation from the object of its affection (integrated with the geographical motif in "Libi vemizraḥ") is also derived from the conventional thematic stock of Arabic love and friendship poetry (Ratzaby, "Studies" 343–44). Halevi transposed this complex of themes in various lyrics closely in which the land of Israel replaces the figure of the beloved or friend as the displaced object of the poet's desire. A parallel may be found in the lyrics of Judah's contemporary, the Hispano-Arabic poet Abū Isḥāq ibn Khafāja (d. 1139). In one of Ibn Khafāja's poems about the charms of his native Valencia the poet imagines an urban garden (and by extension the city and al-Andalus) as a captivating beauty, thereby merging the figures of the beloved and a cherished place. Line 3 of the text also plays on the opposition between East and West:

A garden in al-Andalus has
    unveiled beauty and a lush scent.

The morning glistens from its teeth
    and the night is overshadowed by its scarlet lips.

When the wind blows from the East
I cry: O how I long for al-Andalus! (136)

What, then, is new and distinctive to Andalusi-Hebrew poetry in the topos "My heart is in the East"? Chiefly, the text testifies to a complete realignment or reorientation of the conventional rhetorical opposition between East and West in which the prestige of the latter (al-Andalus) is preferred over the former (Christian Spain or the Muslim East). As noted above, the reformulation of the motif in "Libi vemizraḥ" reverses that conventional rhetorical polarity and thereby attempts to do away with the poet's own considerable investment in al-Andalus. But because of the Andalusi-Jewish elite's unremitting attachment to Spain, the displacement of West by East in this celebrated poem acquires a deeper cultural as opposed to strictly personal significance. Reorientation of the poet's imagined geography can be adduced from other lyrics composed as Halevi restlessly anticipated the sea breezes that would finally carry him on to Palestine:

This wind of yours, O West, is all perfume . . .
Rebuke the east wind that whips up the sea . . .
(Schirmann, *Hebrew Poetry* 2:504; trans. Carmi 350–51; Saperstein 308–11)

Even without additional reference to the religious and secular verse he composed after 1125, the details of Halevi's biography recovered from the Cairo Geniza and the exposition of religious ideas in the *Kitāb al-khazarī* attest that the poet was no longer receptive to the notion that al-Andalus properly stood at the center of the Jewish universe. Accordingly, the altered bearings of "Libi vemizraḥ" (in which East is seen as ontologically and spiritually superior to West) represent more than the transformation of a literary topos. The poem's fixation on Jerusalem/the land of Israel as the locus of meaning signifies nothing less than the attempted cultural reorientation of a devotee "whose only hope is to go East" (letter to Ḥalfon ben Nethan'el ha-Levi in Goitein, "Autographs" 408–12).

What is the reader to make of the intertextual relationship between the poems discussed above? Seemingly conscious transformations of elements of courtly verse into poetic expressions of piety do constitute an essential aspect of the transvaluation of the language, imagery, and style of Halevi's earlier verse. Here the reader uncovers language and images "absorbed and transformed," to recall Kristeva's definition of intertextuality,[3] from a lyric poetic discourse, desecularizing its frequently desacralizing references to biblical texts with quickened allusions to expressions of religious desire. If we think of the relationship between the texts as reflective of a broader cultural problem, an intertextual reading of the relevant passages of the poems supports the impression that the reformulation of a conventional theme in "Libi vemizraḥ" (East replacing West/land of Israel replacing Spain) represents not only a transformation of a homologous text but also subversion of the cultural system of the Jews of eleventh- and twelfth-century al-Andalus.

The poetry discussed to this point represents only one dimension of Halevi's rewriting of the language of the dominant Andalusi-Jewish cultural paradigm. The theoretical critique of the Hebraicized Arabic prosodic forms of the Andalusi school articulated in Halevi's Arabic "Treatise on Poetic Meters" (Schirmann, "Judah Halevi's Treatise" 319–22) and the parallel passage on language, prosody, and music in the *Kitāb al-khazarī* (Baneth and Ben-Shammai 77–83) center on a typological distinction between a "native (Hebrew) poetics" and an Andalusi-Hebrew tradition modeled on Arabic (Brann 97 ff.; Rosen, "Strophic Trend" 315–28). The poet continued to employ Andalusi prosodic forms even as he was awaiting transport from Alexandria to Palestine (e.g., Brody and Habermann 1:67–68, 112–14; 2:258–60). However we now know that Halevi did not use them exclusively but began to adopt in practice an alternative poetics. The so-called puritanical, strophic trend in Halevi's later verse represents the poet's ultimate attempt to reject Andalusi poetics, not by falling silent as Ibn Parḥon reports, but by replacing it with an intrinsic Hebrew model. Two nonquantitative, syllabic muwashshahs (Ratzaby, "Me-oṣar" 172; Brody and Habermann 2:29–31) dedicated to Egyptian notables represent Halevi's most iconoclastic poetics in content as well as form because they eschew the conventional amatory prelude (*nasīb*) before the panegyric (Rosen-Moked, "Girdle Poem" 50–51) and conclude with Hebrew rather than colloquial Arabic or Romance kharjas. Halevi's metrical experimentation, including his employment of syllabic meters, provides further textual evidence of the poet's turn to an "unorthodox" Hebrew poetics.

Work on the second edition of the *Kitāb al-khazarī*, subtitled *Kitāb al-radd wa l-dalīl fī l-dīn al-dhalīl* (Book of Refutation and Proof: On the Abased Faith) also dates from the period between 1125 and 1140. In this version, the Khazar king of the title is a generic monotheist anxious to discover the correct form of worship in which to express his belief in the one God. Interviewing representatives from each of the three monotheistic traditions, the Khazar monarch quickly dispatches his Christian and Muslim mentors as well as an especially sterile philosopher in order to devote himself to absorbing the engrossing stuff of rabbinic tradition from the Jewish scholar. A comparison with *Ramon Llull's thirteenth-century *Book of the Gentile and the Three Wise Men* (Bonner 1:91–304), whose dialogic structure resembles the *Kitāb al-khazarī*, is enlightening. Llull's philosophically minded gentile engages

Jewish, Christian, and Muslim scholars respectively in fair-minded, fully conceived intellectual encounters. By contrast, the Khazar king of Halevi's *Kitāb al-khazarī* embraces rabbinic Judaism over the other traditions almost at the outset, affording the Jewish scholar the opportunity to deepen his spirited exposition of his tradition at length. Accordingly, Halevi is frequently read as a defender of rabbinic tradition or as a severe critic of the twelfth-century Aristotelian trend typified by the Andalusi-Arabic poet and philosopher Ibn Bājja (d. c. 1139).

A recent reading of the *Kitāb al-khazarī* makes a convincing case that the final edition of the text is designed to undermine the attachment to Sefarad among the culturally sophisticated Jews (Berger 216 ff.). The Khazar king, whose voice is more central to the structure and meaning of the text than is commonly assumed (Brann 106–14), criticizes the sterility and hypocrisy with which the Andalusi Jews dutifully recite the canonical prayers for the land of Israel. Furthermore, in response to the scholar's discourse on the metaphysically perfect properties of the land of Israel, the Khazar king shrewdly notes that the Jews neglect observance of their sacred law unless they reside there (Baneth and Ben-Shammai 57–58). This approach to the *Kitāb al-khazarī* further explains why (apart from its parallel in Halevi's biography) the Jewish scholar announces in the epilogue that he is going to Palestine; it is possible to lead the fully realized Jewish life the Khazar king seeks only in that land (Baneth and Ben-Shammai 227–29).

A significant corpus of poems composed between 1125 and 1140, Halevi's "instrincally Hebrew" revisionist prosody and poetics, and the second edition of the *Kitāb al-khazarī* represent the convergence of what can be called a nation-centered poetry, poetics, and thinking. The *Kitāb al-khazarī* rejects the intercultural context and discourse of twelfth-century philosophical inquiry; the new Hebrew verse and poetics attempt to replace Hebrew lyric poetry whose subjects and prosody are the product of the Andalusi Jews' interaction with Arabo-Islamic civilization with an intrinsic poetics whose verse is preoccupied with the individual's spiritual quest and the historico-religious predicament of the community. Together, these nation-centered discourses signify a concerted attempt to recast two highly regarded forms of Andalusi-Jewish culture – poetry and philosophy/theology – and thereby transform the most critical effects of the Judeo-Arabic synthesis on the Jews of al-Andalus. They further appear to signify a repudiation of the lyric world and multireligious, multiethnic, multilingual Iberia painted by María Rosa Menocal (45).

Yet Halevi never completed this revisionist project and did not, could not, altogether break with Andalusi culture. Although the poet's devotion to Palestine and Jewish piety certainly undermined his prior attachment to al-Andalus/Sefarad and its culture, he remained steeped in the consciousness of al-Andalus and its discursive languages. Lyrics with Neoplatonic underpinnings, seemingly frivolous Egyptian poems, and the poet's lifelong embrace of the quintessentially Andalusi muwashshah form in secular and liturgical poetry (Sáenz-Badillos and Targarona 185–94) all demonstrate the continuity of Halevi's later work with Andalusi tradition. For all its acclaim as a document of Jewish piety and apologetics, the *Kitāb al-khazarī* identifies Halevi as an earnest reader of Shiite thought in general and its Ismāʿīlī branch in particular. Far from developing an intellectual and devotional structure of thought and experience internal to Jewish tradition, as some argue, Halevi applied Ismāʿīlī terminology and concepts about group pride (*ʿaṣabiyya*) to his construction of Israel and he enlisted Neoplatonist methods in articulating the *Kitāb al-khazarī*'s peculiar view of Jewish tradition (Wasserstrom 128, 133; Pines).

Judah Halevi's cultural production after 1125 initiated formal and thematic shifts in the discourse of the culture, such that his lyrics, poetics, and epistemology represent a partial rewriting of the dominant Judeo-Arabic paradigm and its supposedly excessive identification with al-Andalus/Sefarad. At the same time, the languages of Andalusi culture continued to dominate Halevi's lyrics and thinking and the poet remained bound emotionally to his Andalusi roots. One of his final lyrics marks the pilgrim-poet's painful leave-taking of the last of his two Andalusi travel companions in Egypt:[4]

It seemed to me easy to take leave of Isaac,
   Yet my heart skips and quakes for him.

Yea, it quits its place on account of Solomon
   Who has gone off leaving me alone,

I despair of ever seeing my brethren and friends,
   For he is the last of all my companions from Spain.

NOTES

1. Jarden, *Liturgical Poetry* 4:941 (l. 3), 946 (l. 4); Brody and Habermann 1:10–11 (ll. 7–8); Schirmann, *Hebrew Poetry* 2:504 (ll. 1, 7). In the last instance, the east wind is signified by the Hebrew *qadim.*
2. For example, Schirmann, *Hebrew Poetry* 2:501–2; trans. Goldstein 140–41; and Sáenz-Badillos and Targarona 500.
3. Jonathan Culler, *The Pursuit of Signs: Semiotics, Literature, Deconstruction* (Ithaca, 1981).
4. The poet Isaac Ibn Ezra and the India trader Abū l-Rabīʿ (Solomon) ibn Gabbai; text: Brody and Habermann 1:13 (no. 11, ll. 5–10).

BIBLIOGRAPHY

Abramson, Shraga. "A Letter of Rabbi Judah ha-Levi to Rabbi Moses ibn Ezra" [Hebrew]. *Ḥayim Schirmann Jubilee Volume.* Ed. Shraga Abramson and Aaron Mirsky. Jerusalem, 1970. 397–411.

Baneth, David H., and Haggai Ben-Shammai, eds. *Kitāb al-radd wa l-dalīl fī l-dīn al-dhalīl (al-Kitāb al-khazarī).* Jerusalem, 1977.

Berger, Michael S. "Toward a New Understanding of Judah Halevi's *Kuzari.*" *Journal of Religion* 72 (1992): 210–28.

Bonner, Anthony, ed. and trans. *Selected Works of Ramon Llull.* 2 vols. Princeton, 1985.

Brann, Ross. *The Compunctious Poet: Cultural Ambiguity and Hebrew Poetry in Muslim Spain.* Baltimore, 1991.

Brody, Heinrich. *Mivḥar ha-shira ha-ʿivrit.* 2nd edn. Leipzig, 1923.

Brody, Heinrich, and A. M. Habermann, eds. *Dīwān des Abū l-Ḥasan Jehuda ha-Levi.* 4 vols. 1930. Rpt., Farnborough, 1971.

Brody, Heinrich, and Dan Pagis. *Moshe ibn ezra: Shirei ha-ḥol.* 3 vols. Berlin, 1935–77.

Burrell, David B. *Knowing the Unknowable God: Ibn-Sina, Maimonides, Aquinas.* Notre Dame, 1986.

Carmi, Ted. *The Penguin Book of Hebrew Verse.* New York, 1981.

Cohen, Gerson D. *Sefer ha-Qabbalah by Ibn Daud: The Book of Tradition.* Philadelphia, 1967.

Edwards, Robert. "Exile, Self, and Society." *Exile in Literature.* Ed. Maria-Ines Lagos Pope. Lewisburg, 1988. 15–31.

Fleischer, Ezra. "On the Sources about Rabbi Judah Halevi's Youth and the Beginning of His Connections with Moses ibn Ezra" [Hebrew]. *Qiryat sefer* 61 (1987): 893–910.

"Yehuda Halevi: Remarks Concerning His Life and Poetical Œuvre" [Hebrew]. *Israel Levin Jubilee Volume.* Ed. Reuven Tsur and Tova Rosen. Tel Aviv, 1994. 241–76.

Goitein, S. D. "Autographs of Judah ha-Levi" [Hebrew]. *Tarbiz* 25 (1956): 393–412.

"Judaeo-Arabic Letters from Spain (Early Twelfth Century)." *Orientalia hispanica: Sive studia F.M. Pareja octogenario dicata.* Ed. J. M. Barral. Leiden, 1974. 331–50.

A Mediterranean Society: The Jewish Communities of the Arab World as Portrayed in the Documents of the Cairo Geniza. Volume 5, *The Individual.* Berkeley, 1988.

Goldstein, David. *The Jewish Poets of Spain.* New York, 1982.

Hamori, Andras. "Lights in the Heart of the Sea: Some Images of Judah Halevi's." *Journal of Semitic Studies* 30 (1985): 75–83.

On the Art of Medieval Arabic Literature. Princeton, 1974.

"Reading a Hebrew Lyric with a Hispano-Arabic Background." *Edebiyāt,* n.s., 3 (1989): 119–28.

Ibn ʿAqnīn, Joseph. *Inkishāf al-asrār wa-ẓuhūr al-anwār.* Ed. Abraham S. Halkin. Jerusalem, 1964.

Ibn Ezra, Moses. *Kitāb al-muḥāḍara wa l-mudhākara.* Ed. and trans. Abraham S. Halkin. Jerusalem, 1975.

Ibn Ḥazm. *Ṭawq al-ḥamāma fī l-ulfa wa l-ullāf.* Ed. Ṣalāḥ al-Dīn al-Qāsimī. Baghdad, 1986.

Ibn Khafāja, Abū Isḥāq. *Dīwān ibn khafāja.* Ed. Muṣṭafā Ghāzī. Alexandria, 1960.

Ibn Parḥon, Solomon. *Maḥberet he-ʿarukh.* Ed. S. G. Stern. 1844. Rpt., Jerusalem, 1970.

Ibn Saʿīd, ʿAlī ibn Mūsā al-Maghribī. *The Banners of the Champions: An Anthology of Medieval Arabic Poetry from Andalusia and Beyond.* Trans. James A. Bellamy and Patricia Owen Steiner. Madison, 1989.

Rāyāt al-mubarrizīn wa-ghāyāt al-mumayyazīn. Ed. al-Nuʿmān ʿAbd al-Mutaʿālī al-Qāḍī. Cairo, 1973.

Jarden, Dov. *Divan shmuel hanagid: Ben tehillim.* Jerusalem, 1966.

The Liturgical Poetry of Rabbi Yehuda Halevi [Hebrew]. 4 vols. Jerusalem, 1978–85.

al-Maqqarī. *Nafḥ al-ṭīb min ghuṣn al-andalus al-raṭīb.* Ed. Iḥsān ʿAbbās. 8 vols. Beirut, 1968.

Menocal, María Rosa. *Shards of Love: Exile and the Origins of the Lyric.* Durham, 1994.

Monroe, James T., and David Swialto. "Ninety-three Arabic Harjas in Hebrew Muwassaḥs: Their Hispano-Romance Prosody and Thematic Features." *Journal of the American Oriental Society* 97 (1977): 141–65.

Pines, Shlomo. "Shiʿite Terms and Conceptions in Judah Halevi's *Kuzari.*" *Jerusalem Studies in Arabic and Islam* 2 (1980): 165–251.

Ratzaby, Yehuda. "Iggeret me-rabbi yehudah ha-levi le-rabbi ḥabib." *Gilyonot* 28 (1953): 268–72.

"Me-oṣar ha-piyyut we-ha-shira." *Sinai* 14 (1950): 170–80.

"Studies in the Nature of Hebrew Poetry in Medieval Spain" [Hebrew]. *Barukh Kurzweil Memorial Volume.* Ed. M. Z. Kaddari, A. Saltman, and M. Schwarcz. Tel Aviv, 1975. 306–53.

Rosen(-Moked), Tova. *The Hebrew Girdle Poem (Muwashshaḥ) in the Middle Ages* [Hebrew]. Haifa, 1985.

"The Strophic Trend in Yehuda Halevi's Poetry: An Alternative Poetics?" [Hebrew]. *Israel Levin Jubilee Volume.* Ed. Reuven Tsur and Tova Rosen. Tel Aviv, 1994. 315–28.

Sáenz-Badillos, Ángel. "The Liturgical Muwassaḥ of Yehuda Halevi" [Hebrew]. *Israel Levin Jubilee Volume.* Ed. Reuven Tsur and Tova Rosen. Tel Aviv, 1994. 185–94.

Sáenz-Badillos, Ángel, and Judit Targarona. *Yehuda Ha-Levi, poemas: Introducción, traducción y notas.* Madrid, 1994.

Saperstein, Marc. "Halevi's West Wind." *Prooftexts* 1 (1981): 306–11.

Scheindlin, Raymond P. *The Gazelle: Medieval Hebrew Poems on God, Israel, and the Soul.* Philadelphia, 1991.

Wine, Women, and Death: Medieval Hebrew Poems on the Good Life. Philadelphia, 1986.

Schirmann, Ḥayim. *Hebrew Poetry in Spain and Provence* [Hebrew]. 4 vols. Jerusalem, 1959.

"Judah Halevi's Treatise on Meters" [Hebrew]. *Studies of the Research Institute for Hebrew Poetry* 6 (1945): 319–22.

"Poets Contemporary with Ibn Ezra and Halevi." *Studies of the Research Institute for Hebrew Poetry* 2 (1936): 186–92, 328–33.

Stern, Samuel M. "Imitations of Arabic Muwashshaḥāt in the Hebrew Poetry of Spain" [Hebrew]. *Tarbiz* 18 (1947): 166–84.

Wasserstrom, Steven M. *Between Muslim and Jew: The Problem of Symbiosis under Early Islam.* Princeton, 1995.

Weiser, Asher, ed. *Ibn ʿezra ʿal ha-tora.* 3 vols. Jerusalem, 1977.

Yahalom, Yosef. "Poetry and Society in Egypt: An Examination Based on the Attitude to Judah Halevi's Secular Poetry" [Hebrew]. *Zion* 45 (1980): 286–98.

CHAPTER 13

PETRUS ALFONSI

Lourdes María Alvárez

Petrus Alfonsi, an Andalusian Jew who converted to Christianity early in the twelfth century, was just one of the many scholars of his time who lived both in and between Jewish, Christian, and Islamic cultures and took upon themselves the task of acting as a bridge between these traditions. Alfonsi's education in Arabic science, philosophy, and particularly astronomy – and his level of erudition was not particularly extraordinary given the standards in Islamic Spain – gave him something of great value to communicate to Christian Europe. He explains his project: "[I]t is proper that all those who have drunk of any philosophical nectar love each other, and that anyone who might have anything rare, precious, and useful which is unknown to others should impart it generously to others, so that in this way everyone's knowledge may both grow and be extended in time" (Tolan 172–73). As a *converso* he sought to convince the Jews of their error in rejecting Jesus; as an Andalusian intellectual, he brought missionary zeal to the dissemination of Islamic and Jewish learning among the Christians of Europe.

Alfonsi lived in a period of great change. The latter half of the eleventh century heralded an enormous shift in the balance of power around the Mediterranean. Christian forces made significant advances both on the Iberian Peninsula, where the Islamic Taifa states were divided and weakened, and in Sicily, which in 1091 fell to the Normans. While these conquests diminished the political presence of Islam in Europe, perhaps paradoxically they also opened up Christian Europe to Arabic philosophical, scientific, medical, astronomical, and literary cultures. Not only had vast libraries like that of Toledo come into Christian hands, but the conquered population of Mozarabs, Andalusian Jews, and Mudejares produced a profound cultural impact: Mudejar architecture, thousands of Arabic loanwords, and new cultural forms such as the troubadour lyric – strongly suggestive of the Arabic and Hebrew strophic poetry (muwashshahs and zajals) born and popularized in al-Andalus.

This intense intercultural contact in Spain and Sicily coincides with the beginnings of Christian Europe's new "hunger of spirit," an awareness of, and yearning for, knowledge of every sort. Certainly this twelfth-century "renaissance" is also a product of important social and economic developments throughout Europe, including the rise of institutions such as the university and increased prosperity. Yet the translators' centrality in nourishing this cultural awakening is beyond question. They not only brought Europe the untold treasures of Islamic civilization but also transmitted the wealth of Greek learning that had been lost to Europe for many centuries.

The terrain had been prepared by several translations of Arabic astronomical and mathematical treatises, dating to the mid-tenth century.[1] Jews were prominent in this movement; in the polyglot and multicultural world of Islamic Spain, they had often found themselves translating, mediating, and negotiating between Arabic and Hebrew. In the twelfth century they not only played a crucial role in translating Arabic works into Latin but also actively promoted and disseminated Islamic sciences throughout Europe.

By the mid-twelfth century, the efforts of the early translators, who worked in relative isolation, had given rise to schools and centers established to translate methodically – and relatively quickly – an enormous corpus of material.[2] The appetite for these translations was inextricably linked to the generalized cultural renewal of the times; each translated text bred the desire for others. Petrus Alfonsi must be counted among those pioneering translators.

His name was Moses Sefaradi until his conversion in 1106, an event he describes in the prologue to his apologetic work, *Dialogi contra Iudaeos*. The baptism – celebrated in Huesca in 1106 – not only marked his personal transformation but was also deeply resonant of the cultural shifts and interactions of the times. Only ten years earlier Huesca had been under Islamic rule; what was now the cathedral was then the great mosque. In a ceremony attended by Alfonso I "the Battler" of Aragon, who served as his baptismal sponsor, Moses took the name Peter, whose feast day it was, and the name Alfonso, after his sponsor.

Other than his own account of his conversion, we have few details of Alfonsi's life. His place of birth is unknown. It is unclear whether he was originally from the Huesca region or was one of the many Andalusian Jews who moved there seeking refuge from the persecution of the recently installed Almoravid government. Alfonsi seems to have held a position of respect and leadership in the Jewish community, perhaps as the chief rabbi of the area. Not only does he himself claim to have carried weight among Jews in matters of interpretation, but another source calls him "magnus rabinus apud judaeos" (Lacarra, *Pedro Alfonso* 10). The king's participation in his baptism also lends credibility to this idea.

After his conversion he traveled to England – perhaps to escape the repudiation of his former coreligionists – where he was known as a "magister" of liberal arts, especially astronomy. Among his pupils was Walcher, the prior of the monastery at Malvern. Alfonsi also seems to have taught in France. He is thought to have returned to Aragon by 1121, for he is listed as a witness in a land transaction that year in Saragossa. Another document places him in Tudela in 1142. The date and place of his death are also unknown.

Writing *Dialogi contra Iudaeos* shortly after his conversion, Alfonsi demonstrated his zeal to put his knowledge of Jewish and Islamic theology in the service of proving the superiority of Christianity. At the same time, he was painfully aware of the ways in which Christian Europe lagged behind Islamic Spain in science, technology, and philosophy. Thus, Alfonsi passionately promoted Arabic science and astronomy in particular: through his teaching, his translation of al-Khawārizmī's astronomical tables, and his *Epistola ad peripateticos*, a tract addressed to "those in all parts of France most diligently engaged in the teaching of knowledge" (Tolan 172). He is best known for the *Disciplina clericalis*, his most literary and in many ways enigmatic work, which brings together sayings and maxims from a variety of philosophers and Arabic and Jewish proverbs and folklore. Both the *Dialogi* and the *Disciplina* circulated widely throughout medieval Europe, as is attested by the large number of extant manuscripts: seventy-nine in the case of the *Dialogi* and seventy-six for the *Disciplina* (183, 199).

There is persuasive evidence to suggest that Alfonsi's labors of instruction and translation go far beyond the four works of unquestioned attribution. Although the texts are lost, there are references to three more dialogues: the first on the seven liberal arts; the second on religions, laws, and beliefs; and the third, titled *De humano proficuo*, on man's superiority to other created beings.[3] Although the former mosque in Huesca was ultimately displaced by a new cathedral and then destroyed, Alfonsi's act of conversion – in itself an act of translation – and his subsequent writings would reverberate throughout Europe for centuries.[4]

DIALOGI CONTRA IUDAEOS

In his prologue to the *Dialogi contra Iudaeos*, Alfonsi addresses the work to those Jews who rebuked him for his apostasy. He chafes at the accusations that he has abandoned Judaism to adopt a more permissive Christian rule, or that he has badly misinterpreted Scripture, or worse yet, that he has cynically sought material gain among the Christians. His decision to write in Latin, rather than Hebrew or Arabic, however, gives support to the suspicion that this work was instead a gesture to prove the sincerity of his conversion. Like the Jewish anti-Christian tracts in Hebrew and other works of religious polemic that invoke the convention of a dialogue of persuasion, the *Dialogi* is more concerned with bolstering the convictions of those who already agree with its author than with winning new converts.

Alfonsi's status as a *converso* is employed not only to provide a motive for writing the work but as a powerful rhetorical strategy.[5] Structured as a dialogue between his two selves, the Jewish Moses and the Christian Peter, this autobiographical fiction – indeed, a sort of confession – loads his ostensibly rational prose with moments of emotion. For example, the repeated references to "your doctors" seem to underscore and reenact Alfonsi's own rupture with them. Naturally, he exploits his intimate knowledge of the Hebrew Bible and Talmud to bolster his arguments, and he even appeals to Hebrew philology to prove the triune nature of God (*DI* 107–13).[6] Arguing against what he sees as slavish adherence to the letter, rather than the spirit, of the Torah, and echoing many of the Karaite arguments about the spuriousness of the Talmud, Alfonsi asserts the importance of adopting an allegorical reading of the parts of the Bible that are illogical or nonsensical if read literally (*DI* 29). For him, Christianity's more flexible and figurative mode of interpretation is a major point in its favor, and ultimately one of the main reasons for his claim that it is more logical.

The *Dialogi* begins with Moses's invitation to Peter to give the reasons for his conversion to Christianity. As in the prologue, Alfonsi portrays himself as an accidental interlocutor, who responds to questions posed by others, rather than as the initiator of the conversation. Whether this is simply a convention or Alfonsi sincerely felt compelled to answer his critics in the Jewish community, there is no reticence in his systematic attack on Jewish practice and belief. Islam, he dispatches quickly; he seems to include it for the sake of completeness, but it is clearly not the focus of his concern.

Moses asks that they base their discussion on the Hebrew Torah. Peter accepts this restriction, saying: "I greatly desire to slay you with your own sword" (*DI* 10).[7] Moses imposes the further condition that Peter develop and supplement his scriptural arguments with "natural reason" (*naturae rationem* [15]). The book, divided into twelve chapters, begins with an elaborate and multipronged attack on Judaism (chaps. 1–4), then quickly refutes Islam (chap. 5), and concludes with a defense of Christianity (chaps. 6–12). The largely civil tone of the discussion is occasionally marred by charges of stupidity, irrationality, and stubbornness, but there is none of the invective that would characterize later anti-Jewish works, such as Peter the Venerable's *Adversus Iudaeorum inveteratam duritiem*, written just a few decades later. Alfonsi's dialogue concludes somewhat equivocally: Moses has accepted the logic of Peter's arguments but, at the same time, seems to cling obstinately to beliefs he has agreed are mistaken. Apparently logic is insufficient to effect a conversion; grace is also necessary. Peter prays that the Holy Spirit will bring Moses to the truth.

One of the overriding themes of the *Dialogi* is establishing a logical proof of Christianity that is independent of sacred texts. Yet the animated digressions on Arabic science often wander far afield of the point they seek to prove; in those passages there is a clear sense of a common quest for truth and knowledge that unites Moses and Peter. Yet the philosophical discussions serve a double purpose here, one that we see echoed in his later work. If philosophy can be used to confirm the truth of revealed religion, then there is no conflict between speculative philosophy and religion. In this, Alfonsi anticipates the efforts of Ibn Ṭufayl, Averroes, Maimonides, Albertus Magnus, and other twelfth-century philosophers who would much more explicitly defend the harmony between religion and philosophy.

Despite his civil tone and commitment to rational discourse, Alfonsi's invocation of the Augustinian trope of confession and conversion, the act of exposing one's former errors and mistakes – here in the person of the *converso* – is the seed of the pattern of escalating the charges leveled at the Jews. Whereas the *Dialogi contra Iudaeos* provided Christian Europe with far more detailed and reliable accounts of Jewish and Islamic practices and beliefs than had previously been disseminated, it also leveled a new and damaging accusation at the Jews.[8] Earlier writers concluded that the Jewish involvement in the crucifixion of Christ was an element in God's plan of salvation or that the Jews had simply failed to recognize the long-awaited Messiah. Alfonsi asserts that they knowingly and willfully killed Christ, and led many people into error by claiming he was a magician born of a prostitute (*DI* 58). Alfonsi concludes: "Certainly, the envy of the Jews and their malice were the cause of Christ's death, moreover the death of Christ is the cause of their captivity" (*DI* 59). Alfonsi's confession – his condemnation of his former belief – brings him grace but it sets in motion a process that culminates in the expulsion of the Jews from Spain.

SCIENTIFIC WORKS AND THE *EPISTOLA AD PERIPATETICOS*

Alfonsi's efforts to bring Arabic science, particularly astronomy (and what we would now call astrology), to Christian Europe are sometimes obscured by his limitations, and by the accomplishments of his students, who quickly surpassed him and achieved lasting renown. Nonetheless, Alfonsi's translations of al-Khawārizmī's astronomical tables represented a significant improvement over the existing level of knowledge. Yet his eagerness to convert Arabic astronomy into terms accessible to Latin scholars – which included creating new Latin terminology when he felt it was necessary – led him to numerous errors, including the most serious one: replacing the Arabic (lunar) calendar with the Julian (solar) calendar without accounting for difference between them, thus rendering his lunar tables useless. Still, even in his failure, he was successful in sparking the interest of other scholars; within ten years Peter Abelard completed a new and much improved translation of al-Khawārizmī.

In the *Epistola ad peripateticos* Alfonsi lays out the usefulness of, and the interdependence between, the seven liberal arts. For him, the greatest of these is astronomy, because "the sun, the moon and other planets exercise their powers in earthly things and many things are affected by them" (Tolan 179). The seasons, weather, tides, and harvests can be predicted using astronomy, so too "the proper times for cauterizing, making incisions, puncturing abscesses, bloodletting . . . and also the hours in which fevers are to end" (174). Thus his text serves a dual purpose: "to give us a perpetual name after our death, and that we might rouse into life a knowledge of this art" (176–77).

Alfonsi's distinctive position on grammar is worth noting: "This cannot be counted among the seven liberal arts, since it is neither knowledge subject to proof nor is it in every language the same, but in each one different" (173). Surely Alfonsi – who moved between Arabic, Hebrew, Latin, and a number of different vernaculars – was acutely aware of the arbitrariness of language, yet his downplaying of grammar may also be a reaction against the claims made for the primacy and sacredness of Arabic by Muslims, or of Hebrew by Jews. By contrast, Christianity never staked its truth claims on the sacredness of the language of its Scriptures but rather on the revelation of "the word incarnate."

DISCIPLINA CLERICALIS

In an irony reminiscent of Petrarch – who found fame not in his dense Latin writings but in the vernacular poems he wrote for diversion – the "perpetual name" that Alfonsi sought came not so much from his scientific or religious writings but from the *Disciplina clericalis*. If in the *Dialogi contra Iudaeos* logic and philosophy "prove" the truth of Christian teaching, in the *Disciplina clericalis* Alfonsi asserts that the wisdom of the philosophers will lead the human spirit "to follow that path in the world which will lead it to the kingdom of heaven" (Hermes 103). The philosophers he cites are Greek, Arab, and Jewish – their pedigree actually gives them greater authority in a Europe dazzled by the learning of the "East." Yet the interest of the *Disciplina* lies not in its aphorisms but in their illustration with fables, verse, and animal tales drawn from Arab and Jewish folklore and oral tradition, and the ambiguities opened up by these fictions.

The *Disciplina clericalis* is not a translation of a preexisting work. Rather

Alfonsi gathered together material from both Arabic and Hebrew sources, organizing the Latin version in a frame-tale structure. Although his composition is original, the use of tales to illustrate and enliven didactic works was already a feature of Arabic literature, perhaps best exemplified in the widely known and much admired *Kalīla wa-dimna*.[9] For the most part Alfonsi is rather vague about his sources. Although he ascribes some aphorisms directly to Enoch, Balaam, Luqmān, Plato, or Aristotle, most of the maxims and stories have no more attribution than "a philosopher said," "the story is told that," or "once upon a time." Much critical attention has focused on remedying this "problem" and identifying Alfonsi's sources, as well as listing later works that drew on his. However, the oral nature of these traditions with their myriad variations often make such a textcentric approach a fruitless task: the "chain" of transmission is more like a web or a tapestry of versions. In any case, Alfonsi's vagueness is purposeful, for the authority of these maxims comes not from a particular philosopher but from their universality, their manifest good sense.

As occurs in *Kalīla wa-dimna* and in later frame tales such as Ibn Zabarra's *Sefer shaʿashuʿim* (Book of Delights) and Don Juan Manuel's *Conde Lucanor*, and to an even more exaggerated degree in Juan Ruiz's *Libro de buen amor*, the juxtaposition of stories with the intention of "mollienda et dulcificanda" [softening and sweetening] (Hermes 104) the underlying lesson and aiding remembrance of a moral often seems actually to undermine the stated purpose. Alfonsi sometimes pairs rather suggestive – if not disturbing – stories with common, almost banal bits of advice. For example, the oft-repeated admonition to test one's friends (i.e., a friend in need is a friend indeed) is illustrated with two tales: that of the half friend, followed by that of the whole friend. A dying man – an Arab, specifies Alfonsi – asks his son how many friends he has. One hundred, the son replies. The old man urges his son to test his friends to see which ones are really loyal, for despite his age the father has won only half a friend. The father suggests that the son present himself at a friend's house with a bloody sack filled with animal remains asking the friend's help in hiding the body of a man he has just killed. The son promptly learns that his "friends" draw the line at abetting a murder; only the father's half friend is willing to help.

In another section of the book, Alfonsi presents a series of humorous stories about the wiles of women. The "teacher" here hesitates to tell these tales, for fear that the naive reader will associate him with the immoralities they describe, but, prodded by the student, he agrees. After hearing several stories of women's trickery and deceit, the student says he takes them to be a warning against marriage. The teacher disagrees with this interpretation, for not all women are evil. Could it be a parody, as some modern critics have suggested? Or is Alfonsi simply a naively medieval – in the pejorative sense – moralist intentionally misread by those more interested in the tales than in the morals they seek to teach?

Is the exaggeration of the story of the half friend really only intended as an aide-mémoire? Is the principle of testing one's friends really still valid when taken to such an extreme? Is friendship to be placed above legal and religious strictures against murder? Is a ruse such as this a respectful way to treat a friend? The question here and in many of the seemingly contradictory exempla of the other medieval frame-tale narratives is whether the questioning of fixed principles of advice is inadvertent, an unavoidable consequence of the interpretative possibilities opened up by stories. While the frame often seeks to determine and fix an interpretation – in this case the pupil and the master discuss the meaning of the story – the disjunction between a sententious aphorism and a story that intends to "prove" is unavoidable. At the same time, if one looks at wisdom literature through the ages, it seems that often the contradiction itself is the true message. Aphorisms in praise of speech are juxtaposed with those that favor silence, those that recognize the power of riches with those that urge its disdain: underlying the contradictions is a call to exercise judgment, a kind of wisdom that cannot be encapsulated in a maxim.

The popularity of the *Disciplina clericalis* grew in the thirteenth century when mendicant preachers, following the example of Jacques de Vitry, began using it as a source for stories to enliven their sermons. The traditions found in Alfonsi's book would be found in many later books: the *Libro de buen amor*, *Castigos y documentos para bien vivir*, *Libro del caballero Zifar*, *Libro de los buenos proverbios*, and so on, although given the pervasiveness of these stories, especially throughout Spain, it is not always possible to determine whether the *Disciplina* played a direct role in their transmission. As fictional narrative continued to gain ground, the stories were freed from their role as instruments of moral instruction, and writers such as Boccaccio and Cervantes embellished them and enshrined them as part of the not quite so Western canon.

NOTES

1. See Millás Vallicrosa 79–115 on early Latin translations of Arabic scientific works.
2. Iohannes Hispalensis, archbishop of Toledo (1152–66), established the renowned school of translators in Toledo. He sponsored translations of Ibn Sīnā (Avicenna), Algazel, and Ibn Gabirol (Avicebron), as well as an impressive number of Arabic astronomical and astrological works, hermetic works, and alchemy. It was in Toledo that Gerard of Cremona (c. 1114–87) translated Greek authors (Ptolemy,

Aristotle, Euclid, Galen) into Latin through Arabic versions and brought Europe Arabic works in philosophy, mathematics, medicine, astronomy, astrology, and alchemy (d'Alverny 453–54). Although earlier studies credited Archbishop Raymond with establishing the school, d'Alverny (444–46) argues convincingly against this theory. In the thirteenth century the Toledo school, especially under the aegis of Alfonso X, gained renown for its translations into Castilian. Sicily was also a hub of translation activity, although more focused on direct translations from Greek into Latin.

3. See Charles Burnett, "Las obras de Pedro Alfonso: Problemas de autenticidad," *Estudios*, ed. Lacarra, 313–48, for an exhaustive examination of works associated with, and attributed to, Alfonsi.
4. The former mosque was used as a cathedral for several centuries. In 1273, however, almost two centuries after its "conversion" to Christian use, King James I declared that it was unseemly to use a building constructed in the service of Islam. He set in motion the construction of a new cathedral, but the "tainted" building remained in use through the first third of the fourteenth century. Ironically, the new cathedral, which took centuries to complete, was strongly marked by the work of Mudejar and Morisco artisans.
5. In the centuries that followed, it became almost de rigueur to have *conversos* argue the Christian side in Jewish–Christian disputations. In that of Paris (1240) the Christian side was held by Nicholas Donin, a former Jew. The Barcelona Disputation of 1263 had the *converso* Pablo Christiani lead the Christian side. In the protracted disputation of Tortosa (1413–14) the Christian position was stridently expounded by the *converso* Maestro Hieronymus de Sancta Fide (born Joshua Lorki). By the fifteenth century *conversos* were arguing against Jews from positions of great power, as witnessed in the case of Pablo de Sancta María, the archbishop of Burgos, formerly Rabbi Solomon ha-Levi, who played a pivotal role in the tragic fate of Spanish Jewry.
6. All references are to the Latin text of Mieth's edition of the *Dialogi* (*DI*). Translations are my own.
7. It is interesting to note that Jewish disputations against Christianity often used New Testament sources. See del Valle.
8. Peter the Venerable appears to have relied heavily, though not exclusively, on Alfonsi's work in composing his *Contra Iudaeos* (d'Alverny 428–29 n. 27). Though ultimately moved to sponsor translations of Islamic material to lend weight and credibility to his Christian apologetics, Peter the Venerable's activities also introduced much previously unknown information about Islam.
9. *Kalīla wa-dimna* comes out of a literary tradition that goes back to Sanskrit, then makes its way through Persian, into the celebrated and widely disseminated Arabic version of Ibn al-Muqaffaʿ. It was translated into Castilian and twice into Hebrew. One of the Hebrew versions was translated into Latin under the title *Directorium humanae vitae, alias parabolae antiquorum sapientium* by Juan de Capua, an Italian Jew converted to Catholicism. That Latin translation spawned a host of new translations into European vernaculars.

BIBLIOGRAPHY

d'Alverny, Marie-Thérèse. "Translations and Translators." *Renaissance and Renewal in the Twelfth Century.* Ed. R. L. Benson and G. Constable. Oxford, 1982. 421–62.

del Valle, Carlos, ed. *Polémica judeo-cristiana: Estudios.* Madrid, 1992.

Ferruolo, Stephen C. "The Twelfth-Century Renaissance." *Renaissances before the Renaissance.* Ed. Warren Treadgold. Stanford, 1984. 114–43, nn. 197–201.

Hermes, Eberhard, ed. and trans., P. R. Quarrie, English trans. *Disciplina clericalis.* Berkeley, 1977.

Hilka, Alfons, and Werner Söderhjelm, eds. *Disciplina clericalis.* Heidelberg, 1911.

Jones, Joseph Ramon, and John Esten Keller, trans. *The Scholar's Guide: A Translation of the Twelfth-Century* Disciplina clericalis. Toronto, 1969.

Lacarra, María Jesús. *Pedro Alfonso.* [Saragossa], 1991.

Lacarra, María Jesús, ed. *Estudios sobre Pedro Alfonso de Huesca.* Huesca, 1996.

Lacarra, María Jesús, ed., Esperanza Ducay, Spanish trans. *Disciplina clericalis.* Saragossa, 1980.

Mieth, Klaus-Peter, Latin edn., Esperanza Ducay, Spanish trans. *Diálogo contra los judíos.* Huesca, 1996.

Millás Vallicrosa, José María. *Nuevos estudios sobre la historia de la ciencia española.* Barcelona, 1960.

Tolan, John. *Petrus Alfonsi and His Medieval Readers.* Gainesville, 1993. Includes Latin/English edn. of *Epistola ad peripateticos.* 163–81.

CHAPTER 14

IBN QUZMĀN

Amila Buturovic

Though celebrated as the outstanding composer of zajal – the strophic form that uses vernacular Arabic of al-Andalus – Ibn Quzmān has by and large remained an enigmatic and neglected poetic figure. We know little about his life: what has been passed on to us is a series of fragmented references found primarily in his diwan. At the outset, this is quite ironic, because Ibn Quzmān's presence haunts almost all of his 149 zajals, regardless of their themes. Unexpectedly and frequently his voice breaks through the poetic frame, alerting the reader to his proximity. Ibn Quzmān enters a poem sometimes as its character and sometimes as his "real" self, further distracting the reader from an empathic response.

Ibn Quzmān's life spans the period of Almoravid domination of the peninsula. In a panegyric dedicated to Almoravid leader Yūsuf ibn Tāshfīn for the victory gained against the Christian forces at the battle of Zallaka in 1086, he mentions himself in a satirical reference to the great event. Although the reader at first experiences a sense of awe before a crucial military victory, Ibn Quzmān disrupts this sensation by drawing attention to himself through a facetious autobiographical remark:

What a day that was!
Many people were then gathered,
and whatever happened to the victors happened.
In my father's testicles I was and did not see
But the one who did narrated the story to me. (no. 38)

Ibn Quzmān died in 555/1160, when his native city of Córdoba was besieged by the Almohads, whose stated mission was to rid al-Andalus of the corruption of the Almoravids, their North African Berber predecessors.

Although linked to Córdoba by both birth and residence, Ibn Quzmān tells us about his trips to Seville, Granada, Málaga, Almería, and Valencia. Most of these travels were prompted by either a search for patronage or trouble with the authorities (nos. 78, 124). Yet Ibn Quzmān portrays himself as infinitely wanton and as refusing to deprive himself of the worldly joys that the Almoravids considered, at least officially, taboo. According to al-Ahwānī, "the major preoccupations of Ibn Quzmān's life are money, wine, and love" (*Zajal* 82):

Except for mine,
there is no kingdom but yours, O Sulaymān,
and only the Abbasids and the Umayyads
could compare with me. (no. 11)

Although we have no proof that the diwan is entirely autobiographical, external sources (al-Maqqarī, Ibn Saʿīd, Ibn Khaldūn, al-Marrākushī) indicate that Ibn Quzmān carries many real experiences into his poems, adding or subtracting unconfirmed details.

It is to be noted, however, that in the context of the diwan at large Ibn Quzmān's hyperbolic expressions of joy are satirically charged. In numerous zajals he shows awareness of the ruler's disapproval of indulgence of any kind. In zajal 47 Ibn Quzmān writes:

I said what I had in mind: that is my excuse
Here I make a stop and my zajal ends.
You are the Almoravids, so I know the story,
You have never liked any extravagance.

Throughout the diwan, Ibn Quzmān hews to his mission of bringing to light and satirizing what people around him dare not mention in public. The targets of his attacks are all the "hypocrites" of Andalusian society – officers, rulers, *fuqahāʾ*, and prostitutes. He spares no one. His poetic ambition is to listen, observe, and differentiate. His purpose is to transform images and sounds into a poetry that will fascinate, entertain, embarrass, and pave the way to a necessary change. But in order not to criticize others and spare himself, he behaves as a nonconformist, rebuking the religious authorities and violating their law, for which he is arrested and punished on several occasions (nos. 39, 41).

Ibn Quzmān's rebelliousness is closely linked with the Almoravid presence in his homeland. The Andalus he knows from experience is the Andalus of the Almoravids. Yet his life seems to be one of self-inflicted displacement and perpetual nostalgia toward the Taifa world he himself never directly knew. In satirizing the Almoravids – implicitly and explicitly – Ibn Quzmān creates a sentimental bond with the Taifa culture the Almoravids have sought to eliminate through political and social means. The two worlds – the Taifa and the Almoravid – function as conflicting metaphors in Ibn Quzmān's poetry, the former standing for cosmopolitanism and the latter for provincialism.

Although the Almoravids' promotion of linguistic, cultural, and religious homogeneity is motivated by an ambition to restore and safeguard Islamic values on the peninsula, Ibn Quzmān reads their quest as an intrusive force of centralization and assault on cosmopolitan diversity characteristic of the party kings. As an antithesis to the Almoravid goal, Ibn Quzmān writes poetry that in both style and form decentralizes meaning. Very little is fixed in his verse: the ideas, tropes, and language escape uniformity. They are at once eclectic and fragmentary. In that sense, while highlighting his own multicultural tendencies, Ibn Quzmān alienates the Almoravid value system designed to singularize meaning in the post-Taifa Andalusian society. Indeed, it seems that all his poetry carries a didactic importance expressed at two levels of critique: as an ethnocultural clash between North African Berbers and Andalusian Arabs, and as a social mismatch between the nomadic values of the newcomers and the urban, multicultural values of Andalusian cities.

In more general terms, Ibn Quzmān's poetry has lent itself to several critical perspectives. Some have dealt with its formal aspects and the linguistic features of Andalusian Arabic. Others have addressed links between medieval Arabic and European literary styles. Further, this poetry has been considered as a text documenting the socioaesthetic values of twelfth-century al-Andalus. And, in a more intrinsic examination of their content, Ibn Quzmān's zajals have been explored for their thematic movements.

The messages conveyed in Ibn Quzmān's poetry appear most effective when viewed in the context of the zajal form through which they are delivered. What form could so excellently serve the purpose of criticizing the Almoravids than one to which they could relate neither aesthetically nor linguistically? The zajal, which came to life at the intersection of Hispano-Arab cultures, was the perfect poetic tool, and Ibn Quzmān used it ingeniously. In the prologue to his diwan, written in impeccable classical Arabic, he strategically expresses his intention of employing vernacular language and the local poetic form rather than the Arabic of the religious and literary elite:

> When I acquired a perfect freedom in the art of composing zajals and when my natural talent responded easily to its strange charms, the foremost leaders in this art became my suites and my attendants, because I reached in it mastery which no one had reached before me, and a technical virtuosity whose fame has spread far and wide. *I established the principles of the art and made it difficult for dull brains to engage in it.* (Nykl, *Hispano-Arabic Poetry* 269, emphasis mine)

As stated earlier, zajals constitute the greatest bulk of the diwan, and are the poet's main claim to fame. The zajal is generally associated with three thematic orientations: panegyric, bacchic, and amatory. Ibn Quzmān's zajals conform to this tradition, but they also introduce certain stylistic devices that make his art highly original. Probably the most outstanding is his narrative method. Related most commonly in the first-person form, Ibn Quzmān's poetic narratives dynamically unfold through a series of incidents, each of which pertains to its own time, setting, and characters. Unable to anticipate the sequence of events, the reader is always guessing what will come next. Transitions from one episode to another go almost unnoticed, though the narration often juxtaposes unrelated incidents in the poet's life. This ability to form a unity out of fragmented space-times places Ibn Quzmān among extraordinary literary artists.

But the feature that distinguishes his poetic legacy best and contributes greatly to the high quality of his narrative style is the employment of vernacular language. A unique blend of classical and colloquial Arabic and Romance, this language is used not only to meet the demands of the zajal form but to distinguish the poet among other great authors of Arabic literary heritage. Indeed, Ibn Quzmān tells us of his familiarity with the great men of letters: al-Jāḥiẓ and Ibn Dāʾūd al-Iṣfahānī (no. 95); Jarīr (no. 52); Abū Tammām (nos. 52, 95, 104); al-Mutanabbī (no. 52); Ibn Baqī (nos. 16, 165); Abū Nuwās, for whom he seems to have special admiration (nos. 63, 123, 178); and so on. Furthermore, the prologue to the diwan cited earlier shows Ibn Quzmān's excellent knowledge of classical Arabic.

The choice of vernacular Arabic and the zajal, therefore, was not arbitrary. It associates Ibn Quzmān with a particular sociohistorical context to which he felt strong sentimental ties. For Ibn Quzmān, the diversity of al-Andalus embodies every desire and inspiration a poet can have; indeed, almost nowhere in his diwan does he express a desire to explore the world beyond al-Andalus. His aesthetic world begins and ends with al-Andalus. Furthermore, Ibn Quzmān likely chose the zajal for ideological reasons. Bakhtin reminds us that vernacular language encourages diversity and change, and challenges fixed order and the control over consciousness. It empowers the "unofficial" forces to destabilize the hegemony of the "official" discourse.[1] In Ibn Quzmān's case, by opposing the Andalusian dialect that thrived on intercultural borrowings to the censored Almoravid expression that denied any form of interculturalism, he establishes the underlying dialectic of dulce et utile in most of his zajals. To illustrate, Monroe observes of a vivacious zajal in which the Romance word *vino* is used:

> The use of the Romance words *vino, vino* produces a comic effect on the one hand, but it should also be remembered that the twelfth century witnessed the birth of increased intolerance and persecution of the Mozarabs. In associating himself with the traditionally Christian theme of wine-drinking like Abū Nuwās before him, Ibn Quzmān is flaunting the vices of the society's most despised outcasts in the face of false piety. Since the Romance words in this poem furthermore appear in the rhyme, their comic effect and foulmouthed realism, or better, negative idealism, receive even stronger emphasis. (43)

Thus, Ibn Quzmān's verse is a powerful social commentary. Posited as a challenge to the rigid values imposed yet not always practiced by the Almoravids, it addresses the gap between the ideal and the real. The "ideal," initiated by the Almoravids as a resuscitation of "true" and "pure" Islam in al-Andalus after the chaotically tolerant party kings, soon proved to be a utopian goal. Though many radical measures indicated that the Almoravids meant business – such as introducing a literal interpretation of Maliki law, charging with heresy any promotion of rational sciences (including kalam), persecuting non-Muslims, and even burning al-Ghazālī's books on account of their intellectual elitism – their religious zeal started to give way to a more moderate and integrated lifestyle (al-Marrākushī 255). The reality of Andalusian city culture gradually seeped into the pores of the Almoravid military edifice, wooing many committed warriors to its easygoing premises. In that sense, Ibn Quzmān's zajals poetically portray what Ibn Khaldūn later speculates to be the main reason for the Almoravid fall: nomadic tribal solidarity collapsing in the luxury of Andalusian sedentary culture because it succumbed to, rather than eradicated, the local modus vivendi, and because it imposed, but did not live up to, the rigid Malikite values (2:296–371). Therefore, if one adopts Ibn Khaldūn's perspective, the Almoravids, though set to purify Andalusian Islam from al-Andalus itself, failed. And Ibn Quzmān, engaged poet that he is, describes this failure as it actually unfolds.

Let us now turn to a brief examination of the three thematic movements in Ibn Quzmān's zajals: praise, wine, and love.

ON PRAISE

Since the process of Almoravid consolidation in al-Andalus involved removing the indigenous aristocratic families and forming an Almoravid military elite, literary patronage by the royal court greatly diminished. The men of letters were forced to break into the austere disposition of the new elites and enchant them with poetry they could hardly understand (al-Shaqundī 51–52). Ibn Quzmān is aware of the gap between the two sides, and learns to act accordingly. Cognizant of the new rules, he injects his zajals with sharp satire: in many instances, he composes *madīḥ* in a very bookish manner, offering little in originality but plenty in correctness. And, as in the praise of the Zallaka battle quoted above, these praises are rarely spared his sardonic wit. Commenting again on a military victory, in zajal 38 he says:

What a bad joke, what a vicious game!
The battlefield was silent and the armor wept.
Oh, don't tell me that story again,
for I'm sure I'll wet my bed at night.

Yet as if to clarify that praise of military accomplishment is demanded by the trade, Ibn Quzmān often communicates that his personal self and his professional commitment to writing good panegyrics should be kept apart. For example, in spite of hyperbolic descriptions of Almoravid military aptitude, Ibn Quzmān admits that privately he is not impressed by it at all. Moreover, in zajal 86 he claims that he understands nothing of war affairs and does not need them in life ("If it had to do with good poetry or a zajal, I would give my opinion!"). Confirming that panegyrics are primarily intended to support livelihood, Ibn Quzmān seems ready to accept that professional etiquette may at times superimpose an alienated poetic identity.

Since for Ibn Quzmān writing *madīḥ*s means business and not pleasure, he shows both respect and disrespect for the object of his praise: the former by complying with the literary demands of composing a fair panegyric, and the latter by dismissing a priori his patrons' ability to distinguish a witty panegyric from a boringly proper one. One such *madīḥ* is in zajal 135:

The moment has come to begin the praise:
he has a gentle and handsome face,
honest intentions he always fulfills:
conceived as ideas, they soon become practice.

The inflexible promotion of hegemonic culture turns out to be the favorite target of Ibn Quzmān's panegyrics. Here, he masterfully captures the societal paradoxes resulting from the Almoravid austerity and lack of literary taste. While he dutifully commends the Almoravids' commitment to "true" Islam, he wittily condemns their inability to safeguard it. But his observation of that gap is not merely passive: rather, it is a blunt provocation due to which his poetry is scorned and subjected to censure. In zajal 22 he exclaims:

Those who are afraid of the faqih
have no skill at all
I truly respect him but mainly avoid him
Whore be the mother of the one who takes no drink
even if he carries Ghazālī on his head.

In this twofold assault on Almoravid etiquette – scorning nondrinkers and showing respect, albeit waywardly, for al-Ghazālī, the persona non grata of the time – Ibn Quzmān challenges their hypocrisy. Though dimmed by public displays of morality, sinful pleasures, after all, are shared by everyone. Blunt in zajal 94, Ibn Quzmān instructs all wine consumers on how they should behave when confronted by a faqih or imam while practicing the illegal enjoyment:

You shall see when you ask me:
Have you drunk wine?
I will say: "Indeed I have,
and that, from a very big glass!"

Due to the nature of the Almoravid cause, religion often strays into the sections on praise. Most often, Ibn Quzmān rejects legalistic exaltations. Yet regardless of antisharia statements that he flaunts in the face of the authorities, Ibn Quzmān respects true piety in other people and is tolerant of other religions. In many zajals Ibn Quzmān discusses his attitude regarding Christianity, toward which he seems to be quite benevolent (e.g., nos. 40, 129, 130). In zajal 40 he observes the Christian New Year, saying that he will wear his best clothes and have a fiesta with his friends,[2] which in this context probably carries political implications. Furthermore, his own commitment to spiritual exercise is expressed in touching terms. Several poems speak of his abstinence from drinking during Ramadan. While we see him enjoy the harvest season during which he joins large groups of people in the celebration of making and consuming wine (no. 50), we also witness his respect for this religious holiday and its rituals. Typical of Ibn Quzmān, however, is a stubborn resistance to succumb to an obligatory observation of the ritual fast. In zajals 119 and 136, the celebration of the end of Ramadan is important because wine consumption will promptly return:

Hurrah, drunkards,
for the sake of the Prophet, gang!
This is the time when
the month of fasting ends! (no. 136)

In another zajal he urges his boon companions to join him in drinking because Ramadan is about to arrive. He says:

Where are you, drunkards,
where are you all?
Whosoever has wine to pour,
my advice to you is empty the cups and keep what remains,
for the days will come
when that little will be craved. (no. 137)

In verses such as these, Ibn Quzmān describes with enchantment and enthusiasm the hectic but merry atmosphere of Andalusian cities. In fact, he dedicates a series of zajals (nos. 8, 82, 85) to this theme, offering in each a different but equally picturesque description of various aspects of the holiday. This highly emotional series reveals the sense of awe that *al-ʿīd* evokes in most Muslims:

[El] alba, [el] alba es dulce, en un dia,
Such is tomorrow and such is the evening.
Give me your hand to kiss,
to put a hundred kisses on it.
God rewards the one who observes
and follows the custom. (no. 82)

It is difficult to associate such sentiments with Ibn Quzmān the cynic. Yet it seems that much of his verse is geared toward shattering our confidence about either his true or literary self. Our understanding of Ibn Quzmān ebbs and flows, and we often find ourselves at the mercy of his unpredictable imagination and even less predictable expressions thereof.

ON WINE

Wine may very well be Ibn Quzmān's favorite theme. Closely linked to his notion of happiness, this theme is treated through various poetic tropes. Like his great bacchic predecessor Abū Nuwās, Ibn Quzmān has created intricate tropes to reproduce both the sensational and visual experience of wine. Several of his zajals are dedicated exclusively to bacchic themes (e.g., nos. 60, 136, 160), while others rarely omit it. Moreover, as occurs with many other authors, Ibn Quzmān often associates love with wine, partly to bond emotions with intoxication but also to satirize the Almoravid prohibition of both "vices" in the public realm. Thus, numerous amatory prologues combine the two themes (nos. 16, 22, 23, 37, 45, 53, 71): the sweet pain caused by the beloved is cured in wine, the joy of being with the beloved is celebrated in wine, sharing happiness and sorrow comes through wine, and so on.

I have a beloved and a smooth wine,
Don't tell anybody about this! (no. 45)

or,

I drank to him, my greatest desire,
then lifted my sleeves and danced to the music.
And while everyone around started remembering God,
I myself, amidst visions and jugs, slipped into deep drunkenness.
(no. 37)

Ibn Quzmān's descriptions of wine itself constitute a colorful spectrum of images and associations. Most often he calls it *raqīq* – smooth, gentle, mild (nos. 45, 56, 71) – and also *asfar* – golden, pale (nos. 29, 56, 71). He gives it various names, confirming not only his fluency in bacchic terminology but its clear popularity in his homeland:

"You know its names?" and he'll say, "No!"
You say, "Come, I will load your ears with them!
They are: *qahwa, mudām* and *ṭilā',*
then, *ḥumayya, khandarīs, rāḥ*!" (no. 94)

A seductive sound effect produced by drinking wine and its gentle splashing against the glass is achieved in zajal 96:

The wine in the glass is moving: pour, pour [*ṣub, ṣub*];
drinking it, the lips do: sip, sip [*'ub, 'ub*];
while the gorge, swallowing it, goes: gulp, gulp [*dub, dub*].

This onomatopoeia is just one of the successful sound reproductions Ibn Quzmān creates by using both the Romance and Arabic, confirming his mastery in achieving original aesthetic effects (García Gómez, *Todo Ben Quzmān* 3:325–564). Wine verses, as stated earlier, are often construed along with love verses, making the transitions among the thematic movements remarkably smooth. In that sense, his insistence that love and intoxication are frequently two sides of the same coin allows for a further exploration of bacchic themes under the guise of love.

ON LOVE

Ibn Quzmān's amatory verse lacks mystical dimension, nor does it belong exclusively to any specific literary trend. In the expression of his sentiments, Ibn Quzmān is highly individualistic, mostly illicit, and discouragingly unpredictable. Love in many of his poems is fastidiously calculated and utterly elusive. Indeed, it is colored with everything: coarseness, idealism, courtesy, machismo. Ibn Quzmān seems to be at home with all.

First narrativizing love with highly meditative poignancy, then stripping it down to mere carnal pleasures, Ibn Quzmān reveals himself to be an elusive lover. A closer look at the diwan confirms that for this great hedonist, love is not a serious matter. Most of the time he scorns simple emotionalism, chastity, and sentimental dependence. His amatory aspirations are cynically instinctive and brutally pragmatic, targeting both men and women. He openly mocks courtly lovers and scoffs at those who ache too much: "Spare me the method of Jamīl and 'Urwa!" exclaims Ibn Quzmān, opting for a more philandering lifestyle:

I'm amazed at lovers
satisfied with just one kiss.
My ways are not their ways.
That's not my path or pick.
O bacchic love, rise and come.

He hardly distinguishes between male and female lovers, taking equal pleasure in both. In zajal 30, he admits

My failure in life you already know,
but only thus will I spend my life.
If among people there is someone
who prefers either sodomy or adultery,
I am certainly the one who likes them both.

In his view, love should be free of frustrations imposed by oaths and futile promises. These are never to be trusted, because the vicissitudes of love and the fickleness of lovers are known far and wide. The comic effect generated by this libertine vision of relationships and the meaning of love is compounded by the association of love affairs with other matters in life. Humor, which is generated by shocking juxtapositions of different concerns (e.g., religion, business, wine), consistently reminds the reader that Ibn Quzmān may be portraying a lifestyle that is a rule rather than an exception.

Furthermore, the effect of such juxtapositions is amplified by the usage of unfolding narratives related as if the poet himself were unaware of their outcome. In zajal 20, for example, the plot is successfully developed in a semi-dramaturgic fashion built around several dialogues: a beautiful girl has been verbally seduced by the poet and has agreed to spend the night with him. When he realizes he has no sleeping robe for her, he sets forth in search for one. Alas, he is short of money. But a solution is promptly found: he swiftly composes a panegyric, sells it to Abū l-Qāsim the grammarian, and with the money he earns, he buys a robe for his guest. In the end, everybody benefits: the girl gets her robe, Abū l-Qāsim his praise, and Ibn Quzmān the girl. Unavoidably, he congratulates himself for his genius:

Yes! You may hear what I said in that praise;
I will read it to you – and you'll wish to applaud me.

Manifestly, such coarse fusion of eroticism and politics functions as a sardonic ridicule of Almoravid ethical ambiguity. In zajal 90 Ibn Quzmān goes one step further: while describing a love affair with a married Berber woman, he amuses the reader with an account of pornographic proportions. The images are a grotesque eroticization of Berber culture: Ibn Quzmān likens the erect penis in his pants to a pitched tent, the beauty of the Berber woman to a *conejo*. The term *conejo* (rabbit) is used in an erotic context that, given the long history of punning between *conejo* and various terms for female genitalia, might correspond to the more blatant term "pussy."[3] Ibn Quzmān then compares her game with his erection to "a chick [who] desired to hide in the nest." The purpose of the affair is also to "make a cuckold of the man who is her husband." The atmosphere is comic, sexually explosive, and morally inverted. In many ways, it functions as a carnivalesque metaphor of disorder and renewal with the intention of purifying language "from dogmatism, intolerance . . . from the single meaning and the single level."[4]

As stated earlier, Ibn Quzmān readily offers his love to both sexes, and his openness about it indicates a tacit societal acceptance of such practices. At a deeper level, however, this "bisexuality" is linked to the issue of prostitution in al-Andalus. In several zajals he makes somewhat misogynist statements caused by his confusion with the female sex. For example, in zajal 89 he says:

Women hold respect for nothing –
not for contracts nor for accords.
Their paradise is confusion –
until they defeat the lover.
And you see only puzzles –
and you see only swindles,
until the things become uneasy –
and they have no mercy on your distress.

For the lofty Ibn Quzmān the female enigma may create a mess of his reputation, so he avoids "serious business" with the opposite sex (no. 21). Rather, he frequents brothels and indulges in sex for money. Yet, cynic that he is, he cannot help but inject his stories of prostitutes with a criticism directed against the apparent political paradox: although brothel life thrives, he is continuously rebuked for his lax lifestyle. Although sex is for sale at large, he is forced to flee from the *fuqahā'*.

Love often permeates his descriptions of physical beauty, and though these are stereotypical aesthetic references, the synaesthetic associations highlight the originality of Ibn Quzmān's poetic skill. All senses seem to be equally titillated when one reads the following stanza from zajal 115:

They say: "Be patient and wait for her!"
"This patience, is it flat or is it round?
And what color is it, friend?" "Perhaps green,
or yellow, or like the aloe of Almería."

The whole series of rhetorical ornaments reveal Ibn Quzmān's tendency to vivify his love poetry so that it detaches him from the archetypes and helps him form a distinctive poetic diction. The aftermath is a poetry fraught with images conveyed through various literary figures. Metaphors and similes constitute the core of love motifs, and have diverse qualities and functions. For example, in zajal 134 Ibn Quzmān tries to define the beauty of his beloved:

Are you an emerald, or a pearl?
Cinnamon or, perhaps, amber?
Are you a candy or maybe sugar?
The daily sun, another moon,
or a combination of this all?

Such disparate images concentrate on the poet's admiration for the beloved. The effect is a sequence of associations invoked as the poet halts before the beloved's beauty, so that the reader's attention is focused more on the poet than on the countenance of his beloved. This kind of metaphorical illustration that highlights the effect rather than the cause is cosmically charted as a continuous cycle of love and life.

What kind of musk is this? What scent?
From this magic others are created.
The moon courts with the daily sun,
and Mercury lapses before Mars. (no. 132)

In many respects, these cyclical movements encapsulate the interconnectedness of Ibn Quzmān's themes: love is linked to praise, praise to wine, wine to love. Together they are among the necessities in life that cannot and should not be denied. In that sense, Ibn Quzmān views the world as a complex and fluid tapestry of different experiences, norms, languages, and peoples. The Andalus he eulogizes in his poetic ideals is the one that embraces this kind of diversity. The Andalus he rejects but sings of is the one that denies it. It is perhaps this stubborn commitment to celebrate a possible world by criticizing the real world in a unique poetic blend of burlesque, cynicism, and lyricism that prompted García Gómez to place Ibn Quzmān "among the most prominent poets of the Middle Ages" (*Poesía* 81).

NOTES

1. Mikhail Bakhtin, *Rabelais*, trans. H. Iswolsky (Bloomington, 1984), 435–37.
2. Menéndez Pidal interpreted such verses as strong evidence of the "Euro-Arabic character of zajal," with which he supported his theory on the literary interconnectedness of the two worlds.
3. The word used is most likely Romance *conejo*, although García Gómez transliterates it as *conecho* and/or *qinaj*, failing to determine its meaning (*Todo Ben Quzmān* 3:395–96). Several lexicons establish the origin of *conejo* in *cuniculus* (see, e.g., Roque Barcia, *Primer diccionario general etimológico* [Barcelona, 1902], 1:990; Martín Alonso Pedraz, *Enciclopedia del idioma* [Madrid, 1958], 1:1170). In the *Diccionario crítico etimológico castellano e hispánico* (Madrid, 1980), Corominas

suggests a possible Mozarab origin of the word, though he is not conclusive about it (173–74). In all dictionaries, however, the primary meaning given is "rabbit." Its feminine version, *coneja*, is metaphorically explained as "a woman who copulates frequently" (as in "breeds like a rabbit"). As an extension of that metaphorical phrase, the *Gran diccionario de la lengua española* (Barcelona, 1996) lists "female sexual organ" as a derivative meaning. This etymology seems to be quite different from Latin *cunnus*, which is a specific reference to a vagina/vulva (see James Noel Adams, *The Latin Sexual Vocabulary* [London, 1982], 80–109). Being a pun, *conejo* is semantically ambiguous. Some have suggested "bunny" as an English term that can be used in an eroticized sense, but the less literal English slang translation as "pussy" more closely approximates the double entendre in English.

4. Bakhtin 317.

BIBLIOGRAPHY

ʿAbbās, Iḥsān. *Taʾrīkh al-adab al-andalusī.* Beirut, 1971.

al-Ahwānī, ʿAbd al-ʿAzīz. "ʿAlā hāmish dīwān ibn quzmān." *Revista del Instituto Egipcio de Estudios Islámicos en Madrid* 18 (1972–73): 182–245.

al-Zajal fī al-andalus. Cairo, 1957.

Bajraktarevic, Fehim. "Ibn Kuzmān." *Encyclopaedia of Islam.* 1st edn. (supp.). Leiden, 1938. 91–92.

Calvente, A. R. "Jarchas, moaxajas, zejeles (II)." *Al-Andalus* 41 (1976): 147–78.

"Jarchas, moaxajas, zejeles (IV)." *Al-Andalus* 43 (1978): 173–80.

Colin, Georges S. "A. R. Nykl: El cancionero de Ibn Guzman." *Hesperis* 16–17 (1933): 165–68.

"Ibn Kuzmān." *Encyclopaedia of Islam.* 2nd edn. Leiden, 1980–. 3:849–52.

Corriente, Federico. "Again on the Metrical System of Muwashshah and Zajal." *Journal of Arabic Literature* 17 (1986): 34–49.

Gramática, métrica y texto del cancionero hispanoárabe de Aban Quzmān. Madrid, 1980.

"The Meters of the Muwashshah: An Andalusian Adaptation of ʿArūḍ: A Bridging Hypothesis." *Journal of Arabic Literature* 13 (1982): 76–82.

García Gómez, Emilio. "Discusión de 96 pasajes de Ben Quzmān." *Al-Andalus* 41 (1976): 240–338.

"Un eclipse de la poesía en Sevilla: La época almorávide." *Al-Andalus* 10 (1945): 285–343.

"Estudio del *Dār aṭ-ṭirāz*: Preceptiva egipcia de la muwashshaha." *Al-Andalus* 27 (1962): 21–104.

"Una extraordinaria página de Tīfāshī y una hipótesis sobre el inventor del zéjel." *Etudes d'orientalisme dédiées à la mémoire de Lévi-Provençal.* Paris, 1962. 2:517–23.

Poesía arábigoandaluza: Breve síntesis histórica. Madrid, 1952.

"Sobre algunos pasajes difíciles de Ben Quzmān." *Al-Andalus* 33 (1973): 249–318.

"Sobre un posible tercer tipo de la poesía arábigoandaluza." *Estudios dedicados a Menéndez Pidal.* Madrid, 1951. 397–408.

"Sobre una propuesta inglesa de correcciones al texto de Ben Quzmān." *Al-Andalus* 43 (1978): 1–50.

Todo Ben Quzmān. 3 vols. Madrid, 1972.

"Tres interesantes poemas andaluces conservados por Ḥillī." *Al-Andalus* 25 (1960): 287–311.

Gorton, T. J. "The Metre of Ibn Quzmān: A 'Classical' Approach." *Journal of Arabic Literature* 6 (1975): 1–29.

"Textual Problems in Ibn Quzmān." *Arabica* 24 (1977): 269–90.

Hoenerbach, Wilhelm. "La teoría del 'zejel' según Ṣafī al-dīn Ḥillī." *Al-Andalus* 15 (1950): 297–334.

Hoenerbach, Wilhelm, and Helmut Ritter. "Neue Materialen zum Zacal." *Oriens* 8 (1950): 266–75.

Ibn Khaldūn. *The Muqaddimah: An Introduction to History.* Trans. F. Rosenthal. 3 vols. London, 1967.

Ibn Sanā' al-Mulk. *Dār al-ṭirāz fī ʿamal l-muwashshaḥat.* Ed. Jawdat al-Rikābī. Damascus, 1977.

Kratchkovsky, Ivan Y. *Among Arabic Manuscripts.* Trans. T. Minorsky. Leiden, 1953.

Lévi-Provençal, Évariste. "Du nouveau sur Ibn Quzmān." *Al-Andalus* 9 (1944): 347–69.

al-Maqqarī. *Nafḥ al-ṭīb min ghuṣn al-andalus al-raṭīb (Analectes sur l'histoire et la littérature des arabes d'Espagne).* Ed. Reinhart Dozy, Gustave Dugat, Ludolf Krehl, and William Wright. 2 vols. 1855–61. Rpt., Amsterdam, 1967.

al-Marrākushī. *Al-muʿjib fī talkhīṣ akhbār al-maghrib.* Casablanca, 1978.

Menéndez Pidal, Ramón. *Poesía árabe y poesía europea.* Madrid, 1941.

Monroe, James T. *Hispano-Arabic Poetry.* Berkeley, 1974.

Neuvonen, Eero K. "La negación qaṭṭ en el Cancionero de Ibn Quzmān." *Studia Orientalia.* Societas Orientalis Fennica 17, 9 (1952): 1–12.

Nykl, A. R. "Algo nuevo sobre Ibn Quzmān." *Al-Andalus* 12 (1947): 123–26.

"Bibliographische Fragmente über Ibn Quzmān." *Der Islam* 25 (1938): 101–33.

El Cancionero del sheih, nobilisimo visir, maravilla del tiempo, Abū Bakr Ibn ʿAbd al-Malik Aben Guzman. Madrid, 1933.

Hispano-Arabic Poetry and Its Relations with the Old Provençal Troubadours. Baltimore, 1946.

Mukhtārāt min al-shiʿr al-andalusī. Beirut, 1949.

al-Shaqundī. *Elogio del islam español.* Trans. Emilio García Gómez. Madrid, 1934.

Stern, Samuel M. *Hispano-Arabic Strophic Poetry.* Ed. L. P. Harvey. Oxford, 1974.

Tuulio, Oiva J. "Ibn Quzmān: Edition critique partielle et provisoire." *Studia Orientalia.* Societas Orientalis Fennica 9, 2 (1939–41): 1–137.

CHAPTER 15

IBN ZAYDŪN

Devin J. Stewart

Writing in the fourteenth century, the renowned literary critic al-Ṣafadī recorded a current definition of the ultimate *ẓarf,* "sophistication" or "elegance," a quality highly prized and contested in Arab social and literary circles throughout premodern times. The true sophisticate is one who "wears robes of white and rings of carnelian, recites the Qur'an according to the reading of Abū ʿĀmr, knows the sacred law according to the tradition of al-Shafii, and relates the poetry of Ibn Zaydūn" (al-Maqqarī 3:566). This recipe-in-a-nutshell for the attainment of social polish reflects the high aesthetic regard in which Ibn Zaydūn's poetry has been held in the Arabic literary tradition. Often described as a master of passion and longing, Ibn Zaydūn is generally held to be the outstanding Arab poet of al-Andalus and ranks among the most illustrious love poets in all Arabic literature. His stormy love affair with Wallāda, the daughter of the Umayyad caliph al-Mustakfī, takes its place alongside the Eastern stories of Laylā and Majnūn, Buthayna and Jamīl, as a classic tale of passion and separation that lives on in the Arab imagination and figures prominently, if in bowdlerized version, in modern schoolbooks. Ibn Zaydūn's poetry also seems to capture the essence of Andalusian poetry at large, shining in two areas considered characteristic fortes of Andalusian literature: the description of gardens and the relatively unstylized presentation of emotion and experience. In its forthrightness, Ibn Zaydūn's work recalls that of his contemporary Ibn Ḥazm.

Abū l-Walīd Aḥmad, son of ʿAbd Allāh ibn Aḥmad ibn Ghālib ibn Zaydūn, was born in 394/1003 to an aristocratic Arab family claiming descent from the Banū Makhzūm clan of Quraysh, the tribe of the prophet Muhammad. He spent his youth and early career in Córdoba, capital of the crumbling Umayyad caliphate and then of the Jahwarid dynasty. His father, ʿAbd Allāh, a prominent jurist and notable under the patronage of the Umayyad caliphs, died in 405/1014, when Ibn Zaydūn was still quite young. Little is known of Ibn Zaydūn's early years and studies. He was probably raised by his maternal grandfather, Abū Bakr Muḥammad ibn Muḥammad

(d. 433/1042), who held positions as judge in Sālim and then as market inspector in Córdoba. Ibn Zaydūn presumably studied under his grandfather as well as his father's associate, the famous judge Abū l-ʿAbbās ibn Dhakwān. Nevertheless, the only figure the sources mention explicitly as his teacher is Abū Bakr Musallim ibn Aḥmad ibn Aflaḥ (d. 432/1041), a grammarian and lexicographer who also taught poetry and belletristic prose works.

Ibn Zaydūn lived at a time when princes and ministers wrote poetry and a well-turned phrase could make or break a career. As the Umayyad caliphate disintegrated, al-Andalus experienced, along with increased political fragmentation, an impressive cultural flowering of which Ibn Zaydūn was a product and in which he took part. Few ages and regions could boast such rulers as the learned Abbadid poet kings of Seville, al-Muʿtaḍid (d. 460/1068) and his son al-Muʿtamid (d. 488/1095). When political turbulence in al-Andalus attained new heights with the final collapse of the Umayyad caliphate in 422/1031 and the establishment of several independent principalities, the party kingdoms, Ibn Zaydūn was well equipped for success. In an age of eloquence, he was never at a loss for words. An official in Seville recounted the lasting impression Ibn Zaydūn had made at the funeral of a female relative. Ibn Zaydūn received the throng of attendees conveying their condolences graciously, thanking each one individually and never using the same phrase twice. The medieval chronicler expresses amazement at the facility that enabled Ibn Zaydūn to improvise the more than one thousand expressions of thanks that the chronicler estimates the occasion would have necessitated (al-Ṣafadī 11; al-Maqqarī 3:565–66).

Closely associated with the Jahwarid rulers Abū l-Ḥazm and his son Abū l-Walīd, Ibn Zaydūn was in all probability instrumental in the foundation of their rule, for the historian Ibn Khāqān labels him "leader of the Cordoban revolt and the rise of the Jahwarid regime" (79). When Abū l-Ḥazm took power in 422/1031, he appointed Ibn Zaydūn into the new government and sent him as ambassador to the neighboring Andalusian kingdoms. Ibn Zaydūn's skill as a poet and composer of elegant epistles served him well in this position for many years, but he suffered a grave setback in about 432/1041 as the result of plotting by enemies at court. Accused of illegally confiscating another man's property, he was incarcerated and ended up spending five hundred days in prison. He wrote to his teacher Abū Bakr Musallim and his companion Prince Abū l-Walīd ibn Jahwar, complaining of being surrounded by common criminals and pleading for help. He also wrote his most eloquent epistle, *al-Risāla al-jiddiyya* (The Serious Epistle), to Abū l-Ḥazm ibn Jahwar, entreating his sovereign's forgiveness. Its literary merit notwithstanding, the letter failed to evoke Abū l-Ḥazm's sympathy, but, presumably with the help of Abū l-Walīd, Ibn Zaydūn finally succeeded in escaping prison and fled to

Seville. There, he was received with favor at the court of the Abbadid ruler al-Muʿtaḍid.

Shortly before the end of his reign, Abū l-Ḥazm pardoned Ibn Zaydūn and allowed him to return to Córdoba, though the exact circumstances under which this happened are unclear. When Abū l-Ḥazm died in 435/1044 and his son Abū l-Walīd became king, Ibn Zaydūn marked the occasion with an elegy for Abū l-Ḥazm congratulating Abū l-Walīd on his accession to the throne. He soon regained his positions, and once again served as Jahwarid ambassador to the Andalusian courts. Several years later, backbiting at court persuaded him to leave Córdoba once more, abandoning his ambassadorship in the midst of a mission to Valencia and returning to Seville in 441/1049. He then served as vizier and ambassador under the Abbadids for the next two decades, through the remainder of al-Muʿtaḍid's reign and into the reign of al-Muʿtamid. Under the latter, he had the opportunity to return to his native city when the Abbadids captured Córdoba, presumably with Ibn Zaydūn's help, and made it their new capital. Ibn Zaydūn died in 463/1070, shortly after returning to Seville to quell a revolt there. His son Abū Bakr continued to serve al-Muʿtamid in numerous positions, including those of governor of Seville and supervisor of the mint, until he died in 484/1091.

Ibn Zaydūn's best-known poetry is his love poetry, and that is associated with the figure of Princess Wallāda, the accomplished daughter of the Umayyad caliph al-Mustakfī, who had reigned for only two years (414/1023–416/1025) before being dethroned and assassinated. Refined, intelligent, and witty, Wallāda became a leading figure in Cordoban society and hosted what was probably the most important literary salon in the capital. She composed poetry and critiqued that of others, and was the object of many poets' and nobles' affections. Her position extended beyond literary circles and gave her a decided influence on the Cordoban politics of the day.

Scholars have noted Wallāda's independent spirit and boldness, and some, probably overgeneralizing the situation, have taken these as evidence that Andalusian women enjoyed much greater social and sexual freedom than their Eastern Arab counterparts (Viguera 711–13). Wallāda's poetry, if it can be taken as her work, certainly corroborates the view that she was quite unreserved. She supposedly had the following verses embroidered in gold on the left and right flaps of her robe:

> By God, I am fit for greatness, and stride along with great pride.
> I allow my lover to reach my cheek, and I grant my kiss to him
> who craves it.

According to Ibn Zaydūn, it was she who suggested their first secret rendezvous:

Wait to visit me when darkness gathers,
For I find that night will keep our secret best.
Were the sun affficted with the love I feel for you,
It would not shine, nor the moon rise, nor the stars traverse the sky.

In its presentation to modern audiences, Ibn Zaydūn's relationship with Wallāda has often been romanticized, omitting mention of jibes and insults the two are reported to have directed at each other. On one occasion, for example, Wallāda accused Ibn Zaydūn of focusing his affections on one of her slave girls, a talented singer:

If you did justice to our love, you would not desire nor prefer my slave girl.
Nor would you forsake a fertile branch, in its beauty, and turn to a branch devoid of fruit.
You know that I am the Moon in the sky, but you burn, to my chagrin, for Jupiter.[1]

On another occasion Wallāda rebuked Ibn Zaydūn for blaming her. She implies that he was engaged in a homosexual relationship with a servant named ʿAlī:

Ibn Zaydūn, despite his virtue, slanders me unjustly, though I am not at fault.
When I approach him, he looks askance at me, as if I were about to castrate ʿAlī.

In other verses, Wallāda openly insults Ibn Zaydūn perhaps in response to his complaints of her infidelity:

They call you the "Sixer"; and your life will leave you before this nickname does:
Sodomite and buggered you are, adulterer, pimp, cuckold, and thief!

Other obscene verses are attributed to her:

Ibn Zaydūn's backside swoons for the rods in men's pants.
Were it to spy a penis atop a palm tree, it would swoop down on it like a vulture.[2]

Nykl refrains from translating these verses, but maintains that they, together with an amorous relationship Wallāda pursued with the poetess Muhja, reveal the thorough corruption of Wallāda's soul. He contrasts her perfidy and utter baseness to Ibn Zaydūn's nobility of thought (111–13). It should be said, however, that Ibn Zaydūn himself did not shy away from using rude language, particularly in his attacks on rivals for Wallāda's affections.

After experiencing Wallāda's devotion, Ibn Zaydūn fell out of favor with her and subsequently became the object of her intense animosity. This undoubtedly had something to do with her relationship with the vizier Abū ʿĀmir ibn ʿAbdūs, Ibn Zaydūn's most powerful rival at court, who subsequently became Wallāda's lover. Indeed, the two were probably responsible for Ibn Zaydūn's imprisonment by Abū l-Ḥazm ibn Jahwar. Ibn Zaydūn was denounced not, as some have suggested, for plotting to restore the Umayyads, but for allegedly appropriating the property of one of Ibn ʿAbdūs's freedmen. This would explain the epithet "thief" that Wallāda applies to him in the verses above. Ibn Zaydūn's rivalry with Ibn ʿAbdūs and others for Wallāda's affections figures prominently in his poems. When Ibn ʿAbdūs made advances toward her, Ibn Zaydūn wrote a poem warning the rival to keep his distance, including these verses:

> You have aroused the lion sleeping in his lair, stirring him from his rest.
> And you continue to extend him the hand of provocation, though he holds back.
> Beware! Beware! For the nobleman rejects insult and is angered thereby!
> The fierce viper's silence does not prevent him from striking.

Later, when Wallāda had already turned her attentions to Ibn ʿAbdūs, Ibn Zaydūn composed these verses playing on the vizier's nickname, the Mouse.

> Wallāda would be such a noble prize for a collector,
> if she could but differentiate between a veterinarian and a druggist.
> They said, "Abū ʿĀmir now embraces her."
> I replied, "Moths are often drawn close to the fire."
> You have blamed us for being succeeded by him
> with the one we love, yet there is no shame in this.
> It was a tasty meal; we ate the sweetest morsels,
> and left some for the Mouse.

In *al-Risāla al-hazliyya* (The Comic Epistle) Ibn Zaydūn voiced his most biting satire of his rival. This fictitious reply from Wallāda to Ibn ʿAbdūs recounts that the latter sent a former lover as a go-between in an effort to win Wallāda's affections. The messenger describes Ibn ʿAbdūs in unrealistically flattering terms, claiming for him the utmost beauty, grace, intelligence, wealth, wit, and other accomplishments. Wallāda, commenting that the messenger would not have been as enthusiastic unless she herself were bored with Ibn ʿAbdūs, angrily rejects the offer, barely restraining herself from violence –

"but the shoe is ready should the scorpion return!" – and then launches into a tirade listing Ibn ʿAbdūs's true qualities: "You are deformed by birth . . . unsurpassed in stupidity, cruel by nature, hard of hearing, boorish in response, despicable in appearance, clumsy in coming and going . . . endowed with putrid breath, possessed of abundant defects, and renowned for your vices! Your speech is a stutter, your conversation a mutter, your discourse a clutter! Your laugh is a cackle, and your gait a scamper! Your wealth is beggary, your religion heresy, and your learning braggery!" She then upbraids him for his impudence in supposing that she could even consider the likes of him: "Should I do with you what ʿAqīl ibn ʿUllafa did to al-Juhanī, who came to ask for his daughter's hand, when he smeared his behind with oil and sat him on an anthill?!" Then she asks how she could turn away from all the available noblemen to someone "whose pond is a trickle and whose well has gone dry, whose energy is gone and whose remaining strength enables him to do nothing but fart?!" (Ibn Zaydūn 634–79).

Despite the ugly exchanges between the two lovers, Wallāda inspired Ibn Zaydūn's most heartfelt and immortal verse. His *Nūniyya,* a fifty-two-verse qasida rhyming in *-īnā* that expresses longing for the lost days of bliss with Wallāda, is by far his best-known poem and one of the most famous love poems in all of Arabic literature.

Morning came – the separation –
substitute for the love we shared,
for the fragrance of our coming together,
falling away . . .

We poured for one another
the wine of love. Our enemies seethed
and called for us to choke
– and fate said let it be.

The knot our two souls tied
came undone,
and what our hands joined
was broken.

We never used to give a thought
to separation, and now, for us
to be together again
is beyond our dreams . . .

To give up hope, we thought,
might bring relief. But it only
made desire for you
burn deeper.

You left. We went our way,
ribs still scorched –
longing for you –
tears still welling in our eyes.

When our secret thought
whispered in your ear,
sorrow would have crushed us,
had we not held on to one another.

Our days turned
in losing you and darkened,
while nights with you
glowed,

When life bounded
free in the intimacy we gave,
when the meadows of our pleasure
were pure,

When whatever we wished
we gathered
from the boughs of loving,
bending near.[3]

Many poets composed *muʿāraḍa*s (imitations in the same rhyme and meter) of the *Nūniyya*, both during the author's life and afterward. Ṣafī al-Dīn al-Ḥillī (d. 749/1349) composed an elegy for the Ayyubid ruler al-Malik al-Mu'ayyad ʿImād al-Dīn based on it in the form of a *mukhammas* (stanzaic poem of the form *aaaab ccccb*). Indeed, the *Nūniyya* became so emblematic of longing and exile that anyone who memorized the poem, it was rumored, would surely die far from home (al-Ṣafadī 12–13). When the Egyptian poet-laureate Aḥmad Shawqī was exiled to Spain in the early twentieth century, he expressed his longing for his homeland in yet another *muʿāraḍa* of the *Nūniyya*.

Another of Ibn Zaydūn's most famous poems is the *Qāfiyya* – rhyming in *āqā* – that describes a garden in the suburb of al-Zahrā', outside Córdoba. The poet had supposedly returned there after fleeing Córdoba because he could not bear the separation from Wallāda and wanted to be near her in any way possible. Overcome with emotion, he recited:

From al-Zahrā'
I remember you with passion.
The horizon is clear,
the earth's face serene.

The breeze grows faint
with the coming of dawn.
It seems to pity me
and lingers, full of tenderness . . .

Today, alone,
I distract myself with flowers
that attract my eyes like magnets.
The wind roughhouses with them
bending them over.

The blossoms are eyes.
They see my sleeplessness
and weep for me;
their iridescent tears overflow
staining the calyx.

In the bright sun
red buds light up the rose bushes
making the morning
brighter still.

Fragrant breaths come from the pome
of the waterlilies,
sleepyheads with eyes
half-opened by dawn.

Everything stirs up the memory
of my passion for you
still intact in my chest
although my chest might seem
too narrow to contain it . . .

In times gone by
we demanded of each other
payments of pure love
and were happy as colts
running free in a pasture.

But now I am the only one
who can boast of being loyal.
You left me
and I stay here,
still sad, still loving you.[4]

An outstanding example of the description of gardens and natural beauty for which Andalusian literature is famous, the *Qāfiyya* brings into high relief the interaction between the poet's mood and his natural surroundings, a feature found in Eastern Arabic poetry as well but carried to new heights by Ibn Zaydūn and Ibn Khafāja, the "gardener" poet. Besides his love poetry, Ibn Zaydūn wrote traditional panegyrics for Abū l-Ḥazm and Abū l-Walīd ibn Jahwar, and the Abbadids al-Muʿtaḍid and al-Muʿtamid. His elegies for Abū l-Ḥazm ibn Jahwar, his wife, al-Muʿtaḍid, al-Muʿtaḍid's wife, and daughter, though elegant, lack the passion of the *Nūniyya* and the *Qāfiyya*. An exception is the deeply moving elegy he recited at the tomb of his friend, the judge Abū Bakr ibn Dhakwān (d. 435/1043). Ibn Zaydūn in later years also exchanged a series of riddle poems playing on the names of species of birds with al-Muʿtamid and the jurist Abū Ṭālib al-Makkī.

Ibn Zaydūn's love poetry has proved the most enduring facet of his opus. The sustained congruence between the themes and motifs of Arabic and medieval Romance love poetry, especially that of the troubadours, suggests more than a coincidental relationship, and, as the leading representative of the Arabic love poetry tradition in al-Andalus, Ibn Zaydūn's poetry merits special attention in this regard. In it, we find many of the typical features of European courtly love poetry. Common points include the conception of the love bond as a pact, often likened to a religious devotion, the tension between concealing and divulging the "secret" of love, and the concept of loyal service to the beloved. The cast of characters surrounding the lover and the beloved, including in particular the "denouncer," who threatens to expose the lovers and break up their tryst, and the "blamer," who reproaches the lover for allowing his passions to carry him away, also shows a strong resemblance. Although research to date has not settled questions of the extent and modes of Arabic literary influence on medieval Romance love poetry, the evidence as it stands is suggestive and points quite decidedly to al-Andalus (see Boase; Menéndez Pidal).

Ibn Zaydūn's poetry can best be described as neoclassical. He excelled in the qasida genre, and his extant poetry includes only two *musammaṭ*s, stanzaic poems resembling the popular muwashshah but differing somewhat in strophic pattern and devoid of colloquial language. He strove to follow the methods of the classical masters and has been called the West's al-Buḥturī. Indeed, it appears that he especially admired al-Buḥturī among earlier Arabic poets for the simple elegance and natural flow of his poetry, and al-Ṣafadī even suggests that the *Nūniyya* was intended as a *muʿāraḍa* of a poem by al-Buḥturī (13). Yet Ibn Zaydūn aspired to compose excellent prose as much as poetry, and often expresses this dual conception of ideal literary talent in his own writings. In these statements he holds up as paragons not only the poets al-Buḥturī and Abū Tammām but also the prose writers al-Jāḥiẓ and the famous secretaries al-Faḍl ibn Sahl[5] and Jaʿfar al-Barmakī. It is assuredly these Eastern figures that he strove to emulate in his own work.

Ibn Zaydūn's most famous prose works are *al-Risāla al-jiddiyya* and *al-Risāla al-hazliyya.* Their high literary value in the East is indicated by the fact that the Egyptian litterateur Ibn Nubāta (d. 768/1366) wrote an extensive commentary on *al-Risāla al-hazliyya* and al-Ṣafadī (d. 764/1363) wrote an equally substantial commentary on *al-Risāla al-jiddiyya.* Five other epistles by Ibn Zaydūn are extant. One, mentioned above, is addressed to Ibn Zaydūn's teacher asking for help in getting released from prison. Another asks al-Muẓaffar Sayf al-Dawla, the prince of Valencia, for financial help. In the *ʿĀmiriyya* (Epistle to Abū ʿĀmir), Ibn Zaydūn writes from Córdoba to his friend Abū ʿĀmir ibn Maslama in Seville after escaping prison, asking him to intercede with al-Muʿtaḍid on his behalf. The remaining two are addressed to al-Muʿtaḍid himself. Little attention has been paid to Ibn Zaydūn's history of the Umayyad caliphs in Spain, the *Kitāb al-tabyīn fī khulafāʾ banī umayya bi l-andalus* (The Exposition: On the Umayyad Caliphs in al-Andalus), modeled on the *Kitāb al-taʿyīn* (The Designation) on the caliphs of the East by the famous historian al-Masʿūdī (d. 345/956). Al-Maqqarī cites a passage from the work concerning the judges appointed in Córdoba by al-Dākhil, the first Umayyad caliph in al-Andalus (3:182). Though the work has not been published, it is extant in manuscript (Brockelmann supp. 1:485).

Like his poetry, Ibn Zaydūn's prose is classicizing. Particularly in *al-Risāla al-jiddiyya,* he avoids the constant use of *sajʿ*, rhymed and rhythmic prose, which had become the fashion among court secretaries during the tenth century and is found in other contemporary literary works such as the *Maqāmāt* of al-Hamadhānī (d. 398/1008) and the *Risālat al-tawābiʿ wa l-zawābiʿ* (Treatise of Familiar Spirits and Demons) of Ibn Shuhayd (d. 426/1035). Instead, he prefers the use of structurally parallel cola without rhyme and often without metrical equivalence in final phrases, more in the manner of al-Jāḥiẓ and other early authors. In *al-Risāla al-hazliyya,* however, Ibn Zaydūn uses a great deal of true *sajʿ*, with rhyming and rhythmically parallel phrases. Ibn Zaydūn's prose is also classicizing in its assiduous references to recherché proverbs and aphorisms, pre-Islamic lore, Qurʾanic narratives, and earlier poetry. In some passages these erudite allusions are so frequent as to border on the pedantic, rendering the text cumbersome and breaking its flow. One passage of *al-Risāla al-jiddiyya* recounts crimes for which the punishment Ibn Zaydūn has endured in prison might actually be fitting:

> If I had been commanded to bow down to Adam and refused; if Noah had told me "Board (the Ark) with us" and I had answered, "I will take refuge on a mountain which will protect me from the water"; if I had ordered a palace to be built so that I might ascend to the God of Moses; if I had prayed to the Calf . . . led the elephant for Abraha; ridden out to defend the caravan at Badr; retreated with one third of the men at the Battle of Uḥud . . . claimed that the oath of fealty to Abū Bakr was a chance

mistake . . . tore the skin that the hand of God had blessed; sacrificed the hoary-headed man with the sign of prostration on his brow; paid as a dower to Qaṭāmi 'Three thousand, a slave, a singing girl, and a blow to ʿAlī with a poisoned sword' . . . (688–93)

These allusions, a small fraction of those present in the original text, refer first to episodes appearing in the Qur'an, involving Satan, Noah's son, Pharaoh, the Golden Calf, and Abraha, the Ethiopian ruler of Yemen who led an attack on Mecca before the Prophet was born. The other references are to battles that took place between the early Muslim community and the pagan Quraysh during the Prophet's lifetime and then to the first four caliphs, the last three of whom were assassinated. *Al-Risāla al-hazliyya* includes much longer passages listing tidbits of pre-Islamic lore that stand in marked contrast with the brilliant and elegant opening of the epistle. It should be noted that Ibn Zaydūn's extant prose works probably represent only a tiny fraction of his original production; he must have written hundreds of elegant epistles in the course of his long career as minister, ambassador, and courtier.

The concomitance of fantastic cultural production and political fragmentation that characterized al-Andalus of Ibn Zaydūn's lifetime is perhaps rivaled only by that of the more famous Italian renaissance. As ambassador to the courts of the party kingdoms and leading minister for the Jahwarids of Córdoba and the Abbadids of Seville, Ibn Zaydūn was able to live a life to which the Eastern poet al-Mutanabbī could only aspire, where eloquence translated directly into noble charges and political prominence. His career was that of a genius in turbulent times, of a man thrust into the midst of political conflicts by his command over words. It is telling that Ibn Zaydūn died on a negotiation mission, having been sent to use his powers to quell a revolt in Seville. Although later generations have paid more attention to his love poetry, it is clear that in Ibn Zaydūn's literary corpus, love, sex, exile, and longing all intertwine in a fascinating narrative of intrigue and struggles for power. His literary attacks and parries attest not only to his keen observation and power of expression but also to his deep engagement in the complex political conflicts of his times.

NOTES

1. The poetess here refers to the slave girl, punning on the word Jupiter, *al-mushtarā* (more often *al-mushtarī*), which also means "the one that has been bought."
2. The scandalous effect of the verses is magnified by the fact that the phrase translated here as "vulture" refers to the mythical birds mentioned in sura 105, which God sent as a scourge of Abraha's Ethiopian forces when they attacked Mecca.

3. Trans. Michael Sells, ll. 1, 5–7, 11–16 (in the order used in Ibn Zaydūn, *Dīwān*, ed. Karam al-Bustānī [Beirut, 1975], 9–13).
4. From *Poems of Arab Andalusia*, trans. Cola Franzen from the Spanish versions of Emilio García Gómez (San Francisco, 1989), pp. 34–37, ll. 1–2, 5–9, 14–15.
5. Not, as ʿAlī ʿAbd al-ʿAẓīm holds, Sahl ibn Hārūn (761 n. 2).

BIBLIOGRAPHY

ʿAbd al-ʿAẓīm, ʿAlī. *Ibn Zaydūn: ʿAsruh wa-hayātuh wa-adabuh.* Cairo, 1955.

Boase, Roger. "Arab Influences on European Love-Poetry." *The Legacy of Muslim Spain.* Ed. Salma Khadra Jayyusi. Leiden, 1992. 457–83.

Brockelmann, Carl. *Geschichte der arabischen Litteratur.* Leiden, 1937–49.

Cantarino, Vicente. *Casidas de amor profano y místico: Ibn Zaydūn, Ibn ʿArabī.* Mexico, 1977.

"Dos aspectos de la soledad arábigo andaluza." *Homenaje a Sherman H. Eoff.* Madrid, 1970. 59–78.

Cour, Auguste. *Un poète arabe d'Andalousie: Ibn Zaidoûn.* Constantine, 1920.

Ibn Bassam. *al-Dhakhīra fī maḥāsin ahl al-jazīra.* Vol. 1. Cairo, 1939.

Ibn Khāqān, al-Fatḥ. *Qalāʾid al-ʿiqyān fī maḥāsin al-aʿyān.* Tunis, 1966.

Ibn Nubāta al-Miṣrī. *Sarḥ al-ʿuyūn fī sharḥ risālat ibn zaydūn.* Ed. Muḥammad Abū l-Faḍl Ibrāhīm. Cairo, 1957.

Ibn Zaydūn. *Dīwān ibn zaydūn wa-rasāʾiluh.* Ed. ʿAlī ʿAbd al-ʿAẓīm. Cairo, 1957.

Jayyusi, Salma Khadra. "Andalusī Poetry: The Golden Period." *The Legacy of Muslim Spain.* Ed. Salma Khadra Jayyusi. Leiden, 1992. 317–66.

Karrū, Abū l-Qāsim Muḥammad. *Shawqī wa-ibn zaydūn fī nūnīyahtihimā.* Tunis, 1956.

LeComte, G. "Ibn Zaydūn." *Encyclopaedia of Islam.* 2nd edn. Leiden, 1954–. 3:973–74.

Lug, Sieglinde. *Poetic Techniques and Conceptual Elements in Ibn Zaydūn's Love Poetry.* Washington, D.C., 1982.

al-Maqqarī. *Nafḥ al-ṭīb min ghuṣn al-andalus al-raṭīb.* Ed. Iḥsān ʿAbbās. 8 vols. Beirut, 1988.

Marchand, B. "Un Muwaššaḥ d'Ibn Zaydūn." *Arabica* 25 (1978): 10–17.

Menéndez Pidal, Ramón. *Poesía árabe y poesía europea, con otros estudios de literatura medieval.* 3rd edn. Buenos Aires, 1946.

Nykl, A. R. *Hispano-Arabic Poetry and Its Relations with the Old Provençal Troubadours.* Baltimore, 1946.

al-Ṣafadī, Khalīl ibn Aybak. *Tamām al-mutūn fī sharḥ risālat ibn zaydūn.* Ed. Muḥammad Abū l-Faḍl Ibrāhīm. Cairo, 1964.

Viguera, María J. "*Aṣluḥu li l-maʿālī*: On the Social Status of Andalusī Women." *The Legacy of Muslim Spain.* Ed. Salma Khadra Jayyusi. Leiden, 1992. 709–24.

CHAPTER 16

IBN ṬUFAYL

Lenn Goodman

Abū Bakr ibn Ṭufayl (d. 1185/6) was born in Guadix, northeast of Granada, in the early twelfth century. He was trained in medicine and studied philosophy in the tradition of the iconoclastic Muslim thinker Ibn Bājja, although he never met this founding figure of Andalusian philosophy. His work as a physician placed him in court circles, and he became secretary to the governor of Granada and then to the governor of Ceuta and Tangier, a son of ʿAbd al-Mutammim, who had been the lieutenant and chief military commander of Ibn Tūmart, the founder of the Almohad dynasty. Ibn Ṭufayl became court physician to the Almohad sultan Abū Yaʿqūb Yūsuf (r. 1163–84) and may have served as a qadi under Abū Yaʿqūb's regime. The ruler was a lover of learning who gathered books in unprecedented numbers from all parts of his dominions and sought out scholars and thinkers as ornaments to his court. He genuinely enjoyed the philosopher's company, and they spent hours, sometimes days, together in conversation. Ibn Ṭufayl is even named in one source as a vizier, or chief minister. He probably did not hold that rank, but his influence with the sultan was immense.

Informally, Ibn Ṭufayl served as a kind of culture minister, introducing many men of learning and science at the court. Among them was the young Ibn Rushd (Averroes), whom he presented to Abū Yaʿqūb around 1169, and for whom he obtained the assignment that made his protégé in time far more celebrated than he. The historian al-Marrākushī relates how Ibn Ṭufayl sang his praises before the Commander of the Faithful, and how the caliph asked Ibn Rushd about the philosophers' views on the burning issue of the world's eternity or creation. Ibn Rushd was hard-pressed to respond, since the Almohad regime was well known for its doctrinal stringency, and the philosophers of Islam were committed, by their Aristotelian rigor, to the eternity of the universe. Most treated scriptural accounts of creation as allegories of the eternal emanation of the cosmos from its divine source and surrogates for the subtler truth: that God timelessly caused the world's ordered but eternal motion. Al-Ghazālī, whom legend made the teacher of Ibn Tūmart, had declared the philosophers of Islam atheists for their denial of creation. An eternal world, as al-Ghazālī reasoned in his polemic, *Tahāfut al-falāsifa* (The Incoherence of the Philosophers), would have no need of God (89, 110, 154).

The young Averroes feigned ignorance at the caliph's questioning but was soon put at ease by hearing Ibn Ṭufayl and the monarch discuss the issue between themselves with learning and sophistication. He joined the conversation and was sent home with a robe of honor and a splendid new mount as tributes to his élan. This interview, we are told, was the first official notice taken of Ibn Rushd's talents. Later, at Ibn Ṭufayl's instance, he was commissioned to write the commentaries on Aristotle that eclipsed the fame of his sponsor and his patron alike. Ibn Ṭufayl had excused himself from the project on the grounds of his age and his commitment to another important work (al-Marrākushī 174–75). When Ibn Ṭufayl retired as court physician in 1182, he was succeeded by Ibn Rushd. But he continued to enjoy the favor of the caliph, and of his son when Abū Yaʿqūb died in 1184, of wounds received at the siege of Santarém in Portugal. Ibn Ṭufayl died at Marrakech the following year.

The intellectual work Ibn Ṭufayl cited in excusing himself from the project that would become Averroes's monumental three-tiered commentary on the Aristotelian corpus was solidly grounded in the natural sciences. He was deeply versed in traditional Islamic law and lore, but also in the philosophical tradition that Muslim thinkers had built up on the foundations of Greek philosophy, known to them through the Arabic translations, paraphrases, and commentaries on the works of Plato, Aristotle, Galen, the pagan Neoplatonists and Peripatetics.

Apart from his work as a physician and his authorship of two medical treatises and a correspondence with Averroes about the latter's medical work, the *Kulliyāt* (Book of Generalities), Ibn Ṭufayl was a key figure in the "Andalusian Revolt" against the authority of Ptolemaic astronomy, following up on suggestions made by Ibn Bājja. This early movement of criticism in astronomy raised grave problems about the Ptolemaic system that were taken seriously by Maimonides, among others, but would not be answered adequately until the Ptolemaic system was overthrown by Galileo and Copernicus. Much as the work of explicating Aristotle was left to be executed by Ibn Rushd, the Andalusian Revolt in astronomy was carried forward by Ibn Ṭufayl's friend and disciple al-Biṭrūjī (see Sabra).[1] But Ibn Ṭufayl wrote several works on "natural philosophy" that are no longer extant, including a philosophical treatment of the soul, which al-Marrākushī saw in Ibn Ṭufayl's own hand.

The important task to which Ibn Ṭufayl obliquely referred, however, centered on metaphysics. At the heart of his metaphysical project was his philosophical fable *Ḥayy ibn Yaqẓān* (Alive, Son of Awake), the story of a self-taught philosopher of perfect intelligence, growing up on an equatorial island without parents, language, or culture, who discovers for himself all phases of knowledge from the technical and physical to the spiritual truths underlying scriptural religions. Tracing the inquiries and discoveries of such a mind – unguided but also unblinkered by tradition – Ibn Ṭufayl believed, could elucidate the truths of philosophy and mysticism and help compose the now century-old quarrel between religion and philosophy in Muslim lands.

As his talk with the Commander of the Faithful on the day of Ibn Rushd's "discovery" made clear, Ibn Ṭufayl knew well the issues that divided the theologian al-Ghazālī (1058–1111) from the Neoplatonizing Aristotelians al-Fārābī (c. 870–950) and Ibn Sīnā (980–1037). In *Ḥayy ibn Yaqẓān* he sought a conciliating synthesis of the Islamic speculative tradition with al-Ghazālī's Sufi-influenced recasting of Islamic mysticism and pietism.

Ḥayy ibn Yaqẓān builds on the famous Floating Man thought experiment of Avicenna. The title is taken from one of the allegories Ibn Sīnā wrote while imprisoned in the castle of Fardajān near Hamadān and refers to the living human intelligence, aroused by the ever wakeful active intellect, the hypostasis by which God communicates his truth to the human mind, and indeed imparts all order and intelligibility to nature. In the Floating Man argument, recurrently used in Avicenna's nonallegorical writings, the philosopher seeks to demonstrate the substantiality of the human soul, that is, its independence or self-sufficiency, by calling on his reader to conceive himself suspended in space, isolated from all sensations, even from all sensory contact with his own body. One would still, he argued, have self-consciousness. Since one conceives of one's own awareness without positing the body or any bodily sensation, the idea of the self is not logically dependent on that of any physical thing. The soul, then, is not just the "tuning of the lute" that will vanish when the instrument is broken, but is a primary given, a substance (see Goodman, *Avicenna* 149–63). The argument was refined and simplified when Descartes recast it in epistemic terms: I can abstract from the supposition of all external things, but not from the supposition of my own consciousness.

Ibn Ṭufayl gave the argument a social twist, transposing the fictive situation from one of sensory deprivation to one of cultural isolation. Although his narrative does draw on the Romulus and Remus sort of motif, proposing a fallow doe as the nurse of the castaway or neophyte Ḥayy ibn Yaqẓān, Ibn Ṭufayl's real purpose is to show what the human mind can know with no help other than its divinely imparted nature – its receptivity and active penchant for inquiry and discovery, the inquiring mind that al-Ghazālī had claimed for himself and that Aristotle had set down as a premise when he opened the *Metaphysics* with the words "All men by nature desire to know."

What Ibn Ṭufayl's thought experiment reveals is that language, religion, and tradition are not necessary conditions for the emergence of a perfect mind. Indeed, human culture will more likely impede than promote the progress of such a mind. This negative conclusion of Ibn Ṭufayl's reflections amounts to a powerful indictment of social institutions in general and of institutional Islam in particular. The indictment is underscored when his story is compared with a scrap of Alexander romance preserved in Arabic at the Escorial (See García Gómez; Pastor 127–56; Hawi 259–60).

The earlier story has Alexander reaching an island where he sees a splendid statue bearing an inscription, which a learned man, after much demurral, deciphers for him. The inscription tells the story of the man in whose honor the statue had been erected. He had been cast away in infancy, despite his royal birth, but was miraculously borne by the waves to an island refuge, where a deer had nourished him. He had, however, acquired no such profound wisdom as Ḥayy ibn Yaqẓān would garner, until he was visited by another human being, who, sheerly by chance, proved to be his father, and who taught him the ways of civilization.

The hesitancy of the aged sage to decipher the inscription suggests that its content was in some way subversive; and we can readily see why, since the implication is that without culture and convention there would be no wisdom or religion. Ibn Ṭufayl's thinking brings him to just the opposite conclusion: there is indeed a natural religion, the content of which is represented in the ultimate wisdom reached by Ḥayy ibn Yaqẓān. But that wisdom is not the mere counterpart of the many and mixed messages of the world's traditions. Tradition and inspiration may find common ground in the end, but their needs and their thrust are often at odds; and tradition must ultimately be regarded as the lesser of the two, a concession to the weaknesses of the common mind but an obstacle to the strengths of the insightful. This devastating critique is delivered with a kind of backhand stroke, but it does not remain tacit. It is spelled out by Ibn Ṭufayl in passages that describe the encounters between the perfected Ḥayy ibn Yaqẓān and the members of a society governed by a prophetically revealed religion that is a "thinly veiled" generic counterpart of Islam.

Ibn Ṭufayl begins the story of Ḥayy ibn Yaqẓān by relating two narratives of his origin suggestive of the rival scientific and religious accounts of the nature and origin of man. The scientific version ascribes Ḥayy's origin to spontaneous generation, relying heavily on the precise characteristics of the matter in which the new organism would take shape. The traditional account resorts to fable, positing a human society and a human drama in which a royal infant is conceived but cast away, like Moses in the bulrushes, to be borne by a providential current to an uninhabited island. In both accounts, chance plays a role. But in the naturalistic version chance becomes the opportunity of nature; in the fabular version, which repeatedly echoes Qurʾanic language, chance becomes the plaything of providence, anthropomorphically addressed.

Ibn Ṭufayl is careful to avoid saying that the two stories contradict each other. Those who tell one story do deny the other. Yet neither account can exclude reference to the imparting of life, spirit, and intelligence, "the spirit which is God's" (Qurʾan 15:28–29, 32:6–9, 38:71–72) and indissoluble from the body, not only in the purview of the senses but also for the mind (Ibn Ṭufayl 106–7).

Ḥayy, like Aristotle's ideal of all men, has an innate desire to know. Nursed and nurtured by his doe foster mother, learning to rely on her and trust in her care, he grows more independent and focuses his desires and aversions, much in the manner of the Stoic accounts of moral development (see Cicero *De finibus* 3.5–7). He learns shame, jealousy, emulation, and covetousness – childhood conditions, in Ibn Ṭufayl's thinking. By adolescence he has reached the age of practical reason, making clothes and weapons for himself, having tired of waiting for horns to sprout on his head and of fighting losing battles with the wild animals of his island. As his foster mother weakens with age, he learns to care for her and discovers the active side of the love that had been the mere passive dependency of youth.

When the doe dies, he tries to restore her, but then realizes that the vital spirit has fled and that the body that remains is without its ruling principle. Ontogeny recapitulates phylogeny as Ḥayy ibn Yaqẓān discovers fire and uses it to provide himself with light and to cook his food. He associates its power with the missing life principle of his doe mother. He dissects the bodies of animals and uncovers the workings of their anatomy and physiology. At twenty-one he begins to think seriously about metaphysics.

Ḥayy discovers the organic form and unity of the cosmos, the distinction between matter and substantial forms, and the ultimate cause of all that he observes, working immanently, through the nature of things, as is figured forth in the language of the Qurʾan (8:17), where God informs his prophet of the unseen dimensions of a battle: "When you shot it was not you who shot but God."

Advancing independently in the same path as the philosophers, Ḥayy observes the retrograde motion of the planets and discovers for himself proof of the world's finite size. If there were an infinite magnitude, then removing a finite part of it would either make it finite or leave it infinite; if the former, then two finite quantities combined would form an infinite; if the latter, then one infinity exceeds another, which is impossible (Ibn Ṭufayl 129).

The classic standoff between Greek eternalism and the creationism of the scriptural traditions, which had been a source of discomfort for the young

Averroes when he first met the Almohad sultan, is recapitulated as an antinomy (it will become the first of Kant's four antinomies of pure reason) in the speculative reasonings of Ḥayy ibn Yaqẓān: if the world is eternal, then its age would be infinite and, so, subject to the same paradoxes that beset a world of infinite size – was the world less than infinite in age a year ago? But if the world was created out of nothing a finite time ago, then (recapitulating Aristotle's reasoning) there was a time before which there was no time. And the very notion of *before which* implies that this too was a time and that the notion of a first moment of time is incoherent.

Ibn Ṭufayl's resolution of the antinomy is sharp rebuke to al-Ghazālī, who had held not only that the two accounts were irreconcilable but that the eternalism of the Aristotelian philosophers of Islam was incompatible with their would-be theism – that it made them atheists in spite of themselves, since no meaning could be found for their notion that God was somehow author of the universe, unless it was the case that the world need not have existed; no meaning can be found for the idea that the world need not have existed, unless there was a time before which the world did not exist. But Ibn Ṭufayl accepts the philosophers' claim that there is such a meaning, that a cause need not precede its effect in time but might be prior to it ontologically, as the condition of its existence. For Ibn Ṭufayl sees the sense of the philosophers' reasoning, which cautions, in effect, that the idea that God precedes the world's creation temporally is only a crude way of envisioning divine transcendence, which actually has the effect of enmeshing God in temporality rather than elevating him above it.

The upshot of the great impasse over creation versus eternity, Ibn Ṭufayl concludes, is that on either account – that of the philosophers, who prided themselves on their science (for eternalism left no room for exceptions to the eternal rule of causal laws), or that of scriptural monotheists (who sustained God's free governance of the universe with the idea that God chose to create, with no prior condition or constraint) – natural theology will still flourish. A scriptural appeal to the world's dependence on the act and choice of God, or an Aristotelian appeal to the Prime Mover – either leads to the recognition of a God who is incorporeal and unimaginable yet governs the world.

Ibn Ṭufayl's truce between scriptural religion and Aristotelian philosophy did not hold even in the Islamic West. Responding to al-Ghazālī's *Tahāfut al-falāsifa*, Averroes sought a line of demarcation between the claims of philosophy and the aims of mass religion (see his *Faṣl al-maqāl* [Decisive Treatise]). But within the territory still held by philosophy he maintained the eternity of the cosmos, arguing in *Tahāfut al-tahāfut* (The Incoherence of the Incoherence), his riposte to al-Ghazālī, that it was not the eternalism of the philosophers but the sophistries of al-Ghazālī that were incoherent.

Yet Ibn Ṭufayl's resolution did appeal to Maimonides. The eternalism of the philosophers, he argued, resulted in an unintended and untenable determinism, which, if taken at face value, would render change as well as choice impossible. The radical contingency that the *mutakallimūn* (Islamic dialectical theologians) ascribed to the world and all things in it led to an equally untenable occasionalism, which left every event to the immediate agency and arbitrary discretion of God. Maimonides argued, taking his cue from Ibn Ṭufayl, that we cannot settle the matter demonstratively one way or the other. But that does not leave us without reasons to guide us. Creation, he argues, is both more probable and preferable to eternity, more probable because strict emanation, unguided by the sort of will or grace that we humans can grasp only in volitional terms, does not seem capable of differentiating divine simplicity into the multiplicity we observe; preferable because it makes more sense to speak of an author of the world if we think of the world as something that need not have existed, that once did not exist, but now does exist and has the nature it has because of the act of God.

The reasons are al-Ghazālī's but the moderation and sympathy for the philosophers are Ibn Ṭufayl's: the philosophers are not atheists; their arguments do work, although the eternity of the world is a postulate of theirs more problematic than they may care to acknowledge, not an axiom and still less the outcome of an apodictic demonstration. But the alternative too is problematic since creation posits a volitional side to God that strict monotheists know – as al-Ghazālī knew when he described a form of monism as the ultimate grade of monotheism – to be undifferentiable ultimately from the divine wisdom.

The discovery of God, as Ibn Ṭufayl's fiction is meant to show, is the discovery of man's vocation, salvation, and felicity. It is also the discovery of the meaning of perdition:

> If there is a Being Whose perfection is infinite, Whose splendor and goodness know no bounds, Who is beyond perfection, goodness, and beauty, a Being such that there is no perfection, no goodness, no beauty, and no splendor that does not flow from Him, then to lose hold of such a Being and having known Him to be unable to find Him must mean infinite torture, as long as He is not found. (Ibn Ṭufayl 137)

The project of the Sufis and the Neoplatonic philosophers is the same: pursuit of gnosis. The perdition and paradise of the Qurʾan are but images by which mystic contemplation and its loss are figured forth as bliss or torment, to an audience not yet initiated into such intimate experience of the Divine, and perhaps not capable of it.

Ḥayy ibn Yaqẓān discovers his own vocation before he knows what men in general are or what societies are like. He promptly sets about to pursue it, recognizing in such spiritual felicity the sole avenue and content of immortality.

He devises his own, natural Sufi discipline. His discipline is ascetic, to minimize the distractions of the body that would call him away from concentration on God's unity. For Ḥayy ibn Yaqẓān knowledge is obligation, and to know what manner of being he is and where he is situated in the cosmos is to know how he must live. There is a definite directionality to the scheme, and that directionality is clearly Platonic. There are some resemblances that Ḥayy must minimize. It is the spiritual that he, and the human beings whose situation he models, must maximize.

Eating, drinking, and other bodily functions were distractions, but necessary to the maintenance of the vital spirit, which in turn enabled Ḥayy to emulate the celestial bodies. This meant three things. First, to be like the stars he must adopt a role of stewardship over nature: he must not only minimize the demands of his body and interfere to the least degree possible with the fufillment of every natural project set forth for living beings by God, but he must actively care for all natural kinds, to emulate the governance and benevolent influence of the stars, "never allowing himself to see any plant or animal hurt or sick, encumbered or in need without helping it if he could" (146).

Second, "Ḥayy made sure always to be clean" (146). Here Ibn Ṭufayl appeals to the emulation of the stars to assimilate the toilet of Ḥayy ibn Yaqẓān not only to the ablutions of Islam but further, to the courtly sparkle ascribed to philosophers like Avicenna and prescribed by the courtly ethical philosopher Ibn Miskawayh, whose emphasis on dressing well, as a component of the virtue of personableness, al-Ghazālī had rejected in favor of simple dress and minimal attention to such externals (see Goodman, "Morals").

Finally, Ḥayy must emulate the motions of the heavens, whose perfection visibly manifests their adoration of God's absolute perfection, as Aristotle had argued. Ḥayy does this by spinning in place and circling his island – in effect recreating the rituals in which Muslims circumambulate the Kaaba in the rites of pilgrimage and Sufi devotees spin to reach the ecstasy of vertigo in the practice of the *dhikr*, the whirling invocation of the name and thought of God, aimed at focusing consciousness on God alone by blotting out all sensory things and all promptings of imagination.

But it was in pure meditation, "submersion," obliterating the externality and otherness of the personality itself, leaving only "the One, True Identity" of the necessarily existent, that Ḥayy found his highest and most perfect emulation, the end to which all his other activities must be means. Even the whirling of the *dhikr* must here be left behind as a vestige of physicality, and stewardship itself becomes a distraction from the perfect ecstasy that the self-taught philosopher now seeks, as Muhammad had done, in a cave. Practice of the discipline that his three forms of mimesis enjoined allows Ḥayy to become a mystic capable of sustaining his gnostic contact with the Divine.

With great labor the goal is achieved: "From memory and mind all disappeared . . . And with the rest vanished the identity that was himself" (Ibn Ṭufayl 149).

His return to self confuses the mind and leads him to confound his own identity with the object of his knowledge, a pantheistic fusing of identities that Islam had battled among extremist Sufis and that Avicenna had battled among philosophers, blaming Porphyry, for example, for taking the mind's "contact" with the active intellect to entail the identity of the two (see Goodman, *Avicenna* 163–72). "This specious thinking might well have taken root in his soul, had not God in His mercy caught hold of him and guided him back to the truth. He then realized that he never would have fallen prey to such a delusion unless some shadows of the physical or taint of sensory things still lurked within him. For 'many', 'few', and 'one'; 'singularity' and 'plurality'; 'union' and 'discreteness', are all predicates applicable only to physical things" (Ibn Ṭufayl 150). Ibn Ṭufayl's Plotinian line of argument allows him to show that the very categories of unity and difference themselves pertain exclusively to the sensory world, that in the spiritual or intellectual world the question of difference of the perfected human soul with the divine simply does not arise.

Similarly, Ibn Ṭufayl deploys Plotinus's idea that the intellectual realm (Nous) is a "one/many" against Plotinus's own quest for the divinization of the soul, preferring Plato's more modest goal of *homoiosis theō* (becoming like unto God), "to the extent that this is possible," echoing the very qualification Plato himself had used. And he relies on Ibn Bājja's reconciliation of the individual immortality of Avicenna (and al-Ghazālī) with the loss of individuality in the disembodied or ecstatic soul, seemingly demanded by Plato's intellectualist arguments for immortality and by the Sufi theme of *fanā'*, dying unto self. True again, he holds, the ecstatic transcends mere selfhood. But in so doing, what he leaves behind are the limitations of the ego, not the consciousness of individuality. The disembodied soul retains the individuality of its intentionality even when it is at one with all other souls.

To Ibn Bājja's idea of diversity in unity Ibn Ṭufayl contributes the image of the community of immortal souls, which here becomes part of Ḥayy ibn Yaqẓān's ecstatic vision, his first direct encounter with other beings that are not merely like him, as are the celestial bodies, but of his own kind:

> Passing through a deep trance to the complete death-of-self and real contact with the divine, he saw a being corresponding to the highest sphere . . . neither identical with the Truth and the One nor with the sphere itself, nor distinct from either . . . at the pinnacle of joy, delight and rapture, in blissful vision of the being of the Truth, glorious be His majesty.
>
> Just below this, at the sphere of the fixed stars, Ḥayy saw another . . . like the form

of the sun appearing in one mirror, reflected from a second. . . . Thus for each sphere he witnessed a transcendent immaterial subject, neither identical with nor distinct from those above, like the form of the sun reflected from mirror to mirror with the descending order of the spheres . . . until finally he reached the world of generation and decay, the bowels of the sphere of the moon.

Here too was an essence free of matter, not one with those he had seen – but none other. Only this being had seventy thousand faces. In every face were seventy thousand mouths; in every mouth, seventy thousand tongues, with which it ceaselessly praised, glorified, and sanctified the being of the One who is the Truth. (152–53)

Functionally, as Ibn Bājja would argue, we have unity here. But the individualities remain distinct, each enjoying the reward of its own quest, in communion with the highest, and in community with one another. Reflection from mirror to mirror both preserves and differentiates the intellectual reality that is imparted from above or beheld from below.

At the level of individual creatures and created species, refraction might be a more fitting metaphor than reflection. But, in keeping with Ibn Bājja's argument, the unity of all disembodied souls does not compromise their Avicennan individuality. And their Platonic inviolability does not render them identical with – nor yet different from – the Divine. For, in the Plotinian terms that Ibn Ṭufayl adopts as the framework of his metaphysic, all being is by participation in the reality, unity, and goodness of the Divine, and the being that God imparts to creatures is never merely identical with his own; yet also never, while it endures, wholly isolated from it. To lose contact with God absolutely would be to be annihilated. But even the souls of the damned do not undergo quite that fate. Rather, like "mirrors covered in rust," they are alienated from the light that might have given fulfillment to their being. This alienation is their "torture and ineradicable agony" (153).

Only as a mature and practicing mystic does Ḥayy ibn Yaqẓān first encounter another living human being, in the person of the anchorite Absāl, a philosophical refugee from an inhabited island long ruled under the laws of a scriptural religion. Absāl, like the theologian of Voltaire's *Philological Dictionary,* has studied many tongues, in his quest for subtlety and sophistication in the exegesis of scripture. Absāl becomes eager to teach Ḥayy to speak, hoping to impart knowledge and religion to him. But what he learns, of course, is that Ḥayy already knows the truth, of which his own religion bears the mere symbols.

Ḥayy, for his part, readily recognizes the true intentions behind the symbolic representations used by the prophet of Absāl's faith. He willingly "accepts" it, fufilling the formal conditions so welcome to the Islamic ideal of proselytization. But as their acquaintance deepens, it is clear that Absāl is the convert and disciple, and Ḥayy, the teacher.

As Absāl tells his friend about his own society, Ḥayy finds two things incomprehensible. First, the prophet uses symbols to portray the divine world, "allowing mankind to fall into the grave error of conceiving the Truth corporeally." Second, besides mandating rituals that Ḥayy would have granted, the prophet also allows the "amassing of wealth and overindulgence in eating, leaving men idle to busy themselves with inane pastimes and neglect the Truth." And when Ḥayy saw all the provisions of the Law had to do with money, sales, and penalties, he was "dumbfounded" at the emphasis on what he considered inanities (161–62).

Ḥayy determines to accompany Absāl to his own island, hoping "that it might be through him" that these people will be saved. The irony of Ibn Ṭufayl's allowing his hero to expect to "save" a populace already in receipt of a religion indistinguishable from Islam would not have been lost on a Muslim audience.

On their arrival, there is great interest in Ḥayy's novelty but when the neophyte philosopher settles down to teach the people, "they recoiled in horror from his ideas" (163). In the end, Ḥayy "saw 'every faction delighted with its own' (Qur'an 23:55, 30:31)" and realized that their appetites and passions made them incapable of following in his footsteps. Reluctantly, he concludes that symbols and restrictive laws are the best that the mass of men are capable of receiving. Admittedly, symbols can be mistaken for the truth itself and the minimal restrictions of a civil and criminal code are readily taken as the substance of righteousness and fulfillment of God's will. But such confusions are a necessary evil. For without the prophet's wise condescension to the moral and intellectual inadequacies of humanity and the weaknesses of human culture, even worse confusions of spirit and depravities of character than those the Candide-like Ḥayy observed would take hold. Ḥayy and Absāl return to their isolated island and continue their devotions "until man's certain fate overtook them" (165).

Ibn Ṭufayl believes that "moral rules, apprehended as ideas first, and then rigorously followed as laws, are and must be for the sage only. The mass of mankind have neither the force of intellect to apprehend them clearly as ideas, nor the force of character to follow them strictly as laws." With rare exceptions, the hearts of human beings are "corroded by their possessions" (163). Yet Ibn Ṭufayl, unlike Ḥayy ibn Yaqẓān and Absāl, did not abandon society but continued to live in it, if not wholly of it. And his work voices a clear, if indirect, invitation to any like-minded spirit, to pursue the higher spiritual path and the supererogatory moral path, which the prophet of Islam wisely saw were beyond the reach of most men.

But the generality of the invitation should not be overlooked, even in the setting of the Arabic *risāla* form, the intimate essay in the guise of a letter to a disciple, in which the narrative of *Ḥayy ibn Yaqẓān* is couched. Much in the spirit of Plotinus, alienation itself becomes an invitation to transcendence to the rare individuals who are capable of it.

NOTE

1. Another figure in the Andalusian Revolt was Ibn al-Haytham (d. c. 1040). Al-Biṭrūjī's *Kitāb fī l-hay'a* (On the Principles of Astronomy) was translated into Latin by Michael Scot, whose version was published with critical comparison to the Arabic original by Carmody (Berkeley, 1952). A Hebrew version by Moses Ibn Tibbon (1259) was translated into Latin by Kalonymus ben David (Venice, 1531).

BIBLIOGRAPHY

al-Biṭrūjī. *On the Principles of Astronomy.* New Haven, 1971.

Conrad, Lawrence, ed. *The World of Ibn Ṭufayl: Interdisciplinary Perspectives on Ḥayy ibn Yaqẓān.* Leiden, 1996.

García Gómez, Emilio. "Un cuento árabe fuente común de Abentofail y de Gracián." *Revista de archivos, bibliotecas y museos* 30 (1916): 1–67, 241–69.

al-Ghazālī. *Tahāfut al-falāsifa.* Ed. Maurice Bouyges. 2nd edn. Beirut, 1962.

Goodman, L. E. *Avicenna.* London, 1992.

"Ibn Bajjah." *History of Islamic Philosophy.* Ed. S. H. Nasr and Oliver Leaman. London, 1996. 1:294–312.

"Matter and Form as Attributes of God in Maimonides' Philosophy." *A Straight Path: Studies in Honor of Arthur Hyman.* Ed. R. Link-Salinger. Washington, D.C., 1988. 86–97.

"Morals and Society in Islamic Philosophy." *Companion Encyclopedia of Asian Philosophy.* Ed. Indira Mahalingam and Brian Carr. New York, 1997. 1000–24.

Hawi, Sami S. *Islamic Naturalism and Mysticism: A Philosophic Study of Ibn Ṭufayl's* Ḥayy ibn Yaqẓān. Leiden, 1974.

Ibn Rushd. *Faṣl al-maqāl mā bayna al-sharī'a wa l-hikma min al-ittiṣāl.* Trans. George F. Hourani as *On the Harmony of Religion and Philosophy.* London, 1976.

Tahāfut al-tahāfut (The Incoherence of the Incoherence). 2 vols. Trans. Simon van den Bergh. London, 1954.

Ibn Ṭufayl. *Ḥayy Ibn Yaqẓān.* Trans. L. E. Goodman. 3rd edn. Los Angeles, 1991. The standard Arabic edition is that of Léon Gauthier (Beirut, 1936); Gauthier published his first French translation in 1900. The work was translated into Hebrew by Moses Narboni (1349), into Latin (from the Hebrew) by Pico della Mirandola (late fifteenth century), by the younger Edward Pockocke (from the Arabic, 1671), by Spinoza's friend Johann Bouwmeester (1672), and by Simon

Ockley (1708). There are also Russian and German translations and a 1904 English version of selected passages.

al-Marrākushī. *The History of the Almohades.* Ed. Reinhart Dozy. Rpt., Amsterdam, 1968.

Pastor, Antonio. *The Idea of Robinson Crusoe.* Watford, 1930.

Sabra, A. I. "The Andalusian Revolt against Ptolemaic Astronomy: Averroes and al-Bitruji." *Transformation and Tradition in the Sciences.* Ed. Everett Mendelsohn. Cambridge, 1984.

CHAPTER 17

IBN ʿARABĪ

Alexander Knysh

Muḥammad ibn ʿAlī ibn Muḥammad ibn al-ʿArabī, as he styled himself in his writings, or Muḥyī l-Dīn ibn ʿArabī, as he was known to Eastern Muslims, was born in Murcia in 560/1165, at the beginning of the Almohad reign. Following the death of the local ruler Ibn Mardanīsh, Ibn ʿArabī's father, a high-ranking Arab official at the Murcian court, moved to Seville to take a post in the Almohad sultan's administration. There, in the capital of the Almohad state, the young Ibn ʿArabī was schooled in the traditional Islamic sciences including the Qur'an and Qur'anic exegesis, hadith, jurisprudence, adab, and kalam. He studied with the best Andalusi ulama of his epoch and quickly mastered all the major fields of Arabo-Islamic knowledge.

Little is known about that early period, which Ibn ʿArabī subsequently dismissed as a mere prelude to his all-important mystical life (Austin, *Sufis* 24; Addas, *Ibn ʿArabī* 45–51). There is some evidence that he was employed as a secretary at the chancery of the governor of Seville, although the exact circumstances of his worldly career cannot be ascertained. In Ibn ʿArabī's own words, he led the carefree life typical of wealthy young men of noble Arab stock (Addas, *Ibn ʿArabī* 55–56).

Still in his teens, he experienced a Sufi conversion precipitated by a heavenly voice commanding him to abandon his ungodly ways and to devote himself to the service of God. Deeply shaken by this episode, Ibn ʿArabī renounced the world and entered the Sufi path. He abruptly parted company with his refined friends and social peers and turned to the ragtag ascetics and "God's fools," whom members of his aristocratic class as well as established Maliki ulama dismissed as worthless beggars, bumpkins, and tricksters.

Unmindful of repeated admonitions and occasional ridicule, Ibn ʿArabī remained faithful to his new brethren in God, whom he later praised in his biographical writings and memoirs (Austin, *Sufis* passim). His subsequent life bears ample testimony to the sincerity and finality of his conversion. Following the example of his Sufi friends, Ibn ʿArabī immersed himself completely in ascetic practices and pious meditation. We witness him practicing constant invocation of God, night vigils, fasting, retreats, and pious meditation. Parallel to ascetic exercises, he studied classical Sufi works.

On his own account, Ibn ʿArabī soon acquired all the knowledge he could from the sheikhs of Seville and its environs and began to crisscross the Iberian Peninsula in search of renowned spiritual tutors. His quest brought him to the Maghrib, where he met many outstanding Sufi masters from the mystical school of the great North African saint Abū Madyan (d. 594/1197).[1] In Ibn ʿArabī's own words, he soon surpassed his Maghribi teachers in degree of spiritual attainment as well as in mastery of the Sufi tradition (Ibn ʿArabī, *Futūḥāt* [O.Y.] 3:119; Austin, *Sufis* 30; Addas, *Ibn ʿArabī* 179–80, 346–50). It seems probable that the claims of the precocious Andalusi Sufi offended certain established Maghribi masters who dismissed him as an upstart. Although he later highly praised his Western Sufi masters (Boase and Sahnoun 47–54), Ibn ʿArabī, like many of his compatriots, must have eventually found the intellectual and spiritual horizons of Western Islamdom too narrow for his ambitions.

In 598/1201, Ibn ʿArabī set out on a pilgrimage to Mecca. He never returned to his Andalusi homeland, which was constantly shrinking in the face of the Christian Reconquista. By the time of his departure, Ibn ʿArabī had written some sixty works on esoteric sciences, Sufi practice, and pedagogy, none of which brought him wide fame.[2] His talents came to full bloom in the Muslim East, where he wrote most of his works, including his controversial masterpieces: *Fuṣūṣ al-ḥikam* (Bezels of Wisdom) and *al-Futūḥāt al-makkiyya* (Meccan Revelations).

Once in the East, Ibn ʿArabī continued to search for renowned scholars and Sufis. His itinerary included the Hejaz, where he spent several years, Palestine, Syria, Iraq, and Anatolia (Addas, *Ibn ʿArabī* 346–62). Throughout, Ibn ʿArabī was accompanied by a small group of devoted disciples, who later served as propagators and interpreters of his teachings (Profitlich; Gril, "Kitāb al-inbāh"). Apart from hadith studies, which he pursued until his last day, Ibn ʿArabī taught his own works to the Sufis and scholars of the Holy Cities, Konya, Sivas, Aleppo, Baghdad, and Damascus. His stay in the Hejaz following his arrival from the West (598/1202–601/1204) was especially productive. He wrote many small treatises and began the major project of his life, the monumental *Futūḥāt al-makkiyya*, which a Western scholar described as "the Bible of esotericism in Islam" (Corbin 73).

Ibn ʿArabī's profound knowledge of the Islamic tradition, allied with his high reputation as a spiritual master, won him a large and enthusiastic following that included a number of Muslim sovereigns who provided the sheikh and his disciples with material support. In Syria, Ibn ʿArabī enjoyed the generous patronage of its Ayyubid rulers, while in Anatolia he was cultivated by the local Saljūq sultans and their courtiers. Among the latter was the father of Ibn ʿArabī's most consequential disciple, Ṣadr al-Dīn al-Qūnawī (d. 673/1274), who spread the sheikh's metaphysical ideas among Persian-speaking scholars.[3] While in Anatolia, Ibn ʿArabī wrote many Sufi works and trained numerous disciples. In addition, he counseled the sultan of Anatolia Kaykaūs on religious and political issues and addressed to him a famous letter of practical advice (*Futūḥāt* 4:547–48; cf. Austin, *Sufis* 42–43; Addas, *Ibn ʿArabī* 277–79). Yet, unlike many ulama who were anxious to be admitted to the royal entourage, Ibn ʿArabī avoided close contacts with secular authorities. Although he accepted royal patronage, he neither amassed a fortune nor entered the service of any Muslim ruler.

From 620/1226 until his death in 638/1240, Ibn ʿArabī resided in Damascus, where he enjoyed the protection of its Ayyubid rulers and of influential religious officials, some of whom became his disciples. Thanks to these connections, Ibn ʿArabī was given free hand in promulgating his esoteric teachings despite the occasional protests of some local ulama, such as the belligerent Sunni preacher Ibn ʿAbd al-Salām (d. 660/1262), who spurned Ibn ʿArabī's claims to supreme sainthood and divine inspiration.[4] The more controversial aspects of Ibn ʿArabī's teaching, however, were confined to a close circle of friends and disciples. Only upon his death did his esoteric works begin to gain wider circulation, antagonizing many conservative ulama. Dismayed at the bold theosophical ideas advanced in these works, they accused their author of heresy and delusion, thereby setting in motion a torrid theological controversy that has not entirely abated up to the present day.

In Damascus, Ibn ʿArabī composed his most famous work, *Fuṣūṣ al-ḥikam* – a brilliant, if extremely opaque, reflection on the nature of prophethood and religious belief, which he lavishly laced with monistic metaphysics and exegetical paradoxes. At about the same time, Ibn ʿArabī completed a final recension of his magnum opus, the *Futūḥāt*. The end result was a colossal book of 560 chapters – both the author's spiritual diary and a comprehensive summa of Islamic esotericism, theology, jurisprudence, and ritual. With the two major projects of his life successfully accomplished, Ibn ʿArabī passed away peacefully, surrounded by his disciples and family. His domed shrine in one of the suburbs of Damascus still attracts his admirers from far and wide.

IBN ʿARABĪ'S DOCTRINE

Ibn ʿArabī's legacy consists, in his own estimation, of some 250–300 works although some modern scholars credit him with twice this number (Yahia

1:37–50, 109–11). Their length varies from two-page pamphlets to multi-volume monuments such as the unfinished Qurʾanic commentary and the *Futūḥāt*. Even more perplexing for investigators is the wide variety of subjects and fields of knowledge that Ibn ʿArabī discussed in his writings.[5] To complicate things further, Ibn ʿArabī often treated traditional Islamic themes from a peculiar angle determined by his monistic vision of God and the world. In other words, he was less interested in these subjects for themselves than for their relevance to the set of mystical and metaphysical insights that he wanted to illuminate, thereby furthering his main purpose.

Neither in the *Fuṣūṣ* nor in the *Futūḥāt* did Ibn ʿArabī provide a succinct and final account of his basic tenets (Chodkiewicz, *Illuminations* 45). On the contrary, he seems to have been deliberately elusive in presenting his monistic doctrine. In a sense, this elusiveness constitutes the very crux of Ibn ʿArabī's discursive method, which urged him to couch his favorite motifs in the terminology and imagery of traditional Islamic sciences, playing on the symbols and conventions of contemporary Muslim culture. In conveying his elusive mystical insights and subtle experiences, Ibn ʿArabī made skillful use of "symbolic images that evoke emergent associations rather than fixed propositions" (Hodgson 2:224).

Although he was familiar with the syllogistic reasoning practiced by the *falāsifa*, he always emphasized that, in the final account, it fell short of capturing the dizzying dynamic of the relationship between God and the cosmos (see, e.g., "Kitāb al-isfār" 2:7). Ibn ʿArabī was also opposed to a blind imitation of earlier authorities, which he considered to be a sign of spiritual and intellectual immaturity (al-Ahl 139–40). In an attempt to overcome the perceived inadequacy of syllogistic argumentation and the slavish dependence on the wisdom of earlier scholars, Ibn ʿArabī turned to shocking antinomies and breathtaking paradoxes meant to awaken his readers to what he viewed as the "real" state of affairs in the universe. No wonder his work strikes us as a mishmash of seemingly disparate themes and topoi operating on parallel discursive levels from exegesis to poetry and mythology to jurisprudence and speculative theology. Such are some major features of Ibn ʿArabī's discursive method that account for the difficulties one encounters in interpreting his writings.

Recent studies of Ibn ʿArabī have called in doubt his esotericist credentials and his perceived disregard for the "externals" of the sharia (Morris, "Ibn ʿArabī's 'Esotericism'"; Chodkiewicz, *Ocean* passim). Supporters of this revisionist approach argue – justly it seems – that Western scholarship has been by and large neglectful of the exoteric facets of Ibn ʿArabī's work, especially his abiding interest in the study of hadith, fiqh, and the minutiae of Islamic ritual. To counterbalance this one-sided approach, the revisionist scholars emphasize the "exoteric" and conventional character of many of Ibn ʿArabī's "esoteric" treatises.

Compelling as this view may appear, it need not obfuscate Ibn ʿArabī's overriding concern for the inner aspects of Islamic revelation as well as his consistent reliance on abstruse symbols and intricate allegories.[6] On closer scrutiny, one discovers that even in his seemingly exoteric works Ibn ʿArabī remained faithful to his esoteric method, viewing quite traditional issues through the esoteric prism of his *Weltanschauung*.[7]

The findings of the revisionist scholars notwithstanding, Ibn ʿArabī's admirers and detractors continue to focus on the esoteric ideas of the *Fuṣūṣ* rather than on the more traditional (and admittedly less controversial) aspects of his vast legacy. Unsurprisingly, therefore, for the general Muslim and Western reader, Ibn ʿArabī remains primarily the author of the *Fuṣūṣ al-ḥikam* – an abstruse and elliptical work that examines the status of prophecy vis-à-vis sainthood as well as Ibn ʿArabī's other favorite themes, such as the perfect man, the "myth of microcosmic return" (Hodgson 2:222–27), the divine self-revelation in the empirical universe, the two aspects of the divine will, and allegoric exegesis. Although the *Futūḥāt* is, on balance, more representative of Ibn ʿArabī's outlook, it is too lengthy, technical, and unstructured to attract anyone but the most devoted investigator. Hence, in evaluating Ibn ʿArabī's contribution to Islamic intellectual history, his students in the East and the West still rely primarily on the *Fuṣūṣ*, which has become the object of some hundred and fifty commentaries (as well as innumerable refutations).

It would be inappropriate to give a detailed analysis of Ibn ʿArabī's *Fuṣūṣ* in a volume on Andalusi literature, especially since it was written long after his departure for the Muslim East. To gain a better idea of this controversial work, one is advised to consult a superb English translation of the *Fuṣūṣ* by Ralph Austin. As for the discursive specificity of this work, suffice it to say that here more than anywhere else Ibn ʿArabī "integrally combined the contrasting approaches of earlier Islamic intellectual traditions that had focused respectively on spiritual disciplines and contemplation, intellectual and scientific inquiry, and the elaboration of scriptural and prophetic teachings" in ways that were "never really repeated or adequately imitated by any subsequent Islamic author" (Morris, "How to Study" 73).

This statement captures the very essence of the author's method in the *Fuṣūṣ* – a work that strikes us as a maze of seemingly disparate theological and metaphysical propositions cast in opaque mythopoetic parables, exegetical paradoxes, poetic puzzles and puns, and ambiguous terminology.[8] Paradoxically, the discursive windows through which Ibn ʿArabī sought to highlight the various facets of his monistic worldview leave their peculiar imprint on the very ideas and experience Ibn ʿArabī endeavors to convey. Hence in the *Fuṣūṣ* it is practically impossible to separate the content from the form. This is not to say that an experienced reader cannot nail down the few constantly reemerging motifs that inform Ibn ʿArabī's entire discourse. Yet, one can never be sure that in the process of reformulation these motifs retain their original meaning intact. The goal of this deliberately devious discourse is to "carry the reader outside the work itself into the life and cosmos which it is attempting to interpret" (Hodgson 2:315).

Further adding to the reader's predicament is the way the elliptical and ambiguous text of the *Fuṣūṣ* forces him to engage in a perpetual decoding of its intended import. In the absence of a clearly defined referential framework (which is further aggravated by the ambivalence of the Arabic pronominal suffixes, whose referents are not always readily evident), one has to draw on one's educational background, world outlook, and subconscious intuition in reconstructing Ibn ʿArabī's convoluted argument. According to James Morris, Ibn ʿArabī's esoteric texts "are meant to function as a sort of spiritual mirror, reflecting and revealing the inner intentions, assumptions and predilections of each reader . . . with profound clarity" ("How to Study" 73). It is, therefore, hardly surprising that each Islamic century produced ever new interpretations of the *Fuṣūṣ*, though in the end several authoritative trends within this interpretive tradition triumphed over continued creativity and innovation. Given Ibn ʿArabī's open-ended discursive strategy, one can see why these numerous interpretations have failed to exhaust the potential of his polyvalent text.

This is not the place to detail Ibn ʿArabī's metaphysical doctrine. Suffice it to say that he viewed the world as a product of God's self-reflection that urged God to show himself in the things and phenomena of the material universe as in a mirror. This idea scandalized many ulama, who accused Ibn ʿArabī of admitting the substantial identity of God and world – a concept that contravened the doctrine of divine transcendency held dear by Islamic monotheism. In Ibn ʿArabī's system, God is not the absolutely otherworldly and impregnable entity of the mainstream Muslim theologians, who consequently came to view the Sufi thinker as the founder of the heretical doctrine of oneness of being (*waḥdat al-wujūd*), understood as pantheism (Austin, *Bezels* 25–27).

THE ANDALUSI PERIOD OF IBN ʿARABĪ'S WORK

The narrative strategies and theological tenets brought to fruition in the *Fuṣūṣ* and the *Futūḥāt* were already evident in Ibn ʿArabī's Andalusi writings that focus on, among other themes, the perfect human individual (*al-insān al-kāmil*), monistic metaphysics, and the mystical path to spiritual and intellectual perfection. In contrast to the obscurity of Ibn ʿArabī's later work, in his early writings these topics are treated in a more lucid way that allows a better insight into the origins and evolution of his thought.

In several treatises written between 590/1194 and 598/1201,[9] Ibn ʿArabī set out to explore the role of the perfect man as a metaphysical reality that links the diametrically opposed aspects of the unique divine Absolute. Neither an animal nor an angel, the perfect man is placed between the world of corruption and the world of immutability, as he combines in himself the characteristics peculiar to both realms. Indispensable for God's innate desire for self-knowledge and self-realization, the perfect man was seen by Ibn ʿArabī as the very cause and the ultimate goal of creation.

One, however, should not assume that, in Ibn ʿArabī's teaching, the perfect man is a sheer metaphysical abstract devoid of any tangible implications for the Muslim community. On the contrary, Ibn ʿArabī explicitly identified him with the supreme Sufi gnostic (*ʿārif*) and saint (*walī*) of the age, the spiritual pole (*quṭb*), handpicked by God to be the guide of humankind. Ibn ʿArabī considered this semidivine, if quite concrete, individual to be identical with the eschatological world-restorer, the Mahdi, who, in accordance with the Muslim tradition, was to appear at the end of time to reestablish Abrahamic religion in its primeval purity and to pave the way for the final advent of the Qurʾanic Jesus, the harbinger of the final hour (Ibn ʿArabī, *ʿAnqāʾ mughrib*; Chodkiewicz, *Sceau*; cf. "Mahdī," *EI*²). Although in these early writings Ibn ʿArabī was rather vague as to the identity of this divinely guided figure, later on he unambiguously declared himself "the seal of Muhammadan sainthood" (*khātam al-wilāya al-muḥammadiyya*) on a mission to revivify the Islamic religion and prepare the community of the faithful for the eventual arrival of Jesus (Ibn ʿArabī, *Futūḥāt* [O.Y.] 1:44–46; Ibn ʿArabī, *Dīwān* 26, 50, 259, 293, 334; Addas, *Ibn ʿArabī* 98–106; cf. Morris, "End of Time" 119–47).

Ibn ʿArabī's interest in the eschatological role of the Sufi *walī* may have been excited by the messianic speculations of the renowned Andalusi Sufis Ibn Barrajān (d. 536/1141) and Ibn Qasī (d. 546/1151), who are frequently quoted in Ibn ʿArabī's works (Addas, *Ibn ʿArabī* 73–79). These speculations, in turn, reflected the messianic and eschatological expectations rife among the Western Muslims of the age (Ibn Khaldūn 2:187–200).

On the theoretical level, both Ibn Barrajān and Ibn Qasī considered perfected Sufi gnostics (and not the ulama) the Prophet's natural heirs, destined to guide to salvation the Muslim community, overcome as it was by corruption, materialism, and moral decay. Furthermore, both masters prophesied darkly about the impending rise of "the just and upright one," "the awaited pious man," untainted by widespread degradation, whose advent was predicted in many eschatological hadith.

Ibn ʿArabī's Sufi predecessors did not limit themselves to theorizing, but sought to implement their doctrines in real life by laying claims to political as well as religious leadership (*imāma*). On the eve of his death Ibn Barrajān was recognized as imam in one hundred thirty villages around Córdoba (al-Shaʿrānī 1:15), whereas Ibn Qasī, encouraged by his enthusiastic disciples (*murīdūn*), proclaimed himself the Mahdi of the epoch and led a fully fledged (and initially successful) rebellion in the Algarve against the decaying Almoravid state from 539/1144 to 546/1151 (Dreher). Significantly, more than forty years after Ibn Qasī's death, in 590/1194, his son presented Ibn ʿArabī with a copy of his father's only surviving work *Khalʿ al-naʿlayn* (The Removal of the Sandals), on which Ibn ʿArabī later wrote a commentary (Addas, *Ibn ʿArabī* 77–79). Ibn ʿArabī was also familiar with Ibn Barrajān's ideas, which he studied with his favorite Sufi master, ʿAbd al-ʿAzīz al-Mahdawī (Addas, *Ibn ʿArabī* 76, 158).

It is, therefore, hardly surprising that Ibn ʿArabī's works from the Andalusi period display his intense fascination with the metaphysical and eschatological role of the Sufi gnostic. The metaphysical aspects of this role are examined in Ibn ʿArabī's early treatises, which focus on the status of the perfect man as God's vicegerent (*khalīfa*) on earth (Nyberg; Knysh). The eschatological implications of human vicegerency were discussed in *ʿAnqāʾ mughrib fī khātam al-awliyāʾ wa shams al-maghrib* (The Fabulous Gryphon: On the Seal of the Saints and the Sun Rising in the West), which contains cryptic prognostications (based on numerology and allegorical exegesis) regarding the time and the circumstances of the rise of the awaited Sufi Mahdi.[10] In yet another early work, *Mashāhid al-asrār al-qudsiyya* (The Contemplation of the Sacred Mysteries), Ibn ʿArabī provided a vivid account of the contemplative states that God bestows on his most perfect *awliyāʾ* in recognition of their elect status (Addas, *Ibn ʿArabī* 157–67). This peculiar mixture of the Neoplatonic metaphysics à la Ikhwān al-Ṣafāʾ and al-Ghazālī, of the Sufi theory of *wilāya*, and of the messianic tendencies peculiar to Ibn Barrajān and Ibn Qasī left its indelible mark on Ibn ʿArabī's mysticism, setting it apart from contemporary Sufi doctrines.

Closely allied to the notion of the perfect Sufi saint is another major theme prominent in Ibn ʿArabī's Andalusi writings. It has to do with the means for the Sufi saint to attain the uppermost degree of spiritual realization and can be defined as mystical ethics and pedagogy. Here, as in his treatment of other subjects, Ibn ʿArabī remained faithful to his allegorical method. Thus, in *Mawāqiʿ al-nujūm* (The Positions of the Stars), written in Almería in

595/1199, Ibn ʿArabī presented the traditional "way stations" (maqamat) of the Sufi path in symbols borrowed from contemporary astrology as he spoke of "the spheres of Islam, *īmān*, and *iḥsān*" and of the subtle correspondences between the Sufi stations and states and the zodiacal signs.

Ibn ʿArabī was careful not to disclose his messianic claims to anyone but his closest followers. His discretion helps explain why this espouser of potentially disruptive ideas managed to avoid conflicts with secular authorities during his lifetime. Ibn ʿArabī's apolitical stance and single-minded preoccupation with visionary experiences and inner life at the expense of wordly activity may account for the fact that at a time when Sufism became increasingly institutionalized, he founded neither a mystical *ṭarīqa* nor a popular Sufi school (al-Taftazānī passim).

IBN ʿARABĪ'S POETRY

The picture of Ibn ʿArabī's work would be incomplete without mentioning his poetry. His poetical production from the Andalusi period was, by and large, entirely subordinate to his metaphysical and ethical views as well as the theory of world-restoring sainthood outlined above. This illustrative poetry bears eloquent testimony to his facility with versification and impressive command of rhyme and meter as well as his skillful use of the lexical resources of the Arabic language. Yet, aside from several short *qiṭʿa*s (occasional poetic lines), his poems can hardly be treated as independent works of art. We are rather dealing with mere poetical illustrations that overflow with quotations from, and allusions to, the Qur'an, the Sunna, and Islamic mythology.

Ibn ʿArabī's independent poetical works, *Tarjumān al-ashwāq* (The Interpreter of Desires) and the *Dīwān*, were composed (or at least committed to writing)[11] after his departure to the Muslim East. The latter is a vast collection of poems and occasional verses that mirror the major themes of Ibn ʿArabī's mysticism, such as prophetology, sainthood, occultism, letter magic, mystical ethics, monistic metaphysics, and esoteric exegesis. In several passages from the *Dīwān* Ibn ʿArabī unequivocally proclaimed himself the seal of Muhammadan sainthood who was sent by God to restore the original meaning of the sharia and to "breathe the spirit back into Islam" (Morris, "End of Time" 121; cf. n. 38). Typical in this regard is the following passage from the *Dīwān*:

> I know very well the contents [of the message] that I have brought
> you
> And I am not the one who has doubts about it or
> follows blindly [earlier authorities]
> We hold our own [independent] position on every single issue

And we have true knowledge about what is concealed [*al-ghayb*]
and what is evident [*mashhad*]
I am entrusted with your guidance and it is in me
that the imamate is vested
I am the seal of the saints in the same way as
Muhammad is the seal of the prophets
I am, however, a specific and limited seal,[12] not the
seal of universal sainthood, for this one belongs
exclusively to Jesus, to whom divine help has been granted. (293)

Some verses from the Andalusi period of Ibn ʿArabī's life feature in his famous adab work *Muḥāḍarat al-abrār wa-musāmarat al-akhyār* (The Conversations of the Pious and Table Talks of the Best Men). Among them is a poignant reflection on the transience of life composed during his visit to the ruins of *Madīnat al-Zahrāʾ, a formerly magnificent caliphal palace near Córdoba, destroyed by the Berber mercenaries at the beginning of the fifth/eleventh century.

These [crumbling] houses are kindled by the last
streaks of the declining sun
Not a single dweller you see around, only
emptiness
Mourning [over the ruins] are birds who have come
here from afar
Now they sing, now they fall silent
I asked one of them, whose song filled my
heart with anguish and sorrow,
"What are you crying and complaining about?"
It said: "I cry over the time [*dahr*]
that is gone and is never to return." (1:259–60; cf. Pérès 127)

The themes and imagery invoked in this verse (i.e., nostalgia, the relentless flow of time, and the abandoned dwellings), as Ibn ʿArabī himself acknowledged elsewhere in the *Muḥāḍarat* (2:69–70), is typical of classical Arabic poetry (Sells, *Desert Tracings*). The same is true of the imagery and topoi in the *Tarjumān al-ashwāq* – a collection of love poetry inspired by one ʿAyn al-Shams Niẓām, a daughter of Ibn ʿArabī's teacher, whom he met during his stay at Mecca in 598/1202. Although in the introduction to the *Tarjumān* Ibn ʿArabī urged his readers not to treat his verses as simple love poems, but as allusions "to divine inspirations (*wāridāt ilāhiyya*), the spiritual visitations (*tanazzulāt rūḥāniyya*), and the correspondences [of our world] with the world of angelic intelligences,"[13] some ulama were unconvinced of the sincerity of his caveat. Goaded by their suspicions and accusations of licentiousness, Ibn ʿArabī wrote a commentary on the *Tarjumān* in which he unraveled his true intentions, stressing the allegorical nature of his love poetry (Ibn ʿArabī, *Dhakhāʾir al-aʿlāq*).

> Whenever I mention traces of abandoned
> encampments or [deserted] dwellings, or
> [forlorn] lodgings
> As I say "her" or "oh!" or, as the case may be,
> "isn't it?" or "why does it?"
> Or as I say "she," or "he," or "they [men],"
> or "they [women]," in the plural, or "they [both]"
> Or as I say, in my verses, "fate has brought me
> to the Najd" or "to the Tihāma"
> Or as I say "clouds burst out crying" or
> "a flower smiled"
> Or when I call on the caravan drivers who are headed
> for Banāt al-Ḥājir or Wurq al-Ḥimā[14]
> Or when I refer to "the shining moons setting in
> their howdahs" or "the suns, or young ladies,
> rising like stars above the horizon" . . .
> Or "full-bosomed and shapely women who appear like
> suns" or "like marble statues"
> Whenever I name something I have just mentioned or
> the like of it, one should consider all this to be
> But the divine mysteries and the pure and sublime
> lights which the heavenly host unveiled
> To my heart and the hearts of those who, like me, have
> attained the status of the true knowers
> [Whatever I mention refers] to the sacred and exalted
> quality [*ṣifa*] that testifies to the veracity of my claims
> So detach your mind from the externals and seek
> the hidden truth until you learn!
>
> (Nicholson 13; cf. Yahia 1:12–13)

NOTES

1. See "Abū Madyan," *Encyclopaedia of Islam*, 2nd edn. (Leiden, 1980–) (hereafter *EI*²); Austin, *Sufis* index; Urvoy 53; Addas, "Abū Madyan."
2. See, e.g., Ibn al-Abbār no. 1023; for a list of Ibn ʿArabī's works from that period, see Yahia 1:100–3.
3. For the dissemination of Ibn ʿArabī's ideas in Eastern Islamdom, see Corbin 69–71, 224; Chittick, "Ibn ʿArabī" 50; Chittick, "Rūmī" 77–79; Addas, *Ibn ʿArabī* index.
4. For details, see my *Ibn ʿArabī in the Later Islamic Tradition: The Making of a Polemical Image in Medieval Islam* (Albany, 1999).

5. According to Yahia, Ibn ʿArabī's legacy can be classified under ten general rubrics: exegesis, hadith, metaphysics, esotericism, theology, mystical ethics, fiqh, history, poetry, and works that defy any categorization. Seventy-five percent of Ibn ʿArabī's overall literary output falls under esotericism and mystical ethics.
6. See my article "Ramz" in *EI*^{2}.
7. See Winkel. Winkel's conclusions, however, are skewed by his partisan drive to portray Ibn ʿArabī as an exoteric scholar.
8. For discussions of Ibn ʿArabī's narrative strategies, see Sells, "Garden" and "Mirror"; Austin, *Bezels* 16–21; Morris, "Ibn ʿArabī's 'Esotericism'" and "How to Study." For the so-called mythic-visional style of writing current among medieval Muslim mystics and poets, see Hodgson 2:225–27 and 311–15.
9. E.g., *al-Tadbīrāt al-ilāhiyya* (The Divine Dispositions), *ʿAnqāʾ mughrib* (The Fabulous Gryphon), *Kitāb al-isrā* (Book of Ascension), *Inshāʾ al-dawāʾir* (Description of the Encompassing Circles), *Risāla fī l-wilāya* (Epistle on Sainthood).
10. This work was analyzed and translated by Gerald Elmore in his unpublished Ph.D. dissertation, "The Fabulous Gryphon: Ibn al-ʿArabī's *ʿAnqāʾ mughrib*" (Yale University, 1995).
11. Some verses in the *Dīwān* date from the Andalusi period of Ibn ʿArabi's career, e.g., the poem addressed to the Almerian Sufi al-Ghazzāl (46).
12. I.e., the seal of Muhammadan sainthood, whose authority is confined to the Muslim community.
13. Quoted in Corbin 138; cf. Nicholson 4.
14. Localities in the Hejaz.

BIBLIOGRAPHY

Addas, Claude. "Abū Madyan and Ibn ʿArabī." *Muhyiddin Ibn ʿArabī: A Commemorative Volume.* Ed. Stephen Hirtenstein and Michael Tiernan. Brisbane, 1993. 163–80.

Ibn ʿArabī ou La quête du soufre rouge. Paris, 1989.

al-Ahl, ʿAbd al-ʿAzīz. *Muḥyī al-dīn ibn ʿarabī: Min shiʿrih.* Beirut, 1970.

Austin, Ralph W. *The Bezels of Wisdom.* New York, 1980.

Sufis of Andalusia. 2nd edn. Berkeley, 1977.

Boase, Roger, and Farid Sahnoun. "Excerpts from the Epistle on the Spirit of Holiness." *Muhyiddin Ibn ʿArabī: A Commemorative Volume.* Ed. Stephen Hirtenstein and Michael Tiernan. Brisbane, 1993. 44–72.

Chittick, William. "Ibn ʿArabī and His School." *Islamic Spirituality: Manifestations.* Ed. S. H. Nasr. New York, 1991. 49–79.

"Rūmī and *waḥdat al-wujūd.*" *Poetry and Mysticism in Islam.* Ed. Amin Banani and Georges Sabagh. Cambridge, 1994. 70–111.

The Sufi Path of Knowledge. Albany, 1989.

Chodkiewicz, Michel, ed. *Les illuminations de la Mecque.* Paris, 1989.
An Ocean without Shore. Albany, 1993.
Le sceau des saints. Paris, 1986.
Corbin, Henri. *Creative Imagination in the Sufism of Ibn ʿArabī.* Princeton, 1969.
Dreher, Joseph. "Das Imāmat des islamischen mystikers Abūlqāsim . . . Ibn Qasī (gest. 1151)." Inaugural-Diss., Bonn, 1985.
"L'imâmat d'Ibn Qasīà Mértola." *Mélanges de l'Institut Dominicain d'Etudes Orientales* (Cairo) 13 (1988): 195–210.
Gril, Denis. *Le dévoilement des effets du voyage.* Combas, 1994.
"Le Kitāb al-inbāh ʿalā ṭarīq Allāh de ʿAbdallāh Badr al-Ḥabashī." *Annales islamologiques* 15 (1979): 87–164.
Hodgson, Marshall G. S. *The Venture of Islam: Conscience and History in a World Civilization.* 3 vols. Chicago, 1974.
Ibn al-Abbār. *al-Takmila li-kitāb al-ṣila.* Ed. F. Codera. Madrid, 1886.
Ibn ʿArabī. *ʿAnqāʾ mughrib.* Ed. M. ʿA. Ṣubayḥ. Cairo, 1954.
Dhakhāʾir al-aʿlāq. Ed. M.ʿ A. al-Kurdī. Cairo, 1968.
Dīwān ibn ʿarabī. 1855. Rpt., Baghdad, 1963.
al-Futūḥāt al-makkiyya. 4 vols. 1867. Rpt., Beirut, 1968.
al-Futūḥāt al-makkiyya (O.Y.). Ed. ʿU. Yaḥiā. 4 vols. Cairo, 1972–.
"Inshāʾ al-dawāʾir." Nyberg 1–38.
"Kitāb al-isfār." *Rasāʾil ibn al-ʿarabī.* Hyderabad, 1948. 2:1–63.
Kitāb al-isrā ilā maqām al-asrā. Ed. S. al-Ḥakīm. Damascus, 1988.
Muḥāḍarat al-abrār wa-musāmarat al-akhyār. 2 vols. Beirut, n.d.
"al-Tadbīrāt al-ilāhiyya." Nyberg 103–240.
Ibn Khaldūn. *The Muqaddimah: An Introduction to History.* Trans. F. Rosenthal. 2nd edn. 3 vols. Princeton, 1967.
Knysh, Alexander. *Mekkanskiye otkroveniya.* St. Petersburg, 1995.
Maḥmūd, Zakī Najīb. "Tarīqat al-ramz ʿinda ibn ʿarabī." *al-Kitāb al-tidhkārī: Muḥyī al-dīn ibn ʿarabī.* Cairo, 1969. 69–104.
Morris, James Winston. "At the End of Time." Chodkiewicz, *Illuminations* 119–47.
"How to Study the 'Futūḥāt': Ibn ʿArabī's Own Advice." *Muhyiddin Ibn ʿArabī: A Commemorative Volume.* Ed. Stephen Hirtenstein and Michael Tiernan. Brisbane, 1993. 73–89.
"Ibn ʿArabī's 'Esotericism': The Problem of Spiritual Authority." *Studia Islamica* 71 (1990): 37–64.
Nicholson, Reynold Alleyne. *The Tarjuman al-ashwaq.* London, 1911.
Nyberg, Henrik. *Kleinere Schriften des Ibn al-ʿArabī.* Leiden, 1919.
Pérès, Henri. *La poésie andalouse en arabe classique au XI siècle.* Paris, 1953.
Profitlich, Manferd. *Die Terminologie Ibn ʿArabī's im "Kitāb wasāʾil al-sāʾil" des Ibn Saudakīn.* Freiburg, 1973.
Sells, Michael. *Desert Tracings: Six Classic Arabian Odes.* Middletown, 1989.
"Ibn ʿArabī's 'Garden among the Flames': A Reevaluation." *History of Religions* 23(1984): 287–315.

"Ibn ʿArabī's 'Polished Mirror': Perspective Change and Meaning Event." *Studia Islamica* 67 (1988): 121–49.

al-Shaʿrānī. *al-Ṭabaqāt al-kubrā.* 2 vols. Cairo, n.d.

al-Taftazānī, Abū l-Wafāʾ. "al-Ṭarīqa al-akbariyya." *al-Kitāb al-tidhkārī: Muḥyī al-dīn ibn ʿarabī.* Cairo, 1969. 295–353.

Takeshita, Masataka. *Ibn ʿArabī's Theory of the Perfect Man.* Tokyo, 1987.

Winkel, Eric. "Ibn ʿArabī's *Fiqh*: Three Cases from the Futuhat." *Journal of the Muhyiddin Ibn ʿArabī Society* 13 (1993): 54–74.

Urvoy, Dominique. "Littérature et société dans la Séville musulmane." *Séville: Vingt siècles d'histoire.* Ed. B. Lavallé. Bordeaux, 1992. 37–56.

Yaḥia, ʿU. *Histoire et classification de l'œuvre d'Ibn ʿArabī.* 2 vols. Damascus, 1964.

CHAPTER 18

RAMON LLULL

Gregory B. Stone

Ramon Llull – *vir phantasticus* (crazy man); *doctor illuminatus* (enlightened doctor); *arabicus christianus* (Arabic Christian); *philosophus barbatus* (bearded philosopher); "founder of Catalan prose and one of Catalonia's greatest medieval writers" (Bonner in Llull, *Doctor* 45); "author of a vast number of works – 265 according to the latest catalogue of works – on countless subjects and in numerous literary forms" (45); "the first European to write prose novels on contemporary themes" (1); author of the million-word *Book of Contemplation* (written first in Arabic – all of Llull's Arabic writings have been lost or were destroyed – then in Catalan) – was able "to elaborate a theory of the universe which, of all medieval theories, came closest to a general hypothesis which should explain all observable phenomena" (Hillgarth 17). Furthermore, Llull, who is also recognized as one of the founders of the European study of Near Eastern languages, established in 1276 an Arabic language school in Miramar on Majorca, and in 1311 he successfully petitioned the Church Council of Vienne to establish chairs of Arabic at the Universities of Paris, Louvain, and Salamanca.

If Llull is less known today than he perhaps ought to be, this fall into relative obscurity is a rather recent phenomenon. As Peers remarked concerning Llull's fame through the eighteenth century, "there really were those who could take seriously the refrain: 'Tres sabios hubo en el mundo, / Adán, Salomón y Raymundo' [There have been three wise men in the world / Adam, Solomon, and Ramon], and there were even those who could quote the notorious remark, attributed to one Père Rossell, that the Old Testament was the work of God the Father, the New Testament of God the Son, and the writings of Ramon of God the Holy Spirit" (402). Llull's reputation for multifaceted accomplishment became so enormous that by the middle of the nineteenth century he had become "the discoverer of nitric acid, of a Great Elixir, even of America!" (409). The following remarks emphasize Llull's approach to Islam and certain of his works that most clearly show significant affiliations with the Arabic tradition.

LIFE, MISSION, TOLERANCE

Llull was born on Majorca in 1232, just three years after James I of Aragon had captured the island from the Arabs, who had held it for three centuries. Llull's father, probably a noble, was a member of the conquering army. Llull himself, in his teens and twenties, was a courtier and seneschal for James's son, the future James II of Majorca.

Despite the Reconquest, in Llull's youth the majority of Majorca's population remained Muslim – although most Muslims, save for a few who had been of service to James I, were soon dispossessed, impoverished, or enslaved. Llull grew up witnessing firsthand the conflict that accompanies linguistic and religious difference. This cultural diversity was the chief determining element of Llull's life's project, summed up by this wish expressed by one of the characters in Llull's *Book of the Gentile and the Three Wise Men*: "Ah! What a great good fortune it would be if . . . we could all – every man on earth – be under one religion and belief, so that there would be no more rancor or ill will among men, who hate each other because of diversity and contrariness of beliefs and sects! And just as there is only one God, Father, Creator and Lord of everything that exists, so all peoples could unite and become one people" ("Prologue," *Selected Works* 1:116).

Llull's solution to the problems posed by cultural difference was the institution of a unified global culture. In practical terms, this aim entailed, for Llull, the conversion of Muslims and Jews to Christianity. In *Blanquerna*, conversion is not a matter of "saving souls," of turning Jews from error to truth, but rather a matter of pacifying one's world, of bringing Jews and Christians into accord on a common ground of shared belief. Llull's assault against cultural alterity was, in his mind, only a necessary means for the establishment of cultural unity.

Llull's insistence on turning diversity into identity, his inability to let others remain other, is an idea that nowadays we abhor. But we should not confuse Llull's position with intolerance or ethnocentrism. Llull refuses to assert the intrinsic superiority of Latin, European, and Christian to Arabic, Hebrew, African, Islamic, and Jewish culture. But, unlike twentieth-century intellectuals, Llull did not take seriously the future possibility of a harmonious world founded on diversity. Having witnessed only the combination of cultural difference and violence, Llull did not believe that cultural difference and peace could ever coexist; since peace was his overriding goal, universal assimilation was, in Llull's view, the only real option.

Llull's tolerance toward Islam and Judaism reaches its height in his *Book of the Gentile and the Three Wise Men*. First written in Arabic, then in Catalan and Latin, the book is meant, Llull says, "for entering into union with and getting to know strangers and friends" (*Selected Works* 1:304). Depressed with thoughts concerning the inevitability of his death, a character called the Gentile (a pagan, who does not believe in the One God) follows a path into a clearing in the forest, where he encounters three wise men – a Jew, a Muslim, and a Christian. Each of the three takes his turn giving a philosophical account of his religious doctrines. The Gentile, persuaded by their reasonings, announces that henceforth he will worship God. But which of the three monotheisms does the Gentile deem to be more true than the others? Just where we expect a Christian polemicist would assert the superiority of his belief, Llull finishes with an open-ended question, as the Gentile, right on the verge of announcing which religion he will choose, is silenced by the three wise men:

> But before the three wise men left, the Gentile asked them in astonishment why they did not wait to hear which religion he would choose in preference to the others. The three wise men answered, saying that, in order for each to be free to choose his own religion, they preferred not knowing which religion he would choose. "And all the more so since this is a question we could discuss among ourselves to see, by force of reason and by means of our intellects, which religion it must be that you will choose. And if, in front of us, you state which religion it is that you prefer, then we would not have such a good subject of discussion nor such satisfaction in discovering the truth."
> (1:300–301)

Llull is more interested in representing the three monotheisms sharing a common discursive ground than he is in a polemical insistence on the superiority of Christianity's claim to truth.

Although it is fair to call Llull a "missionary," he is not usually a propagandist, a proselytizer, or a religious zealot. This is quite clear in a proposal that the eighty-year-old Llull makes to Frederick III of Sicily in his *Liber de participatione christianorum et saracenorum.* Llull advocates the following as part of what can only be called a cultural exchange program between Europe and North Africa: "that well-educated Christians familiar with the Arabic language go to Tunis to let Muslims see the truth of their faith, and that well-educated Muslims come to the kingdom of Sicily to discuss their faith with wise Christians. And perhaps by such means there might be peace between Christians and Muslims . . . and they would not try to destroy each other" (*Opera latina* 16:246, trans. mine).

In some of Llull's writings this tolerance toward Islam seems to wane, and on occasion he advocates armed crusades.[1] However, one ought at least to consider the context in which these endorsements are presented. The apparent call-to-arms in Llull's *Phantasticus,* for instance, is situated in a chapter called "On Order"; Llull's point is that the Church's "two swords" (intellectual and corporeal power) ought only to be deployed in the right order, that verbal combat must take priority over physical combat (*Opera latina* 16:28). As Llull says elsewhere, "strength of mind is nobler and greater than strength of body" (*Blanquerna* chap. 50, 190). Only nonviolent crusading is Christ-like – a position asserted in *Blanquerna* by none other than the sultan of Babylon: in a letter to the pope, the sultan, after noting that Christians are attempting to hold the Holy Lands "by force of arms," writes that he "marvelled that the Pope and the Christians worked not after the manner of Jesus Christ and the Apostles . . . for this cause, he said, God willed not that they should possess the Holy Land beyond the seas" (chap. 80, 323). For Llull, the only legitimate conquest is discursive.

On one hand, Llull's effort to replace physical combat with the verbal construction of a new world is an infliction on others of a discursive power ultimately more destructive of alterity and more pernicious than military action. Llull seems to suggest, as Machiavelli would later assert, that true dominion over others requires their internal acquiescence to a system of ideas. On the other hand, Llull's attempt literally to disarm Christian crusaders is a noble effort to transform the nature of Europe's relations with others, to propose as an alternative to the "corporeal sword" a "mental sword" – a repudiation of violence is perhaps best represented in a famous episode from the *Vita coaetanea*, the remarkable autobiography that Llull dictated to his disciples in 1311, about four years before his death.[2] The episode is normally taken at face value, as narrating an actual happening in Llull's life, but it is perhaps best read in an allegorical key.

Before turning to the episode, some biographical background is necessary. In his early thirties, the *Vita* tells us, Llull, a dissolute troubadour, irreligious chivalric courtier, and the majordomo of the future king of Majorca's household, was "about to compose and write in his vulgar tongue a song to a lady whom he loved with a foolish love" (*Selected Works* 1:11). But Llull, enraptured by a mystical vision of Christ crucified, was unable to finish his courtly love song. This scene repeated itself for several nights; subsequently, Llull renounced his former life and dedicated himself to serving God through (1) converting unbelievers to Christianity even at the price of martyrdom;[3] (2) writing the world's best refutation of the errors of the unbelievers (1:13); and (3) instituting monasteries "in which selected monks and others fit for the task would be brought together to learn the languages of the Saracens and other unbelievers" (1:13).

As training for his threefold mission, Llull spent nine years in a hermitlike intense study, especially of Arabic theology, philosophy, language, and literature. The *Vita* tells us that in order to learn Arabic, Llull acquired a Muslim slave. After the period of study, an incident occurs that reads much like an allegory for relations between Europe and the Islamic world. With little provocation, simply having heard that the slave had blasphemed the name of Christ, "Ramon, impelled by a great zeal for the Faith, hit the Saracen on the mouth, on the forehead, and on the face. As a result the Saracen became extremely embittered, and he began plotting the death of his master" (1:16–17). "Ramon" here stands less for Llull than for Western Christendom in general, and Ramon's violence against the Muslim is not so much an anecdote from Llull's biography as it is a metaphor for two centuries of military crusades waged by the West against the Near East. The slave eventually attacks Llull with a sword. Ramon manages to survive the attack, and he imprisons the slave while mulling over the proper punishment. On one hand, Ramon hesitates to put the Muslim to death, "for it seemed harsh to kill the person by whose teaching he now knew the language he had so wanted to learn, that is, Arabic" (1:17). For thirteenth-century European society, deeply indebted to the philosophical language of the Arabs, violence against Islam was just such a betrayal of that culture under whose tutelage it had been educated. On the other hand, Ramon fears that he must be merciless, "knowing that from then on [the Muslim] would not cease plotting his death" (1:17). To this point the episode has represented the relations between Europe and the Arabic world in a twofold manner. First, despite its having perhaps acquired a position of material (military) mastery, Europe remains the "student": it was raised to its present level of culture and civilization by learning from the Arabs. Second, Europeans and Arabs are presently caught up in a cycle of violence that was instigated by Europe's striking the first blow (the excessively cruel First Crusade of 1096, leading to the Christian army's genocidal capture of Jerusalem in 1099). And now the situation seems to be, from the European perspective, at an impasse. For Europe to do nothing, to follow the course of a nonviolent pacifism, would be to put itself in jeopardy. Yet for Europe to respond in kind to the latest act of violence would only perpetuate the unending cycle of retaliation. The impasse is resolved, to Ramon's relief, by a sort of miracle or deus ex machina: "When on the way back [Ramon] made a slight detour to visit his captive, he found that he had hanged himself with the rope with which he had been bound . . . Ramon therefore joyfully gave thanks to God . . . for keeping his hands innocent of the death of this Saracen" (1:17).

The Muslim's suicide is the symbolic wish-fulfillment of Llull's lifelong dream. Llull did not aim to destroy Islam; rather, he wished that it would destroy itself. Llull was willing to assist in this suicide, but the real agent of Islam's death would be a force whose genesis was within Islam itself – Arabic rationalist philosophy. The "suicide" of Islam would be its rationalistic zeal for Truth so strong that it could even be turned against the revelations of the Prophet (as Nietzsche once said, "Truth kills; it even kills itself"). Llull's missionary project was an attempt to capitalize on Arabic rationalism, to persuade non-Christian intellectuals who had given up their own creeds that Christian doctrine was not demonstrably irrational. Philosophy, for Llull, is an expedient instrument at the service of Llull's primary aim of global unification. Indeed, in *Blanquerna* it is Philosophy himself who, learning that his sister Faith "had journeyed among the Saracens, and . . . had found men learned in philosophy that believed not in the articles of the Saracens," insists that the time is right for the West to use *falsafa* against its native culture: "The time has come wherein our knowledge [Philosophy] is exalted; the unbelievers demand necessary demonstrations and reasons, and refuse credence to aught beside. It is time for us to go, and make use of the science which we have . . . Very great is the doubt which the sages of the Saracens have in their belief; the Jews are in doubt by reason of the bondage wherein they live" (chap. 44, 165).

Llull learned Arabic not so much to further the transmission of Arabic thinking into Europe (that transmission had been going strong for two centuries), but rather to further the continuation in the Arabic world of the tradition of rationalist *falsafa* (a tradition that was perhaps already defunct, with the death of Ibn Rushd [Averroes] in 1198). Llull made himself into, among other things, an Arabic writer; he was not an Arabist whose project was to translate from Arabic into Latin (when he did translate, it was from his own Arabic works, works that he initially intended to be read by Arabs). Indeed, among his very first works is a compendium, written in Arabic, of the logical and rationalist writings of al-Ghazālī (Llull conveniently failed to mention that al-Ghazālī himself was, in questions concerning metaphysics, no rationalist but rather had written expositions of the *falāsifa*'s ideas in order to question them). Llull's strategy in writing Arabic *falsafa* was twofold: to increase among Muslims the number of rationalists (hence, Llull presumed, doubters), and to introduce into *falsafa* the notion that the basic doctrines of Christianity (the Trinity and the Incarnation) were in accord with a rational understanding of metaphysical reality. Llull's aim was to reverse the direction of the one-way flow of philosophical ideas; to return to the Arabs – but with a difference – the gift (or, the poison) that they had brought to Europe.

Convinced that believers never drop their beliefs when faced with others' claims to have better beliefs, Llull concentrated most of his efforts on devising an apparently belief-free technique for demonstrating what is real, a technique that he called the Great Universal Art of Finding Truth (and which, the *Vita* says, was revealed to him in a divinely inspired illumination). The Art is a way to discourse about reality without recourse to the Scriptures of Judaism, Christianity, or Islam. Starting with what Llull called the Absolute Principles (nine qualities of God that all three monotheisms agree on, such as Goodness,

Greatness, Eternity, etc.), the Art assigns to each Absolute Principle an alphabetic notation (Goodness = B, Greatness = C, Eternity = D, etc.). Llull then posits that there are nine Relative Principles (difference, concordance, contrariety, etc.), which are also assigned the same nine letters of the alphabet (difference = B, concordance = C, contrariety = D, etc.). Various other sets of nine principles are also denoted by the same nine letters (for instance, under the rubric "Questions and Rules," one finds that "whether?" = B, "what?" = C, "of what" = D, etc.). Llull provides geometrical figures and tables that help one manipulate the various letters of this *ars combinatoria*. Llull's claim is that anything real, any true proposition, can ultimately be reduced to one of the possible permutations that result from combining the letters of this alphabet; and conversely, that if something cannot be so reduced, it should be considered unreal or untrue. Llull adapted his Art to virtually every field of study known to the Middle Ages, thereby insisting on the fundamental unity of all knowledge. The Art is not without analogy to twentieth-century structuralism in its claim that all the diverse particulars of a system are reducible to a single basic structure of relations (but, whereas structuralism treats a given system – myth, for instance – as an autonomous whole, having no necessary relation to other systems, Llull's Art is a "system of systems," all of which are regarded as sharing the same fundamental structure). Llull refined, revised, complicated, and simplified his Art throughout his life, and it is the foundation (sometimes imperceptible) of all his writings.[4] Llull thought that by emptying his intercourse with non-Christians of any apparent Christian bias, he could subtly persuade the non-Christian to accept the Art as an expression of universal (not culturally relative) Truth. Then, after gaining the non-Christian's goodwill, Llull would demonstrate that the doctrines of the Trinity and the Incarnation are in accord with permutations of the principles of the Art and therefore are not demonstrably unreal, untrue, or irrational.

THE HERMENEUTIC SPIRAL: *THE BOOK OF THE LOVER AND THE BELOVED*

In our century, Llull's most popular work has been *The Book of the Lover and the Beloved*. Originally appearing as a book within the book *Blanquerna*, completed around 1283, *The Book of the Lover and the Beloved* has been treated, by both medieval and modern readers, as an independent work in its own right. The book consists of 366 brief "verses" written in an allusive, enigmatic, and lyrical prose – one for each day of the year, including leap year.[5]

In reading *The Book of the Lover and the Beloved*, one can usually begin by positing that the "Lover" represents a human being and the "Beloved" represents "God/Christ" (but see Menocal 66–68 for a critique of this scheme). Yet we soon realize we are instead being asked to entertain various senses and to multiply meanings. As Llull tells us in the prologue, "each verse suffices for contemplating God a whole day" (5) – signifying that if we hasten to apply a ready-made meaning to these verses we are using Llull's book improperly.

What, for instance, is the meaning of verse 116? "A bird was singing on a branch, saying 'I will give a new thought to the lover, who will give me two.' The bird gave the new thought to the lover, and the lover gave two to the bird to lessen his torments. But the lover felt his pains of love increase" (*Doctor* 204). Johnston glosses this verse in a reasonable manner, making it into a familiar moral lesson: it is an "illustration of the paradox that 'less is more' in love: more concern for the beloved is less painful to the lover" (*Book* 47). In his edition, Johnston translates "thought" (in Llull's Catalan, *pensament*; in Llull's Latin, *cogitatio*) as "care" (in the sense of concern or worry), and his reading is this: the lover, trying to lessen his pain, trades two units of care for one unit of care, only to find out that his pain has instead increased. Implied in Johnston's gloss is that the less you care for, are concerned with, or reflect upon God, the more you are tormented.

This reasonable reading by no means exhausts the verse's sense. We may, for instance, regard the exchange between bird and lover as a hermeneutic fable – the "bird" representing poetic language (as birds often do in the troubadour tradition that is one of Llull's sources), the "lover" representing a reader or would-be exegete. The bird offers up something unitary or onefold that generates in return something duplicitous or double. The bird offers something like metaphor, a new thought that cannot be reduced to, or explained away by, already established systems of meaning. The bird offers to the lover a unitary utterance that is as yet still pure signifier (something not unlike the very verses of Llull's book prior to our acts of glossing). The lover, a reader, responds with something twofold. Perhaps the lover responds to the bird's gift of metaphor by splitting it into "form" and "content," "vehicle" and "tenor," "signifier and signified," thereby clarifying and rendering reasonable the new thought by turning it into an illustration of the same old thought. But such exegesis, which the reader had hoped would lessen the pain of incomprehensibility, in fact leaves one unfulfilled, sensing that there is something more from which one is now excluded. Alternately, perhaps the reader responds to poetic language not by splitting it in two but rather by doubling it, by multiplying its meanings, glossing the new thought with a plurality of senses.

Indeed Blanquerna (who within the fiction of the novel is the supposed author of *The Book of the Lover and the Beloved*) explicitly asserts that his aim is to accustom the reader to the habit of producing glosses. Blanquerna learned this, he says in the prologue, from studying the writings of the Sufis: "a Saracen had told him that the Saracens had certain religious men, among whom the most highly considered were those called 'sufis,' and that these men had words of love and brief examples which aroused great devotion in men. *These are words which require exposition, and by their exposition the understanding rises up higher*, and carries the will with it, increasing its devotion" (189, emphasis added). According to this formulation, we do not, before approaching such verses, already possess in our understanding the requisite system of meanings ("old thoughts") that will enable us to read; rather, "exposition" (interpretation) in some sense precedes our understanding, which is itself in some sense produced by our interpretations.

But how can we explain poetic language before we understand it? Earlier in *Blanquerna* Llull poses the issue, a version of the problem of the "hermeneutic circle," in terms of a reciprocal relation between the understanding (the intellect) and the will (desire): "the understanding comprehends that which the will loves, and the will loves that which the understanding comprehends" (chap. 66, 257). We understand that which attracts us, and we are attracted to that which we understand. This seems to be a circle that we cannot enter, since, in our initial encounter with an unfamiliar object, we will neither be attracted nor understand. Llull suggests beginning simply by beginning, by deciding to love the unfamiliar, by daring to posit, before it is intelligible, a meaning. Such a loving, ungrounded interpretation generates an understanding, which in turn generates a greater desire to interpret, which itself generates a richer understanding, and so on, in an ever widening hermeneutic spiral. Hence our intellect or understanding is not something prior to our interpretations; rather, it is something that grows out of them and that is generated, in the first instance, by our poetic language.

As the prologue suggests, Llull was inspired to write *The Book of the Lover and the Beloved* after studying Sufi mysticism. The influence of Sufism is manifest, first, in Llull's affinity for certain basic Sufi attitudes. One such attitude is an openness to finding truth in other religious doctrines and cultural traditions – a universalism that seems to be a potential sense of *The Book of the Lover and the Beloved*'s verse 90: "The lover said to the beloved, 'Many are the paths by which you come to my heart, and reveal [*representava*] yourself to my eyes, and my words name you by many names, but the love by which you both mortify and give life to me is one, and one alone'" (*Doctor* 200). This thought is not without relation to the Sufi tradition, for "it became almost commonplace for Sufis to argue that even idolaters, who fell down and worshipped stones, were really worshipping the true God: for they were worshipping the best approximation they could find to the Truth" (Hodgson 401). Llull proclaims himself to be the source of his own authority (as Sufis, such as

Abū Yazīd al-Bisṭāmī, often do). Contrary to prevailing medieval European practice, Llull rarely cites authorities; instead, Llull's fictional worlds are populated with characters who, in seeking the truth, invariably turn to reading books by Llull.

Llull, without formal education or official affiliation with the Church, asserts that he, and *anyone* for that matter, is entitled to proclaim the truth. Llull is the layperson par excellence: having no degree in philosophy, he presumed not just to teach, but radically to redesign the curriculum, at the University of Paris; having no position in the Church, he presumed to tell the pope how the world ought to be reformed by the propagation, not of Holy Scripture, but of Llull's own writings. In thus wresting away authority from an elite class of professional "knowers," Llull is the most important European precursor of such proto-Renaissance figures as Dante and Meister Eckehart, both of whom insist on the layperson's right to say, "I am the Truth."

FICTIONING TRUTH: *THE BOOK OF THE BEASTS*

Another work popular with modern readers is *The Book of the Beasts*, which, like *The Book of the Lover and the Beloved*, initially appeared as part of a lengthy novel – in this case, Llull's *Felix, Or the Book of Wonders* (completed around 1289). Felix, the novel's protagonist, after speaking briefly with some holy men, "went to the place where the beasts were about to elect a king" (*Doctor* 247). At this point Felix is forgotten, as the text recounts the political actions of this community of animals – a story whose plot (which has been compared favorably with Orwell's *Animal Farm*) is advanced by a series of embedded fables. The fables themselves are drawn from various sources, but above all from the Arabic tale collection *Kalīla wa-dimna*.

Among the elements that make *The Book of the Beasts* unique in the history of Western literature is that Llull does not treat fables as illustrations or examples of some extrafictional or extralinguistic truth. Narratives, for the beasts, are not fictional representations of a reality that is outside fiction; rather, they are instruments by which the beasts perform actions. Indeed, one of Llull's main aims (not only here, but throughout his writings) is to challenge the notion that the "verbal" and the "real" are two entirely separable domains. In *The Book of the Beasts* he does this by undermining the idea that there is a frame separating an "outside" (the real world, truth) from an "inside" (the fictional world, language).

Llull dismantles the dualism of *res* and *verbum* by placing things that we might assume ought to be outside the frame inside and things that we think ought to be inside outside. The beasts themselves, for instance, are not "inside" the frame of *The Book of the Beasts*; they are not, like the animals in a medieval bestiary (nor even like Orwell's animals) fictional allegories for the more real "outside" that is the human world. The beasts are the ones who tell fables, not the ones about whom fables are told. Llull exploits this device in ways that are sometimes dazzling. When he first comes upon the beasts, for instance, Felix overhears the bear, the leopard, and the lynx debating whether the lion or the horse ought to be elected king. At a certain point in the debate Dame Reynard the fox interrupts to tell a story about some humans who were debating the election of a bishop. At a certain point in *that* story one of the humans makes the following astonishing statement that situates him no longer inside the frame but rather outside it: "If the lion is king, and the bear, the lynx, and the leopard disagree with his election, there will forever be ill will toward the king; and if the horse is king, and the lion commits some wrong against the king, how will the horse get his revenge, if he is not as strong as the lion" (249). These out-of-place words, belonging to the debate taking place outside the frame concerning the beasts' election of a king and not to the debate taking place inside the frame concerning the humans' election of a bishop, represent a "curious instance of the characters in a story within a frame story referring to the characters in the frame story" (249 n. 8).

This intentional deconstruction of the boundaries between an outside reality and a fictional inside is reiterated. When *The Book of the Beasts* first opens, for instance, Felix is a character *within* its narrative ("Felix went to the place where the beasts were about to elect a king"); there is no frame separating Felix's world from that of the beasts. Yet at the end of *The Book of the Beasts*, Felix is outside the book, as he has somehow been transported to a different level of reality: "Here ends *The Book of the Beasts*, which Felix brought to a king so that he might learn" (288). We are left with a contradiction: Felix is outside the book of which he is inside. This duplicity applies above all to Llull himself, for he is a constantly recurring character in his own works (*Blanquerna*'s "Ramon the Fool," for instance). Llull even goes so far as to use, as one of the fables told by one of the animals, a version of Llull's own *Vita* (the very story of Llull and his Muslim slave discussed above). Llull's life (which we might think ought to be the outermost outside) thus turns up inside the frame, as a fable; at the same time, what is inside the frame – the fable – is more real than fictional.

The point of this play in *The Book of the Beasts* is to suggest what Llull elsewhere explicitly asserts – that the "reality," "truth," or "essence" of humankind is not distinct from the fictions of humankind; we become what our fictions make us (see Stone). This mutual relation of truth and language leads Llull to what is perhaps the most stunning of his formulations: his redefinition of the true essence of the human species. Whereas the whole Aristotelian and medieval tradition had defined man as rational animal, in his *Ars brevis*

Llull says, "homo est animal homificans" [man is a manificting animal]. Llull reiterates, also in the *Ars brevis,* this utterly original definition: "Man is that being whose function is to manifict" (*Selected Works* 1:628). This *fic* is the *fic* of *fictio,* of making, of fiction, of language, fables, discourses, disputations. So we may prefer a translation such as "Man is an animal who, fictionalizing, makes man." Our essence is *man-ifiction,* "making man"; what is most real about humans is that humans make their reality through fictioning. Language or fiction is not some domain separable and distinct from the truth or reality of humankind. It is this idea – that we are what we say we are – that energized Llull's activity of writing meant to make his contemporaries other than what they were.

NOTES

1. See Kedar for an account – emphasizing Llull's endorsement of violence – of the "incongruities" in Llull's position on crusading.
2. See *Doctor* or *Selected Works* for an English translation; for the Latin text, see *Opera latina* 8:271–309.
3. There is an apocryphal story, still widely circulated as fact, that Llull died a martyr, stoned to death in a public square in Algeria for loudly proclaiming Christianity's superiority. See *Selected Works* 1:43–44 for the actual circumstances of his death and for an explanation of the origin of the legend.
4. For detailed treatments of the Art, see Pring-Mill; Yates, *Lull*; Carreras y Artau.
5. See the Johnston edition for Llull's original Catalan and Latin texts and a modern English translation; there is also a modern English translation by Eve Bonner in *Doctor Illuminatus.*

BIBLIOGRAPHY

Batllori, Miquel. *Ramon Llull en el món del seu temps.* Barcelona, 1960.

Carreras y Artau, Tomás, and Joaquín Carreras y Artau. *Historia de la filosofía española: Filosofía cristiana de los siglos XIII al XIV.* 2 vols. Madrid, 1939–43.

De Courcelles, Dominique. *La parole risquée de Raymond Lulle: Entre le judaïsme, le christianisme et l'islam.* Paris, 1993.

Hillgarth, J. N. *Ramon Lull and Lullism in Fourteeth-Century France.* Oxford, 1971.

Hodgson, Marshall G. S. *The Venture of Islam: Conscience and History in a World Civilization.* Vol. 1. Chicago, 1974.

Johnston, Mark D. *The Evangelical Rhetoric of Ramon Llull: Lay Learning and Piety in the Christian West around 1300.* New York, 1996.

The Spiritual Logic of Ramon Llull. Oxford, 1987.

Kedar, Benjamin Z. *Crusade and Mission: European Approaches toward the Muslims.* Princeton, 1984.

Llull, Ramon. *Blanquerna.* Trans. E. A. Peers. 1926. Rpt., New York, 1987.

The Book of the Lover and the Beloved. Ed. and trans. Mark D. Johnston. Warminster, 1995.

Doctor Illuminatus: A Ramon Llull Reader. Ed. and trans. Anthony Bonner. Princeton, 1993.

Nova edició de les obres de Ramon Llull. Majorca, 1990–.

Obres essencials. 2 vols. Barcelona, 1957–60.

Obres de Ramon Llull. Ed. Salvador Galmés et al. 21 vols. Palma de Mallorca, 1906–50.

Obres selectes de Ramon Llull. Ed. Anthony Bonner. 2 vols. Palma, 1989.

Raimundi Llulli opera latina. Ed. F. Stegmüller et al. Vols. 1–5. Palma, 1959–67. Vols. 6ff. Turnhout, 1975–.

Selected Works of Ramon Llull. Ed. and trans. Anthony Bonner. 2 vols. Princeton, 1985.

Maalouf, Amin. *The Crusades through Arab Eyes.* New York, 1984.

Menocal, María Rosa. *Shards of Love: Exile and the Origins of the Lyric.* Durham, 1994.

Palou, Sebastian Garcias. *Ramon Llull y el islam.* Palma de Mallorca, 1981.

Peers, E. Allison. *Ramon Lull: A Biography.* London, 1929.

Pring-Mill, R. D. F. "The Analogical Structure of Lullian Art." *Islamic Philosophy and the Classical Tradition: Essays Presented to Richard Walzer.* Columbia, S.C., 1972. 315–26.

El microcosmos lul.lià. Palma de Mallorca, 1961.

Probst, J. H. "Ramon Lull, philosophe populaire catalan et franciscain." *Criterion* 3 (1927): 182–210.

Sala-Molins, Louis. *La philosophie de l'amour chez Raymond Lulle.* Paris, 1974.

Southern, R. W. *Western Views of Islam in the Middle Ages.* Cambridge, Mass., 1962.

Stone, Gregory B. "Ramon Llull vs. Petrus Alfonsi: Postmodern Liberalism and the Six Liberal Arts." *Medieval Encounters* 3 (1997): 70–93.

Turner, William. *History of Philosophy.* Boston, 1903.

Urvoy, Dominique. *Penser l'Islam: Les présupposés islamiques de l'Art de Lull.* Paris, 1980.

"La place de Ramon Lull dans la pensée arabe." *Catalan Review* 4 (1990): 201–20.

Yates, Frances A. *Giordano Bruno and the Hermetic Tradition.* Chicago, 1964.

Lull and Bruno: Collected Essays. Vol. 1. London, 1982.

CHAPTER 19

IBN AL-KHAṬĪB

Alexander Knysh

The great Andalusi polymath and statesman Abū ʿAbd Allāh Muḥammad ibn ʿAbd Allāh ibn Saʿīd al-Salamānī, better known as Lisān al-Dīn ibn al-Khaṭīb, was a bright star in the pleiad of great minds of his age, which consisted of such luminaries as ʿAbd al-Raḥmān and Yaḥyā ibn Khaldūn, Ibn Marzūq, Ibn Baṭṭūta, and Ibn Zamrak.[1] He was born in 713/1313 in the town of Loja of a family of Arab notables, whose members had traditionally been employed in the religious and civil service of Andalusi rulers (al-Maqqarī 5:50). When Ibn al-Khaṭīb was only several weeks old, his father was invited to take a high post at the court of the new emir of Granada, Ismāʿīl I (r. 713/1314–725/1325), and the family moved to the capital. In Granada, Ibn al-Khaṭīb received an excellent education under the guidance of the best scholars of the epoch, whose biographies he gratefully included in his works (al-Maqqarī 5:189–251, 350–603). He studied a broad variety of subjects: Arabic language and grammar, sharia and exegesis, adab and poetry, medicine and *falsafa*, history, and Sufism. Ibn al-Khaṭīb's breadth of background is mirrored in a dazzling multiplicity of the topics treated in his writings. His vast knowledge, noble pedigree, and the high post of his father, combined with his unique literary talent and extraordinary memory, destined him for a splendid career at the Granadine court.

In 741/1340, Ibn al-Khaṭīb suffered a severe personal crisis, when his father and elder brother were killed in the battle of Ṭarīf (Salado). Fortunately, despite Ibn al-Khaṭīb's young age, his former teacher Ibn al-Jayyāb, vizier of the emir Yūsuf I (r. 733/1333–755/1354), decided to appoint Ibn al-Khaṭīb his personal secretary. Upon Ibn al-Jayyāb's untimely death of plague in 749/1349, Ibn al-Khaṭīb became head of the royal chancery with the title of vizier.[2] He was put in charge of the emir's diplomatic correspondence and was occasionally sent as ambassador to Andalusi and Maghribi rulers. In addition, he was responsible for formulating and editing royal decrees and edicts, which he later collected in the book *Rayḥānat al-kuttāb wa-nujʿat al-muntāb* (Sweet Basil of the Secretaries and the Provision of the Seekers) and which, along with his diplomatic epistles, were praised by the historian al-Maqqarī as the pinnacle of literary perfection (5:404–46). To these functions he later added those of master of the royal household, which in his own words gave him full authority over the financial, military, administrative, and political affairs of the Granadine court and state as a whole (*Iḥāṭa* 1:22, 2:17–18). Ibn al-Khaṭīb retained all these posts and titles under the new emir Muḥammad V al-Ghanī bi-llāh (from 755/1354 to 760/1359), his former disciple and confidant. Moreover, it appears that Ibn al-Khaṭīb was instrumental in ensuring the young emir's ascent to the throne and soon became his right-hand man (Bencheneb 76). He further distinguished himself by successfully accomplishing an important diplomatic mission to the Marinid ruler Abū ʿInān, who, impressed by Ibn al-Khaṭīb's spirited panegyric, pledged to support the Granadine emir in his struggle against the Reconquista (Ibn al-Khaṭīb, *Iḥāṭa* 1:23–24). From then on, Ibn al-Khaṭīb invariably steered Granada's foreign policy toward a closer cooperation and, in the long run, union with the powerful Marinid state (Ibn al-Khaṭīb, *Taʾrīkh al-maghrib* p. "lām").

When in 760/1359 Muḥammad V was deposed by his half brother Ismāʿīl and a group of disloyal courtiers and narrowly escaped with his life, Ibn al-Khaṭīb, as doyen of the deposed regime, landed in prison with his property confiscated by the new ruler. However, he was soon released thanks to the interference of the Marinid sultan Abū Sālim and joined his fugitive sovereign in his Maghribi exile. In Fez they were welcomed by Abū Sālim and his retinue, which featured such consequential figures of Western Islamdom as Ibn Marzūq and ʿAbd al-Raḥmān ibn Khaldūn (Ibn al-Khaṭīb, *Iḥāṭa* 1:25–27; Arié 108–9). After a brief stay in Fez, Ibn al-Khaṭīb asked the emir's permission to tour his vast realm. His colorful impressions of this trip are described in a travelogue (*riḥla*) titled *Nufāḍat al-jirāb fī ʿulālat al-ightirāb* (The Shaking of the Bag: On the Diversion of the One Who Travels Abroad) – a mine of illuminating information on the political and cultural life of the Marinid Far Maghrib with an informative excursus into its recent history (al-Tiṭwānī 114–40).

Ibn al-Khaṭīb finally settled in a quiet town of Salé, which he had visited on an earlier diplomatic trip to Morocco. He spent almost two years there, immersed in writing and pious meditation yet not neglectful of his mundane interests. With a generous monthly stipend of five hundred silver dinars awarded to him by Abū Sālim he lived a life of ease. His calm was shattered by the sudden death of his wife, whom he bemoaned in moving elegies. Ibn al-Khaṭīb's residence in Salé was a rare occasion for nurturing his personal predilection for Sufi spirituality.[3] While in Salé, Ibn al-Khaṭīb frequented local Sufi lodges and cemeteries and was favorably received by Salé's most popular *walī*, the reclusive Ibn ʿĀshir (al-Nāṣirī 30–32; "Ibn ʿĀshir," *EI*[2]). At the same time, his luxurious lifestyle drew the criticism of a local notary whom Ibn al-Khaṭīb rebuffed in a lengthy treatise against the men of this legal profession (Turki).

Ibn al-Khaṭīb's seclusion ended in 763/1362, when Muḥammad V regained his throne with the help of the Marinid sultan. Ibn al-Khaṭīb returned to Granada to assume his former post at the head of the civil and military authority (*dhū l-wizāratayn*) of the Granadine kingdom. Soon after his return to the capital, he ran afoul of the able commander of the Maghribi volunteer troops stationed in Granada, Yaḥyā ibn ʿAlī, whom he viewed as a rival. In an effort to maintain his undivided control over the state politics and the military, Ibn al-Khaṭīb launched a series of intrigues aimed at besmirching the reputation of this general in the eyes of the ruler. His efforts led to the expulsion of Yaḥyā ibn ʿAlī and his supporters, leaving Ibn al-Khaṭīb the sole senior executive of the Granadine state (Arié 205). In a similar vein, he disposed of the ambitious Maghribi émigrés, the Marinid prince Ibn Yaflūsīn and the ex-vizier Masʿūd ibn Masāy, although this time he was driven by the desire to please the Marinid sultans of Fez (Ibn al-Khaṭīb, *Taʾrīkh al-maghrib* pp. "lām" and "mīm"; Arié 440).

His intense scheming aroused the hatred of the emir's courtiers sympathetic with the banished Maghribi émigrés and, moreover, alienated his friends and disciples. In a drive to secure his undivided influence on the emir, Ibn al-Khaṭīb did not hesitate to trample even his most loyal friends. Thus, when Muḥammad V showed favor to the Maghribi vizier ʿAbd al-Raḥmān ibn Khaldūn, who had successfully accomplished a delicate diplomatic mission to the court of Peter the Cruel of Seville, Ibn al-Khaṭīb's envy sent his old friend packing to the Maghrib in 766/1365 (Arié 441; Ibn al-Khaṭīb, *Iḥāṭa* 1:30; "Ibn Khaldūn," *EI*²).

In the meantime, his position at the Granadine court began to erode due to the intrigues and hostile rumors instigated by his disciples and aides Ibn Zamrak and Ibn Farkūn, who joined hands with his powerful enemy, the grand qadi of Granada, ʿAlī al-Nubāhī. The former two secretly craved their teacher's position, whereas the latter was offended by Ibn al-Khaṭīb's mystical ideas expounded in the *Rawḍat al-taʿrīf* as well as his leniency toward those whom the qadi condemned as "heretics" (al-Maqqarī 5:118–22). More important, the emir, already in his forties, began to resent the vizier's overbearing control over the affairs of the state as well as his single-minded loyalty to the Marinids, which, in the emir's mind, was detrimental to Granada's own interests (Bencheneb 77).

Apprehensive of the emir's growing displeasure, Ibn al-Khaṭīb entered into secret negotiations with the Marinid sultan ʿAbd al-ʿAzīz, who resided in Tlemcen. Having secured the sultan's support, Ibn al-Khaṭīb left the capital in 773/1371 with his youngest son, ʿAlī, on the pretext of inspecting fortresses in the western part of the Granadine kingdom. Instead, he headed for Gibraltar, from where he set sail for the Maghribi coast (Ibn al-Khaṭīb, *Iḥāṭa* 1:33–36).

Ibn al-Khaṭīb's sudden departure infuriated his enemies, especially Ibn Zamrak and al-Nubāhī, who hastened to accuse him of treason. The latter also declared him a heretic who had belittled the reputation of the Prophet, espoused the "atheistic" teachings of the *falāsifa*, and propagated the incarnationist doctrine (*ḥulūl*) of the monistic Sufis. Shortly after Ibn al-Khaṭīb's escape to the Maghrib, al-Nubāhī issued a fatwa that called for the destruction of the vizier's works and the confiscation of his property. The books were put to torch in Granada's market square. The qadi then sent Ibn al-Khaṭīb a letter exposing the vizier's alleged "abominations" and excommunicating him from the community of the faithful. The ad hominem nature of this letter, which apart from heresy and desertion accused Ibn al-Khaṭīb of venality, unscrupulousness, and detraction from the reputation of living and deceased scholars, suggests that al-Nubāhī had a personal grudge against the disgraced vizier. This impression is corroborated by his reference to the instances of Ibn al-Khaṭīb's unsolicited interference with, or disregard for, legal rulings and criminal verdicts meted out by al-Nubāhī.

Stung by these accusations, Ibn al-Khaṭīb wrote a refutation of his detractor titled *Khalʿ al-rasan fī l-taʿrīf bi-aḥwāl abū l-ḥasan* (Giving Free Rein to the Exposition of the Condition of Abū l-Ḥasan), in which he ridiculed al-Nubāhī as an impish, apelike dwarf, grossly ignorant of the nuances of the Islamic tradition. His ungenerous treatment of the qadi contrasts sharply with Ibn al-Khaṭīb's earlier portrayal of al-Nubāhī as the greatest scholar of the epoch (*Katība* 146–53; *Iḥāṭa* 1:40–41).

At al-Nubāhī's instigation, Muḥammad V demanded that the sultan ʿAbd al-ʿAzīz either extradite or execute his heretical protégé. Unconvinced by al-Nubāhī's accusations, the Marinid sultan declined the request as motivated by personal hatred. Although the Marinid ruler died soon afterward, Ibn al-Khaṭīb continued to enjoy the patronage of vizier Abū Bakr ibn Ghāzī, who became regent on behalf of ʿAbd al-ʿAzīz's minor son. The new ruler and his retinue moved to Fez, where they received another letter from the Nasrid emir demanding the extradition of the fugitive vizier. Ibn Ghāzī's blunt refusal to grant his request infuriated Muḥammad V and may have contributed to his decision to support the opponents of Ibn Ghāzī and his young ward, whom the Granadine emir had deliberately cultivated at his court. With his military and political support the rebels soon gained the upper hand in the dynastic struggle that ensued and proclaimed Abū l-ʿAbbās Aḥmad al-Marīnī the new sultan.

With Ibn Ghāzī no longer by his side, Ibn al-Khaṭīb was left face to face with the victors who owed their triumph to the Granadine emir and were eager to repay their debt. They threw the disgraced vizier into prison until the arrival of a delegation from Granada headed by Ibn al-Khaṭīb's disciple-turned-enemy Ibn Zamrak, who had served as vizier since the former's escape to the Maghrib. Upon the delegation's arrival in Fez, the new sultan ordered a public hearing of Ibn al-Khaṭīb's case, which was conducted by a council of scholars loyal to him as well as the members of the Granadine delegation. Undaunted by the intimidation and torture, Ibn al-Khaṭīb protested his innocence and flatly denied the accusations of heresy and unbelief leveled at him by Ibn Zamrak. His plight was aggravated by the fact that the person in charge of the trial was his old enemy Sulaymān ibn Dā'ūd, whom Ibn al-Khaṭīb had denied a lucrative post in the Granadine military a few years earlier (al-Maqqarī 5:110–11).

Although some ulama pronounced Ibn al-Khaṭīb guilty of heresy, the vote was far from unanimous and no conclusive decision was reached by the council. Ibn al-Khaṭīb was sent back to prison, where he was strangled in the night by thugs sent by the vizier Sulaymān ibn Dā'ūd, who acted in collusion with Ibn Zamrak's Andalusi delegation. The next morning (the end of 776/May–June 1375), his body was buried at Bāb al-Maḥrūq in Fez. Unsatisfied, his vengeful enemies exhumed his body and threw it on a bonfire, whereupon his charred remains were finally laid to rest. Soon after Morocco wrested its independence from France (1956), a modest mausoleum was erected over his grave under the orders of the Moroccan king Muḥammad V (al-Nāṣirī 80, 141).

A detailed account of Ibn al-Khaṭīb's last ordeal was left by ʿAbd al-Raḥmān ibn Khaldūn, who remained his friend and admirer despite the brief alienation that occurred between them at Granada. At the close of his narrative, Ibn Khaldūn quotes the poignant verses that the imprisoned vizier reportedly composed on the eve of his assassination:

> We travel far away, albeit the dwellings are near
> Although we have a message to deliver, we remain speechless
> Our breath suddenly stopped
> As if a loud prayer was followed by a silent recitation
> Of noble ancestry we were, but, alas, we have turned into a stack
> of dry bones[4]
> We used to feed others, but lo, now we ourselves are food [for
> worms]
> We were like shining suns that travel high in the sky above,
> But, lo, the suns have set and been lamented by the [orphaned]
> stars

Many a warrior armed with the sword was felled by a rain of
sharp-pointed arrows
Many a lucky one was suddenly failed by his good fortune
Many a young nobleman, who used to don the royal mantle, was
put in his grave wrapped in rags
So, tell the enemies: "Yes, Ibn al-Khaṭīb is gone, but is there
anyone who will not be gone one day?"
And tell those of you who rejoice at this news: "Only he who
thinks he will never die can rejoice on a day like this!"

(Ibn al-Khaṭīb, *Dīwān* 1:185; cf. al-Maqqarī 5:111–12)

IBN AL-KHAṬĪB'S LEGACY

Ibn al-Khaṭīb's work provides ample evidence of his unusual versatility and places him squarely among Islam's greatest polymaths. In a vast corpus of an estimated sixty works he treated such diverse subjects as history, biography, the art of government, politics, geography, poetics, theology, fiqh, Sufism, grammar, medicine, veterinary medicine, agriculture, music, and falconry (al-Maqqarī 7:97–102). His literary heritage was popularized by the great champion of Andalusi culture al-Maqqarī (d. 1041/1632),[5] who dedicated the second part of his monumental historical and literary encyclopedia *Nafḥ al-ṭīb min ghuṣn al-andalus al-raṭīb wa-dhikr wazīrihā lisān al-dīn ibn al-khaṭīb* (Breath of Perfume from the Tender Branch of al-Andalus and an Account of its Vizier Lisān al-Dīn ibn al-Khaṭīb) to the Granadine vizier (1:15). With the first European edition of al-Maqqarī's work in 1855, Ibn al-Khaṭīb was introduced to the European reader. From the outset, European scholars tended to focus on his historical writings, which are indeed a real mine of variegated information on the kingdom of Granada and its Andalusi predecessors.[6] Of these writings, three have received the lion's share of scholars' attention: *al-Lamḥa al-badriyya fī l-dawla al-naṣriyya* (Flash of Moonlight: On the History of Granada), a political history of the Nasrids of Granada (634/1237–897/1492) up to 765/1364 arranged according to the dynastic principle; *al-Iḥāṭa fī akhbār gharnaṭa* (Comprehensive Book on the History of Granada), which, in addition to dynastic history, provides detailed biographies of the celebrities connected with Granada from the earliest days of the Muslim conquest up to Ibn al-Khaṭīb's own time; and, finally, *Kitāb aʿmāl al-aʿlām fī man būyiʿa qabl al-iḥtilām* (Deeds of the Great: On Those Who Came to the Throne before Reaching Maturity), a general Muslim history in three parts dealing with the central lands of Islam, al-Andalus, and the Maghrib respectively, which Ibn al-Khaṭīb started in Tlemcen between 774/1372 and 776/1374 and completed shortly before his death (Dunlop, *Arab Civilization* 146; Arié 179–80). In these and other works,[7] Ibn al-Khaṭīb made extensive use of the historical and biographical writings of his predecessors, especially Ibn al-Qūṭiyya, Ibn al-Ṣayrafī, Ibn Ḥayyān, Ibn ʿIdhārī, Ibn Abī Zarʿ, Ibn Saʿīd al-Maghribī, Ibn al-Abbār, Ibn Bashkuwāl, and Ibn al-Zubayr, whose contribution he readily acknowledged.[8]

In addition to the biographies of Granadine notables in his historical works, Ibn al-Khaṭīb compiled specialized biographical dictionaries of Andalusi literati, which were patterned on Ibn Bassam's *al-Dhakhīra* (Treasury), al-Fatḥ ibn Khāqān's *Qalāʾid al-ʿiqyān* (Gold Necklaces) and *Maṭmaḥ al-anfus* (The Desire of Souls), Ibn Diḥya's *al-Muṭrib* (The Delightful), and Ibn Saʿīd's *al-Ḥulla al-siyarāʾ* (The Garment of Pure Silk) in propagating the achievements of Andalusi litterateurs among Eastern Muslims.[9] In one such work, *al-Katība al-kāmina* (A Troop in Ambush), written toward the end of his life, Ibn al-Khaṭīb revised the earlier laudatory biographies of some of his friends-turned-enemies from the *Iḥāṭa*, presenting them in unfavorable light. This collection of 103 biographies in florid rhymed prose is arranged according to the professional background of the men of letters treated in it: the preachers and the Sufis; the Qurʾan reciters and instructors; the judges; and the functionaries in the royal chancery.[10] By citing selected poetic pieces from the works of his predecessors, Ibn al-Khaṭīb implicitly attempted to convey his own standard of good poetic taste as well as his personal sympathies and antipathies (17).

His concern for proper poetic style and imagery is even more pronounced in his poetic anthology *al-Siḥr wa l-shiʿr* (Enchantment and Poetry), which was designed by the author as a guide to good poetry and literary taste and featured numerous excerpts from the occasional, descriptive, and ascetic poetry by distinguished oriental authors: Abū l-ʿAtāhiya, Abū Nuwās, Ibn al-Rūmī, Ibn al-Muʿtazz. On the occidental side, Ibn al-Khaṭīb gave preference to Ibn Rashīq, al-Muʿtamid, Ibn ʿAmmār, Ibn al-Labbāna, Ibn Sahl, and Ibn Ḥamdīs (Arié 454). He was also fond of the indigenous poetic forms such as zajal and muwashshah, the best samples of which he collected in a special anthology titled *Jaysh al-tawshīḥ* (The Striking Army of Stanza Poetry) (see Stern).

Ibn al-Khaṭīb's own poetry, especially at the early stage of his career, displays his intimate knowledge of, and dependence on, the work of the great court poets of the Muslim East, namely, Abū Nuwās, Abū Tammām, and al-Mutanabbī. The themes and genres of his poetic works are also quite traditional: description of nature (*waṣf*), court panegyric (*madḥ*), love lyric (*ghazal*), lamentation (*rithāʾ*), satire (*hijāʾ*), epigram (*taḥakkum*), wine poetry (*khamriyya*), and ascetic and devotional poems. He also composed political and didactic verses that lavishly adorn his historical works and travelogues. Much of his poetic output, which had been dispersed throughout his vast corpus of writings, was only recently gathered under one cover (*Dīwān*).

A great master of rhymed prose (*sajʿ*), Ibn al-Khaṭīb collected the most elegant and involved samples of his diplomatic correspondence with the Maghribi rulers as well as the royal edicts he had edited in the anthologies *Kunāsat al-dukkān* (The Sweeping of the Shop) and *Rayḥānat al-kuttāb*, which served as models for occidental Muslim diplomats and writers for centuries to come. His diplomatic epistles range from the transparently lucid and concise to the deliberately equivocal and obscure – evidence of the author's remarkable ability to adapt to rapidly changing political circumstances and shifting diplomatic alliances.

Although an impeccable and refined *sajʿ* runs like a red thread across the texture of Ibn al-Khaṭīb's entire literary production, his mastery of this form reaches its culmination in his "assemblies" (maqamat), the stylistic and imaginative sophistication of which often verges on preciosity. In a sense, Ibn al-Khaṭīb was a resuscitator of this long-neglected genre (Arié 448), although his interpretation of it was quite distinct from that of its classical exponents, al-Hamadhānī and al-Ḥarīrī– the Islamic precursors of the picaresque novel. In Ibn al-Khaṭīb's *Khaṭrat al-ṭayf fī riḥlat al-shitāʾ wa l-ṣayf* (The Trembling of the Apparition: On Travel in Summer and Winter) we find neither a picaro nor a traditional picaresque plot. Rather, we witness a typical Muslim travelogue (*riḥla*), in which the author recounts, in meticulous and colorful detail, the sultan's trip across his Andalusi domain. The exquisitely refined narrative of this "geographic" maqama is put in the mouth of the courtly companion of the royal traveler – an astute observer of the customs, landscape, and cultural characteristics of his native country (ʿAbbādī). The rhymed prose of the maqama is interspersed with poetic quotations and rare pieces of erudition that, in line with the exigencies of adab literature, are designed both to entertain and to edify. Here, as in many other of Ibn al-Khaṭīb's works, we observe a hybridization and intertwining of several traditional genres and trends of medieval Arabic literature – a fact that alerts us to the inherent limitations of conventional taxonomy.

In his other maqamat, *Mufākharat mālaqa wa-salā* (Boasting Match between Málaga and Salé) and *Miʿyār al-ikhtiyār* (The Preferred Measurement), Ibn al-Khaṭīb draws an extended comparison between the respective merits of Andalusi and Maghribi cities. In the latter work, written during his stay in Salé, in the "passages that are eminently balanced" and marked by "the [skillful] choice of synonyms and the [smooth] progression of rhythmical units," Ibn al-Khaṭīb brings forth the advantages of the Nasrid metropolis against its less sophisticated and spectacular Maghribi counterpart and – perhaps unwittingly – evinces his "secret preference for . . . his Andalusi homeland" (Arié 450). The influence of the maqama genre is evident in Ibn al-Khaṭīb's other works, such as *Muthlā al-ṭarīqa fī dhamm al-wathīqa* (The Exemplary Path: On the Condemnation of the Notaries), which, in the rather ungenerous remark of a contemporary investigator, accounts for an unfortunate combination of "the exuberance of expression with the poverty of idea and of the search for an exquisite and rare word with the banality of the theme" (Turki 170).

Much more typical of the *riḥla* genre in its traditional sense, as established by Ibn al-Khaṭīb's famous compatriot Ibn Jubayr (d. 614/1217) and developed by another Andalusi, Ibn Rushayd (d. 721/1321), is his work with the odd name, *Nufāḍat al-jirāb fī ʿulālat al-ightirāb*. Composed during the vizier's first exile to the Maghrib following the aforementioned coup d'état, it provides unique information about places in the Far Maghrib visited by the author. Apart from the usual poetic quotations and melancholic reflections on the transience of life inspired by the sight of ancient ruins, this work abounds in illuminating descriptions of local notables, politics, historical monuments, cemeteries, mosques, *madrasa*s and *ribāṭ*s, which makes it a precious source for the historical geography of medieval Morocco. Typical of this genre is the following vivid description of Bedouin life in the Sahara desert cast in the usual florid and sonorous *sajʿ*:

> The sun descended and waned, then [suddenly]
> melted and plunged headlong into the lap of the
> twilight. Finally, after the hardship
> we had endured and the arduous labor we had
> accomplished – we could enjoy the award of a
> long-awaited rest. So we dismounted next
> to the tents that arched [on the horizon]
> like the camel's hump – the tents
> with tangled ropes, whose mounds were crowded
> like the [houses] of a city made of wool.
> It was a city, whose hearths were camel dung,
> whose walls were acacias, and whose vegetation
> was not free from mud.
> In its vicinity [we found] the ponds overflowing
> with water, the dwellings full of people, the
> meadows intricately embroidered [with herbage],
> and the swift streams that arched their silver bosoms.
> Then the sheikh [of the tribe] appeared;
> he greeted us and talked to us eloquently and
> with great affection. He was a mature man,
> whose hair was whitened by his age . . .

[Fa-zālat al-shams wa-mālat//thumma sālat
wa-nhārat//fī ḥijr al-maghrib wa-nhālat//
wa baʿada laʾyi mā balaghnā//wa-min al-kadd
faraghnā//wa-minḥat al-rāḥa tasawwaghnā//
wa-nazalnā bi-izāʾi khiyām//istadārat fī
sanam//wa-qad ishtabakat ḥibāluhā//
wa-tarāṣṣat jibāluhā//. . .] (al-Tiṭwānī 1:128)

In returning to the maqama genre, mention should be made of Ibn al-Khaṭīb's *Maqāmāt al-siyāsa* (Maqamat on Politics) (al-Maqqarī 6:431–45) that brings out the political spectrum of his multifaceted literary work. This short treatise on the art of government was shown by D. M. Dunlop to be a paraphrase of the *Book of the Greek Testaments Extracted from . . . the Politics of Plato* by the Tulunid historian Aḥmad ibn Dāya[11] – about a certain king of the ancient Greeks, who leaves his "testament to his son, together with the parallel testaments of other fathers" ("Work" 52–53).

In the *Bustān al-duwal* (Garden of the States), Ibn al-Khaṭīb moves away from this classical prototype and presents the functioning of the state government in the allegory of the garden of ten trees. Each tree corresponds to an institution or constituency of the monarchical state: the sultanate, the vizierate, the chancery, the judgeship and religion, the police, the governorship, the ministry of war including the navy and the cavalry, the royal entourage, including the physicians, astrologists, veterinarians, royal hunters, falconers, boon-companions, chess players, poets, and musicians, and, finally, the tree of the commoners, who constitute the bulk of the sultan's subjects. The divisions and subdivisions of each institution are, in turn, allegorized as the tree's branches, roots, trunk, bark, leaves, blossoms, and so on. The well-being of all the trees is dependent on the tree of the sultanate. Although ingenious, this conceit is too schematic to add to our understanding of the real Andalusi state in Ibn al-Khaṭīb's epoch.

To gain a better insight into the realpolitik of the Granadine court, one should look to Ibn al-Khaṭīb's chronicles and biographical collections, which provide a wealth of concrete data absent from his theoretical writings on the art of government. Ibn al-Khaṭīb's chronicles are often compared unfavorably with the monumental history of the Maghrib by his great contemporary Ibn Khaldūn. Although he may have lacked Ibn Khaldūn's analytical depth, Ibn al-Khaṭīb succeeded in furnishing a lively picture of Andalusi history, whose actors are real, down-to-earth individuals driven by the universal human impulses of hatred, passion, love, fear, and greed. This vivid and at times openly subjective historiography deliberately discards the appearance of historical objectivity, boldly proclaims the personal sympathies and antipathies of its author, and passes candid judgments on historical figures. In his historical works Ibn al-Khaṭīb focuses on the underlying motives, intellectual and moral qualities, and strengths and weaknesses of the characters whose outward actions had previously been the sole subject of traditional Islamic historiography (Bencheneb 59).

Ibn al-Khaṭīb's vision of historical process receives its most mature articulation in his *Aʿmāl al-aʿlām*, which was scarcely completed before his death. To Ibn al-Khaṭīb, the history of the Muslim states of the East and the West provides valuable lessons to be learned by every ruler and statesman, especially because of history's tendency to repeat itself in broad outlines as well as in details. This repetition, in the vizier's view, is determined by the recurrent patterns of human responses to similar historical circumstances, which, in turn, answer to their position in the five-stage class structure he establishes through a perceptive analysis of historical phenomena.

The activities of the five social strata (*ṣinf*; pl. *aṣnāf*) are seen as turning around the office of the sultan, which is equally beneficial to everyone and therefore held sacred by all his subjects. This outward propriety, however, quickly vanishes at the time of succession, when the sultanate becomes the bone of contention of the three politically active groups – that is, the rapacious and unscrupulous courtiers, the aristocratic adventurers and princely pretenders, and the materialistic and ignorant masses (*awbāsh*) – each pursuing its vested interests. The other strata – the apolitical government officials and administrators, the retiring religious scholars and jurists, and the idealistic ascetics and mystics – remain aloof and passively accept the outcome of the wicked court politics. As the struggle over succession unfolds, all dynastic principles and rights, not to mention elementary human decency, are overshadowed by the base instincts of greed, vanity, self-aggrandizement, and political expediency (Hoenerbach, *Islamische Geschichte* 33–34; "Historiador" 54–56).

The complex interplay of these social forces and their egoistic instincts, combined with the passivity and aloofness of the others, determine the course of human history. Remarkably, the masses, which had been almost totally absent from the historical scene in earlier dynastic chronicles, are allotted a substantial, if not entirely independent and invariably negative, role in Ibn al-Khaṭīb's *Aʿlām* – a fact that can be explained by the vizier's aristocratic disdain for *profanum vulgus* (Hoenerbach, "Historiador" 57). Ungrateful and hard to please, they hate and vilify the ruler, even when he acts for their own good. This "deaf, dumb, and mindless" mass (Hoenerbach, *Islamische Geschichte* 68–69) never comes to the rescue of its royal benefactor in times of crisis and takes gleeful delight in his downfall.

The ignorant populace falls easy prey to sedition by all manner of troublemakers and is quick to rebel against the legitimate government at the first sign of its weakness. In analyzing the causes of the rebellious spirit of the Andalusi populace, Ibn al-Khaṭīb offers a remarkably "modern," almost "positivistic explanation" (Hoenerbach, "Historiador" 51–52). The vizier's scheme includes three major factors: (1) the geopolitical – the mountainous terrain and relative isolation of some provinces vis-à-vis the central government; (2) the psychological – the stiff-necked, obdurate, and undisciplined character of the Andalusi Arabs and Berbers; and (3) the circumstantial – the destabilizing and intrusive presence of the Christian states of the north. Curiously, Ibn al-Khaṭīb all but ignores the role of religion and messianic movements in instigating large-scale social and political transformations – the role that is so critical to Ibn Khaldūn's understanding of historical process (Ibn Khaldūn 2:192–220).

At the same time, Ibn al-Khaṭīb agrees with his Maghribi colleague in discerning several distinct cycles that dominate the evolution of Muslim dynasties. Thus, he describes the Umayyad state in al-Andalus as a living organism or plant, which developed from a small sprout to a full-grown tree that blossomed, bore fruit, and eventually withered. This Machiavellian concept of social and political organization, based on the empirical observation of human activities and psychology, implicitly deemphasizes the fideistic belief in the arbitrary will of God as the sole cause of historical process that had been taken for granted by earlier Islamic historians (Hoenerbach, "Historiador" 61).

Ibn al-Khaṭīb's political ideal rests on the notion of a legitimate dynastic rule supported by an all-powerful vizier personified by the great Almanzor (Ibn Abī ʿĀmir al-Manṣūr), who, ruling with the iron fist on behalf of the minor caliph, revived the decaying caliphal state and forestalled the impending anarchy (Hoenerbach, *Islamische Geschichte* 32).

The political views of Ibn al-Khaṭīb display remarkable parallels with those of his younger contemporary on the Christian side, Pero López de Ayala – a professional court functionary who served under five kings of Aragon. In his *El rimado de palacio* Ayala summarizes his ideas regarding the politics and internal life of the Spanish courts and provides a number of theoretical observations that bear close resemblance to the conclusions reached by his Muslim counterpart. Like Ibn al-Khaṭīb, Ayala singles out five "estates" (*estados*), which form the foundation of the monarchical state (Hoenerbach, *Islamische Geschichte* 16–17, 37–38): the courtiers and the king's confidants (*priuados del rey e los sus allegados*); the generally apolitical officials of the royal administration; the noble adventurers driven by political ambitions; the aloof men of religion who serve as the king's counselors and the judiciary (cf. Ibn al-Khaṭīb's ulama and *fuqahāʾ*); and the townsfolk and petty bourgeoisie (who correspond to Ibn al-Khaṭīb's *awbāsh*, yet, in Ayala's work, are described in positive terms) (Hoenerbach, "Historiador" 56).

Despite these striking resemblances, there are a few differences also. Whereas Ayala is generally optimistic regarding the human character and condition and even tries to improve them in the pious sermons included in *El rimado*, Ibn al-Khaṭīb takes a much more disillusioned view of mankind. He seems to resign himself to human imperfection and to accept the cyclical notion of history with its vicious circle of rebellion, anarchy, cowardice, treachery, and mayhem.

Unlike Ibn Khaldūn, who was preoccupied primarily with establishing the general laws and stages of historical progression, the Granadine vizier was more concerned with the role of the human factor in history – a concern that makes his approach complementary, not inferior, to that of the Maghribi thinker. His pessimistic world outlook must have been influenced by his own tragic experiences, especially his eventual disgrace after long years of faithful service at the Granadine court. Yet, unlike Ibn Khaldūn, who judiciously withdrew from active political life into a legal career ("Ibn Khaldūn," *EI*²), Ibn al-Khaṭīb did not learn from his misadventures and remained loyal to the familiar courtly environment after his escape from al-Andalus. For this loyalty he eventually paid the ultimate price.

NOTES

1. See respective articles in *Encyclopaedia of Islam*, 2nd edn. (Leiden, 1954–) (hereafter *EI*²).
2. For the office of the vizier in the Granadine administration, see Arié 198–208.
3. Ibn al-Khaṭīb's views of Sufism and its various trends are laid out in his *Rawḍat al-taʿrīf bi l-ḥubb al-sharīf* (Garden of Instruction: On Chaste Love) – a work in which he treats Sufism as a sympathetic outsider rather than as a practicing Sufi. See Santiago Simon.
4. A pun based on the ambiguity of the word *ʿiẓām*, which means both "nobility" and "bones."
5. See "al-Makkarī," *EI*².
6. See, e.g., Simonet; Müller; for further references see al-Warāgilī 16–18.
7. I.e., *Ṭurfat al-ʿaṣr fī dawlat banī naṣr* (The Wonder of the Age: On the History of the Nasrid State) (no longer extant), *ʿĀʾid al-ṣila* (A Revision of the Continuation), following the *Kitāb ṣilat al-ṣila* (Continuation of the Continuation) by Ibn al-Zubayr (d. 708/1308), and *Raqm al-ḥulal fī naẓm al-duwal* (The Ornamentation of the Garments: On the Organization of States).
8. al-Tiṭwānī 76–78; for these Andalusi authors, see articles in *EI*².
9. Among the works of this genre are *al-Tāj al-muḥallā* (The Adorned Crown), *al-Iklīl al-ẓāhir* (The Flowery Wreath), and *al-Niqāya baʿad al-kifāya* (The Selection from the Sufficient Amount). See Ibn al-Khaṭīb, *Katība* 17–18.
10. This structure was apparently borrowed from the poetical anthologies of al-Fatḥ ibn Khāqān; see *EI*².
11. See *EI*².

BIBLIOGRAPHY

ʿAbbādī, Aḥmad. *Mushāhadāt lisān al-dīn ibn al-khaṭīb fī bilād al-maghrib wa l-andalus.* Alexandria, 1958.

Arié, Rachel. *L'Espagne musulmane au temps des Nasrides (1232–1492).* Paris, 1973.

Bencheneb, Saadedine. "Mémoires, tableaux historiques et portraits dans l'œuvre de Lisān ad-Dīn Ibn al-Khaṭīb." *Revue d'histoire et de civilisation du Maghreb* 2 (1967): 54–85.

Dunlop, D. M. *Arab Civilization to A.D. 1500.* Beirut, 1971.

"A Little-Known Work by Lisān al-Dīn Ibn al-Khaṭīb." *Miscelanea de estudios árabes y hebraicos* (Granada) 12 (1959): 47–55.

Hoenerbach, Wilhelm. "El historiador Ibn al-Jaṭīb: Pueblo-gobierno-estado." *Andalusia islámica* 1 (1980): 44–63.

Islamische Geschichte Spaniens. Zurich, 1970.

Ibn Khaldūn. *The Muqaddimah: An Introduction to History.* Trans. F. Rosenthal. 2nd edn. 3 vols. Princeton, 1967.

Ibn al-Khaṭīb. *Dīwān lisān al-dīn ibn al-khaṭīb.* Ed. M. Miftāḥ. 2 vols. Casablanca, 1989.

al-Iḥāṭa fī akhbār gharnāṭa. Ed. M. ʿInān. 2nd edn. 4 vols. Cairo, 1973–77.

al-Katība al-kāmina. Ed. Iḥsān ʿAbbās. Beirut, 1963.

al-Lamḥa al-badriyya. Ed. Muḥibb al-Dīn al-Khaṭīb. 2nd edn. Beirut, 1978.

Rawḍat al-taʿrīf bi l-ḥubb al-sharīf. Ed. M. al-Kattānī. Rabat, 1970.

Sharḥ raqm al-ḥulal fī naẓm al-duwal. Ed. ʿAdnān Darwīsh. Damascus, 1990.

Ta'rīkh al-maghrib al-ʿarabī. Edn. of pt. 3 of Ibn al-Khaṭīb's *Aʿmāl al-aʿlām.* Ed. M. al-ʿAbbādī and M. al-Kattānī. Casablanca, 1964.

Lévi-Provençal, Évariste. *Histoire de l'Espagne musulmane.* Edn. of pt. 2 of Ibn al-Khaṭīb's *Aʿmāl al-aʿlām.* Rabat, 1934.

al-Maqqarī. *Nafḥ al-ṭīb min ghuṣn al-andalus al-raṭīb.* Ed. Iḥsān ʿAbbās. 8 vols. Beirut, 1968.

Müller, M. *Beiträge zur Geschichte der westlichen Araber.* Munich, 1866.

al-Nāṣirī, J. *Ibn al-khaṭīb bi-salā.* Salé, 1988.

Santiago Simon, Emilio de. "¿Ibn al-Jaṭīb, místico?" *Homenaje a don José Maria Lacarra de Miguel.* Saragossa, 1977. 3:217–28.

Simonet, Francisco. *Descripción del reino de Granada bajo la dominación de los Naseritas.* Madrid, 1861.

Stern, Samuel M. "Two Anthologies of Muwaššaḥ Poetry: Ibn al-Ḫaṭīb's *Ǧayš al-tawšīḥ* and al-Ṣafadī's *Tawšīʿ al-tawšīḥ.*" *Arabica* 2 (1955): 150–92.

al-Tiṭwānī, Muḥammad. *Ibn al-khaṭīb min khilāl kutubih.* Tétouan, 1954.

Turki, ʿAbd al-Majīd. "Lisān al-Dīn Ibn al-Khaṭīb (713–76/1313–74), juriste." *Arabica* 16 (1969): 155–211, 280–329.

al-Warāgilī, Ḥasan. *Lisān al-dīn ibn al-khaṭīb fī āthār al-dārisīn.* Rabat, 1990.

8 Monreale Cathedral, exterior of apse

THE DUAL HERITAGE IN SICILIAN MONUMENTS

D. F. Ruggles

The architectural monuments of Norman Sicily reflect a dual heritage. While Monreale's cathedral (built 1174–82) and Palermo's Capella Palatina (c. 1140) served Christian religious purposes and communicated their message of salvation via figural representation, their program of ornamentation revealed a continuing interest in dazzling surface embellishment that was the legacy of Islamic visual culture. The predilection for domes on squinches, the patterned geometrical manipulation of brick and tile, and the use of hanging *muqarnas* (stacked niches that fill corners and disguise the transition from the vertical to the horizontal plane) in architectural interiors are examples of the persistence of the Islamic decorative aesthetic. La Zisa Palace, whose patron was William II (r. 1166–89), was one of many garden palaces and pavilions built by local Muslim craftsmen. Its halls featured a fountain with water pouring over a textured chute (*chadar*), the entirety crowned by a *muqarnas* half-dome, and stucco inscriptions in Arabic on the walls that praised the palace as paradise on earth. Gardens, interior fountains, and mural inscriptions were characteristic of Islamic palaces and demonstrate how easily Sicily's Norman rulers adapted to the comfortable and luxurious Arab style of living.

The cathedral of Santa María Nuova at Monreale is a large basilica with an attached cloister. Its apse exterior is adorned with interlacing stilted arches that frame blind inner arches, resting on slender colonnettes. The textured terracotta and glazed-tile decoration of the enframing bands anticipates the Mudejar churches of Spain (*Mudejar Teruel) and was the product of Muslim artisans working in a largely unchanged ornamental tradition for a Christian patron. The structure of the building served Christian liturgy, but its skin was Islamic and reflected the mixed ethnic and religious population of Sicily under Norman rule.

PART IV

TO SICILY

CHAPER 20

POETRIES OF THE NORMAN COURTS

Karla Mallette

The Normans seized Muslim-controlled Sicily during the eleventh century and established the "Kingdom of the Two Sicilies" (that is, the island on one hand and the southern tip of the Italian mainland on the other), a state that blended Muslim, Eastern Christian, and Western Christian institutions and cultural influences, and culminated during the reigns of Roger II (1130–54), William I (1154–66), and William II (1166–89). William II left no heir to the throne, and on his death the state was thrown into confusion as battles over succession erupted. In 1198, after nineteen years of civil unrest during which various Norman and German contenders battled for control of Sicily, four-year-old Frederick II, the son of German king Henry VI and Roger's daughter Constance, was crowned king of Sicily.

The Norman state was strong, and many of its institutions survived the interregnum between William II and Frederick. However, cultural production in Sicily came to a temporary end. At the court of Frederick II, Sicilian culture would be brilliantly revived. The historical relationship between Sicily and the Muslim world and the prestige attached to the Arabic scientific tradition made that tradition particularly appealing to Frederick. He brought translators and learned men to Sicily from other lands; scientific texts were imported for translation, then exported to other European cities. He circulated a series of philosophical questions to Arabic scholars. His original letter does not survive, but we possess the responses written by Ibn Sabʿīn (see Amari, "Questions," for a translation of a substantial portion of this text). He consulted Muslim texts and falconry experts for his treatise *De arte venandi cum avibus.* Although the Sicilian court did not produce as many translations from the Arabic as Toledo, Frederick's efforts to import, translate, and assimilate Arabic scientific texts, and then disseminate them to other courts in Christian Europe, made Sicily an important center for the diffusion of the Islamic sciences to the Christian world.

The Siculo-Italian poets whom literary historians generally term the

"Scuola Siciliana" represent the most splendid cultural achievement of the era of Frederick II. These poets wrote the first significant literary works in an Italian vernacular. They have typically been seen as a link between the early Romance vernacular tradition, represented by the Occitan troubadours and the French trouvères, and the Italian *dolce stil nuovo* poets of the late thirteenth century; and certainly the Sicilians did respond explicitly to the courtly love tradition established by earlier poets. However, a complex local cultural and literary history, which is properly viewed as a chapter of the complex history of Arabic literature in Europe, preceded them in this place where one hundred years earlier a circle of poets had written in praise of the Sicilian monarch Roger II in Arabic. It was at that Sicilian court, both officially Christian and intuitively Arabic, that al-Idrīsī had composed one of the most remarkable geographic studies of the Middle Ages, a work Roger had commissioned in Arabic, making no effort to commission a Latin translation for either local consumption or export to Christian Europe. The royal palaces and, as in Mudejar Spain, even the churches of Norman Sicily were adorned with Arabic inscriptions.

Reminiscent too of the cultural texture of al-Andalus, a city like Palermo in the last quarter of the twelfth century had a thriving population of Jews, including a circle of poets writing in the Hebrew Andalusian style – the surviving body of poems includes muwashshahs, as well as imitations of Judah Halevi. Curiously, the knowledge we have of that Arabized Jewish universe comes from the reports of a certain Anatoli ben Joseph, who like many other travelers bound for other places (famously Ibn Jubayr, of course) would have left us sparkling portraits of Sicily. Anatoli, a native of Marseilles, would have also found common ground of a different sort with another group of immigrants to Palermo, the poets and other Languedocians who found refuge from the destruction of the Provençal courts. It was in such a complex environment that the invention of an Italian literary vernacular and the inauguration of a poetic movement using that vernacular as its medium took place during the years of Frederick's rule, and marked an endpoint in the literary history of Norman Sicily.

Most of the Siculo-Arabic poetry of the Norman era that we possess was preserved in the anthology made by ʿImād al-Dīn (d. 1201), *Kharīdat al-qasr wa jarīdat al-ʿasr* (The Virgin Pearl of the Palace and the Register of the Age). The majority of the poetry that ʿImād al-Dīn collects consists of *madīḥ* (panegyrics) written in praise of Roger II. ʿImād al-Dīn displays an ambivalent attitude toward the poets of Roger's court: on more than one occasion, he cuts a work short with a curt refusal to cite any more poetry in praise of the infidel. But the preponderance of *madīḥ* demonstrates that the Christian king of Sicily was sufficiently interested in the poetry of Muslim Sicilians to have appreciated and materially supported poets who wrote in tribute to him.

ʿImād al-Dīn reproduces a section of a poem by ʿAbd al-Raḥmān ibn Abī al-ʿAbbās al-Kātib, known as al-Aṭrābanishī (i.e., from Trapani), describing and celebrating one of Roger's royal parks, a fishing preserve located in the outskirts of the capital city, Palermo. This fragment is generally considered to be the loveliest of the Siculo-Arabic poems of the Norman era:

> Favara of the two seas! you have gathered together desires
> [in you] life is pleasant, [your] view is majestic . . .
>
> The oranges of the island when they blossom
> are like fire blazing in branches of chrysolite
>
> The lemons are like the yellow [complexion] of a lover
> who, having spent the night in the torment of distance, laments
>
> And the two palm trees like two lovers who choose
> as protection from the enemy, a castle well-fortified against them
>
> . . .
>
> Oh two palms of the two seas of Palermo, may you always drink
> of the sustaining rain, and may it not be cut off
>
> May you take pleasure in the passage of time, and may it bestow
> upon you
> all desires, and may events [be so gentle as to] lull you to sleep
>
> By God, may [your] shade protect the people of love
> for in the safety of your shade, love is shielded.
>
> (For the Arabic text, *Biographical Dictionary* 55)

The poet's delicate description of the garden and the pool has helped to make this the best-known of the poetic works of Norman Sicily, translated numerous times, and, in the words of a modern scholar, "almost the symbol of Muslim Sicily" (Gabrieli 1:26–27; see also Amari, *Storia* 3:778–80; Corrao 164–67). The repeated use of dual nouns grants al-Aṭrābanishī's description of Roger's pleasure garden an intimate, even amorous tone. The excerpt chosen by ʿImād al-Dīn opens with a reference to the "two seas" (*baḥrayni*) of Favara; the poet speaks throughout of the two seas and of two palm trees, "like two lovers." Modern scholars have speculated that the poet's references to two bodies of water indicate that there were originally two ponds in the park, though traces of only a single pond remain. However, it seems more likely that the poet blends Qur'anic imagery (see sura al-Raḥmān, with its description of the "two gardens" of paradise) and conventions from love poetry ("the people of love" is a common turn of phrase in love songs) to produce an idealized representation of Sicily and its ruler.

It is tempting to speculate that the evocation of the two lovers was intended to call to the reader's mind the characteristic of Norman Sicily most often remarked by Muslim observers: the cohabitation of Muslim and Christian populations under the rule of a Christian king.[1] This notion is reinforced by al-Aṭrābanishī's closing invocation to the two palms to protect the "people of love" (*ahl al-hawā*). The word I have translated as "people" is typically used to refer to a tribe, a nation, a group of people linked by some ethnic or national identity. Who, during the twelfth century, were the "people" of Sicily?

The Normans who invaded Sicily a century earlier adapted many of the institutions of Muslim Sicily, rather than eradicate and replace them. Repressions of Sicilian Muslims did occur during the Norman period: uprisings in 1161 and again in 1189 culminated in the massacre of Muslims, and Muslims emigrated from Sicily in substantial numbers throughout the twelfth and thirteenth centuries. However, the Normans embraced Islamic ideas of government and Arabic culture with enthusiasm, a policy that produced the extraordinarily syncretic culture of twelfth-century Sicily. Sicilian coinage, for instance, continued to bear Arabic inscriptions throughout the Norman period. The architecture of Norman Sicily integrated Muslim and Christian elements; architectural inscriptions are found in Arabic as well as in Greek or Latin.

The Sicilian monarchs adapted many of the customs of Muslim kings, among them the use of *ʿalāma*s, Arabic royal titles. Indeed, ʿImād al-Dīn makes reference to Roger II's royal title in his brief introduction to al-Aṭrābanishī's poem, using the word *al-muʿtazziyya* to describe the park, in turn referring to Roger II's *ʿalāma*: *al-Muʿtazz bi-llāh*, "the one who exults in the glory of God." Other references to the *ʿalāma*s of the Norman rulers are found in an Arabic inscription in the palace known as La Zisa, in Palermo. Work on La Zisa began during the reign of William I, Roger's son. Michele Amari has argued convincingly that its name is an Italian corruption of the Arabic *al-ʿazīz*, "the mighty" (*Epigrafi* 67–72). This theory is supported by an Arabic verse inscription in a large room on the ground floor of the palace, which concludes with the line "This is the earthly garden (or paradise) which comes into sight; that is the *Mustaʿizz*, and this is the *ʿazīz*" (81). Amari argues that this line plays on the *ʿalāma* of William II (son of William I): *al-Mustaʿizz bi-llāh*, "the one who has become powerful in God"; and it is on this basis that Amari speculates that the second William had a hand in finishing work on the palace (82). William's title is drawn from the same etymological root (*ʿz*) as Roger II's title, as is the name of the building itself, which is also given in the closing verse of the inscription. The continuity of the building with the ruler, and of that ruler with his grandfather, would be underscored for those visitors who knew the mottoes of the Norman monarchs of Sicily, who could connect *al-Muʿtazz* (from Roger's royal title) with *al-Mustaʿizz* (from William's), and those two figures with *al-ʿazīz*.

The historical awareness demonstrated by this poetic inscription illustrates one of the more remarkable aspects of Norman court culture: its occasional flashes of self-consciousness, and more precisely its Sicilian self-consciousness. Because Sicily is an island, and because it was occupied and ruled from various mainlands between antiquity and the modern age, it could be understood to be an extension of any one of those mainlands in response to the political realities of the moment (see Varvaro 18). During the Norman period, connections with the Italian and the North African mainlands, and with the Greek archipelago and mainland, were maintained. But the Normans, unlike the Arabs who ruled Sicily before them or the French or Spanish who ruled after them, did not attempt to supplant and replace existing cultural forms, which in some measure explains the seamless Arabization made visible by details such as the Norman *ʿalāma*s.

Rather than negotiate a tie between Sicily and a single mainland, the Normans conceived of Sicily as a discrete geographic, political, and cultural entity: they exploited the indigenous cultural traditions they found on the island. The inscription at La Zisa – a lucid summation of the might of the Siculo-Norman dynasty – and al-Aṭrābanishī's delicate description of the royal park at Favara represent two of the most triumphant and articulate moments of Sicilian self-celebration. If the Siculo-Norman experiment had endured, it might have produced more such literary and architectural monuments. But the Golden Age of the Norman era, measured from the first year of Roger II's reign (1130) to the end of William II's (1189), lasted no longer than an individual's lifespan. And when the Norman rule ended, the desire to see Sicily as a discrete land ended as well, and the ties that linked Sicily to Christian Europe were to become primary.

During Frederick II's reign (1198–1250), the attitude of the Sicilian state toward Muslims both within and outside Sicily shifted significantly. Frederick displayed a genuine admiration for the scientific and political culture of the Arabic-speaking world. At the same time, he negotiated much closer ties to mainland Europe than the Norman rulers of Sicily had; he was crowned German emperor in 1211 and Roman emperor in 1220. The activities of the Siculo-Italian poets during the years of his reign constitute a parallel attempt to stress the ties between Sicily and the European mainland. The conventional nature of their poetry, their willingness to work largely within the boundaries established by earlier Romance vernacular poets, demonstrates a

Romanizing trend remarkable in a kingdom where, a century earlier, court poetry had been written in classical Arabic. And the containment of Sicily's Muslims in a ghetto city on the Italian mainland signals the growing perception of Muslims as an alien and threatening segment of the Sicilian population, always present in Norman Sicily but never so boldly articulated.

The Siculo-Italian poets wrote from the margins of Latinate culture. The Sicilian court had not, before the era of Frederick II, played a role in the evolution of Romance vernacular culture; the Latin production of the Sicilians was limited to a handful of chronicles, epic poems, and translations from the Greek and Arabic. When the Sicilian poets began to write in an Italian vernacular, poets writing in the langue d'oc and langue d'oïl had already explored the psychological and social implications of the drama of courtly love from every angle and for several centuries. The best-known and most accomplished of the Siculo-Italian poets, Giacomo da Lentini, acknowledges and problematizes the Sicilians' belated relation to the Romance vernacular tradition in his poem "Amor non vole." In the opening verses, he alludes to the difficulty facing the Siculo-Italian poets, complaining that one of the fundamental conventions of the lyric love tradition – invocation of the beloved to have mercy on the lover and to accept his amorous advances – has been exhausted through overuse. Giacomo illustrates this difficulty later in the poem through a pair of lapidary images:

Ogni gioia ch'è più rara	Every delight that is more rare
tenut'è più prezïosa	is held to be more precious
ancora che non sia cara	even though it is not of more value
de l'altr'è più grazïosa;	it is more gracious than another;
ca, s'este orïentale,	for, if it is oriental,
lo zafiro assai più vale,	the sapphire is worth that much more,
ed à meno di vertute . . .	though it has less power . . .
'Nviluti li xolosmini	Cheapened are the turquoises
di quel tempo ricordato,	of that remembered age,
ch'erano sì gai e fini,	that were so gay and fine,
nullo gioi non à trovato.	no one found delight [in them].

(For the Italian text, see Panvini 11–12)

With these two images, Giacomo introduces an example of something believed to be more precious, because more rare (the oriental sapphire), and an example of something cheapened by overuse (the turquoise). Writing in the 1950s, the scholar Antonino Pagliaro solved a puzzle that had troubled critics by identifying the gem Giacomo describes in verses 31–34 (the word that he uses, *xolosmini*, is related to the Armenian word for turquoise, and seems to have been transliterated and transmitted through the Arabic alphabet), and traced Giacomo's intimation that the color and quality of the turquoise can degenerate with the passage of time, unfamiliar in Christian Europe, to the Arabic lapidary tradition.

The association of the gems and the lapidary learning of the Orient with both rarity and value is central to Giacomo's discussion of his relation to the Romance vernacular lyric love tradition. However, at the same time that Giacomo and the Siculo-Italian poets worked to forge an Italian literary vernacular, the status and living conditions of Sicilian Muslims were changing radically. In 1224 Frederick began to deport Muslims from the island and resettle them in Lucera, a town on the Italian mainland, a move undertaken primarily to remove a source of civil unrest from the island. The Muslim colony, however, proved a dynamic economic success: the citizens of Lucera manufactured arms and wood inlays; they cultivated the surrounding countryside, which had been underworked because underpopulated; and they provided a standing army on which Frederick drew for his most demanding military ventures.

Lucera would remain, throughout Frederick's life, a point of contention in his battles with the Church. Frederick himself, perhaps disingenuously, cited the colony as evidence of his fidelity to the Church, asserting that he had labored long and hard to isolate the Muslims in Lucera and worked to promote their conversion to Christianity once the colony was established (see, e.g., Huillard-Bréholles and Luynes, vol. 4, pt. 2, p. 831; Matthew of Paris 349). Still, Frederick's critics often mentioned Lucera when questioning his allegiance to the Church. In his 1239 excommunication order against Frederick, Pope Gregory claims that in Lucera the king "made the buildings in which the divine name was worshipped into places where cursed Muhammad is adored" (Huillard-Bréholles and Luynes 5:288). Frederick bickered with the pope in particular regarding attempts to send priests to Lucera to convert the Muslims. Pietro Egidi, author of the most complete study we have of Muslim Lucera, notes that the conversion of the citizens would have reduced the antagonism between them and their Christian neighbors "which fomented the military spirit in them," would have increased the pope's power in southern Italy, and would have deprived Frederick of a valuable agricultural workforce (631): Frederick had clear and compelling political motives for preserving the difference between the Muslim colony and the surrounding countryside, and more complex and ambiguous cultural ones. His practice of spending time in this ghetto of his own making, reputedly lounging in oriental splendor in the midst of a harem, reflects paradoxes and ambivalences characteristic of Frederick.

During Frederick's reign, original Arabic literary production in Sicily, which had continued under Roger, ceased. At the same time, an emphasis on communication of Arabic scientific culture to the Christian world was consolidated and the Sicilian court was second only to Toledo in its cultivation of translations – and, as in Toledo, Arabized Jews played a crucial role in the process. While with the deportations to Lucera the last Sicilian Arabic communities were eliminated, and Frederick's cultural policy from some perspectives demonstrates a perception of Arabic culture as something "foreign," contemporary anecdotes reveal that Frederick was not only an adept speaker of Arabic but considered himself so skilled an Arabist that, reputedly, he would personally vet some of the translations he commissioned (among which Maimonides' work was a particular favorite). As Sicilian king, he inherited an intimate proximity to this culture, and strove to exploit its advantages, while isolating and minimizing the potential dangers.

Perhaps Giacomo's discussion of the gems of the East can be read to reflect the new Sicilian attitude toward Muslims. "If it is oriental, the sapphire is worth that much more," Giacomo writes, echoing the valorization of "oriental" culture as foreign and precious. This statement reads like a sly reminder of the Sicilian poet's advantage as a resident of a kingdom that grants him access to the East and its intellectual and material treasures. However, Giacomo goes on to undermine the value of the "oriental sapphire": "Every delight that is more rare," he writes, "is held to be more precious, even though it is not of more value . . . For, if it is oriental, the sapphire is worth that much more, *though it has less power.*" Despite popular opinion, the sapphires from the East are not "more precious": it is the distance they traverse that compels the undiscerning to see them as valuable. Again, Giacomo's mention of the "turquoises of that remembered age," with its reference to the Arabic lapidary tradition and its use of an Arabizing Sicilian name for the gem, evokes the value of the stone only to question it: "Cheapened are the turquoises of that remembered age, that were so gay and fine." During an earlier period, turquoises possessed the power to enchant the observer. Time has dimmed the charm of the gem, however; what once seemed so appealing no longer can seduce.

The "remembered age" to which Giacomo alludes is ambiguous. Its most obvious referent is the vaguely defined era of the poets who have written before him, who have exhausted the strategy of invoking the beloved for mercy, just as time exhausts the beauty of the turquoise. However, the phrase may have another level of reference: the poet may intend to bring to mind the age when Arabic was the primary cultural tongue of the Sicilian court, when Muslim scientists introduced new ways of thinking about the natural world (like the property here attributed to the turquoise) and Muslim poets honored a Christian king in Arabic. In both these lapidary references, a stone represented as having some connection with the Muslim world is held up at one moment as uniquely valuable and exposed as a sham in the next. It is noteworthy that Giacomo sets this pair of lapidary references, first celebrating the wealth of the "Orient" and then questioning it, at the center of a poem addressing his relation to the Romance vernacular tradition of Christian Europe.

References like these to the learning and the material wealth of the Arabic-speaking world are not common in Siculo-Italian poetry, and those seeking explicit Arabic ties to Sicilian poetics will be disappointed. The Romanized Sicilians' access to the Arabic world, a product of both the history of Muslim–Christian cohabitation in Sicily and the economic and cultural ties maintained with Arabic states by Frederick II, had been and remained an important aspect of the Sicilian cultural situation; and the Sicilian cultural situation in turn influenced the evolution of Siculo-Italian poetics. Furio Brugnolo, discussing the evolution of what he terms the Sicilian "cultural project," affirms that Sicilian poetry openly takes the works of the Provençal troubadours as its model and does not explicitly respond to an appreciable degree to other literary influences. However, the convergence of cultural influences in Sicily seems to constitute "a factor of capital importance from the historical point of view, since it confirms what had been revealed time and again by other kingdoms (think of the Plantagenet court of Henry II of England, or the Castilian court of Alfonso X): *that the decisive push toward the development and consolidation of the new vernacular literatures is attested precisely there where there is greater interaction between different languages and cultures*" (272–73, emphasis added).

In northern Italy, where the conflict between linguistic cultures was not nearly as marked, the earliest vernacular poets wrote in Occitan and in Franco-Veneto. But the Italian literary vernacular was invented by these Sicilians who wrote from a land where cultural identity was more problematic, and, as the persona of Frederick exemplifies, one of profound equivocation vis-à-vis Arabic culture. At the same time, the Sicilians' urge to differentiate themselves with the established Romance vernacular tradition was powerful enough to produce a new vernacular altogether.

Brugnolo identifies the "interaction between different languages and cultures" as a crucial element in the formation of Romance vernacular culture. A close reading of the cultural history of Sicily, taking into account in particular the developments that preceded the emergence of a literature in an Italian vernacular, allows us to fine-tune Brugnolo's observation. Cultures converged in Norman Sicily from the outset, but Romance vernacular literature did not emerge as a result: the culture of the Norman court integrated Arabic, Eastern Christian, and Western Christian elements, and court poets wrote in Arabic. During the reign of Frederick II, the linguistic and cultural affiliations of the royal court shifted. Frederick's diplomatic and cultural activities indicate an attempt to maintain and exploit his connections with the Arabic-speaking world, but he worked simultaneously to segregate the Muslim population within Sicily: the "Kingdom of the Two Sicilies" became not only geographically but also culturally and ethnically divided. And as the role of Arabic culture in Sicily was circumscribed, the Western Christian tradition came to assume a more primary position. These developments – the maintenance of valued cultural connections with the Arabic-speaking world outside Sicily, the distance established between Muslim and Christian populations within Sicily, and the growing hegemony of Latinate Christian culture in Sicily – allowed Sicilian Christians of Frederick's era both access to Arabic culture and leverage to manipulate it. Not only cultural convergence but more importantly the containment of Arabic culture constitute a necessary prerequisite for the emergence of an Italian vernacular culture in Sicily.

NOTE

1. For example, see the remarkable description of Sicily written by Ibn Jubayr, who visited the island during the reign of William II, Roger's grandson.

BIBLIOGRAPHY

Amari, Michele. *Le epigrafi arabiche di Sicilia.* Ed. Francesco Gabrieli. Palermo, [1971?].

"Questions philosophiques addressées aux savants musulmans par l'Empereur Frédéric II." *Journal asiatique*, 5th ser., 1 (February–March 1853): 240–74.

Storia dei musulmani di Sicilia. Ed. Carlos Alfonso Nallino. 3 vols in 5. Catania, 1933–39.

A Biographical Dictionary of Sicilian Learned Men and Poets. Ed. Iḥsān ʿAbbās. Beirut, 1994.

Brugnolo, Furio. "La scuola poetica siciliana." *Storia della letteratura italiana.* Ed. Enrico Malato. Rome, 1995. 265–337.

Corrao, Francesca Maria, ed. *Poeti arabi di Sicilia.* Milan, 1987.

Egidi, Pietro. *La colonia saracena di Lucera e la sua distruzione. Archivio storico per le province napoletane* 36 (1911): 597–694; 37 (1912): 71–89, 664–96; 38 (1913): 115–44, 681–707; 39 (1914): 132–71, 697–766.

Folena, Gianfranco. "Cultura e poesia dei siciliani." *Storia della letteratura italiana.* Ed. Emilio Cecchi and Natalino Sapegno. Milan, 1965. 1:273–347.

Gabrieli, Francesco. "Ibn Hamdis." *Delle cose di Sicilia.* Ed. Leonardo Sciascia. Palermo, 1980. 1:21–48.

Huillard-Bréholles, J. L. A., and H. de Albertis de Luynes, eds. *Friderici Secundi historia diplomatica.* 6 vols. Turin, 1963.

Ibn Jubayr. *Riḥlat ibn jubayr.* Beirut, 1964.

The Travels of Ibn Jubayr. Trans. R. J. C. Broadhurst. London, 1952.

al-Idrīsī. *Opus Geographicum.* Naples, 1970.

Matthew of Paris. "Ex Mathei Parisiensis Cronicis maioribus." *Monumenta Germaniae Historica,* Scriptores, vol. 28. 1888. Rpt., Stuttgart, 1975.

Norwich, John Julius. *The Normans in Sicily.* London, 1992.

Pagliaro, Antonino. "Inviluti sono li scolosmini . . ." *Nuovi saggi di critica semantica.* Messina, n.d. 199–212.

Panvini, Bruno, ed. *Le rime della scuola siciliana.* Florence, 1962.

Schirmann, Jefim. "Hebräische poesie in Apulien und Sizilian." *Mitteilungen des Forschungsinstituts für hebräische Dichtung.* Berlin, 1933. 95–147.

Stern, Samuel M. "A Twelfth-Century Circle of Hebrew Poets in Sicily." *Journal of Jewish Studies* 5 (1954): 60–79, 110–13.

Varvaro, Alberto. *Lingua e storia in Sicilia.* Palermo, 1981.

CHAPTER 21

IBN ḤAMDĪS AND THE POETRY OF NOSTALGIA

William Granara

In the year 1078 at the age of twenty-four, ʿAbd al-Jabbār ibn Ḥamdīs, the scion of a Muslim family that had inhabited Sicily for generations, left his homeland and set out in pursuit of fame and fortune. He had lived his youth in the splendor of a privileged class of landed gentry. But the times were changing: by the beginning of the third Islamic century in Sicily, internal strife was tearing apart the Muslim community. War, disease, and destruction were wreaking havoc on the land, while the hordes of Norman armies lay in wait, preparing to carve their name on Sicilian history. As political stability and economic security declined, so too did the courtly atmosphere of the princely palaces in which poets like Ibn Ḥamdīs could pursue lucrative and prestigious careers.

Since the opportunities for a promising professional poet, particularly a court panegyrist, were to be found elsewhere, Ibn Ḥamdīs chose temporary exile, first to al-Andalus and then to North Africa, to make his fame and fortune as a poet-warrior. Like all good native sons of Sicily, Ibn Ḥamdīs had every intention of one day returning home. But the return to his beloved homeland would never come to pass. The pain and regret he suffered would be a constant theme in much of his poetic œuvre throughout his long life. In the sixty years he lived following his departure from Sicily, Ibn Ḥamdīs witnessed the destruction of Muslim Sicily by the Norman armies, the fall of Muslim principalities to the Reconquista in Spain, civil wars, plagues, the death of most of his relatives, and finally, his own blindness at the end of his life.

One of the ironies in the history of Muslim Sicily is that Arabo-Islamic culture did not come to a halt with the end of Islamic political domination. The fruits of two centuries of planting and cultivating a civilization were vigorously reaped by the Norman princes who moved into the furnished palaces of their predecessors and built their new kingdom on the foundations of a well-developed Muslim state. The religious and cultural tolerance that eventually became the hallmark of the court of Roger II allowed Arabic and

Islamic institutions to survive and prosper. But this turn of events undoubtedly left a bitter taste in the mouth of Ibn Ḥamdīs, whose vicious invectives against the Norman infidels stand in sharp contrast to the Arab historians, poets, and scholars who lavished praise and blessings on their great Norman benefactors.

Fated never to return to his homeland, Ibn Ḥamdīs took it upon himself to become Sicily's poet-in-exile, its premier émigré. His verses variously echoed the voice of the itinerant memoirist, wandering minstrel, panegyrist and eulogist, chronicler and historian, town crier, and holy warrior. He sought to become the conscience of *dār al-islām*, the Muslim community, and took every occasion in his poetry to remind Muslims of their glorious victory in Sicily, and at the same time urge his compatriots to continue in their jihad. In a poem written to his native Syracuse as it offered its last resistance to the invading Normans, Ibn Ḥamdīs appropriates the language and imagery that recalls pre-Islamic Arabic battle poetry (416–17, no. 270). He concludes:

> This is God's country! If you abandon its spaces,
> your aspirations on earth will be shattered.
> Your glory will end in humiliation and exile,
> and your unity will be cast off by separation.
> The land of others is not your land,
> nor are its friends and neighbors yours.
> Can the land of another replace your land?
> Can a milkless aunt take the place of a mother?
> O friend, whose love follows my love
> just as the second rains follow the first rains –
> chain yourself to the country which is your beloved homeland,
> and die in your own abode.
> Reject the thought of experiencing exile,
> as the mind refuses to try out poison. (ll. 17–23)

The thirteen years (c. 1078–91) that Ibn Ḥamdīs spent in al-Andalus were critical to his formation as a poet, since this was, so to speak, his first professional stint in exile. Yet he could not have felt completely alien in al-Andalus, given the similarity of its cosmopolitan culture to the one he had left in Sicily. He thrived in an environment that was cultivated by and celebrated in Arabic poetry. We know that his diction, imagery, themes and structures, as well as his poetic temperament, developed a particular Andalusian flavor. Yet conspicuously absent from his diwan are the muwashshahs and zajals very much in vogue in al-Andalus at the time. In a time and place where traditional, mainstream Arabic poetry was competing with these popular, innovative genres, one wonders why such a public and celebrated poet like Ibn Ḥamdīs limited himself to composing verses that were, in the words of Francesco

Gabrieli, "irreproachable classical craftsmanship of a rigorously traditional type" ("Sicilia" 115).

But Ibn Ḥamdīs's poetic conservatism was both deeply psychological and consciously political, and far more comprehensive and encompassing than Gabrieli's description. It was a complex conservatism that incorporated elements of the various "classicisms" of the age: he steadfastly adhered to the spirit of the tradition defined by its appropriation of the language, imagery, themes, and formal units of the classical qasida, a vision that had incorporated the worldview of the pre-Islamic poets to that of later Islamic poetic successors. Thus the poetry of Ibn Ḥamdīs reflects a keen awareness of where Arabic poetry had been and where it was going, as well as of contemporary issues in Arabic literary theory and criticism. He was clearly influenced by the poets still called "modernist" (*al-muḥdathūn*) who flourished in the urban centers of the Abbasid empire and whose innovations in the form, content, and imagery of Arabic poetry often rendered quaint and obsolete the conventions of a Bedouin/desert literary tradition. In Ibn Ḥamdīs's liberal use of certain rhetoric devices (antithesis and paronomasia), as well as other aspects of his style, we can see clearly his predilection for the so-called modern and a pronounced proclivity toward the theories and styles of Abū Tammām (d. 850), al-Mutanabbī (d. 965), and al-Buḥturī (d. 897).

Those who have studied Ibn Ḥamdīs's diwan are united in their focus on a select number of poems that have come to be called *ṣiqilliyya*s (Sicilian poems). They agree that these poems are the finest of his œuvre for their lyrical quality and bring out the best in Ibn Ḥamdīs's craft. These poems share the common theme of Sicily as paradise lost in which we experience Ibn Ḥamdīs's Sicily-centered worldview. They are constructed on a central theme of opposition: Sicily (homeland) versus exile. This includes subsets of temporal oppositions – youth versus old age; morning versus evening (lightness versus darkness); black, curly hair versus white, thinning hair – and spacial oppositions – familial pastures versus hostile terrain (fertility versus barrenness); celestial versus subterranean (stars of victory versus graves of defeat).

While these pairs of oppositions, rhetorically expressed in the liberal use of paronomasia and antithesis, echo a long continuum of themes and images that permeate classical Arabic poetry from its pre-Islamic Bedouin beginnings up to the latest innovations of the poet's own time, they also express vividly the personal experiences of one man's exile, the struggle with his guilt and betrayal, and his quixotic quest to return Sicily to Islam, all of which would endure a lifetime.

The theme of *al-ḥanīn ilā l-awṭān* (nostalgia for one's home[land]) dominates many of the *ṣiqilliyya*s of Ibn Ḥamdīs. Like most other themes in Arabic poetry, *al-ḥanīn ilā l-awṭān* traces its origins to the pre-Islamic qasida, sometimes as a motif expressed in a line or two, or sometimes as a theme within a larger segment, such as the amatory preface (*nasīb*). Ibn Ḥamdīs works this theme into his poetry in its native, Bedouin (pre-Islamic, classical) expression. As seen in the verses cited below, the poet fashions the images of animals, such as the lion, gazelle, dove, and especially the camel, that most vividly convey the painful languishment over separation from the natural habitat. And, in keeping with the literary times, Ibn Ḥamdīs integrates this motif into various themes and formal units (*aghrāḍ*), especially the elegy (*rithāʾ*).

In a tripartite poem best described as a lament on lost youth, Ibn Ḥamdīs begins by contrasting the joys of youth to the anxieties of old age via a series of oppositions: joy (of youth)/anxiety (of old age); illness/cure; white/black (hair); moist/parched (land); and thunder/lightning (3–4, no. 2). The end of this first segment introduces the next, raising the level of anticipation:

> I spent the night in darkness,
> and lo! the first sign of dawn brought light. (l. 10)

What follows reveals that "light" here is "consciousness" and "memory," brought about from an awakening from the deep slumber of exile, that has forced the the poet to remember. The second segment contains other classical *aṭlāl* motifs, such as the loss of youth (*faqd al-shabāb*) and the weeping over abandoned ruins (*al-bukāʾ ʿalā al-aṭlāl*), and the memory of the proverbial sacred ground of both pre-Islamic Arabs and early Muslims, a metaphorical reference to Sicily.

Ibn Ḥamdīs's use of universal themes of the classical qasida enables his Arab audience to share emotionally and poetically in his own personal experience. The third segment of the qasida is the remembrance of Sicily, the major theme of the poem. Yet even in this final segment, the poet does not disengage from the *nasīb*. On the contrary, he appropriates its images and recaptures its moods in order to re-create himself as the lover standing over the abandoned abodes.

> For them my heart harbors a burning fire
> bringing chronic ailment to my body.
> There stand abodes where cruel twists of fate
> prowl like wild wolves,
> where I used to accompany the lions in their thickets
> and the gazelles in their coverts.
> Beyond you, O sea, I have my paradise
> where I donned the robes of blessing, not of despair.
> Whenever I seek a morning there,
> you grant me instead only an evening.

If I could be given my desire –
since the sea stands in the way of reunion –
I would sail the sea with the moon as my boat
until in it [i.e., Sicily] I would embrace the sun. (ll. 17–23)

In coming to terms with the Sicily, now distant in time and in space, whose abodes have been effaced by Fate, the poet accepts his own destiny. At the same time he will defy and challenge it with his poetry. Although returning to Sicily may be as difficult as reaching the sun mounted on the crescent moon for a ship, the poet will nonetheless continue on his literary *raḥīl.* As long as he lives, and as long as he writes poetry, Sicily will be his muse: his beloved (*ḥabīb*); his abandoned abode (*aṭlāl*); the destination of his journey (*raḥīl*); the subject of his elegy (*rithāʾ*); the object of his praise (*madḥ*); the spirit of his wine song (*khamriyya*); and the recipient of his boast (*fakhr*). The power of his poetry lies in what Suzanne Stetkevych terms "the increasing freedom of manipulation of the traditional images and structural components of the classical *qaṣīda* and his increasing ability to fuse the literary past and political present into a new and cohesive literary statement" (232).

Ibn Ḥamdīs exercised this poetic freedom in two elegies, one to his father and the other to a daughter. In each, the poet describes the occasion of the announcement of the news of death. The emotional effect of the coming of the bearer of such news is heightened by the fact that the poet is in exile, far from the deceased. Although neither elegy can be defined strictly speaking as a *ṣiqilliyya,* each nonetheless demonstates how Ibn Ḥamdīs appropriated traditional literary genres to fashion his poetics of exile.

These two elegies were written far apart in time: the elegy to the father was written not long after the poet left his homeland, whereas the piece to his daughter, whose own daughters he mentions in the poem, contains a line in which he refers to himself as a man of eighty. In a sense they complement each other, serving as beginning and end to his long life in exile. Moreover, in the elegy to his father, Distance is the villain; in the elegy to the daughter, the villain is Time.

The elegy to the father (522–24, no. 330) is an occasional piece (*qiṭʿa*) that begins with a customary gnomic introduction (*muqaddima ḥikamiyya*) on the vicissitudes of fate. The elegy proper starts with a prayer for rain:

May God water mercifully the grave of my father
with the clouds of early morning and late afternoon,
and may his spirit separate from his body
and go to the land of repose and comfort. (ll. 7–8)

He follows this with verses that extol the qualities for which the deceased is to be remembered, and then the effects that his passing will have on the bereaved, that is, the poet/exile. The monotheme of the deceased is in keeping with medieval critics' views on the elegy, which they regarded as a subject too solemn to have an amatory preface. Also, the singing of the praises of the deceased holds true to the accepted view that since the elegy was a kind of panegyric, the praise was appropriate to the occasion and it added a soothing, consoling contrast to the verses of anguish and loss (*tafajjuʿ*) contained in the poem. This contrast between the praise of the deceased and the anguish over his loss intensifies the poem's overall emotional impact. Once again, we see simultaneously Ibn Ḥamdīs's loyalty to the traditions of classical poetry and his adherence to the prescriptions of the literary theorists.

However, what distinguishes this poem are the passages that bear Ibn Ḥamdīs's personal stamp as Sicily's premier émigré and court eulogist:

> The announcement of his death has come to me in a foreign land.
> How frightening it is to hear of such a calamity!
> It has reddened the clear white color of my tears,
> and turned to white my long black curls.
> It is as though living in a land of exile
> erases all remembrances of one who has been exiled.
> I kept an image of him in my heart,
> and kept close to me his distant soil.
> I wailed like a bereaved mother for this noble man,
> my only consolation is my verses. (ll. 12–16)

Then, by appropriating the pre-Islamic motif of the morning of separation (*al-bayn*), Ibn Ḥamdīs tells his personal story as though he were reciting extemporaneously:

> I will forget everything except the day of separation,
> when our eyes revealed our secrets.
> A long time passed as we bade each other farewell,
> with pearly tears rushing down our cheeks.
> Here I stand barefoot over [Time's] embers
> with the passing of [my father].
> I went to a land of bitter exile,
> while he went to a land of sweet repose. (ll. 19–22)

The verses that follow bring the elegy full circle. Having taken consolation in the celebration of his life, the poet completes his mourning ritual and cries that the losses will remain with him forever:

> I am one remaining in deep grief after him,
> shedding tears of blood over him.
> I have cried for my father for hours on end,
> and the signs of my grief appear on my face.

My anguish continues to blaze,
my tears continue to flow.
My soul as long as it continues to be
will meet the same fate as he. (ll. 30–33)

The elegy to the daughter (364–67, no. 245) reveals a poet more somber in his grief and more philosophical in his resignation to fate. Whereas the tone of the first elegy was one of sharp pain, that of the second is melancholic and introspective. This is reflected in the greater number of verses and the longer metrical scheme. This difference in emotional tone between the poems is perhaps explained by the fact that the death of his father had a stronger connection to the poet's exile, in time and in place. It was an integral part of his breaking away. That of his daughter came much later, having given him time to reflect and reconcile.

A gnomic introduction conveys both universal and personal themes:

We live our days in slumber while arrows are pointed at us,
and we are both nurtured and delighted with the bitterness of colocynth.
Death has dedicated itself to people unaware;
it seizes them off guard, morning and evening . . .
Anguish is a heavy burden for an old man,
how I wish its weight were on the neck of a younger man.
I have returned to remembering the inevitability of death,
with its long history of treachery and deceit. (ll. 1–2, 15–16)

The bulk of the elegy proper narrates the sad story of how rumors of Ibn Ḥamdīs's death reached his daughter. Then, having completed the rites of mourning for him, she died soon thereafter. The cursing of fate mixes with the poet's feeling of guilt:

A killing sadness has struck you because of my death.
Could it be that death has found you because of me? (l. 33)

The poem's final line is a reiteration of the sense of guilt:

By your saintly patience I seek forgiveness for the gravity of my sins.
Your excellence compensates my depravity, your forebearance my ignorance. (l. 40)

What is particularly striking and poignant about the elegy is that the exiled, homeless, uprooted poet uses images of land to bring the poet and listener back to the psychological, emotional, and poetic state of the abandoned abode as the confluence of his pain and consolation, and his guilt and redemption. Line 20 resonates a motif in prophetic tradition (hadith) and line 28 brings home the theme of *al-ḥanīn ilā l-awṭān*:

My little plant which I planted for Reward, I have moved to
another part of me,
and shaded her with my protection . . .
Word of your death has come to me and rekindled the flames of
my grief,
like the fires in a forest dense with trees . . .
I see myself as a stranger crying over a stranger,
as though we were both yearning for a homeland and family.
(ll. 20, 22, 28)

After several verses that describe the despair of the bereaved, including that of her young daughters, "chicks of doves left in their nest and spotted by the eagle," Ibn Ḥamdīs reappears in the guise of poet-as-abandoned-lover. The elegy ends in an *aṭlāl*-like segment, with a prayer for rain:

May the verses of poetry gush tears for you,
like the tears of doves on the branches of tamarisk trees.
May every wild cow hovering around your grave in the desert cry
for you
because your eyes are beautiful as theirs.
May these tears water the tomb of Kifāḥ on a moist land
with rain that has on fertility the same effect as drought.
(ll. 36–38)

From his position in the mainstream of "modernist" Arabic poetic practice, Ibn Ḥamdīs looks both backward and forward: backward in appropriating such stock phrases and images as the *aṭlāl* theme, the dove, the wild cow, and rain to give structure and emotional effect to his poems; and forward by his characteristic manner of manipulating the language, imagery, and formal units of the traditional qasida to create a distinctively "Sicilian" lyrical quality.

By the end of their second century in Sicily, the Muslims saw the completion of the jihad campaign, political stability, and economic and commercial prosperity. However, the house of al-Ḥasan ibn ʿAlī al-Kalbī succumbed to fratricide and irrevocable political divisions that resurrected Arab–Berber rivalries and tensions between older- and newer-generation immigrants from North Africa. How could Ibn Ḥamdīs reconcile the fond memories of gallant, sacred jihad, of green pastures and a life of ease with the bitter awareness of Muslim Sicily's internal weakness and self-destruction? On a personal, emotional level, he would attach his own bitter life experiences and personal losses onto the ever present themes of the Arabic qasida, in both its traditional forms and its variations and permutations. It was especially the *aṭlāl* (the weeping over the abandoned abode), the *raḥīl* (the desert journey), and the *rithā'* (elegy) that gave voice to the private persona of the poet.

But to address the wider public, and to express the realities of Muslim

Sicily to a weary, skeptical public who came to view their golden age as a thing of the past, there was the need for literary venues wider than the *aṭlāl* and *raḥīl* and the images and emotions they were able to provoke.

The tension between Sicily as paradise and paradise lost undoubtedly haunted and challenged the memory of Ibn Ḥamdīs. The luster and sanctity of Islamic jihad had long faded in Sicily. In its place emerged what the Spanish historian Américo Castro has described as "the constant oscillation between antagonism and the sharing of a common life between the Christian and Muslim peoples" (475).

To reconcile memories of antagonism with the sharing of a common life, Ibn Ḥamdīs once again tapped the vast resources of Arabic poetry to give shape and voice to his memories, and to tell the story of Sicily as he saw it. In two noteworthy poems, we see his appropriation of the wine song genre (*khamriyya*) and the battle poem to poeticize two variations on the Sicilian theme. Both poems are unequivocally *ṣiqilliyya*s, both were written in the later years of his life, and both were written with the explicit intention of evoking memory itself.

The wine song and the battle poem both have their origins in the pre-Islamic qasida, as either motifs or whole segments. Both are often part of the boast (*fakhr*) theme of the qasida, and each developed its own corpus of vocabulary and imagery. By the time Ibn Ḥamdīs came to write his poetry, both had long since evolved into separate genres and preferred literary forms for expressing the *dār al-islām* and the *dār al-ḥarb*, that is, the Muslim and non-Muslim worlds. With the Islamic prohibition of wine, the wine song became the vessel that held all the fruits forbidden to Muslims. It often included the Islamic poet's fantasies and dalliances with his Christian neighbor who not only was permitted wine, but celebrated it. On the other hand, the battle poem, built on the language and imagery of the pre-Islamic Arab qualities of bravery in the face of an enemy tribe, took on Islamic tones as it embodied the virtues of Islamic jihad.

The first of these two poems (180–83, no. 110) begins with a gnomic introduction whose lament on lost youth and fate's twists ends with an allusion to the poet's life of alternating war and peace:

> I exhausted all of the energies of war;
> and I carried on my shoulder the burdens of peace. (l. 4)

Inserting a wine song between the gnomic introduction and the remembrance segment, Ibn Ḥamdīs poeticizes a fond memory of the Sicily of his youth, of his days of unrestricted pleasure, and a time in which coexistence with Christians yielded rewards. It is a memory that accommodates both pure innocence and sheer licentiousness:

A cloistered nun unlocked her convent,
  and we were her night visitors.
The fragrance of a liquor brought us to her,
  one that revealed to your nose her secrets . . .
I placed my silver on her scale,
  and from the jug she poured her gold.
We offered betrothal to four of her daughters,
  so that pleasure might deflower their innocence.
(ll. 12–13, 16–17)

Ibn Ḥamdīs ends the wine song segment with the image of a dancer, playing a tambourine, whose outstretched leg he likens to a candlestick, and who possesses the power both to give light and take it away. Both the nun and the dancer, with their power to intoxicate and give light, and thus stimulate the memory, are metonyms for Sicily. And, like all that is good in his life – Sicily, wine, pleasure – this evening of sensual intoxication must end in an abrupt awakening, the darkness of passive memory transformed into the light of active remembering. Fate as deus ex machina appears on the morning after and casts its sobering reality over the poet's reimaging of Sicily:

I remember Sicily, as agony stirs in my soul
  all remembrances of her.
An abode for the pleasures of my youth, now vacated,
  once inhabited by the noblest of people.
For I have been banished from paradise,
  and I long to tell you its story.
Were it not for the saltiness of tears
  I would imagine my tears as her rivers.
Twenty years old I laughed out of youthful passion.
  Now at sixty I cry for her crimes. (ll. 32–36)

In a poem written as a memorial to his hometown of Syracuse (274–76, no. 157), Ibn Ḥamdīs draws on the traditional themes of the battle poem to tell the painful story of the town's defeat. Although the poem can be more properly called an occasional piece, its intoductory verses echo the classical qasida in all its poetic glory:

In times of great stress we urge on our camels
  whose feet carry us through the vast wastelands,
frightening the beautiful-eyed wild cows scattered in the desert,
  whose eyes remind us of beautiful maidens,
virgins – you see their exceptionally rare beauty,
  in harmony with and exemplars of their own species.
O reproacher, let me unleash my tears, for in my utmost patience,
  I have found nothing to prevent them.

I am a man resigned to a sorrow
  that has left a scar in his heart.
I always thought my homeland would return to its people,
  but such thinking was wrong, and I am now in despair. (ll. 1–6)

Ibn Ḥamdīs wants to draw his Muslim audience into the cause of its co-religionists, standing valiantly on the frontiers of the Empire in defense of the Faith. The poet liberally uses the embellishing rhetorical devices that came to characterize the "new" poetry (*badīʿ*) of the early Abbasid age. By constructing pairs of oppositions with the frequent use of paronomasia and antithesis, Ibn Ḥamdīs creates a world of "us" versus "them" (the self versus the other): mosque versus church; noble Arab versus barbarian; lion versus wolf. To express more poetic, abstract oppositions, Ibn Ḥamdīs emulates the style of Abū Tammām, whose panegyric poems to the Abbasid caliphs on the occasions of their victories over Byzantium two and a half centuries earlier set new standards for battle poetry:

How often the flash of a pointed sword you imagined in the thick
    of battle,
  like the twinkling of stars on a dark night,
alone among the edges of the swords of knights,
  whose thrusts separate heads from their helmets.
I never imagined that the heat of fire would turn cold
  as it hit the dry branches of palm trees in the heat of day.
(ll. 17–19)

Since the poem was written after the defeat of the Muslims, the task of composing verses vaunting the Muslims' bravery and strength, while mocking the enemy, barbaric and weak, must indeed have been challenging. The verses contain a mixture of historical fact and fantasy, but it was not the historical reality of Sicily that Ibn Ḥamdīs wished to sing. It was rather the symbol of Sicily, metaphor for all that Islam was capable of achieving. The affixing of Muslim Sicily onto the continuum of the Arabic poetic tradition, his likening its heroes to the hero-warriors of the classical qasida, and his suggestion that the Muslim Sicilians' raids on Calabria were as noble and valiant as the Abbasid caliphs' thrusts into Byzantium: these were the poetic commemorations of a fallen homeland.

Among the *ṣiqilliyya*s of Ibn Ḥamdīs is a panegyric written to Tamīm ibn al-Muʿizz (d. 1108), prince of Mahdiyya (modern Tunisia) and member of the Berber Zirid ruling family that was granted autonomy by the Fatimids when they moved the seat of their government to Egypt in 967. The Zirids eventually lost control of much of what had been under Fatimid control, but their great contribution to the Islamic *umma* was their military resistance to Norman aggression. Ibn Ḥamdīs arrived at the court of Tamīm in the last years of Muslim rule over Sicily and worked as court poet to this last Arab patron of Muslim Sicily. By now a seasoned poet of notable accomplishment, Ibn Ḥamdīs was able to draw on his vast repertoire to compose a panegyric, not only to his employer, but to the man who might liberate his homeland.

This poem (28–33, no. 27) is an ostentatious display of poetic virtuosity that draws in all the elements of classical, modern, and neoclassical poetry to create an epic hero for a falling nation. The transition between the gnomic introduction and the panegyric sections rests on the motif of the phantom of separation that allows the poet to disengage from the *aṭlāl/raḥīl* state of mind and at the same time keep his memory or consciousness focused on the past. Among these verses and through his selective imagery, Ibn Ḥamdīs conveys alternating feelings of angst and suffering.

> Have the leanness of my body and the whiteness of my forelocks
> altered my appearance so that [the phantom] does not visit?
> If whosoever is absent counts the months of his exile,
> then I have counted eons upon eons for mine.
> How many resolutions sincere as swords
> have been drawn from their sheaths by the hands of false hope.
> I have in the skies of the East a constellation that shines
> whenever I reach for its highest stars.
> I have become so accustomed to my exile from it,
> that the number of days add up quickly, as though counted in the palm of the accountant. (ll. 23–27)

The poet once again constructs Sicily and his exile from it onto the poetic universe of the *aṭlāl/raḥīl*, and once again the dynamic of the retrogressive and progressive nature of his poetry is at work. His use of old themes will allow him to map Sicily onto the Arabic poetic universe. Sicily at this point in the poem is still an abstraction, embodied as a poetic motif, his muse, the abandoned abode, the destination of his journey.

The second segment of the poem, the panegyric proper, is divided into two parts, separated by an interlude that bewails Sicily's fate in blunt language. In the first part of the panegyric, the poet uses standard celestial imagery and wine song motifs to express both the qualities of the prince and the poet's personal relationship with him. But then the interlude comes as an abrupt shift, a narrative segment that has the effect of a rude awakening with which the poet jolts his audience to the painful, larger narrative of what Sicily has become. The nostalgic longings for a paradise lost give way to an unusually sharp invective against the victorious enemy and censure for the divided compatriots who failed to save the homeland:

> If my country were free, I would go to it with a resolve
> that considers journeying to it an absolute necessity.
> But my country, how can I release it from captivity,
> while it sits in the clutches of the usurping infidels?
> If these dogs have prevailed by consuming my lands,
> it is only because our veins were blocked.
> It was a time when my compatriots destroyed each other, obeying civil strife,
> in which every woodsman lit a bonfire.
> The passions this strife aroused were such
> that they guided them in opposing directions.
> Kinsfolk showed no mercy to their own people,
> as swords dripped with the blood of kin. (ll. 36–41)

The poet will resume his panegyric but on a different note. In contrast to the celestial, abstract qualities of Tamīm that followed logically and poetically the soft, feminine themes of the *aṭlāl/raḥīl*, Ibn Ḥamdīs recasts his panegyric in the earthy, masculine language and imagery of the battle poem that sing Tamīm's qualities of a strong, resolute, righteous holy warrior. The verses are replete with classic supernatural images and motifs of the warrior-hero, with language that speaks loudly and moves quickly:

> If they go to fight in the fiercest of battles,
> they unleash thunderbolts from the clouds of their hands.
> On the days of piercing lances, they have strong hands
> that deliver the lion's liver to the fox in their attack.
> They have stallions that gallop through enemy territory,
> whose neighing prolongs the wailing of mourning women,
> with the stallions' ears pointed beneath their swords,
> just like the pens of writers made pointed by sharpening.
> (ll. 44–47)

In later verses Ibn Ḥamdīs conjures images of holy war, thus giving an aura of sanctity and righteousness to his patron(s).

> While some people stray from the path of guidance,
> they are guided from straying by the shiniest stars . . .
> When they are not attacking the Normans,
> they would enter on the inside of ships, on the backs of sturdy horses.
> They would die the death of glory in the thick of battle,
> while cowards die in the arms of beautiful women.

They stuffed pillows with the dust from holy war,
which they will recline upon in their graves. (ll. 52, 55–57)

He ends the panegyric segment as he did the gnomic introduction, on a personal note, the sorrowful theme of nostalgia for the homeland, the distinctive feature of his *ṣiqilliyya*s:

Is there not in God's protection an abode in Noto
upon which the clouds pour forth their abundant rains?
I fashion its memory in my mind at every waking moment,
and I draw forth for it the drops of gushing tears.
I yearn like the old she-camels for a homeland,
to which the abodes of lovely maidens are drawing me.
Whoever leaves a homeland but whose heart remains in it,
hopes for the return of the repentant heart to its body.
(ll. 59–62)

Ibn Ḥamdīs's life was not unlike that of the pre-Islamic poet who moved from place to place, weeping over abandoned abodes, and longing to return to something that would never be. His life experiences and his poetic temperament fit neatly into the qasidic mold. He had no need to venture out of the literary mainstream to find his means of expression.

The presence of Sicily as paradise lost cast a strong and distinctive shadow over all the poems in which he worked this theme. The "traditional" nature of his Sicilian poetry was certainly in keeping with the traditional nature of most aspects of Arabo-Islamic culture in Sicily. It was the reflection of a frontier mentality that sought identity in being, in the main, being more Arab, more Islamic, more orthodox, more Maliki, more conventional than the free-thinking urban centers of Córdoba, Cairo, and Baghdad.

The venerated tradition of the classical qasida, its universality and immortality, and above all, its ability to survive the vicissitudes of literary time and perpetually reinvent itself appealed to Ibn Ḥamdīs. It was on the solid foundations of the qasida that he sought to construct an epic and build a memorial to his beloved Sicily. The memory of a Sicily that was quickly slipping out of reach could be preserved only through the immortal qasida, the canon par excellence of Arabic literature, and not through the muwashshah or the zajal, which must have seemed too temporal, too local and light-hearted for such an important subject.

In a poem written to recall the memory of Bedouin traveling companions, Ibn Ḥamdīs uses the occasion to extol the virtues of the pure Arab of the desert, mixing pre-Islamic and Islamic themes. In a moment of emotional intensity, the poet deftly shifts to the first person and enters into the battle scene and into the panoply of virtuous qualities.

We are the people of the frontier whose teeth smile at war
whenever war makes its frowning [threatening] face . . .
We launched an attack on the enemies of God in their own abode,
in a ship that was submerged in death's abyss.
It floated around the infidels and made for us against them,
a protective shield like birds hovering in a circle in the sky . . .
Akin to war, and erected for its cause,
these ships, filled with lions, floated on the water.

(ll. 18, 27–28, 30)

It is the appeal to Bedouinness, to Arabdom, and to Islam that gives the qasida its universality and immortality, and one that Ibn Ḥamdīs makes his own in order to historicize, mythicize, and poeticize Sicily. And true to form, he ends the poem on a personal note, first by conjuring up the image of the phantom of separation, and then signing off with his customary insignia:

Oh, what a wonder a visit whose phantom visited their eyes,
in which, out of drowsiness, there was delusion.
The phantom weakened my feet as I stopped at the traces,
whenever it is moistened, it is struck.
A vast land and its bounty has sent me the sweetness of its fragrance,
without which I would be plunged into distress . . .
I long for my lands in whose earth
rest in peace the bones and joints [remains] of my people,
Just like a strong camel, led astray in the dark of night,
moaning with longing to return to its homeland.
The full bloom of youth has wilted in my hands,
but my mouth still mutters the memory of my youth.

(ll. 42–44, 46–48)

NOTE

A longer version of this study, accompanied by Arabic texts, appears in *Edebiyāt* 9 (1998): 167–98.

BIBLIOGRAPHY

ʿAbbās, Iḥsān. *al-ʿArab fī ṣiqilliya.* Cairo, 1959.
Muʿjam al-ʿulamāʾ wa l-shuʿarāʾ al-ṣiqilliyyīn. Beirut, 1994.
Ahmad, Aziz. *A History of Islamic Sicily.* Edinburgh, 1975.

Amari, Michele. *Biblioteca arabo-sicula.* Leipzig, 1857.
Storia dei musulmani di Sicilia. 3 vols. Ed. Carlos Alfonso Nallino. Catania, 1933–39.
Arazi, Albert. "*al-Ḥanīn ilā l-awṭān* entre la Jahiliyya et l'Islam: Le bedouin et le citadin reconciliés." *Zeitschrift der deutschen morgenlaendischen Gesellschaft* 143 (1993): 287–327.
Bouyahia, Chedly. *La vie littéraire en Ifriqiya sous les Zirides.* Tunis, 1972.
Castro, Américo. *The Spaniards: An Introduction to Their History.* Berkeley, 1971.
Gabrieli, Francesco. *Ibn Ḥamdīs.* Mazara, 1948.
"Sicilia e Spagna nella vita e nella poesia di Ibn Ḥamdīs." *Dal mondo dell'Islam.* Naples, 1954. 109–26.
Ibn Ḥamdīs. *Dīwān.* Ed. Iḥsān ʿAbbās. Beirut, 1960.
Ibn al-Qattāʿ. *al-Durra al-khaṭīra fī shuʿarāʾ al-jazīra.* Ed. Bashīr ʿal-Bakkūsh. Beirut, 1995.
al-Iṣfahānī, al-ʿImād al-Kātib. *Kharīdat al-qaṣr wa-jarīdat al-ʿaṣr: Qism shuʿarāʾ al-maghrib.* Ed. Muḥammad al-Marzūqī et al. Tunis, 1966.
al-Mālikī, Abū Bakr ʿAbd Allāh. *Kitāb riyāḍ al-nufūs.* Ed. Ḥusayn Muʾnis. Cairo, 1951.
Monroe, James T. *Hispano-Arabic Poetry.* Berkeley, 1974.
Rizzitano, Umberto. "Ibn Ḥamdīs." *Encyclopaedia of Islam.* 2nd edn. Leiden, 1954–. 3:782–83.
al-Sanūsī, Zayn al-ʿĀbidīn. *ʿAbd al-Jabbār Ibn Ḥamdīs: Ḥayātuh wa-adabuh.* Tunis, 1983.
Stetkevych, Suzanne Pickney. *Abū Tammām and the Poetics of the ʿAbbāsid Age.* Leiden, 1991.

CHAPTER 22

MICHAEL SCOT AND THE TRANSLATORS

Thomas E. Burman

Less than a century after Michael Scot's death in about 1235, Dante placed this translator and scientist, who passed his last years at the Sicilian court of Frederick II, in the *Divine Comedy*, where, rather than being praised for his important Arabic-to-Latin translations, he was unpleasantly consigned to punishment among the sorcerers in hell's eighth circle (*Inferno* XX, 115–17) – and this is only the most vivid instance of his posthumous reputation as a magician and alchemist. Yet it was through the intensely active intermediation of such restless souls as Michael that a vast quantity of Arabic writing was made available to Latin-Christian thinkers in the twelfth and thirteenth centuries. Indeed, just as the creative energy of the Hellenized East had flowed into Arabic civilization itself only through the intercession of a peculiar assortment of pagan, Jewish, Christian, and convert translators in the Islamic heartlands, so Arabic scholarship's considerable impact on medieval European culture required a similar class of cosmopolitan linguists of whom Michael Scot is thoroughly representative in both his labors and his misleading posthumous fame.

As a translator, Michael specialized in Arabic works of natural philosophy. In this he was typical of the movement as a whole. It is true, of course, that works of adab such as *Kalīla wa-dimna*, and religious works such as the Qur'an itself, and even the *ʿAqīda* (Creed) of Ibn Tūmart found their translators. Nevertheless, the great bulk of the translations from Arabic into European languages (including Hebrew) in the Middle Ages concerned science and philosophy: mathematics, astronomy, biology, medicine, physics, metaphysics, psychology. Indeed, what inspired the many wandering European scholars to come to the regions where European Christendom overlapped with the House of Islam, and to work industriously there either alone or with bi- or multilingual natives, was that love of natural philosophy so characteristic of the renaissance of the twelfth century and the Scholastic period. As was the case of the Greek- and Syriac-to-Arabic translation movement of earlier centuries, the practical scientific works – on medicine, say, and algebra – preceded the less obviously practical works on metaphysics and psychology. Yet by Michael's lifetime, European thinkers were clearly interested in the whole range of Greek and Arabic philosophical and scientific works.

By the time Michael Scot became active as a translator in the early thirteenth century, the Arabic-to-Latin translation movement was already a century and a half old. As with most of his predecessors – Robert of Ketton (fl. 1136–57), Plato of Tivoli (fl. 1134–45), Herman of Carinthia (fl. 1138–43), Gerard of Cremona (1114–87) – we know little of his life before he suddenly appeared in Toledo as the translator of al-Biṭrūjī's *Kitāb fī l-hay'a* (On the Principles of Astronomy) in 1217, and we are not much better informed about his later career. Though his name would suggest Scottish or Irish origins, there is, Minio-Paluello has pointed out, no other clear evidence that he was from the British Isles, though there was a long tradition of British scientific translators (Ketton, Adelard of Bath, Robert Grosseteste). That we first find him working in Spain is hardly surprising either, for though Latin Christendom and the Islamic world also bordered each other in both Sicily and the Crusader states, the most ancient and enduring frontier area was Iberia, and it was here that the great majority of translations were made.

We next hear of Michael in 1220–21 when he was living in Bologna and engaged, it would seem, in medical investigations. A few years later the papacy had obtained for him nonresidential benefices in Britain, and it was in this period that he seems to have drawn the attention of Frederick II, perhaps beginning to accept his patronage later in the decade. This too is part of a larger pattern in the history of the translation of Arabic works into European languages: where the twelfth-century translators were often beneficed clerics encouraged in their work by important churchmen, thirteenth-century translation was often royally underwritten. Frederick II's younger contemporary Alfonso X of Castile (1252–84) was the patron of a remarkable number of Arabic-to-Castilian translations. The majority of his translators were Jewish, some working in teams, and the range of the translations was broader, including works on chess, and a version of Muhammad's Night Journey (*Liber scale Machometi*). Yet his project was very much in line with the twelfth-century movement in which works on science predominated.

Things were very similar at Frederick II's court. The king-emperor himself had a very real interest in natural philosophy, as the list of scientific questions that he submitted on one occasion to Michael suggests. Jewish scholars in his entourage studied Aristotle's works, Ibn Rushd's commentaries, and the *Almagest.* Michael himself, like such twelfth-century translators as Dominicus Gundisalvi and the Jewish convert Petrus Alfonsi, composed original scientific works, in his case fairly rudimentary compendia on natural philosophy, and he clearly worked on these at Frederick's court, though they were likely begun elsewhere. Furthermore, Michael probably completed some of his translations, such as his version of the portion of Ibn Sīnā's *Shifā'* on animals (*De animalibus*), which was dedicated to Frederick in 1232, at the Sicilian court. He was presumably still attached to Frederick's court when he died.

In addition to the translations of al-Biṭrūjī's *Kitāb fī l-hay'a* and Ibn Sīnā's *De animalibus*, Michael also translated the Arabic version of Aristotle's *De animalibus*, as well as Ibn Rushd's *Great Commentary on the De caelo* and, very likely, his *Great Commentary on the De anima*, both of these existing in dozens of manuscripts. He may also have translated other of Ibn Rushd's commentaries such as the great commentaries on *The Physics* and *The Metaphysics*, but these attributions are by no means certain, nor are the claims for his translation of a number of other scientific and philosophical works.

His original works – consisting primarily of a trilogy of elementary handbooks on natural philosophy called *Liber introductorius*, *Liber particularis*, and *Physionomia* – had a much smaller impact, each existing in only a handful of manuscripts. While based in part on Arabic sources, these works were clearly intended for beginners. Together they cover an impressive range of disciplines: astrology, geography, climatology, medicine, music, anatomy, physiology. Other original works attributed to him include a commentary on Sacrobosco's *Spheara* (an important Latin astronomical work), a few other works on natural philosophy, and a collection of alchemical and magical works (*Ars alchemie*, *Lumen luminum*, *Geomantia*, *Experimenta necromantica*) that, authentic or not, helped establish his reputation as a magician and alchemist.

The impact of the translations of Michael Scot and the other medieval translators was enormous. The vast corpus of Greek and Arabic Aristotelian works that were made available to Latin thinkers revolutionized education and systematic thought of all sorts. The seven liberal arts (grammar, rhetoric, dialectic; arithmetic, geometry, astronomy, music) had long been studied in European schools, but dialectic and the more scientific disciplines had been seriously neglected. By the middle of the thirteenth century, this curriculum had been transformed into a thorough-going course on Aristotelian natural philosophy studied through the lens of the comprehensive commentaries of Ibn Rushd and other Arab thinkers. Because of the peculiar organization of medieval European universities, which first appeared in the early years of the thirteenth century, all students – including those who would go on to advanced courses in civil and canon law, medicine, and theology – first made their way through this highly Arabized set of Aristotelian studies. The great theologians, canon lawyers, and theoretical physicians of the later Middle

Ages were all, in the first instance then, masters of Arab-Greek Aristotelian thought.

These facts make it all the stranger that for Dante, and for Europe generally for many centuries after his death, Michael Scot was memorable not for the seminal role he played in transforming Western thought but for a series of alchemical and magical works that may or may not have been his. In this he is also representative of many of the other translators who labored at the hard business of making Arabic works speak in Western languages. Not only does little information about most of them survive from the Middle Ages itself, but they and their labors have received surprisingly little attention from modern scholars, not only in the synthetic works on medieval European history, but even in works on the intellectual history of the Middle Ages. Despite the fact that medieval and later Western civilization was, to a substantial degree, built on the foundation of irreplaceable translations – the Vulgate, Boethius's versions of Aristotle's logic, the Latin *Almagest*, the Latin Averroes, the Latin *Canon* of Ibn Sīnā – the creators of these translations receive very little attention outside the small circle of specialists who study medieval translation. They have become, as Walter Berschin has observed, "anonymous carrier[s] in the transmission of knowledge whose name[s] scarcely interest anyone" (191).

This modern disregard for translators, which George Steiner and others have commented on, is doubtless rooted in modern notions of creativity that see the work of translation as both passive and inevitable. Yet the translations that Michael and his fellow interpreters produced were nothing if not intensely active work, and they certainly were not inevitable. The whole process of translation, from deciding what texts to translate to producing a final version, was one that required remarkable initiative and energy on the part of translators, and to fail to perceive this in Michael Scot and the other translators is to misapprehend seriously the role they played in offering Arabic culture to medieval Europeans.

This individual initiative clearly reveals itself even in the willingness to travel so far in search of these Arab books and to undergo the rigors of learning Arabic already alluded to, but the act of choosing which texts to translate is a particularly important and creative aspect of it. In some cases patrons clearly had a hand in deciding what was translated, but since most patrons did not know Arabic or much about what texts were available, the translators themselves surely exercised considerable agency here as well, and Michael Scot was no exception. His translations of Ibn Rushd's commentaries, which recent scholarship has dated to the mid-1220s, were made at a point when he had no clear patron, but seems to have been living on his ecclesiastical benefices. It seems, therefore, that Michael was himself largely responsible for deciding to undertake these translations, and in so doing he played a central role in introducing to Latin-Christian thinkers the expositions of Aristotle that would be so widely consulted that their author eventually would be known simply as the Commentator. It is notable that this contribution appears to have been grasped by his contemporaries, for Roger Bacon, who was no admirer of Michael Scot, saw him as the initiator of the study of Averroist thought in medieval Europe.

Some of the further importance of these decisions about texts can be grasped when it is remembered that Ibn Rushd had died less than three decades before Michael completed these first Latin versions of his works, and that al-Biṭrūjī's *Kitāb fī l-hay'a* was as recent, having been written sometime after 1185. In reality, therefore, Michael was in these cases translating virtually contemporary Arabic works, and, though many of the works translated in this period were far older, this was not at all uncommon. Michael and the other translators often chose, therefore, to make available the most innovative and interesting works of Arab philosophy. Al-Biṭrūjī's treatise attempted to use new mathematical methods to resuscitate the old concentric cosmology of Aristotle, while Ibn Rushd's enormous contributions in stripping Aristotle's thought of the Neoplatonic overlay that had so long obscured it need no retelling here. Synthetic works on medieval intellectual history still too often allege that Islamic civilization's role in the history of systematic Greek thought was primarily the custodial one of preserving it for later, creative use by Latin thinkers. The works of Ibn Sīnā, Ibn Rushd, and Maimonides clearly go far beyond safekeeping, and in choosing to translate their works into Latin, often very soon after their lifetimes, Michael Scot and the other translators introduced Latin Europe to a contemporaneously vital philosophical tradition.

But it is not just in choosing which works to translate that the likes of Michael Scot exercised lively initiative. They did likewise in the actual process of translation. Recent scholars, such as Charles Burnett, have shown that while word-for-word translation came to predominate there was originally a fairly wide range of approaches to the translation of scientific works, from strict verbatim rendering to "intelligent adaptation." Though his translation method has not been studied very thoroughly, it appears that Michael Scot's approach fell somewhere near the middle of this spectrum. Soon after his death, Michael – like not a few of his predecessors – came to be ferociously criticized as a translator. Roger Bacon and Albertus Magnus vividly questioned Michael's competence as a translator and scientist, though the latter made extensive use of his translation of Aristotle's *De animalibus*. Nevertheless, as Aafke M. I. van Oppenraay has recently argued, on the basis of an analysis of his translation of that same work, Michael not only knew Arabic extremely well, but translated it both faithfully and carefully without falling into slavish word-for-word translation. He frequently abbreviates for clarity's sake, sometimes to the extent of replacing a whole phrase with an adjective: "lā tantaqilu min makān ilā makān" [they do not move from place to place], for example, becomes "immobiles." He also adds clarifying words to aid his reader: "li-annahu yadhhabu madhhabayn" [because it goes two ways] becomes "quoniam vadunt per duas vias contrarias" [because they go two *contrary* ways] (van Oppenraay 125–26).

His translation of al-Biṭrūjī's *Kitāb fī l-hay'a* exemplifies much the same approach. Although he does follow the Arabic syntax closely, when the Arabic seems too terse, Michael adds clarifying phrases, as in the following portion of the treatise where al-Biṭrūjī introduces a long quotation from Ptolemy: "wa-dhalika anna-hu yaqūlu fī l-jumla al-thāmina min al-maqāla al-ūlā wa-maʿa mā dhakarnā fa-qad yanbaghī an . . ." [And this is what he says in the eighth section of the first tractate, "and together with what we have related, it is necessary that . . ."]. Michael's version (which contains a misreading of *al-thāmina* [eighth] as *al-thālitha* [third]) reads this way: "Et hoc quia ipse dicit (in collectione tertia, tractatus primi) hoc scilicet et cum eo quod narrauimus, tunc pertinet quod . . ." [And this is because he says (in the third section of the first tractate) this, to wit "and with that which we have narrated, it then follows that . . ."]. The added *hoc scilicet* [this, to wit] helps make clear to the Latin reader where the quotation begins. He also does not hesitate to adopt in Latin a very different construction than found in the Arabic so as to make his version more idiomatic. Michael transforms the typically Arabic "wa-jamʿ mā taḥtahū min al-aflāk [y]uḥarraku" [and all of what is beneath it in the way of heavens is moved] into the rather different but very natural Latin phrase "et omnes celi inferiores eo moventur" [and all the heavens beneath it are moved]. When he believes it will serve his readers to abbreviate the text substantially, he does this too. At one point al-Biṭrūjī cited a series of Qur'anic verses about God's throne (*ʿarsh*) and chair (*kursī*) in connection with a discussion of how God is the the self-mover who moves all. In his translation, Michael passes over these examples entirely (al-Biṭrūjī 2:5, 125, 123; Michael Scot 71, 90).

The overall impression, then, is of a conscientious and energetic translator doing his best to provide his audience with a readable text. In so doing, it seems clear that Michael, like many of his predecessors, was more than willing to turn to experts for assistance. The colophon to his al-Biṭrūjī translation of 1217 mentions the assistance of one *Abuteus levita* (Abuteus the Levite), though it is not clear what sort of help he provided. Some have contended that this Abuteus, an Arabic-speaking Jew who later converted to Christianity, was his cotranslator: this work, then, like many others in this period, would have been the result of a team translation. Van Oppenraay's opinion, however, is that Michael worked largely alone, turning when necessary to experts, such as

Abuteus, for clarification of difficult passages. Whatever the role that Abuteus played, Michael's collaboration with him is another example of the active initiative exercised by the translators. Concerned to make their texts accessible to Latin readers, they sought out whatever help was available, working in pairs when necessary, or simply consulting with native speakers and scholars when difficult words or concepts had to be given Latin form. Perhaps the most striking example of this is Robert of Ketton's studious reliance on Qurʾanic commentaries in his Latin version of the Qurʾan so that his Latin text is, as I have argued elsewhere, heavily influenced by traditional Muslim Qurʾanic exegesis.

Dante's portrayal of Michael Scot as a magician suffering in hell captures, therefore, the complexity and cultural importance of Arabic-to-Latin translation, as well as the ambivalence of medieval Europe about the whole enterprise. Dante certainly was aware of the great influence of Arabic thought on European culture in his day. Indeed, he had read widely in the scholastic philosophy and theology of such thinkers as Aquinas and Albertus Magnus, whose thought had been profoundly shaped by Ibn Rushd and Maimonides. What is more, his own conception of hell and heaven was probably influenced by Western versions of Muhammad's Night Journey. It was surely clear to him, then, that translators such as Michael Scot had accomplished a remarkable feat of alchemy: they had extracted from the feared and deeply admired Arab-Muslim civilization powerful intellectual currents that they then transformed, almost magically, into equally powerful Latin-European ideas and texts. This linguistic and cultural alchemy, however, was a dangerous thing. Arab-Aristotelian ideas were essential to the great Thomist synthesis of the thirteenth century – a synthesis that Dante surely embraced – but the conflicts between the so-called Latin Averroists who sought to teach pure Aristotelian thought in the faculties of arts and the religious authorities who saw this as undermining Christian teaching make clear that these same Arab-Aristotelian ideas were often seen as a corrosive solvent that might destroy Christian society. The workers of this Arabic-to-Latin alchemy were almost bound to be viewed with ambivalence, and in Dante's great poem such a reputation often earned one a place in the infernal regions.

BIBLIOGRAPHY

Berschin, Walter. "Übersetzungen des XIII. Jahrhunderts ins Lateinische." *Geist und Zeit: Wirkungen des Mittelalters in Literatur und Sprache. Festschrift für Roswitha Wisniewski zu ihrem 65. Geburtstag.* Ed. C. Gottzmann and H. Kolb. Frankfurt am Main, 1991. 191–200.

al-Biṭrūjī. *Kitāb fī l-hayʾa.* Ed. Bernard R. Goldstein. *Al-Biṭrūjī: On the Principles of Astronomy.* 2 vols. New Haven, 1971.

Burman, Thomas E. "*Tafsīr* and Translation: Traditional Arabic Qurʾān Exegesis and the Latin Qurʾāns of Robert of Ketton and Mark of Toledo." *Speculum* 73 (1998): 703–32.

Burnett, Charles S. F. "Literal Translation and Intelligent Adaptation amongst the Arabic–Latin Translators of the First Half of the Twelfth Century." *La diffusione delle scienze islamche nel Medio Evo Europeo.* Ed. B.-M. Scarcia Amoretti. Rome. 1987. 9–28.

"Michael Scot and the Transmission of Scientific Culture from Toledo to Bologna via the Court of Frederick II Hohenstaufen." *Micrologus* 2 (1994): 101–26.

"Some Comments on the Translating of Works from Arabic into Latin in the Mid-Twelfth Century." *Orientalische Kultur und europäische Mittelalter.* Ed. A. Zimmermann and I. Craemer-Ruegenberg. Berlin, 1985. 161–71.

"The Translating Activity in Medieval Spain." *The Legacy of Muslim Spain.* Ed. Salma Khadra Jayyusi. Leiden, 1992. 1036–58.

"Translating from Arabic into Latin in the Middle Ages: Theory, Practice, and Criticism." *Editer, traduire, intepréter: Essais de méthodologie philosophique.* Ed. G. Lofts and P. W. Rosemann. Louvain-la-Neuve, 1997. 55–78.

Daiber, Hans. "Lateinische Übersetzungen arabischer Texte zur Philosophie und ihre Bedeutung für die Scholastik des Mittelalters." *Rencontres de cultures dans la philosophie médiévale: Traductions et traducteurs de l'antiquité tardive au XIVe siècle.* Ed. J. Hamesse and M. Fattori. Louvain-la-Neuve, 1990. 203–50.

d'Alverny, Marie-Thérèse. "Les traductions à deux interprètes, d'arabe en langue vernaculaire et de langue vernaculaire en latin." *Traduction et traducteurs au Moyen Age: Actes du colloque international du CNRS organisé a Paris . . . les 26–28 mai 1986.* Ed. G. Contamine. Paris, 1989. 193–206.

"Translations and Translators." *Renaissance and Renewal in the Twelfth Century.* Ed. R. L. Benson and G. Constable. Cambridge, Mass., 1982. 421–62.

Kennedy, Philip F. "Muslim Sources of Dante?" *The Arab Influence in Medieval Europe.* Ed. D. Agius and R. Hitchcock. Reading, 1994. 63–82.

Menocal, María Rosa. *The Arabic Role in Medieval Literary History: A Forgotten Heritage.* Philadelphia, 1987.

Michael Scot. *De motibus celorum.* Trans. of al-Biṭrūjī's *Kitāb fī l-hayʾa.* Ed. Frank Carmody. *Al-Biṭrūjī, De motibus celorum: Critical Edition of the Latin Translation of Michael Scot.* Berkeley, 1952.

Minio-Paluello, Lorenzo. "Michael Scot." *Dictionary of Scientific Biography.* New York, 1974. 9:361–65.

Thorndike, Lynn. *Michael Scot.* London, 1965.

van Oppenraay, Aafke M. I. "Quelques particularités de la méthode de traduction de Michel Scot." *Rencontres de cultures dans la philosophie médiévale: Traductions et traducteurs de l'antiquité tardive au XIVe siècle.* Ed. J. Hamesse and M. Fattori. Louvain-la-Neuve, 1990. 121–29.

9 Santa María Mediavilla

MUDEJAR TERUEL AND SPANISH IDENTITY

D. F. Ruggles

While the shift from Muslim to Christian rule in Aragon in the twelfth century was a major political upheaval, the identity and religion of the resident population remained relatively static due to protective royal edicts that guaranteed rights such as the practice of religion and freedom of movement. Thus, in 1365, approximately 235,000 Mudejares (Muslims under Christian rule) still lived in Aragon. Despite plague, emigration, and conversion, even as late as the fifteenth century a census documented a Muslim population of 11 percent in Aragon and 10 percent in the city of Teruel.

The Mudejares were skilled in construction and built several churches in Teruel, of which the remains of four survive. Santa María Mediavilla, which dates to 1342, replaced an earlier Romanesque church to which a Mudejar tower was attached in 1258. The tall, rectangular, brick tower that spans the street is decorated with panels of interlacing arches, bricks set in a sawtooth pattern, framed *ajimez* (paired) windows, and green and white glazed tile that was the specialty of the Mudejar potters of Teruel. The Tower of San Martín was built in 1315 in the area that had been the intra-muros Muslim quarter after the conquest. It too consists of a tall rectangular block arching over the street, ornamental brickwork, and glazed ceramics. The surface of the majestic tower is crisply textured, colorful, and gleams in the sunlight.

The Teruel towers follow the model of larger Almohad minarets such as the Mosque of Ḥasan in Rabat (1195–96), the Kutubiyya Mosque in Marrakech (1197), and the Mosque of Seville (1184–95). The Almohad minarets' surface decoration of blind, polylobed, interlacing arches can be traced to the *maqṣūra* arcade surrounding the mihrab

10 Tower of San Martín

of the Great Mosque of Córdoba. The leap from structural arches at Córdoba to facade ornamentation in the Almohad minarets was architecturally far more daring than the transformation from minaret to church tower; however, the latter was a dramatic ideological leap.

Why did the Teruel patrons choose an overtly Islamic decorative vocabulary for their churches? To posit that Mudejar artisans were employed because they were the most skilled and that the Mudejar practice of working in inexpensive brick was a necessity in a region lacking good supplies of stone is an argument that assumes passivity on the part of the church patrons. The church fathers could certainly have invited artisans from León, whose late thirteenth-century stone cathedral on the French-dominated pilgrimage route to Santiago embraces the Gothic style of French cathedrals such as Reims. The fact that they did not do so indicates that the selection of Mudejar was deliberate. Whereas the Gothic style was employed at León because it was French, in Teruel the Mudejar style was employed because it was not. French Gothic and its political associations were rejected in favor of Mudejar, despite its evident Islamic roots, because it signified regional culture and an emergent Spanish identity.

PART V

MARRIAGES AND EXILES

CHAPTER 23

THE MOZARABS

I

H. D. Miller

In November 1982, during a brief stop in Toledo, Pope John Paul II was greeted by representatives of that city's surviving Mozarabic community and presented with a tenth-century prayer book. It is not known whether John Paul, an amateur linguist of some note, opened this artifact of Christian fidelity, written in a characteristically Andalusi-Arabic hand, and read its first line: "bi-smi llāhi r-raḥmāni r-rahim" [In the name of God, the Merciful, the Compassionate].

This manuscript was a fitting gift for the first visit by a reigning pontiff to Spain. Given by the descendants of a people with a complex, hybrid identity and received by the literal successor of the men who helped extinguish important features of that identity, it was freighted with meaning and irony. That it survived to the present day, when so many other Iberian Arabic texts were willfully destroyed, is remarkable. That 3,300 descendants of the Mozarabic culture that produced it still proudly call themselves Mozarabs is astonishing. One would have assumed that Mozarabs, as a group, had disappeared sometime before Cardinal Cisneros, seized by a revisionist's mania for antiquities, attempted to revive their dead liturgy in the early sixteenth century. Yet there they were, in Toledo, in 1982, still in the same place they were last seen nearly six hundred years earlier, still wearing the tattered shreds of their historical identity. For the modern Mozarabs, with their culture long abandoned and their traditional languages gone – Arabic banished from Iberia five hundred years earlier, and the Mozarabic Romance dialect extinct – all that persists of that earlier identity is an ancient Latin liturgical rite – an un-Arabized religious remnant of a pre-Muslim Visigothic past, now sustained with regular but poorly attended masses in the Toledan cathedral's Mozarabic chapel – and the belief that their foreparents once remained proudly Christian on an almost entirely Muslim peninsula.

Nine hundred years earlier, John Paul's predecessor, Gregory VII, would have understood the symbolism of a prayer book written in Arabic script. What it represented would have been more aggressively apparent in 1082: a concrete, immediate threat to the hegemony of his Roman rite rather than a symbolic relic of a radically different past. Gregory had understood that the Arabocentric, Arabophilic culture of the Iberian Muslim had become, in many ways, the culture of the Mozarab, and that the ancient Visigothic-Mozarabic rite was the emblem of that culture. He recognized it, and he actively sought to eliminate it by banning what he called the "superstitio Toletanae," the ancient liturgy, and by encouraging the influence of French Cluny in the court of Alfonso VI as a way of ensuring the predominance of the Roman rite. But for the Mozarabs of Toledo the ban of the rite, formalized by the Council of Burgos in 1080, would remain merely theoretical, even after Alfonso had rejected the results of an ordeal by fire, kicking the Mozarabic book back into the holy judicial blaze; theoretical after Alfonso conquered Toledo in 1085 (on the exact day Gregory died); and still theoretical after the installation of the French clergy in the church hierarchy of newly taken Toledo – theoretical because Alfonso and his successors were forced by the threat of mass emigration, by the potential loss of an economically valuable minority, to allow Mozarabs to resist the reformist impulses of the Church. What was not theoretical was the potential emigration of Mozarabs. It happened in 1085, when some Mozarabs had elected to follow the defeated Muslim ruler of Toledo, al-Qādir, into exile rather than give up their rite and culture. Only by winking at the continued practice of the ancient rite in the six parishes of Toledo set aside specifically for Mozarabs was Alfonso able to prevent a larger emigration and attract Mozarabic settlers from the south.

With a degree of religious tolerance assured, Mozarabic culture in Toledo thrived in the twelfth and thirteenth centuries as Christians from al-Andalus fled north to avoid Almoravid religious repression. Jews and Muslims, most famously the qadi of Toledo, also converted to Christianity, becoming "New Mozarabs" in the process. Even many of the European Christians who came to Toledo, predominantly Franks and Castilians, married into Mozarabic families or voluntarily adopted Arabic culture, becoming what Mikel de Epalza calls "Neo-Mozarabs" (151). The common bond that held these Mozarabs, Neo-Mozarabs, and New Mozarabs together and distinguished them from Muslims and Jews was their adherence to the Visigothic-Mozarabic rite.

Why, in a volume devoted to the history of Arabic literature in al-Andalus, is it necessary to discuss the doctrinal disputes and convolutions of the Roman Church? The Mozarabic rite is the marker of the Mozarab, the single characteristic that distinguishes Mozarabism from Arabism. As a minority, Mozarabs are different not because they adopted Arabic culture, but because they remained Christian after the cultural shift to Arabism, when every incentive – economic, political, and social – argued for conversion to Islam. Even when the pressure for total submission, *islām*, was greatest, as it must have been during the zenith of the Cordoban caliphate, they retained a sliver of Latinity. At its smallest, that fragment was the practice of the Mozarabic rite. Later, when Muslim rule was replaced by Christian rule, they continued to practice the Mozarabic rite until both it and their culture ceased to exist, finally overwhelmed by the vitality of Roman Christianity and Spanish culture in the fourteenth century. This dogged persistence in their Visigothic brand of Christianity is why Epalza has called them "an emblematic minority," cited by historians and mythmakers as examples of both Islamic tolerance and Christian endurance in the face of adversity.

It is best to see Mozarabism not as the simple predominance of Arabic culture over Latin culture, but as an arc of culture, in which the two principal elements are mixed in varying proportions at various points. Alvarus's famous ninth-century complaint against young Christian men who mimic Muslim fashions and write fluent Arabic poetry is a marker of the changing Mozarabic mix, from predominantly Latinate to predominantly Arabic. Likewise, the rapid decrease in the writing of Arabic-language legal charters in Toledo at the end of the thirteenth century is a marker of the final shift away from the Arabic back to the Latinate. This is not to say that the two elements exist in isolation inside the Mozarab, one unaffected by the other. Nor is it an attempt to say, as many have done, that the Arabic, the Semitic, was finally and completely eradicated from Christian Spain. Instead it is to speak in general terms, without trying to unravel the complex web of cultural influences and counterinfluences. Only a few scholars have honestly attempted to separate and identify these individual strands. Thomas Burman has written eloquently on eleventh- and twelfth-century Mozarab intellectuals – Christian *mutakallimūn* – fully conversant with both the Christian Gospels and the Qur'an, able to employ the technical language of kalam and sound Latin theology while writing religious polemic and apologetic in either sacred language (168–81).

The polymorphous, hybrid nature of Mozarabic culture is obvious in the various bilingual artifacts that have survived: the bilingual epigraphs on tombstones; the Latin signatures on Arabic legal documents; the Arabic glosses in Latin texts; a twelfth-century Latin–Arabic glossary intended for teaching Mozarabs their own sacred language. And although it might be possible to see traces of the Muslim Near East in the archway of a medieval church, or in a particular chord progression in a Spanish song, or in the facial features of Beatus's illuminated saints, it is harder to see just how these things fit together with each other. How then are we to understand the historical phenomenon of Mozarabism? What is it that justifies our calling all of these diverse items "Mozarabic"? Is it the mother culture of the artist or the style of the artifact that gives the name?

II

Hanna E. Kassis

The name "Mozarab" derives from an Arabic word meaning "Arabized."[1] For the purposes of this essay I use the term "Mozarab," irrespective of the alternative etymological explanations proposed for it, in reference to the Arabic-speaking Christians of the Iberian Peninsula. These comprised members of the indigenous population of the peninsula before the conquest in 711 – Romano-Iberians and Goths – as well as, very likely, migrant Christians from other parts of the Islamic world. To these two groups may be added Christians of Muslim origin who appeared in large part only after the collapse of Muslim power in the peninsula, and those Christians of non-Arabic descent, Castilians and Franks, who adopted Mozarabic customs after the fall of Toledo in 1085 (Epalza 151). In discussing the literature of the Mozarabs, I limit my investigation to works written in Arabic.[2] There is no evidence to support a hypothesis that the Mozarabs were involuntarily Arabized by the conquerors. On the contrary, opponents of the rapid Arabization of the Mozarabs imputed the reason for the demise of Latin Christian culture to the laxity of their coreligionists and their diffidence toward the preservation of their heritage as they willingly embraced the language and culture of the Arabs. In addition to the fact that the governed adapt themselves to the language and culture of the ruler, it may be argued that the growing primacy of Arabic among non-Muslims, Christians and Jews alike, was in part due to the presence in that language of a body of secular literary expression (adab) that was accessible to the ordinary person without religious commitment.

Whether lured or impelled, the Mozarabs had acquired the language, customs, and other social practices of the Arabs at the latest by the middle of the ninth century. Primary attestation of this fact is to be found in the writings of Alvarus, one of the leading opponents of Arabization and acculturation in the ninth century. Closing his *Indiculus luminosus*, the treatise in which he justifies the martyrs of Córdoba, Alvarus bemoaned the great pleasure Christians found in reciting the poetry and narratives of the Arabs, and the ease with which they abandoned Latin in favor of Arabic (*Spaces). But if indeed there was a rich poetic tradition among the Mozarabs, as Alvarus claims, we regretfully have nothing but a very minuscule trace of it, and that from a period later than Alvarus's. For example, Ibn Saʿīd, followed by al-Maqqarī, speaks briefly of the presence of the Mozarabic poet Ibn al-Mirʿizzī al-Naṣrānī (al-Mirgharī, according to al-Maqqarī) in the court of al-Muʿtamid ibn ʿAbbād, citing a few lines of his poetry, including a poem written in conjunction with his presentation of the gift of a female hunting dog to al-Muʿtamid (Ibn Saʿīd 1:269; al-Maqqarī, *Analectes* 2:350–51; al-Maqqarī, *Nafḥ* 3:521).

The extant textual evidence demonstrates that it was the clergy who were largely responsible for the intellectual and literary activity of the Mozarabs in al-Andalus, whether in Latin or in Arabic, and that their work dealt primarily with religious and ecclesiastical matters. But while the Mozarabs continued to manifest an intellectual vitality in spite of their domination by a religion other than their own, they did not achieve the intellectual or literary stature of Andalusian Jews. Nor did their intellectual output compare at any time with that of their Christian coreligionists in the Near East. Nothing was produced by the Mozarabs to compare to the writings of Theodore Ibn Qurrah or Yaḥyā ibn ʿAdī. Nor do we find a Christian, even writing in Latin, of the caliber of John of Damascus, writing in Greek. Moreover, the literary output among Christians of the Near East included adab, a genre that according to the evidence so far before us was almost completely lacking among the Mozarabs.

The pioneering work in the study of the Arabic literature of the Mozarabs is that of Francisco Simonet, who charted the path toward a history of the Mozarabs and their literature. To this should be added Heinrich Goussen's attempt at a systematic study of this literature; Georg Graf's assembly of the references to Mozarabic literature in his study of Arabic Christian literature; Ángel González Palencia's compilation of the archival documents of the Mozarabs of Toledo in the twelfth and thirteenth centuries (*Mozárabes*), and what was perhaps the first inclusion of the Mozarabs in the study of the literature of al-Andalus (*Historia*); and van Koningsveld's recent writings that have advanced attention to Mozarabic literature and its possible periodization. Despite these studies, there remains a degree of uncertainty regarding the identity of the authors of the few extant works and, in some cases, the exact dates of their composition.

There appear to be two types of Mozarabic literature: works that were commissioned by the caliph, and others, noncommissioned, initiated to satisfy the needs of the Mozarabic community itself. Among the commissioned works only two are extant. The first, and for a long time the best-known work by a Mozarab, is often referred to as *Kitāb al-azmān* (The Córdoba Calendar), a liturgical calendar and almanac that has survived in a fourteenth-century Arabic text transcribed in Hebrew characters, as well as in a later Latin version. The author is named Abū l-Ḥasan ʿArīb ibn Saʿīd al-Kātib, in the Arabic source, or *Harib filii Zeid episcopi*, in the Latin version. Both Ibn Saʿīd, quoted by al-Maqqarī, and the Latin version indicate that the book was commissioned by the caliph al-Ḥakam II (r. 961–76).

The caliph's concern with Christian feasts, to the extent that he would commission the writing of a liturgical calendar, may be seen as the result of his interest in assembling information about the beliefs and practices of his non-Muslim subjects. This is evident from the fact that he obtained a translation of (or commentary on) the Jewish Talmud (Ashtor 1:364–65). The constant cross-references in the liturgical section of the book to equivalent feasts and celebrations in the Near East and Egypt suggest that links did in fact exist between the Christians of al-Andalus and their confrères in the eastern Mediterranean Muslim world.

Another work translated for the library of al-Ḥakam II was Orosius's *History*. According to Ibn Juljul, as quoted by Ibn Abī Uṣaybiʿa (d. 1269), the Byzantine king "Armanius" (Romanus, the Byzantine coemperor with Constantine Porphyrogenitus) sent ʿAbd al-Raḥmān III many gifts, including an illuminated copy of the Greek text of Dioscorides' botanical treatise, as well as the Latin text of Paulus Orosius's *Historiarum adversus paganos* (translated as *Taʾrīkh al-ʿālam* [Universal History]). Ibn Juljul states that the Byzantine emperor indicated that "the book by Dioscorides will only be of benefit if there is a person [to translate it] who has a mastery of Greek and knowledge of the identity of the medications. If such a man exists in your country you shall reap, O King, the benefits of the book." Ultimately, Dioscorides' work was translated, during the reign of al-Ḥakam II (Ibn Khaldūn 2:169), by the caliph's Jewish physician, Ḥasdai Ibn Shaprut, assisted by the monk Nichola, who was sent by the Byzantine emperor for the purpose at the caliph's request (Ibn Abī Uṣaybiʿa 494; Sayyid *k–ka* [xx–xxi]; Badawi 11).

Another instance of the writing of a "world history" is preserved, albeit in fragments, in the archives of the mosque of Qayrawan. It was identified by Levi Della Vida as typically Mozarabic on calligraphic grounds, as well as by the presence of Latin glosses in the margins and the occasional use of western Mediterranean forms of orthography in which short vowels are prolonged (124). In its present form, the beginning of the text is missing, and the work opens with a segment of biblical history (Saul's disobedience and his replacement by David), and concludes with the arrival of the Muslims in al-Andalus. Unlike the history of Orosius, the style is occasionally less than refined and major events in world history are omitted.

The majority of the noncommissioned works that were composed primarily for the benefit of the Mozarabic community comprise translations of segments of the Christian Scriptures and canon law, as well as treatises of polemics and proselytization. The earliest and perhaps most widely utilized of this genre was the Christian Bible. As the Christians of al-Andalus became increasingly Arabized, the need for the translation of their sacred Scriptures into Arabic ensued. How soon after the Muslim conquest such translations appeared is subject to debate. There is a suggestion that the earliest translation of the Christian Bible into Arabic in al-Andalus took place within a short period after the Muslim conquest. This claim is first made by Rodrigo Ximenes (d. 1237), bishop of Toledo during the reign of Alfonso VIII, who identifies the translator as Juan, the "glorious and saintly" bishop of Seville "whom the Arabs call Saʿīd al-maṭrān" (Jiménez de Rada 77; Tisserant, "Feuille" 325). The same claim is repeated in the *Primera crónica general*, which dates from the reign of Alfonso X the Wise (Menéndez Pidal 326), and subsequently by Juan de Mariana (3). There is even mention of the existence in the Escorial of a copy of the translation (Simonet, "Estudios" 55), but this work is now regrettably lost and there is no mention of it in Casiri's otherwise complete catalog of the manuscripts in the Escorial compiled after the fire of 1671, which consumed a large portion of the Arabic collection of that library.

Although the possibility of the existence of a translation of the Bible into Arabic by Bishop Juan of Seville is not contested, the dates of the translator are not certain. Simonet, followed by Tisserant, dates Bishop Juan to the ninth century and places him in the company of those prelates who attended the Council of Córdoba in 839 (Simonet, *Historia* 320; Tisserant, "Feuille" 327–28).

The earliest extant translations of the Scriptures in al-Andalus date from the tenth century. These comprise the complete text of the four Gospels (two strands of translation) and the Book of Psalms (two renderings in prose and another in verse). With the exception of the recently edited rendering in verse (Urvoy, *Psautier*), all these remain in manuscript. We also have fragments (dated 15 March 1115) of Paul's Epistles to the Laodiceans (Tisserant, "Version"), and to the Galatians (Tisserant, "Feuille"). To these variant extant biblical texts we should also add the text cited by Vincentius in his compilation of the compendium of canon law (see below). The text of the Scriptures he employed differs from both of the two preceding strands. Similarly, it is different from that utilized by Ibn Ḥazm, who, it is quite evident, had access to yet another complete text of the New Testament, which included (in the order presented by Ibn Ḥazm) the four Gospels, the Book of Acts, Revelation, seven Catholic Epistles (he refers to them as *al-qānūniyya*), and fifteen Epistles of Paul (2:20). There is no doubt that Arabic translations of the remaining books of the Christian Bible existed as well. But despite this activity, the variety of extant texts demonstrates that although a desire for an

Arabic rendering of the Scriptures undoubtedly existed, it failed to produce a text that was universally accepted by the community.

The need for an Arabic translation of the Bible, against the background of the sacral status reserved for Latin in the Western Church, was rationalized by reference to the Scriptures themselves. In his introduction to the prose version of the Book of Psalms (Vatican MS), one of the translators advocates the necessity of using the vernacular (Arabic in this case) as the language of prayers, lectionaries, and exegesis. He cites Scripture (Paul's 1 Cor. 14) in a manner that lends support to his reasoning:

> The Apostle [Paul] said, "If a believer utters his prayers in his own tongue, he benefits himself with the spiritual gifts. Whosoever instructs the community (*al-jamāʿāt*) and proclaims and interprets to them in his own tongue, realizes the spiritual benefits both for himself and the community." The Apostle further said, "I wish you all to speak in your own tongue. But more than that I want you to understand the interpretation of the prophecies."

One of the three extant texts of the Book of Psalms was rendered in poetry (*rajaz* meter) by Ḥafṣ ibn Albār al-Qūṭī, a descendant of the vanquished Visigoths (Dunlop, "Ḥafṣ" 147–51), in 989. Ḥafṣ mentions that his work is a translation of Jerome's interpretation (Urvoy, *Psautier* 17 [l. 63]) rendered in poetry (15 [l. 24]), most likely in Mozarabic Latin. The author was not unknown to his Muslim contemporaries (Ibn al-Qūṭiyya 31), and his work appears to have had some circulation outside the confines of the Mozarabic community. It was cited by Moses Ibn Ezra in his discussion of the complexity of translation (42 [23b]) as well as in his examination of the problem of "opposites" and "synonyms" (*aḍḍād* and *muqābala*) in poetry (244 [128a]; Dana 235–36). Ḥafṣ's translation of the Book of Psalms may also have been part of a larger collection of biblical translations he carried out, as may be attested by the reference made by Ibn Gabirol to *Kitāb al-qūṭī* (Book of the Goth) (36 [Arabic], 85 [English]) from which he quotes a short passage from the Book of Proverbs (19:19). On the other hand, *al-Qūṭī* may simply be an appellation (*kunya*) applied to any one of many descendants of the Goths. In this case, Ibn Gabirol's reference would be to yet another Mozarabic translation of Scriptures so far unrecovered. It must be borne in mind that this poetic rendering (the *urjūza*) is simply a translation, albeit in poetry, that should not be taken for more than what it is, an aesthetic rendering and not an indicator of a critical spirit (Urvoy, "Culture" 275). But, in spite of this judgment, Ḥafṣ's name and work continued to be known centuries later. A thirteenth-century (?) polemicist known only by his toponymic appellation as al-Qurṭubī cites several passages from a lost work in prose by Ḥafṣ in which he discusses such religious issues as fasting, feasts, the Eucharist, the use of salt in the ritual purification of houses, and symbolic gestures such as marking oneself with the sign of the cross (422–31).

The two renderings of the Psalms in prose (still in manuscript and under edition by this author) demonstrate a degree of independence in translation. Each relies on Jerome's Vulgate and one, as we have pointed out, puts forth an argument in favor of reading and recitation in the vernacular (Arabic). But in spite of their similarity, they remain distinct from each other.

A remark at the beginning of Luke's Gospel indicates that the translation of the extant four Gospels (currently under edition by this author) was carried out by a Mozarab named Isḥāq ibn Bilashku (Velázquez) of Córdoba in the year 946 (Taeschner 92; Kassis, "Arabicization" 153). In his text, as well as in that of another manuscript (Madrid) that represents a different strand of translation, each of the four Gospels is preceded by an introduction drawn from the writings of Jerome. In addition, Ibn Bilashku's work concludes with a lectionary (appointed readings from the Gospels) arranged according to the calendar of the feasts of the Church, as well as an essay on the means of determining the dates of the beginning of Lent and of Easter.

The best-preserved work of Mozarabic literature in Arabic is the codex of canon law that has been dubbed the [*Hispana*] *Sistemática mozárabe* (Díez 587ff.; Kassis, "Christians" 412–19). The text – and it is obvious that we have the original unique manuscript – was written by a priest (*qiss*) named Binjinsiyus (Vincentius) for al-Usquf ʿAbd al-Mālik, a bishop about whom nothing is known. But although we have no information about the bishop, his see, or his ethnic origin, we have some details about Vincentius. In a colophon to book 8 of the manuscript (Escorial MS 1623), he alludes to his own position as canonist and, perhaps, as *qāḍī al-naṣārā* in his region:

> I would have managed to stay there [at another bishop's manse] a month or more to copy personally what I needed except for my judicial obligations and those of the congregation which God had entrusted to me; I am alone in the judiciary.
>
> (lawlā rutbatī (fī) al-sharīʿa wa-thaqāf al-jamāʿa allatī qalladanī allāh amrahā wa-anā waḥdī fī l-sharīʿa.)

The manuscript contains a code of canon law for use by the Arabic-speaking church in al-Andalus and is assembled in ten books, each of which is called a *muṣḥaf*. Each *muṣḥaf* is divided into chapters (*rasm*). A colophon to book 7 sets the date of the completion of the work to that point as 16 October 1087 of the Spanish era, that is, 1049 of the common era. Another colophon to book 8 already cited indicates that the date of completion to that point was the first Sunday in Lent, presumably of the following year, 1050.

The text is clearly an independent Arabic parallel to the Latin *Hispana systematica*, and not a translation of it (Kassis, "Christians" 415). It appears that while the Latin and Arabic texts shared a common purpose, they were developed independently: the compiler Vincentius and his team were creative jurists rather than mere translators. There is no doubt that at times the order of the two texts is similar (particularly in book 10), but the predominant picture is one of divergence rather than agreement. Moreover, there is variance in the manner in which the text is cited. The order of each entry in the Latin *Hispana systematica* was that of the text followed by the reference. By contrast, the structure of each entry in our Arabic text appears to parallel that of Muslim traditions (the structure of entries of hadith literature): first the source is cited (*isnād*), then the substance (*matn*). There is no evidence to suggest that the codex was anything more than a unique internal document prepared by a jurist priest for his patron bishop. The few duplicate folios found separate from the main document (Urvoy, "Note" 235–36) could be nothing more than the work of one of the several clerical emissaries sent by Vincentius to scour the various episcopal archives in search of material for his compendium.

The codex is strictly ecclesiastical in content: "Who should not be admitted into the priesthood" (book 1), "Concerning monasteries and convents" (book 2), "Rules governing the ordering of church councils and synods" (book 3), "Baptism and the order of the cult" (book 4), "Marriage" (book 5), "The clergy and the religious education of the public" (book 6), "Calling councils and synods by the king who is a believer in the Trinity, and combating heresies" (book 7). The remaining three books deal more with dogma than with order: "Concerning the oneness and omnipotence of God" (book 8), "Repudiating heresies and heretics" (book 9), and "Averting the worship of idols" (book 10). In the context of marriage, the codex contains a reference to zajal, which the priests were not permitted to attend (Kassis, "Christians" 418). However, there is nothing in the text to indicate that the term refers to the specific type of poetry that came to be known by that name. Sections of book 9 revive the Gothic invective against Jews and Judaism.

The dominant style of these noncommissioned works tends to be of lesser quality, in syntax and vocabulary, than those commissioned by al-Ḥakam II, which are barely distinguishable from contemporary non-Christian Arabic literature. Undoubtedly, a number of Latin (and Greek) terms pertaining to the specifics of the Christian liturgy and practice, which have no equivalent in Arabic, had to be incorporated into the vocabulary of the Mozarabs. These terms are particularly evident in Vincentius's compendium of canon law (Simonet, "Estudios" 529–34; Kassis, "Christians" 417–18), where the degree of Islamicization is more pronounced than in any other document. But it is rather curious that purely Islamic expressions should be employed by the Christian jurist as well as by the translators of the Scriptures.

There are many illustrations of this point. At the simpler level, for example, the divine name is often followed, in the Islamic style, by the formula *ʿazza wa jalla*, and the similarly innocuous expression *aʿūdhu bi-llāh* is used throughout. Similarly, in Vincentius's compendium, the priest is referred to as an imam (pl. *ayimma*); borrowing from Hebrew, he is occasionally referred to as *al-qūhin* or *al-kūhin*; unnamed heretics are called *khawārij*, their partisans are called *shīʿa*; curiously, the collection of canons of St. Martin of Braga is called *al-muwaṭṭaʾ*, the title of Imam Mālik's compendium that held sway over al-Andalus. The translators of the documents so far mentioned use the Qurʾanic name Yaḥyā for John the Baptist as well as for the disciple and author of the fourth Gospel, while refraining from using ʿĪsā instead of Yasūʿ. Other Qurʾanic terms employed include *ḥawārīy* for "disciple," *al-zabūr* for the entire collection of the Psalms, and *sūra* for an individual psalm.

But the borrowing and utilization of Islamic modes of expression go even deeper. The opening page of the introduction to the Gospel of Matthew in one of the Gospel manuscripts (Madrid) begins with the Christian invocation "bism al-āb wal-ibn wal-rūḥ al-quddūs" [In the name of the Father, etc.]), while the text of the Gospel itself, as well as subsequent Gospels and their introductions, begins with the Muslim *basmala*. Similarly, seven of the ten books of Vincentius's compendium of canon law begin with the same invocation. The use of the *basmala* was not uncommon in Christian writings. But it is rather curious that, in his compendium, Vincentius places it on the lips of Recared, the Visigothic king, as he inaugurated the Third Council of Toledo (book 7, chapter 1).

The use of Qurʾanic expressions, or ones that resembled them, was not uncommon in these Christian writings. Following the *basmala* in books 2 and 3 of his compendium, Vincentius adds the Qurʾanic expression "wa-huwa ḥasbī wa-niʿma l-wakīl" [He (i.e., God) is sufficient for me; he is the fairest custodian] (al-Imrān, v. 173). In book 2, chapter 16 (folio 135v) of the same work, a pre-Islamic Iberian metropolitan, Galestine, addressing the bishops of Galicia, is reported by Vincentius to have described nonbelievers as "al-kāfirūn alladhīna lā yuʾminūna billāhi wa-la yawmi l-ḥisāb" [the disbelievers who do not believe in God, nor in the day of reckoning]. In book 2, chapter 17 (133v), Pope Leo, who sat on the papal throne before the rise of Islam, counsels forgiveness of sins and acceptance of a repentant sinner into the fold of the church, as God himself is merciful. Vincentius phrases the papal speech as follows: "li-annahu al-ghafūr al-raḥīm alladhī wasuʿat raḥmatuhu al-samāwāti wal-arḍ" [For he is the Forgiving, Merciful, whose mercy encompasses the heavens and the earth]. While some of these passages are not direct quotations from the Qurʾan, their Qurʾanic tenor is obvious to those who are acquainted with the text and vocabulary of that sacred book.

The incorporation of Qurʾanic material is not limited to the work of the jurist priest Vincentius. The introduction to the Book of Psalms in one of the manuscripts (British Museum) concludes with a clearly Islamic formula: "wa-allāh aʿlam wa-aḥkam waḥdahu lā sharīka lahu rabb al-ʿarsh al-ʿaẓīm" [God alone is All Knowledgeable, All Wise, having no associate, Lord of the Great Throne]. The expression "waḥdahu lā sharīka lahu" is part of a phrase used extensively in Islam and, in a sense, is understood to repudiate what is perceived to be Christian dogma. Similarly, "rabb al-ʿarsh al-ʿaẓīm" is a Qurʾanic expression widely used in Muslim devotions.

There are strong indications of the existence of other Mozarabic literary documents. These include the translation of some of the works of Jerome and Isidore of Seville as well as polemical and other works. Such documents, however, are regrettably lost and are only alluded to or included in the writings of others. For example, Ibn Juljul lists *kitāb al-quruwāniqa* (vocalization is uncertain), Jerome's *Chronica*, as one of the sources he had studied and examined in preparation for his own work (3). Furthermore, in his biography of Galen, he quotes a passage from the *Etymology* of St. Isidore (41; Sayyid *lh* [xxxv]). It is quite likely that an Arabic translation of these works existed at one time but was lost. To this should be added a translation of an unnamed work by Eunomius, the Arian bishop of Cyzicus (d. 394). Translating the first canon of the Council of Constantinople (381), the compiler of book 4 of the compendium of canon law (folio 240v) mentioned earlier says, "Every heretical group [*firqa khārija*] shall be anathematized, particularly the book of Eunomius or Eunomian, which I have translated from Greek to Arabic without a book" [alladhīn (*sic*) tarjamtuhu min al-rūmī fī l-ʿarabi bilā kitāb].

Another work that appears to have been lost is a history of the kings of the Franks that al-Masʿūdī says he came across in Cairo in 947–48. According to al-Masʿūdī, the book was presented to al-Ḥakam II by ʿUrmāz (undoubtedly, an erroneous transcription of *ghudimāru*, Godemaro, also known as Gondemaro or Gotmar), the bishop of Gerona who appears to be its author (2:7). He had earlier traveled to Córdoba (in 940) as the emissary of Sunyer, son of Guifred the Frank (Shunyīr ibn Ghīfrīd al-Ifranjī), lord of Barcelona, in the company of Ḥasdai Ibn Shaprut, emissary of al-Ḥakam II. The passage preserved by al-Masʿūdī is too short to give any indication of the nature of the work. It simply states that "their [the Franks'] first king was *qulūduyu* (Clovis), who was Christianized by his wife *ghurṭila* (Clotilde)."

Polemical literature is concentrated in Toledo, which had fallen into Christian hands in 1085. Our best illustration of this peculiar genre is a work written by an unnamed priest from Toledo. It is lost as a separate work but is preserved in the equally polemical response written by al-Qurṭubī. The Muslim author rebuts an assault on Islam by the unknown Christian priest who addressed his work, titled *Kitāb tathlīth al-waḥdāniyya* (The Threefold Nature of the Oneness [of God]), to some Muslims of Córdoba. It appears that al-Qurṭubī was prompted to respond to the book of the unknown Christian writer in view of the fact that the latter, not having received any response from the Muslims of Córdoba to his treatise, had assured himself of the triumph of his argument and had boasted about the superiority of the Christian doctrine over that of Islam. In the course of composing his refutation, al-Qurṭubī cited specific passages of the Christian text, thus preserving a work that is otherwise lost.

It has been suggested, in reference to other works of polemics, that it was not uncommon for an author to fabricate an argument by a hypothetical opponent in order to refute it (Turki 80). This may very well have been the case with a work, purportedly of Mozarabic authorship, preserved by a Muslim writer named al-Khazrajī (Burman 63). And it would be quite plausible in the case of al-Qurṭubī were it not for the fact that both the knowledge of Christian trinitarian theology and the virulence of the attack on Islam and its teachings contained in the passages from the Christian source preserved by al-Qurṭubī are such that they are unlikely to have originated from a devout Muslim.

In the course of his refutation of *Kitāb tathlīth al-waḥdāniyya,* al-Qurṭubī cites two earlier treatises on Christian theology. One of these works, titled *Kitāb al-masā'il al-sab' wa l-khamsīn* [The Fifty-seven Treatises], is by an unknown author. The other work, *Muṣḥaf al-ʿālam al-kā'in* [Book of the Actual World], is by an author named Aghushtīn (Augustine), a Mozarabic polemicist active during the middle of the twelfth century (Burman 80–84). The purpose of citing these works, of course, was not to adopt the views of either Aghushtīn or the unknown author, but rather to show the uncertainty of the Christian position and demonstrate what al-Qurṭubī evidently perceived as a latent contradiction in the statement of the elements of the Christian faith.

With the weakening and collapse of the Andalusian caliphate at the beginning of the eleventh century, the position of the Mozarabs became increasingly tenuous, worsening as the Muslims themselves grew weaker militarily and socially. Some Mozarabs were exiled to Morocco by the Almoravid ruler ʿAlī ibn Yūsuf following their ill-fated treachery in 1124. Others migrated to regions of the peninsula under Christian rule. Throughout this period of instability, the need for a means of understanding the Latin vocabulary, which was becoming ever more remote from these fully Arabized Christians, became urgent. It is, perhaps, against this background that we must place the much debated *Glossarium latino-arabicum* (Seybold; Koningsveld, *Glossary*; Chalmeta 249), an alphabetized Latin glossary with Arabic equivalents.

As Muslim power further declined in al-Andalus, especially following the defeat of the Almohads at Las Navas de Tolosa in 1212, so did intellectual life. With the exception of the kingdom of Granada, where a rich body of literature was created, intellectual life in al-Andalus began to decline rapidly. Muslims then living under Christian rule – Mudejares, and later Moriscos – gradually began to write their religious documents in Spanish, rather than Arabic, though sometimes employing Arabic characters (Aljamiado). The Mozarabs fared no better. What their literary achievement may have been during this period remains to be discovered. There is evidence of some writing activity (in Arabic) by Mozarabs living in Toledo after the fall of that city to Alfonso VI in 1085 (González Palencia, *Mozárabes*), although this is limited to short texts of a nonliterary nature. This is not to say that the intellectual activity of the Mozarabs was lost in the process of their migration or exile. The survival of such activity, at least among the Mozarabs living in exile in Morocco, is well attested in a debate recorded by al-Wansharīsī in his compendium of *fatāwā*, or legal responses (11:155–58). Although there is no trace of writing enterprise, the details of the debate itself are quite informative. In his report, al-Wansharīsī records that during the second half of the thirteenth century, an unnamed priest from Marrakech, undoubtedly a descendant of the Mozarabs who had been exiled during the preceding century, was engaged in a debate with Ibn Rashīq, a Muslim poet from Murcia, then in Christian hands. The subject of the debate was a challenge issued by al-Ḥarīrī for someone to add a fourth line to three he had written in one of his maqamat. As no one had succeeded in meeting the challenge, the priest asked Ibn Rashīq for the reason why no one had ascribed to the maqamat the quality of inimitability (*iʿjāz*), an attribute reserved for the Qurʾan. Furthermore, while neither al-Ḥarīrī nor anyone else had claimed *iʿjāz* for the maqamat in spite of the fact that no one had been successful in imitating them, would that not cast a shadow of a doubt, argued the priest, on the fundamental affirmation of the uniqueness of the Qurʾan, where *iʿjāz* is seen as evidence of divine revelation? The priest was quick to insist that he himself did not question the Muslim affirmation nor did he make any claim in favor of the inevitable conclusion regarding the uniqueness of the maqamat.

Neither Ibn Rashīq, with whom he debated, nor the meticulous and strict al-Wansharīsī, who recorded the debate, found fault with the priest's language. At no time had he called into question the divine origin of the Qurʾan. What is remarkable in this account is the priest's outstanding acquaintance not only with the maqamat, but with the details of the discussion surrounding them. It is evident that his literary acumen was superior to that of Ibn Rashīq.

Some decades after the fall of Granada in 1492, a treatise on a Christian topic, written in Arabic by a pseudo-Christian, appeared: *Kitāb mawāhib thawāb ḥaqīqat al-injīl* (Book of Rewards of the Truths of the Gospel). The text, still in manuscript (under edition by L. P. Harvey), was written in the middle of the sixteenth century by a Muslim who either was forced into conversion to Christianity or feigned being a Christian. Not without justification, this document would be treated as the work of a Morisco rather than a Mozarab. But, regardless of the sincerity of the author, it was presented and treated as a Christian document, and may therefore be considered as an illustration of the literary achievement of the "New Mozarabs," to use Epalza's classification.

Writing after the fall of Granada in 1492 and in the atmosphere of extreme cultural humiliation, the author forged an archaic Arabic script (block letters) in an attempt at archaization. The text states that when the Holy Spirit descended on the Disciples of Christ at Pentecost, a revelation came down to *al-ṣāliḥa al-ʿadrāʾ maryam* (the Virtuous – or Blessed – Virgin Mary). The extant text contains the Virgin's response to eight questions addressed to her by Peter. The questions and responses, the text claims, were recorded by James, son of Zebedee, but written down by his own disciple, Shamʿūn ibn ʿAṭṭār al-Aʿrābī, presumably our author. The entire purported revelation was in Arabic. The questions ostensibly put to the Virgin Mary by Peter pertained defensively to Islam and the Arabs but were couched in a Christian framework and vocabulary. It was not until the middle of the sixteenth century that Rome, having confiscated the original text written on lead tablets, finally declared it a forgery.

Not only was this text the last piece of religious literature purporting to be Christian and written in Arabic; it was, perhaps, the last piece of any literature written in Arabic on the Iberian Peninsula. Although the Mozarabic liturgy and, with it, the distinct identity of the Arabic-speaking Christians within the wider community of faith had been brought to an apparent end in the eleventh century by Alfonso VI, it was not until the middle of the sixteenth century that the viability of Arabic as a language of Christian (as well as pseudo-Christian) intellectual productivity in al-Andalus came to a full stop.

NOTES

1. There are disputed explanations for this etymology: among them that it comes from the active participle *mustaʿrib*, or, conversely, that it relates to the passive *mustaʿrab*.
2. The Latin writings of Mozarabic Christians living in al-Andalus are included in Juan Gil's compendium of non-Arabic Mozarabic literature. I also do not treat

here the complex matter of the bilingual muwashshahs and their kharjas, often identified as some of the earliest bits of the Mozarabic literary corpus, nor do I address the accompanying issue of the Hispano-Romance dialect sometimes called "Mozarabic" used as a daily language by both Christians and Muslims at various points in Andalusi history. Both of these latter items are discussed in more detail elsewhere in this volume. See especially *Language, *Music, *Spaces, and *Muwashshah.

BIBLIOGRAPHY

Ashtor, Eliahu. *The Jews of Muslim Spain.* 3 vols. Philadelphia, 1973.

Badawi, ʿAbd al-Raḥmān. *Taʾrīkh al-ʿālam: al-Tarjama al-ʿarabiyya al-qadīma.* Beirut, 1982.

Burman, Thomas. *Religious Polemic and the Intellectual History of the Mozarabs, c. 1050–1200.* Leiden, 1994.

Casiri. *Biblioteca Arabico-Hispana escurialenis recensio et explantio Michaelis Casiri.* 1760–70. Rpt., Osnabrück, 1969.

Chalmeta, Pedro. "Mozarabs." *Encyclopaedia of Islam.* 2nd edn. Leiden, 1954–. 7:246–49.

Collins, Roger. *Early Medieval Spain: Unity in Diversity, 400–1000* (*New Studies in Medieval History.* 2nd edn. Basingstoke, 1995.

"Literacy and the Laity in Early Mediaeval Spain." *The Uses of Literacy in Early Mediaeval Europe.* Ed. Rosamond McKitterick. Cambridge, 1990. 109–33.

Dana, Joseph. "Poetics in *Kitāb al-Muḥāḍara wa l-Mudhākara* by Moshe ibn Ezra and its Sources in Arabic Books of Poetry and Criticism." Diss., University of Tel Aviv, 1977.

Díez, Gonzalo Martínez. *La colección canónica hispana.* Vol. II, *Colecciones derivadas.* Madrid, 1976.

Dozy, Reinhart. *Le Calendrier de Cordoue.* New edn. accompanied by a prologue and an annotated French trans. by Charles Pellat. Leiden, 1961.

Dunlop, D. M. "Ḥafṣ b. Albar: The Last of the Goths?" *Journal of the Royal Asiatic Society* (1954): 139–51.

"Sobre Ḥafṣ ibn Albar al-Qūṭī al-Qurṭubī." *Al-Andalus* 20 (1955): 211–13.

Epalza, Mikel de. "Mozarabs: An Emblematic Christian Minority in Islamic al-Andalus." *The Legacy of Muslim Spain.* Ed. Salma Khadra Jayyusi. Leiden, 1992. 149–70.

Gil, Ioannes. *Corpus scriptorum muzarabicorum.* 2 vols. Madrid, 1973.

González Palencia, Ángel. *Historia de la literatura arábigo-española.* 2nd edn. 1945. Trans. Ḥussain Monés. *Taʾrīkh al fikr al-andalusi.* Cairo, 1955.

Los mozárabes de Toledo en los siglos XII y XIII. Madrid, 1926–30.

Goussen, Heinrich. *Die christlich-arabische Literatur der Mozaraber.* Leipzig, 1909.

Graf, Georg. *Geschichte der christlichen arabischen Literatur.* Vol. 1, *Die Übersetzungen.* Vatican City, 1944. Rpt., 1959.

Ibn Abī Uṣaybiʿa. *ʿUyūn al-anbāʾ fī ṭabaqāt al-āṭibbāʾ*. Ed. Nizar Riḍā. Beirut, 1965.

Ibn Ezra, Moses. *Kitāb al-muḥāḍara wa l-mudhākara.* Ed. Abraham S. Halkin. Jerusalem, 1975.

Ibn Gabirol, Sulayman. *Kitāb iṣlāḥ al-akhlāq ʿalā raʾy afāḍil al-ḥukamāʾ al-mutaqaddimīn (The Improvement of Moral Qualities).* Ed. and trans. Stephen S. Wise. New York, 1902. Rpt., 1966.

Ibn Ḥazm. *al-Fiṣal fī l-milal wa l-ahwāʾ wa l-niḥal.* 5 vols. Cairo, 1964.

Ibn Juljul. *Ṭabaqāt al-aṭibbāʾ wa l-ḥukamāʾ*. Ed. Fuʾād Sayyid. Cairo, 1955.

Ibn Khaldūn. *Kitāb al-ʿibar.* Beirut, 1960. Reissued 1983. 14 vols. The division by volume (*qism*) is that of Ibn Khaldūn.

Ibn al-Qūṭiyya. *Taʾrīkh iftitāḥ al-andalus.* Ed. Ibrāhīm al-Abyārī. Beirut, 1982.

Ibn Saʿīd al-Maghribī. *Kitāb al-mughrib fī ḥulā al-maghrib.* Ed. Shawqī Ḍayf. 3rd edn. 2 vols. Cairo, 1978.

Jiménez de Rada, Rodericus Ximenius. *Opera.* 1793. Rpt., Valencia, 1968.

Kassis, Hanna. "The Arabicization and Islamization of the Christians of al-Andalus: Evidence of Their Scriptures." *Languages of Power in Islamic Spain.* Ed. Ross Brann. Bethesda, 1997. 136–55.

"Arabic-Speaking Christians in al-Andalus in an Age of Turmoil: Fifth/Eleventh Century until A.H. 478/A.D. 1085." *Al-Qantara* 15 (1994): 401–22.

Koningsveld, P. van. "Christian Arabic Literature from Medieval Spain: An Attempt at Periodization." *Christian Arabic Apologetics during the Abbasid Period (750–1258).* Ed. Samir Khalil Samir and J. S. Nielsen. Leiden, 1994. 203–24.

The Latin–Arabic Glossary of the Leiden University Library. Leiden, 1977.

Levi Della Vida, Giorgio. "Un texte mozarabe d'histoire universelle." *Etudes d'orientalisme dédiées à la mémoire de Lévi-Provençal.* Paris, 1962. 1:175–83. Reproduced in *Note di storia letteraria arabo-ispanica.* Ed. Maria Nallino. Rome, 1971. 123–32, with Nallino's ed. and Italian trans. of the Arabic text on 133–92.

al-Maqqarī. *Nafḥ al-ṭīb (Analectes sur l'histoire et la littérature des arabes d'Espagne).* Ed. Reinhart Dozy, Gustave Dugat, Ludolf Krehl, and William Wright. 1855–61. 2 vols. Rpt., Leiden, 1967.

Nafḥ al-ṭīb min ghuṣn al-andalus al-raṭīb. Ed. Iḥsān ʿAbbās. 8 vols. Beirut, 1968.

Mariana, Juan de. *Historia general de España.* Vol. 7. English trans.: *General History of Spain, from the first peopling of it by Tubal, till the death of King Ferdinand.* London, 1699.

al-Masʿūdī. *Murūj al-dhahab wa-maʿādin al-jawhar.* 4 vols. with an index by Yūsuf Asʿad Dāghir. Beirut, 1978.

Menéndez Pidal, Ramón, ed. *Primera crónica general: Estoria de España que mandó componer Alfonso el Sabio y se continuaba bajo Sancho IV en 1289.* Madrid, 1906.

Navarro, María Ángeles. *Risāla fī awqāt al-sana: Un calendario anónimo andalusí.* Granada, 1990.

al-Qurṭubī. *Kitāb al-iʿlām bi-mā fī dīn al-naṣārā min al-fasād wa l-awhām wa-iẓhār maḥāsin dīn al-islām wa-ithbāt nubūwat nabīyinā muḥammad ʿalayh aṣ-ṣalāt wa l-salām.* Ed Aḥmad Ḥijāzī al-Saqqā. Cairo, 1980.

Sayyid, Fuʾād. See *Ibn Juljul z–m [vii–xlviii].*

Seybold, Ch. F. *Glossarium latino-arabicorum.* Berlin, 1900.

Simonet, Francisco Javier. "Estudios históricos y filológicos sobre la literatura arábigo-mozárabe." *Revista de la Universidad de Madrid,* 2nd ser., 1 (1872–73): 292–310, 546–61; 2 (1872–73): 55–68, 523–44.

Historia de los mozárabes de España. 1897–1903. Rpt., Madrid, 1984.

Smith, Colin. *Christians and Moors in Spain.* Vol. 1, *711–1150.* Warminster, 1988.

Taeschner, Franz. "Die monarchianischen Prologe zu den vier Evangelien in der spanischen-arabischen Bibelübersetzung des Isaak Velasquez nach der münchner Handschrift cod. arab 238." *Oriens Christianus* 32 (1935): 80–99.

Tisserant, Eugène. "Une feuille arabo-latine de l'épître aux Galates." *Revue biblique* 19 (1910): 321–44.

"La version mozarabe de l'épître aux Laodicéens." *Revue biblique* 19 (1910): 249–53.

Turki, ʿAbd al-Majīd. "La lettre du Moine de France." *Al-Andalus* 31 (1966): 73–83.

Urvoy, Marie-Thérèse. "La culture et la littérature arabe des chrètiens d'Al-Andalus." *Bulletin de littérature ecclésiastique* 92 (1991): 259–75.

"Note de philologie mozarabe." *Arabica* 36 (1989): 235–36.

Le Psautier mozarabe. Toulouse, 1994.

al-Wansharīsī. *al-Miʿyār al-muʿrib wa l-jāmiʿ al-mughrib ʿan fatāwā ahl ifrīqiya wa l-andalus wa l-maghrib.* Vols. 1–13. Ed. Muḥammad Ḥajjī et al. Rabat, 1981.

CHAPTER 24

THE ARABIZED JEWS

Ross Brann

In the Muslim East, a literary intellectual of Arabic and Persian traditions might well earn the honorific *dhū l-lisānayn* – one who commanded the two principal languages in which Islamic culture was then conducted, preserved, and transmitted. Members of the Muslim *oikoumēnē* of a different order and a singular socioreligious condition, the Jews of al-Andalus also esteemed cultural literacy in two languages, one of which was Arabic. Moses Ibn Ezra's (d. c. 1138) epistolary lyric to Abū Ibrāhīm (Isaac) Ibn Barun (eleventh century), the author of a comparative grammar and lexicon, *Kitāb al-muwāzana bayn al-lugha al-ʿibrāniyya wa l-ʿarabiyya* (Book of Comparison between the Hebrew and Arabic Languages), and Judah Halevi's (d. 1141) rhymed-prose salute to Ibn Ezra, the venerable dean of Andalusi-Jewish letters, among many texts expressing similar sentiments, unambiguously set forth the Andalusi Jews' cultural ideal valorizing Arabic as well as Hebrew learning. Other texts authored by these figures bespeak a more complex and ambivalent sense of the Jews' multiple cultural loyalties.

The literary culture of the Arabized Jews of al-Andalus represents, among other things, a particular instance of the general development of the Jews under Islam during the Middle Ages. Afforded economic opportunity, religious freedom, and social integration in the defined role of "protected people," Jews were also caught up in the intellectual stimulation and challenges of Islamic civilization. The principal means by which the Jews of Islam west of the Iranian plateau gained access to the economic and social domain of Islam as well as its cultural realm was their apparently swift adoption of Arabic as the language of everyday life, an accommodation that also saw them employ Arabic as their primary although not sole literary language. Structural affinities between Judaism and Islam as well as their unique historical experience and distinctive consciousness seemed to make for a relatively smoother cultural transition for the Jews than the more numerous and less uniformly urban Christians of al-Andalus. Yet, if the process of Arabization produced similar results for the Jews of North Africa and the Muslim East, we must direct our attention to what was specific about the literary culture of the Jews of al-Andalus, that is, the cultural life of Jewish elites whose material prosperity, involvement in Andalusi public affairs and administration, communal responsibilities and significance in Jewish history belie their genuinely small numbers (Wasserstein, "Jewish Elites" 103).

Arabization of the Jews in the Muslim East led to fundamental changes in the articulation of Jewish culture during the ninth and tenth centuries, especially in the fields of law, liturgy, and theology, as evidenced in the foundational accomplishments of Saadiah ben Joseph al-Fayyūmī (d. 942), the eminent head (*ga'on*) of one of the rabbinical academies in Iraq, and in the work of North African scholars such as Isaac Israeli, Judah Ibn Quraysh, and Dunash Ibn Tamīm. But the Arabized Jews were arguably nowhere as open to participation in the wider culture nor as productive in remaking Jewish culture as in al-Andalus from the mid-tenth through the mid-twelfth centuries. Not only did Andalusi Jews deepen the engagement with Arabic verse and adab works, scientific learning, mystical piety, and speculative thought, but they also composed poetry and wrote metaphysical works and scientific studies of general interest in Arabic. By the middle of the eleventh century, their contribution to scientific tradition was impressive enough to warrant review in Ṣā'id al-Andalusī's (d. 1069) *Ṭabaqāt al-umam* (Categories of Nations), where the grammarian Jonah Ibn Janāḥ (b. c. 990) is said to have possessed "an immense knowledge of Arabic and Hebrew," and the erudite courtier Abū l-Faḍl Ibn Ḥasdai (Saragossa, eleventh century) is credited with having "learned with precision the Arabic language, its rhetoric, and the composition of poetry" (88–90), a judgment corroborated by Moses Ibn Ezra, who refers to him as having "a perfect mastery of poetry and sermonic discourse in Hebrew and Arabic" (68 [38b]).

Andalusi Jews, including a woman named Qasmūna, composed Arabic poetry sufficiently noteworthy to be transmitted by al-Maqqarī in his presentation on the literary merits of the people of al-Andalus (3:522–30). Collections of Andalusi-Arabic lyrics include verses of at least eleven Jewish poets. Abū Ayyūb ibn al-Mu'allim, a physician and scholar of religious law who "performs sorcery in both languages [i.e., Arabic and Hebrew]," according to Moses Ibn Ezra (78 [42b]), is represented in Ibn Sa'īd's anthology, *Rāyāt al-mubarrizīn wa-ghāyāt al-mumayyazīn* (Banners of the Champions and Standards of the Elite) (134–35; Stern, "Arabic Poems"). Ibrāhīm ibn Sahl al-Ishbīlī (d. 1251) was an important Andalusi-Arabic poet and courtier of Jewish origin who converted to Islam. Some Arabic poems composed by Jews did not find their way into collections of Arabic verse and did not survive. For example, Joseph Ibn Nagrila (d. 1066) relates that as a young lad he received a little set of Arabic poems from his father, Samuel Ibn Nagrila (Samuel the

Nagid), for him to master (Jarden 66). Indeed, the great Andalusi historian Ibn Ḥayyān presents the elder Ibn Nagrila as follows: "He wrote in both languages, Arabic and Hebrew. He knew the literatures of both peoples. He went deeply into the principles of the Arabic language and was familiar with the works of the most subtle grammarians" (Ibn al-Khaṭīb 1:438; Schippers, *Spanish Hebrew Poetry* 54–55). Joseph seems to have followed his father's example, for Moses Ibn Ezra observes that "after Hebraica, his knowledge was greatest in Arabic lore, its language, poetry, popular songs, history, historiography and traditions" (66 [35a]). It is worth noting that al-Maqqarī also reports of Andalusi Jews engaged in the study of Arabic grammar, although he does not mention either Ibn Nagrila in this regard but Ibrāhīm ibn Sahl (5:69).

Other sources and texts also seem to establish individual Jews as participants in a shared Andalusi cultural experience. Reports of individuals such as Abū l-Naṣr al-Manṣūr, apparently a Jewish musician employed at the Umayyad court of al-Ḥakam I (d. 822) (Ashtor 1:66–67; al-Maqqarī 3:124–25), indicate the involvement of Andalusi Jews in the general cultural life during the ninth century, more than a century before we are able to speak of an Andalusi-Jewish literary culture. Solomon Ibn Gabirol, a literary intellectual of the eleventh century, is best known to Jewish history as a philosophically minded Andalusi-Hebrew poet. But apart from his resplendent collection of Hebrew devotional poems and singularly original (secular) diwan, Ibn Gabirol appears as a writer of Arabic speculative and ethical works. *The Source of Life* (Lat. *Fons vitae*; Heb. *Meqor ḥayyim*), whose original is lost, is expressly devoted to general philosophy with barely a mention of concerns specific to Judaism; *Iṣlāḥ al-akhlāq ʿalā rāʾy afāḍil al-ḥukamaʾ al-mutaqaddimīn* (Improvement of the Moral Qualities), which was copied in Arabic script, treats ethical issues associated with each of the five senses. Biblical proof texts are cited, but only in support of the philosophical presentation (Wise; Tobi 294). According to recent discoveries from the Cairo Geniza, Ibn Gabirol may well have authored a collection of Arabic aphorisms that has survived only in Hebrew as *Mivḥar ha-peninim* (Choice Pearls) (Ben-Shammai). Similarly, Moses Maimonides (b. 1138) significantly contributed to several fields of medical research, and his youthful clarification of philosophical terminology, *Maqāla fī ṣināʿat al-manṭiq* (Treatise on the Art of Logic), appears to have been addressed to a Muslim dignitary and scholar of religious law (Kraemer, "Maimonides" 77–78).

In the final analysis, however, Andalusi-Jewish culture is not remembered for the few Arabic works authored by Jews and directed to a general, as opposed to a specifically, Jewish audience. More particularly, the Jews of al-Andalus turned from a narrowly traditional, rabbinic homiletic and legal intellectual regimen to strictly rationalist methods of studying their own heritage. They cultivated an ambitious program of Arabic-language, Hebrew, and Bible-centered studies (grammar, philology/lexicography, textual exegesis, and systematic theology) that far eclipsed the first efforts in this field undertaken during the ninth and tenth centuries in Iraq, Palestine, and North Africa. Although many important Arabic texts from this period have been lost, fragments discovered in the Cairo Geniza provide us with sufficient material to speak of established circles of philologists, grammarians, exegetes, pietists, and philosopher-theologians who contributed surpassing Arabic-language philological and grammatical studies on Hebrew, commentaries on the twenty-four books of the Hebrew Bible, and devotional and systematic philosophical reflections on Jewish belief. With the exception of Moses Maimonides, who spent the first part of his life in al-Andalus before fleeing to the Maghrib, none were polymaths on the order of Ibn Ḥazm, at least according to the reckoning of extant works. But Andalusi-Jewish scholars commanded every learned discipline of the period: the aforementioned Samuel the Nagid (966–1056) was a grammarian, exegete, talmudic scholar, and an Arabic and Hebrew poet; Isaac Ibn Ghiyāth (d. 1089), the preeminent rabbinic authority of the talmudic academy at Lucena, was a grammarian, exegete, and Hebrew poet; Judah Halevi, a physician, theologian, and Hebrew poet; and Abraham Ibn Ezra (d. 1164), a mathematician, astronomer, grammarian, philosopher, exegete, translator/adaptor, and poet, and among the first intellectuals profoundly involved in Arabic learning to write exclusively in Hebrew.

Arabic works by these and other figures attained canonical status in Jewish tradition, largely through Hebrew adaptations produced for the benefit of communities beyond *dār al-islām*. Notable among these translated texts are Baḥya Ibn Paquda's manual of Jewish piety, *al-Hidāya ilā farā'iḍ al-qulūb* (Book of Direction to the Duties of the Heart), Jonah Ibn Janāḥ's two-part Hebrew grammar, *Kitāb al-luma*ʿ (Book of Radiance) and *Kitāb al-uṣūl* (Book of Hebrew Roots), Judah Halevi's enthusiastic defense of rabbinic Judaism, *Kitāb al-radd wa l-dalīl fī l-dīn al-dhalīl/al-Kitāb al-khazarī* (Book of Refutation and Proof: On the Abased Faith/The Khazarian Book), and *Dalālat al-ḥā'irīn* (Guide of the Perplexed) by Moses Maimonides. On account of these works and their liturgical and secular Hebrew poetry, the Andalusi Jews' literary legacy came to be deemed the most significant manifestation of Jewish culture under Islam, the cultural products of what was later deemed the Golden Age.

What is the significance of the Andalusi Jews' engagement with and participation in Arabo-Islamic culture and the particularly Jewish purposes to which they applied the language and intellectual and spiritual agenda of the dominant culture? Andalusi-Jewish literary culture across the disciplines is typically presented as a reflection of Arabo-Islamic "influence" (e.g., Halkin, "Judeo-Arabic Literature"; Vajda; Dana, "Influence"; Schippers, *Spanish Hebrew Poetry* 2–3), or as an imitative, competitive, or defensive reaction to the Jews' minority status as *dhimmīs* within the Muslim polity of al-Andalus (Schippers, "Arabic"; Ratzaby 331–32). Developments in Judeo-Arabic poetics and in Hebrew language and Bible-centered studies at the center of the Andalusi-Jewish curriculum are frequently portrayed as apologetic or polemical in nature if not altogether accommodating toward the prestigious and appealing majority culture. In particular, Moses Ibn Ezra, the author of four Arabic works on Andalusi-Jewish poetics and cultural history (two of which have come down to us), is singled out for embracing Arabo-Islamic cultural norms to the point of literary assimilation (Allony).

For all their apparent differences, these approaches share a set of reflexive assumptions about the significance of the Jews' Arabization in al-Andalus. It is, after all, far easier to describe texts and identify their ties to Arabic sources as "influences" and "reactions" borne out of the Jews' minority status than to attempt a more nuanced conceptualization of the Jews' complex interaction with Arabic culture in al-Andalus. So long as the Arabo-Islamic culture and society of al-Andalus are couched almost exclusively in terms of religious identity, it will always appear as though the Jews were marginal, on the outside looking in, overwhelmed by, reacting to, and dependent on the dominant majority culture. It follows according to the most extreme formulation of this approach that their Judeo-Arabic culture will seem the symbiosis of "two wholly separate cultures" (Blau, *Emergence* 35) – a culture by Andalusi Jews that happens to be written in Arabic, a linguistic accident, as it were, in which the language of discourse implies little about cultural identity. If we insist on reading everything the Jews wrote in terms of a religious identity consciously in opposition to Islam, we can conjure plenty of evidence from polemical and theological texts, liturgical poetry, and occasional writings to reinforce a sense of the Jews' otherness and their separation from fellow speakers, readers, and writers of Arabic in al-Andalus. I do not mean to minimize that sense of otherness or the historical experience that informed it. But such conscious reflections on their religious and literary identity in al-Andalus, although highly significant, account for only part of the cultural reality and may reflect, among other things, a sense of intellectual and religious embattlement and the Jews' unease over their linguistic, cultural, and social assimilation whose dangers were all too apparent (Kraemer, "Andalusian Mystic" 62).

From the middle of the tenth century until the dislocation of the Jewish communities of al-Andalus under the Almohads (c. 1145), a clear division of linguistic functions is said to have prevailed in the making of Jewish culture: Hebrew was reserved almost exclusively for literary-aesthetic functions (i.e., for devotional and secular poetry, and ornate, formal rhymed prose) and Arabic for various communicative functions (Drory, "Words" 61–63). Even Hebrew literary intellectuals such as Solomon Ibn Gabirol and Judah Halevi, who professed ideological commitments to Hebrew, were swept along by the reality of life in a society dominated by the compelling power and appeal of Arabic learning, as well as by the ease of expressing themselves in the spoken language of their country.

Texts seemingly resistant to one of the dominant Arabo-Islamic cultural paradigms and taken as evidence, say, of Jewish pietism, dissatisfaction with life in a Muslim society, or contention with Islam were also written in Arabic and are equally reflective of the way that language is embedded in their own textual experience and inner consciousness. That is the ironic significance of the reticulation of Ibn Paquda's work of Jewish ethics and stinging social critique (*al-Hidāya ilā farāʾiḍ al-qulūb*; Safran) with Sufi terms and ideas (Goldreich), or the inventive Judaizing intersection of Judah Halevi's aforementioned defense of rabbinic Judaism (a work religiously critical of the Aristotelian worldview associated with Ibn Bājja's philosophy) with conceptual elements and terminology of Ismāʿīlī (Shiite) tradition (Pines; Lobel). Even in the restricted domain of Jewish law (in the form of responsa, talmudic treatises, synthetic legal commentaries, and systematic digests of halakah), the Arabic language served as a mediator of Arabo-Islamic culture and the point of interface between Arabo-Islamic and Jewish culture (Goitein, "Interplay"; Libson 235). Rather than viewing the Jews' Arabization as a sign of external "influence," perhaps we can take it as evidence of their circumscribed cultural convergence within the multiethnic, multireligious configuration of Andalusi society.

Counter to models treating Andalusi-Jewish culture as self-contained and segregated, as an expression of the Jews' minority status, or as their defensive reaction to Arabic influence, the impulse to produce and consume Arabic and Hebrew culture has been studied as a sign of the ambiguity and conflict central to Andalusi-Jewish identity (Scheindlin, "Rabbi"; Brann, *Compunctious Poet*). It has also been presented as evidence of a simultaneous cultural closeness and distance (Wasserstein, *Rise and Fall* 216, 219), and a symbiotic cultural duality of Jewish and Arabic elements cultivated by Andalusi-Jewish elites (Scheindlin, *Gazelle* 3–6; Goitein, *Jews and Arabs* 131–67). Another of the more considered interpretive paradigms put forward speaks of "literary contacts" and "cultural interference" producing Judeo-Arabic including Andalusi-Jewish culture (Drory, "Literary Contacts").

These approaches have the benefit of moving literary history beyond notions of the "influence" one culture exerts on another, especially when it comes to the complex relationship among majority and minority cultures. Nevertheless, the literary historians' principal focus on texts tends to call attention to instances of direct literary influence or outright imitation (Drory, "Literary Contacts" 278–79), especially as literary activity is reflected in new poetic styles, literary genres, or specifically appropriated analytic methods and discursive terminologies.

If we set out to determine what Andalusi Jews were reading, say Jonah Ibn Janāḥ as a student of al-Sībawayhī or al-Mubarrad, Ibn Paquda as a reader of al-Muḥāsibī, or Solomon Ibn Gabirol, the Neoplatonic thinker and poet, as a possible devotee of *Rasāʾil ikhwān al-ṣafāʾ*, we are certain to find ourselves drawn to traces of texts, to specific literary models and their "contacts" and "influences," because what an author reads always conditions and informs what he thinks and writes. Such an approach, however unavoidable for the literary historian or the historian of religion, essentializes textual traces and inadvertently obscures the internalization of culture through language – in this case, the internal processing of Arabic that preceded and then accompanied the consumption and production of Arabic texts among the Jews of al-Andalus. Accordingly, the Andalusi Jews' own literary output is not only textual evidence of their literary contacts or conscious efforts at grafting the stuff of Arabo-Islamic culture onto their own tradition but also the resultant end product of the otherwise undetectable process of their Arabization.

Before the emergence of their literary culture in the mid-tenth century, the Jews of al-Andalus had been speaking Arabic for generations and thereby came to think in and view the world through the medium of that language. As Frantz Fanon put it, "to speak a language is to take on a world, a culture" (38). Because language structures reality through preexistent cognitive ingredients thereby informing the experience of its speakers (Berger and Luckman), Andalusi-Jewish culture cannot be reduced to the studied, conscious application of Arabo-Islamic terminology, discursive forms, and modes of thought to the essence of Jewish tradition. Rather, their literary culture also represents their instinctive, creative refraction of the language, forms, and substance of Arabo-Islamic learning in the form of a Jewish subcultural adaptation and thus amounts to textual evidence of the Jews' occasionally shared participation in Andalusi intellectual life.

Apart from their specifically religious observances, practices, beliefs, and their distinctive sense of history, the Jews' Arabization fully integrated them into the pluralistic Andalusi scene. Arabic language and culture not only surrounded the Jews in the speech and writings of their Muslim (and

Christian) neighbors so as to influence them as cultural others; but also and more pertinently, Arabic was the linguistic medium central to the Andalusi-Jewish experience. Indeed, it was the agency responsible for their intellectual and social integration, which along with their full participation in the political economy of al-Andalus and their inspired attachment to the country they called Sefarad marked them as Andalusis.

Led by a class of international merchants with an acute interest in the life of the mind, the Jews' thorough social and economic integration fostered relationships with Andalusi Muslims, the details of which have been preserved in the documents of the Cairo Geniza and studied by S. D. Goitein in his magisterial *Mediterranean Society* (see also Constable 54–62, 85–96). Surviving accounts of cultural liaisons involve physicians, scientists, and philosophers where the field of knowledge was decidedly interconfessional. That is the context of Moses Maimonides' notice of having "read texts" "under the guidance" of one of Ibn Bājja's pupils (2:268). Reports of several close cultural encounters have also been transmitted in historical and literary sources, giving us a glimpse of the nexus between the Jews' socioeconomic integration and their participation in Andalusi culture. Ibn Bassam relates that a Jew named Joseph Ibn Isḥāq al-Isrāʾīlī apparently belonged to a literary circle led by the distinguished poet Abū ʿĀmir Ibn Shuhayd. The master poet is said to have appreciated the Jew's intelligence and literary talent, especially after he bested a Muslim in a poetic contest (1:233; Ashtor 3:98). In *Ṭawq al-ḥamāma* (The Dove's Neckring), Ibn Shuhayd's close friend Ibn Ḥazm mentions his fraternizing visits with a Jewish physician and herbalist in Almería (67). Of course, such encounters could be contentious rather than collegial. Ibn Ḥazm reports in *al-Fiṣal fī l-milal* (Book of Schisms and Sects) having had exchanges of both varieties with Jewish scholars, including his meetings with Samuel Ibn Nagrila (1:152–53).

Moses Ibn Ezra's abundant references to the Qurʾan in *Kitāb al-muḥāḍara wa l-mudhākara* (Book of Conversation and Deliberation) indicate that Andalusi Jews had ready access to this material and learned from it. On occasion, they even called on such knowledge in surprisingly frank discussions with Muslims, as demonstrated by Ibn Ezra's famous and implicitly polemical exchange with a "great Islamic scholar" on the problem of translating the Ten Commandments and the *Fātiḥa* (Opening) respectively (Rosenthal 19; Ibn Ezra 42–44 [24a]]). The account of this episode tacitly presents the Hebrew Bible as a kind of "Jewish Qur'an," a construct made explicit elsewhere when Ibn Ezra refers to the Hebrew Bible as *umm al-kitāb*, *nuṣūṣ*, or simply *qurʾān* (28 [15b], 254 [133b], 54 [29a]).

Another compelling illustration of the Andalusi Jews' direct intellectual engagement with Muslims is available in Joseph Ibn ʿAqnīn's (b. Barcelona, twelfth century) *Inkishāf al-asrār wa-ẓuhūr al-anwār* (Revelation of the Secrets and the Appearance of the Lights), a philosophical commentary on the biblical Song of Songs replete with references to Arabic poetry and speculative thought. Ibn ʿAqnīn relates an incident involving the Andalusi-Jewish physician Abū l-Ḥasan Meir Ibn Qamniʾel in which Ibn Qamniʾel witnessed another Jewish physician present an exoteric view of the Song of Songs before the Almoravid emir Ibn Tāshfīn. Appalled at what he viewed as an ill-informed colleague's foolish performance, Ibn Qamniʾel interceded to convince the emir of the sacred text's properly spiritualized reading. His preferred hermeneutic approach proved to be *taʾwīl* (490), the interreligious method familiar to Muslims, Christians, and Jews alike. Other examples could be offered, but in each of these instances Andalusi Jews can be observed "speaking the same language" as their Muslim informants, counterparts, and interlocutors, regardless of the differing contexts and subject matters at hand. By "speaking the same language," I mean not merely Arabic but various representative Arabo-Islamic discursive languages and idioms put to use in the elaboration of Jewish culture.

The reports of close cultural encounters and the literary activity across the disciplines briefly surveyed permit us to identify the Jews of al-Andalus as part-time members of a larger linguistic community without impermeable religious boundaries. They spoke the Andalusi dialect of Middle Arabic, wrote in various stylistic registers (shifting along the continuum of Arabic multiglossia), differing from their Muslim neighbors in supplementing their speech and writings with Hebrew (and Aramaic) loanwords of obvious religious significance and in their preference for writing Arabic in the Hebrew script (Goitein, *Mediterranean* 1:16; Hary 77). That language as well as religion and ties to place served as principal emblems of the Arabized Jews' self-definition is suggested in works Maimonides composed after leaving Spain. Where his usage differs from the closely related Egyptian Maghribi Arabic, Maimonides refers to the Andalusi dialect with the phrase *ʿindanā fī l-andalus* (Blau, "Maimonides"). Maimonides' practice appears to illustrate the secondary linguistic grounding of the concept of *waṭan*, the attachment to homeland that may have transcended religious community (Goitein, *Mediterranean* 2:274; Constable 57).

The interpretative paradigm outlined represents the Arabized culture of the Jews of al-Andalus as a rereading and rewriting of their tradition in Arabic according to the literary and cultural conventions of that language. They were doing what comes naturally and authentically – reflecting on their religious tradition through their spoken language according to the preferred intellectual methods and literary models of their time and place. Looked at in this way, the consequence of the Jews' Arabization was the deep penetration of

Arabic discursive vocabulary, literary genres, the conceptual frameworks of adab and *ḥikma* along with the absorption of the aesthetic, rhetorical, and philosophical values of Andalusi Arabo-Islamic culture.

How exactly did Arabic play out in the inner and intellectual life of the Andalusi Jews and what consequences followed for the articulation of Andalusi-Jewish culture in Arabic and Hebrew? S. D. Goitein frequently observed we are almost entirely in the dark about Jewish existence under Islam, including a detailed picture of linguistic and cultural practice, before the tenth century by which time Jewish society, institutions, and culture had already been radically reshaped (*Jews and Arabs* 89–90). The available textual evidence suggests that a relatively small group of Andalusi-Jewish elites emerged during the middle of the tenth century. The figure usually associated with the appearance of an elite class of producers and consumers of Jewish culture in al-Andalus is Ḥasdai Ibn Shaprut (d. 975), a physician, secretary, and diplomat at the court of ʿAbd al-Raḥmān III (Ṣāʿid al-Andalusī 88–89) also known for supposedly collaborating on an Arabic translation of a Greek pharmaceutical treatise. Ibn Shaprut's status at the Umayyad court doubtlessly contributed to his unparalleled authority within Andalusi-Jewish society for whom he is said to have established al-Andalus as an independent center of Jewish communal authority, learning, and culture (Ibn Ezra 56 [30a–b]). He further engaged in ambitious intercommunal correspondence with or on behalf of the Jews of other lands, notably the Khazars of the Caucasus region (incidentally the subject of considerable interest on the part of the Jews of al-Andalus), the ecumenical authorities of the Jewish community in Iraq, and the wife of the Byzantine emperor. Ibn Shaprut thus established a pattern of looking after communal interests, fostering literary patronage and in some cases religious scholarship that served as a model for high-minded Jewish courtiers during the period of the party kings: the inimitable Samuel Ibn Nagrila (Zirid Granada), Abraham Ibn al-Muhājir (Abbadid Seville), and Abū l-Faḍl Ibn Ḥasdai (Hudid Saragossa), who ultimately converted to Islam.

Apart from research in mathematics, astronomy, geography, and medicine, the Andalusi Jews' first surviving literary endeavors in specifically Jewish areas of cultural enterprise were apparently conducted in Hebrew rather than Arabic. Ibn Shaprut's own secretary, Menaḥem Ibn Saruq, for example, compiled a dictionary of biblical Hebrew in Hebrew and drafted ornate Hebrew epistles for his patron. Interest in language as the object of rational inquiry was the impetus for compiling the dictionary, and it was clearly dictated by the Arabo-Islamic as well as the specifically Jewish cultural environment. Critical factors were the challenges posed to Jewish literary intellectuals by biting Muslim criticism of biblical anthropomorphisms and penetrating questions about the reliability of the text as an authentic Scripture, sectarian conflict between contending Rabbanite and Karaite versions of Judaism, and the Arabo-Islamic investment in elegant poetic expression and style as signs of the religiously perfect properties of Arabic. Thus, the self-proclaimed purpose of Ibn Saruq's *Maḥberet* (Dictionary) is "to demonstrate the elegance of Hebrew" (1 [l. 17]).

It is clear that Andalusi-Jewish literary intellectuals consciously cultivated Hebrew language and biblical studies (as well as Hebrew poetry; see below) to set themselves apart from other Andalusis. But regardless of their cultural ideology and professed linguistic commitments, the questions Ibn Saruq and all Andalusi-Jewish literati asked indicate they were thinking in terms of Arabo-Islamic categories. In this instance, the concept of *ṣaḥot ha-lashon* (precision and beauty of language), the Hebrew parallel of the Arabic terms *faṣāḥa* and *balāgha*, had become pivotal to the Andalusi Jews' understanding of their religious culture. The rabbis of classical Judaism certainly held the view that the Hebrew language was unique, but until Saadiah Gaon's Hebrew grammar *Kitāb faṣīḥ lughat al-ʿibrāniyyīn* (Book of Elegance of the Language of the Hebrews) presented the language and style of the Hebrew Bible as intrinsically eloquent and elegant (Drory, *Emergence* 175–76), its implications had never been systematically explored nor its consequences fully pursued in a cultural program such as the Andalusi Jews conceived and practiced.

Earlier tenth-century Maghribi scholars such as David ben Abraham al-Fāsī (*Jāmiʿ al-alfāẓ* [Compilations of Words]) and Ibn Quraysh (*Risālat yehuda ibn quraysh* [Epistle of Judah Ibn Quraysh]) conducted Arabic-language comparative philology in researching biblical Hebrew. But the redoubtable Ibn Saruq ordained that the language of research remain the language of tradition, as though it were possible to confine the study of Jewish texts to a Jewish language within a hermetically sealed Jewish framework. Similarly, Ibn Saruq was among the first to compose Hebrew poetry on social themes, dedicating several poems to his patron Ḥasdai Ibn Shaprut. The traditional form and prosody of Ibn Saruq's verse would soon give way to a new model inspired by Arabic, yet its subject matter already represents the poet's and patron's assimilation to the sociocultural environment of the Umayyad court. Classical literary Hebrew was to serve as the principal sign of the Andalusi Jews' newfound aesthetically minded literary identity, an identity that makes sense only in the context established by Arabic culture and Muslim society.

If Arabic-language scientific research, philosophical and theological works, and the interpretation and dissemination of Jewish law proliferated, broadening the areas of interaction between Arabo-Islamic and Jewish culture, why did Ibn Saruq's party staunchly oppose referring to Arabic in analyzing Hebrew (Sáenz-Badillos, *Tešubot* 88 [Hebrew])? Apparently, the problem for the traditionalists rested on the religious implications of comparative method. They would not consciously equate Arabic, the language of divine revelation for Muslims, with Hebrew, the holy language of Scripture for Jews.

The arrival in Córdoba of Dunash ben Labrat (tenth century), a savant and poet from the Muslim East who joined Ibn Shaprut's entourage, seems to have catalyzed debate over the place of Arabic learning and language in the articulation of Andalusi-Jewish culture. Just as committed to Hebrew language studies as their conservative counterparts, those who championed comparative grammar and philology sought a balance between Hebrew and Arabic learning that meant finding the proper function for each in Andalusi-Jewish cultural life (Drory, "Words" 56–63). An epigram attributed to Dunash ben Labrat captures that balance with poetic symmetry: "Let your Garden be the Books of the Pious, your Paradise the books of the Arabs" (93). Ben Labrat's essential contribution to this initial stage in the development of Andalusi-Jewish literary culture was twofold. He assailed Ibn Saruq's philological method and insisted on the necessity and advantage of recourse to Arabic cognates and morphologies (Sáenz-Badillos, *Tešubot* 88 [Hebrew]); he also devised a means for transposing the quantitative meters of Arabic poetry to Hebrew that had long since lost the phonological distinctions between long and short vowels. Ibn Saruq's students took issue with the prosodic innovation as with comparative philology, but it quickly caught on among a Jewish aristocracy reared on the sensory and imaginative pleasures of Arabic verse.

Here was a defining moment in Andalusi-Jewish literary history: from this point on, the form, structure, and style of Hebrew poetry were inextricably linked to Arabic; and the next generation of grammarians and exegetes not only utilized their intimate knowledge of Arabic as Ben Labrat had done but readily expressed themselves in Arabic as a principle language of Jewish culture. Moses Ibn Gikatilla (eleventh century), the author of Arabic language works on Hebrew grammar and biblical exegesis whom Moses Ibn Ezra commends as a learned authority and the foremost connoisseur of discourse and poetry in "both languages" (68 [35b]), explains that the grammarians simply had to employ Arabic in order thoroughly to investigate and explain the details of Hebrew because this was the language everyone understood (Nutt 1). And Arabic was not nearly so foreign as some would have it. In Jonah Ibn Janāḥ's words: "for Arabic, after Aramaic, is the language which most resembles ours" (8).

The most significant methodological advance belonged to Judah Ḥayyūj (d. c. 1000), the first grammarian to realize that the Arabic system of triliteral roots applied to Hebrew. Without explicitly explaining his method, Ḥayyūj put this insight to use in *Kitāb al-afʿāl fī ḥurūf al-līn* (Weak and Geminative Verbs in Hebrew), a work that served as the basis for subsequent research on the behavior of Hebrew. The limitations of Ḥayyūj's method and the unfinished business of his work emboldened Hebrew grammarians of the next generation when a group led by Samuel Ibn Nagrila in Granada aligned itself against a rival party in Saragossa headed by Jonah Ibn Janāḥ. Grammar and philology, of course, were not abstract sciences in this scriptural community any more than among the classical Arabic grammarians of Basra and Kufa. Rather, their raison d'être was to serve as the principal hermeneutic tools for enlightened scriptural exegesis. In any case, the seemingly arcane and decidedly contentious controversies among Hebrew grammarians indicate the extent to which rereading the biblical text had become a matter for rational debate. We can appreciate the significance of such disputes in another way as well. In the contested spaces of Andalusi-Jewish religious, literary, and intellectual life, scholars engaged one another's philosophical, philological, and exegetical assumptions and positions by using all of the discourses and methods developed in Arabo-Islamic culture. Whereas the divergence of these discourses and the rifts within and among their partisans were sources of anxiety for Andalusi Jews, the literary historian discerns in their variety an unmistakable sign of cultural vitality.

Drawing on the tools of Hebrew grammar and philology, Andalusi exegetes engaged the biblical text in a fundamentally new way. They too frequently disagreed over textual explications or the nuances and limits of their method. For instance, Judah Ibn Balʿam (end of eleventh century), a philologist (e.g., *Kitāb al-tajnīs* [Book of Paronomasia]), grammarian (*Kitāb ḥurūf al-maʿānī* [Book of Particles]), and exegete (*Kitāb al-tarjīḥ* [Book of Decision] on the Torah; *Nukat al-miqra'* [Niceties of Scripture] on the Prophets and Writings), directs polemical barbs at Isaac Ibn Ghiyāth's commentary on Ecclesiastes (*Kitāb al-zuhd* [Book of Asceticism]). He also levels withering attacks against Moses Ibn Gikatilla, whose grammatical (*Kitāb al-tadhkīr wa l-ta'nīth* [Book of Masculine and Feminine]) and exegetical works were apparently very influential as well as controversial, but survive only in fragments and in numerous citations preserved in the Hebrew canonical biblical commentaries of Abraham Ibn Ezra. Ibn Gikatilla's literary sensibility as a reader of Scripture is especially noteworthy in the history of Andalusi-Jewish letters. He departed radically from tradition in his historicizing treatment of biblical prophecies and in approaching the Book of Psalms as prayers and poems rather than prophecies (Simon 113–44). In Ibn Gikatilla's reading of the biblical text, one recognizes an Andalusi's attention to the aesthetic qualities of language and style within a rationalistic conceptual framework that are the signs of adab and *ḥikma* respectively.

Does recognizing that the work of the grammarians and exegetes signals a contest over meaning between the Jews and Muslims (and frequently among the Jews themselves) completely account for the significance of their efforts to appreciate the refined style of the Hebrew Bible? Or can we identify in the venture of the grammarians, lexicographers, and exegetes additional evidence of how Arabo-Islamic norms and values penetrated the inner life of Andalusi Jews through the Arabic language, transforming the way they perceived and experienced language itself? An inspired illustration of this transformation is Moses Ibn Ezra's comment on a biblical simile (Lam. 4:7, "Her elect were purer than snow, Whiter than milk," or according to a variant reading, Song of Songs 4:3, "like a scarlet thread are your lips"). Finding the turn of phrase particularly lovely, the poet-critic exults, "Were Lamentations (or the Song of Songs) to challenge (the Book of) Ecclesiastes with this verse, it would prevail thereby!" (258 [134a–b]; Dana, *Poetics* 151). The distinctive literary sensibility evident in Ibn Ezra's enthusiastic remark reminds us that appreciation of beauty and the experience of literary pleasure are culturally determined categories, as conventional as language, and therefore emblematic of the Andalusi Jews' new internalized aesthetic.

A recurrent theme of literary life was the Andalusi Jews' abiding belief in the singularity of their cultural identity predicated on their fidelity to *ṣaḥot ha-lashon.* Ibn Janāḥ and Moses Ibn Ezra, for example, aver that the Jews of al-Andalus were descended from the Jews of Judaea. The Andalusis saw themselves as heirs to the Judaeans' superior guardianship over the Hebrew language as asserted in a talmudic interpretation (ʿEruvin 53a) of a biblical source (ʿObadiah v. 20) (Ibn Janāḥ 6; Ibn Ezra 54–55 [29a–b]). Noble lineage and their claim to an incomparable cultural tradition distinguished the Andalusis markedly from Jewish communities of other lands – an Andalusi-Jewish variation on the Arabic topos *faḍāʾil ahl al-andalus*:

> There is no doubt at all that the inhabitants of Jerusalem, from whom we – members of the Spanish exile – are descended, were more knowledgeable in rhetorical eloquence and in rabbinic tradition than the residents of other cities and towns.
>
> (Ibn Ezra 54 [29b])

Reflecting on the history of Andalusi-Jewish letters, Moses Ibn Ezra thus identifies historical and intrinsic factors that account for the revival of interest in classical Hebrew and the reemergence of biblicizing literary Hebrew style. On one hand, Ibn Ezra attributes the renascence to the Jews' intimate knowledge of Arabic and ascribes its success to Ḥayyūj's detection of the triliteral root; on the other hand, the discovery of that fundamental "inner principle" reveals the handiwork of Providence (56 [29b]).

As in other cultural undertakings, historically minded literary intellectuals attempted to find precedents in biblical Israel for their contemporary interests in poetry, philosophy, and other cultural endeavors – a recovery process that neatly converged with their focus on the Hebrew Bible as the stylistic and linguistic basis for Jewish cultural life. Take musical performance and theory for example. Grounded in the musical theory developed by the Ikhwān al-Ṣafāʾ and al-Fārābī, works such as Moses Ibn Ezra's *Maqālat al-ḥadīqa fī maʿnāl-majāz wa l-ḥaqīqa* (The Garden: On the Figurative and the Literal), a philosophical examination of the poetic language of the Hebrew Bible, and Joseph Ibn ʿAqnīn's *Ṭibb al-nufūs* (Hygiene of the Soul), a compendium of ethical aphorisms from Jewish and non-Jewish sources, contain passages devoted to the importance of music in Judaism going back to the Levites in the Temple service.

No discussion of the Arabized Jews of al-Andalus would be complete without reference to their Hebrew verse and its intimate relationship with Arabic poetry and its poetics. How does their Hebrew poetry, the Andalusi Jews' sovereign literary achievement, fit into the scheme of circumscribed cultural fusion suggested in this essay? The most obvious examples of the complex process of literary appropriation by Andalusi-Hebrew literary intellectuals are Dunash ben Labrat's arabicizing quantitative prosody, contrefaction (*muʿāraḍa*) of the prosodic and melodic patterns of Arabic muwashshahs and incorporation of Arabic kharjas in Hebrew muwashshahs, intertextual references to Andalusi-Arabic poets as well as poets from the Muslim East, Hebrew translations of Arabic lyrics by al-Mutanabbī, Abū Nuwās and others, and Hebrew devotional poetry informed by the language and conceptual framework of Islamic piety (Scheindlin, "Ibn Gabirol's Poetry"). Linguistically, Arabic loan translations along with outright Arabisms of syntax and morphology strongly impressed the character of medieval Hebrew in Spain (Sáenz-Badillos, *History* 232 ff.). And Arabic superscriptions were even employed in the Andalusi-Jewish poets' Hebrew diwans. These items represent only the most accessible and immediate layer of the Jews' Arabization as manifested in their Hebrew literary activity.

Beyond these direct appropriations and practices, the Jews' Arabization is evident in Hebrew poetry in more subtle but no less significant ways. Like Arabic, Andalusi-Hebrew poetry is stylized in form and conventional in content. Its language is the classical Hebrew analyzed by the grammarians, some of whom were inspired by their high regard for the aesthetic properties of the language to practice a Hebrew artistry as poets. The forms, rhetorical style, genres, themes, and the formulation of motifs of the Hebrew lyric were all patterned after the Arabic verse that served as its background (Schippers, *Spanish Hebrew Poetry*; Levin). Poetic tradition was thus initially embodied in a preexistent canon: monorhymed and strophic Arabic poetry. It is not a coincidence that the four authoritative poets of the school, Samuel the

Nagid, Solomon Ibn Gabirol, Moses Ibn Ezra, and Judah Halevi, for all their manifest differences of temperament and style, were each masters of Arabic learning.

How much of the arabicizing aspects of Hebrew poetry can we ascribe to the poets' internalization of the form, structure, and style of Arabic verse with which the Hebrew poets were on such intimate terms? How much can we attribute to the poets' purposeful tinkering in their workshops, that is, applying Arabic conventions to the cherished biblical Hebrew they knew by rote? Perhaps the only way to begin to answer these questions is to say that Hebrew poetry in al-Andalus, its genres and their conventions, arose out of the dialectical relationship between a well-established yet still evolving Arabic tradition on one hand and its own emergent subcultural process on the other, a process that promoted biblical Hebrew as the linguistic sign of Andalusi-Jewish literary identity. The initial dependence of the Hebrew lyric on its Arabic model therefore seems at once more conscious, studied, and defensive than any area of literary activity conducted in Arabic, the Jews' spoken language.

Although Hebrew verse shared its poetics with Arabic, the languages carried different textual associations and allusions and generated different imaginative experiences for the Hebrew poets and their audience specific to Jewish history and the biblical text. Notwithstanding the literary historians' appreciation of the deep and seemingly subordinate relationship between Hebrew poetry and Arabic poetry and poetics, perhaps the nascent embrace can be defined as an operation of translation from Arabic to Hebrew. Translation theorists Susan Bassnett and André Lefevre observe:

> Translation is, of course, a rewriting of an original text. All rewritings, whatever their intention, reflect a certain ideology and a poetics and as such manipulate literature to function in a given society in a given way. Rewriting is manipulation, undertaken in the service of power, and in its positive aspect can help in the evolution of a literature and a society. Rewritings can introduce new concepts, new genres, new devices and the history of translation is the history also of literary innovation, of the shaping of power of one culture upon another. (ix)

According to this broad understanding of translation, the process of conveying meaning from one language-based poetic system into another language involves an appropriation for distinctly ideological purposes. It certainly appears that the Andalusi Jews' rewriting of the original content of Arabic poetry and poetics into the target language of biblical Hebrew involves such a manipulation. Hebrew poetry (and to a certain extent the grammarians' research on biblical Hebrew) not only signals the Jews' defensive, imitative response to the overwhelming appeal of Arabic but also is an emptying of Arabic into Hebrew – a transaction that created a poetry to serve as an expression of the poets' self-confidence as Andalusi Jews (Brann, "Power").

Hebrew poetry therefore functioned as a "discourse of power" in more than one sense: it was a sign of the Andalusis' ascendance over other Jewish communities, of the elites' control of the discourse of Jewish culture, and a subversive appropriation of Arabic culture for Jewish ideological purposes.

The culture of the Arabized Jews of al-Andalus did not come to nearly as abrupt an end as the community itself. Rather, the Jews' association with Andalusi learning was sufficiently powerful that refugees from Almohad persecution sought to carry on their traditions in Toledo where Arabic continued to serve as a spoken language. Abraham Ibn Dāʾūd's (twelfth century) *Sefer ha-qabbalah* (Book of Tradition) transmits a vignette about Samuel Ibn Nagrila's first appointment to public office in Zirid Granada (Cohen 71–72). The youthful Samuel is said to have been tucked away in a Malagan spice shop when the high-ranking *kātib* Ibn al-ʿArīf "discovered" his surpassing stylistic skill and masterful knowledge of adab. The tale, which draws on an Andalusi-Arabic account regarding al-Manṣūr (Ibn Abī ʿĀmir) preserved by al-Maqqarī (Stern, "Life" 135–38; al-Maqqarī 1:399), serves as a sign of the sociopolitical reasons for the high esteem Arabic continued to enjoy among Jews in its transplanted context through the thirteenth century (Assis).

The Jewish literary intellectuals of al-Andalus were by turns participants in a shared cultural experience and socioreligious outsiders. The contingent, situational nature of both their participation and their marginality in Andalusi society and culture illuminates the problem of the various components of Andalusi-Jewish culture in relation to Arabic, moving us away from viewing "contact" or "conflict" as the only viable paradigms accounting for the role of Arabic in the Jews' literary identity and cultural consciousness. In the ongoing conversation involving Jewish and Arabo-Islamic elements in the articulation of Andalusi-Jewish culture, Arabic language and learning can be valorized and Islam resisted or contested.

BIBLIOGRAPHY

Allony, Nehemiah. "The Reaction of Moses ibn Ezra to ʿArabiyya." *Bulletin of the Institute of Jewish Studies* 1 (1973): 19–40.

Ashtor, Eliahu. *The Jews of Moslem Spain.* 3 vols. in 2 with new introduction and bibliography by D. J. Wasserstein. Philadelphia, 1992.

Assis, Yom Tov. "The Judeo-Arabic Tradition in Christian Spain." *The Jews of Medieval Islam: Community, Society, and Identity.* Ed. Daniel Frank. Leiden, 1995. 111–24.

Bassnett, Susan, and André Lefevre, eds. *Translation, History, and Culture.* London, 1990.

Ben-Shammai, Haggai. "New Fragments from the Arabic Original of *Mivḥar ha-peninim*" [Hebrew]. *Tarbiz* 60 (1991): 577–91.

Berger, Peter L., and Thomas Luckman. *The Social Construction of Reality: A Treatise in the Sociology of Knowledge.* New York, 1967.

Blau, Joshua. *The Emergence and Linguistic Background of Judaeo-Arabic.* 2nd edn. Jerusalem, 1981.

"Maimonides, al-Andalus, and the Influence of the Spanish-Arabic Dialect on His Language." *New Horizons in Sephardic Studies.* Ed. Yedida K. Stillman and George K. Zucker. Albany, 1993. 203–10.

Brann, Ross. *The Compunctious Poet: Cultural Ambiguity and Hebrew Poetry in Muslim Spain.* Baltimore, 1991.

"Power in the Portrayal: Representations of Muslims and Jews in Judah al-Ḥarīzī's *Taḥkemoni.*" *Princeton Papers in Near Eastern Studies* 1 (1992): 1–22.

Brody, Heinrich, and Dan Pagis. *Moshe ibn ezra: Shirei ha-ḥol.* Berlin, 1935–77.

Cohen, Gerson D. *Sefer ha-Qabbalah by Ibn Daud: The Book of Tradition.* Philadelphia, 1967.

Constable, Olivia Remie. *Trade and Traders in Muslim Spain: The Commercial Realignment of the Iberian Peninsula, 900–1500.* Cambridge, 1994.

Dana, Joseph. "The Influence of Arabic Literary Culture on the Judeo-Arabic Literature of the Middle Ages as Reflected in Moses Ibn Ezra's *Kitāb al-muḥāḍara wa l-mudhākara*" [Hebrew]. *Sefunot,* n.s., 5 (1991): 21–36.

Poetics of Medieval Hebrew Literature According to Moses Ibn Ezra [Hebrew]. Jerusalem, 1982.

Drory, Rina. *The Emergence of Jewish-Arabic Literary Contacts at the Beginning of the Tenth Century* [Hebrew]. Tel Aviv, 1988.

"Literary Contacts and Where to Find Them: On Arabic Literary Models in Medieval Jewish Literature." *Poetics Today* 14 (1993): 277–302.

"'Words Beautifully Put': Hebrew versus Arabic in Tenth-Century Jewish Literature." *Genizah Research after Ninety Years: The Case of Judaeo-Arabic.* Ed. Joshua Blau and Stefan C. Reif. Cambridge, 1992. 53–66.

Dunash ben Labrat. *Shirim.* Ed. Nehemiah Allony. Jerusalem, 1947.

Fanon, Frantz. *Black Skin, White Masks.* Trans. Charles Lam Markmann. New York, 1967.

Goitein, S. D. "The Interplay of Jewish and Islamic Law." *Jewish Law in Legal History and the Modern World.* Ed. B. S. Jackson. Leiden, 1980. 61–77.

Jews and Arabs: Their Contacts through the Ages. New York, 1974.

A Mediterranean Society: The Jewish Communities of the Arab World as Portrayed in the Documents of the Cairo Genizah. Vols. 1–5. Berkeley, 1976–88.

Goldreich, Amos. "Possible Arabic Sources of the Distinction between 'Duties of the Heart' and 'Duties of the Limbs'" [Hebrew]. *Te'uda* 6 (1988): 179–208.

Halkin, Abraham S. "Judeo-Arabic Literature." *The Jews: Their Religion and Culture.* Ed. L. Finklestein. 4th edn. New York, 1971. 121–54.

"The Medieval Jewish Attitude toward Hebrew." *Biblical and Other Studies.* Ed. A. Altmann. Cambridge, Mass., 1963. 233–48.

Hary, Benjamin H. *Multiglossia in Judeo-Arabic, with an Edition, Translation, and Grammatical Study of the Cairene Purim Scroll.* Leiden, 1995.

Ibn ʿAqnīn, Joseph. *Inkishāf al-asrār wa-ẓuhūr al-anwār.* Ed. Abraham S. Halkin. Jerusalem, 1964.

Ibn Bassam. *al-Dhakhīra fī maḥāsin ahl al-jazīra.* Ed. Iḥsān ʿAbbās. 8 vols. Beirut, 1979.

Ibn Ezra, Moses. *Kitāb al-muḥāḍara wa l-mudhākara.* Ed. Abraham S. Halkin. Jerusalem, 1975.

Ibn Ḥazm. *al-Fiṣal fī l-milal wa l-ahwāʾ wa l-niḥal.* 5 vols. in 2. Cairo edn. 1899–1903. Rpt., 1964.

Ṭawq al-ḥamāma fī l-ulfa wa l-ullāf. Ed. Salāḥ al-Dīn al-Qāsimī. Baghdad, 1986.

Ibn Janāḥ, Jonah. *Kitāb al-lumaʿ (Le livre des parterres fleuris).* Ed. Joseph Derenbourg. Paris, 1886.

Ibn al-Khaṭīb. *al-Iḥāṭa fī akhbār gharnāṭa.* Ed. Muḥammad ʿAbd Allāh ʿInān. 2 vols. Cairo, 1973.

Ibn Paquda, Bahya. *al-Hidāya ilā farāʾiḍ al-qulūb.* Ed. A. S. Yahuda. Leiden, 1912.

Ibn Saʿīd, ʿAlī ibn Mūsā al-Maghribī. *Rāyāt al-mubarrizīn wa-ghāyāt al-mumayyazīn.* Ed. al-Nuʿmān ʿAbd al-Mutaʿālī al-Qāḍī. Cairo, 1973.

Ibn Saruq, Menaḥem. *Maḥberet.* Ed. Ángel Sáenz-Badillos. Granada, 1986.

Jarden, Dov, ed. *Divan shmuel hanagid: Ben tehillim.* Jerusalem, 1966.

Judah Halevi. *Kitāb al-radd wa l-dalīl fī l-dīn al-dhalīl (al-kitāb al-khazari).* Ed. David H. Baneth and Haggai Ben-Shammai. Jerusalem, 1977.

Kraemer, Joel L. "The Andalusian Mystic Ibn Hud and the Conversion of the Jews." *Israel Oriental Studies* 12 (1992): 59–73.

"Maimonides on the Philosophic Sciences in His Treatise on the Art of Logic." *Perspectives on Maimonides: Philosophical and Historical Studies.* Ed. Joel L. Kraemer. Oxford, 1991. 77–104.

Levin, Israel. *The Embroidered Coat: The Genres of Hebrew Secular Poetry in Spain* [Hebrew]. 3 vols. Tel Aviv, 1994–95.

Libson, Gideon. "Halakhah and Law in the Period of the Geonim." *An Introduction to the History and Sources of Jewish Law.* Ed. N. S. Hecht et al. Oxford, 1996. 197–250.

Lobel, Dianna Nicole. "Between Mysticism and Philosophy: Arabic Terms for Religious Experience in Yehudah Halevi's Kuzari." Diss., Harvard University, 1995.

al-Maqqarī. *Nafḥ al-ṭīb min ghuṣn al-andalus al-raṭīb.* Ed. Iḥsān ʿAbbās. 8 vols. Beirut, 1968.

Moses Maimonides. *The Guide of the Perplexed.* 2 vols. trans. with an introduction and notes by Shlomo Pines and introductory essay by Leo Strauss. Chicago, 1963.

Nutt, John William, ed. *Sheloshah sifrei diqduq.* London, 1870. Rpt., 1968.

Pines, Shlomo. "Shiʿite Terms and Conceptions in Judah Halevi's Kuzari." *Jerusalem Studies in Arabic and Islam* 2 (1980): 165–251.

Ratzaby, Yehuda. "Arabic Poetry Written by Andalusian Jews" [Hebrew]. *Israel Levin Jubilee Volume.* Ed. Reuven Tsur and Tova Rosen. Tel Aviv, 1994. 329–50.

Rosenthal, Franz. *The Classical Heritage in Islam.* Trans. Emile and Jenny Marmorstein. Berkeley, 1975.

Sáenz-Badillos, Ángel. *A History of the Hebrew Language.* Trans. John Elwolde. Cambridge, 1993.

Tešubot de Dunaš ben Labrat. Critical edn. and Spanish trans. Granada, 1980.

Safran, Bezalel. "Bahya ibn Paquda's Attitude toward the Courtier Class." *Studies in Medieval Jewish History and Literature.* Ed. Isadore Twersky. Cambridge, Mass., 1979. 154–96.

Ṣāʿid ibn Aḥmad al-Andalusī. *Kitāb ṭabaqāt al-umam.* Ed. Louis Cheikho. Beirut, 1912.

Scheindlin, Raymond P. *The Gazelle: Medieval Hebrew Poems on God, Israel, and the Soul.* Philadelphia, 1991.

"Ibn Gabirol's Religious Poetry and Sufi Poetry." *Sefarad* 54 (1994): 110–42.

"Rabbi Moshe Ibn Ezra on the Legitimacy of Poetry." *Medievalia et Humanistica,* n.s., 7 (1976): 101–15.

Wine, Women, and Death: Medieval Hebrew Poems on the Good Life. Philadelphia, 1986.

Schippers, Arie. "Arabic and the Revival of the Hebrew Language and Culture." *Jews under Islam: A Culture in Historical Perspective.* Ed. Julie Marthe-Cohen. Amsterdam, 1993. 75–93.

Spanish Hebrew Poetry and the Arabic Literary Tradition: Arabic Themes in Hebrew Andalusian Poetry. Leiden, 1994.

Simon, Uriel. *Four Approaches to the Book of Psalms: From Saadiah Gaon to Abraham ibn Ezra.* Trans. Lenn J. Schramm. Albany, 1991.

Stern, Samuel M. "Arabic Poems by Spanish-Hebrew Poets." *Romanica et Occidentalia: Etudes dédiées a la mémoire de Hiram Peri.* Ed. Moshe Lazar. Jerusalem, 1963. 254–63.

"The Life of Samuel the Nagid" [Hebrew]. *Zion* 15 (1950): 135–45.

Tobi, Yosef. "A Second Manuscript of *Kitāb iṣlāḥ al-akhlāq* by Solomon ibn Gabirol" [Hebrew]. *Hebrew and Arabic Studies in Honour of Joshua Blau.* Jerusalem, 1993.

Vajda, Georges. "Judaeo-Arabic [Judaeo-Arabic Literature]." *Encyclopaedia of Islam.* 2nd edn. Leiden, 1954–. 4:303–7.

Wasserstein, David J. "Jewish Elites in al-Andalus." *The Jews of Medieval Islam: Community, Society, and Identity.* Ed. Daniel Frank. Leiden, 1995. 101–10.

The Rise and Fall of the Party Kings: Politics and Society in Islamic Spain, 1002–1086. Princeton, 1985.

Wise, Stephen S., ed. and trans. *The Improvement of the Moral Qualities by Solomon Ibn Gabirol.* Rpt., New York, 1966.

CHAPTER 25

THE SEPHARDIM

Samuel G. Armistead

The descendants of Hispanic Jews exiled from Spain in 1492, who have retained their Spanish language and an awareness of their Iberian cultural heritage down to the present day, are, in a sense, the last representatives of the distinctive, multiethnic, trireligious society that developed and flourished in al-Andalus and later in Christian Spain during the Middle Ages. Their links to that culture and distant time can still be found in certain features of their modern heritage. Together with their continued use of the Spanish language, the religious poetry of the great masters of Golden Age Hebrew literature continues to echo, in Spanish translation, in the sacred verse of the Sephardim; the metrics of Sephardic didactic poetry and of oral lyric songs, in a number of instances, still faithfully reflect medieval Hispanic models; many Judeo-Spanish *romances* perpetuate, in both meter and subject matter, the verse and the narratives of medieval Castilian epics and their early balladic derivatives; and the Judeo-Spanish ballads still embody a few striking evocations of a medieval Hispanic trireligious society, whose memory has all but disappeared from similar oral poetry sung today on the Iberian Peninsula. On the following pages, I review the vernacular literature of the Sephardic Jews, stressing, wherever possible, the continuity between the Hispanic past and later literary and linguistic developments.

The Hispanic Jews who fled from al-Andalus to the Christian north after the Almoravid invasion (1091–1147) were probably bilingual, speaking both colloquial Hispano-Arabic and Mozarabic, the archaic Hispano-Romance dialect spoken throughout Muslim Spain during the early Middle Ages. Learned individuals were, of course, also conversant in Hebrew and in classical Arabic. During the early years of their residence in Christian territory, some Jews may perhaps have developed a distinctive form (or forms) of Jewish Spanish but, as Laura Minervini (*Testi*) has eloquently shown, by the fifteenth century, Spanish Jews wrote and undoubtedly also spoke a language that was very similar, if not essentially identical, to that of their Christian neighbors. During the first century after the diaspora, the language of exiled Hispanic Jewry must have experienced a time of great fluidity, in which various different regional dialects would compete for influence: this would be a "crucial period in the formation of the Judeo-Spanish *koiné* . . . The first texts of the Diaspora period show a deep reshaping of the communicative habits of the Sephardim" (Minervini, "Formation"). We must conclude that, in many of their characteristics, the modern Judeo-Spanish dialects, rather than being heirs to any putative and distinctive medieval Jewish Spanish, are largely – though by no means completely – a product of linguistic patterns that evolved after the exile (Révah).

Characterized by lexical and phonological archaisms, nonstandard usage, and regionalisms (including significant contributions from Portuguese), these dialects have continued to be spoken in two areas, at opposite extremes of the Mediterranean world: in the Balkans and the Near East (Bosnia, Macedonia, Bulgaria, Romania, Greece, Turkey, Israel), on one hand, and in various towns in northern Morocco, on the other. The Eastern communities developed a number of distinctive regional forms, whereas the North African towns, in close proximity one to another, spoke similar, if not altogether identical, dialects.[1] Both geographic branches of Judeo-Spanish attest to the survival of numerous phonological and lexical features characteristic of medieval Spanish. Both dialects also exhibit many Hebraisms, especially in religious writing (Bunis, *Lexicon*), but, in everyday speech, there are far fewer Hebrew loans than, for example, in Yiddish. The major postdiasporic lexical borrowings in the East are from Turkish (plus relatively few from Greek and south Slavic), while the North African dialect – the most intensely Arabized of any Romance language – has been notably enriched by massive loans from Maghribi colloquial Arabic, even involving the conservation of numerous distinctive features of Arabic phonology. The vast majority of the many Arabisms in both geographic branches of Judeo-Spanish came in by way of Turkish in the East and from North African colloquial Arabic in the West, while the number of peninsular Arabisms exclusive to Judeo-Spanish is insignificant (Armistead, "Linguistic Problems").

The exiles of 1492 included many men of great learning. In Balkan and eastern Mediterranean lands, the Sephardim were to encounter native Jewish communities where learning and literature were held in high esteem (Weinberger). Hebrew presses serving a Sephardic readership were soon established in the major centers of the Eastern diaspora. But the Sephardim were Spaniards as well as Jews and they brought with them into exile an intense interest in contemporary Spanish literature. To such tastes respond the Hebrew translations of Fernando de Rojas's *Celestina*, composed in Italy by Joseph ben Samuel Ṣarfati in 1507–8 (McPheeters) and of the first part of Garci Ordóñez de Montalvo's *Amadís de Gaula*, by Jacob ben Moses Algabbai, printed in Istanbul, between 1534 and 1546 (Sholod). Even in the mid-seventeenth century, individual Eastern Jews could still be found who maintained a lively interest in Golden Age Spanish literature (Menéndez Pidal, "Catálogo" 1053–54), but, to the Eastern communities especially, the peninsula became ever more remote and, despite the continued arrival of *conversos* bringing news and texts from contemporary Spain, literary preferences were developing in very different directions from those of the distant homeland.

Patrimonial Judeo-Spanish literature – literature with possible connections to the medieval Hispano-Jewish past – can be divided into the following categories: (1) Bible translations and liturgical writings; (2) biblical commentaries; (3) writings on Jewish doctrine and practice; (4) didactic strophic poetry (*coplas*); (5) drama; (6) oral literature (*CLS*). In the late nineteenth century, with the opening of Eastern Jewry to the West, Sephardic literature acquired various modern, Western, and previously unfamiliar genres: journalistic writings, essays, poetry by individual authors, novels – original works, as well as translations from Hebrew, French, Italian, German, Greek, English, Turkish, and Russian – and the vast majority of dramatic works. (Here we allude only to the origins of Sephardic drama, which may or may not have distant antecedents in earlier tradition.)[2]

BIBLICAL TRANSLATIONS AND LITURGICAL WRITINGS

Various Judeo-Spanish translations of the Bible, of the Pentateuch, and of individual books were published in the Sephardic East. Starting in 1540, we have an edition of the Psalms printed in Istanbul and, from 1569 on, various biblical books were published in Salonika. Here the anonymous translator may well be following some medieval Jewish-Spanish preexpulsion archetype (*CLS* 35). Destined for pious home reading, the vehicle for these translations is Ladino, a peculiar modality of Judeo-Spanish, which faithfully follows the syntax of a Hebrew (or Aramaic) original, producing a syntactic calque of the text being translated. Reserved for biblical renderings and certain liturgical texts (e.g., the Haggadah), this sacred language suggests a peculiar and decidedly non-Romance subtext (Séphiha, *Deutéronome* and *Structure*). The Ferrara Bible, printed in Italy in 1553, forms part of this same tradition. Here is the first phrase of Genesis 1:4 in Hebrew (Elliger and Rudolf), in the Ladino text of Ferrara (Lazar), and in the 1569 Catholic rendering of Casiodoro de Reina, which exhibits normal Spanish syntax:

vayar' elohim et ha'or ki ṭov.
y vido el Dio a la luz q*ue* buena.
y vio Dios que la luz era buena.
[And God saw the light, that it was good.]

The first full translation of the Bible, staying close to its antecedents, was a bilingual Hebrew-Ladino edition published in Istanbul by Abraham Asá, between 1739 and 1745. Besides Bible translations, complete and partial Judeo-Spanish renderings of Hebrew daily and festive prayers, as well as numerous translations of the *Pirke abot* (Sayings of the Fathers) and the especially beloved Passover Haggadah were published in many centers in the Sephardic East, as well as in Italy. These and other initiatives to render the holy texts, commentaries, and moralistic works in Judeo-Spanish respond to the growing perception by community leaders of a cultural, linguistic, and religious crisis among their less learned coreligionists: many Sephardim were no longer able to read or comprehend Hebrew. According to Abraham Asá, in the introduction to his translation of the Pentateuch (1739): "el hamon ha-ʿam no continaban a meldar el Arbaʿ we- ʿesrim" [the common people were no longer reading the Bible] (*CLS* 40). To understand the law, to read on the Sabbath and on holy days, is a moral duty and, ideally, Judaism involves a lifelong, ongoing process of education. The loss of the holy language thus represented a grave crisis that called for vigorous remedial action. There is here, despite the radically different conditions under which they practiced their faiths, a curious parallel between the linguistic situation of the Sephardim, living in the religious freedom of their Ottoman exile, and the Morisco crypto-Muslims, who, during the sixteenth century, continued to live in Spain, under severe Inquisitorial surveillance: both were rapidly losing a working knowledge of their holy languages and, in both cases, religious leaders felt called upon to respond to such critical conditions by creating Spanish renderings of the sacred texts and commentaries to strengthen or even keep their religion intact.

Responding to such a "mancanza de pueder entender el senso de las oraciones" (inability to understand prayers), numerous Hebrew piyyutim (hymns or liturgical poems) were translated (or, following a process of contrafaction, were adapted) into Judeo-Spanish. Elena Romero puts the known corpus of such poetry at more than eighty texts, some in unique renderings and others in various different translations of the same Hebrew piyyut (*CLS* 69–70). Together with hymns written by Sephardic liturgical poets after the exile, liturgical poetry in Spanish translation includes famous compositions by great poets of the Hispano-Hebraic Golden Age: among others, Judah Halevi, Solomon Ibn Gabirol, Moses Ibn Ezra, Abraham Ibn Ezra. Judeo-

Spanish versions of such great spiritual compositions as Halevi's *Mi khamokha* (Who Is Like unto Thee?) and Ibn Gabirol's *Keter malkhut* (Royal Crown) came to be included in the vernacular repertoire, together with those of other important preexpulsion poets: Baḥya Ibn Paquda and Shem Tob Ardutiel – the great Don Santo de Carrión, author of the *Proverbios morales* – whose lengthy *vidduy* (confession) was translated several times and became part of the Sephardic Yom Kippur service (*CLS* 73–74, 77–78; Zemke, *Critical Approaches*).

BIBLE COMMENTARY

The eighteenth century can be considered the Golden Age of Judeo-Spanish literature. The 1700s saw a sustained effort to create an exhaustive, encyclopedic commentary on the Bible, written in the vernacular and thus available to all members of the Sephardic communities. These were the years that also saw a vigorous flowering of didactic, paraliturgical poetry in Judeo-Spanish and, from 1700 on, we also have the first known manuscript copies of traditional ballad poetry, which had undoubtedly been sung in oral tradition, without solution of continuity, since before the diaspora. We witness, then, a renewed and variegated interest in literary productivity during the 1700s. In the area of biblical commentary, the great Sephardic achievement is the *Meʿam loʿez* (literally "From a people who speak a strange language"), a multivolume encyclopedia of biblical exegesis and lore, whose gradual creation, starting in 1730, lasted through to the end of the nineteenth century. Jacob Khuli, the first author of this monumental multigenerational work, sounds a familar note in explaining his motivations for creating the *Meʿam loʿez*:

> muy pocos son los que saben meldar un pasuk a las derechas . . ., siendo no entienden lashón ha-kodesh y afilú los que saben los vierbos, no entienden lo que quitan por la boca y de día en día se van apocando el meldar y olvidándose la ley de la ğente y los rižos del ğudezmo. (*CLS* 83–84)

> (Few are those who know how to read a biblical verse correctly . . ., since they do not understand Hebrew and, even if they know the words, they do not understand what they are pronouncing and they gradually limit their readings, forgetting the people's religion and the laws of Judaism.)

The *Meʿam loʿez* was created in response not only to an alarming, progressive decline in the knowledge of Hebrew, but also to even more alarming intrareligious tensions growing out of the debacle of Sabbatean messianism in the late seventeenth century, a catastrophe that shattered Jewish communities throughout Europe, leaving them riven with dissension (Nehama, vol. 5; Scholem). If similar disasters were to be avoided, the Sephardic faithful would have to be educated in religious matters and in a language they could read. Initially, the *Meʿam loʿez* reflected these concerns, but over the years, as commentaries on more and more biblical books saw publication, the work transcended its immediate purposes and became a revered, beloved source of rabbinical knowledge, moral lessons, legends, stories, anecdotes, popular wisdom, combining instruction with entertainment. The successive authors (J. Khuli, Isaac Magriso, Isaac Argüeti, Menaḥem Mitrani, and others) were constantly plagued by the problem of how to finance the publication of their large-format volumes. Elena Romero divides the *Meʿam loʿez*'s long and convoluted editorial history into three epochs: an initial, classical period (1730–77), a transitional stage (1851–70), and, finally, a new epoch (1882–99) (*CLS* 86–102).[3] The *Meʿam loʿez* also had its imitators (one, the *Meshivat nefesh* [Delight of the Soul], published in Istanbul, 1743–44, comments on Ibn Gabirol's *Azharot* [Exhortations]) and there were numerous other commentaries published in the late nineteenth and early twentieth centuries, but the *Meʿam loʿez* will remain as the masterpiece, the revered Sephardic encyclopedia of religious knowledge.

DOCTRINE AND PRACTICE

The great religious codifier, Joseph Caro, constitutes a living bridge between medieval Spain and the Sephardic diaspora. Born in Toledo in 1488, he compiled his *Shulḥan ʿarukh* (The Set Table) at Safed in 1564–65, drawing on distinguished medieval predecessors – Isaac al-Fasi and Maimonides among them. There were several Judeo-Spanish translations and adaptations of Joseph Caro's work. The prolific Moses Almosnino's classic *Regimiento de la vida*, written in Salonika and printed there, in Hebrew letters, in 1564 (and in Amsterdam, in Latin type, in 1729), is still essentially in the contemporary peninsular language and can hardly rank as postdiasporic Judeo-Spanish literature, but, even so, it cannot go unmentioned here. Note how, for all his learning, Jacob Khuli, in his introduction to the *Meʿam loʿez*, though full of admiration, confesses to having difficulty in reading Almosnino's Spanish: "sus ablas son muy seradas" (Zemke, "On Almosnino"). As with the other genres we have seen, translations of works on halakic practices and moral precepts (*musar*) were an absolute necessity for "los que no saben lashón más que ladino" (*CLS* 110). Together with numerous original works by postdiasporic Sephardic authors, there are translations of, or commentaries on, various works by medieval masters: Maimonides' *Sefer ha-miṣvot* (Book of Good Deeds); Ibn Paquda's *Sefer ḥovot ha-levavot* (Duties of the Hearts); Isaac

Aboab's *Menorat ha-ma'or* (Candlestick of Light) (*CLS* 108, 112). The *Pele yoʿeṣ* (The Wonderful Counselor), written in Hebrew by Eliezer Papo (Istanbul, 1824) and translated by his son, Judah ben Eliezer Papo (Vienna, 1870–72), offers a splendid vignette of the intimate, popular context in which such moralistic works were to be and undoubtedly were read in Sephardic communities of the Balkans and the Near East:

Cada año que lo melde en su caza con su familla, shabatot y moʿadim y nochadas largas de invierno; que se acožgan el vezindario y que lo melden ǧuntos. Las mužeres que saben meldar que acožgan las amigas y parientas y que lo melden con ellas. (*CLS* 115)

(Each person should read [this book] in his home, with his family, on Saturdays and on feast days and on long winter evenings; neighbors should gather together and read it together. Women who know how to read should gather their friends and their relatives and read it with them.)

Moralistic literature was, of course, not solely prescriptive, but included numerous lengthy narratives and short stories, pertaining to biblical personages and medieval patriarchs. Such is the Hebrew *Sefer ha-yashar* (Book of the Righteous), preserved in a seventeenth-century Judeo-Spanish manuscript translation and in later printings from Salonika and Istanbul, which included, among other legends and *midrashim* (commentaries), a lively account of Joseph's adventures, with the emotionally charged, traditional scene – shared with the Muslim tradition – in which Potiphar's wife, Zelikha, invites her critical (and hypocritical) friends to a banquet, where the handsome Joseph appears in all his splendor:

Y asentaron a comer en caza de Zelikhah. Y despues que comieron, les dieron a cada una una çidra, y les dieron un cuchío a cada una que mondara la çidra. Y encomendó Zelikhah que vistieran a Yosef con paños buenos, y que lo truxeron delantre de ellas. Y vino Yosef visto delantre de ellas, y miraron todas las muǧeres en Yosef y vieron a su ermozura, que no quitavan los ožos de él. Y se cortaron todas las muǧeres las manos que estavan mondando las çidras, que se inchiron todas las çidras de sangre; y no supieron si se cortaron, mirando la ermozura de Yosef. (Lazar, *Joseph* 280)[4]

(And they sat down to dine in Zelikha's house and, after they had eaten, [the servant girls] gave each lady a citron and a knife, so they could peel the fruit. And Zelikha commanded them to dress Yosef in beautiful clothing and bring him out before her guests. And Yosef came into view before them and all the women looked upon Yosef and saw his beauty and could not take their eyes off him. And all the women cut their hands as they were peeling the fruit and all the citrons were covered with blood and they did not know they had cut themselves, for looking at Yosef's beauty.)

Other Judeo-Spanish renditions of important medieval Hebrew compilations include the *Sepher Yosippon* (or *Sepher Yoseph Bin Gorión*), printed in

Hebrew, in Constantinople, in 1510, and translated into Judeo-Spanish by the great Bible translator and editor Abraham Asá, and published in Constantinople, in 1743 (with several subsequent reprintings) (*CLS* 130–31; Toaff). The famous – and controversial – story collection *Sepher Ben Sirá* (Alphabet of Ben Sira) was first printed in Hebrew, in Constantinople, in 1519, and is known in a Judeo-Spanish manuscript fragment from the Cairo Geniza and in a series of nineteenth-century printings (*CLS* 125, 139–40; Romero, "Versión" and "Versiones"). There is also a late Judeo-Spanish version of the widely known medieval exempla collection, usually called the *Sendebar*. The translation by Yakov Abraham Yoná, *Sentipa el filósofo* – published in his *Trezoro*, Salonika, 1910 – is, I believe, based on a modern Greek chapbook, rather than on any of the numerous different redactions that circulated in Europe and the Near East during the Middle Ages (Epstein; Lacarra).

DIDACTIC STROPHIC POETRY (*COPLAS*)

As we have already seen, the eighteenth century witnessed a notable flowering of Judeo-Spanish literature. At earlier stages, literary production consisted largely of translations, but – while these continued to be written – the 1700s saw the development of original literary works written in Judeo-Spanish. The monumental and plurisecular *Me'am lo'ez* is certainly the best example in prose. But the eighteenth century also gave us the earliest known documentation of what may be considered the quintessential genre of Judeo-Spanish poetry: didactic, narrative, strophic poetry, inspired by events from the Jewish past, as well as by contemporary history.[5] This is primarily written poetry, in some cases by known authors, which, all the same, frequently enters oral tradition and, in traditionalized form, may be sung side by side with oral ballads and lyric poetry, but, unlike these latter forms, usually sung by women, the *coplas* will primarily be favored by men. The *coplas* offer us an impressively extensive and diverse body of material, which, until relatively recently, had remained essentially unknown. Thanks to the erudition of Iacob Hassán and Elena Romero, this vast repertoire of poetry has been cataloged, edited, and studied.

Romero estimates the extant corpus at around four hundred different text types (represented by up to two thousand primary texts) (*CLS* 145). Though the first known versions date from the very beginnings of the eighteenth century, it seems quite probable that the *copla* tradition may go back, with no break in continuity, to important medieval antecedents, such as, for example, Shem Tob de Carrión's *Proverbios morales* and the anonymous *Coplas de Yosef* (*CLS* 147; González Llubera; Lazar, *Joseph*). In this regard, some of the *coplas*' diverse strophic arrangements offer significant, if only indirect, evidence.

Here, occasionally, we find examples of the late medieval 6 + 6 syllable *arte mayor* verse (Clarke 288). More important, for our purposes, is the survival, in the *coplas*, of the 7 + 7 syllable *redondilla* strophe (rhymed *abab*) used in Shem Tob's *Proverbios* and abundant zajal- and *villancico*-like arrangements (*aaab*), undoubtedly harking back to medieval Spanish and Hispano-Arabic antecedents (Frenk 309–26). Interesting, too, in this regard, are rhymes such as *tortura/rogadera* and *soñaba/ariba*, where rhyme depends only on a penultimate consonant + a final vowel, inevitably recalling the homioteleutonic rhyme characteristic of Semitic prosody (*CLS* 153–55).

The *coplas*' subject matter is far ranging. Many, of course, are geared to the yearly cycle of religious festivals, so there are *coplas* for Purim – with the valiant heroine Esther playing an essential part – as well as for Passover, Hanukkah, Shavuot (Harvest), Simḥat Torah (Rejoicing of the Law), Sukkot (Tabernacles), Tu bi-Shebat (Arbor Day), and, of course, for the Sabbath. Thematically, numerous *coplas* concern general Jewish topics – the Creation of the World; Adam and Eve; the Patriarchs: Abraham, Isaac, Jacob; the Twelve Tribes; Joseph and his adventures; Moses and the Exodus; the Destruction of the Temple; the Maccabees – but many other *coplas* fulfilled a historiographic function (*noticierismo*) that, in medieval Spain, was reserved for the epic and later for the *romances*: to report, record, and comment on contemporary events. Many *coplas* thus concern relatively recent happenings – mostly in the Balkans and the Near East but also in Morocco – of particular interest to the Sephardim: an earthquake in Istanbul, disastrous fires in Salonika, the fall of Sultan Abdul Hamid, the subsequent political liberalization and modernization (*CLS* 163–64; Hassán, "Cantar"). Other *coplas* concern diverse aspects of Sephardic life: dirge-like *coplas* (*qinot*); admonitory songs (*coplas de castiguerio*); *coplas de aliyá* on returning ("going up") to the Holy Land; *coplas del felek* (Turkish for "fate, destiny"), humorously commenting on the late nineteenth-century modernization of Sephardic culture. The masterpiece of *copla* literature, Abraham Toledo's vast *Coplas de Yosef ha-Çaddiq* (The Righteous Joseph), first printed in Constantinople, in 1732 (four later reprintings), embodies a total of 595 strophes and consists of mostly octosyllabic assonant quatrains (*abab*), though the zajalesque pattern (*aaab*) also occurs (Hassán, "Visión" 37; Lazar, *Joseph*). Though this is a learned poem of known authorship, characteristic features of oral poetry are quite frequently in evidence: for example, verses shared with *romances*, minstrel formulas, binary synonymic constructions ("Y seax bivos y sanos"), indications of the musical *makams* to which certain passages are to be sung (*CLS* 158–62; Hassán, "*Coplas de Yosef*"; Armistead, "Three" 41–43). Exemplifying the influence of Balkan traditional poetry on the *coplas*, Judah Kalʿí's *Coplas de las flores* (Flower Poem) is probably inspired by a Greek song in which various flowers engage in a debate about their respective virtues (*En torno* 189–93).[6]

DRAMA

The late nineteenth and early twentieth centuries saw a great production of dramatic literature in Judeo-Spanish. Most of these works fit perfectly into the category of "Adopted Literature" modeled on Western European genres (Hassán, "Visión"; Romero, "Más teatro"). Only in certain very early plays, or in plays closely connected with religious festivals, like those about Queen Esther (Romero, *Teatro*), do we perhaps perceive, on the analogy of the Yiddish *Purimspiel*, a distant echo of late medieval antecedents, such as the Provençal *Esther* poem, by Crescas del Caylar (c. 1327), that was doubtless composed to be read (or perhaps performed?) during Purim (Meyer and Neubauer; Silberstein). Particularly interesting in this regard is the recently discovered *Pyesa de Yaakov Avinu* (The Play of Our Father Jacob), by Moses Samuel Konfino, published in Bucharest, in 1862, to date the oldest known Judeo-Spanish play (Bunis, "*Pyesa*"; Armistead, "Additional Note").

ORAL LITERATURE

A very rich oral literature has survived among Spanish-speaking Jews, both in the Eastern communities and in North Africa. The following genres have been documented: narrative ballads (*romansas*); lyric songs (*cantigas*); cumulative songs, prayers, and medicinal charms; riddles (*endevinas*); proverbs (*refranes*); and folktales (*consejas*).[7] In almost every case, a rich repertoire of text types going back to prediasporic medieval antecedents now shares the stage with other items borrowed more recently from peoples among whom the Sephardim settled after their exile. For instance, while many Judeo-Spanish ballads have indisputable medieval antecedents, others are obvious translations from modern Greek; North African Jewish wedding songs perpetuate the same synonymous parallelism (*amigo/amado*, "friend/ beloved"; *garrido/lozano*, "sprightly/proud") already present in the medieval Castilian and Galician lyric (Alvar, *Cantos*), while some Eastern quatrains are direct translations from Greek (*En torno*); riddles and proverbs likewise attest to both medieval and postdiasporic components.[8] The medieval character of the Judeo-Spanish ballad tradition was eloquently evoked (in 1922) by the great Spanish philologist Ramón Menéndez Pidal, the first critic to approach the problem from the comparative perspective of modern scholarship:

> When we listen to the *romances* of the Jews from Moroccan cities, so similar to versions preserved in the oldest broadsides [*pliegos sueltos*] and song books [*cancioneros*], we seem to be hearing the voices of Spaniards from the time of the Catholic kings, as if Tangier, Tetuán, Larache, Alcazarquivir, and Xauen were old Castilian cities,

plunged by enchantment into the depths of the sea, that allow us to hear the songs of their ancient inhabitants, bewitched there . . . more than four hundred years ago.

(Menéndez Pidal, *Estudios* 335–36, my translation)

Menéndez Pidal's appraisal is indubitably correct, as has been repeatedly confirmed by subsequent scholarship. Yet all the ballads are not medieval. A number of Judeo-Spanish ballads were composed after 1492: some were brought to the Sephardic communities by *conversos* who left Spain or Portugal during the 1500s or 1600s; others were obviously composed in the diaspora communities; many modern ballads were brought to Morocco by Spanish settlers in the early twentieth century; yet others, in the East, were taken over from the Greek ballad tradition. *Los siete hermanos y el pozo airón* was sung by Sephardim in Salonika, but is unknown in the peninsular tradition. In its style and its formulistic diction, it seems very much like any other traditional *romance*, but it turns out to be a faithful formula-by-formula rendition of a Greek ballad, *Ho stoichioméno pēgádi* (The Haunted Well). Here, as an example of Sephardic oral narrative poetry, is a synthetic version, based on published and unedited texts in our own collection and at the Archivo Menéndez Pidal in Madrid:

Ya se van los siete hermanos,	Now the seven brothers depart;
ya se van para Aragó.	now they depart for Aragón.
Las calores eran fuertes;	The heat was intense;
agua non se les topó.	they found no water.
Por en medio del camino,	On the road they were traveling,
toparon un poǧo airó.	they found a deep well.
Echaron pares y nones;	They threw lots;
a el chico le cayó.	it fell to the youngest.
Ya lo atan con la cuedra;	Now they tie him to the rope;
ya lo echan al poǧo airó.	now they lower him into the well.
Por en medio de aquel poǧo,	Halfway down that well,
la cuedra se le rompió.	the rope broke.
La agua se les hizo sangre;	The water became blood for them;
las piedras culevros son;	the stones are serpents;
culevros y alacranes,	serpents and scorpions,
que le comen el corasón.	to eat out his heart.
Ya atornan los sex hermanos,	Now the six brothers turn back,
amargos de corasón.	bitter at heart.
– Asperadvos, mis hermanos,	"Wait, my brothers!

quiero dezir una razón:	I would speak a word to you:
Si vos pregunta la mi madre,	If my mother asks you,
la diréx: ¡atrás quedó!	tell her: 'He remained behind!'
Si vos pregunta el mi padre,	If my father asks you,
le diréx: ¡al poğo airó!	tell him: 'In the well!'
Si vos pregunta la mi mujer,	If my wife asks you:
¡bivda mueva ya quedó!	'She has just become a widow!'
Si vos preguntan los mis hijos,	If my children ask you:
¡güerfanicos muevos son!	'They have just become orphans!'"[9]

One of the most striking instances of the medieval character of Judeo-Spanish traditional ballads is their continued recollection of the trireligious Iberian society that the Sephardim left behind when they began their multi-secular peregrination through Mediterranean lands and beyond. So, *La expulsión de los judíos de Portugal*, one of the ballads sung until recently by Moroccan Jews, evokes the welcome accorded a Spanish princess who is to become queen of Portugal:

Ya me salen a encontrar	Now three marvelous religions
tres leyes a maravilla:	come out to welcome me:
Los cristianos con sus cruces,	The Christians with their crosses,
los moros a la morisca,	the Moors in Moorish garb;
los judíos con sus vihuelas,	the Jews with their *vihuelas*,
que la ciudad estrujía.	that made the city ring.

Similar descriptions survive in other *romances* in Morocco and in the East, while in the modern oral tradition of Spain and Portugal the memory of medieval Iberian trireligious symbiosis has been almost totally forgotten (Armistead, "Memory"). Another medieval component in the modern oral tradition is the numerous Christian elements present in Judeo-Spanish ballads (*En torno* 127–48). The Sephardim learned their ballad repertoire from their Christian neighbors during the late Middle Ages and, together with the songs, they also acquired the many Christian components that survive in their oral poetry even today, five hundred years after their departure from the Iberian Peninsula.

NOTES

1. For Eastern Judeo-Spanish, see Crews, *Recherches*; Luria; Révah; Sala, *Estudios* and *Phonétique*; Wagner, *Sondersprachen*. For Morocco, Bénichou, "Observaciones" and "Notas"; Benoliel; Wagner, "Zum Judenspanischen."

2. Concerning "modern" Judeo-Spanish literature, see *CLS*, and for the theater, Romero, *Teatro*, *Repertorio,* and "Más teatro." Note also Hassán's "Literatura." *CLS* is the single most important source for the study of written literature in Judeo-Spanish.
3. There are two partial editions of the Judeo-Spanish original: Gonzalo Maeso and Pascual Recuero, and Cynthia Crews's rigorously edited "Extracts." Pascual Recuero (*Antología*) edits stories found in the *Me'am lo'ez* and Molho (242–94) includes a selection spanning the years 1730–1899. There is a twenty-volume Hebrew translation (or rather, an adaptation) of the *Me'am lo'ez*, by Shmuel Yerushalmi (1967–81) (*CLS* 105), which in turn has been partially translated into English by A. Kaplan and others. I have seen the translations of Judges, 1 Samuel, and Song of Songs. The *Me'am lo'ez* has been the subject of substantial scholarly contributions. Note, for example, Domhardt; Goldberg; and Wiesner.
4. McGaha gives an English translation of the original Hebrew text (96); concerning the traditional motif, see Armistead, "Three," 43–45.
5. Concerning the *coplas*, see the pathbreaking studies of Hassán, "Coplas de Purim"; Hassán and Romero; Romero, "Coplas de Tu-bišbat," "Coplas sefardíes," *Coplas sefardíes*; *Bibliografía*; Romero and Carracedo; also Attias.
6. Parallels in Near Eastern and medieval Western literatures are legion. See, for example, Steinschneider; Ethé 226–29; Walther; Segre 73–81.
7. As starting points, for ballads, see Armistead et al., *Romancero*; Bénichou, *Creación*; *FLSJ*. For lyric songs, Alvar, *Cantos* and *Endechas;* Hemsi 191–340; Weich-Shahak. For cumulative songs and prayers, Pedrosa, "Plurilingüismo" and *Dos sirenas* 187–220. For medicinal charms, Armistead, "Judeo-Spanish . . . Poetry in the United States" 369–72. For riddles, Armistead and Silverman, "Nueve adivinanzas." For proverbs, Carracedo and Romero. For folktales, Haboucha. For overviews, Armistead, "Judeo-Spanish . . . Poetry in the United States" and "Littérature."
8. For postdiasporic features, see, for example, *En torno* 149–239; Armistead and Silverman, "Sephardic Folkliterature" and "Nueve adivinanzas"; Armistead, "Eyebrows"; Armistead, Haboucha, and Silverman. Textual evidence for the Sephardim's acquisition of Near Eastern and Balkan features has been amply confirmed by studies of the music to which Judeo-Spanish ballads are sung. See, especially, Israel J. Katz's studies.
9. See Armistead, "Greek Elements," and *En torno* 154. The motif of the *pozo airón* is, however, of very ancient peninsular origin, concerning which José Pedrosa has now uncovered new and dramatic evidence ("*El pozo airón*").

BIBLIOGRAPHY

Alvar, Manuel. *Cantos de boda judeo-españoles.* Madrid, 1971.
Endechas judeo-españolas. 2nd edn. Madrid, 1969.
Armistead, Samuel G. "An Additional Note on Jewish-Spanish Joseph Narratives." *Romance Philology* 49 (1995–96): 276–77.

"'Eyebrows like Leeches': Balkan Elements in a Judeo-Spanish Song." *La Corónica* 24 (1995–96): 91–103.

"Greek Elements in Judeo-Spanish Traditional Poetry." *Laografia* 32 (1979–81): 134–64.

"Judeo-Spanish Traditional Poetry: Some Linguistic Problems." *Zeitschrift für Romanische Philologie* 108 (1992): 62–71.

"Judeo-Spanish Traditional Poetry in the United States." *Sephardim in the Americas: Studies in Culture and History.* Ed. Martin A. Cohen and Abraham J. Peck. Tuscaloosa, 1993. 357–77.

"La littérature orale des juifs sépharades." *Cahiers de littérature orale* 44 (1998): 93–122.

"The Memory of Tri-Religious Spain in Judeo-Spanish Traditional Poetry." *Proceedings of the Howard Gilman International Colloquium: The Spanish–Jewish Interaction.* Tel Aviv, forthcoming.

"Near Eastern and Balkan Elements in Sephardic Oral Literature." *Proceedings of the Tenth British Conference on Judeo-Spanish Studies.* Ed. Annette Benaim. London, 1999. 1–20.

"Three Jewish-Spanish Joseph Narratives." *Romance Philology* 49 (1995–96): 34–52.

Armistead, Samuel G., et al. *El romancero judeo-español en el Archivo Menéndez Pidal (Catálogo-índice de romances y canciones).* 3 vols. Madrid, 1977.

Armistead, Samuel G., Reginetta Haboucha, and Joseph H. Silverman. "Words Worse Than Wounds: A Judeo-Spanish Version of a Near Eastern Folktale." *Fabula* 23 (1982): 95–98.

Armistead, Samuel G., and Joseph H. Silverman. "Nueve adivinanzas de Estambol: Colección Milwitzky." *Sefarad* 58 (1998): 31–60.

"Sephardic Folkliterature and Eastern Mediterranean Oral Tradition." *Musica Judaica* 6 (1983–84): 38–54.

Attias, Moshe. "Judeo-Spanish 'Coplas de Purim'" [Hebrew]. *Sefunot* 21 (1958): 331–76.

Bénichou, Paul. *Creación poética en el romancero tradicional.* Madrid, 1968.

"Notas sobre el judeo-español de Marruecos en 1950." *Nueva revista de filología hispánica* 14 (1960): 307–12.

"Observaciones sobre el judeo-español de Marruecos." *Revista de filología hispánica* 7 (1945): 209–57.

Benoliel, José. "Dialecto judeo-hispano-marroquí o hakitía." *Boletín de la Real Academia Española* 13 (1926): 209–33, 342–63, 507–38; 14 (1927): 137–68, 196–234, 357–73, 566–80; 15 (1928): 47–61, 188–223; 32 (1952): 255–89.

Bunis, David M. *A Lexicon of the Hebrew and Aramaic Elements in Modern Judezmo.* Jerusalem, 1993.

"*Pyesa di Yaakov avinu kun sus ižus* (Bucharest, 1862): The First Judezmo Play?" *History and Creativity in the Sephardi and Oriental Jewish Communities.* Ed. Tamar Alexander et al. Jerusalem, 1994. 201–52.

Carracedo, Leonor, and Elena Romero. "Refranes publicados por Ya'acob A. Yoná." *Sefarad* 41 (1981): 389–560.

Casiodoro de Reina and Cipriano de Valera. *La Santa Biblia.* Buenos Aires, 1951.

Clarke, Dorothy Clotelle. *A Chronological Sketch of Castilian Versification.* Berkeley, 1952.

CLS = Romero, Elena. *Creación literaria en lengua sefardí.* Madrid, 1992.

Crews, Cynthia M. "Extracts from the *Me'am Lo'ez* (Genesis), with a Translation and a Glossary." *Proceedings of the Leeds Philosophical and Literary Society: Literary and Historical Section* 9, 2 (1960): 13–106.

Recherches sur le judéo-espagnol dans les pays balkaniques. Paris, 1935.

Domhardt, Yvonne. *Erzählung und Gesetz: Deskriptive und präskriptive Hermeneutik mit Blick auf den Me'am Lo'ez des Rabbi Jakob Kuli.* Bonn, 1991.

Elliger, K., and W. Rudolph et al. *Biblia Hebraica Stuttgartensia.* 4th edn. Stuttgart, 1990.

En torno = Armistead, Samuel G., Joseph H. Silverman, and Israel J. Katz. *En torno al romancero sefardí.* Madrid, 1982.

Epstein, Morris. *Tales of Sendebar.* Philadelphia, 1967.

Ethé, Hermann. "Neupersische Literatur." *Gundriss der Iranischen Philologie.* Ed. Wilhelm Geiger and Ernst Kuhn II. Strassburg, 1896–1904. 212–300.

FLSJ = Armistead, Samuel G., Israel J. Katz, and Joseph H. Silverman. *Folkliterature of the Sephardic Jews.* 3 vols. Berkeley, 1971–94.

Frenk, Margit. *Estudios sobre lírica antigua.* Madrid, 1978.

Goldberg, Arnold. *Me'am Lo'ez: Diskurs und Erzählung in der Komposition: Ḥayye Sara, Kapitel I.* Frankfurt am Main, 1984.

González Llubera, Ignacio. *Coplas de Yoçef.* Cambridge, 1935.

Gonzalo Maeso, David, and Pascual Pascual Recuero, eds. *Me'am Lo'ez: El gran comentario bíblico sefardí.* 4 vols. Madrid, 1964–74.

Haboucha, Reginetta. *Types and Motifs of the Judeo-Spanish Folktales.* New York, 1992.

Hassán, Iacob M. "Un cantar sefardí sobre el naufragio de 1638." *El siglo XVII hispanomarroquí.* Ed. Mohammed Salhi. Rabat, 1997. 311–31.

"Las coplas de Purim." Diss., Universidad Complutense, 1976.

"Las *Coplas de Yosef* y la poesía oral." *Balada y lírica.* Ed. Diego Catalán et al. Madrid, 1994. 270–82.

"La literatura sefardí culta: Sus principales escritores, obras y géneros." *Judíos, sefarditas, conversos: La expulsión de 1492 y sus consecuencias.* Ed. Ángel Alcalá. Valladolid, 1995. 319–30.

"Visión panorámica de la literatura sefardí." *Hispania Judaica.* Vol. II, *Literature.* Ed. Josep M. Solà-Solé et al. Barcelona, 1982. 25–44.

Hassán, Iacob M., and Elena Romero. "Quinot paralitúrgicas." *Estudios sefardíes* 1 (1978): 3–57.

Hemsi, Alberto. *Cancionero sefardí.* Ed. Edwin Seroussi et al. Jerusalem, 1995.

Katz, Israel J. *Judeo-Spanish Traditional Ballads from Jerusalem.* 2 vols. New York, 1972–75.

"The Musical Legacy of the the Judeo-Spanish *Romancero.*" *Hispania Judaica.* Vol. II, *Literature.* Ed. Josep M. Solà-Solé et al. Barcelona, 1982. 44–58.

"The Sacred and Secular Musical Traditions of the Sephardic Jews in the United States." *Sephardim in the Americas: Studies in Culture and History.* Ed. Martin A. Cohen and Abraham J. Peck. Tuscaloosa, 1993. 331–56.

Lacarra, María Jesus. *Sendebar.* Madrid, 1989.

Lazar, Moshe. *Joseph and His Brethren: Three Ladino Versions.* Culver City, 1990.

Lazar, Moshe, ed. *The Ladino Bible of Ferrara (1553).* Culver City, 1992.

Luria, Max A. *A Study of the Monastir Dialect of Judeo-Spanish.* New York, 1930.

McGaha, Michael. *Coat of Many Cultures: The Story of Joseph in Spanish Literature 1200–1492.* Philadelphia, 1997.

McPheeters, Dean W. "Una traducción hebrea de *La Celestina.*" *Homenaje a Rodríguez-Moñino.* 2 vols. Madrid, 1966. 1:399–411.

Menéndez Pidal, Ramón. "Catálogo del romancero judío-español." *Cultura española* 4 (1906): 1045–77; 5 (1907): 161–99.

Estudios sobre el Romancero. Ed. Diego Catalan. Madrid, 1973.

Meyer, Paul, and A. Neubauer. "Le roman provençal d'Esther par Crescas du Caylar, médecin juif du XIVe siècle." *Romania* 21 (1892): 194–227.

Minervini, Laura. "The Formation of the Judeo-Spanish *Koiné.*" *Proceedings of the Tenth British Conference on Judeo-Spanish Studies.* Ed. Annette Benaim. London, 1999. 41–52.

Testi giudeospagnoli medievali (Castiglia e Aragona). 2 vols. Naples, 1992.

Molho, Michael. *Literatura sefardita de Oriente.* Madrid, 1960.

Nehama, Joseph. *Histoire des israélites de Salonique.* 7 vols. in 4. Salonika, 1935–78.

Pascual Recuero, Pascual. *Antología de cuentos sefardíes.* Barcelona, 1979.

Pedrosa, José M. *Las dos sirenas y otros estudios de literatura tradicional.* Madrid, 1995.

"Plurilingüismo y paneuropeísmo en la canción tradicional de *El buen viejo.*" *Romania* 113 (1992–95): 530–36.

"*El pozo airón*: Dos romances y dos leyendas." *Medioevo Romanzo* 18 (1993): 261–75.

Révah, Israel S. "Formation et évolution des parlers judéo-espagnols des Balkans." *Ibérida* 6 (1961): 173–96.

Romero, Elena. *Bibliografía analítica de ediciones de coplas sefardíes.* Madrid, 1992.

"Las coplas sefardíes: Categorías y estado de la cuestión." *Actas de las Jornadas de Estudios Sefardíes.* Cáceres, 1981. 69–98.

Coplas sefardíes: Primera selección. Córdoba, 1998.

"Coplas de Tu-bišbat." *Poesía: Reunión de Málaga de 1974.* Málaga, 1976. 276–311.

"Más teatro francés en judeoespañol." *Sefarad* 52 (1992): 527–40.

Repertorio de noticias sobre el mundo teatral de los sefardíes orientales. Madrid, 1981.

El teatro de los sefardíes orientales. 3 vols. Madrid, 1979.

"Versiones judeoespañolas del libro hebreo medieval de los relatos de *Ben Sirá.*" *History and Creativity.* Ed. Tamar Alexander et al. Jerusalem, 1994. 177–87.

"Una versión judeoespañola de *Los relatos de Ben-Sirá* según un manuscrito de la Guenizá de El Cairo." *Sefarad* 57 (1997): 399–428.

Romero, Elena, and Leonor Carracedo. "Poesía judeoespañola admonitiva." *Sefarad* 37 (1977): 429–51.

Sala, Marius. *Estudios sobre el judeo-español de Bucarest.* Mexico City, 1970.

Phonétique et phonologie du judéo-espagnol de Bucarest. La Haye, 1971.

Scholem, Gershom. *Sabbatai Ṣevi: The Mystical Messiah.* Princeton, 1973.

Segre, Cesare. "Le forme e le tradizioni didattiche." *Grundriss der Romanischen Literaturen des Mittelalters* 6 (1968): 58–175.

Séphiha, Haïm Vidal. *Le ladino (Judéo-espagnol calque:) Deutéronome.* Paris, 1973.

Le ladino (Judéo-espagnol calque): Structure et évolution d'une langue liturgique. 2 vols. Paris, 1979.

Sholod, Barton. "The Fortunes of *Amadís* among the Spanish Jewish Exiles." *Hispania Judaica.* Vol. II, *Literature.* Ed. Josep M. Solà-Solé et al. Barcelona, 1982. 87–99.

Silberstein, Susan Milner. "The Provençal Ester Poem Written in Hebrew Characters c. 1327 by Crescas de Caylar: Critical Edition." Diss., University of Pennsylvania, 1973.

Steinschneider, Moritz. "Rangstreit-Literatur." *Sitzungsberichte der Philosophisch-Historischen Klasse der Kaiserlichen Akademie der Wissenschaften* (Vienna) 155, 4 (1908): 1–87.

Toaff, Ariel. *Cronaca ebraica del Sepher Yosephon.* Rome, 1969.

Wagner, Max Leopold. *Sondersprachen der Romania.* Ed. Heintz Kröll. 4 vols. Stuttgart, 1990.

"Zum Judenspanischen von Marokko." *Volkstum und Kultur der Romanen* 4 (1931): 221–45.

Walther, H. *Das Streitgedicht in der lateinischen Literatur des Mittelalters.* Munich, 1920.

Weich-Shahak, Susana. "Childbirth Songs among Sephardic Jews of Balkan Origin." *Orbis Musicae* 8 (1982–83): 87–103.

Weinberger, Leon J. *Anthology of Hebrew Poetry in Greece, Anatolia, and the Balkans.* Cincinnati, 1975.

Wiesner, Christa. *Jüdisch-Spanisches Glossar zum Me'am Lo'ez des Iacob Kuli: Genesis und Exodus bis Teruma.* Hamburg, 1981.

Yerushalmi, Shmuel. *The Book of Judges: Me'am Lo'ez.* Trans. and adapt. Nathan Bushwick. New York, 1991.

The Book of Samuel I: Me'am Lo'ez. Trans. and adapt. Y. G. Weiss and Moshe Mykoff. New York, 1991.

The Book of Shir HaShirim: Me'am Lo'ez. Trans. and adapt. Zvi Faier. New York, 1988.

Zemke, John M. *Critical Approaches to the "Proverbios morales": An Annotated Bibliography.* Newark, 1997.

"On Almosnino's *Regimiento de la vida* (Salonika, 1564)." Forthcoming.

CHAPTER 26

THE MORISCOS

Luce López-Baralt

TIMES OF TEARS

"We are not in times of grace, but of tears." Thus the sixteenth-century Spanish crypto-Muslim Baray de Reminŷo sums up the emotional situation of Spain's last Muslims prior to their final expulsion in 1609. The statement is echoed throughout the literature of these hybrid Spaniards who had to resort to transliterating the Spanish language of their oppressors with the Arabic script of the once flourishing al-Andalus. Another Morisco author, who chose to hide his identity under the pseudonym "El Mancebo de Arévalo," depicts the Mora de Ubeda, an old Muslim woman, "weeping at the fate of the Muslims" as she relates how she lost all her relatives and possessions during the 1492 siege of Granada.

Muhammad himself is seen in Morisco literature to cry over al-Andalus's fate. In MS 774 of the Bibliothèque Nationale de Paris Ibn ʿAbbās recounts in an *aljofor* (prophecy) that the Prophet, after his evening prayer, looked over the setting sun and cried. Pressed to explain his sorrow, Muhammad answered: "I have wept because my Lord has shown me an island called Andalusia, which will be the most distant island populated of all of Islam, and which will be the first from which Islam will be thrown" (Sánchez Álvarez 252).

Spanish Morisco literature constitutes a collective effort to preserve the community's Islamic identity against the overwhelming difficulties of Inquisitorial Spain. All the remnants of Muslim culture – religious ceremonies, language, personal names, regional apparel, even the festive dance of the *zambra* – had been strictly forbidden by a succession of official edicts throughout the sixteenth century. Many Moriscos fled to Muslim countries, while those who stayed in Spain were forcibly baptized. But some of the most adamant Muslims, now "officially" Catholic, went underground. From the midst of these crypto-Muslims came the combative yet sorrowful authors we have been quoting.

The underground Moriscos tried to preserve their cultural heritage from oblivion and, in rewriting their classical literature "del arabí en aljamí" – from Arabic to Spanish in the Arabic script – they ended up reinventing themselves as authors and readers. The result was a profound innovation in Arabic belles lettres, Islamic religious treatises, and even practical works (medical books, itineraries) the Moriscos had inherited from their ancestors. Consider the legend of the hero Buluquía, who travels through time and space to meet an as yet unborn prophet named Muhammad. The story, which an anonymous Morisco translated into Spanish in MS VIII of Madrid's Biblioteca de Estudios Árabes,[1] is extant in its original Arabic version in both the *Thousand and One Nights* and al-Thaʿālibī's *Qiṣaṣ al-anbiyā'* (Stories on the Prophets). But it is one thing to have enjoyed the Muslim legend and its delight in *mirabilia* in the open spaces of a Moroccan or Syrian medieval marketplace and quite another to have heard it in the hushed silence of the Spanish crypto-Muslims' clandestine dwellings. Anwar Chejne rightly proposes that even Arabic literature of entertainment (adab), when translated by the Moriscos, served the purpose of cultural self-affirmation in the face of extinction. If the painfully exact translations of the Moriscos could take on such new meanings, the underground testimonial literature was still more original and more engaged – and more hybrid as well.

TO LOSE A LANGUAGE, TO INVENT A LANGUAGE

The underground Spanish Muslims were torn between the Islamic and Spanish aspects of their legitimate cultural heritage that had become incompatible in Renaissance Spain. The Moriscos who stayed in their motherland had to accept cultural integration into an official, monolithic Catholic "Spanishness." They had either to bury in oblivion or to force into clandestinity the Islamic ingredients of their national identity. Many ended up being culturally hybrid, because the slow deterioration of their Islamic heritage did not always give way to a complete identification or a profound knowledge of Catholic culture. Even the Spanish name that now came into vogue for Muslims – "Moriscos" – acquired a negative social innuendo.

Moriscos faced a new dilemma with the final expulsion decreed by Philip III in 1609: they had not been allowed to be bona fide Spaniards in their native land, but they did not have the time to become full-fledged Muslims in the first decades of their exile in Barbary either. They thus suffered two different processes of acculturation. In their new adoptive countries they had to relearn their long-forgotten Arabic and acquire a deeper knowledge of their religion, by now reduced mostly to superficial rituals.

Their literary saga, which roughly encompasses the sixteenth century, began in earnest when the benevolent capitulations of the Catholic monarchs, made after the fall of Granada, were violated. The sustained effort of preserving the remnants of the Moriscos' cultural identity is, ironically, really a Renaissance phenomenon – perhaps a Renaissance *à l'envers*, for no other European nation has produced such a peculiar literary corpus as Spain did during its supposed "classical" period. Those manuscripts we have recently begun to discover and decode allow us to witness with singular pathos the extinction of a people, as well as their efforts to hold back the inevitable historical forces about to descend on them.[2]

The Morisco authors were the antichroniclers of a vanishing world. Their first tragedy was the loss of the Arabic language. For Muslims, praying in the sacred tongue of the revelation is an essential part of the religious ritual. Thus Ottmar Hegyi observes that the authors of clandestine texts clung to their Arabic characters less for secrecy than for the sacred dignity of the Arabic characters. Crypto-Muslims deeply resented having to use for their treatises "aljamí," or Aljamiado (from the Arabic *'ajamiyya,* meaning foreign tongue).[3]

A high-ranking sharif, Ibn ʿAbd al-Rafīʾ al-Andalusī, describes how his father taught him the Arabic alphabet and the first notions of Islam when he was six years old. His testimonial gives us privileged access to a crypto-Muslim home and forces us to share the fear the youngster must have felt when his father quietly approached him one day with a wooden slate in his hand. Ibn ʿAbd al-Rafīʾ assures the reader that after many years of exile in Barbary he can still see the slate graphically inscribed in his memory. The father starts to write the "letters of the Christians" on the slate and goes over them with his son. Every time the child repeats one of these "foreign" signs, the father, with gentle yet authoritative patience, shows him corresponding Arabic signs. "Ours are like this," he whispers in the startled child's ear (Turki 117). Al-Rafīʾ ends up having to memorize a double alphabet neatly inscribed in a double column. He learns immediately that he is in the midst of a dangerous academic task: he must keep his father's teachings strictly to himself. Not even his mother should have access to the delicate curving Arabic signs on the wooden slate. He remains alone, memorizing his ominous lesson, when suddenly his mother bursts into the room and scolds him: "What was your father teaching you?" "Nothing," mutters the child, starting his life of duplicity as a crypto-Muslim.

Not all crypto-Muslims had the same scholarly tenacity – or the same good luck – as Ibn ʿAbd al-Rafīʾ. The Morisco Francisco de Espinosa alleged in his Inquisitorial trial that "he knew no more words in Arabic than *El handurila dela bradamin hurrazmin,* and that he did not even know what they meant" (García Arenal 103). Of course the accused could have been disguising his Islamic knowledge to avoid incrimination, but in fact the Aljamiado manuscripts denounce a similar situation. When Arabic is briefly quoted, it usually contains grammatical errors. Even the Mancebo de Arévalo, whom his collaborator Baray de Reminŷo describes as a "scholarly young man . . . very expert and educated in the reading of Arabic, Hebrew, Greek, and Latin, and in *aljamiado* most conversant" (Harvey, "Manuscrito" 65), seems to have had a quite modest literary and religious culture, as shown by his linguistic errors in these languages (Harvey, "Mancebo" 33). When his Morisco friends, ignorant of Arabic, beg the young man for instruction in the language, he "helps" them with this outrageous "lesson," whose original opacity we respect in the translation:

> I wished to collect certain Arabic similes in *Aljamiado* because some of my friends asked me why it was that in Arabic in certain passages sometimes one said *Allāh*, other times *Allāhu*, and other times *Allāhi* . . . one is to understand that saying *Allāh* without any other appearance [addition] is to speak in absolutes. *Allāhu* is to take current [*sic*, no doubt meaning "to speak"] in order to invoke some saying . . . as though to say "merciful" or "mercy." Saying . . . *Allāh* is like that man who suddenly wishes to entrust himself to *Allāh*; he goes directly to *Allāh* instead of asking his *alrraḥma* or pity. The man who says *Allāhu* goes more slowly in seeking . . . pity.
>
> (López-Baralt, *Islam* 178–79)

Despite the difficulties, the crypto-Muslims refused to forget Arabic. In the momentous year of 1492 the fall of Granada and the expulsion of the Jews permitted the nationalization of Spanish territory, while the discovery of America opened the peninsular culture to unexpected horizons. But 1492 was also the year that Antonio de Nebrija published the first *Gramática de la lengua castellana*. The humanist thought that his Spanish *Gramática*, based on Quintilian and Diomedes, would serve the unity of his recently founded nation, which quickly proclaimed Castilian its official tongue. But within a few years the underground Moriscos had translated the Arabic grammar *Jurrumiyya* or *Muqaddima* of Muḥammad al-Sanhājī ibn al-Jurrūm, born in Fez (1273–1339). The anonymous Aljamiado rendition of the popular opuscule, extant in Junta MS XII, probably anteceded the first European editions and Latin translations of the text.[4] The clandestine manual may have been the Moriscos' fierce answer to Nebrija's *Gramática*, and one can only wonder how many crypto-Islamic children – the future authors of our Aljamiado texts – used it in the secrecy of their homes in their struggle to remain bilingual.

Aljamiado literature was indeed so mestizo in its linguistic outlook that when the first manuscripts were discovered in the eighteenth century, scholars did not know what to make of them. Confused by texts written in the Arabic script but that were not extant in the Arabic tradition, researchers like Silvestre de Sacy thought they must have been written in "some of the languages spoken in Africa, or perhaps in Madagascar" (630).

But the Morisco texts were not only linguistically hybrid. They also rethink Spain from the Islamic point of view. The texts are written, as the Spanish saying goes, "al revés de los cristianos" [inverting Christianity]. They force us to get acquainted with a concept of Spain the fundamental cultural, religious, and social values of which have been inverted: Islam is the true religion, Muhammad is the Prophet of God, and we should pray to Allah. But the same proselytistic Morisco authors were already so immersed in Spanish mainstream culture that they quote from it constantly, thus offering us a strange mise-en-scène for authors like Lope de Vega and Góngora. Some, like the anonymous author of MS S-2 of the Biblioteca de la Real Academia de la Historia, felt so European in their Islamic refuges that they adopted some racist attitudes of their former enemies toward the Islamic community.

THE CANON

Proselytistic manuscripts constitute the bulk of sixteenth-century Islamic Spanish literature. The Mancebo de Arévalo describes in his *Breve compendio* a visit he paid to ʿAlī Sarmiento, an illustrious *ʿalīm* (Muslim sage) from Granada. Sarmiento, already one hundred years old and infirm, had been so afflicted by the fall of the city that he moved to the outskirts of town to avoid the insults his fellow Muslims were subjected to. The Mancebo went to his house in the company of two Morisco friends and was quite impressed when he heard Sarmiento formally lecture the newcomers from a homemade pulpit (*almimbar*): "he stood at his house's *almimbar,* and with the very same tunic he used to wear when he greeted the Kings of Granada during . . . festive occasions, he began preaching" (Harvey, "Manuscrito" 73–74).

Our chronicler remained optimistic: he assures us in the prologue of his opus magnus that he will write yet another *Tafsira* "when this land is free" (Narváez, "'Tafsira'" 34) – that is, when Spain is liberated from the Christians. But he must have felt doubt: almost all the Moriscos he meets in Granada believed the worst was yet to come. He interviews the survivors again and again, and his modern attitude reminds María Teresa Narváez, the *Tafsira*'s editor, of that of a journalist *avant la lettre.* In the lament of Yūse Banegas, a "great" Arabist, recorded by the Mancebo, the long-muted voices of the vanquished Islamic community are allowed to describe historical events from their own point of view:

> My son, I do not weep for the past, for from the past nothing returns, but I weep for what you will see if you [stay] on this island of Spain . . . And what most hurts is that the Muslims will imitate the Christians, and will not refuse their dress nor dodge [spurn] their food. Pray to his kindness that . . . they pay no attention to their law

with their hearts . . . If the fathers belittle the religion, how will the great-great-great grandchildren praise it? If the king of the conquest keeps not his words, what awaits us from his successors? (Harvey, "Yūse" 300–2)

The crypto-Muslim authors also attacked Christianity theologically. The anonymous author of MS 5302 of the Biblioteca Nacional de Madrid first depicts Jesus' gestation and birth, which seem to him as normal as those of any other human being: "[Jesus] stayed in [Mary's] womb for nine months and then left it through the same place where Adam's sons leave it" (fol. 5r).[5] He states that Allah is uncreated, that he does not eat, drink, or sleep, unlike Jesus (fol. 6r). The depiction of the crucifixion is startling: "[Jesus] was afraid . . . he complained . . . and implored [God] that he be excused from experiencing the process of death. And he asked God to let him rest, and an angel came to comfort him . . . So how can he be God, as you Christians claim, when he needed such . . . consolation from the Almighty?" (fol 13v).

Muhammad is unsurprisingly celebrated as the true prophet of the crypto-Islamic community. Consuelo López-Morillas's *Textos aljamiados sobre la vida de Mahoma, el Profeta de los moriscos* offers a splendid collection of Aljamiado texts depicting the Prophet's sacred genealogy and miracles. According to the profusely copied *Kitāb al-anwār* (Book of Lights),[6] the Prophet inherited from Adam and the religious prophets who preceded him a miraculous light that shone on his forehead as a sign of his future role as the spiritual leader of the Muslims.

A most moving testimony concerns the Inquisition. The anonymous informer, who writes from the safety of Tunisia, seems to know that he is writing for posterity:

Thanks . . . be given to our merciful Lord, who plucked us out of the midst of these Christian heretics . . . [for] every day their abhorrence grew greater in their hearts, and it was necessary that one show oneself as they demanded, for if it was not done, [we] were taken to the Inquisition, where for following the truth we were stripped of our lives, properties, and children; for in a trice a person was thrown into a dark prison, as black as their evil designs, where they would be left for many years as the property was consumed . . . and the children, if they were small they were put out to rear, to make of them, like [the Christians], heretics; and . . . some said that [we] all should be put to death, others that we should be castrated [by cauterization] in a part of the body so that [we] might not engender children and so die out by degrees.
(López-Baralt, *Islam* 238)

Almost all aspects of life were rewritten by Morisco authors. A veritable *Kāma Sūtra*-like erotic treatise advises the male reader how to make love in the context of Islamic religious law. The mysterious author wrote his work around 1630, when he was already a refugee in Tunisia. His manual, extant in a long miscellaneous manucript of the Biblioteca de la Real Academia de la Historia of Madrid,[7] was written for the first generation of Moriscos already born in exile. They were in the process of relearning Muslim religion and law, and this Morisco author, particularly cultured in Islamic matters, decided to give them a hand. His Spanish codex includes memoirs of his days in Inquisitorial Spain and of his own deportation to Africa, as well as an Italian-like novella.

The Spanish *Kāma Sūtra* is its most astonishing chapter. Since the refugee believes that sex can lead to everlasting contemplation of God, he gives his male readers detailed instructions on how to pray while making love. This ritual and prayerful sexual union is unimaginable in Christian tradition. St. Augustine teaches in his *De bono coniugali* that coitus, even when performed in legitimate marriage, is invariably tainted with original sin. In his *Summa theologica* Thomas Aquinas argues that a couple can escape the inherent sin of the marriage act only by detesting its pleasure. Ignoring this tradition, part of his own Spanish legacy, our author offers his fellow Spanish Moriscos an unforgettable lesson:

> When the husband is ready for penetration, he should introduce his member and rub it against the vagina, as to further excite both himself and [his partner]. He should say *biçmi yllahi* [in the name of God] when proceeding to introduce his member. The penetration has to be performed lovingly and gently . . . [He] should delay his climax until he is sure that both partners reach it at the same time: much love is attained when [the sexual union] is performed this way . . . In the moment of spilling his seed [ejaculation] he should pray . . . [and after the act] he should say in his mind, without moving his tongue, [another] silent prayer. (López-Baralt, *Kāma Sūtra* 368–69)

The secret Islamic community taught its members not only how to make love but also how to die. A symbolic skull describes what it had been like for him to surrender his soul:

> ʿAzrail [the Angel of Death] descended upon us brandishing fire and received our souls with a blast of fury. He took my *al-ruh* [soul] from me [tearing it apart] from joint to joint and from vein to vein until he forced it all the way to my throat. Then he knocked it with a terrifying club of fire. I felt such pain . . . that I can only compare it to the experience of being skinned alive. I . . . have been lying here . . . for three hundred years now and I still feel the pain in my throat from the pulling out of my soul. (Vespertino Rodríguez 344)

After such eschatological struggle, many Moriscos had the relief of learning that there awaited them an Islamic paradise inhabited by black-eyed houris of ravishing beauty, with a gaze that would turn salty waters sweet.[8]

The crypto-Muslim imagination exploited another literary genre *pro domo sua.* When the Turpin Tower, the old minaret of the mosque, was demolished in 1580 in order to expand the cathedral, a lead box was discovered, containing "prophetic" inscriptions in Spanish and Arabic dealing with the end of the world. Fifteen years later, lead tablets written in angular Arabic characters (so as to look antique) and crude Latin were found in Sacromonte, Granada. These thin tablets had been made to appear to belong to the first century, and included several books – *The Great Mysteries Seen by St. James, Enigmas and Mysteries Seen by the Virgin*, among others – attributed to Tesifón Ebnatar and his brother Cecilio Enalrabí, putative disciples of St. James the Apostle, the future patron saint of Spain (Cabanelas). The archbishop of Granada, Pedro Vaca de Castro, enthusiastically ordered the lead tablets (*plomos*) excavated. The find, according to Harvey ("Moriscos" 8), caused as much uproar as the Dead Sea Scrolls have in our own day. The texts describe Christ and the Virgin Mary, who is snatched up into heaven on a mare (a coarse version of Muhammad's ascent on the *burāq*) and who replies to St. Peter's inquiries concerning sixteenth-century Granada and the importance of the Muslims in those late years. A long theological dispute followed, and although the relics were authenticated by peninsular scholars in 1600, they were finally moved to Rome and declared heretical (Godoy y Alcántara 47).

The *plomos* implied a diplomatic (and truly desperate) attempt to synthesize the Christian and the Islamic religions on the eve of the final expulsion in 1609. In them, the Islamic phrase "there is no god but God and Muhammad is his prophet" becomes "Lā illāha ila allāh, wa-yasūʿ rūḥ allāh" [there is no god but God and Jesus is the spirit of God]. Alonso del Castillo and Miguel de Luna, who took part in the "official" translations of the tablets, may in fact have been their authors. The false chroniclers and the Turpin Tower manuscript might be seen as theologically naive and as failing to halt the Morisco expulsion and to lend dying Islam some last prestige, but they set a literary precedent of the Aljamiado prophecy genre.

One of the most colorful prophecies, by an anonymous author and extant in MS 774 of the Bibliothèque Nationale de Paris, declares that discord will break out "between the two kings, adorers of the cross and the eaters of pork . . . and Allāh . . . will send a king who shall be called Ahmad" (López-Baralt, *Islam* 205–6). The Turks will aid the Spanish Muslims and Sicily, Majorca, Ibiza, and Spain will be returned to Islam. The captured king of the Christians will be sent to Valencia and become a Muslim.

The details of the triumph are startling:

> When the Christians see that, they will gather in the city of the river. Over them will come three Muslim kings, and they will enter the city by force of arms, and all three shall eat at one table, and afterwards they will bless one another; one will move into

the area of Monkayo [*sic*], the other into the area of Çuera [*sic*], and the other into the area of Himça (which we believe signifies Seville). And when the Christians see that their king is captive they will turn Muslim . . . And the Muslims shall be conquerors, with the power of Allah *taʿālā* [praised be he]. (206)

TO BE SPANISH, TO BE EXILED

Morisco literature is not always so clearly pro-Islamic. The Spanish Islamic minority, after generations underground, was already becoming culturally hybrid while still in Spain. Most arrived in Barbary not only as baptized Christians, but immersed in the Castilian culture of their social milieu, which they usually knew better than their own long-lost Islamic civilization. The reader must read cautiously between the lines to grasp the underlying anguish and divided loyalties.

Although the process of hybridization of the Spanish Muslim culture had begun earlier, the fall of Granada brought the crisis. When the Mancebo de Arévalo describes his visit to ʿAlī Sarmiento, he subtly slips in a damaging piece of information about his much admired "onrrado *ʿalīm*": "He had a *conducta* [safe-conduct] from King Ferdinand . . . After the fall of Granada there was not a Moor left that was as rich as he, because he stayed on such good terms [en tanta gracia] with the Christian king and with his prelates, that he could have whatever he wished" (Harvey, "Manuscrito" 72–73). The young chronicler then copies for posterity the text of the royal decree in his own *Breve compendio.* This document, dated 1499, provides ʿAlī and his descendants a permanent status of civil and religious liberty. Harvey suspects that the price for such unheard-of generosity must have been high; ʿAlī might well have served as an informant for the Christian monarchs ("Yūse" 299).

Ginés Pérez de Hita argues in his *Guerras civiles de Granada* that the Venegas or Vanegas, originally from Fez, were among the Andalusians who helped deliver Granada into the hands of the Catholic monarchs. Their collaboration brought them benefits including the right to bear arms and land endowments. Morisco manuscripts confirm the chronicler's assessment. Yūse Banegas lost all his family except a daughter during the siege of Granada. Yet he enjoys a solid social and economic position, lives in an "ornamented farmhouse" [*adornada alquería*], and has his freedom to practice Islam expressly guaranteed. Harvey explains his situation by yet another safe-conduct that, this time, Abū l-Qasim Venegas, Yūse's possible relative, possessed – a decree similar to the one King Ferdinand gave ʿAlī Sarmiento ("Yūse" 298). The Mancebo dealt with double-crossers during his fact-finding trip to southern Spain. Yet they helped deepen the young chronicler's knowledge of Islam, thus preparing him for his future life as a combative crypto-Muslim.

The Mancebo himself admits to leading a double life, this time in favor of his secret Islamic community. His own mother had been a Christian for twenty-five years, and we can well imagine the subtle treasons and anguished secrecy that must have characterized the young writer's childhood. No wonder he has no qualms about "spying" for Islam as an adult. He admits to a curious "theological" experiment in which he pretends to be a Christian and confesses the same sin to different priests:

> It happened to me in Jaén, in order to test this [situation] to try three Christian [priests] in one day, and on one single sin, and each one of them gave me his own sort of absolution. The wise men of the Moors [*ʿalīmes*] give the penance in measure of the sin, according to its gravity. (Harvey, "Mancebo" 29)

In all likelihood, the Mancebo's life must have passed in one long act of *taqiyya* – in times of extreme distress, Muslims can pretend to practice a different religion while keeping Islam in their hearts. Many Moriscos did. The presumed perpetrators of the hoax of the lead tablets of Sacromonte and the manuscript of the Turpin Tower feigned to be sincere Christians, and Miguel de Luna even held the post of official translator of King Philip II. After the lead tablet debacle, he devised a another literary fraud: he pretended in his *Verdadera historia del Rey Don Rodrigo* to have "discovered" an ancient manuscript by the Muslim historian Tarif Abentarique in the Escorial. Luna "translated" the Arabic text into Spanish, and thus his *Verdadera historia* constitutes the "true history" of the peninsula's colonization by the Arabs. As expected, the Muslims were more enlightened than their Christian counterparts. Our pseudohistorian manages to launch a thinly veiled but nonetheless terrible invective against his own employer, King Philip II, again in a desperate effort to prevent the expulsion of his brethren by dignifying their Islamic heritage. Today the *Verdadera historia* constitutes a disturbing piece of literary fiction, even more so because Luna received Catholic last rites before dying.

The literary preferences of the Moriscos were even more openly conflicted than their religious and cultural loyalties. In their cultural resistance, they must have felt that they should not identify too closely with their oppressors' belles lettres. Yet they did. The Mancebo de Arévalo casually quotes from Islamic authorities like al-Ghazālī, Ibn Rushd, Ibn ʿArabī, and even the mysterious ʿUmarbey. But he hides the names of authors he is even more familiar with. Gregorio Fonseca demonstrates that the young scholar randomly attributes to Islamic authorities bits of wisdom belonging to Kempis's *Imitatio Christi*. There is no evidence in the Mancebo's texts that he read any Islamic authority in depth. His Arabic was probably defective and possession – let alone formal study – of Islamic books was strictly forbidden in his native Spain. So it is not surprising again to come upon another passage – this time in the *Tafsira* – in which the hybrid scholar usurps a European text and passes it as his own. Narváez identifies it as being taken from Fernando de Rojas's prologue to *La Celestina.*[9] She confronts both texts, Rojas's and the Mancebo's, and concludes that the Morisco chronicler transcribed excerpts from Petrarch's *De remediis utriusque fortuna* into Aljamiado. Despite his obstinate pro-Islamic commitment, the Mancebo uses Rojas's agnostic prologue to ponder a senseless, cruel universe. Perhaps the Morisco author knew that the author of *La Celestina* was a *converso* of Jewish origin and identified with his religious tragedy. The Mancebo himself testifies that he had close Jewish friends who commiserated with him over the crypto-Muslims' collective bereavement.

Another crypto-Muslim, Taybili, oscillated between the endeavors of his struggling Islamic community and eager acquisition of Spanish books. He too quoted from *La Celestina* in a long literary work he wrote in Tunisia. When in Spain, Taybili went by the name of Juan Pérez, and few might have suspected that the anxious bibliophile with expertise in the literary avant-garde was a closet Muslim.

> I remember being in the *feria* [bazaar or market] of Alcalá de Henares, where the famous university is. It was back in 1604, and as I was strolling by the main street [with a friend], we arrived at a bookshop – they had very authentic and well-provided bookshops there at the time – and since I am so inclined to reading I entered and asked for the *Césares* by Pedro Mexía, for the *Relox de príncipes* and the *Epístolas* by [Antonio de] Guebara [Guevara] and for some other recent releases. I bought six books in all.
>
> (Bernabé Pons, *Cántico* 153)

Juan Pérez's companion counters that such new releases cannot compare with the tales of *Caballero Febo*, *Amadís de Gaula*, *Palmerín de Oliba*, and *Don Belianís de Greçia.* A young student in the bookshop, who was listening to Juan Pérez's friend's taste in chivalric literature, exclaims: "We have a reborn Don Quixote in here!" One wonders how Taybili (who was at the same time Juan Pérez) would have reacted when reading Cervantes's best-seller and realizing that the masterpiece had "really" been written in Arabic by the "true historian" Cide Hamete Benengeli, and that it was one of his own people – a Morisco Aljamiado – who took to the task of "translating" Don Quixote's adventures from the Arabic.

These troubled souls writing from the underground to save their Islamic national identity could not resist imitating and translating for posterity the literary pieces of their religious enemies. Álvaro Galmés de Fuentes points out that the *Historia de los amores de París y Viana*, an old chivalrous novel of European origin, whose heroes are the daughter of the dauphin of France and the noble knight Paris, received a careful Aljamiado reforging during the sixteenth century.

Even when they stuck to their pro-Islamic proselytism, the Moriscos expressed themselves not only in Spanish but in its most characteristic poetic meters. It is odd indeed to hear Muhammad praised in the octosyllabic rhythm of the old peninsular ballads or *romances*: "O Muhammad, nuestro amparo / Nuestro muro y defensor / Refugio de nuestras penas / Y en nuestras tinieblas sol" [Oh Muhammad, our refuge / Our fortress and defender, / Refuge of our sufferings / And sun in our darkness] (Chejne 134). Taybili mocks the Eucharist – in the even more sophisticated hendecasyllables of Italian origin that made Renaissance poets like Garcilaso and Góngora so famous. In the most sacred moment of the Mass, the priest "dixe çiertas raçones sosegado / con que diçen que Dios luego desciende, / y en la hostia se mete y comprehende" [calmly says some words, / by which they say God descends, / and introduces himself in the host and constitutes it] (Bernabé Pons, *Cántico* 208).

The crypto-Muslims arrived in their new Islamic homelands plagued with these contradictions. One of Cervantes's characters, the Morisco Ricote, describes his experience as an exile who opted to return home secretly:

> All of us were punished with exile; a mild and merciful penalty in the opinion of some, though to us it was the most terrible that could be inflicted. Wherever we are we weep for Spain . . . In Barbary and in all those parts of Africa where we hoped to be received, entertained and welcomed we are worst treated and abused . . . For now I know by experience the truth of the saying, that the love of one's country is sweet.
>
> (Cervantes, *The Adventures of Don Quixote*, trans. J. M. Cohen [Baltimore, 1950], bk. 2, chap. 54, p. 819)

The secret manuscripts testify that the fictional Ricote's experience was often true to history. The author of the Spanish *Kāma Sūtra*, in the testimonial chapters of his miscellaneous opus magnus, confesses that upon his arrival in Tunisia, even though Muslims like Citibulgaiz and Uthmān Day had been generous, "there were [also] some wicked people." He then silences himself and tries to explain away his hasty remark by blaming his Morisco brethren for their misfortune: "Enough! It was our own fault because we failed to follow the truth. Enough! Because in any case we were finally able to hear the *tawḥīd* [unity of God], celebrated in the open" (López-Baralt, "Angustia" 51–52). He explains the new trials of the Moriscos in their adoptive homeland as "in atonement of our sins" and advises his saddened fellow Spaniards to come to terms with their new tormentors amicably (51–53). Yet despite his conciliating attitude – he is suggesting the use of *taqiyya à l'envers* – the exile exclaims concerning the Tunisians: "I just cannot believe that anyone would mean evil for his own blood and nation" (53). A tacit acceptance of his destiny as a perpetual *apátrida* (landless man) underlies his disconsolate statement.

Perhaps that is why he dares to write one of the most polycultural texts of the Spanish Islamic literary corpus. He admits to having been reacculturedin Islam once in Tunisia, and, as a confessed parvenu, he delights in dropping the names of Muslim authorities: Aḥmad Zarrūq, al-Ghazālī, Asbag. But he seizes the opportunity to evoke his Spanish classics – as usual, without mentioning them by name. His text is interspersed with the sophisticated poetry of Garcilaso, Góngora, Quevedo, as well as the popular *romancero*. He even describes attending in his lost Spanish homeland the plays of Lope de Vega – whom he quotes by heart. But the best surprise is that the playwright's Petrarchan sonnets grace the Spanish *Kāma Sūtra* and even bring it to a dramatic close.

Our exiled chronicler identified so closely with Spanish literature that it is not an exaggeration to call him a "maurophile Moor." He adapts to his own fiction the cliché of the gallant but false Morisco in vogue in Spanish Renaissance literature. Our author should have known that the dreamlike Zaide and Abenámar had nothing to do with his own despised brethren. But he cannot resist the temptation of becoming, at least for a moment, a "true Spaniard" and goes on to evoke Daraja, the Alhambra, and the Torres Bermejas in his idealized novella.

Again the exiled author dreams of the impossible when he assumes another very "Spanish" trait in his prose: racism. Being "noble" in his homeland depended not only on an undisputed lineage, but on being able to boast of *pureza de sangre* (purity of blood). No one of social standing could have Morisco or Jewish blood. Lope de Vega and many other Spanish authors often joked at the expense of the mestizo social pariahs. The Morisco must have been a victim of these slurs while on the peninsula. But in Tunisia he wants to forget his former humiliation and writes a novella in which one of the characters boasts of his "[pure] blood and illustrious ancestry" (López-Baralt, "Angustia" 56).

Like most crypto-Muslims, the refugee from Tunisia seems incapable of fully identifying with either of his two nationalities. Like other Morisco authors – his fellow *lloradores* – he hates Spain's political and religious repression, yet he secretly feels Spanish and in his incurable nostalgia celebrates his lost country's rich literature – even identifies with some of its prejudices. Like most crypto-Islamic Moriscos, he is a sincere Muslim and is grateful for his benefactors' reception in Africa. Yet he resents the native Tunisian population that made the Moriscos feel like perpetual foreigners.

Reading Spanish Islamic literature is a sobering experience. Many Moriscos wrote not only to preserve their Islamic heritage but to come to terms with their conflicted identity. Although the task was insurmountable, the Moriscos did succeed in sharing with future generations testimony of their conflict, explored in an intensely polycultural, uniquely Hispano-Muslim literary corpus.

NOTES

1. Previously known as the Biblioteca de la Junta de Estudios Árabes, abbreviated here as Junta.
2. The clandestine manuscripts began to be discovered long after the expulsion of 1609: in 1728 several codices hidden inside the column of a house in Ricla turned up; and in 1884 a substantial collection was discovered under a false floor in a demolished house in Almonacid de la Sierra in Saragossa. In the last ten years many more manuscripts have surfaced. Furthermore, not all the Morisco texts in Europe's libraries are properly cataloged.
3. Although the technical term has been generally applied to the entire secret literary corpus of the last Muslims of Spain, some Moriscos wrote in the Arabic language and even in Spanish using the Latin script both before and after exile in Barbary. Gerard Wiegers prefers to refer to Morisco literature as "Islamic Spanish literature" ("Yça Gidelli" 2).
4. Martín Martínez de Cantalapiedra used the *Jurrumiyya* to teach Arabic in Salamanca around 1560–64, when St. John of the Cross was a student at the prestigious university.
5. A study, by Edil González Carmona, from the University of Puerto Rico, is under publication by the *Revue d'histoire maghrebinne* (Tunisia).
6. María Luisa Lugo edited the whole corpus of this Aljamiado legend, together with two Arabic originals (diss., University of Puerto Rico, 1995).
7. After I published *Un Kāma Sūtra español* in 1992, two more manuscripts of the treatise came to my attention (see López-Baralt, *Un Kāma Sūtra español: El primer tratado*).
8. I am quoting from MS S-2 of the Biblioteca de la Real Academia de la Historia.
9. Her study is under publication in the *Bulletin of Hispanic Studies.*

BIBLIOGRAPHY

Bernabé Pons, Luis. *Bibliografía de la literatura aljamiado-morisca.* Alicante, 1992.
El cántico islámico del morisco hispanotunecino Taybili. Saragossa, 1988.
Cabanelas, Darío. *El morisco granadino Alonso del Castillo.* Granada, 1965.
Cardaillac, Louis. *Morisques et chrétiens: Un affrontement polémique (1492–1640).* Paris, 1977.
Chejne, Anwar. *Islam and the West: The Moriscos.* Albany, 1983.
Epalza, Mikel de. *Los moriscos antes y después de la expulsión.* Madrid, 1992.
"Moriscos et andalous en Tunisie au XVIIe siècle." *Recueil d'études sur les moriscos andalous en Tunisie.* Ed. Mikel de Epalza and R. Pétie. Tunis, 1973. 150–86.
Fonseca, Gregorio. "Relación y ejercicio espiritual sacado y declarado por el Mancebo de Arévalo en nuestra lengua castellana." Diss., Oviedo, 1987.
Galmés de Fuentes, Álvaro, ed. *Actas del coloquio internacional sobre literatura aljamiada y morisca.* Madrid, 1978.
Historia de los amores de París y Viana. Madrid, 1970.

García Arenal, Mercedes. *Los moriscos.* Madrid, 1975.
Godoy y Alcántara, José. *Historia de los falsos cronicones.* Madrid, 1968.
Harvey, L. P. "The Literary Culture of the Moriscos, 1492–1609: A Study Based on the Extant Manuscripts in Arabic and Aljamía." Diss., Oxford, 1958.
"El Mancebo de Arévalo y la literatura aljamiada." Galmés de Fuentes 21–48.
"Un manuscrito aljamiado de la Biblioteca de la Universidad de Cambridge." *Al-Andalus* 22 (1958): 49–74.
"The Moriscos and *Don Quixote.*" University of London, King's College. 11 November 1984.
"Yūse Banegas: Un moro noble en Granada bajo los Reyes Católicos." *Al-Andalus* 21 (1956): 297–302.
Hegyi, Ottmar. "El uso del alfabeto árabe por minorías musulmanas y otros aspectos de la literatura aljamiada, resultante de circunstancias históricas y sociales análogas." Galmés de Fuentes 147–64.
Iversen, Reem. "En busca de una alfombra de oración: Una carta desesperada de un morisco de Tórtoles." Forthcoming.
López-Baralt, Luce. "La angustia secreta del exilio: El testimonio de un morisco de Túnez." *Hispanic Review* 55 (1987): 41–57.
"La estética del cuerpo entre los moriscos o de cómo la minoría perseguida pierde su rostro." *Le corps dans la société espagnole du XVIe et XVIIe siècles.* Ed. Agustín Redondo. Paris, 1990. 35–348.
Islam in Spanish Literature: From the Middle Ages to the Present. Trans. Andrew Hurley. Leiden, 1992.
Un Kāma Sūtra español. Madrid, 1992.
Un Kāma Sūtra español: El primer tratado erótico de nuestra lengua (Mss. S-2 BRAH *Madrid y Palacio 1767).* Madrid, 1995.
"El oráculo de Mahoma sobre la Andalucía musulmana de los últimos tiempos en un manuscrito aljamiado-morisco de la Biblioteca Nacional de París." *Hispanic Review* 52 (1984): 41–57.
López-Baralt, Luce, and Awilda Irizarry. "Dos itinerarios moriscos secretos del siglo XVI: El ms. 774 París y el ms. T-16 BRAH Madrid." *Homenaje a Álvaro Galmés de Fuentes.* Madrid, 1985. 547–82.
López-Morillas, Consuelo. *The Qur'an in Sixteenth Century Spain: Six Morisco Versions of Sura 79.* London, 1982.
Textos aljamiados sobre la vida de Mahoma, el Profeta de los moriscos. Madrid, 1994.
Lugo, María Luisa. "Hacia la edición crítica del 'Libro de las luces': Una leyenda aljamiada sobre la genealogía de Mahoma." Diss., University of Puerto Rico, 1995.
Narváez, María Teresa. "El Mancebo de Arévalo, lector morisco de *La Celestina.*" Forthcoming.
"'La Tafsira' del Mancebo de Arévalo: Transcripción y estudio del texto." Diss., University of Puerto Rico, 1988.
Nykl, A. R. "Aljamiado Literature: El Rrekontamiento del Rey Alisandere." *Revue hispanique* 77 (1929): 409–611.

Oliver Asín, Jaime. "Un morisco de Túnez, admirador de Lope: Estudio del ms. s-2 de la Colección Gayangos." *Al-Andalus* 1 (1933): 409–56.

"El *Quijote* de 1604." *Boletín de la Real Academia Española* 28 (1948): 89–126.

Pérez de Hita, Ginés. *Guerras civiles de Granada.* 2 vols. Madrid, 1913.

Sacy, Silvestre de. "Notice et extraits des mss. de la Bibliotèque Nationale." *Journal de savants* 4 (1797): 626–947.

Sánchez Álvarez, Mercedes. *El manuscrito misceláneo 774 de la Biblioteca Nacional de París.* Madrid, 1982.

Turki, ʿAbd al-Majīd. "Documents sur le dernier exode des andalous en Tunisie." Epalza, *Recueil* 114–27.

Vázquez, Miguel Ángel. "Un morisco muere ante nuestros ojos: El jadiz y leyenda de Silmán al-Farsi." *Le v° centenaire de la chute de Grenade (1492–1992).* Ed. A. Temimi. Zaghouan, 1993. 733–45.

Vespertino Rodríguez, Antonio. *Leyendas aljamiado-moriscas sobre personajes bíblicos.* Madrid, 1983.

Wiegers, Gerard. *Islamic Literature in Spanish and Aljamiado: Yça of Segovia (fl. 1450), His Antecedents and Successors.* Leiden, 1994.

"Yça Gidelli (fl. 1450), His Antecedents and Successors: A Historical Study of Islamic Literature in Spanish and Aljamiado." Diss., Rijksuniversiteit, 1991.

PART VI

TO AL-ANDALUS, WOULD SHE RETURN THE GREETING

THE *NŪNIYYA* (POEM IN N) OF IBN ZAYDŪN

Morning came – the separation –
substitute for the love we shared,
for the fragrance of our coming together,
falling away.

The moment of departure
came upon us – fatal morning.
The crier of our passing
ushered us through death's door.

Who will tell them
who, by leaving, cloak us
in a sorrow not worn away with time,
though time wears us away,

That time that used
to make us laugh
when they were near
returns to make us grieve.

We poured for one another
the wine of love. Our enemies seethed
and called for us to choke
— and fate said let it be.

The knot our two souls tied
came undone,
and what our hands joined
was broken.

We never used to give a thought
to separation, and now, for us
to be together again
is beyond our dreams.

How I wish I knew –
and I have given your rivals
no satisfaction – if ours
have won a share from you.

Keeping faith in you,
now you are gone,
is the only creed we hold,
our religion.

What is our fault
that you cool the envier's eye,
satisfying one who takes
pleasure in our misfortune?

To give up hope, we thought,
might bring relief. But it only
made desire for you
burn deeper.

You left. We went our way,
ribs still scorched –
longing for you –
tears still welling in our eyes.

When our secret thought
whispered in your ear,
sorrow would have crushed us,
had we not held on to one another.

Our days turned
in losing you and darkened,
while nights with you
glowed,

When life bounded
free in the intimacy we gave,
when the meadows of our pleasure
were pure,

When whatever we wished
we gathered
from the boughs of loving
bending near.

Oh the good times spent with you –
God bless them with a gentle rain.

You were for our spirits
the fragrance of basil.

Do not imagine
that distance from you
will change us,
as distance changes other lovers.

We sought, by God,
no other in your place,
nor do our hopes
turn us another way.

Night-traveler, lightning,
go early to the palace
and offer a drink to one
who poured us her pure love freely,

And ask if thoughts of us
trouble a lover
as the memory of her
possesses our troubled mind.

O fragrant breath of the east wind
bring greetings to one,
whose kind word would revive us
even from a distance.

Will she not, through the long
pass of time, grant us consideration,
however often, however
well we plead?

Fostered in royalty
as if God shaped her from musk
(and we mere humans
from clay),

Or formed her in pure silver
and crowned her
with gold, unalloyed,
new creation and glory.

When she bends,
her necklace weighs her down –
bracelets bruise her skin
so tender!

Within her veils
she is the nursling of the sun
though it touches her
barely.

As if on the curve
of her cheek, the star
of Venus were graven,
amulet and charm.

What harm is it
we are not of her station.
In love, and it is enough,
we are equal.

O garden where our gazes
gathered rose and sweetbriar
unveiled soft and tender
by young amours!

O life, in whose brilliance
we were granted our wishes,
each and every kind,
drawing out our pleasure!

O the good times gone by
when we strolled in splendor,
adorned in its robes,
long folds trailing!

We cannot name you.
In station you transcend
all names, freeing us
of the obligation.

You are unique, the one and only.
Your qualities cannot be shared.
We are left to describe you
as best we can.

O garden never dying,
your lote tree and spring of Kawthar
are now for us the tree of skulls
and the drink of the damned.

Did we not spend the night,
making love our third companion,

when our good luck weighed
on our informer's eyes,

Two secrets
hidden in the whisper of darkness,
until the morning's tongue
was about to reveal us.

No wonder we recalled
sadness forbidden
to prudent minds,
our patience gone and forgotten.

We read our sorrow,
that dawn of parting
as Qur'an, reciting it by heart
from the verse of patience.

We can find no drink
like loving you –
even as it quenches
it leaves us thirsting more.

Nothing can divert our gaze
from the horizon
of the beauty of your star.
Bitterness cannot turn us from it.

Not by choice did we
withdraw from so near!
Time's twist, destiny
turned us against our will.

As the wine is mixed
and sparkles, and singers
perform their trance of song,
we ache for you.

The passing round of the cup of wine
brings out in us no mark of repose
the sound of a lute,
no forgetting.

Be true to our vow
as we have been.
The noble give back,
loyally, as given.

If from its towering course the night's
full moon bent toward us,
she would not (forgive the thought)
stir out desire.

I am left sad, keeping the faith
though you have shut
me out. A phantom
will be enough, memories suffice.

Though in this world
we could not afford you,
we'll find you in the stations
of the last assembly, and pay the price.

A response from you
would be something!
If only what you offered
you gave.

God bless you
long as our love for you still burns,
the love we hide,
the love that gives us away.

(Translated by Michael Sells)

INDEX